M000167435

Creating
Social
Democracy

Sweden and Northern Europe, 1988

CREATING SOCIAL DEMOCRACY

A Century of the
Social Democratic Labor Party in Sweden

Edited by
Klaus Misgeld, Karl Molin,
and Klas Åmark

THE PENNSYLVANIA STATE UNIVERSITY PRESS
University Park, Pennsylvania

First published as *Socialdemokratins samhälle: SAP och Sverige under 100 år*
by Tiden (Stockholm)
Copyright © 1988 Författarna

This English translation and revised edition © 1992
The Pennsylvania State University

Library of Congress Cataloging-in-Publication Data

Socialdemokratins samhälle. English
    Creating social democracy : a century of the Social Democratic
Labor Party in Sweden / edited by Klaus Misgeld, Karl Molin, and
Klas Åmark ; translated by Jan Teeland.
    p.   cm.
    Translation of: Socialdemokratins samhälle.
    Includes bibliographical references and index.
    ISBN 0-271-00868-7 (cloth). — ISBN 0-271-00931-4 (pbk.)
    1. Sveriges socialdemokratiska arbetareparti—History.   2. Sweden
—Politics and government.   3. Socialism—Sweden—History.
I. Misgeld, Klaus, 1940–   .   II. Molin, Karl, 1944–   .
III. Åmark, Klas, 1944–   .   IV. Title.
JN7995.S86S5913   1992
324.2485'072–dc20   92-8857
                                                                        CIP

All rights reserved
Printed in the United States of America
Published by The Pennsylvania State University Press,
Suite C, 820 North University Drive, University Park, PA 16802

Translation from Swedish by Jan Teeland of English ETC

It is the policy of The Pennsylvania State University Press to use acid-free paper for
the first printing of all clothbound books. Publications on uncoated stock satisfy the
minimum requirements of American National Standard for Information Sciences—
Permanence of Paper for Printed Library Materials, ANSI Z39.48–1984.

Contents

Foreword

The Research Council of the Labor Movement Archives and Library initiated the project, "The Social Democratic Labor Party and the Development of Swedish Society over 100 Years," and has actively followed the progress of the project from its commencement in January 1987. Over a number of years the Research Council and a wide circle of scholars carried on discussions in which the central research areas were established and new questions for examination were outlined. In addition, the council and the authors conducted seminars in which they thoroughly examined drafts of most of the chapters and discussed the organization of the project.

The project itself and the translation into English have been funded by The Bank of Sweden Tercentenary Foundation. Lars Wessman, director of the Labor Movement Archives and Library, has had overall responsibility for the management of the project. A committee, chaired by Professor Rudolf Meidner and including Lars Wessman, the author Sven Lindqvist, and senior research fellows Karl Molin, Klas Åmark, and Klaus Misgeld, was formed to supervise the project work.

The planning and disposition of the project were carried out with the assistance of Karl Molin and Klas Åmark as scientific experts. In addition to their contributions to the volume, Karl Molin and Klas Åmark together with Klaus Misgeld have edited the book and written the Introduction. The librarian Marie Hedström compiled the Bibliography. Jan Teeland (English ETC) has taken on the difficult task of translating the very diverse contents of the book (with the exception of Tim Tilton's and Gøsta Esping-Andersen's contributions, which were originally written in English).

For the American edition, Klas Åmark has written an Afterword summarizing developments in Sweden and in Swedish Social Democracy after 1988, and Karl Molin has composed the Historical Orientation, which presents the Swedish Social Democratic Labor Party (SAP) to a non-Swedish readership.

Contributors have had access to minutes and other internal material from the SAP, the Social Democratic parliament group, and the LO up to 1968, and occasionally from subsequent years (as a matter of practice, the SAP, the parliament group, and the LO permit research in their records except for those relating to the last twenty years). The Labor Movement Archives and Library has also assisted with archive material, past and present conference and other organization publications, and access to relevant literature.

The perspective of the last few decades is a rather short one for a historical work, and a longer view, together with access to new source material, might lead to the revision of certain conclusions presented in the book—an observation borne out by the new Afterword. However, for a total picture it is important that the authors carried their investigations into present-day issues and expressed, if cautiously, views concerning future developments.

Finally, we would like to thank everyone who has read the book in manuscript and provided valuable comments: university seminar participants, people active in politics and trade unions, and individual scholars.

Rudolf Meidner,
Chairman of the Research Council of the Labor Movement
Archives and Library

Lars Wessman,
Project Director and Director of the
Labor Movement Archives and Library

Stockholm, 30 September 1988 and 1 March 1991

Klaus Misgeld, Karl Molin, and Klas Åmark

Introduction

Olof Palme once used the image of a snail to describe reformist Social Democracy. He liked the self-irony in the metaphor and also thought it revealed important aspects of his own party's character. The snail image, which originated with the German author Günter Grass, can also be appreciated when we reflect upon the party's history.* One thinks, for example, of the creature's pace. Many who have been eager to reach the goals they believe they see so clearly have found the pace insufferably slow. Some have tried to teach the snail to leap, while others who are settled have been bothered by its constant and dogged movement. One also recalls the snail's muscular foot and its mobile antennae. Every observer of the snail understands that an important connection exists between the two: the antennae take the bearings for future destinations, while, with its knowledge of the terrain, the foot chooses the most appropriate route.

To this extent the image of the snail lends itself well to illustrating important points for research in Swedish Social Democracy. One such point concerns the pace and direction of reformist progress. To obtain a perspective on tempo increases and periods of stagnation, downhill slopes and culs-de-sac, comparisons with other countries would seem to be the obvious method. Another important subject for research is the relationship between the ideological program and concrete day-to-day political issues. What role have larger visions played? Have they really provided direction, or has the task of finding short-term solutions to acute problems been of overriding importance?

More difficult, but no less exciting, is to contemplate another characteristic of the snail, namely that it is androgynous—each individual con-

---

*Olof Palme at the Social Democratic Youth Conference, 12 June 1975. See O. Palme 1987, 29–32, where Palme uses Günter Grass's snail metaphor to describe (in German) social democracy (G. Grass 1972; in Swedish 1973).

tains both sexes. A snail would find it difficult to understand the struggle for equality between men and women. Could the same be said for Social Democrats? Yes, historically, and we would add that this is equally true of other Swedish parties. More important, we think this is an area requiring exposure to historical analysis. We need to know more about the attitudes of reformism toward gender-bound division of work in society and toward women's demands for equal influence in society and in politics.

When planning this anthology of essays on the history of the SAP, we had hoped to shed more light on these issues, so well encapsulated by the image of the snail: the development of Swedish reformism in a comparative international perspective; the relationship between political program and practical politics; and the party's position regarding issues of equality between the sexes. Hence the contributors were asked to consider these questions in their essays.

Historical perspective is critical to any discussion of such important themes, and it provides a lens through which these chapters on Social Democratic policy can be viewed. Such a presentation is particularly relevant at the moment for several reasons. The party was founded one hundred years ago and has both reflected and affected the radical transformation that Swedish society has undergone during the period. At a time when Sweden was an agrarian society the Social Democratic Labor Party appeared—the first Swedish political party in a modern sense, with a permanent mobilizing and activating organization. When industrial society was facing a profound crisis at the beginning of the 1930s, the Social Democratic Labor Party won political power and also demonstrated its ability to use it. Today, with the focus on structural change in the economy, adaptation to European integration, and ecological problems, the party is still a leading political force in the country. An attempt to summarize what we know about the party's development during the last tumultuous century should be of general interest.

Over recent decades research on Swedish Social Democracy has been lively, but it has been dominated by chronological and thematically limited points of departure. So there is much to be gained by research that addresses and analyzes central problems within a broader chronological framework. To achieve this, teamwork has been required, with the participation of scholars from different disciplines and with varying scientific points of departure. One important lesson learned from this project is that conceptions of history, evaluations of various kinds of sources, and ideas about presentation are not the same among the different disciplines, and that no one, not even historians, has exclusive rights to the writing of history.

Contributions to the present anthology encompass three large subject areas: economic policy, social and welfare policy, and party structure and activities. Two additional essays are also included. One deals with the party's international policies—internationalism and peace efforts occupy a pivotal position in Social Democratic self-awareness (Alf W. Johansson and Torbjörn Norman: Chapter 11): the other is concerned with the role of ideology in SAP politics and in Swedish political thinking in general (Tim Tilton: Chapter 13).

The essays on economic policy—which is at the heart of and provides the springboard for Social Democratic policy in general—discuss three central issues: the party programs and implemented economic policies (Villy Bergström: Chapter 5), cooperation and conflict within the labor movement, that is, between the party and the trade union movement (Klas Åmark: Chapter 3), and agricultural policy (Clas-Erik Odhner: Chapter 6). The latter contribution also is based upon personal experience.

Five essays deal mainly—although not exclusively—with the party's social and welfare policies and with changes in social realities. Areas such as family policy (Ann-Sofie Ohlander: Chapter 7) and education (Bo Lindensjö: Chapter 10) are investigated. Housing policy is examined on both national (Thord Strömberg: Chapter 8) and local levels (Peter Billing, Lars Olsson, and Mikael Stigendal: Chapter 9). The latter contribution also takes up power relations and local politics in Malmö. The fifth of these essays is devoted to Social Democratic welfare policies (Gøsta Esping-Andersen: Chapter 2).

The essays on the party's organization and rise to power are written from various points of view. How the party's inner structure has changed is analyzed in one essay (Gullan Gidlund: Chapter 4); in another, party strategies and tactics in its pursuit of power are discussed (Göran Therborn: Chapter 1). The third essay concentrates on party discipline (Karl Molin: Chapter 12).

At the core of Social Democratic politics has always been a universalist welfare policy, so those questions impinging upon or illuminating this area have had priority in this book. Consequently, important topics such as culture and the environment have been treated indirectly if at all. Such omissions are also due to the fact that we are dealing with one hundred years of party existence; political issues and policy areas that are of vital interest today have not necessarily played a significant role in the past—at least not explicitly. This does not mean, of course, that these issues are uninteresting.

The task of the contributors, then, has been to summarize and discuss previous research in their respective areas. In addition, they have complemented previous scholarship with new research—to a much greater degree than we had initially anticipated. There is a significant amount of original research included in this book.

How have we managed the three selected central aspects of the party's history? It might seem as if the common themes have been rather buffeted about by the centrifugal forces generated by different research temperaments working with thirteen different subject areas. However, the book was never meant to provide a full and exhaustive examination of the subjects; it was intended to provide historical material and intellectual inspiration for future research and discussion. And with this we think it has largely succeeded: consider, for example, the divergent views on the relationship between program and practice. Tilton and Esping-Andersen strongly emphasize the ideological continuity in the party's actions, whereas Lindensjö and Ohlander assert a near absence of unequivocal programmatic lines. Therborn reveals the significance of tactics, while Bergström draws a composite picture of a party that sometimes ignores its program and sometimes permits it to play a leading part. The book also contains debates on the international perspective and on women's struggles.

The book summarizes developments within the various subject areas and discusses specific problems. At the same time, it contributes to another, more extensive debate in which the main issue can be formulated along the following lines: Are developments in society generally determined by long-term structural changes, which are basically the same in all Western capitalist countries, or are national political forces primarily responsible for development? Politicians usually stress the importance of politics, especially when times are good and they are in power themselves. Scholars are often more skeptical, but in the contributions to this book there is a tendency to award political actors an important role.

One possibility for those wishing to assert an independent significance for politics is to demonstrate elements in societal development that are not to be found in an international pattern nor able to be placed in inherited national structures. Such an element in Swedish society is presented in this book (especially in the essays by Esping-Andersen and Tilton)—namely, the union of equal distribution of welfare and high economic effectiveness. In Swedish social policy as it has been shaped since the 1930s, there is a preventive aspect that, together with an active labor market policy, is meant to be favorable to both the individual and the economy. This "productivist" welfare policy seems to be a unique phenomenon created by Swedish Social Democracy, and crucial for its "people's home," the notion that society should embody the characteristics of a home.

Another way to approach the question of the significance of politics is to try to find in the course of history palpable changes that can be ascribed to the influence of politics. The basic assumption here would be that structures dominate in certain periods, politics in others. From the perspective of a century, which is the view applied in the present volume, the decade of the 1930s stands out as a period in which politics were truly important, especially in contrast to the preceding decade of political impotence. Per Albin Hansson's first government demonstrated a forcefulness and resolution previously unseen. What happened then has been described in many ways: as the historical compromise between labor and capital; as the integration of the working class into industrial society; as the victory of parliamentary democracy over dictatorship. However, of almost equal import was that the power and strength of will evinced by the new government fostered new belief in the possibilities of politics to change social reality.

In historical writing about the Swedish Social Democratic Labor Party, the 1930s are often presented as a high-water mark. The decade was preceded by ideological conflicts, parliamentary incompetence, and a lack of alternatives to liberal economics. It was followed by continued work along the lines initiated, but also by a new uncertainty about the party's position regarding the market economy. Given this, the 1930s indeed appear as a golden decade. Objections to this picture of the decade may be justified. Even those who recognize the enormous psychological and political importance of the Social Democratic line of action may find its role in economic development exaggerated. It may also be thought that other historical demarcations are of equal importance.

Finally, one should be aware of the risk of creating heroes through focusing on the actors, of raising competent predecessors to the status of lesser gods. To remind us that we live in a world where controlled anxiety and not heroism is the best we can hope for, we have our German snail. Günter Grass cautions, "Of course you understand, children, that the word paradise makes my snail anxious. It is even afraid of those who pave the way for a paradise, and [responds by] drawing itself into its shell." With its pro-

nounced pragmatism and antitotalitarian attitudes, the Swedish snail certainly shed this anxiety; it too crept into its shell at the advance of dictatorships. What was remarkable, although not supernatural, was that it was
able to hold its antennae high, sound new bearings, and embark upon a
decisive and resolute march. For the Swedish people it showed the way
toward a society that was not a paradise, but measured in earthly terms,
fairly good.

Karl Molin

Historical Orientation

The following is a short introduction to the development of the Swedish political system during the last one hundred years. Emphasis is placed on constitutional developments and the growth of, and changes in, political parties. The aim here is to summarize key political developments that have shaped the growth of Social Democracy in Sweden in order to present a general background for the chapters that follow.

THE 1880s: ROYAL POWER QUESTIONED

When the Swedish Social Democratic Labor Party (SAP) was formed in 1889,* the Swedish political system was controlled by stable conservative forces. The bicameral Riksdag had existed since the 1860s, replacing the old parliament of the estates (with four chambers for the nobility, priests, burghers, and farmers, respectively). The right to vote for representatives to the Riksdag was restricted according to income and wealth. The First (upper) Chamber had developed into a haven for higher officials, large landowners, and big businessmen, while the Second (lower) chamber became dominated by farmers. Ruling power lay with the king in accordance with the constitution of 1809, and the king used his royal prerogative to appoint the cabinet. Taxation, however, lay in the hands of the Riksdag.

*"SAP" is an acronym for *Sveriges Socialdemokratiska Arbetareparti*. The term Social Democratic was generally adopted during the 1880s by those North European workers parties that wanted to indicate a Marxist inspiration. Related parties in Latin countries such as France and Italy (even Germany before 1891) preferred the term Socialist. The term Social Democracy refers both to those visions for a better society that unfolded within the Social Democratic Labor Party and to the labor movement itself, including its social and cultural as well as political activities.

In many respects the 1880s was a decade that heralded changes. Popular engagement in politics grew through a nationwide debate on protective tariffs in agriculture. In the Riksdag, groups resembling political parties began to appear. The king's right to single-handedly appoint a government, was increasingly challenged by parliamentarians who thought that the government ought to reflect opinions in the Riksdag. The 1880s was also the decade when structural changes in society accelerated. The number of employees in the crafts and manufacturing industries doubled during the last three decades of the nineteenth century, whereas the proportion of the population earning a living in agriculture dropped from three-quarters to one-half. The percentage of those living in cities increased from under 10 percent to over 20 percent.

A large proportion of the cities' workers was excluded from politics through the voting regulations. Even though increased wages raised somewhat the number of people entitled to vote, in the 1908 election to the Second Chamber 65 percent of all men over twenty-one were still unable to meet the income requirement. For this group, the Social Democratic Labor Party offered hope.

THE NEW PARTY

When it was formed in 1889, the Social Democratic Labor Party was a loose umbrella organization for trade unions, political organizations, and health and burial funds. The party's first representative in the Riksdag was the journalist Hjalmar Branting, elected to the Second Chamber in 1896. The following year the party drafted its first comprehensive program, but it did not elect its first chair until 1907, when Branting was chosen by a broad majority. He remained chair of the party until his death in 1925.

Two political demands dominated party propaganda during its first decade. Predictably, one was universal suffrage; the other, an eight-hour workday. Early in the new century, a third demand was added to the party's list: disarmament. Interest in this question had been stimulated by the reform of the defense forces carried out in 1901, when compulsory military service was introduced. All male citizens had their liberties infringed upon by the required period of military training. Consequently, antidefense agitation grew.

THE EMERGENCE OF A MULTIPARTY SYSTEM

An initial step toward universal suffrage was taken in 1909. The Riksdag approved a new voting law that gave all men an equal say in the election to the Second Chamber. Other rules governed the election to the First Chamber: its members were appointed by regional political assemblies chosen in the general election. In these elections a plutocratic guarantee was retained, which meant that the vote of the very rich was worth forty times that of the poor. Of greater long-term importance, however, was the abolition of the system of majority vote in districts with a single representative. Instead, a modified proportional system was introduced when the election districts were enlarged. The concrete effect of this was that the importance of individuals diminished. Parties took over the nomination of candidates and campaigning, and more parties had a real chance of entering into the political assemblies.

The 1911 election to the Second Chamber, the first election under the new rules, did not lead to any drastic changes in the formation of parties. Three parties dominated the scene. The Liberal party,* standing for universal suffrage, social reform policies, and a moderate reduction of defense costs, received 40 percent of the vote. The Conservative party,** wishing to circumscribe democratization, strengthen defense, and preserve traditional values, obtained 31 percent of the vote. The Social Democrats received 28.5 percent of the vote.

PARLIAMENTARY BREAKTHROUGH

The struggle between the king and the Riksdag over power to form a government reached a breaking point in August 1905, when the ninety-year-old union with Norway was exposed to a fatal attack from the Norwegian opposition. One minister, who was supported by King Oscar II, submitted

---

*Frisinnade Landsföreningen (literally the National Association of Freethinkers/"Libertarians"—referring mainly to people from Free churches) split with the national party, the Liberal party, in 1923 but joined forces again in 1934 as Folkpartiet, or the Liberal party. As of 1990 the party has been known as Folkpartiet Liberalerna.

**The National Association of Voters. In 1938 it was called the National Conservative Organization (Högerns riksorganisation); it changed its name in 1969 to Moderata samlingspartiet (the Conservative party).

a bill including his set of conditions for dissolution but was turned down by the Riksdag and subsequently was forced to resign. The new government was clearly dependent upon the Riksdag's support and not the king's, and under the authority of the Riksdag the union was dissolved.

The king, however, refused to accept as a parliamentary precedent this loss of power, and his position had strong support within the political Right. Two ideals of government confronted each other in this struggle. The Liberals, and in particular their leader, Karl Staaff, took as their model the English House of Commons parliamentarism. The Conservatives' ideal was the Germany of Kaiser Wilhelm; they wanted to award to the Swedish monarchy something of the power and authority of the German kaiser and wished to draw clear boundaries for the development of democracy.

In February 1914 the conflicts led to a dramatic outburst. A government led by the Liberal party (which after the election of 1911 was the Riksdag's largest), with the support of the Social Democrats, presented a proposal for specific reductions in defense spending. Spurred on by conservative advisers and his militant queen (granddaughter of Kaiser Wilhelm I), the king gave a speech in the courtyard of the Stockholm Palace in which he rejected the Liberal government's defense policy. He had, in effect, disavowed his own government on the most important issue of the day. There was little his opponents could do. Workers organized counterdemonstrations in support of the Liberal prime minister, but he chose to resign. He was replaced by a Conservative caretaker ministry.

That the right wing and the king were still powerful political forces was further underscored by the election to the Second Chamber in March 1914. The Liberals lost 8 percent of their electorate and thirty-two mandates, while the Conservatives made considerable gains.

1917: THE SOCIAL DEMOCRATIC LABOR PARTY SPLIT

Through the election of 1911 the Social Democratic Labor Party had become an important political force, but the party was still incapable of achieving concrete political results on its own. Cooperation was necessary, and the reform-minded Liberal party was the obvious choice for a partner. However, every cooperative endeavor placed definite demands on the Social Democrats' ideological emphasis. Concerted effort in support of a national, nonrevolutionary reform policy was a prerequisite for agreements with the Liberals, but this was no simple requirement for a party that had long functioned as a radical discussion club, in which views varied from revolutionary anarchism to moderate reformism. Branting tried to unify the party behind a practical reform policy that could attract wide support in the Riksdag.

Efforts by the party leadership to pursue a practical reform policy in cooperation with the Liberals forced a confrontation with the radical left wing of the Social Democrats. The radical faction, which wanted to destroy capitalism rather than reform it and to abolish military defense, was compelled to leave the party in the spring of 1917. Members of this faction formed their own party, which would later become the Swedish Communist party.

PARLIAMENTARY BREAKTHROUGH AND THE VOTING RIGHTS REFORM

The year 1917 was a critical period for Swedish politics. The new radical left-wing party participated in the election that year, as did another newcomer, the Agrarian party,* which addressed itself to the rural population. Both parties won seats in the Riksdag, and, together with the three older parties, they formed a party structure that would remain basically the same until 1988 when yet another party, the Green party, would enter the Riksdag.** The election in 1917 was epoch-making also in that it ended the conflict between different constitutional ideals. The election results, which entailed heavy losses for the Conservatives, led to strong demands for a change of government. The king and the Conservatives were anxious to avoid a parliamentary precedent and consequently refused any change. After protracted negotiations in which royal powers were successively relinquished, a left-wing government was formed based on the Riksdag's two largest parties, the Social Democrats and the Liberals. This was the decisive breakthrough for the parliamentary principle in Swedish politics.

But the victory of parliamentarianism did not mean that the Riksdag be-

*From 1943, the Rural party–Agrarian party (Landsbygdspartiet-Bondeförbundet); from 1957, the Center party.

**The Green party lost its seats in the Riksdag in the election of 1991, and two small bourgeois parties came in: the Christian Democrats, propagating conservative values, and the right-wing populist Ny Demokrati (New Democracy).

came the only center of political power. The king and his court would continue to play a significant role, particularly in questions of defense and foreign policy. Even more important was that the state bureaucracy, dominated by permanent officials who tended to be conservative, continued to exercise influence over both the making and implementing of decisions.

The advent of a Liberal–Social Democratic government, however, meant that the suffrage issue was at last near a solution. This government put forth a conclusive motion on universal and equal franchise. Influenced by the revolutionary currents in Europe—not least by the dissolution of the German kaiserdom—the Conservatives accepted the principle of universal suffrage. In 1919 the Riksdag gave women the right to vote. It also abolished the graded scale for voting in elections to municipal assemblies and, indirectly, to the First Chamber. Thereafter, the only difference between the chambers was that the First had a longer mandate period and a successive turnover and thus came to represent a somewhat older electorate.

THE 1920s: POWERLESSNESS AND INTERNAL CONFLICTS

Cooperation between the Social Democrats and the Liberals also extended to the second of the Social Democrats' three demands—the eight-hour workday. A law on delimiting the workday was adopted by the Riksdag in 1919 and came into effect on 1 January 1920. Thereafter, cooperation between the two left-wing parties was dissolved and replaced by a division into blocs. On the one hand were the "socialist" parties—the Social Democrats and the Communists. On the other hand were the "bourgeois" parties—the Conservatives, the Liberals, and the Agrarian party. This new division thereafter became (and continues to be) the most important borderline in Swedish politics.

Throughout the 1920s the bourgeois bloc was the strongest, but the three parties had different views on important issues and consequently could never form a government with a firm majority in the Riksdag. From 1920 to 1932 eight different governments attempted to put through their proposals by seeking support from the Right or the Left. These weak minority governments were unable to make and implement reforms.

The improvements in the Swedish people's economic and social conditions that took place in the 1920s were due more to the increased success of the Swedish export industry than to decisions of the Riksdag. In 1920 a wholly Social Democratic government did appoint one committee to study nationalization and another to investigate the introduction of industrial democracy. However, the party did not have sufficient political force to achieve its aims; neither did it have any clear ideas on how to conduct short-term economic policies. During those brief periods in the 1920s when the SAP was in government, the party's policies were rather conventional and defensive.

In the middle of the decade several of the leading moderate, reformist members of the SAP died, among them party chair Branting. Internal conflicts flared up again. Per Albin Hansson, the legendary "founding father" of Swedish Social Democracy, became the new party leader. During these early years, however, he vacillated between positions and had difficulties asserting his views. Before the election of 1928 the party published a program containing radical elements such as a stiffer inheritance tax. The result was heavy reverses for the party, with a loss of fourteen mandates. After an internal settlement in the autumn of 1929, the party gathered its forces around a program aimed at practical reforms within the framework of a capitalist society. Disarmament would be postponed. The party would pursue policies not only aimed at the workers, but designed to include the entire population. The foundations were laid for the so-called *folkhem* policy, which was meant to serve the entire people rather than only the working class and to regard democracy rather than socialism as its ultimate goal.

THE 1932 ELECTION VICTORY: THE CRISIS PROGRAM

The election of 1932 was greatly colored by the economic depression, with its high unemployment and market crises in agriculture. In 1930 the Social Democrats had put forward a comprehensive program for combating the crisis, featuring extensive employment relief programs and state unemployment insurance. The crisis program became a trump card in the election campaign, which ended in victory for the Social Democrats. The party was now able to form its own government. However, the decisive victory for the Social Democrats came in 1933, when the new government succeeded in reaching a settlement with the Agrarian party on the crisis program. The price the Social Democrats had to pay involved a program of support for domestic farming that entailed, among other things, a higher price for butter as well as a tax on margarine.

This "horse trading" with the Agrarian party initiated fruitful cooperation in the Riksdag, and after the 1936 election cooperation expanded into government coalition. A vigorous majority had been created, and a number of important social and political reforms could be enacted—among them, unemployment insurance, improved pensions, statutory vacations, and state subsidies for housing construction. Altogether, the 1930s reform period confirmed a general belief in the responsibilities and potential of the state in economic and social life. Business cycles should be balanced, the industrial infrastructure improved, and social problems eliminated.

The reform policies gained the voters' approval. In the local elections of 1938, the Social Democrats were supported by 50.4 percent of the voters. Many thought that parliamentarism had landed in a stalemate that favored the Social Democrats. They had mobilized the working class, and as long as that class encompassed a majority of the population the party would have a firm hold on the nation's political development. The tasks confronting the opposition seemed hopeless; Per Albin Hansson raised the question of whether a permanent multiparty coalition government might not be the best solution to the problems of parliamentarism.

UNCERTAIN MAJORITY

Developments during World War II confirmed Hansson's speculations, to a degree. The Agrarian party had been included in the government since 1936, and in December 1939 a national coalition government that included the Conservatives as well as the Liberals was formed. At the same time, the Social Democrats' unique position among the electorate was confirmed: in the national elections of 1940, the party received a record-high 53.8 percent of the vote. In the first postwar election, the socialist parties (the Social Democrats and the Communists) retained their strong position, but a shift in the proportion of votes in the socialist bloc benefited the Communists. In the local elections of 1946 Communists won 11.2 percent of the vote, their highest total ever.

But the notion of a constant Social Democratic hegemony would be proved false. In only one election during the postwar period (1968) did the Social Democrats receive over half of the votes. Up to 1976, the party's portion hovered around 45 percent. To have a majority in the Riksdag the SAP was dependent upon support from others. Most often this support came—more or less reluctantly—from the Communists, whose voter support had dropped rapidly to just over 4 percent. The possibility of a change of government loomed largest before each election and drove the Social Democrats to seek parliamentary settlements with one of the bourgeois parties and to avoid moves that could mobilize antisocialist opinion. From 1951 to 1957 cooperation between blocs was secured through coalition between the SAP and the Agrarian party.

REAPING THE HARVEST AFTER WORLD WAR II

The Social Democrats welcomed the peace with high hopes of a society characterized by full employment, just distribution of production profits, improved efficiency, and more democracy in business and industry. The postwar period was to reap the harvest of socialism. Reform policies were facilitated by favorable economic cycles. Swedish production had not been disturbed by the war, and Sweden could now sell paper, wood products, steel, and ships all over the world. Economic policies in these circumstances concentrated on two basic questions: How could full employment be combined with stable price levels, and how should reduced wage differentials and increased social security be combined with economic efficiency? Debates on these questions were intense, not only between the government and the political opposition but also between the party and the trade union movement.

A number of social and political reforms were carried out. Among the most important were the universal child allowance (1947), obligatory health insurance (1955), and the National Supplementary Pension Scheme, or ATP (1959). Housing shortages in the cities posed more difficult problems. Encouraging housing construction by means of state subsidies proved insufficient. However, a temporary balance was achieved in the housing market in the 1960s through a central government campaign that produced about 100,000 new flats annually.

During the first decades after the war, a comprehensive agreement was developed on the labor market. Chairs of the LO, the Swedish Confederation of Trade Unions,* and the SAF, the Swedish Employers' Confederation, traveled around the United States together giving talks about "the Swedish model." One of the structural prerequisites for the agreement was the tradition of locating industries in small communities in the countryside, which facilitated contact and mutual understanding across class boundaries.

CONSTITUTIONAL REFORM

In 1969, after fifteen years of inquiries and party-political controversies, the Riksdag approved a thoroughgoing revision of the Swedish constitution, Europe's oldest written constitution, which had been in place since 1809. The revised constitution put into law the parliamentary system, but it abolished the bicameral structure that had existed since the 1860s. The Riksdag would now consist of a single chamber, with 349 representatives elected directly by the people. The election system distributed Riksdag seats in strict proportion to the number of votes cast for parties—those parties that received at least 4 percent of the vote.

The time span between regular elections was shortened from four to three years. The new rules followed the principle that the will of the people should be rapidly and accurately reflected in the composition of the Riksdag, and that the composition of the Riksdag should in turn determine the color of the government. In practice this meant that even a very small shift in the electorate could result in a change of government. A party would need to obtain only 4 percent of the vote to gain representation in the Riksdag. The Social Democrats' hold on the government became even more uncertain.

In 1974 the revised constitution of 1969 was replaced by an entirely new one. In addition to new regulations governing the Riksdag and the electoral system, the 1974 constitution also included a list of fundamental freedoms and rights. The order codified in the new constitution is a democracy operating through political parties. The substance of election activities resides in parties, and in the Riksdag they have the responsibility for ensuring that election results are reflected in the composition of the government. The constitutional debates that preceded the reform stressed the significance of political parties in ongoing debates and in the political activation of the

*"LO" is an acronym for _Landsorganisationen_, the Countrywide Organization. It was formed in 1898 to coordinate trade union policies.

citizenry. In acknowledgment of the importance of political parties, the 1965 Riksdag decided to introduce state support for those parties represented in the Riksdag. At present this subsidy constitutes the most important source of income for the parties.

THE NEW RADICALISM OF THE 1970s

Olof Palme became the leader of the Social Democratic Labor Party and prime minister in 1969. At that time, many people considered the system of social security nearly complete. What remained to be done was in the nature of refinements. Future reforms would focus on increasing both equality and industrial democracy. Sweden was on the threshold of economic democracy, according to some radical groups within the party and in the trade union movement.

In the mid-1970s two reforms were carried out that aroused great expectations. The law on employment protection (1973) guaranteed wage earners protection against unwarranted dismissal. The law on codetermination (1976) gave trade unions the opportunity to participate in important decisions in companies. It was understood, however, that the concrete implementation of this right would be determined through negotiations between the parties involved. But within the private sector few such negotiations have been concluded, and so the practical consequences of the law on codetermination remain limited.

However, it was the proposal for the wage earners' funds that had the greatest political impact during the 1970s. It all began in 1976 when the LO congress supported a proposal transferring a portion of company profits to funds that, via the purchase of stocks, would place wage earner representatives on company boards. This was a strategy for gradually transferring economic power into the hands of wage earners. Opposition from the bourgeois parties and from industrial and employer organizations was solid. However, in 1983 the Riksdag approved the creation of five investment funds that, until 1990, would be established using portions of industrial profits and that would function according to normal market principles. The effects of these funds on power relations within business and industry may confidently be described as negligible.

The struggle over this attempt to realize economic democracy confirms an old lesson: that reforms of the power structure within business and industry do not attract widespread engagement, not even among workers, whereas bourgeois countercampaigns can easily expand into mass movements.

NEW QUESTIONS, ELECTION FAILURE, AND RETURN

One important element in the political landscape of recent decades has been the proliferation of new issues requiring innovative thinking on the part of all the parties, including the Social Democrats. Among the new issues are regional development policy, questions of gender equality, and environmental policies. The SAP has tried to convince the public that the party favors development of sparsely populated regions, equality for women, and stiffer protective environmental regulations, but its concrete results have not been sufficient to convince activists in each field.

Dwindling support for traditional Social Democratic policies, difficulties in creating a positive profile in the new issues, and a simultaneous transformation within the electorate involving a shift from class-voting blue-collar workers toward opinion-voting white-collar workers have made the SAP's political position complicated and uncertain. In 1976, after forty-four years in government, the party lost an election. A bourgeois three-party coalition government consisting of the Conservative, Liberal, and Center parties was formed. It was, however, hampered by difficult internal disputes, particularly over the issue of nuclear power.

After another election defeat in 1979, the Social Democrats were returned to power in 1982. The country's economy was in trouble, and, as in 1932, the new government took office with a detailed program in hand. It acted decisively and had some success, most notably in maintaining low unemployment. Other problems, however, such as low productivity, high cost levels, and high inflation, were blamed on the government. Its methods of solving problems were similar to traditional bourgeois policies, and this caused internal conflicts and continual disputes with the LO.

The election of 1991 gave the Social Democrats only 37.6 percent of the votes, their worst showing since 1928, and a bourgeois four-party government took over. In addition to the three parties of 1976, the Christian Democrats—newcomers in the Riksdag—joined the coalition.

TRAUMA

What the people of Sweden recall more than anything else from recent decades is not political strife and economic crises but one single, inexplicable act: the murder of their prime minister. Olof Palme was killed on the night of 26 February 1986 when, together with his wife and without security guards, he strolled home from a movie. For many, the shot that killed him signaled the end of an era: the secure and orderly "people's home" had been razed to the ground, and with it the dream of Sweden as a sanctuary for freedom and human solidarity.

AB	Stockholms län (county)
C	Uppsala län
D	Södermanlands län
E	Östergötlands län
F	Jönköpings län
G	Kronobergs län
H	Kalmar län
I	Gotlands län
K	Blekinge län
L	Kristianstads län
M	Malmöhus län
N	Hallands län
O	Göteborgs och Bohus län
P	Älvsborgs län
R	Skaraborgs län
S	Värmlands län
T	Örebro län
U	Västmanlands län
W	Kopparbergs län
X	Gävleborgs län
Y	Västernorrlands län
Z	Jämtlands län
AC	Västerbottens län
BD	Norrbottens län

Administrative regions (counties) in Sweden and their main cities.

Göran Therborn

1

A Unique Chapter in the History of Democracy: The Social Democrats in Sweden

THE EXCEPTIONALISM OF THE SAP

Swedish Social Democracy has occupied a position of parliamentary power during this century without parallel in the history of modern democracy. As of the 1991 election, the SAP had led the government of Sweden for fifty-six out of the seventy years of parliamentary elections with universal suffrage—80 percent of the period of democratic government in Sweden. For forty consecutive years Sweden had a Social Democratic prime minister, and for thirty-eight years (57 percent of the democratic period) the Social Democrats were the sole governing party. In the parliamentary elections from 1921 to 1985 the SAP attracted an average of 44.8 percent of the voters, and from 1944 to 1985, 45.7 percent. In five elections the party has received more than half of the total votes: in the local and indirect First Chamber elections of 1938, 1942, and 1962, and in the Second Chamber elections of 1940 and 1968.

What has been exceptional is the combination of these components of political power: government leadership, majority rule, and number of

Table 1.   Party Power in Developed Parliamentary Democracies.

	Years	A %	B	C	D	E	F
SAP	53	79	40	38	19^1	44.8	45.7
Best other workers' parties	40^2	62^2	23^3	37^3	25^5	43.4^4	45.8^5
	37^3	57^3	18^4	25^5	16^3	43.1^5	45.4^4
Best bourgeois parties	52^6	98^8	41^8	51^{13}	43^{13}	44.7^9	46.1^9
	42^7	86^6	36^{10}	40^9	33^8	43.4^7	45.1^{12}
	15^{13}	76^{13}	23^{11}	33^8	32^7	42.0^{13}	44.7^8

Sources: Thomas Mackie and Richard Rose, *The International Almanac of Electoral History* 2nd ed. (London: 1982); *Journal of Electoral Studies*, 1983–88.

A   =   Government leadership by year and percent of time since the introduction of parliamentary democracy (at least for men) up to mid-1988
B   =   Number of years of uninterrupted government for same period
C   =   Number of years of sole government, same period
D   =   Number of years of majority government, same period
E   =   Average percentage of votes during the same period
F   =   Average percentage of votes during the postwar period (from 1944 in Sweden, 1943 in Australia and New Zealand)

Notes:
  1. Majority at elections for upper and lower houses. SAP has had its own majority in the lower house only in 1940–44, during the coalition government.
  2. Socialdemokratiet in Denmark.
  3. Det Norske Arbeiderparti (DNA), Labor Party of Norway.
  4. Austrian SPÖ.
  5. Australian Labour Party.
  6. Belgian Christian Social Democrats.
  7. Conservative Party of Great Britain.
  8. Japanese Liberal-Democrats (Liberals prior to the party merger at the 1958 election).
  9. Irish nationalist party, Fianna Fáil.
  10. Italian Christian Democrats.
  11. Australian Liberal Party.
  12. West German Christian Democrats.
  13. Canadian Liberal Party.

votes. There are parties that have succeeded in one or another of these aspects, but no other has even approached success in all. The facts above become even more remarkable when one considers that they were obtained in a multiparty system with proportional representation. Table 1 compares the SAP and other successful parties in developed democracies on the basis of various criteria, covering a period ending with the summer of 1988.

Among labor parties the other two Scandinavian Social Democrats, the

Austrian Social Democrats, and the Australian Labour party have come closest to the SAP. However, if one examines government and voter influence, the gap becomes much larger. In number of votes, the Australian and Austrian parties are comparable to the SAP, but the former has been in government for only twenty-five years (29 percent of the democratic period beginning in 1901) and the latter for only twenty years (30 percent). The Norwegian and Danish Social Democrats have led governments for many years but show a much weaker voter base: 38.3 percent on average for the DNA (the Norwegian party) from 1956 to 1985, and 37.2 percent for Social-demokratiet (the Danish party) from 1920 to 1988. Both have lost a great deal of support since the 1960s; 40 percent is now considered a great success for the DNA and 30 to 33 percent for the Danish Social Democrats. The bourgeois parties have demonstrated a motley pattern internationally. The most successful—those with high figures in both government and vote columns—have been the Japanese Liberal-Democrats, the Irish nationalist Fianna Fáil, the Canadian Liberals, and the Conservatives in Great Britain. Thus the SAP has occupied a unique position not only in Sweden, not only in comparison with other labor parties, but also within the framework of international parliamentary democracy. Remarkably, this phenomenon has received very little attention; it has scarcely been subjected to any systematic research.[1]

A Key Position in the Party System

A party can attain a dominating position in a democratic political system in two ways: through being especially representative nationally or through having a key position in the party system. By "nationally representative" I mean that, according to majority opinion, the party is closely associated with the nation and the national interest—albeit not unanimously and seldom on its own; but the association is strong enough to give the party a certain advantage over its competitors. A key position in the party system involves occupying a central place in relation to various interest coalitions, either between parties in a multiparty system or between interest groups in a pluralist two-party system. The SAP's power rests on both.

The SAP acquired its national representativeness during the 1930s, a position that was consolidated during the war years. It was underlined by the voters very clearly in elections from 1938 to 1942, when in three consecutive elections the party obtained an absolute majority—50.4, 53.8, and 50.3 percent—and the bourgeois parties expressed a basic consensus with social democracy. The national interest that the SAP primarily represented at that time was the small, peripheral nation-state's interest in remaining outside of all international conflicts. An official expression of this interest can be found in a statement motivating the coalition between the Agrarian party and the SAP in 1936: "In a time of anxieties and upheavals in the lives of people and nations, when democratic and parliamentary forms of government are repressed or threatened by dictatorships, it has seemed more than usually urgent to secure popular self-government in our country by creating the broadest possible basis for the work of the government."[2]

Since then, safeguarding the national interest, expressed in strict armed neutrality, has been closely associated with the Social Democrats. The Conservative and Liberal parties have sometimes been deemed intrinsically "unreliable" as regards the policy of neutrality—for instance, in questions concerning NATO in the 1940s and 1950s, and the Common Market in the 1960s. One of the effects of this has been the caution and discretion displayed by the Conservatives in the Swedish EC debates during the 1980s. Olof Palme and his party's clear opposition to the American war in Vietnam could not, however, be utilized by the bourgeois opposition. Yet the SAP's national representativeness was acquired with a policy that was not uncontroversial in the international social democracy of the 1930s, and would hardly be considered uncontroversial today. It involved dissociation from support for the Spanish republic (even though fundraising was permitted and organized), rejection of antifascist cooperation (both in the peoples' front with the Comintern and in the League of Nations), a very restrictive refugee policy, and outward accommodation to Nazi Germany. Power has its price.[3]

In addition, the national interest, as formulated during the politically calamitous years worldwide at the end of the 1930s, also had a social component. In Sweden national policy became a social welfare policy, and this was greatly due to Alva and Gunnar Myrdal's 1934 book *Kris i befolkningsfrågan* (Nation and Family, 1941). This book, more than any other single factor, transformed the population issue into one of social policy and from social policy into national policy. Social reforms thereby became a national interest—the expanded reproduction of the "tribe." All the bourgeois parties became engaged in this; behind the Population Commission of 1935 and the Population Enquiry of 1941 lay ardent political opinion, and the inquiries expressed very broad social policy ambitions.[4] However, the connection between national and social policy favored social democracy. Social security has become a part of the Swedish national identity, and the Social

Democrats have demonstrated greater and more steadfast social engagement than the other parties.

The Swedish bourgeoisie has never had one dominant party, but rather two or more equally strong competing parties. Prior to 1991, the three-party coalition governments of 1976 and 1979 were the only bourgeois majority governments in Sweden since the national government during the dissolution of the union with Norway in 1905. None of these governments remained for a whole election period. On the left the SAP has always had at least one small party, from which passively or actively it has been able to elicit support when needed. After establishing itself above the 40 percent mark during the 1930s, the SAP has since occupied a key position as a large, dominating middle party in the Swedish party system. For one or two of the smaller bourgeois parties, an arrangement with the SAP often has been preferable to the uncertain prospects of a bourgeois majority. If none of the bourgeois parties has been so inclined, support from the left-wing party has usually been sufficient to give an SAP government a parliamentary majority.

The role of bearer of national interests and its position in the Swedish party system go far to explain the SAP's internationally unique position of power. But how did the party achieve this, and how did it succeed in retaining this role and this position for so long?

SWEDISH CLASS POLITICS

The Workers' Party and Class Politics

Needless to say, the history of Sweden's Social Democratic Labor Party must also be studied in terms of class analysis.[5] If one makes a systematic international comparison—to the extent this is possible—one finds that Sweden, Finland, and Denmark have had the most class-oriented politics; in other words, in these countries more than in any others class membership has explained party (block) voting, and in these countries the voting differences between manual workers and others have been greatest. Other countries with clear class-influenced politics include Norway, Austria, Australia, New Zealand, and, in the 1950s, Great Britain.[6] Class voting has diminished over recent years and manual labor has become more questionable as a class criterion, but in relative terms the difference regarding class-denoted politics between Sweden and other countries has nonetheless grown. Since 1973 (and Glistrup and his Danish tax revolt) class differences in voting behavior have been greater in Sweden than in Denmark, while similarities to England and West Germany have lessened during the 1970s and 1980s.[7]

The pronounced class character of Swedish party politics may seem paradoxical for several reasons. Class separation in Sweden is not especially prominent; indeed, Sweden is one of the least unequal countries in the world.[8] Thus the SAP's position as a recognized legitimate representative of the Swedish nation and as governing party for many years might lead one to the conclusion that its support has been socially evenly distributed. Such is not the case.

One side of class politics has been the Social Democrats' comprehensive mobilization of the working class. In the elections of 1948 and 1956–1968, SAP received about 70 percent of workers' votes; the two labor parties together received about 75 percent. As far as one knows a higher degree of class mobilization has never been achieved for any party or left wing in democratic elections anywhere under comparable conditions. From 1982 to 1985 the SAP collected 65 percent of workers' votes, and the VPK (Vänsterpartiet Kommunisterna, the Left Party Communists) received 5 percent.[9]

The Mobilization of the Working Class

Why has class politics been such a force in Sweden and in the Nordic countries? The answer to that question must be sought primarily in the relation between the workers' class formation and the growth of the party system. Of decisive importance in this respect are two structural determinants and a temporal one. The first structural determinant is relatively self-evident: the more pronounced the class situation is, the more clearly capitalistic wage labor is separated from personal services or independent work; the more directly farmers come into contact—and conflict—with capital and market forces, the stronger are the tendencies toward class organization—and among the different types of class organizing is included organizing by political class. The other structural determinant is possibly not as obvious, but it is at least as significant: the nature of the state's relationship to its inhabitants. The stronger and more uniform the state, the more direct and legitimate its organization of the population—including its boundaries vis-à-vis populations in other areas across state borders—the more propitious is the situation for political class organizing. A centralized state with a well-functioning state bureaucracy, state church, secure national borders, and an ethnic composition in the population consistent with state boundaries promotes class parties and class politics because such circumstances reduce the need for and the latitude for other forms of collective organization.[10]

Conscious and articulated class politics began with the modern labor movement, which arose during a relatively short historical period despite enormous cross-national differences in capitalist development and political circumstances. The period extended from the Franco-Prussian War and the Paris Commune of 1871 to World War I. Class mobilization was successful in part because at the time of international organizational efforts, the working classes in the respective countries had not been mobilized previously, either because the political system had engaged only the establishment or because the economic system had yet to engender a modern working class.

Conditions in Sweden during this foundation period were uncommonly propitious for the development of a socialist labor movement. In Swedish agrarian society there was already a tradition of collective self-organization and a certain amount of independence in relation to the powers-that-be. In central and northern Sweden conflicts with timber companies had drawn lines of demarcation against capital even before any sizable industrial working class had been formed. Guild traditions were fairly weak in the overwhelmingly agrarian Sweden, and new companies were—remarkably for the time—often owned by absent capitalists and run by employed managers. In other words, the relations and conflict of interest between capital and labor were distinct early on in Sweden. Industrialization was scattered, but the lack of large concentrations of companies and workers was more of an advantage for the latter's class organization. Very large companies like those in the United States and Germany gave power and resources to capital, which the workers then could not oppose.[11]

The Swedish state was an institution of officials, politically and socially antiquated but a fairly effective, correct, and uncorrupted state of law. It did not have any sort of attached patronage system as in the United States or Italy. Its borders were generally recognized, except for the fragile dynastic union with Norway, and it possessed an empire neither in mind nor in substance. Nationalist or imperialist mobilization was not possible other than in temporary, basically defensive national manifestations such as the farmers' march, which in February 1914, turned to the king with their concerns for the national defense and royal political power. The state church was part of officialdom and as such could not organize the new working class; the same was true of its Lutheran counterparts in the other

Nordic countries and in northern Germany. The evangelical movement did organize workers, but each of the many competing denominations was too weak to organize its own labor movement after Catholic or Calvinist models. Locally, religious organizing could attain some significance,[12] and a certain evangelical labor-liberalism continued in the Liberal party until the conflicts over the ATP (General Supplementary Pensions) scheme. Ture Königsson, whose defection from the Liberal party's line decided the parliamentary majority in favor of ATP in 1958, was a religious labor-liberal.

Prior to the advent of social democracy no mass politics existed in Sweden. The SAP was Sweden's first political party in the modern sense—that is, it was something more than a club of members of the Riksdag. Thirteen years after the formation of the SAP, Sweden's second political party was created: Frisinnade Landsföreningen (National Liberal Organization). The working class and the vast majority of the population were virtually excluded from politics. In the election of 1887, at the peak of the tariff conflict, 4.9 percent of the population over twenty years of age voted.[13] In contrast to several other countries, including (to a degree) Denmark and Norway, the Swedish Social Democrats were not faced with competing political loyalties among members of the working class. The trade union movement grew simultaneously with social democracy, decisively stimulated by political agitation.

Under these political conditions Sweden underwent an industrialization that was remarkably rapid and unique in Western Europe. The number of workers employed in the mining, manufacturing, and building sectors rose by 14.8 percentage points (of total employment) between 1880 and 1910. The closest comparisons to this in Europe were Belgium with an increase of 10.2 percentage points and Germany with 6.1 from 1882 to 1907. With 24.7 percent of the total labor force employed in these sectors in 1910, Sweden placed in the bottom half of Western Europe—below Belgium, Switzerland, Great Britain (all around 45 percent), Germany (39 percent), and the Netherlands (32.8 percent)—but the social/economic dynamic generated a favorable political situation. Proletarianization meant that the relation between the company owner and family assistants on the one hand and employed workers on the other changed from 1.23:1 to 0.78:1 between 1880 and 1910.[14]

Within the framework of a given relationship between class formation and the party system, the classes' size, socioeconomic unity, and development play an important role. At the first parliamentary election with an expanded electorate in 1911, when the Social Democrats scored their first

electoral victories, social group III (basically manual workers and their families) contributed 43 percent of the votes. The SAP received 28.5 percent.
The introduction of universal suffrage did not change the social composition
of the electorate. In 1917 social-statistical group III comprised 47.6 percent
of the voters; in 1921, after the establishment of universal suffrage, the
figure was 47.9 percent. Recipients of poor relief were still denied the right
to vote, and election participation dropped heavily. Nondomestic workers
outside agriculture—in a broad sense, the most easily organized working
class—comprised one-third of the voters during the 1920s and 1930s. Social group III became a majority of the electorate only after 1928. It remained so until the modern electoral surveys during the 1950s, but social
group III's voting strength peaked in 1940, when it comprised 54.7 percent of the electorate, and the SAP and the SKP (Sveriges Kommunistiska
Parti, the Swedish Communist party) together received 57.3 percent of the
votes.[15] According to election researchers' recent surveys, the proportion of
workers among the voters remained fairly stable up to and including the
election of 1976—half or a bit more; it then dropped to 43 percent in 1985.
Industrial workers constituted at that time 18 percent of the total electorate—the same number as "middle-bracket white-collar workers."[16]

There are indications that the Swedish working class was more uniform
economically than its counterparts in other countries. An investigation
commissioned by the Swedish Metal Trades Employers Association for internal use shows, for example, that in 1930 in the Swedish manufacturing
industry the wages of unskilled workers were 81 percent of those of skilled
workers. In Germany, the comparable figure was 70 percent; in England,
65 percent; in France, 66 percent; and in Switzerland, 76 percent.[17]

Just before and during World War I the SAP caught up with its mentor
party, the German SPD, and with the Danish Social Democrats in voter
mobilization. The SAP went from 30.1 percent of the votes in the spring of
1914 to 36.4 percent in autumn 1914 and 31.1 percent in 1917, when an
even 8 percent for the Social Democratic Left party gave 39.1 percent to
both parties together. With its unbroken acceleration between 1914 and
1917, before the end of the war the Swedish labor movement had established itself as one of the strongest in the world.[18] During this time, political mobilization of the working class was more than matched by union
mobilization. In 1907 Sweden had, together with Denmark, the most comprehensive trade union organization in the world. Failure in the general
strike in 1909 sank the Swedish trade union movement under the Danish,
Australian, German, and English levels. However, membership rapidly be-

gan to recover, and the LO (the Swedish Trade Union Confederation) regained its 1907 figures in 1917.[19]

Two labor parties on the periphery of industrial capitalism progressed faster than the SAP during their foundation periods: the Australian Labour party and the Finnish Social Democrats. Both countries had half-colonial status and lacked dominant internal political authorities and an entrenched upper class. However, neither in Australia nor in Finland could the early successes of the labor movement be preserved and consolidated. In both cases the reasons have to do with international and interstate conflicts and their domestic political effects—or, putting it another way, with the international overdetermination of the class struggle and class mobilization.[20]

In 1917 the SAP became Sweden's largest political party. In parliamentary elections after the advent of universal suffrage in 1921 to 1928, the SAP and the other labor parties received an average of 44.5 percent of the votes. Only the Australian results are comparable (44.6 percent). In other countries the labor movement achieved at best 40.2 percent (in Austria).[21] During the 1920s the SAP alone received 37.8 percent, a figure exceeded only by Labour in Australia and the Social Democrats in Austria. In contrast to the latter, the SAP did not confront an equally strong or larger bourgeois party. Even in the right wing's best and the left wing's worst election in 1928, the SAP was 7.6 percentage points ahead of the largest bourgeois party, the Conservatives.

The organizing efforts of Swedish trade unions went steadily forward during the 1920s. This progress from the initial postwar enthusiasm was unparalleled internationally; by 1930 Swedish union organization was matched only by Australia and Denmark.[22] By the 1930s the Swedish working class became what it has remained: the world's most unionized.[23]

The Middle-Class Alternatives

Several sister parties have sometimes been more successful outside the working class than the SAP—for example, the Norwegian Labor party with white-collar workers (up to the mid-1960s), farmers, and fishermen.[24] When it was about the same size as the SAP, the West German Social Democratic party attracted more support from both the white-collar and private business sectors in elections to the federal parliament from 1969 to 1980.[25] From 1982 to 1985 workers (including pensioners and non-wage-earning family members) comprised about 60 percent of the SAP's electorate, whereas workers comprised only about 50 percent of the Austrian Social Democratic voters from 1976 to 1983.[26]

Little attention has been paid to the SAP's relative limitations outside the working class, and a concrete explanation is not easy to find. The SAP has never been a socially isolated labor party, and its limitations do not seemingly correspond very well with the remarkably high degree of union organization among Swedish white-collar workers, nor with the important role that Social Democratic cadres have played and still play within the salaried employees movement, from Sigfrid Hansson, Harald Adamsson, and Valter Åman to Lennart Bodström and Björn Rosengren. One reasonable explanation could lie in the following composite hypothesis. First, class theory makes it reasonable to assume with Adam Przeworski and John Sprague (see note 1) that class organization and class politics have a price, that there is a "trade-off" between support from the working class and support from the middle class and the petite bourgeoisie. In other words, politics that win support from one class do so at the expense of diminished or static support from the others. And this is because classes, in addition to a certain amount of common concerns, have different interests and social perspectives. Despite its strategic and tactical openness, the SAP has been clearly stamped as a labor party, a label reinforced by its ties with the LO, the Swedish confederation of trade unions, and collective affiliation. In 1956 workers (and their families) comprised 75 percent of SAP voters.[27]

Second, social integration among the large classes, the Swedish tradition of the people standing together against the powers-that-be, can be expressed politically in ways other than through voting for the SAP. The most accessible alternative has been the development of and support for analogous social democratic policies in other parties. The Agrarian party/Centre party, the Liberal party, and sometimes even the Conservatives should be viewed in this perspective—as social reform parties.

Third, the Swedish party system has provided the progressive middle class with a close alternative to social democracy. In Germany and Austria liberalism has always been weak. The same has not been true of Norway, but after liberation from Sweden, the Norwegian *Venstre* (Left) fell apart and became increasingly a marginal liberal phenomenon. The same development was also occurring in Sweden when the Liberals split on the question of prohibition. However, with the liberal reunification in the Folkpartiet (the Liberal party) in 1934 liberalism renewed its influence on Swedish politics, even if party leader Bertil Ohlin never succeeded in becoming prime minister. By 1956 Folkpartiet had become the main white-collar workers' party (40 percent of its support; the SAP had 26 percent).[28] The transformation of the Agrarian party into a radical popular movement during the 1930s, with the farmers union organization (RLF) and its youth organization (SLU) in the vanguard, limited the SAP's appeal in rural areas. The Norwegian Agrarian party remained more of a *kulak* (propertied farmers) party.[29]

The strong class character of Swedish politics should lead us to expect political changes from the deindustrialization of Sweden after 1965. Between then and 1985 industrial employment fell in absolute terms by 18.9 percent, a decline only exceeded by Belgium, Britain, and Holland. So far the expected political effects have hardly materialized, no doubt due to the existence in Sweden of (by and large) maintained full employment and a high proportion of public sector jobs. But in the longer run, increasing strain on traditional SAP organization and on stable class cleavages is to be expected.

The Meaning of Class: Popular Movements and the Political Agenda

The nature of class politics in Sweden and in Scandinavia in general is quite special and is most simply summarized in terms of a popular movement. The labor movement did not arrive by itself in Sweden (and Scandinavia); it arose unplanned as a part of a whole wave of new popular movements. Aside from the labor movement the most important were the evangelical and the temperance movements. In 1878 what quickly became the largest evangelical organization, the Mission Covenant church, was founded, and the following year the temperance movement, IOGT (the International Order of Good Templars), was imported from the United States. In 1881 August Palm arrived from Denmark, and in 1883 the other large temperance organization was created, the Swedish Blue Ribbon Association. The temperance movement was in the middle of the popular movement spectrum: its activists came from evangelical organizations, and it supplied the labor movement with many union cadres and members of the Riksdag. Up until World War I, it was also the largest popular movement. The links between the popular movements were sometimes strikingly direct and short. IOGT was introduced into Sweden by the former Baptist preacher Olof Bergström.[30] The labor movement's most outstanding figure, Metal Workers chair Ernst Blomberg, was a Good Templar like many other local initiators and organizers in the iron and metal industries.[31] Of the members of the Second Chamber of the Riksdag elected in 1911 and 1917, 64 percent were members of the Temperance Society; in 1949 the figure was still high—41 percent. Among Social Democratic members of the Riksdag, organized teetotalers dominated in numbers. Between 1911 and 1920 the proportion never dropped below 84 percent, and in the left-wing Social Democratic group in 1917 all were teetotalers.[32] These figures must be seen in light of the fact that, at its peak in 1910, the temperance movement encompassed about one-tenth of the total adult population.[33]

Popular movements embrace a number of common features that have strongly colored Swedish politics in general and popular class politics in particular. All popular movements have endeavored to awaken, organize, educate, and transform people and to change their lives and living conditions. "Movement" in this connection takes on a special meaning: a collective, tightly woven *organization*. Another aspect of popular movements has involved self-organized, collective educational activities in the form of study circles, which originated among Good Templars in Skåne but spread throughout other movements as well. ABF (Arbetarnas Bildningsförbund, the Workers Educational Association) soon became the foremost example of these educational circles. This popular movement tradition tends to give to politics a reformatory, educational orientation and a collective organizational form. It also couples class and popularism in a way that gives both a good deal of latitude.

Traditions can have an explanatory function only to the extent that they are reproduced. The Swedish popular movement tradition received the necessary reinforcements during the 1930s. The farmers and their youth groups created their own popular movement, and the LO expanded enormously. The unionizing of the white-collar segment began during a period of Social Democratic power and was influenced by the workers' trade union movement. Key white-collar organizers included prominent Social Democrats Sigfrid Hansson and Valter Åman.

Particularly noteworthy and politically important was the mass organization of the youth of the popular classes. After its formation in 1917 the SSU (Social Democratic Youth organization) rapidly increased its membership, even though its initial numbers were low. In 1925 the SSU had 21,000 members; in 1928, 42,000; in 1931, 64,000; and in 1934, 100,000, at which it remained until its undramatic decline began around 1950.[34] At the same time, the farmers' youth organization, SLU, grew from 20,000 in 1930, 60,000 in 1934, 87,000 in 1939, and 97,000 in 1942 to 115,000 in 1949.[35]

By international standards, the Swedish political organizing of youth groups was unparalleled. At its best, the Austrian Socialist Youth organized 38,000 members (1923).[36] The Norwegian AUF reached a peak of 33,000 members in 1938,[37] which, translated into Swedish population figures, would be about 70,000, a fair bit under the SSU's maximum of 106,000 in 1937. (Immediately after the war in 1946, the AUF temporarily exceeded the SSU with 52,000 members—translated into Swedish terms, about 110,000.)[38] The Danish Social Democratic youth association membership never exceeded 27,000 (1937), which in Sweden would correspond to 45,000. Denmark's SLU, Venstres Ungdom, numbered 45,000. In Finland the Social Democrats were loosely organized, and their youth organization had only 5,000 to 6,000 members in the 1930s, or 9,000 to 10,000 in terms of Swedish population size. The Finnish farmers' youth organization was, however, somewhat larger than the SLU in relative figures, but Finland was much more agrarian than Sweden.[39]

The vigor and longevity of popular movement traditions in Sweden are grounded in the combination of two conditions. Popular movements are first and foremost a rural phenomenon, markedly weaker in larger cities.[40] During the 1930s SSU membership had a borderline in towns with twenty thousand inhabitants; above that, membership density was just over one-third of the national average.[41] Rural areas were large in Sweden: the rural population first became less than half of the entire population between 1930 and 1935. Between 1945 and 1950 the populations of administrative urban areas became larger than those of rural districts, but the city population did not reach over half of the national population until 1957.[42]

Thus popular movements can be viewed partly as an expression of Sweden's very late and protracted urbanization and partly as a modernized continuation of the time-honored independence and self-organization of the Swedish countryside, previously expressed in "the estimable agrarian estate" (of propertied farmers) with its village communities, parish representatives, churchwardens, jurymen, and members of the Riksdag.

The Social Democratic labor movement soon moved into the center of the field of popular movements. In 1911, when the temperance movement was at its zenith, the Social Democrats were its strongest representatives in the Riksdag.[43] After the "democratic breakthrough" at the end of 1918 the Liberals, who were the other classic popular movement party, suffered setbacks and party splits. The "*frisinnade*," who represented the popular wing of liberalism, carried only 9.8 percent of the votes in the 1932 parliamentary elections. After 1930 the evangelical religious movement began to fade, having stagnated during the 1920s,[44] while the labor movement grew rapidly, along with the new agrarian movement.

The tradition of popular movements connects class politics—and thereby social democracy—with roots that go deep into the history of the Swedish people. This tradition suffuses the typical features of Swedish class politics: little spontaneity or militancy in word and action, but competent organization, thorough preparation, caution, willingness to negotiate, stubbornness, and perseverance.

Class politics also involves a particular *political agenda*, one occupied with economic and sociopolitical questions concerning production, distribution, and power. For a labor party, such an agenda is of course a great advantage. Party members have gathered around precisely such questions in which, moreover, the working class and more or less closely associated social strata can make their numbers felt in democratic social systems. Despite both real and potential conflicts over compromise or struggle, reform or revolution, class politics have had a unifying, adhesive, and strengthening effect on the working class and on the labor movement. Other types of agendas have had another dynamic. Foreign and defense policies stopped the two first labor governments in the world, the Australian and the Finnish. Differing views of defense and the world situation divided Swedish Social Democrats in 1916 and 1917[45]—and finished off the Second International. Nuclear energy issues caused the Swedish Social Democrats to forfeit the elections of 1976 and 1979. Because of Sweden's geopolitical situation, with Finland as a buffer against the east and Denmark and Norway against the south and west, and because of the disarming of religious issues between an increasingly empty state church and a fragmented and early-waning evangelical movement, it has been difficult for political questions other than those having to do with class to occupy the center stage of politics.

LEADERSHIP AND PARTY POLITICS

We have now placed the SAP in the international party history of democracy and in modern Swedish class history from a comparative perspective, and have thereby taken a measure of the party's parliamentary power and basic preconditions. We have identified the prerequisites and contexts for the party's power and influence. However, prerequisites and possibilities can be bungled, utilized well or badly. Positions once achieved can be lost. In other words, we must also look at how the party and its leadership have *acted*—what choices they have made between different alternatives.

In this context power and influence are not meant to be seen in any

programmatic sense and therefore are not evaluated from any ideological,
point of departure. Power and influence refer exclusively to the SAP's actual power in government and in the Riksdag. In addition to its practical
manageability, this analytical limitation has the advantage of being somewhat uncommon in what are most often ideologically impregnated discussions of Swedish Social Democracy. My attempts to evaluate the
significance of social democracy for Swedish social development appear
elsewhere.[46]

In the history of the SAP we can distinguish five characteristic and vitally
important courses of action taken in order to win and retain power as a
labor party functioning within a democratic framework. The following examples indicate how they were used in important historical situations.

The Two Doors: Initiatives Toward Accord/Accommodation with the Right and the Left

In comparison with costly, short-term revolutionary assessments in other
social democracies at the time, from Norway to Holland and Switzerland,
the Swedish Social Democrats' actions at the end of World War I appear
very constructive for the creation of a parliamentary position of power.
From the vantage point of the experiences of the 1980s, the SAP's actions
from 1917 to 1920 seem to reveal the first important expression of a central
element in Swedish Social Democratic power politics. We can call it ac-
cord/accommodation initiatives, or open-door politics; its opposite is the
politics of isolation or polarization. However, it is important not to confuse
accord initiatives with compromise politics or accord per se. What I refer to
here is a strategy or tactic that is not static and above all not oriented
toward creating agreement between existing views, but toward pursuing
goals in such a way that it is possible for others to accept them and cooperate or join in with them.

In the spring of 1917 and late autumn of 1918 revolutionary feelings
pervaded a significant portion of the Swedish working class and the nation's
soldiers. The ruling powers were alarmed and prepared for revolution.
Considering the failures of revolutions everywhere in 1918 and 1919 (except in Russia), a successful revolution in Sweden was unlikely in retrospect. However, this was difficult to presume in May and June 1917 or in
November and December 1918. Even today it is risky to speculate whether
the SAP could have utilized the situation to make more extensive reforms
than it did, but it is reasonable to claim that, in terms of the party's subsequent parliamentary power, the SAP and LO leadership acted optimally.

The party and LO leadership did not go against the waves of demonstrations and actions but instead became engaged in order to channel them in nonrevolutionary directions. In this way pressure on the undemocratic Right was maintained and sharp demands for immediate democratization were made both in the spring of 1917 and in the autumn of 1918. Party leader Hjalmar Branting and the LO leadership saw to it that neither ultimatums nor any immediate social and economic demands were made, although Per Albin Hansson and most of the younger leaders wished to be tougher. Demands were confined to immediate parliamentary democracy, to be obtained under constitutional forms.

The revolutionary zeal of the spring of 1917 ebbed, and the right-wing Swartz government remained in power until the election in the following autumn when a Liberal–Social Democratic government was formed. However, the right-wing opposition in the First Chamber continued to block democratization in constitutional forms. Only after the revolution in Berlin and under intensive pressure from all sides did the right wing give up, one week before Christmas in 1918. Under revolutionary pressure but without a revolution, and according to the old predemocratic constitution's own dictates, Sweden became democratic. The archbishop and the powerful banker Marcus Wallenberg (the elder) were engaged in the final phase of the process. Social Democrats were the driving force, but in the end nearly all were involved—except property owners and the academic right wing.[47]

An effect of this cooperation was that the SAP rapidly and painlessly became accepted as a legitimate and ordinary government party by the bourgeois majority. This enabled the party to exploit its position as the largest party in the Riksdag. In March 1920 the first purely Social Democratic government took office, with a certain amount of dread discernable in right-wing and royal circles. After the election of 1932 it was parliamentarily obvious, albeit not necessary since the majority was still bourgeois, for the old Conservative leaders, Lindman and Trygger, to instruct the king to appoint a Social Democratic government.[48]

It should be noted that the door was also held open for the Left during the political crises of 1917 and 1918 despite the split in the party in early spring 1917 with the formation of the Social Democratic Left party. This was equally advantageous to the left-wing party and the SAP. Both in June 1917 and in November 1918 revolutionary slogans were issued appealing to the left to cooperate with the SAP and LO leadership.[49] This gesture derived not only from a realistic insight into relative strength; a similar realism and preparedness to cooperate on the part of the left should also be seen in light of the fact that the party split was not due to SAP actions (the SAP and Sweden were neutral in the war) but rather to differing assessments—of the war, of the risk of prowar activism in Sweden, and of the consequences of the war for Swedish domestic politics. Contacts with the left were kept open: with the formation in 1917 of the Workers Committee, SAP leaders personally and directly engaged themselves in the revolutionary currents through participating in the debate on revolution at mass meetings in Folkets Hus (the People's [Community] Hall) and elsewhere, and they did not associate with the powers-that-be. The Social Democratic minority government of 1920 also underlined a willingness to cooperate with the left. Someone who was found guilty of lèse-majesté was given amnesty, as were left-wing socialists sentenced to prison for defamation of the "White" Finnish regent, Mannerheim. Sweden was probably the first country in Europe to establish trade relations with the Soviet Union—in May 1920.[50] Previous electoral cooperation with the Liberals—in a party cartel—was replaced from the 1921 election onwards by cooperation with left-wing socialists and communists.

Although the SAP and the left could not be encompassed in the same party, the SAP obtained almost the best possible left-wing opposition, plus the organized collective return of left-wing socialists and ex-communists in 1923, 1925, and 1937—an inimitable series of events in the history of the labor movement. Even the Nazi-tainted Nils Flyg sent out feelers in May 1940 about returning to the party, but he was rejected.[51]

During the 1930s the tone toward the left became more caustic. The internationally nonaligned "Kilbom" communist faction was reckoned the most dangerous opposition.[52] In 1936 the SAP called a halt to cooperation with the left. Democratic cooperation, implicitly with the Agrarian Party and the liberal *frisinnade*, was a main theme in Per Albin Hansson's agitation. Even more than *folkhemmet* (the idea of the nation embodying the attributes of a "home" for its citizens), national democratic cooperation, to which even the right wing was invited in the 1938 election campaign, was Hansson's slogan after 1933. Typical is the following, from the election campaign of 1934: "We meet the right-wing call for splitting the nation with a call for cooperation among all democratic forces. While the Right and the Bolsheviks speculate in differences, we concentrate on the commonly shared and unifying."[53] The slogan became even more convincing when it was put into action after the election victory in 1936—in the coalition offer to the Agrarian party and in the conciliatory tone directed toward the right wing in 1938.

However, the older generation of Social Democrats did not block openings in either direction. At a party executive meeting after the election of 1944 Hansson said that "cooperation can be sought from both the left and the right. It is a matter of keeping all possibilities open."[54] For the younger generation of Social Democrats, who to a great extent had won their political spurs in the struggle against the communists, such openness was unthinkable.[55] The cold war and the SKP's defense of the Stalinization of Eastern Europe rendered Per Albin Hansson's sentiments unviable for the succeeding generation. Cooperation was sought and reestablished with the Agrarian party. Hansson's views made their way into the changes and the reevaluations of the late 1960s.

The both-doors-open policy likewise characterized SAP actions during the 1970s and 1980s. With the support of the VPK (Left Party Communists), majorities were created for Social Democratic rule in the Riksdag and on county and municipal councils. Agreements with the VPK have been reached over particular issues, but more often they have been subordinated to efforts at cooperation with one or more of the bourgeois parties.

Initiatives for accord/accommodation should not be seen as expressions of general good will. Rather, they should be interpreted as expressing a special philosophy of and strategy for power. The conclusion of the postelection discussion in the party executive in 1936 summarizes the issue: "*P.A. Hansson:* . . . Personally I am of course interested in having a government with the broadest possible base, but without significant concessions on our part. *Wigforss:* None at all!"[56]

Class Politics and LO Politics

The policies of the first Social Democratic governments contained an element of class politics in principle. After having failed in an attempt to mediate a conflict in the building industry, Branting's government made a remarkable intervention in the autumn of 1920 in support of the workers. The SAF's (Swedish Employers Confederation's) blockade of cement to non-SAF building companies was lifted by the government through the application of the Right of Disposal law.[57] The government got away with this. The two following Social Democratic governments fell because of conflicts between the labor movement and the bourgeois parties concerning the Unemployment Commission's actions during partial disputes on the labor market. Most memorable was the third SAP government going to battle in 1926 over an appeal against the commission's decision to send unemployed workers to the Stripa Mine as strikebreakers. The appeal was lodged by the Swedish Communist party and the SAC (Syndicalists). The government interpreted the issue as a fundamental class question and resigned when its support of the appeal was sharply reproved by a parliamentary majority.[58]

Postwar interpretations—basically in terms of the history of ideas—have often overlooked that what was decisive in 1932 and 1933 was not Keynesian expansion versus deflation; that is, public work for the unemployed versus state passivity, deficit financing versus a balanced budget, etc. Rather, the political disputes and settlements of 1933 concerned the extent of protection measures for agriculture and wages for public employees; that is, concrete class issues regarding workers and farmers.[59] Unmediated class politics is hardly to be found in the center of Social Democratic actions after 1933. This should not be taken to mean that the party and its leaders and ministers have relinquished the party's labor or workers party features; but it does mean that class interests are understood in terms filtered through the Federation of Trade Unions, the LO.

Class politics becomes LO politics. They need not stand in opposition to each other, and normally they do not. However, when they do, wage-earner interests not conveyed through organizations take second place. In a discussion in the party executive in 1951 concerning a Coercion Act to halt a labor conflict among nurses (organized outside the LO), the veteran Rickard Sandler stated that "now we have heard through [the health care politician] Torsten Andrée, primarily the employer's views. Would it not be possible also to hear the other side? I hope we shall never be forced to adopt the proposed law."[60] In the official instructions for interpretation of the 1970s legislation on employment protection and on codetermination, the employer was given the expressed right to dismiss employees who participate in a wildcat strike.[61] The class politics mediated by the LO has had a much greater influence on social democracy after the war than before, at least until the introduction of the Wage-Earners' Funds at the beginning of the 1980s.

Socially and politically the LO is unique: socially in its extent in terms of class—69 percent of the working class in 1945, 76 percent in 1950, and 89 percent in 1975;[62] politically in its monolithic Social Democratic cadres—of 317 FCO (local Trades Council) chairs, 311 were Social Democrats in 1958 (there were two communists and four independents). Of executive members in trade unions with over three hundred members, 96 percent in the Metal Workers union were Social Democrats; in Engineering, 92.1 percent; in Municipal, 89.2 percent; in Building, 82.2 percent.[63] Since 1958 the Social Democratic hold on the LO has increased further: for instance, there seems not to have been any VPK delegates to LO congresses during the 1980s.[64]

The infusion of class in the Swedish political system is expressed and reproduced in the initially direct and subsequently LO-mediated class policy conducted by the SAP. The LO showed itself to be more than an interest organization in the 1938 Main Agreement at Saltsjöbaden (the seaside resort near Stockholm, where some of the negotiations were held).[65] At the extra SAP conference in 1967 LO chair Arne Geijer remarked that the LO had a class perspective: "You say that we have begun to get away from class divisions. We have not—we have just as much of a working class as we had before."[66]

In the class politics pursued by the LO lies an important explanation for why the SAP was able to retain government power for such a long time. The party was never given an opportunity to become self-satisfied and conservative. As indicated by Table 2, Social Democratic citizens were more critical of Swedish society after thirty-seven years of more or less unbroken Social Democratic government than they were after sixteen years.

Tactics

The way that the Social Democrats handled bourgeois confusion and their own uncertainty in 1932 and 1933 was tactically masterful. At the discussions in the party executive on 21 September, after a victorious election (which, however, retained a bourgeois majority), the situation was as follows. The SAP's immediate demand was the disbanding of the Unemployment Commission and its replacement with public relief works in accord with market conditions, and the introduction of unemployment insurance. The election results were interpreted as a victory for free trade and gradual

Table 2. Swedish Citizens' Views of Society, 1948 and 1969. (Replies to question: Do you think that Sweden can be described as a class society?)

	Total		Social Democrats	
	1948	1969	1948	1969
Yes	52%	64%	56%	72%
No	32	28	33	21
Undecided	14	7	12	7

Source: SIFO (Swedish Institute of Public Opinion Research), Indikator, August 1969.

elimination of agricultural regulation. The SAP would seek cooperation with the liberal *frisinnade*, and if this proved impossible one leading Social Democrat, Per Edvin Sköld, advised the party to refuse to form a government. Gustav Möller suggested also approaching the Liberals, the only pure pre-Keynesian, economically liberal party in the country. The proposed finance minister, Ernst Wigforss, warned against concessions to the *frisinnade*, but in the executive and election committee he also stressed the need for budget economies. No one except the second-rank politician Henning Leo (and then only in passing) mentioned the Agrarian Party at all.[67]

In fact, virtually everything went against the party leaders' notions in September 1932. The Unemployment Commission remained; a proper unemployment insurance system was postponed. No agreement was reached either with the *frisinnade* or with the Liberals. Protectionism and agricultural controls were expanded. The Agrarian party became the SAP's political partner—on the latter's initiative—and Ernst Wigforss went down in history not as the retrenchment minister but as the first Keynesian.

Yet it would be wrong to say that events "went" counter to what the SAP had concretely planned. The tactical skills of Hansson and Social Democratic leaders lay in their ability to improvise these results, which, even though they departed drastically from party intentions and the party program in the short term, had the crucial advantage of giving the party power in the Riksdag. SAP tactics were developed in and through three different kinds of negotiation with the bourgeois parties conducted simultaneously by the SAP government during the winter and spring of 1933: an official and public discussion to underline the seriousness of the times and its own willingness to cooperate; an informal but also public debate to divide the right-wing opposition; and a series of secret negotiations with individual Agrarian party members through which an agreement was chalked out.[68]

By 1956 relations with the Agrarian party, revitalized in 1951, began to wane. In the directly elected Second Chamber sat a 119-to-112 bourgeois majority, which, however, could be balanced by a 82-to-68 labor majority in the First Chamber. Many coalition party members were tired of each other. The Conservatives and Folkpartiet (Liberal party) did not lie far below the Social Democrats—40.9 percent against the SAP's 44.6 percent in 1956. It was the great political battle of the 1950s concerning the statutory national supplementary pensions scheme, ATP (Allmänna Tjänstepensionen), that would give the Social Democrats a second wind and two more decades in power. ATP was not an easy issue to get through, but the Social

Democrats succeeded by means of a new show of tactics in the grand style, and this time well planned.

Of all the parties, the Agrarian party was least interested in ATP, even though its leader, Gunnar Hedlund, was initially prepared to accept the proposal.[69] Communist support was deemed somewhat tainted and, in any case, would not be sufficient considering power relations in 1956. The bourgeois opposition wanted the question to be put as a referendum, and a proposed constitutional change from 1954 (awaiting final action in the Riksdag after a new election) gave one-third of the Riksdag the right to demand a referendum. The LO thought it unacceptable that social groups already having supplementary pensions should be included in deciding on a general supplementary pension. Tage Erlander and his government felt pressed between already-made constitutional concessions and the LO's unreserved class interests.

The first and most important single move in this situation came when Tage Erlander and Gunnar Hedlund realized that, despite their parties' diametrically opposite views on the ATP question, they shared a common tactical interest, namely to outmaneuver the Conservatives and the Liberals. Hedlund and the Agrarian party leadership wanted to re-form their party into the Center party, and to do this they needed to expand at the expense of both Conservatives and Liberals. Tage Erlander wanted to retain power and carry out ATP; consequently, after the election in 1956, and against considerable resistance, he argued for maintaining the coalition with the Agrarian party a while longer. He wished to prevent a referendum at the behest of a minority, as would be required by the pending constitutional change that the SAP on its own would have difficulties blocking. However, the Agrarian party and the SAP together could call for the referendum to be taken according to the old regulations, which stated that the government determines how the issues should be formulated. On 12 October 1956 Tage Erlander convinced the party executive to agree to continued coalition with the argument that "we cannot postpone the constitutional proposal on a consultative referendum and therefore I daresay that without a coalition government there will be no supplementary pension."

One major point about the partnership with the Agrarian party in the ATP proposition was that there would be three alternatives instead of two. Great care was taken with their formulation. A secret poll taken in Stockholm indicated that if the SAP and LO line was presented as "obligatory" it would fail, but that it would succeed if put in terms of a "legal right," which indeed became the official formulation.[70] The opposition's formulation of its own proposal was largely rejected: words such as "citizen," "stable value," "optional," and "contract" were found unacceptable. Despite Hedlund's protests, however, the opposition was allowed to use the word "voluntary."[71]

How important this vigilance was is difficult to say—presumably not very in regard to the opposition's proposal. Opinion formation remained free: the only thing the government could determine was what would be on the ballots. However, the censoring demonstrated a high degree of tactical awareness: no word was left to chance.

Hedlund and the Agrarian party won the referendum in 1957. Everyone else lost, the Conservatives and Liberals a bit more than the SAP and the Swedish Communist party. In the parliamentary election in 1956, the "Line 1" parties (the SAP and the communist SKP) received 49.6 percent; in 1957 "Line 1" received 45.8 percent. The "Line 2" party, the Agrarian party, had received 9.4 percent in 1956, while its dismissive pension alternative received 15 percent the following year. "Line 3" received 35.3 percent in 1957—5.6 percent points fewer than the Conservative and Liberal total in 1956. (The rest were blank votes.) The Social Democrats had better results in the extra parliamentary election in 1958. The SKP did not participate in all election districts, and the SAP and the SKP together received exactly the same percentage of votes as they did in 1956. The Center party received more votes than its predecessor, the Agrarian party, and the Conservatives and Liberals received only 37.7 percent.

Writing three alternatives into the referendum was tactically ingenious. The Social Democratic line had not failed to win the majority—it was the largest. The only party apart from the SAP and the SKP that had a positive interest in settling the issue of supplementary pensions was the leading but now weakened opposition party, Folkpartiet (the Liberal party). As leader of the opposition it was difficult for Ohlin by himself to reach a settlement with the SAP, but at the same time he was being pressured by left-wing Liberals. After the referendum, the newspaper *Dagens Nyheter* pressed for a settlement with the Social Democrats.[72] In the spring of 1959 ATP got through the Riksdag because the evangelical labor-liberal, Ture Königsson, declined to vote against it.

Thus ATP was secured—but not the expansion of the Swedish welfare state. The election in 1960 was the most polarized of the postwar period—indeed, since the "Cossack" election of 1928. Against the labor movement stood three bourgeois parties, all of which wanted to block social expansion. It should also be recalled that by international standards Sweden was a rather average welfare state in 1960.[73] One of the decisive factors leading to further social expansion was another sophisticated tactical maneuver. In the Social Democratic pension proposal, union organizations had been given the right to remain outside the ATP system if they could negotiate equivalent pensions. As the prominent Social Democrat and TCO (Swedish Confederation of Professional Employees) chair Valter Åman expressed it at a party executive meeting on 2 October 1958: "The majority in TCO are against it being obligatory, so it is a matter of softening up the majority." Torsten Nilsson, minister of social affairs and architect of the final pension scheme, knew what the controversy was about: "I would call it a smoke-screen, all this about withdrawal rights, but you don't spread that about."[74]

Nilsson had done his job well. In the spring of 1960 the SIF (Swedish Industrial Salaried Employees Association) and the SAF (Swedish Employers Confederation) negotiated a supplementary pensions agreement. At the time the SIF had a bourgeois leadership, and it may be presumed that both SIF and SAF were anxious to find a solution outside the system. However, this proved impossible. The SIF joined the ATP system, and previous pension benefits were replaced by a 15 percent pay advance.[75] The "Line 3" argument that ATP would mean significantly reduced real wages was devastated. SAP support rose to 47.8 percent in the election, the highest figure since 1950 and its best parliamentary election since 1940. Erlander later referred to the 1960 election as an "ideological break-through."[76] This breakthrough, which paved the way for enormous social expansion, can also be seen as the triumph of Social Democratic tactics.

Olof Palme's disarming of the nuclear power issue through a referendum with three alternatives also had a tinge of Per Albin Hansson's and Tage Erlander's tactical genius. Palme's referendum erased a new across-the-board issue from the agenda so that the election in 1982 could be won on classic Social Democratic issues. The three alternatives were important in order to avoid associating the Social Democrats with the Conservatives.

Competent Engagement

The SAP established its power in the 1930s with simple, immediate socio-economic reforms, public relief work not below the lowest laborer wages, and a raised basic pension, albeit one not sufficient to live on.[77] Concerns of the time were indicated in the title of the SAP's comprehensive economic motion in 1932, *Crisis Aid for Workers and Farmers*. After World War II, party leaders would look nostalgically back on that time and its issues. From 1945 until the second half of the 1960s at least, leading Social Democrats sometimes sighed over Tage Erlander's comments in 1952: "We now meet . . . no opposition as regards social reforms. . . . We must reckon that in any case Folkpartiet will try on all occasions to offer more than the government."[78] In the party executive on 17 September 1964, Sten Andersson pointed out that "what is difficult is that in all issues the opposition tries to get as close to Social Democracy as possible." While this sheds a light on the history of Swedish social policy that is hardly in accord with the official chronicles, there are two aspects of political power here that warrant attention.

The first is that, historically, Social Democratic power has been bound up with the pursuit of full employment and social security. For Social Democratic leaders this historical parallel has been a tactical resource and an inherited obligation. After the 1966 election failures Erlander made the following comment at a party executive meeting on 1 October: "The most dangerous statement made about us during the whole election campaign was Hedlund's . . . that one did not recognize the Social Democrats. . . . We must form policies and propaganda in such a way that the voters recognize us as bearers of tried and true welfare policies in different forms than before in [our present] changing society." "Work, security, development" became the slogan of the extra party conference, and labor market policies expanded greatly.[79] The election campaign of 1982 was conducted along the same lines, with four pledges: to reestablish the constant value of pensions, abolish waiting days for benefits (benefit restrictions), halt the decline of unemployment insurance, and stop the reduction of state contributions toward local authority child care.[80]

In contrast to several sister parties, the social engagement of the Swedish Social Democrats has never been viewed as well-meaning incompetence. On the contrary, among the economic bourgeoisie the SAP as a rule has enjoyed considerable respect due to its economic expertise and competence. One hundred and fifty "stock market experts" selected SAP finance minister Kjell-Olof Feldt in September 1987 as by far the best conceivable finance minister and cabinet minister. Ingvar Carlsson came second in the prime minister class (after the Liberal party leader). In February 1988, thirty-nine out of one hundred corporate business leaders deemed a Social Democratic government better for the economy than a bourgeois one, even if only eighteen personally preferred a Social Democratic cabinet.[81] In the autumn of 1932 the SAF publication *Industria* had stated that "the new government's vitality is its most prominent feature. Indeed, to an extent this forward spirit overrides intelligence in some of the new men, but the measure of intellectual talent is still on average significant. . . . "[82]

A bourgeois embrace can arouse suspicions in the eyes of the working class. However, it is striking that Swedish Social Democracy's three great classic finance ministers, Ernst Wigforss, Per Edvin Sköld, and Gunnar Sträng, were all economic autodidacts, technically sophisticated as well as deeply rooted in the labor movement. More than respectability on grounds of bourgeois or technocratic kinship, this indicates the ability of popular movement education to safeguard and develop talent. Gunnar Sträng's successor, Kjell Olof-Feldt (who resigned from the cabinet in early 1990), has another background and would have needed a little more time to be able to develop the authority of his predecessors. However, the tradition was carried on in that Feldt was at once one of the party's most controversial figures internally and one of its most popular politicians, externally as well as internally.

In short, Social Democratic power has been maintained historically through demonstrated social-political *and* expert economic knowledge.

Organization

The organization of the SAP is dealt with in another chapter of this book, but the enormous importance of the organization as an instrument of political power must be mentioned here. If the organization's unity, extent, and dynamic are preserved or expanded, then the party may be able to withstand changes in class structure that would otherwise threaten to undermine the party's position. The parties of the new Right (whether they be the so-called Progress parties in Denmark and Norway, Thatcherism in England, or the Reagan revolution in the United States) have achieved their successes from a bourgeois platform, winning over sections of the working class that the old classical Right could never reach.

After the Austrian party, which in 1980 had about 720,000 individual members,[83] the SAP—with 1,207,000 collective and individual members as of 31 December 1986, according to the latest accessible annual report— was the strongest Social Democratic party organization in the world, in relation to the size of the population. As far as is known, only the SAP has continually increased its membership up to the beginning of the 1980s. The Danish and Norwegian parties (the latter also having a Swedish type of collective membership) began to backslide in the early 1950s, and the Austrian party has been stagnating since 1960 with a certain amount of ups and downs.[84]

Since the difficult depression from 1920 to 1922 (with mass unemployment and consequently diminished collective membership), the SAP's membership figures have diminished only in 1946, 1957, 1965, 1968, 1970, 1981, 1984, and 1985, until the late 1980s.[85] Figures dropped slightly in 1946 because of the Communist success in the unions. Reductions in 1957 were probably a symptom of stagnation, which was counteracted by the ATP mobilization. The 1960s was a decade of organizational crisis, but also the period when Social Democratic organizational development in Sweden, in contrast to other countries, made a turnabout and shot ahead again. The Social Democratic youth organization, SSU, reached its nadir in 1962 and has since maintained its late-1950s level. There is no reliable information available on the division between single and collective members, but individual membership should lie between 25 and 30 percent, or around 300,000 to 350,000. From a membership survey taken for the 1968 party conference, we know that the party had 210,000 individual members in 1948, 219,000 in 1957, and 223,000 in 1967. At the same time the total party membership increased from 638,000 to 891,000.[86] The brunt of the party's organizational muscle comes from its grip on the LO, but since the 1960s there have been important economic contributions from the taxpayers through the party subsidies.

The organizational crisis in the 1960s was largely overcome by reactivating the party internally, a process in which the party secretary, Sten Andersson, must have played a major role. Extensive consultative deliberations with party members and even nonmembers began in 1965. Party conferences were given greater weight.[87] The radicalization of the LO and the growth of a young revolutionary opposition, also in large industrial workplaces, stimulated the SAP into strengthening its workplace organizing. First of May demonstrations, a tradition of the Swedish labor movement, were expanded. One of the best indicators of how the SAP's mobilizing abilities were developed over the years is the sale of First of May badges, a symbol of party identification and personal support of the labor movement. Figures for this are available from the 1920s onward, and they are most likely more reliable than assessments of the number of participants in demonstrations (the absolute figures should not be taken too seriously: the badges are bought for many different reasons).

As shown in Table 3, the protracted decade of the 1940s—from 1938 to 1950—constitutes the zenith of party mobilization, followed by the period between 1978 and 1983.

Development in the mid-1980s indicated a certain organizational decline. Party membership at the turn of the year 1987–1988 (1,164,000) lay below that of 1979–1980. Sales of First of May badges dropped in the

Table 3.   SAP Sales of First of May Badges, 1927–1988. (In thousands)

1927	151	1955–60	300	1982	446
1930	170	1961	275	1983	408
1934	338	1962	250	1984	386
1936	388	1963	290	1985	385
1938	425	1964	290	1986	394
1939	494	1966	300	1987	361
1940	408	1967–71	not given	1988	434
1945	431	1972	301	1989	336
1947	481	1973	307	1990	219
1948	476	1974, 1976	318	1991	196
1950	460	1977	387		
1951	324	1978	403		
1952	323	1979, 1981	430		

Source: SAP *Annual Reports* 1916–1991; SAP Party Executive 1989–1991, oral communication.

mid-1980s to below 1977 levels; the increase in 1988 turned out to be only a temporary change. In 1990 and 1991 the sale of May Day badges fell dramatically, down to levels last seen before the party came to power in 1932. After the forced abolition of collective affiliation (under the threat of legislation by the opposition parties to the right and to the left combined), party membership has dropped to a quarter of a million in 1991. Internationally that is still a very respectable figure, but for the SAP it constitutes a major change.

It is possible that in the future the 1980s will be viewed as a turning point in the SAP's history, leading to fewer roots in LO-mediated class politics and a weaker party organization. However, in a comparative perspective, by the end of the 1980s these tendencies still only appeared as small dips in a still-ascendant curve.

LUCK AND SKILL

A winner cannot afford bad luck. Swedish Social Democracy has had the good fortune to reside on the sunny side of politics. When the party celebrated its sixtieth year (1949), party editor and international secretary Kaj Björk departed from the customary sanctimoniousness with a number of sharp observations made on the basis of international experience. "The fundamental fact which differentiates Sweden's Social Democratic Labor Party from almost all other labor parties in Europe, and which is particularly relevant today, is that we have not had a war for 125 years. The advantages of this can hardly be overestimated."[88]

The SAP has had luck not only with geopolitical position. Its delicate balancing act in the autumn of 1918 could have failed, for within the party were forces that could very well have produced a situation similar to Germany's. When Admiral Dyrssen, in charge of the naval station at Skeppsholmen in Stockholm, asked his chief, the Social Democratic minister of the navy, Palmstierna, what he would do if the sailors mutinied, the minister replied, "Shoot half a minute before it is too late."[89] Had Palmstierna and Dyrssen created a civil war in 1918, it is doubtful whether there would have been any sustained logrolling fifteen years later.

The SAP has also had luck in its two major economic crises. In the 1930s the party came to power in the depths of a crisis and was able to ascend with the economic currents. Devaluation in 1931 had given the Swedish export industry such advantages that capital had no further demands of any consequence and therefore little reason to cause problems for the Social Democratic government.[90] The international crisis from 1973 to 1985 seriously affected Sweden relatively late, arriving when the Social Democrats lost power. The party returned just after the international and Swedish economic trough had been reached in 1981.[91]

On the other hand, winners seldom win time after time purely by luck. The historical preconditions for Social Democratic power were unusually favorable in Sweden, but preconditions can be bungled. Even given these extraordinary preconditions and their large portion of luck, the Swedish Social Democrats can be said to have earned their power by their own skills. Domestically the SAP has been consummate in realizing the interests and practical consequences of national and working-class politics, in tactical maneuvers, and in political expertise and organizational strength.

And Their End? A 1991 Postscript

What this past will lead to in the future is uncertain. It gave the SAP a good start into its second century. However, luck rarely stays forever, and skill is like a bayonet: one can do a great deal with it, but one cannot sit on it.

After the elections of 1988, both tactical skill and luck slipped out of the hands of the SAP government. The possibilities of consolidating the broadening and revitalization of the party base inspired by environmental issues, which the party conference of 1987 and the following elections had opened up, were disregarded entirely. Instead the cabinet concentrated on bringing about a middle-class-oriented tax reform, which confused the core electorate without strengthening party appeal among right-wing voters. The inflationary pressures of a uniquely tight labor market and governmental attempts at easing them further aggravated party relations with the working class.

By the spring of 1989 the SAP had lost ten percentage points in the opinion polls in six months, an unprecedented change in the history of Swedish opinion polling. The loss of political touch, or *Fingerspitzengefühl*, continued into the summer of 1991 with a dismissive government attitude—unique in party history—toward the signs of an incipient recession and unemployment. The electoral campaign of 1991 was well conducted, but too much credibility had already been lost, and the government could not use its traditional argument of being the guarantor of full employment.

Luck is now on the side of the members of the bourgeois coalition in the same sense that it was on the side of the Social Democrats in 1932 and in 1982. Now it is the former who take office just as a recession is gaining ground and deepening and who, most likely, will face the electorate shortly after the economy begins to turn. The SAP remains a vigorous force, but it will need to resuscitate all its classical political finesse.

NOTES

1. Important contributions to the explanation of the SAP's success regarding social democracy have, however, been made: Castles 1978; Elvander 1980; Korpi 1981; Esping-Andersen 1985; Przeworski and Sprague 1986; Heclo and Madsen 1987.

2. Quote after Hansson 1938a, 7.

3. But in contrast to the Belgian Social Democrats' change to a policy of neutrality at the end of the 1930s, the Swedish involved no compromise with democracy before the restricted censorship and transport ban was imposed on the communist press during the war. On the Belgian Social Democrats' homage to the "authoritarian state," see Jaak Brepoels, *Wat zoudt gij zonder 't werkvolk zijn? Anderhalve eeuw arbeidersstrijd in België*, vol. 1: 1830–1966. (Leuven, 1977).

4. Hatje 1974.

5. See also Therborn 1986a.

6. *Electoral Behaviour* 1974; *Electoral Participation* 1980; Alford 1967; *Electoral Change in Advanced Industrial Democracies* 1984; *Party Systems in Denmark, Austria, Switzerland, the Netherlands, and Belgium* 1987; Korpi 1983; Holmberg and Gilljam 1987.

7. *Electoral Change in Advanced Industrial Democracies* 1984, 30, 352. I have not been able to obtain recent information from Finland.

8. Swedish income distribution compared internationally in 1986.

9. Holmberg 1984, 94; Holmberg and Gilljam 1987, 184–86.

10. These hypotheses are taken from a work in progress. For a survey of research, see, e.g., *Working-Class Formation* 1986; *Europäische Arbeiterbewegungen im 19. Jahrhundert* 1983.

11. See Therborn 1986b.

12. Jönköping is one example. See Ericsson 1987; cf. also I. Palm 1982. In his explanation of the election setbacks in 1956, Erlander referred to, among other things, "Christian anti-socialist agitation"; see *SAP Executive Minutes* 25 Sept. 1956 (Labor Movement Archives).

13. *State, Economy, and Society in Western Europe, 1815–1975*, 1983, 142.

14. Ibid., vol. 2, 1987, chap. 7.

15. Calculations taken from SOS, Parliamentary Elections.

16. Holmberg and Gilljam 1987, 185, 179. In contrast to the old social group III, "workers" here include shop assistants but not foremen et al. Both the old social group statistics on the voting register and interview investigations reckon pensioners and non-income-earning family members together with those employed.

17. Calculated according to the Metal Trades Employers Association Executive Board *Annual Report* 1933 (Metal Trades Employers Association Archives, Stockholm).

18. Mackie and Rose 1982; *State, Economy, and Society in Western Europe, 1815–1975*, 1983, chap. 3.

19. Kjellberg 1983, 50, 269. Thanks to a continued expansion in the metal industry, the number of workers under collective agreements diminished only insignificantly after the general strike. Most of the leading employers had accepted the workers as a collective. See also Åmark 1986, 227.

20. Alapuro 1988 (read in manuscript 1987).

21. Mackie and Rose 1982.

22. Kjellberg 1983, 50. The Australian and Danish organizing in fact edged over the Swedish. In my conclusion above I have excepted the nonsocialist, Christian, and liberal unions from the German figures (cf. Kjellberg 1983, 302, note); otherwise they would have equaled the Swedish.

23. Ibid., 36.

24. Valen 1981, 106–7. For comparison with Sweden, see Holmberg and Gilljam 1987, 182, 185 (on age specification, which can be useful with reference to international comparability).

25. *Westeuropas Parteiensystem im Wandel* 1983, 22; Webber 1983, 36.

26. Holmberg 1984, 82; Holmberg and Gilljam 1987, 179; Gerlich in *Party Systems in Denmark . . .* 1987, 80.

27. Westerståhl and Särlvik, *Svensk valrörelse 1956* (The Swedish Election Movement, 1956), Department of Political Science, Gothenburg University 1957, 1.

28. Ibid., 2.

29. See also Kjeldstadli 1978.

30. Lundkvist 1977, 203.

31. Lindgren vol. 1 (1938), 16, 224–25.

32. Lundkvist 1977, 175, 177; H. Johansson 1954, 198.

33. Membership figures are taken from H. Johansson 1954, 235; population figures are from *Swedish Historical Statistics*, part 1, *Population, 1720–1967*, 2d ed. (Stockholm: Central Bureau of Statistics, 1969).

34. *SAP Annual Report* 1986, 125.

35. Thunberg 1942, 33; *Bröder låtom oss enas!* (Brothers, Let Us Unite!) 1950, 278, 298, 391.

36. P. Pelinka and Woller 1980, 44.

37. Sogstad 1951, 472. SSU figures are from Lindbom 1952, 345. Contemporaneous SAP surveys indicate a maximum of 104,000 in 1936 (and 1941).

38. Membership figures from Elvander 1980, 185.

39. Organization figures are taken from Dybdahl 1978, 120–22. On a few occasions during the 1940s the Danish Social Democratic youth organization, DSU, reported 30,000 members. Elvander 1980, 185.

40. See, for example, H. Johansson 1954, 148.

41. Lindbom 1952, 338.

42. *Swedish Historical Statistics*, part 1, 48, 66.

43. Lundkvist 1977, 178.

44. H. Johansson 1954, 235.

45. Höglund (1953) and Lindbom (1952) share the same views on this matter.

46. *Sweden Before and After Social Democracy* 1978; see also Therborn 1984, 1986c, 1985, 1986b, 1988; "'Pillarization' and 'Popular Movements': Two Variants of Welfare Capitalism: Netherlands and Sweden," in *Comparative History of Public Policy*, ed. F. Castles (Cambridge, 1989).

47. Andrae 1975; Gerdner 1966; Klockare 1967.

48. Nyman 1955, 72.

49. Andrae 1975, 106; Klockare 1967, 160.

50. *SAP Annual Report* 1920, 30–31.

51. *SAP Executive Minutes* 23 May 1940.

52. Before the election of 1932 G. Möller wrote a vituperative pamphlet on them: *Kilbommarna och socialdemokratin* 1932. In 1934 a group of left-wing socialists, mainly in Gothenburg, joined the so-called Kilbom communists, who then changed their name to the Socialist party. The dangerousness of the party was emphasized in the *Minutes* of the SAP executive committee from 19 Oct. 1935 (Labor Movement Archives). Despite the fact that prior to the election of 1932 he demanded amnesty for the Ådalen workers, Prime Minister Hansson later refused amnesty for the communists who had been sentenced to prison for leading protest meetings in Ådalen in 1931. The members of the military who had killed five peaceful, unarmed demonstrators had already been acquitted by the courts. See B. Norman 1968, 191–92.

53. Hansson 1934a, 3; see also 1934b and 1938b, and the collection of his speeches, *Demokrati* (Democracy) 1935.

54. *SAP Executive Minutes* 5 Nov. 1944.

55. Sven Andersson 1980, 267–69.

56. *SAP Executive Minutes* 25 Sept. 1936.

57. *SAP Annual Report* 1920, 30.

58. The SAP's views are evident in the annual reports of 1923 and 1926.

59. See also Therborn 1984, with references.

60. The Social Democratic parliamentary group's *Minutes* 6 Nov. 1951 (Labor Movement Archives). According to the records, in addition to Sandler only Nancy Eriksson was against the Coercion Act. It was hoped that a settlement could be found under threat of the act without implementation. The opposition was harder, but supporters were also more militant when the government proposed a Coercion Act against ships' officers in 1955: "As union people we cannot vote for the proposition as it can have consequences," declared LO chair Axel Strand (Social Democratic parliamentary group's *Minutes* 18 May 1955).

61. Government proposition 1975/76: 105, 290–92. See also Hydén 1978, 152–153.

62. Kjellberg 1983, 278.

63. An inquiry into the political situation within the executives of FCO organizations, larger trade unions, and TCO committees in 1958 (SAP Office of the Executive, 1959).

64. This assertion is based on a certain amount of personal knowledge and interviews among VPK cadres.

65. The LO had written a draft for the party executive's statement on equality issues for the extra party conference in 1967. In the executive Hjalmar Mehr sharply attacked the draft as

being "rather careless and one-sided" and much too critical of postwar development. Erlander supported Mehr, and the statement was rewritten (*SAP Executive Minutes* 30 June 1967). The party executive's statement to the conference confirms that "there is no doubt that in essential respects, leveling policies have been successful. Equally, continued efforts toward increased equality and toward the abolishment of remaining class boundaries constitute social democracy's perhaps most important task." Arne Geijer was the person reporting for the party executive (he was not present for the executive 30 June meeting), and he maintained a critical position. "Most agree that a certain income leveling occurred up to 1948, but there is great doubt about how development has proceeded since. . . . Indeed, Swedish welfare is . . . incomplete in the highest degree" (*SAP Conference Minutes* 21–23 Oct. 1967, 355, esp. 361).

66. *SAP Conference Minutes*, 21–23 Oct. 1967, 361.

67. *SAP Executive Minutes* 21 Sept. 1932; Executive Committee *Minutes* 19 Sept. 1932.

68. See Therborn 1984, 43–44 with references.

69. Jonasson 1981, 25–27.

70. This survey was reported by Erlander in the executive. *SAP Executive Minutes* 26 Mar. 1957.

71. Sydow (1978, 176–78) relates this from a Social Democratic point of view.

72. See Samuelsson 1983, 225–27.

73. On the election, see Therborn 1983; on social policy, OECD 1985, 21.

74. Social Democratic parliamentary group *Minutes* 11 Feb. 1958.

75. Malmström 1970, 220–22; B. Molin 1967, 115–17.

76. *SAP Executive Minutes* 2 Oct. 1964.

77. The increases in the 1930s did not diminish the pensioners' need for poor relief. In 1923 16 percent of pensioners requested help; in 1941, 18.3 percent. Elmér 1960, 306.

78. *SAP Executive Minutes* 22 Oct. 1952. The same sentiments can be found in Sven Andersson; *SAP Executive Minutes* 9 Dec. 1945; Gunnar Sträng 2 Oct. 1964.

79. Furåker 1976, 17, 61.

80. Askling 1982, 473–75.

81. *Dagens Nyheter* 13 Sept. 1987, 14, and 18 Feb. 1988, 13.

82. Svenska Arbetsgivareföreningen: *Industria*, 1930, 516.

83. Gerlich, in *Party Systems in Denmark* . . . 1987, 82.

84. Elvander 1980, 163; Gerlich, in *Party Systems in Denmark* . . . 1987, 82; Sully 1977, 218–31.

85. *SAP Annual Report* 1986, 119–21. See Appendix: Swedish Social Democratic Labor Party Membership 1889–1991.

86. SAP 1968, 33. Figures for 1987 according to the most recent information were obtained from the party headquarters by the author (1988).

87. Pierre 1986, 206–8.

88. Björk 1949, 233.

89. Palmstierna 1953, 238–39.

90. For further evidence and references, see Therborn 1984.

91. OECD 1987, 44.

Gøsta Esping-Andersen

The Making of a Social Democratic Welfare State

The Swedish welfare state has been endowed with two identities. To the world at large, it is regarded as *the* model of advanced (some might say excessive) social policy; to the Swedish Social Democrats, it stands as the flagship of their achievements over the past century.

It is not surprising that the synonymity between the welfare state and social democracy is so readily invoked for Sweden: the two grew up together. It was under Social Democratic leadership that the famous "Middle Way" was forged, and welfare state institutionalization coincided with five decades of virtually uninterrupted Social Democratic rule. But if we scratch the surface of historical coincidence we will uncover ample evidence that the Swedish welfare state has its roots deeply implanted in historical conditions that precede the birth of the Social Democratic labor movement. The evolution of both occurred in an internationally unique social context.

The Social Democratic strategy has always faced the problem of how to reconcile three dilemmas: the quest for power, the pursuit of equality, and the need for economic efficiency. In the case of Sweden, the conditions for resolving these goals have been especially opportune, and this must be kept in mind when we evaluate the genuine contributions of social democracy.

Most industrially advanced nations are self-proclaimed welfare states, and there is nothing particularly exceptional about the Swedish if we measure achievement in terms of social expenditure commitments or the menu of social programs. Some, like the Dutch and the Danish, spend about the same proportion of the national product on social welfare as do the Swedish; indeed, there are very few programs that do not have a counterpart elsewhere. What is peculiar about the Swedish welfare model is its structuralization and, therefore, it is this which must be analyzed.

The Swedish welfare state certainly imposes heavy burdens on taxpayers, and this clearly does reflect a powerful political commitment to welfare. But the real significance of the costs is structural—namely, that it is a welfare state thoroughly built on principles of universalism, egalitarianism, "decommodification," and efficiency. To uphold such principles in an affluent and increasingly middle-class society, the welfare state cannot escape the burdensome costs that go with guarantees of optimal service and benefit standards. If the principles of universalism and solidarity are to be upheld by the public sector, it is necessary that the market be marginalized. This, in turn, means that the welfare state must satisfy more than basic needs: it must pitch its services to the tastes of a working class that has become prosperous as well as to a discriminating middle-class clientele. Sweden has achieved an average living standard so high that few, if any, citizens would remain content with minimum or even basic standards of social security. Hence, the welfare state is bound to be costly.

The cost structure of a welfare state reflects its priorities. Some equally expensive welfare states target most of their spending on compensating for social ills. The Swedish model is unique in its bias toward a "productivistic" and preventive social policy; it spends relatively little on unemployment benefits but invests heavily in employment, training, job mobility, adult education, the prevention of illness and accidents, and family services. It is a welfare state both designed for and dependent upon the minimization of social need and the maximization of employment. The philosophy is that money spent here creates greater savings elsewhere.

A productivistic social policy may be very expensive, but then the costs of unproductive expenditures remain reciprocally lower. Sweden's peculiar welfare state structure therefore lowers expenditure burdens where others raise them. And by furnishing employment, it increases the number of taxpayers where others reduce them. In the Swedish welfare state, therefore, a large share of welfare costs might well be regarded as investments in economic growth. The distributional effects are certainly impressive; poverty and economic insecurity have been largely eradicated, and Sweden is the indisputable leader in the equal distribution of incomes or in living standards after transfers and taxes. Yet Sweden's most spectacular accomplishments lie outside the conventional measures of welfare: it has been able to sustain full employment; it has substantially diminished the salience of class; and for decades it managed to build a powerful consensus behind its own perpetuation. In this sense, social expenditure must also be regarded as an investment in power. Indeed, the welfare state has been a cornerstone of Social Democratic power.

The Swedish welfare state did not unfold according to a grand Social Democratic design. Too often, the literature depicts its evolution as a deliberate, step-by-step, Social Democratic accomplishment. True, it is a welfare state that shares most of the basic principles enunciated by the labor movement. Yet many of these principles were broadly shared to begin with, and during the fifty-odd years of Social Democratic rule we find floundering and improvisation as well as programmatic coherence. On occasion it may very well be that the policymakers were simply confused. But to assume programmatic coherence is to assume that the conditions for pursuing power, equality, and economic efficiency do not change.

The phases of Swedish welfare state development reflect the ways in which social democracy has struggled to balance these three goals. If we begin with power, it is clear that the Social Democrats always faced a dilemma: total power was never possible on the basis of a democratic, parliamentary strategy. First, by depending on working-class support alone the party would never be able to mobilize a numerical majority; parliamentary control would, therefore, have to rest on coalitions. It follows that the welfare state could never become a purely Social Democratic or working-class project. From *folkhemmet* (People's Home) in the 1930s to the new "middle-class" welfare state of the 1970s, Swedish social reforms have always mirrored underlying political and social coalitions. And, like the welfare state, Swedish Social Democratic power has been premised on class coalitions, not just on working-class mobilization.

In terms of efficiency, the principal constraint lies in the smallness, openness, and export-dependent nature of the Swedish economy. Since the 1920s and 1930s Swedish Social Democracy has been firmly wedded to the principle of full employment through economic growth. Certainly, no one ever believed in an equality of shared poverty. In the accord that was struck between the labor movement and business in the 1930s, labor fully acquiesced to the sanctity of private ownership. On this basis, the Social Democrats' formula for prosperity came to embrace a precarious blend of distributional equality, a productive and flexible labor force, and acceptable profit levels. The Swedish labor movement has been unusually capable of striking a positive-sum deal between equality and profits, between welfare and efficiency. Each phase in welfare state evolution is as much marked by its approach to efficiency as to power.

Equality has certainly always been the central goal, but it constitutes also a means and a third perennial constraint. Most early socialist movements assumed that meaningful equality would have to await the nationalization of, at least, the "commanding heights" of the economy. Swedish Social Democracy abandoned this dogma quite early. In place of the impossible concept of equal rewards, it launched the more practical pursuit of social justice through democratized opportunities, resources, and participation. It put the fight for social citizenship before the final democratization of ownership. With this historical reversal in ideology, Swedish socialist theoreticians could indulge in a peculiar teleological extravaganza: the historical mission of the labor movement was to shepherd Sweden through the successive stages of political, social, and eventually economic democracy.

Social democracy's idea of equality has always been influenced by multiple objectives. An obvious first principle is the promise to eradicate poverty, diminish class differences, and create a more just distribution of opportunities. The main approach to this end in Sweden has not so much been income redistribution as decommodification. Social policy is a means to decommodify the vital areas of consumption, but also to decommodify the status of the worker: the state must guarantee a social wage that adequately substitutes for market incomes.

Paradoxically, equality also came to be a means for efficiency. The success of Swedish Social Democracy owes much to its intellectual capacity to harmonize these seemingly conflicting goals. Equality was not promulgated as merely compatible with efficiency. It became, indeed, a precondition for its optimization: more equally distributed purchasing power is a precondition for macroeconomic performance; family policy is an investment in future human capital; the equalization of resources, such as health or education, is the foundation for optimal labor productivity; solidaristic wage policy and active manpower programs spur industrial modernization; income security helps overcome workers' natural resistance to rationalization; and preventive social policy diminishes human waste and economic costs.

Equality also came to serve a third goal on which, however, the party has been less vocal. Yet there has never been much doubt that equality and solidarity are essential preconditions for labor movement unity and power. Labor movements have always faced two obstacles to organization and unity: the market, and the legacy of precapitalist communities. As participants in the market, people compete, divide, and stratify. And from precapitalist society came the powerful legacy of narrow guild and corporate solidarity, localism, and organic paternalism. Social Democratic power must therefore disestablish the salience of both, and put in their place a universalistic solidarity. When we have defined the realm of equality, we have automatically defined the realm of solidarity. As we shall see, the phases of Swedish welfare state development are marked by distinctly different conceptions of solidarity: from the early "microsocialist" model of solidarity, through a national solidarity of the "little people," to the contemporary (and more problematic) struggle to find a principle of solidarity that embraces wage earners at all levels.

As a system of stratification the Swedish welfare state is unique because of its egalitarian results, but even more because of its capacity to substitute universalist solidarity for the rival solidarity systems that alternative welfare states expound: the class dualisms that are pervasive in the American and even the British systems; the egotistic individualism that the dominant private welfare system cultivates in the United States; or the narrow and fragmentary corporate solidarity that is institutionalized in several European welfare states.

THE PRELUDE TO A SOCIAL DEMOCRATIC WELFARE STATE

Swedish Social Democracy may have celebrated its centennial, but its role in welfare state construction has been significant only during the past five decades. As elsewhere, the nascent Swedish labor movement had no coherent plan for social policy. Until the conclusion of World War I, its energies were concentrated on the problems of trade union recognition and the fight for full parliamentary democracy. Unlike its German, Austrian, and even Danish brethren, it was spared the problematic role of "negative socialism," futilely vetoing conservative, antisocialist reforms. In Sweden the conservative forces were divided, and in this environment there was little scope, indeed, for Bismarckian "social pacifism."

The sporadic social pacifist initiatives that were undertaken were, in turn, hardly occasions for class warfare. Hjalmar Branting, the grandfather of Swedish Social Democracy, chose to support the Bostrom government's pension proposal in 1898 despite finding it seriously flawed. The Swedish socialists did not assume (as did their brethren elsewhere) that bourgeois reformism would lure workers to embrace the class enemy. Party chairman Branting was eager to avoid the image of "negative socialism" and held that even bad reforms could be exploited for future improvements.[1]

Barred from parliamentary power and called upon to redress acute social needs, many early socialists pursued the microsocialist strategy of building their own empires of workers' welfare societies. In Sweden, this approach was never seriously pursued. The trade union movement, for one, expended most of its resources on costly strikes and the uphill task of membership mobilization. Friendly societies (mainly sickness funds) did enjoy some growth,[2] but they were not—as in Germany—a fountain of Social Democratic strength. Swedish Social Democracy always sought national solutions and was therefore drawn to the parliamentary strategy. This meant awaiting the moment in which it could decisively influence legislation.

Until the 1930s Sweden was an international laggard in social security development. Yet the absence of either legislation or fraternal societies was possibly less keenly felt than elsewhere. For one, Sweden's late industrialization was more rural than urban, and it did not compel the massive mobility or social dislocation that prevailed elsewhere. In 1900 only 20 percent of the population lived in urban areas. The local (*bruksamhälle*) industrialist often provided a patriarchical welfare system, and these rural-based workers often maintained small family plots on the side. Even so, the rural areas were mired in poverty. The massive wave of emigration between 1880 and 1914 helped alleviate much of the social misery that accompanied early industrialization.

The rudimentary principles of social policy that emerged in this epoch of social democracy were powerfully influenced by this unique political economy. The Swedish socialists did not confront a hopeless struggle to have their ideals of universalism and solidarity accepted. These principles were already forged in Sweden's peculiar social structure. It was a class system with an extraordinary concentration of capital within a tiny clique of wealthy families, an unusually small middle class, and a mass of workers and small peasants living in the countryside. Inserted in this class structure was a powerful and highly centralized state machinery. The popular masses were divided by very little except geographic distance; poverty was shared by almost all. To a society thus undifferentiated, a broad sense of solidarity came much easier than either individualism or corporatism.

Sweden, therefore, did not need the socialist movement to inject the principle of universal solidarity into social policy. In 1884, before the Social Democratic Labor Party was even formed, the governing Liberal party established a Royal Commission to prepare proposals for workers' insurance. Dominated by reform-minded Liberals, the commission's report actually advocated a pension scheme that is hard to distinguish from the basic *Folkpension* (the people's pension plan) promoted much later by the Social Democrats in both Denmark and Sweden. Its advocacy of basically universal and equal coverage followed simply from the decision to cover "workers and similar persons"; and as was generally acknowledged, this definition fit in practice just about every Swede.[3]

As it turned out, the first pension legislation was delayed until 1913, when the (Liberal) government pioneered the world's first truly universal pension scheme. This instance reflects, once again, how readily the principle of universalism emerged in Sweden. But the debates leading up to the reform also illustrate that the socialists were still groping for a coherent social policy.

The 1913 pension reform was influenced by the Social Democratic leader, Hjalmar Branting, who had a long-standing commitment to the concept of a universal people's pension. Yet he and other Social Democrats were at times also in favor of both voluntary employer plans (with state subsidies) and the kind of worker insurance introduced by Bismarck.[4] The latter model had, in fact, been bitterly opposed by the German socialists for its class-divisive intent, and Branting's research on similar proposals in Austria finally dissuaded him.

Above all, what led the Social Democratic majority to embrace the universalistic model was its acknowledgment of the social and political realities of Sweden: most workers were rural, and worked for employers who could ill afford (and had the power to refuse) social contributions. Moreover, the need for relief was as widespread among the self-employed as it was among workers; and, perhaps most important of all, the Social Democratic Labor Party needed political support from the agrarian classes who, for obvious reasons, had no interest in a social insurance model.[5]

The interwar period saw the Swedish labor movement grow strong; by 1920, the Social Democrats had become the single largest party but remained unable to govern for more than brief, and typically traumatic, interludes. The political system was in flux, but so also was social democracy.

Although considerably more active and creative on the social policy front, the party was still groping for a workable and coherent political formula. It was a party wedged between the radicalism of nationalization and the pragmatism of immediate social reforms. It presented itself in the traditional image of a workers' party, but it never adhered to the Kautsky resolution against cross-class collaboration. Swedish Social Democracy viewed alliances with the Liberals and farmers as potentially necessary and, in principle, positive. For social reasons, the party could hardly avoid pitching its appeals to the rural classes. And, politically speaking, ad hoc alliances with either the Liberals or the Agrarians helped nurture the chronic divisions among the three nonsocialist parties.

As early as 1895, Branting began to promote the "people's party" model.[6] Social democracy as the unity of all the "little people," be they workers or peasants, was formally embraced by the 1911 party conference and program revision; it was reconfirmed in the 1919 "Goteborg program." The nationalization issue was dominant during the 1920s but disappeared with the defeat that followed Minister of Finance Ernst Wigforss's inheritance tax proposal in the 1928 elections.

The 1928 election was a historical watershed in the move toward a party of the common people. It was in this campaign that Branting's successor, Per Albin Hansson, coined the famous *folkhems* (People's Home) model: the emergent Social Democratic state should be like a home, a family, in which solidarity is natural and mutual help instinctive. The People's Home conveys an image of cross-class, national solidarity; it virtually assumes a strategy of building broad political coalitions. Without it, Swedish Social Democracy and its welfare state program would probably not have succeeded in the 1930s. It was not merely a precondition for power, but also the cornerstone of the universalistic social policy model that the Social Democrats inaugurated and maintained so successfully for so many years.

By the 1920s the Swedish Social Democrats had fully realized that a purely working-class party would never attain parliamentary majorities. The "red-green" alliance that made the Social Democratic welfare state possible in the 1930s was premised on a quid pro quo forged with the Agrarian party, until then a major source of opposition to the labor movement. This political deal marked the birth of a wholly new political alignment. Yet in Sweden a cross-class alliance of this sort was not as unthinkable as it would have been in, say, Germany. Sweden already had a legacy of cross-class collaboration from the nineteenth-century struggle for democracy.

SOCIAL DEMOCRACY AS A "PEOPLE'S HOME"

Until the 1930s, the Liberals were the closest thing to a friend that the Social Democrats had. They had participated most actively in the prolonged battle for full democracy, and had supported a cautious reformism. The Agrarian party, in contrast, had been adamantly opposed to social reform, and to the labor movement generally. Accordingly, there is considerable historical irony in the fact that it was with Agrarian support that the Social Democrats were catapulted to power in the 1930s. Indeed, its contribution was as decisive as the strength of the working classes. On the European continent, labor movements were often as strong as that in Sweden or stronger; but they were ghetto parties of the urban working class, unable to broaden their popular base and, as a consequence, less pressed to shelve ideological orthodoxy (such as the commitment to nationalization). They had perhaps the power of numbers, but not the power to govern. They had neither the legitimacy nor the kind of workable policies to confront credibly the economic crisis of the 1930s.

Like Denmark and Norway, Sweden's agriculture was not very labor intensive. It was dominated by family farmers on one side and a mass of precarious peasants on the other, strata that could easily blend into a "little people" identity. But in contrast to Marx's depiction of peasants as a "sack of potatoes," they were educated, well organized, and politically articulate; and they had been active participants in the struggle for democracy. There were two main reasons why Scandinavian Social Democracy came to power in the twentieth century: its capacity to build a red-green coalition with a People's Home welfare policy, and its ability to drop nationalization and, instead, negotiate an accord with business based on Keynesian policies.

The Swedish red-green coalition was modeled on its Danish predecessor. It was premised on a positive-sum deal with price and income subsidies to farmers in return for their support for budgetary reflation, employment promotion, and welfare reforms. At the time, this reform package appeared as a radical historical watershed for Social Democratic politics. But on closer inspection, its principles are hardly at variance with liberal policy elsewhere (as, for example, in the United States).

The Social Democrats' image as the force responsible for the successful solution to the crisis may be more attributable to luck than to achievement. Nevertheless, its welfare program and economic reconstruction policies became a major political asset for Swedish Social Democracy, while it became a liability to labor movements elsewhere. In Germany, as in Britain, the economic crisis brought about a virtual collapse of social security schemes; in Sweden, new schemes were introduced to alleviate the crisis. The net effect, be it warranted or not, was the emergence of a synonymity between the Social Democratic movement, political democracy, economic prosperity, and social welfare.

Social democracy's breakthrough in the 1930s seems the more epochal when we consider the meager record of the previous bourgeois governments' reformism. Until the economic crisis, they had legislated only work accident (1916) and pension insurance (1913); and since the pension scheme had not yet matured, most pensioners were forced to rely on poor relief. Thus, the massive social need that emerged with the economic crisis confronted a wasteland of social protection.[7]

As it happened, the absence of an established conservative reformism was of double political advantage. On one side, the Social Democrats could exploit the tabula rasa situation in the sense that it allowed them considerable freedom to construct the welfare state in harmony with their own basic principles. They were not, as in Germany, France, or Italy, compelled to live with a previously institutionalized apparatus of stratifying insurance that was impossible to change because too many interests were wedded to its perpetuation. On the other side, the paucity of earlier accomplishments helped cast both the Conservatives and the Liberals in the image of parties unconcerned with the people's welfare.

The People's Home package contained three basic ingredients. Aside from agricultural price supports, its centerpiece was a countercyclical full employment program, developed by Wigforss and the Stockholm School economists, and a program for social reform, sponsored by Minister of Social Affairs Gustav Möller. The most remarkable feature of the reflationary policies was not their aggregate scope but the principle that public employment programs paid standard trade union wage. As Lindbeck has argued, the rapid fall in unemployment cannot be ascribed so much to budget deficits (which were indeed quite cautious) as to the positive effect of Hitler's rearmaments program on Swedish exports.[8] Also, the upsurge in exports was aided by an undervalued krona.

It may very well have been luck and circumstance, but the conclusion remains that renewed prosperity benefited all social classes and thus helped institutionalize the legitimacy of both active full employment policy and social democracy itself. It became one instance in which the labor movement could demonstrate its commitment to an efficient economy.

Gustav Möller was the architect of the Social Democratic welfare state. The concept of a "welfare state" has usually been identified with William Henry Beveridge in Britain at the end of World War II. Yet the phrase can be found in Möller's 1928 election program manifesto: "The state should not merely be a night-watchman state, but also a welfare state,"[9] which he defined as "not only a responsibility, but also a duty, to establish guarantees for the well-being of citizens in all aspects."[10] The cornerstones of Möller's 1928 program were better accident insurance; unified, universal health insurance; a universal "people's pension"; the abolition of poor relief; and unemployment insurance.

The program that Gustav Möller launched in the 1930s followed his earlier blueprint, but with decisive modifications. In both implicit and explicit terms, it espoused a symbiosis of equality and efficiency. The principle of universal rights and equal flat-rate benefits, financed through progressive taxation, came to define equality. What departed from his earlier conception was the inclusion of the Myrdals' emphasis on preventive social policy and a bias in favor of employment rather than cash support.[11] This explicitly "productivistic" social policy became Social Democracy's positive-sum solution to the enduring equality-efficiency trade-off.

This was the framework for the battery of reforms that came in the 1930s and 1940s: employment creation and the Manpower Commission (AMS) (1933, 1940, and 1948), the new "People's Pension" (1935 and 1946), unemployment insurance (1934 and 1941), preventive health and social services (1937, 1938, and 1943), family allowances (1935, 1937, and 1947), and rent subsidies (1941, 1942, and 1948). The replacement of poor relief with a more solidaristic assistance plan and the sickness benefit reform were delayed until the 1950s, the latter primarily because Agrarian allies refused to accept the labor movement's proposal for earnings-related cash benefits. A genuine, full-scale active manpower policy was not fully implemented until the 1960s.

This first-phase welfare state was, in reality, rather cautiously universalistic and egalitarian. Many social rights were subject to income testing, although deliberately designed so as to minimize stigma and discretion. And more important, perhaps, benefits were uniformly modest. Herein lies a more implicit compromise with efficiency: the welfare state was meant only to provide a basic minimum, not to engender negative work incentives. However, despite the shortcomings of this first phase, the notion of citizenship as the sole criterion for benefits was firmly implanted. In general, this strengthened solidarity; in particular, it benefited women, since it granted them a modicum of economic independence and strengthened status equality between the sexes.

The edifice that Gustav Möller built in the 1930s and 1940s was therefore rudimentary and signaled no sharp break with the liberal tradition. Above all, it lacked a national sickness benefit system; the prevalence of income testing undercut the ideals of universalism; and benefits were generally too low to offer the level of income security that socialist principles demanded. The burdens of wartime mobilization had temporarily stalled Möller's project, and it was not until the 1950s that major improvements were reconsidered. In 1951 the matter was given some urgency when Möller threatened to resign unless the Social Democratic Labor Party leadership supported his call for a bold new era of reform. The debate illustrates the difficulties Social Democrats had in balancing the constraints of power, economic efficiency, and equality.[12]

A majority in the party leadership objected to Möller's call for a new social policy thrust. The arguments were twofold. One was strategic, namely that the party could not afford to alienate its Agrarian party allies, especially in consideration of upcoming elections. The other was economic. With reference to inflationary pressures and the need to maintain a budget surplus, the majority position held that the status of the economy prohibited costly reforms. Möller's response deserves to be quoted at length since it depicts very well the dilemmas that Social Democratic reformism faced in this era:

> It is said that my proposals imply a new economic policy. I reject this view. Is it really [your] opinion that the only thing of importance is to manufacture a budget surplus? . . . As I listen to the discussion, it is my impression that the party leadership views me as a Social Democrat who is way too old-fashioned. It is as if the party ought to become nothing more than an administrative party. . . . I personally lament the fact that the party leadership is dedicated to the status quo when it comes to social policy.[13]

The early People's Home welfare state reflected the constraints of Social Democratic power, and of its underlying social basis of "the little people": its idea of solidarity was defined in terms of an equality of the floor. As such, the edifice guaranteed a minimal level of security but could not offer much decommodification. Its benefits were too modest to appeal to the Swedish middle class, albeit still small; its real focus was to redress poverty and want among small farmers, peasants, and workers.

The People's Home, then, addressed a historically peculiar era of social democracy, one in which the rural classes defined the notion of equality and held the key to power and in which the Social Democrats tamed higher welfare ambitions for the sake of efficiency. It is precisely because the conditions for power, solidarity, and economic efficiency changed that the Swedish Social Democrats found themselves both capable of and forced to restructure the welfare state.

THE EMERGENCE OF THE "MIDDLE-CLASS" WELFARE STATE

When in the 1950s Herbert Tingsten developed his "end of ideology" thesis, the diagnosis appeared fairly accurate.[14] The Social Democrats were, as Möller's speech suggests, preoccupied with economic stabilization in a period of inflation and balance-of-payments difficulties. In 1949 they had compelled trade unions to freeze wages as part of an unpopular income policy. The party leadership had no policy alternative to the full employment/price stability dilemma. And its ability to launch new bold ideas was circumscribed by its continued dependence on the red-green coalition.

However, the incompatabilities of the People's Home model gained in force and eventually provoked the end to the "end of ideology." The foundations of the People's Home were decaying for political reasons. The Social Democrats' own electoral performance was slipping during the 1950s, and the political salience of the agrarian classes was rapidly diminishing as modern urbanization finally came to Sweden. Finally, it was not a bigger working class that postwar development brought to Sweden, but a rising and more heterogeneous middle class of salaried white-collar strata.

The new class structure compelled political realignment. The Social Democrats had not been ignorant of the new class developments, but had taken them as unproblematic. Typical of this period is an analysis in *Social-demokratisk Skriftserie*,[15] which held that the loss of traditional social prestige, income advantages, and job security together with growing unionization all conspired to "social democratize" the middle classes. Hence, on the basis of this kind of "proletarianization" thesis, the Social Democratic party believed that its conventional working-class appeals would also work admirably among the white-collar electorate. It believed that the bourgeois bloc, and especially the Liberal party, had little hope of winning the middle classes. If the Social Democrats could sustain the red-green coalition, the bourgeois parties would remain split and, as a result, the Liberal party would appear as a utopian alternative to voters.

Reality, however, seemed to refute the assumption that the same old tactics would win over the new classes. The new middle classes were becoming an independent force, quite differentiated and as likely to embrace "bourgeois" as Social Democratic politics. They did unionize rapidly, but within autonomous federations (TCO, the Swedish Confederation of Professional Employees, and SACO, the Swedish Confederation of Professional Associations). To remain in power, the Social Democrats would have to forge a new coalition with a new political formula. The chance presented itself on the issue of a second-tier, earnings-related pension scheme (the ATP pensions). The conflict over the ATP pensions inaugurated both political realignment and the shift from a People's Home to a new "middle-class" regime. In reality, a novel conception of equality, solidarity, and efficiency was in the making.

The ATP pension issue was not just a battle over power, but compelled a reassessment of equality and efficiency. It was the trade union movement, and not the rather fatigued party leadership, that launched the debate. The trade unions' main concern was to equalize pension rights. Since the existing, flat-rate, universal pension guaranteed only modest benefits, most better-off groups had begun to bargain or contract for themselves additional private insurance; civil servants, of course, enjoyed special pension privileges. As a result, the gap was widening between working-class pensioners and those white-collar groups that had additional private sector insurance. Because of its modest benefits, the people's pension was inadvertently nurturing new class divisions; hence, the foundations of universalism and solidarity were in jeopardy. Having failed at the bargaining table, the trade unions persuaded the Social Democratic party that only a legislated, universal, earnings-graduated second-tier pension would resolve these dilemmas of solidarity.

It was the efficiency issue espoused by the trade unions that more than anything else provoked political conflict and realignment. The LO demanded that the ATP pensions be financed through direct contributions and be funded in autonomous, semipublic pension funds. Its motive was to bring a larger share of the capital market under collective decision-making, partly to ensure adequate levels of investment and partly to pursue socially desirable investment goals (such as housing construction).

It was, at first, with no great enthusiasm that the Social Democratic party embraced the ATP proposal. Not surprisingly, the proposal was flatly opposed by the employer associations and all the bourgeois parties. The employers were not opposed to second-tier pensions as such, but insisted on a system of voluntarily negotiated private sector pensions; they refused to entertain any ideas of publicly controlled pension funds. The preference for private sector pensions was preeminent in both the Liberal and the Conservative parties.

The Agrarians found themselves in a particularly precarious position. Their traditional rural constituency saw no advantage in an earnings-related pension for wage earners and advocated, instead, higher flat-rate pensions. But the Agrarian party too had grasped the political significance of class structural change and saw the need to compete for white-collar votes. It decided to rename itself the "Center party." Name change notwithstanding, it flatly refused to support the Social Democratic pension plan and provoked, as a result, the collapse of the increasingly anachronistic red-green, "little people" coalition.

This is not the place to examine in detail the resulting pension struggle. It involved an indecisive national referendum, the resignation of two cabinets, and a climate of prolonged and highly charged political confrontation that shattered any previous "end of ideology" notion. After almost three years of conflict, the Social Democrats finally passed their reform in 1959 with a one-vote majority.[16] The law included a clause of vital importance for the future of the Swedish welfare state. It specified that, initially, only manual workers would be covered; the white-collar workers, organized in the TCO, would decide within one year whether to join or opt for a separately negotiated scheme. Had the latter been the actual outcome, the principle of universalist solidarity would have been dealt a serious blow. As it turned out, the architects of the ATP plan had foreseen this eventuality, and with its emphasis on ample earnings-related benefits it was easily competitive with private sector alternatives. ATP was thus a vehicle for white-collar mobilization.

The Social Democrats' pension victory was a historical watershed because it catalyzed a major political realignment. The party shed its little-people alliance and began in earnest to pursue a new coalition of workers and the salaried middle classes. That the ATP pension helped mobilize white-collar support for a Social Democratic future is evident from subsequent elections.[17] It was a stepping-stone to a new political coalition, and it helped delegitimatize, once again, the bourgeois opposition parties. Not surprisingly, the Social Democratic party soon after abandoned its little people rhetoric and began to label itself the wage-earner party.

A new welfare state model went in tandem with political realignment. The principles of universal solidarity were preserved, but recast: in pensions, as in sickness benefits, unemployment insurance, and indeed all ensuing reforms, coverage was equal and universal, while benefits were tailored to earnings and expectations. The old ideal of equality "of the floor," of a minimalist equality, was surrendered in favor of an equalization "at the top." Rather than impose a working-class welfare state on the new middle classes, the new principle was to extend to workers full membership in a middle-class welfare state. Equality of status is, in this way, premised on middle-class norms, and the new welfare state becomes an avenue of working-class upward mobility. The Swedish welfare state became deproletarianizing.

It was mainly this transformation that caused social expenditures and taxes to grow so explosively in the 1960s and 1970s. Universalism matched with middle-class benefit standards must demand heavy public expenditures. Nevertheless, a genuinely universalistic middle-class welfare state will crowd out private schemes and thus lessen two evils that typically plague the residualist welfare state: first, by crowding out the private sector, government is spared powerful pressures to grant tax privileges to private welfare plans; second, the welfare state will more likely be able to count on middle-class tax loyalty. The net effect is greater welfare state solidarity rather than tax revolts.

By the late 1960s, the middle-class formula was essentially in place within the ever-growing array of income transfers, but social, educational, and health services were rather poorly developed. Their real expansion began in the late 1960s and lasted throughout the 1970s.

The step toward a middle-class welfare state was decisive for social democracy's political future. Denmark is a telling example of how the failure to advance beyond the people's pension model came to haunt Social Democracy: its increasingly dualistic welfare state, burdened with colossal tax expenditures that favored the middle classes' private sector welfare system, faced an explosion of anti-welfare state revolt in the 1970s. Symptomatically, Danish Social Democracy has decayed due to lack of middle-class electoral support.[18]

It is important to realize that the equality embodied in the recast Swedish welfare state is not merely one of status. The decision to upgrade the social wage to reflect normal earnings and middle-class expectations has been one of the single most effective means of combating poverty. With the combination of the flat-rate universal pension and the ATP pension (or the transfer-tested pension supplement that goes to those who do not yet qualify for ATP), it is impossible for anyone to retire with less than 50 percent of the median income. Empirical research has shown that in the 1980s there were no aged poor in Sweden.[19] This contrasts with no less than a 21 percent rate of aged poor in Britain, where the flat-rate pension was never supplemented with a genuinely universal second-tier pension.

Finally, it is clear that the new middle-class welfare state contributes heavily to the reduction of class differences in living standards. Recent analyses of the Level of Living data demonstrate that the Swedish welfare system not only helps improve living conditions continuously over time (and even during the recent economic crisis), but that its thrust is unequivocally to equalize more and more the distribution of welfare across the social classes.[20]

In tandem with welfare state restructuralization, Swedish Social Democracy introduced a gradual change in its approach to efficiency. In the traditional People's Home model, the pursuit of efficiency was largely cast in the conventional liberal mold: work creation rather than unemployment assistance, the prevention of social ills, and the maintenance of full employment through standard Keynesian macroeconomic management. In the People's Home welfare state, social benefits were too modest to threaten the work ethic.

As with the ATP reform, it was also the trade unions that forced upon the Social Democrats a recast economic policy. The catalyst was the wage freeze of 1949–1951, which not only created rifts in the unity of party and unions but also fueled greater wage inequalities and helped subsidize the profits of uncompetitive firms. Incomes policies as a remedy against inflation in a full employment economy threatened to destabilize politics and to block the dynamism necessary in a small, open economy. The Rehn-Meidner model, which combines an active manpower policy with a system of solidaristic wage bargaining in the labor market, was proposed by the LO already in 1951.[21] Its basic principle is to eliminate unproductive jobs and, via retraining and mobility, shift workers to dynamic sectors. As with the ATP question, the Social Democratic Labor Party remained hesitant and was not really committed to an active labor market policy until the 1960s.

Active labor market policy introduced a novel, microlevel supply-side dimension to full employment management. It also gave rise to a new relationship between equality and efficiency. First, the pursuit of a solidaristic wage policy helped shift the focus of equalization from the welfare state to collective bargaining. This obviously helped reconcile the new earnings-graduated (and therefore less redistributive) social security system with the commitment to equality. With a more egalitarian earnings structure, differentiated social transfers would appear less invidious. And as a consequence the burden on the welfare state to provide income redistribution, in addition to universalism and adequacy, would be markedly relaxed.

Second, the active labor market policy combined a new commitment to accelerate economic rationalization and modernization with guarantees of individual job and welfare security. And by helping to move manpower from "sunset" to "sunrise" jobs, the Rehn-Meidner model served not only to reduce the inflationary pressures that come from firms unable to pay prevailing wages, but also to weed out the poorest end of the labor market. In this sense, economic policy paralleled the new principles of social policy, namely to upgrade the lowest social groups to "middle-class" status and to uplift the quality of jobs offered.[22]

Swedish Social Democracy's new policy regime brought in its train a gradual dismantling of the traditional separation between social and economic policy. The pursuit of full employment no longer remained solely the domain of fiscal or monetary policy, but was integrated with welfare policy. And welfare goals such as income equalization were shifted into labor market policy. Housing policy is, perhaps, the clearest example of how social and economic policy merged.

Urbanization came very late to Sweden, but then it came with a vengeance. From a welfare perspective, the housing situation was extraordinarily bad and demanded immediate attention. From an efficiency perspective, the lack of adequate urban housing was an obvious barrier to labor mobility and economic progress. The "Million Program," launched in the 1960s, promised to build one million new units within ten years. Financed largely by the huge pension reserves, this goal was actually attained. Yet if this was a significant Social Democratic success, it was also short-lived. Housing shortages were perhaps alleviated, but at the expense of widespread consumer dissatisfaction with the residential milieu offered in the new, prefabricated satellite communities.

It is debatable whether the active labor market policy actually provided an effective means for noninflationary full employment,[23] but its effects on equality cannot be questioned. The reduction of wage differentials was spectacular during the 1960s and, especially, the 1970s.[24] It is also beyond doubt that accelerated economic change has been heavily biased in favor of "good" jobs. In the emerging service sector, for example, the low end of cleaning, restaurant, and hotel jobs has declined substantially. A recent study shows that, today, the ratio of good to bad jobs in the Swedish service sector is 4:1, compared to 3:1 in Germany and 2:1 in the United States.[25] Solidaristic wage policy prohibits low-paid jobs; active manpower programs provide an opportunity to leave them. The equality that this regime provides also, in principle, nurtures efficiency. It moves labor from low- to high-productivity employment; it eliminates the part of the economy that is most likely to lead to poverty and low incomes. It is thus a method for reducing the burdens on welfare state transfers and services.

With its new welfare state regime, the Social Democratic party re-emerged triumphantly in the politics of the 1960s. The dull years of end-of-ideology thinking had been left behind, and the party could once again proclaim itself the vanguard of equality, democratization, and modernization. The bourgeois opposition remained torn and split, forced to acquiesce to the Social Democratic image of society, as Castles has put it.[26]

The Social Democratic party seemed to be heading toward a successful and politically powerful coalition of its traditional blue-collar core and the new middle strata, a coalition that did not seem to require uncomfortable and negative-sum trade-offs. Yet the logic of coalition-building was new in the sense that it precluded a cross-party alliance. Social democracy became even more dependent on its own capacity to mobilize electoral majorities. If all parties pitch their message in the image of a wage-earner party, however, that alone could not secure social democracy a bright political future. Instead, lasting political dominance must be based on the loyalties that Social Democratic institutions cement. The future of Swedish Social Democracy came to rest more on the welfare state it had built, and less on the one it could promise.

Paradoxically, we can trace both the Social Democratic party's comparative success and its growing difficulties to the nature of the welfare state regime it erected in the 1960s. When more or less fully completed in the early 1970s, the middle-class welfare state gave birth to new incompatibilities for which old solutions were inadequate. It is therefore possible to argue that a third phase emerged in the mid-1970s. In this phase, once again, the issues of power, equality, and efficiency resurfaced.

ECONOMIC DEMOCRACY OR MORE INEQUALITY?

All available data confirm that Swedish Social Democracy enjoyed an electoral breakthrough among the middle classes in the 1960s. Its share of lower- and middle-level white-collar voters jumped to between 52 and 55 percent, and, despite the party's new middle-class profile, the loyalties of the traditional working class did not wane.[27] The new political realignment seemed therefore to be an optimal positive-sum strategy. Public opinion in the 1960s endorsed a new surge of welfare state extensions.

The 1970s, however, showed the new regime to be inherently fragile; the coalition began to turn negative-sum. Electorally, the Social Democratic party lost much of the white-collar support it had gained in the previous decade. Concomitantly, it suffered losses among blue-collar trade union members, and especially disquieting was the party's suddenly weakened capacity to mobilize young, first-time voters.[28] In contrast to the old red-green coalition, the Social Democrats had no cross-party alliance (other than the implicit support of the tiny Communist party) with which they could remain in office despite electoral losses. The losses in 1973 and again in 1976 were not cataclysmic, as they were in Denmark and Norway, but they were enough to unseat the Social Democrats for two terms.

The bases of Social Democratic power thus seemed to be eroding. It is tempting to explain this with reference to the impact of seriously worsened international economic conditions, the two OPEC oil-shocks, and stagflation. Slow growth renders the pursuit of full employment difficult, international instability helps debilitate Swedish export performance, the growing welfare burden becomes more difficult to finance, and distributional tensions become more severe. All of these forces (including also the unanticipated conflict over nuclear energy) surely had an impact, but since the basic incompatibilities were evident prior to the 1973 oil crisis our attention should properly focus on the inherent problems in the model itself. The essential difficulties in the new middle-class regime were tied to the problem of equality and efficiency.

Incompatibilities in the equality-efficiency mix began to surface in the late 1960s. As investment rates declined, the maintenance of full employment appeared in doubt. The active labor market policy had contributed to a major wave of economic restructuralization and rationalization, but the welfare side of this process proved harsher than anticipated. Redundant workers were increasingly reluctant to move to the industrial centers (it often meant moving from the north to a drab housing complex in a southern urban center). A politically more unmanageable symptom was the sudden outburst of unsanctioned wildcat strikes, motivated by plant closures and perhaps also narrowing wage differentials. Swedish workers seemed to be striking against the Swedish model.

Rising worker resistance and declining economic growth compelled a relaxation of the active manpower policy's efficiency aims. The bias of active manpower programs began to shift from worker mobility into expansionary industries to the subsidization of sheltered jobs. The problem of labor market management was further exacerbated by rising inflation. The ill-timed, government-induced recession of 1971–1973 helped contain wage pressures and inflation temporarily—but at the cost of rising unemployment, additional burdens on the active labor market programs, and a subsequent wage explosion in 1974 and 1975. A serious blow to the Social Democrats' legitimacy was the decay of popular trust in its capacity to uphold the promise of full employment. By the mid-1970s, voters actually believed the bourgeois parties to be better guarantors of full employment.

The remedies that were adopted seemed to contradict the efficiency standards that social democracy itself had defined. Decaying industries were subsidized, as were bloated company inventories. It seemed that across the board the management of economic problems imposed heavy fiscal costs. The Social Democratic model had always relied on budget surpluses to counteract inflation in a full employment economy. However, in 1975, the central government deficit reached 4 percent of total expenditure. The maintenance of full employment seemed increasingly expensive, and no longer compatible with dynamic growth.

Nevertheless, the strains emerged much more powerfully on the question of equality. The distributional claims within the Social Democratic coalition became increasingly opposed. On one side, the LO—representing blue-collar workers—demanded a new thrust toward income equalization. This coincided with the assertion of novel egalitarian claims from new left circles and, most decisively, from women. On the other side, there emerged a growing resistance to excessive equalization from both within the more privileged sections of the working class (metal workers especially) and from the new middle class. The dilemma was not just the incompatibility of claims and the lack of economic growth with which to dampen them, but also the growing incapacity of the welfare state to deliver income redistribution. Sweden's new middle-class welfare state remained universalist, granting top-quality social rights that deproletarianized workers while satisfying middle-class tastes. However, these same features blocked serious income redistribution.

In the late 1960s the Social Democrats were bombarded with criticisms for their failure to deliver equality. Caught unprepared, the party scrambled for an adequate response. It established a commission to examine the problem, and party programs now promised a new era of equality. In the trade unions, the solidaristic wage policy was pursued with new vigor; but, whether in the public budget or in collective bargaining, the scope for more redistribution soon proved narrow indeed. The labor movement's new program for economic democracy in the 1970s can only be understood in terms of the dilemmas of equality it faced.

In a welfare state that is both universalistic and middle class, the scope for major income equalization is automatically narrow. Taxation gradually loses its redistributive potential when spending burdens mount. And spending will grow dramatically in a welfare state that grants universal and optimal rights. The Social Democrats' egalitarian thrust in the early 1970s consisted of steepened tax progressivity, the elimination of employee contributions, and the introduction of an array of special transfers to low-income households. Most important of these were housing allowances and special supplements to pensioners not eligible for the ATP earnings-related pension. In a sense, this implied the reintroduction of targeting, but of a new kind: not as a traditional income test, but as an automatic "transfer' test." In this way, universalism would not be jeopardized by the potential stigma of targeted assistance.

In sum, social democracy's response to its novel efficiency-equality problems ended up costing the welfare state more money, and thus required higher taxes. The combined effect of exploding taxes and spending is exactly what most concurrent theories of welfare state crisis claimed would trigger a political backlash.[29] In Sweden, there is little doubt that tax resentments were on the rise, and that the electorate's support for additional welfare program expansions was on the wane. Yet, there was never any serious, or even half-serious, welfare state backlash.[30] The middle-class fabric of the welfare state had been thoroughly institutionalized and thus proved itself immune to right-wing attacks or popular backlash movements. This was evident when in the 1980s the Conservative party adopted a neoliberal program, advocating rollbacks and a residual welfare state alternative. The electorate's response was overwhelmingly negative.

There were no revolts in Sweden against taxing and spending per se.
But, instead of "voice," social democracy faced a growing problem of "exit."
The cause was, ultimately, the incompatibility of distributional claims. The
distributional problem for the Social Democratic party sprang from the
composition of its coalition. From one side, its low-income constituency
(and increasingly women) pressed for more income equality. This pressure
had its roots not only in the traditionally egalitarian thrust of Swedish culture and the rising expectations that had been fueled by the long era of
labor movement power, but also in the logic of the new welfare regime
itself. The underlying egalitarian principle of postwar social democracy was
the elimination of class- and status-based privilege by gradually raising
workers to middle-class status in the welfare state, in the sweeping education reforms of the 1960s and 1970s, and in the labor market. But the new
welfare state promoted earnings-differentiated social benefits, and the solidaristic wage policy, despite its great strides, was chronically weakened by
wage drift. Low-wage workers, and especially women, therefore demanded
a new war on inequalities. And in Sweden, low-income wage earners constitute a tremendously powerful force in the trade union system.

From the other side of the Social Democratic coalition, large numbers of
salaried wage earners, as well as workers in highly profitable industries,
began to express resentment against what they saw as excessive income
equalization and a loss of status. In 1971, for example, the SACO had lost a
major battle over pay against the public sector, and since then the salaries
of government-employed professionals had lagged behind those in the private sector. Similarly, key unions such as the Metal Workers Union
(Svenska Metallindustriarbetareförbundet) felt increasingly cheated in the
solidaristic wage regime. In addition, the forbidding marginal tax rates
seemed to confiscate what was left of traditional middle- and upper-income
earners' pay advantage. Under these conditions, a typical middle-class
household needed two earners in order to uphold the middle-class consumption standard to which it felt entitled.

The evolution of the equality issue began in the trade unions, and only
later did the middle-class resentments surface. In an inflationary environment with high marginal taxes, real wage gains can only be attained with
very high nominal wage hikes. With the 1973 refinancing of social contributions, employers were already burdened with the OECD's highest wage
costs; the 1975 wage increases seemed to price Sweden out of international
competition. It was therefore logical for the LO to press for a tax reform

that would lessen the marginal tax. This, however, would also lessen progressivity. Hence, the tax and transfer nexus of the welfare state could no longer serve ambitious income redistribution projects.

As tax reform was delayed (until 1991), the problem lingered on. And, even if a large part of the growing public expenditure was financed with debt, the tax burden continued to mount. Many other factors can be cited as explanations for the middle-class defections from the Social Democratic party in the 1970s, but the issues of taxation and a perceived excessive income equalization moved a crucial middle-class margin to the right. In short, the system failed at once to satisfy (especially trade unionist) calls for more equality and middle-class demands for less taxation and greater income differentiation. This dilemma was obviously exacerbated by slow economic growth; its resolution certainly could not be found within the realm of conventional welfare policies.

In many ways, the situation in the 1970s came to parallel that of the 1950s. The Social Democrats presided over a set of basic incompatibilities, for which they could offer no positive-sum solutions. The party expended its creative energies on day-to-day problem management.

The trade unions once again took the policy initiative, perhaps because they experienced the contradictions more keenly than did the party; their scope for maneuver was being impaired by declining investments, rising unemployment, and the tensions generated by solidaristic wage policy; bargaining for real wage increases was made close to impossible by the interface of inflation and taxes. The agenda was defined by the rediscovery of Ernst Wigforss's old slogan: "Democracy cannot stop at the factory gates."[31] Under this heading, the LO signaled its intent to renegotiate the class accord that was struck with business in the 1930s. With a series of industrial and economic democracy reforms, the LO wanted to challenge directly the sanctity of ownership prerogatives and, concomitantly, shift the terrain of the distributional struggle.

The shift to industrial codetermination and economic democracy was presented as a bold new era of social democratization: the time had come when social citizenship naturally demanded its economic complement. Rhetorical grandeur notwithstanding, the shift was motivated by necessity. Far from being a long-planned leap into the future, it appeared to most as hastily improvised problem management. Nevertheless, with its call for industrial and later economic democracy, the Swedish labor movement provoked a fundamental alteration of the Swedish political economy. By introducing the principle of citizens' rights directly into private enterprise,

the Social Democratic party found itself in a very difficult climate of ideological polarization.

With a series of reforms, culminating with the famous MBL law (*Medbestämmandelagen*, or worker codetermination), the Social Democrats succeeded in improving job security, health and safety standards, and worker
participation in decision making. These reforms reflect the problems that
faced trade unions from the late 1960s onward: declining rank-and-file cooperation with the active labor market regime, leftist demands for more
equality, and heightened anxiety about job security. The reforms were attractive in the sense that they responded to real concerns yet imposed no
new expenditure burdens on the welfare state; they appeared to be a politically rewarding positive-sum response.

The reforms did not, however, repair social democracy's troubled coalition. For one, they failed to mobilize decisive enthusiasm among wage
earners. More seriously, they explicitly attacked the sanctity of employer
prerogatives laid down in the 1938 Saltsjobaden accords. The labor movement had now declared open war on the rights of private property. The
reforms, as such, were not especially radical, but they were accompanied
by a trade union demand that all issues pertaining to managerial rights now
be subject to negotiation. It was the principle rather than the actual practice that provoked a new hostility and militancy among employers.

The LO's proposal for economic democracy in the form of collective
Wage-Earners' Funds reflects also a blend of necessity and choice. The
proposal, originally authored by Rudolf Meidner (1975) and accepted by
the LO congress in 1976,[32] addressed mainly the issues of equality and
democratization of capital ownership.[33] The plan that was eventually legislated in 1982 reflects the influence of Sweden's changing political and economic realities. Its original focus on equality gave way to an almost exclusive preoccupation with capital formation, social security finances, and
sustained full employment. Economic democracy became an instrument of
economic policy, not of equality and extended social welfare.

The Social Democratic party's defeat in the 1976 elections cannot be
ascribed to one single factor, but there is no doubt that the Wage-Earners'
Funds issue became an electoral liability.[34] Its political management was
extraordinarily clumsy. Furthermore, the Wage-Earners' Funds had pre-
cious little popular backing, even among blue-collar union workers. The
idea had even less support among the new middle classes.[35]

Industrial and economic democracy can be regarded as Swedish Social
Democracy's principal means to resolve its zero-sum problems. Both, how-

ever, clearly fell short of resolving the constraints of power, equality, and efficiency upon which social democracy's future hinges. The politics of "economic citizenship" could not do for social democracy in the 1970s and 1980s, what the ATP reforms did in the 1960s: they have failed to coalesce workers and the middle class, and they have not established a new consensus for the Social Democratic image of society. They have instead helped catalyze open political warfare from both employers and the nonsocialist parties. The maintenance of social democracy on top of a private capitalist economy is a difficult undertaking when there is no acceptable accord between capital and labor.

The politics of economic citizenship have also failed to genuinely address the dilemmas of equality. The Wage-Earners' Funds may help safeguard pensions for the future, but their appearance is that of compulsory savings. They do not appear to respond to workers' demands for more equality, nor to middle-class demands for reduced taxation. In other words, the fundamental distributional dilemma that has plagued the Social Democratic middle-class coalition remains unresolved.

Finally, economic and industrial democracy constitute something of a break with social democracy's historical model for "egalitarian efficiency." The new employment rights and worker codetermination are seen (rightly or wrongly) by management as stifling and inflexible. For rationalizing firms they impose a rigidity that motivates management to seek recourse to traditional welfare programs: the pension system makes it feasible to lay off older workers, and training subsidies become a precondition for hiring young workers. In this sense the welfare state becomes, unwittingly, a tool for managing economic problems to an even greater extent than before.

In reality, then, economic and industrial democracy could not solve the dilemmas of the new middle-class welfare state regime. And indeed the ideological intensity that has surrounded the issue has obscured a policy development of far greater importance, namely the ways in which the upgrading of welfare state services came to serve as the principal employment policy from the late 1960s onward. The origins of this trend lie in two issues that loomed large in the 1960s social policy discussion: the improvement of women's position in society, and greater attention to the quantity and quality of social service delivery. The two concerns were merged in the ensuing explosion of health, education, and social services.

The provision of more services means, in effect, job creation in the public sector. Since the expansion began in the full employment era, it is not possible to ascribe to it the motive of compensating for lack of alternative employment growth. The logic, however, turned social service growth into an employment policy directed almost exclusively at women. From 1965 to 1984 total government employment doubled, from 700,000 to 1.4 million. Almost the entire increase was centered in the social welfare sector (education, health, and social welfare), and women came to occupy more than 75 percent of these new jobs, a large proportion certainly on a part-time basis. The consequences of this growth are far-reaching. First, it has undoubtedly led to a level of service provision that matches the quality of Sweden's transfer system. In this sense, it has consolidated the middle-classness of the welfare state by providing a service network that captures the desires of a middle-class clientele.

Second, the policy of a welfare state monopoly on the provision of social services further immunized it against backlash, especially because many public goods are overwhelmingly consumed by the middle classes. That the welfare state edifice, despite tax conflicts, remained not only legitimate but actively supported by the middle and working classes is clear from the debates and conflicts of the 1980s. In 1981 the nonsocialist coalition proposed a bill to reintroduce waiting days and certification to qualify for sickness benefits. It was no problem for the Social Democrats to mobilize overwhelming opposition to this relatively mild welfare state rollback. During the mid-1980s, the Right abandoned its customary consent to the welfare state and campaigned for residualism and privatization. This earned them a severe electoral defeat in the 1985 elections.

Third, the extension of welfare state employment has permitted an extraordinary growth in female labor force participation, a goal that the Social Democrats could ill afford to ignore. Given the sluggish state of the Swedish economy throughout the 1970s, this would clearly have been difficult to attain otherwise. The welfare state has, in effect, provided the only significant source of job growth over a long era.

The welfare state's two roles as employer and as service provider are interdependent. Services create jobs for women, but services must also exist for women to work in the first place. One of the reasons for this extraordinary female bias is that services for women become jobs for women. However, there is an additional interdependency in the welfare state's strong employment bias. A welfare state like the Swedish needs to maximize the tax revenue base and minimize "unproductive" expenditures. In light of the historical commitment to productivistic social policy, this naturally spurs an all-out effort to generate employment. The expansion of service employment is therefore not merely an isolated phenomenon; it is the expression of a self-reinforcing circular logic inherent in Swedish Social Democratic politics.

In this instance, however, Social Democratic circularity may have turned negative. The underlying motives were clearly female emancipation, equality, and welfare, and they allowed Sweden to post a fantastic increase in female employment during an era when most European nations suffered stagnation and often decline. The result, however, is that the overwhelmingly female bias has created a degree of gender segregation in the Swedish labor market that may very well prove explosive. Women constitute 72 percent of overall government employment; in contrast, their share in manufacturing is 22 percent and in business services, 38 percent.[36] The Swedish labor market may in fact be one of the most sex segregated in the advanced industrialized world.

The ghettoization of women in the public sector may easily confound the disequilibrium problems that face the Swedish welfare state. Indeed, it is threatening to become the major axis of social conflict in Sweden. The basic problem is that taxation has become the precondition for the maintenance and expansion of employment. With almost a third of the labor force in the public sector, and with limited prospects for additional tax revenues, government is forced to hold down public employee salaries. Not surprisingly, the consequence is an explosion of equity struggles between the (largely female) public sector unions and their private sector equivalents.

If the public-private sector axis, overlayed by gender, becomes the major point of conflict—as events in the 1980s certainly suggest—Social Democracy's coalition capacities will be additionally limited. Recent data show that the large white-collar mass is increasingly divided into a Social Democratic core largely composed of (female) public employees, and a backlash core composed of (male) private sector employees.[37] The future of social democracy may hinge on the propensity to marry between the two groups.

CONCLUSION

The Swedish welfare state is usually subject to two kinds of interpretations. One, typified by the work of Walter Korpi[38] and John Stephens,[39] attributes its achievements to the labor movement's unique capacity for power mobilization: social democracy fought successfully against an unwilling opposition and could thus implement its chosen program. This argument does not deny that there may have been a general consensus on many occasions, and even over long periods. The compelling case for this interpretation is that Social Democratic power has been so solid as to compel the opposition into acquiescence—that social democracy became, in fact, hegemonic.

The alternative interpretation unites to a degree pluralists and Marxists. In a recent study, Heclo and Madsen refute the centrality of power and argue that the foundations of the Swedish model lie in the culture of Sweden itself.[40] Its expansion has mainly followed a process of adaptation and creative problem solving. Therborn, representing at this point a structuralist Marxian class analysis, argues that the emergence of the full-scale welfare state had less to do with parliamentarism and party power than with the exigencies of a changing class structure.[41] In other words, both types of analyses conclude that the result would have been similar had Sweden been ruled instead by nonsocialist majorities.

The position taken in this study is eclectic: it deviates from each interpretation, yet fuses arguments of both. It seems evident that many of the principles embodied in Swedish Social Democracy are mere mirror images of features deeply ingrained in Swedish society: the ideals of universalism and solidarity come immediately to mind. It would, in fact, be equally valid to reverse the argument and posit that Swedish Social Democracy owes its success in the first place to the preexisting solidarity that permeated the society in which it emerged and grew; its historical achievement was to invoke what was, essentially, already present. Social democracy, then, may be the natural outcome of Swedish history rather than its great architect.

However, there is also certainly a strong case for a power model. There are specific instances in which the outcome would have been markedly different had the Social Democrats not been so powerful. Such was the case in the ATP pension conflict, for example. The most likely alternative outcome would have been an array of private sector, occupational pension schemes, possibly less universalistic and certainly less under collective control. But what, then, is the basis of Social Democratic power, and when is it of critical significance?

The view taken here is that the power of Swedish Social Democracy has been partly hegemonic and partly conditional upon its capacity to forge positive-sum alliances. Its hegemonic power rests on its capacity to interpret and represent the social structure, and on its institutionalization of social citizenship. Social democracy has constructed a welfare state regime that brought defeat to those who challenged its legitimacy. The middle-class electorate returned to the fold in the 1980s not because the Social

Democrats presented a new policy, or because the party had resolved any of its severe distributional dilemmas, but because the bourgeois governments between 1976 and 1982 could offer no alternative to the Social Democratic logic. Besides being fragile and torn throughout their reign, the bourgeois parties could not claim any greater economic efficiency, nor could they afford tne risk of allowing unemployment or greater inequalities to surface. In that period Social Democratic hegemony blocked the bourgeois parties' chances of mobilizing the middle classes around an alternative political formula.

The second basis of Social Democratic power derived from its capacity at key historical junctures to forge positive-sum class coalitions, and subsequently to strengthen these with positive-sum policies. As a consequence the nonsocialist opposition was simultaneously divided and weakened. Ultimately, the Social Democrats could maintain power because their appeal to solidarity among the different social classes was stronger than the issues that divided them; the full employment welfare state gave social democracy the basis for such an appeal.

If we do not take into account the centrality of solidarity and coalition formation, we cannot understand why social democracy's position has eroded. If the ingrained solidarity of the social structure was the underpinning of Social Democratic success for more than half a century, it may also be the gradual decay of this kind of solidarity that explains its contemporary flux. The instinct of solidarity in Sweden has its historical roots in the homogeneity, uniformity, localism, and, indeed, provincialism of Swedish society. It was never a culture tolerant of "otherness," differentiation, or privilege. The solidarity of the People's Home was viable precisely because Sweden remained undifferentiated, because it did not fully urbanize until after World War II, and because it remained quite isolated from the rest of the world. Unlike the rest of Europe, the Swedes had never been forced to experience foreign powers or peoples (with the marginal exception of the Finns) within their communities. Sweden enjoyed the luxury of modernizing in relative isolation from the rest of the world.

These conditions no longer obtained from the 1960s onward as Swedes came to experience urban anomie, geographic and cultural mobility, and the influx of foreign ethnic and racial cultures and minorities, and as Sweden's once simple class structure was penetrated by the much more complex, differentiated, and cosmopolitan new middle classes. Such structural change makes it much more difficult to arrive at positive-sum solutions to the constraints of equality, efficiency, and power. It is clearly not the welfare state edifice, nor its tax load as such, that has weakened social democracy. Taxes are never popular, but they were tolerated because of loyalty to, and identification with, the welfare state.

The real source of disequilbrium is that equality is a perennial Achilles' heel in the Social Democratic welfare state model. The People's Home represented a very basic kind of equality, one for the "little people." This corresponded quite well to the kind of class structure that then prevailed. The solidarity upon which the Social Democratic coalition was forged was very much nurtured by popular resentments against anything associated with elitism and privilege; the privileged few could in any case be counted on to look out for themselves. With the new "middle-class" model, however, the Social Democrats introduced a new concept of equality: equality at the top. The welfare state was thus recast in the role of the great leveler, an instrument of deproletarianization. The basis for a Social Democratic majority coalition was once again assured, but only to the extent that it leveled social citizenship status and not income differentials. The weakness of the middle-class regime is that it also called for, and depended on, substantial income leveling.

To fully establish the middle-class coalition, the Social Democrats have been compelled to find an acceptable way out of the income equalization dilemma: equalization may be demanded by lower income groups, but it is rejected by higher income groups. The problem is that both groups are necessary ingredients for political power. From the experience of the 1970s and 1980s, it is clear that economic democracy is no positive-sum solution. The Swedish Social Democrats will most likely have to renounce one of socialism's cornerstones and accept the idea that equality can be only a secondary objective.

NOTES

1. Branting, *Tal och skrifter* (Speeches and Writings), 1928, 3:54ff. and 278.
2. Kuhnle 1978.
3. Arbetarförsäkringskommittén, vols. 1 and 2, 1888 and 1889; Elmér 1960.
4. Branting 1909; 1928, vol. 3; Elmér 1960.
5. Branting 1928, 3:246ff.; Tingsten 1967 (1941), 1:200.
6. Branting 1929, vol. 8.
7. Comparative social expenditure data for the 1930s, compiled by the International Labor Office (1933, 1936), show clearly Sweden's international laggard position. Even prior to the 1936 Social Security reforms, the United States spent more than Sweden on social protection.

8. Lindbeck 1975.

9. G. Möller 1928, 5.

10. Ibid., 5; my translation.

11. A. Myrdal and G. Myrdal 1934 (1941); A. Myrdal 1944; and Thomson 1944.

12. The following account is based on the protocol of the Social Democratic party executive meeting of 31 July 1951 (Arbetarrörelsens arkiv och bibliotek, Stockholm).

13. My translation.

14. Tingsten 1955. Herbert Tingsten, a former professor of political science, had been a Social Democrat but left the party. In 1946 he became editor-in-chief of the liberal newspaper *Dagens Nyheter*.

15. No. 4 (1946).

16. The conflict over the ATP pensions is well documented in B. Molin (1967). A brief discussion can also be found in Esping-Andersen (1985).

17. Särlvik 1977; Elvander 1980; Esping-Andersen 1985.

18. A more systematic and detailed comparison of the Scandinavian social democracies can be found in Elvander (1980) and Esping-Andersen (1985).

19. Hedström and Ringen 1987; *Patterns of Income and Poverty* 1988.

20. *Välfärd i förändring* 1984.

21. Rehn 1948.

22. For excellent overviews of the new Swedish economic policies in the 1960s and thereafter, see Martin (1975, 1979, and 1984), Erixon (1984), and *Norden dagen derpå* (1986).

23. Lindbeck 1975.

24. Meidner 1974; *Den produktiva rättvisan* (Productive Justice) 1984.

25. Esping-Andersen, "Post-Industrial Employment Trajectories: Germany, Sweden, and the United States" (Paper presented at the ECPR Workshops, Amsterdam, April 1987).

26. Castles 1978.

27. Esping-Andersen 1985, 126–30.

28. Holmberg and Gilljam 1987.

29. Wilensky 1976; Rose and Peters 1978; Heidenheimer, Heclo, and Adams 1975.

30. Esping-Andersen 1985.

31. Wigforss 1923.

32. Meidner 1978 (1975); LO 1976a.

33. We shall not review the long and complicated evolution of the Wage-Earners' Funds debate here. Some excellent overviews can be found in Åsard (1978) and Pontusson (1984). Meidner's original proposal is available in English (Meidner 1978, 1975), but see also LO (1976a). As Meidner notes, his proposal follows a long history of similar ideas, beginning with Naphtali's (1928) and continuing in the postwar era with the West German Gleitze plan. Closer to home, Meidner's model followed the lead of the Danish Economic Democracy plan, developed by the previous Social Democratic prime minister, Viggo Kampmann (1970). For an overview of comparative economic democracy, see also Esping-Andersen (1985).

34. Petersson 1977.

35. Petersson 1977; Holmberg 1981; Esping-Andersen 1985.

36. M. Rein, "Women in the Social Welfare Labor Market" (Wissenschaftszentrum Berlin, 1985, Mimeographed).

37. Holmberg and Gilliam 1987; Hans Zetterberg, *SIFO Indicator*, no. 3, 1985.

38. Korpi 1978b; 1981.

39. Stephens 1979.

40. Heclo and Madsen 1986.

41. *Sweden Before and After Social Democracy* 1978.

Klas Åmark

3

Social Democracy and the Trade Union Movement: Solidarity and the Politics of Self-Interest

A STRONG LABOR MOVEMENT

By international standards, the Swedish labor movement appears unusually strong, well organized, and unified. Its forty-four years of unbroken rule (1932–1976), the highest degree of union organization in the world since the 1930s, and the close cooperation between the SAP and the LO (Swedish Trade Union Confederation) are usually mentioned as indicative of its strength. However, depictions of the Swedish labor movement's unique power are misleading when its opposition is disregarded. In Sweden there is also an unusually strong, well-organized business and industrial community, inclined toward negotiation, as well as a comparatively weak and fragmented middle class. It is this triad that, especially during the period from 1910 to 1976, provided the basis for the Swedish power system, which has been very much defined by the labor movement's political advantage and by a combination of conflict and cooperation in negotiations, in the labor market, and in politics between the labor movement and business and industry.

The Swedish Landsorganisationen, or LO (Swedish Confederation of Trade Unions), is the large central organization representing the workers trade unions. The LO was formed in 1898 and initially encompassed mainly privately employed workers unions. During the interwar period, public sector unions successively joined the LO. In the beginning the LO was a common defense organization, supporting unions exposed to large-scale lockouts by employers. From the mid-1930s, power became concentrated in the LO and its executive, the Landssekretariatet. After the end of the 1930s, the LO entered into central agreements with the SAF, the Swedish Employers Confederation, regarding negotiation regulations, worker protection, and industrial democracy. From the mid-1950s onward, the LO has conducted central wage negotiations with the SAF.

Swedish employers organized themselves early on. The SAF was formed in 1902 as the central employers organization and from 1907 onward was the dominant organization. Other employers organizations—for example, those in forestry and agriculture, the building trades, and the wholesale and retail trades—later became members of the SAF. The SAF has always been a heavily centralized organization with power markedly concentrated in its chair and managing director. For a long time the SAF tried to promote similar central agreements for all the major branches of industry and resolutely used lockouts to achieve its principal demands.

An important prerequisite for the balance of power in Sweden has been the close collaboration between the SAP and the LO, expressed on an organizational level by the collective affiliation of LO members in the SAP and also by a close and many-faceted practical cooperation.[1] This collaboration has rested on a firm reformist foundation, which has been not just ideological but also built into the respective organizations' operating principles. For the party this has entailed the decisive strategic choice of giving priority to parliamentary power through winning general elections and thereby, according to inter alia the American Marxist Adam Przeworski, choosing to ignore in practice the possibility of developing Sweden into a socialist society.[2]

The LO's corresponding strategic choice has involved not only choosing to negotiate with employers on working conditions,[3] but also accepting certain premises for negotiations, one of which concerns the distinction between the concepts of the labor force and work (or the work process). The labor force is a commodity that is bought and sold in the marketplace, and when this transaction is completed, work can commence at the workplace. The Swedish labor movement was organized from the start around the task of improving the workers' terms when they sold their labor, while power over the work itself was left open. Since the 1890s the instrument for this struggle has been the collective agreement, which gave rise to what I have called open cartels for the purpose of limiting competition within the unions' own ranks regarding price and other terms for selling their labor. Workers in occupations in a particular geographic area or workplace agreed among themselves as to what they would ask for their labor. The cartels were normally open, which meant that everyone who worked within an area covered by the agreement had the right to join a labor union, but the agreement applied to all workers regardless of whether they were organized.[4]

For many Swedish employers this method for limiting competition was well known when they confronted it in the 1880s and 1890s. Even before the trade unions became a real problem for them, they had used the method themselves to limit internal competition in selling goods and services. When the workers began to organize themselves and demanded the drafting of collective agreements, the employers were faced with a strategic choice. Between 1895 and 1910 the strategy of the open cartel succeeded, and it was institutionalized in the SAF (the Swedish Employers Confederation) and in the system of collective agreements. This meant that the employers could decide to utilize those advantages that the contract system gave them—particularly that of industrial peace and the possibilities of calculating long-term labor costs. The SAF gave priorities to calculability and predictability—in other words, what Max Weber called the most important basic principles of modern rational capitalism.[5]

One important condition set by the SAF for acceptance of the collective agreement system, and by extension rights of association and negotiation, was that the LO accept paragraph 23 of SAF's charter. The employers retained the right to lead and distribute work, and to employ and dismiss personnel. The first principle thus expressed the distinction between the labor force and work and gave the employers rights of determination over the latter. The LO has openly challenged this principle only on a few occasions. The second principle involved intervention in the buying and selling of labor, and over this battles have been repeatedly waged.[6]

A critical prerequisite for the LO's successes was, then, that the organized employers in their turn accepted their role in the strategy that made negotiation and the policy of collective agreements possible.

Despite the strong common ground between the SAP and the LO there have been potential conflicts between their respective principles and goals:

	Short-term	Long-term
SAP	Maximizing voters	Parliamentary power
LO	Improved working conditions	Economic power over production

At certain times conflicts have arisen between the long-term goals of the SAP and the short-term goals of the LO. At the beginning of the century, when the SAP wanted to call a general strike for the right to vote, the LO leadership deferred support mainly because they did not want to jeopardize strike funds for a political action. When the LO has reached out toward economic power, in the guise of nationalization, wage earners' funds, or industrial democracy, the party has procrastinated on the grounds of maximizing voters.

In the following, we shall look more closely at how relations between the SAP and the LO have developed over a century, focusing on two issues: strikes and industrial peace up to 1940 and wage policies from 1940 to the present time.

STRIKES IN POLITICS

Strikes and the Party

When a fully formed collective agreement system was established, organized through strong centralized parties, collective bargaining assumed great significance. The negotiations encompassed not only wages but also several other central economic questions such as the wage system, working hours, and negotiation procedures. A great deal was at stake, and powerful organizations with substantial resources at their disposal were pitted against each other. There were many grounds for dispute; solidarity within the open cartels held, and perseverance during open conflicts was often very great. Conflicts over rights of association and negotiation became especially bitter; whereas although disputes over the content of the agreement were many and protracted from the 1890s to the 1930s, they contained relatively little open violence.[7]

The character of the conflicts essentially determined the role of the state in the labor market. The high frequency of conflict and concomitant large economic losses placed heavy pressures on the state to intervene in the labor market, while peaceful interludes primarily cast the state in the role of arbitrator. Only secondarily was the need for open repression demonstrated when the state, and in particular its judicial system, was used to protect the rights and implications of private ownership. The party's double role was also thereby defined in relation to the labor market. As an integral part of the labor movement, the SAP should support the unions in their organizing and struggles; and as legislator and potential representative of state power, the SAP should strengthen arbitration institutions and minimize the social/economic losses engendered by the conflicts.

Labor disputes confronted the trade union movement with two large problems. On the one hand, unions were to obtain the best possible working conditions by successful collective bargaining, especially when negotiations gave way to open conflict. On the other hand, unions should minimize the drain on their resources caused by disputes, which could even threaten their existence—after the general strike of 1909 several unions fell apart. In questions of industrial peace the two branches of the labor movement had partly shared, partly conflicting interests.

During the labor movement's breakthrough phase during the 1880s and 1890s, relations between the party and the trade union movement were at once intimate and ambiguous. Leading party spokesmen regularly intervened in strikes, sometimes as strike leaders, sometimes as members of arbitration courts. Cooperation was not without friction, however, partly because party members thought that many of the spontaneous, minor upheavals were meaningless and doomed to failure from the start. So they intervened to stop such disputes. From the mid-1890s the trade union movement grew very rapidly. The organizations became more stable, and their leadership became more effective. The union representatives took increasingly decisive control over their own organizations and asserted their right of decision making in union disputes. The party's representatives maintained their right to assert the interests of the general public against those of individual groups of workers.[8]

The creation of the LO in 1898 and, several years later, the withdrawal of the demand for obligatory affiliation in the SAP, were held as signs of the trade union movement's independence from the party.[9] However, party leaders could still intervene in conflicts as arbitration judges. A 1906 law concerning arbitration in labor disputes established the Conciliators' Service, and thereby a state agency systematically took over the role of arbitrator. The party's direct participation in labor disputes diminished further.[10]

From the point when the SAP entered the government in 1917, Social Democratic governments have had direct responsibility for industrial peace, with all the ensuing complications. One example of such complications is the major lockout in the building trade in 1920. In the middle of March 1920, the first wholly Social Democratic government had presented an ambitious housing program. On 1 April the SAF ordered a comprehensive lockout in the building industry, which continued for eight months. The Branting government had excellent reasons for wanting the conflict to end and appointed a large commission for arbitration. But the commission's contract proposal was rejected in August by a broad majority of workers, whereas the employers with some hesitation supported it.

The government then intervened directly with its own proposal, which was immediately and almost brutally rejected by the union leadership, despite the negative effects this could have in the coming parliamentary elections. And indeed the election was a setback for the SAP, and the government was forced to resign. However, just before resigning the government intervened again, this time in favor of the workers. By means of confiscating a large amount of cement (with the help of a special wartime law) and offering it for sale, the government broke the material blockade that the SAF had raised at great cost. After this a solution to the conflict was found, one supported by a broad majority of the workers.[11]

During the 1930's another conflict in the building industry landed in the center of politics. In the spring of 1933 an extensive strike broke out among building workers, in part led by communists. This strike was if anything even more inopportune for the Social Democratic government than that of 1920, since the strike blocked important measures in the famous crisis program. The government again actively intervened. When the first arbitration proposal was rejected by the workers, the government itself presented one more favorable to the workers, which they supported after submitting to some pressure from both the party and the LO leadership. This time the employers prevented a settlement.

The dispute became protracted. Early in 1934 a new proposal was presented, one closer to the standpoint of the employers and accompanied by the threat of a comprehensive lockout. The government again pressed for a settlement, this time threatening coercive legislation to back up a mediation proposal before the conflict expanded into a general strike. Confronted by such a double threat, the workers and union leadership were compelled against their will to accept an unfavorable contract proposal.[12]

Labor market conflicts have often created complications in the relations between the SAP and the LO. The party has repeatedly advocated general interests over and above the struggle of individual groups of workers for better working conditions. A gradual shift is apparent: first the party's and then the LO leadership's basic position has gone from supporting disputes to accepting responsibility for general economic development. The more responsibility they have been prepared to take, the more negative they have been to major industrial disputes. The party's task has more and more clearly been to strengthen mediation, even if this has pressed workers into significant concessions.

Legislation and Industrial Peace

From the 1890s to the mid-1930s, more than any other country Sweden was a nation of strikes and lockouts. The high frequency of labor unrest gave rise to lively political debates on questions of industrial peace and to a number of attempts at legislation. One of the central political questions from the beginning of the century to 1928 was the "judicial dispute" or litigations—that is, disputes over how current contracts should be interpreted.

During the decade from 1910 to 1920 the Conservatives made three ambitious attempts to create collective agreement legislation. From the unions' point of view, these proposals contained many unfavorable paragraphs, and the LO, together with the SAP and the Liberals, managed to stop the legislation. Despite this, there was actually a group within the labor movement supporting legislation, but its positive attitude was squelched by the Conservatives' far-reaching and antiunion legislative ambitions.[13]

A marked change had occurred by 1925. The groups in the labor movement favoring legislation began to take the offensive under the leadership of Gustav Möller, minister of social affairs, and Per Albin Hansson's brother Sigfrid Hansson, who was chief editor of the LO's magazine, *Fackföreningsrörelsen* (The Trade Union Movement). Möller thought it especially appropriate to legislate mandatory arbitration in litigations, and he appointed a delegation for industrial peace to investigate this and other related issues. However, the tactical problems of a parliamentary minority soon came to block Möller's ambitions. The Social Democratic government collapsed in 1926, and Carl Gustaf Ekman's Liberal government took over. When the latter decided to create laws for collective agreements and a Labor Court without giving the LO the central role in preparing the legislation that it demanded, the labor movement again united against the proposed legislation, despite major differences within the movement.

When the laws were passed in the spring of 1928 (despite a short protest strike organized by the LO), the forces in favor of the legislation again got the upper hand. The LO's General Council, supported by a broad majority, agreed to appoint members to the Labor Court in the autumn of 1928. The new laws would soon prove to reinforce the collective agreement system and thus the principles of the open cartels—primarily the agreements on sales of labor, industrial peace during the contract periods, and calculability. The laws were stiff against not only workers breaking the peace but also against employers who tried to put themselves above the law or who refused to sign the agreements.[14]

During the decade from 1928 to 1938 the question of "third party" rights was in the center of legislative ambitions and political debate. The Conservative party was again on the march, with a particularly aggressive campaign during the first half of the 1930s directed against the alleged misuse of union dispute measures. Among other things, the Conservatives wanted a law protecting third parties from being drawn into conflicts through blockades, boycotts, threats, and harassment. Especially controversial was the idea that strikebreakers should be "third parties" with the right, guaranteed by the state, to be "neutral" in conflicts and to expect protection from the state against harassment after conflicts.[15]

The Conservative campaigns and grandiose attempts at legislation met with stiff opposition from the LO and its members, particularly regarding the issue of strikebreakers. However, the party leadership believed that certain abuses did exist in the labor market, not least in the building industry, and that because of this there was a need for legislation. The government pursued two lines. The first consisted of a revision of the proposed law on the third parties in order to produce a usable draft relating to certain aspects of the issue. The result was a proposition before the 1935 Riksdag signed by the minister of social affairs, Gustav Möller. The second line was advocated by Prime Minister Per Albin Hansson himself: a broad inquiry on the multifarious issue of industrial peace.[16]

Hansson presented his idea for an inquiry to the LO leadership in December 1934. There was a sharp reaction. He was called to the LO Secretariat the next day to defend his proposal. Despite Hansson's explanation that the inquiry was not directly aimed at concrete legislation, LO's chair Edvard Johansson stated that the LO could not be involved in the inquiry: "The measures already adopted concerning third party rights have created such ferment and animosity among union people that to continue along this line would only damage the trade union movement."[17] Thus it was the strong negative views of the members that were decisive for the LO, not its own basic attitudes toward attempts at legislation. When the Möller proposition was to be dealt with in the Riksdag, the situation facing Edvard Johansson and LO's vice chair Albert Forslund was that the bourgeois parties, who had a majority in the Riksdag, wanted to go further than Möller, so that in effect the proposal was the best of a bad lot for the LO. However, at the last minute the Conservative party decided to vote against the legislation because it did not define the position of strikebreakers. LO leaders now got their chance: they submitted reservations to the committee and sent word to the parliamentary group and the government that they intended to vote against the proposal in the Riksdag since there was no longer any risk that the bourgeois parties would unite on making the law worse. The debate in the Riksdag was long, and pressures from the party leadership heavy. In the end, however, the Social Democratic government did not dare risk pushing the law through against the wishes of the LO and decided to withdraw the proposition.[18]

The actions of the LO leadership in the Riksdag came to determine the fate of the industrial peace inquiry. When Möller contacted the LO to discuss the results of the inquiry, the LO leadership replied that they were not interested in state intervention in the labor market. Instead the LO intended to negotiate on its own with the SAF on the current questions. And so it did. Negotiations ended with the Saltsjöbaden Accords of 1938.[19]

Among other things the Saltsjöbaden Accords contain regulations covering disputes over agreements currently in effect, a prohibition on conflict measures taken for political or religious reasons, and improved employment security, but otherwise little that is concrete. However, the accords became a symbol for cooperation between the SAF and the LO and therefore came to provide the basis for industrial peace on the Swedish labor market and to be one of the most important components of the "Swedish Model."[20]

Thanks to a tactical blunder by the Conservative party, the LO succeeded in keeping both the state and the SAP away from union activities. The free negotiation model was maintained against the will and ambitions of the party leadership, who soon had to accept it.

STABILIZATION POLICY AND THE POLICY OF WAGE SOLIDARITY

With the Saltsjöbaden Accords, the question of industrial peace was struck from the political agenda for four decades. Instead, economic policy came to the fore, giving both branches of the labor movement extremely difficult problems to solve and causing significant rifts both between and within each organization.

The Postwar Program

Problems began to multiply especially after World War II. When the war was nearly over, an extensive inquiry was initiated to shape policy for the anticipated postwar depression. A special working group was formed with representatives from party organizations and the LO, chaired by Wigforss and with LO economist Gösta Rehn as executive secretary, to draw up a labor movement Postwar Program.[21]

This program strengthened the solidarity between the two branches of the labor movement. The program assumed an acute risk for a new postwar depression similar to that of the 1920s. Full employment was consequently given highest priority and was to be maintained through a demand-stimulating Keynesian budget policy in accordance with the 1930s model. Like the Social Democratic crisis policy of the 1930s, this budget policy would directly and concretely favor workers in their struggles to improve their living standards.[22]

The Postwar Program also contained the view of the economy and wages that had played an increasingly important role for the LO since the 1930s. Instead of concentrating on the struggle over the share of wages and profits in the value derived from production, the LO focused more and more on a policy that gave priority to long-term economic growth. The LO leadership thus began to believe that measures for improving efficiency in business and industry lay in the workers' interest. At the same time a democratization of power in companies was called for. The statements of wage policy in the Postwar Program cohered with the LO's intentions too. "Equal Income for Equal Work" was the slogan, mainly referring to workers and small farmers in rural regions, who should earn the same incomes as city workers, and women, who should receive the same wages as men.[23]

Excess Demand and Inflation

Postwar pessimism was soon shown to be unfounded: in fact, the world economy entered the period that has been called the "golden age" of capitalism (1950–1973). Generally high demand created full employment, which was maintained for a long time. The economic and political problems of the time proved to be the opposite of what had been expected: the risk of excess demand and inflation loomed large. Stabilization, which became the central goal of Social Democratic policy, came to expose both branches of the labor movement to great stresses and strains.

For social democracy, stable economic development was synonymous with rapid economic growth. Overuse of the resources of production could have equally negative effects on accumulated growth as underuse. Therefore in the government's economic policy the reduction of excess demand became an even more important element than stimulation in periods of recession, and it was mainly reduction measures that created friction in relations with the LO.[24]

Substantial wage increases that exceeded the levels allowed by economic growth were considered to jeopardize stable economic development. The risk of wage inflation was particularly great because of full employment, which lessened competition between workers and increased competition between companies for labor. One effect of this was that from 1946 wage drifts (wage rises exceeding contract allowances) increased to a level nearly three times as high as that in the period between the wars.[25] In the words of Finance Minister Sköld in 1955: "We are facing one of the most difficult problems of full employment, a strong trade union movement and weak employers."[26]

In that the SAF did not manage on its own to keep wage levels under control, there was a sizable risk that inflation would rise to such heights that stabilization would collapse. The power problem of the wage policy was that, though the party had decisive political power, it was at that time weaker in relation to the bourgeois parties than the LO was in relation to the SAF.[27]

The difficult problem that the interplay between stabilization policy and wage policy confronted both branches of the labor movement with for a long time was formulated with a good deal of insight by Minister of Finance Ernst Wigforss in the financial plan for 1947:

> Nothing can prevent a whole population from granting itself increased monetary income—nothing except the realization that it will not necessarily lead to a real rise in living standards. The difficulty with allowing such an insight to determine actions lies not least in the difficulty of finding one amongst all the recognized norms for a just distribution of the national income. Striving for

social/economic balance is thus conjoined with attempts to find such
mechanisms within economic life which take account of the need to
promote enterprise and thrift, and at the same time, give various
groups of citizens the feeling of receiving their just proportion of the
results of production.[28]

The problems Wigforss pointed to were highlighted by growing inflation
that began in the autumn of 1946. By the beginning of 1947 the Postwar
Program had lost its guiding role in the government's concrete economic
policy. Instead, efforts were made to find a model for an economic policy
within a full employment economy that could combine a stabilization policy
demand for restraints on nominal wage hikes with wage policy demands for
justice and equality. These efforts lasted a decade and had to be carried on
while acute problems were being solved.

Problems with Stabilization and Unity

In the spring of 1947 the government tested the possibility of producing a
common anti-inflation program with a series of conferences, first with other
political parties and then with representatives of business and industry and
interest organizations. These attempts failed.[29] During the wage negotiations in the autumn of 1947, the pressure to raise wages became very
strong despite the LO's call for restraint and the SAF's attempt to central-
ize negotiations in order to keep wage levels down. LO chair Axel Strand
was even able to tell the General Council that the government had told
him that a new, major labor conflict would force it to resign.[30] Experience
from wage negotiations in 1947 demonstrated that admonishments from the
government and LO's leadership did not give concrete results when they
were not accompanied by the language of power. From the LO's point of
view, the problem was that the government did not choose to guarantee
price levels in exchange for union restraints.[31]

When the economic problems became even worse in early 1948, Wigforss immediately had to achieve more effective stabilization. In his view
the basic problem was a significant surplus demand, which was potentially
extremely inflationary. It was necessary to limit purchasing power drastically—the exact opposite of the crisis program's and the Postwar Program's stimulation of demand. The first to acknowledge the government's
demands was the civil service, especially civil servants in TCO (the Swedish Confederation of Professional Employees). The government then
turned to the farmers and the LO, requesting an extension of current contracts and agreements.[32]

This confronted the LO with a difficult solidarity problem, since the same measure had different effects on the various unions and contract areas. The problem had very much to do with the difference between the export industry on the one hand, and domestic market industries and the public sector on the other. The export industry was dominated by flexible wage systems, minimum wages with individual bonuses, and piece-rate systems. The large external demands also created stiff competition between companies for labor, which led to widespread wage drifts. In domestic market industries and the public sector, fixed hourly wages dominated, which made wage drifts impossible at the same time as parts of the consumer goods industry were in a difficult situation.[33]

To the government's demand for an extension, representatives from the export industry replied that they would refrain from the largest potential wage rises. Representatives of unions with fixed wages could argue that they received nothing at all while unions with flexible wage systems, which moreover normally had higher wage levels, received wage drifts anyway. The six-month-long debate finally ended with the trade unions going along with a general extension of contracts. They understood that the only thing they could commonly agree to was what was called an "idiot stop"—that is, wage stoppages for everyone. Since negotiations between the SAP and the Agrarian party over a coalition had collapsed in the middle of October, a refusal from the LO on stabilization would have provoked a government crisis.[34]

In June 1949 the newly appointed coordination minister, Per Edvin Sköld, initiated the next major stabilization measure, aiming to repeat the 1948 decision to prolong contracts. The LO Secretariat agreed that extending contracts was the only method to organize a restrained wage policy. But early on, spokesmen appeared with other views, advocating an adjustment policy that would allow limited increases in wages and prices with the intention of favoring the most exposed groups. The LO Secretariat suggested that the union accept the extension in exchange for guarantees that certain social and political reforms would be speeded up. The General Council first said no, favoring the adjustment policy line. One reason for this reaction was the fear that farmers and white-collar employees would be favored over workers. However, since the LO leadership had pressured these groups' representatives at a roundtable conference, the Secretariat decided to support the government's wage-stop policy through a new extension.[35]

A new agreement was almost at hand when in September 1949 England devalued the pound, and the Swedish government decided to follow with a major devaluation of 30 percent. This changed the prerequisites for the

stabilization policy, which for the government became even more important in order to prevent wage and price rises from ruining the effects of
devaluation. For the LO, the problem prior to devaluation was the relationship with farmers and white-collar workers; after devaluation, the problem concerned the large profits expected by the export industry. However,
it was difficult to get at these profits through wages. Since profits were so
unevenly distributed among companies, a wage policy aimed at devouring
the profits would lead to drastic wage differences between companies and
industries. Better would be a policy in which the government collected
surplus profits in taxes and used the money to subsidize the price rises that
accompanied devaluation. The government firmly refused to follow such a
line.[36]

What won approval in the LO was the adjustment alternative, combining
wage increases for the most exposed groups and an upward adjustment of
price levels. The debate was conducted in a General Council meeting with
representatives of the government in which Per Edvin Sköld acted with
characteristic brusqueness, actively supported by Prime Minister Tage
Erlander and Agriculture Minister Gunnar Sträng. From the union side,
LO economists Gösta Rehn and Rudolf Meidner finally spoke out, arguing
for the adjustment alternative in an occasionally heated polemic against
Sköld. An important argument for Rehn and Meidner was that the government's policy forced the LO into preventing its members from receiving
the wages that employers were willing to pay them.[37]

Within the LO the decision was postponed, and information was requested from the unions about what demands the latter wanted to advance
for their most poorly paid members. In the meantime, the often troubled
prime minister experienced a difficult crisis: if Erlander, the academic,
were to have the LO against him, it would be difficult for him to remain in
his post.[38]

When the unions' demands arrived at the LO, it was evident that even
the very worst-off groups were so many and so large that the adjustment
alternative was impossible to justify. One reason for this was that World
War II caused such a compression of the wage structure that it was next to
impossible to differentiate any one small group of workers with unques-
tionably bad working conditions.[39]

Thus, devaluation created great strains on the labor movement; tensions
multiplied—between the government and the LO and between the LO
leadership and its members, as well as between different unions. Experience of this type of state income policy was clearly negative for all participants, even though the government triumphed in the short term.

Profits, Wages, and Prices

The powerful inflation that followed on the heels of the outbreak of the Korean War in June 1950 created new trials for the stabilization policy. In the face of the workers' demands for wage compensations, Erlander and Sköld (now finance minister) called for restraint.

A lively debate ensued throughout nearly the whole of 1951 between the government/party leadership and the LO around the triad of profits, wages, and prices. The government intervened against the "worst" surplus profits in the lumber industry, requesting union restraints in exchange. The LO then demanded a significantly more extensive suspension of profits and a more active price policy before it would accept modifications.[40] Disputes between the government and the LO again became troublesome. This time it was Finance Minister Sköld who was so distressed at the LO leadership's inability to control the trade union movement that he considered resigning.[41]

The boom period from 1954 onward exposed the inflationary aspects of the new wage policy. The LO's chair, Axel Strand, felt compelled to protest publicly against the government's stabilization policy and its demands for union restraints. The debate between Strand and Sköld was first conducted internally in the parliamentary group, then publicly and with a great deal of notice in the First Chamber in the budget debate in January 1955.

Strand's rather harsh criticism followed the formulation of the problem by Wigforss in 1947. In boom periods the stabilization policy prompted unacceptable wage differences because the profitable export industry awarded its workers substantial wage drifts, whereas fixed hourly wages developed slowly. Consequently the worst-paid workers got the lowest bonuses and now needed substantial compensation, without any lectures from the finance minister. Sköld stuck to his basic opinion that the unions were too strong and employers too weak in an economy of full employment, and hence the government must ensure union restraints.

The critical question was raised by Erlander: If the government allowed wages and prices to rise, would it be possible to cope with the unemployment that would occur when the weaker companies collapsed?[42] In fact, to that question LO economists Gösta Rehn and Rudolf Meidner had a positive and constructive reply. They were given the opportunity to present their model for how stabilization policy and wage policy should be shaped and coordinated at a conference at Harpsund in March 1955. For the first time Erlander agreed with the Rehn model, being convinced by the answer to the question he had posed in the parliamentary group. From 1956 the political prerequisites existed for the government to work with the Rehn model as a basis for its economic policy. The coalition with the Agrarian party had been dissolved, Sträng replaced Sköld as finance minister, Geijer replaced Strand as LO chair, and the SAF forced the LO into centralized wage negotiations. In retrospect, the years from 1957 to 1964 have been considered the stabilization policy's golden age.[43]

Thus it was the LO and LO economists that succeeded in formulating a basic theoretical recipe capable of finding practical solutions to the problems Wigforss had articulated. The basic idea behind this stabilization policy was expressed in the following way by Gösta Rehn in 1951:

> The latter type of stabilization policy can, in contrast to that carried on in Sweden at least up to 1950, be expressed as follows: through a more stringent budget balancing policy so much purchasing power is drained away (actually effective demand) that certain islands of unemployment arise. These shall not be "drowned" through a new flood of purchasing power, but instead should be "showered" by concrete, locally managed, recruitment of labor and measures to encourage labor mobility.[44]

What Rehn meant was that the government's all-too-generous economic policies caused symptoms of excess demand, which had to be attacked with control measures. This created political problems—not least for the LO, whose leadership was forced to exert such pressures to restrain members' wage demands that serious problems of confidence arose.[45]

Women's Wages

At least since the beginning of the century, women's wages in relation to men's have been an issue. For a long time women's wages comprised 50 to 65 percent of those of men. The argument for equal pay was conducted at an early stage from two sides. Radical women demanded equality with men and consequently the same wages for the same work. Conservative male workers also demanded the same pay, on the grounds that an employer who had to pay as much to a woman as to a man would employ men; in this instance, equal pay policy was part of a policy to protect men in competition with women for work.

It took a long time for the LO to take any concerted action to equalize wages. In 1943 a committee was appointed to investigate the question, and from 1944 onward the issue regularly appeared in recommendations from the General Council to unions to raise women's wages. In that year the principle of equal pay for equal work, directed especially at women's wages, was included in the Postwar Program. However, a central agreement between the SAF and the LO to abolish special wages for women was not drawn up until 1960.[46]

Full employment gradually gave women such a strong position in the labor market that their risk of being excluded or pushed out of the market was thought to have disappeared. The abolition of women's wages at the beginning of the 1960s increased the average wage of women workers from about 60 percent of men's to over 90 percent by the 1980s. This happened at the same time as the proportion of working women increased to a very high level by international standards but in the context of an extremely gender-segregated labor market, where typical women's occupations have lower wage levels than those of men despite everything that the LO has been saying for thirty-five years about equal pay for equal work.[47]

THE LABOR MOVEMENT AND THE CRISIS

Inflation and Structural Crisis
The stabilization and wage policy based upon the Rehn model functioned well until the mid-1960s. Thereafter the labor movement was faced with several new very difficult development tendencies. The most obvious was the rate of inflation, the marked increase of which was due mainly to developments on the world market and to rises in oil prices. More difficult to perceive were the first signs of a growing structural crisis, especially in the Swedish staple industries, that broke out in full force in 1977 and 1978.

After 1966 the system of contract agreements and collective bargaining was also greatly complicated by public employees receiving full strike and bargaining rights. The SACO (the Swedish Confederation of Professional Associations) immediately utilized these rights in a large teachers strike. Union-organized middle-class groups henceforth played an increasingly important role in the labor market and in political life. LO ambitions for equity and just distribution received new impetus through comparisons with white-collar workers.[48]

Wage leveling also became a greater priority for the LO, and stabilization was increasingly seen in terms of a leveling policy. The LO's low-paid unions had been assiduously advancing the wage-leveling issue since the end of the 1940s, but the LO did not concretely begin to assert the demands of its low-paid members until the contract negotiations during the second half of the 1960s. This coincided with the SAP's call for increased equality at the party conference in 1967. Both cases were influenced by the general radicalization of politics and societal debate occurring at the time.[19]

The LO's low wage policy widened the gap between itself and the TCO (the Swedish Confederation of Professional Employees) and the SACO (the Swedish Confederation of Professional Associations), politically and in terms of union issues. For the LO to retain its dominance in the negotiation system, white-collar workers had to accept the LO's basic principles: social/economic responsibility, industrial peace, and commitment to raising low wage levels. In practice this presumed total coordination of negotiations for these larger employee collectives. However, this coordination, strongly desired by the LO, was prevented by the white-collar workers. In 1970 the SAF concluded a five-year agreement with white-collar workers in private industry, which took them out of coordination efforts. In the public sector, there were rumblings of a major dispute in the spring of 1971, a situation that had troublesome aspects for the LO. One problem was that public sector employers took the initiative, for example, through a very radical offer to low-paid members early in the negotiations that challenged' the LO's view that the export industry should spearhead wages. Another important new tendency was evident here—the opposition between the private and public sectors.

The LO was also against large, open conflicts, in part because of the risk of direct state intervention in negotiations. Precisely this occurred in 1971 when the SACO and Swedish Federation of Government Officers (SR) strike was met by the state employer with comprehensive lockouts that attracted great attention, even internationally. When the lockout threatened to extend to military officers, Prime Minister Olof Palme chose to apply the Coercion Act.[50]

In the early 1970s the LO had landed back in the problems of the late 1940s, with competition between various groups and organizations threatening to force a wage spiral during a time of high inflation. The problems in the 1970s were even greater, however, particularly because of the high marginal tax rates (direct income tax). The gross increases that would now be necessary in order to raise real wages after taxes were very great indeed. In addition, industrial profits were exceptionally large in 1974 and 1975.

Since the problems and risks facing negotiators in 1974 and 1975 were unusually great, it seemed justifiable to ascertain whether the government could intervene to facilitate wage negotiations. The government's reply came in what was to be known as the Haga Agreements.[51] The parties involved were the SAP, the Folkpartiet (the Liberal Party), the TCO, and the LO, and the result was a tax and wage package. The rate of progressive income taxes was lowered, and this was financed by raised employers contributions, which in turn were deducted from the margin available for pay increases. The LO maintained its principle of disclaiming state income policy, but the Haga Agreements were accepted as a temporary departure in anticipation of a reformed tax system.[52] If the intention of the Haga Agreements was to check wage rises, then they utterly failed. The total increase of labor force costs in 1975 and 1976 was about 20 percent per year.[53]

During the first half of the 1970s the Rehn model declined in relevance. Competition between the wage-earner collectives imperiled stability, high international inflation rendered wage margins more difficult, industrial peace was no longer guaranteed, and the state was forced to intervene in matters of income policy.

Theoretical ideas within the LO did not suffice to produce solutions for the problems of the late 1970s. Since its congress in 1961 the LO had developed a more considered program for state economic policy, in part to deal with the large problems accompanying the structural transformation of industry. However, the LO's reasoning presumed a growth economy. When the crisis landed in Sweden current industrial policy became discredited because of the way the bourgeois government that came to power in 1976 handled it. The Wage-Earners' Investment Funds also became important in the LO's plans for the future. The idea of the funds was launched at the congress in 1971, and the first proposal was presented by Rudolf Meidner and others in 1975. However, the funds were formed to solve problems that arose because large profits were left behind in the most successful companies through the machinations of solidaristic wage policies, not in order to cope with the lack of capital concomitant with the structural crisis.[54]

The party's economic policies under the firm hand of the aging finance minister, Gunnar Sträng, were not especially devoted to solving future problems either. The stabilization policy functioned increasingly badly from the end of the 1960s, partly because of lack of "timing" in countercyclical measures. The traditional Social Democratic policies, oriented to stabilization, growth, and efficiency, were not able to handle the new problems—stagflation, increasing unemployment, etc.[55]

Labor Law Offensive and the Power over Work

In the area of economic policy the labor movement had evident difficulties in formulating a new basic theoretical concept to meet the problems of the 1970s. However, in another area the LO was on the offensive—labor law legislation. This offensive encompassed three main areas:

1. Strengthening *job security* (which included the right to time off for studies, etc.) through, among other things, a law on employment security—a continuation of the struggle dating back to 1906 and 1938 over the employer's right to freely employ and dismiss people. Through legislation the LO obtained better and stiffer regulations than through collective agreements.

2. Strengthening *negotiation rights* through the codetermination law and the law on union representatives. This legislation expanded and reinforced the collective bargaining system. Here too the LO obtained extended negotiation rights at the same time as antistrike regulations were made more stringent so that wildcat strikes would be considerably more difficult to carry out.

3. Improved possibilities for influencing *power over work and production* through the law on board representation, aspects of MBL (the Codetermination Act), laws on the work environment and occupational injury, and the Wage-Earners' Investment Funds. The LO's ambitions were far-reaching, but in the decision-making process preceding the legislation these ambitions were moderated a great deal—not only because of opposition from the SAF and the bourgeois parties, but also because of the actions of the SAP.[56]

The first two groups of laws generally rested on the premises of the Swedish model: parceling off work from the sales of the labor force, and industrial peace. However, the LO's ambitions as regarding power over work and production stretched much further than what was allowed by the first premise. When this boundary was exceeded, it became difficult for the LO to get the party to go along. The SAP was willing to strengthen negotiation institutions and workers' positions as sellers of labor, but the party wanted to avoid compulsory legislation for power over work.

Ways Out of the Crisis

The SAP's second election defeat in 1979 made it clear to the labor movement that the previous economic policy was not sufficient either to win the election or to conduct Sweden out of its crisis. Work to shape a new basic concept for economic policy went on in various places. The LO worked on proposals for wage and industrial policies and the Wage-Earners' Funds, aiming at the 1981 party conference. In the autumn of 1980 the SAP leadership appointed a crisis group consisting of Ingvar Carlsson, Kjell-Olof Feldt, and Leni Björklund (leader of the Stockholm County Council) from the party and Rune Molin from the LO to work out a program for the future. Leading party economists, headed by Erik Åsbrink and Klas Eklund (both would later play an important role in the Department of Finance), formed a discussion and investigation group aimed at influencing future SAP government policy.[57]

On several points a broad unanimity was quickly reached. Industrial profits were too low and had to be allowed to increase—at the expense of wages. The rate of inflation had to be checked by drastic measures of some sort, but the LO's industrial committee opposed devaluation. Wages had to be restrained while total effective demand was stimulated through, for example, a comprehensive state investment program.[58]

The party program, "The Future for Sweden," which was adopted at the conference in 1981, strongly stressed—in contrast to the material produced by the LO—the need for restraints in the public sector. The program also railed against unilateral stimulation of demand. Both public and private consumption was to be restrained to provide room for a considerable increase in industrial investment.[59]

The crisis program, then, was a compromise between the LO's active industrial policy, with strategic state planning on a fairly long-term basis and different types of stimulation of production and efficiency, and a line favoring restraints, which was pursued especially hard by party economists with a certain amount of support from the crisis group.[60] However, at the party conference in 1981 the side supporting restraints was temporarily defeated. At the LO congress of the same year the demand for an active state industrial policy dominated, and the election campaign of the following year was inspired by ideas of expansion.[61]

Party economists argued for a major devaluation. After the election victory they were joined by the party leadership, and the new Social Democratic government initiated its term with a devaluation of 16 percent.[62] This measure was quickly accepted within the party and by the LO, despite the fact that devaluation involved a major reinterpretation of the program. However, devaluation also galvanized the competitive power of Swedish export industries and entailed a rise in the proportion of profits from 22 percent of the value derived from production in 1980 to 34 percent in 1983—historically a very high level. Industrial growth was thus stimulated by means of a vigorous redistribution of the surplus from the wage earners to the companies.

Because companies suddenly received such large profits, the active state industrial policy could be drastically diminished. In their new form, the Wage-Earners' Investment Funds were of little practical importance. The two conditions set by the LO (for instance, at the 1981 conference) for it to accept raised profit levels—an active state industrial policy and the Wage-Earners' Funds, which would exert real influence over companies—played an obscure role in the government's actual policies after devaluation.[63]

The new policies were carried through by the party's real leaders despite the fact that the decisions in both party and LO conferences went otherwise, as did statements in the election campaign. The new basic concept for economic policy was this time formulated by a small group of party economists, probably in close cooperation with Feldt, who developed ideas that were very far from the main lines of the LO debate.

The primary goal of devaluation was to create growth and profits in industry. After the decision to devaluate, it became, if anything, even more important to reduce inflation by restraining wage rises so that industrial competitiveness would not be shattered again. The new policy, which came to be called the "third way," compelled the government to be firm and decisive in keeping wage levels down.*

When comparing the "third way" policies with the 1930s crisis program, the labor movement's Postwar Program, and the Rehn model, it is very striking that the Feldt policy forced the government to place greater demands on the LO and consequently on the majority of party members than the Keynesian economic policy had. Feldt shared the problem of holding wage levels down with Wigforss and Sköld, but the new negotiation struc-

*The policy of the "third way" originally designated a choice between three political and economic strategies when the Social Democrats formed a government in 1982. The three alternatives were: (1) an expansionist crisis policy along the Keynesian lines that were then being tested in France; (2) a liberal economic policy with stiff restraints in order to fight inflation and concomitant high unemployment; and (3) a major devaluation in order to stimulate the Swedish export industry and increase its international competitiveness. This last alternative became Finance Minister Kjell-Olof Feldt's "third way." Later (as earlier in the 1940s and 1950s) the expression came to be used in a totally different sense. The "third way" was presented as the Social Democratic alternative to liberal capitalism and its high unemployment on the one hand, and Eastern Bloc socialism on the other. My reference here is to the term in its original (1982) meaning. See especially Bergström in the present volume.

ture in the labor market complicated the problem. One central difficulty at present is the large proportion of imported goods—even in export industry production—which means that the stimulation of private consumption leads to a drastic weakening in the balance of payments while at the same time doing nothing to benefit the export industry. Hence the government is forced to argue against the very type of policy that had previously contributed to making the labor movement in Sweden so strong. Instead of following a policy that leads to direct advantages for the workers, the government has had to persuade workers to accept not only higher profits and lower real wages but also a lower quality of public services. What the government has been able to offer in exchange has been improved economic growth, high levels of employment by international standards, and a rapidly decreasing budget deficit.[64]

Wage earners' willingness to accept the "third way" can mainly be perceived in their response in wage negotiations, where their belief in the future and convictions concerning the durability of government policy are put to the greatest test. In the finance plans for 1987/88 and 1988/89 the wage rises obtained since 1982 were pointed to as the only significant threat to the new policy. Moreover, wage statistics show that the problem increased during 1987 through a significantly greater wage drift than the government expected.[65]

Since 1982 wage negotiations and settlements have been inordinately contentious and complicated. The most important reason is that various organizations in the labor market have developed strategies tending in different directions. It is not the forms of negotiation that create present-day problems on the labor market; the problems originate in the negotiating parties' policies.[66]

Public employees have repeatedly disregarded one of the premises of the Swedish model, namely industrial peace. Major open disputes were initiated by government civil servants in 1985, and by doctors and nurses in 1986. These disputes provoked discussions about government employees' right to strike.

However, a greater threat to the model has come from the Swedish Employers Confederation. The strategy followed by the SAF since 1907 has been based on, among other things, limiting competition in open cartels, with binding agreements on labor force prices not only with workers, but also between companies. Limits on competition were relaxed in periods of full employment through wage drifts, which allowed a certain amount of competition between companies for labor, using wages as bait. During the

1980s the SAF has expressed in increasingly determined tones the demand that the system of wage negotiation be decentralized. The policy pursued by the Swedish Metal Trades Employers Association in 1988 seems to have aimed at disbanding the central agreements between the SAF and the LO in order to open up competition between industries, while the state agreements have been utilized mainly to preserve industrial peace in local negotiations. In addition, the desire for a great deal of latitude has been expressed—to enable managers to set individual wages in accordance with the slogan, "Wages—A Tool for Management."

Needless to say, this entails a departure from the open cartels principle of limiting competition. Instead, companies developed a new strategy to protect themselves against the harmful effects of competition through binding the most important groups of workers and other employees to the company by means of sundry benefits—increased individual wages, profit sharing, stock purchases subsidized by the company for the employees, etc. This rapidly growing new strategy also makes it even more crucial for the SAF to attack the LO's policy of wage solidarity.[67]

The LO's main line has been to safeguard central and coordinated negotiations and wage solidarity—including its leveling aspect.[68] Difficulties in upholding a solidaristic wage policy have markedly increased during the 1980s. It has been assaulted not only by the SAF but also by public sector employers. The introduction of individual management wage settlements, toward which a crucial step was taken in the 1988 contract negotiations, invites individual wage settlements in the public sector, which is totally alien to the basic principle of wage solidarity—equal wages for equal work. The Social Democratic–run public employers policy has thus directly and openly challenged the core of the LO's wage policy and consequently threatens the unity within the wage-earners collective.[69]

At the same time, strains within the LO have been increasing considerably. One cause of discord is that, as in the 1950s, the different wage systems produce such varying results from the same centrally negotiated contracts.[70]

For the Social Democratic government the problem from the beginning has been wage levels and the annual wage rises. When Finance Minister Feldt thought it necessary to allow profits to rise drastically, it became even more important to keep wage levels down. To accomplish this the government has adopted a number of different measures: direct discussions with the parties involved about wage levels, reforms of marginal tax rates to dampen demands from high-income earners, the proclamation of limits to inflation, and wage ceilings. What we have here in effect are a number of elements in a state income policy.[71]

In summary, neither the LO nor the SAF has kept to the premises of the Swedish model. LO demands have increased its power over work and production, while the SAF, partly in reaction, is proceeding to abandon the policy of open cartels. The situation is further complicated by the independent actions of white-collar groups. Growing oppositions in the labor market and competition between the large wage-earners collectives push up wages and have led to several major conflicts. Both tendencies threaten devaluation policy and thus compel state intervention.

As long as there is disagreement on strategy, the government is continually forced to intervene in the labor market. In the extension of this policy lies a general acceptance of an active state income policy with an expressed program of wage levels and wage structures, and with expanded legislation for negotiation and conflict rights.[72] Thus are the potential oppositions between the two branches of the labor movement thrown open; they are pitted against each other, with the party in the role of employer and the LO in that of a straight employee, with diminished social and economic responsibility.

PREREQUISITES FOR UNITY

Viewed from the perspective of a century, what dominates our picture is the successful cooperation between the SAP and the LO. By international standards this cooperation is also unique, and is one of the primary reasons for the unusual position of power occupied by the Swedish labor movement—within politics as well as in the labor market.[73]

Among the important prerequisites for unity within the labor movement are the party's successful investments in parliamentary power, the LO's strategy of limiting the competition of open cartels, and the institutionalization of that strategy in a centralized collective bargaining system, supported by legislation that reinforces the negotiation system and is directed against those among both workers and employers who do not respect peace obligations involved in the wage settlements nor the duty to negotiate.

On several crucial occasions the labor movement has been confronted with fundamental problems for which new solutions (with strategic implications) have had to be found. In these situations serious disagreements have arisen, between the SAP and the LO and within each organization. What is remarkable is that the LO has successfully defended itself against the most far-reaching party proposals and launched its own solutions, which have also become practical policy. Since the 1920s the LO's defense against the embraces of the party has involved adhering to its earlier policy, which was against active state involvement in the labor market. However, in the 1980s a new situation has arisen as party economists' proposals have become practical party policy. There is no doubt that the LO's influence over government policy has appreciably diminished since 1982.[74] One feature noticeable throughout has been that stiff demands from the party on the LO have aggravated dissension within the LO and led to such virulent protests from members that LO leaders have had good grounds to criticize party policy.

As was asserted at the beginning of this chapter, it is not only the labor movement that has had unique power in Sweden, but also the employers and business organizations. This may seem like a contradiction, but it actually expresses a causal connection. The open cartel strategy creates and demands strong inner cohesion; the centralized wage bargaining system institutionalizes and strengthens solidarity in both camps and gives little latitude to group and special interests. So even the SAF's choice of strategy is an important condition for the strength of the Swedish labor movement.

This choice of strategy rests on the distinction between work and the selling of labor. When the LO seriously prepares to step over the line of demarcation, the SAF feels compelled to review its choice of strategy. This is precisely what happened in the 1960s. Armed with the labor law reforms and proposals for Wage-Earners' Funds, the LO demanded power over work and production. The SAF's reply involved turning away from the central contract system and the open cartels' limits on competition toward a strategy in which companies compete for the most attractive work force and defend themselves by binding key workers more closely to the company with various fringe benefits. It is this strategic reevaluation within both the LO and the SAF that more than anything else threatens the Swedish model—and by extension the strength and unity of the labor movement.

What is remarkable is that Social Democratic government policy after 1982 contained several elements that are directly antagonistic to conditions for unity within the labor movement and the wage-earners collective. As Harry Fjällström (elected LO employee responsible for wage negotiations) claimed in an interview, the large profits in business and industry became after the 1982 devaluation powerful weapons in the hands of corporations, weapons that were used against the labor movement.

The SAP's concentration on parliamentary power places the reformist labor movement in a possibly insoluble dilemma. The growth of a quantitatively extensive middle class has meant that to an extent the SAP's policies must satisfy middle-class and white-collar workers' interests in order for it to win elections and retain parliamentary power—which indeed the SAP has done.[75] Moreover, the growth of the public sector means that parliamentary power makes the party's leading representatives into large and formidable employers. Thus, reformist parliamentarianism means that the party must be able to encompass the interests of employers as well as those of white- and blue-collar workers. Since 1982 the party has deemphasized specific workers' interests as represented by the LO in favor of the interests of employers and white-collar workers.

In conclusion, despite the well-known difficulties involved with making satisfactory prognoses, I would like to point out a few possible tendencies in the development of relations between the SAP and the LO. Cooperation and cohesion between them have so far been strong enough to resist fairly powerful stresses. However, it seems to me that dissensions today are perhaps greater than ever before. An international parallel may illuminate the future course of events.

England and Denmark show two different patterns of splits within the labor movement. In England, right-wing Social Democrats have broken out of the interface between Labor and the TUC and entered into a close, albeit problematic, relationship with the Liberal party at a time when the left wing of the Labor party is strong. In Denmark the ties between the party and the trade union movement have always been weaker than in Sweden. Denmark's party has moved to the right, leaving a gap on the left for a socialist people's party to fill.

Within Swedish Social Democracy, the right wing has normally dominated. However, the policy of the "third way" has indisputably carried SAP policy even more to the right at the same time as relations with the LO have been greatly strained, and divisions within the LO have intensified. If this development should continue, Sweden might be heading toward a Danish solution. Yet both organizational and ideological unity within the Swedish labor movement is so strong that the Danish alternative seems less likely. However, two factors could force developments in such a direction: the SAF could opt for and succeed in decentralizing the wage negotiation system at the same time as the environmental party ("the Greens") tips the balance in the Riksdag and forces the SAP into close cooperation with the Center party or the Liberals.

NOTES

1. See Chapter 4.
2. Przeworski 1985, chap. 1, esp. pp. 23–46. Korpi (1978a) and Esping-Andersen (1985), however, argue that Social Democratic policies can be developed into socialism.
3. Rothstein 1987, 279–99.
4. See Åmark 1986, chap. 2.
5. Åmark 1986, 20–33, 82–83, 89–90. On Weber, see Collins 1986, chap. 2.
6. See note 4 and Schiller 1967 on the December Compromise of 1906; see Schiller 1973 and Eklund 1974, chaps. 12.2 and 3, on paragraph 23/32.
7. Korpi and Shalev 1979; Shorter and Tilly 1974, chap. 12; Casparsson 1966a.
8. Zennström 1983, chaps. 17, 26. See also Lindgren 1938, chaps. 5 and 6, esp. p. 155.
9. Millbourn 1987; Zennström 1983, 233–36.
10. See Westerståhl 1945, 293–309, on the 1906 law.
11. Åmark 1989, chap. 6.
12. Kupferberg 1972.
13. See Westerståhl 1945, chap. 11, for the basic presentation. Eklund 1974, chaps. 11.1 and 11.2, provides a Marxist interpretation, mainly based on Westerståhl.
14. This is based on Sten Andersson's thesis (1990), in which the conflicts within the labor movement and the meaning of the tactical aspects are emphasized in a polemic against Westerståhl 1945 (chap. 12) and Eklund 1974 (chaps. 11.3 and 11.4). The interpretation of the significance of the Labor Court is based on Geijer and Schmidt (1958).
15. Westman 1987, 159–61; Westerståhl 1945, chap. 12; Eklund 1974, chap. 11.5.
16. See previous note and the directives to SOU 1935:66, "Concerning Provision to the People and Industrial Peace," 2, Appendix 1, 31 Dec. 1934.
17. LO Secretariat Minutes 29 and 30 Dec. 1934 (LO Archives). Söderpalm (1980, 28–30) considers the inquiry to be a "breakthrough in . . . the parties getting closer" (29) and sees it as an important stage in the development of cooperation, an assertion which the LO leadership's hitherto unremarked attitude would hardly support.
18. See the Minutes of the Social Democratic parliamentary group, 23 and 31 May 1935 (Arbetarrörelsens arkiv och bibliotek, Stockholm); LO Secretariat, 20 May 1935; Westerståhl 1945, 386–404, esp. pp. 395–97, where the conflicts between the party leadership and LO representatives are covered up. See also Casparsson 1966a, 66–67, and Eklund 1974, 276–81, who closely follow Westerståhl. Earlier research underestimates the conflicts between the party and the LO.
19. The accords were named after the seaside resort of Saltsjöbaden, near Stockholm, where some of the negotiations were held.
20. On the Saltsjöbaden negotiations, see Casparsson 1966b; Söderpalm 1980, 28–36; Schiller 1974, chap. 8. De Geer 1986, 369–72 adds nothing new to the discussion.
21. The Labor Movement's Post-War Programme 1944; K. Molin 1979; Lewin 1967, chap. 3:3; Elvander 1980, 223–29.
22. See, e.g., E. Lundberg 1955, chaps. 2–4 and 9; E. Lundberg 1983, chap. 3. An overview of the debate on the 1930s crisis is found in Fürth 1979, chap. 1.
23. The Labor Movement's Post-War Programme 1944, 15, pt. 10.
24. On stabilization policy in general (which is a recognized economic concept), see the Stablisation Enquiry, SOU 1961:42; Myhrman and Tson Söderström 1982; Lindbeck 1975, esp. chap. 4. Solidarity in wage policy has been treated in several works: see Ullenhag 1971, on union debates; Meidner 1973, on solidarity in wage policy in theory and practice; Hadenius 1976, on the connection between wage policy and centralization within the LO; Åsard 1978,

on the connection between solidaristic wage policy, stabilization and the Wage-Earners' Funds; Martin 1984, on wage policy and the rise of the Swedish model and crisis; Elvander 1988, on wage negotiations and state incomes policy in the 1980s; E. Lundberg 1955 and 1980, on the connections between wage policy and national economic development; Lindbeck 1975, on the Rehn model and economic policy from an economic point of view; SOU 1961:42, on stabilization policy and wage policy; "Wage formation and social/economic stablisation" 1985, for an economic criticism of wage solidarity; Hedborg and Meidner 1984, for a radical plea for solidarity and equality; D. Andersson (1987) for a detailed review of wage leveling and a plea for it to be continued; and the LO's reports on wage policy (1951, 1971b, 1976, 1981a, and 1987).

25. E. Lundberg 1955, 131–34, 400–402. In Sweden, wage drifts refer to wage increases that exceed the amounts laid down both in the central agreements concluded between the SAF and the LO and in the national agreements on branch level. In the postwar period, wage drifts have accounted for about half of the wage rises—the other half being stipulated by the agreements.

26. See Sköld's speech to the parliamentary group, 18 Jan. 1955.

27. See a survey of the academic debates on this problem in Åmark 1984, 54–56.

28. *The Financial Plan 1947*, 12, in B. Levin, *1947 års inflationskonferenser* (The 1947 Inflation Conferences) (Department of History, Stockholm University, 1976, Stencil).

29. Levin 1976; Sköld's notes reproduced in Jonasson 1976, 149–50; Wigforss in the parliamentary group, 10 June 1947.

30. De Geer 1986, 107–9; Hadenius 1976, 72; Strand's introductory speech to the LO General Assembly, 26 and 27 Apr. 1948, in *Minutes* (LO Archives).

31. See Strand's speech at the LO chair's conference, 2 June 1948, in *Minutes* (LO Archive).

32. Wigforss, *Minnen* (Memoirs), 1954, 3:384; Hadenius 1976, 72–73; SOU 1961:42, 370–73.

33. LO 1951, 104–27; *Wage Statistics Yearbook* 1950.

34. LO's General Council, 26 and 27 Apr. 1948; 6, 8, 10, and 11 Nov. 1948; LO's Chair's Conference, 18 Oct. 1948. See Lantz, Chairman of the Joint Unions, at the General Council, 11 Nov. 1948 on the government question.

35. Sköld's notes in Jonasson 1976, 176–77; LO Secretariat 1, 8, and 15 Aug. 1948; 12 Sept. 1948; LO's General Council, 22 Sept. 1948; 2 and 3 Nov. 1948; LO's Chairman's Conference, 14 Sept. 1948.

36. Erlander 1974, 45ff.; LO's General Council, 22 Sept. 1948; 2 and 3 Nov. 1948; parliamentary group, 18 Oct. 1948.

37. LO's General Council, 22 July 1948; parliamentary group, 18 Oct. 1948.

38. Ruin 1986, 64–65, 185–94.

39. LO Secretariat, 31 Oct. 1948; LO's General Council, 2 and 3 Nov. 1948.

40. LO Secretariat, 9 Apr. 1951; 3 and 21 May 1951; 21 Aug. 1951; 5 Nov. 1951; LO's General Council, 26 and 27 Apr. 1951; 23 Aug. 1951; and 9 Nov. 1951; LO's Chairman's Conference, 12 June 1951; 15 Dec. 1951; Labor Movement's Cooperation Committee, 12 Apr. 1951; 4 May 1951; 4 Sept. 1951 (LO Archives).

41. Sköld's notes in Jonasson 1976, 192.

42. Parliamentary group, 18 Jan. 1955, Parliament, Upper House 1955:2, 17–19.

43. See, e.g., Myhrman and Tson Söderström 1982; R. Andersson and Meidner 1973; and Lindbeck 1975, on the government's use of the model. See also E. Lundberg 1981, on Sträng.

44. Citation in Erlander 1974, 237. See also Rehn 1950 and LO 1951, 134–49, esp. 146.

45. See esp. Rehn's PM, 10 Mar. 1955, to the Harpsund conference on the reasons for Strand's speech in the committee report debates in 1955 (LO Archives).

46. C. Carlsson 1986, 162–64; Qvist 1973, 109–11; Sund 1987, 92–99.

47. Qvist 1973, 109–23; Gustafsson and Lantz 1985.

48. Hadenius 1976, 107–12; Nycander 1972.

49. Meidner 1973; Hadenius 1976, 99–106. See also LO 1971b and 1971c, and B. Lundberg 1979, on the debate on equality.

50. Hadenius 1976, 107–12; Nycander 1972.

51. Haga Palace in Stockholm was where the negotiations were held.

52. LO 1976b, 218–23; Hadenius 1976, 112–15; Elvander 1988, 288–92.

53. LO 1981b, 35–45.

54. Åsard 1978, chaps. 4 and 5; Åsard 1985; Öhman 1982, chaps. 4, 11, and 12; Rehn 1980, 45–46.

55. Lindbeck 1975, 63–96; E. Lundberg 1983, 131–56; Myhrman and Tson Söderström 1982.

56. See, e.g., Schiller 1989a; Hammarström 1982. The most important LO reports are those of 1966 and 1971a.

57. H. Bergström 1987, chap. 5.4 and pp. 83–87, on the election defeat in 1979; LO 1981a and 1981c; SAP 1981.

58. LO 1981a; SAP 1981; K-O Feldt, *Kjell-Olof Feldt om economisk politik på 80–talet: Ett handfast och konkret program* (Kjell-Olof Feldt on Economic Policy in the 80s: A Concrete and Resolute Programme), Stockholm, 1982; H. Bergström 1987, chap. 5.4. See also the debate on industrial policy at the LO congress in 1981, in which active state response played a major role. LO, *Congress Minutes* 1981, 2, 917–1101.

59. SAP 1981; see also H. Bergström 1987, chap. 5.4.

60. H. Bergström 1987, 95–97.

61. Ibid., 109–12. However, Feldt continued to argue for restraint; see note 58.

62. H. Bergström 1987, 193–201.

63. Feldt 1984, 32–41, esp. 39; Elvander 1988, 295.

64. Ministry of Finance, *Government Budget Proposals 1987/88, Summary* 1987, 33–39; Feldt 1985.

65. Ministry of Finance, *Government Budget Proposal 1988/89, Summary* 1988, 27–29, and *National Accounts.*

66. See also my interview with H. Fjällström, LO's contracts secretary, 2 June 1988; Elvander 1988, chaps. 2–4 on wage negotiations in the 1980s. Elvander argues that the forms cause the problems; see esp. 364–69.

67. On the SAF's new strategy, see, e.g., Bergman 1986, SAF 1979 and 1986, and Östman 1987.

68. D. Andersson 1987; LO 1986 and 1987; interview with D. Andersson 1987, and with Fjällström 1988.

69. Sjölund 1987; interview with Fjällström 1988.

70. See *Metallarbetaren* (The Metal Worker), no. 48, 1987, on wage developments and wage drifts.

71. Ministry of Finance 1987, 33–39 (See note 64); Elvander 1988, 282–305.

72. See SAMAK 1985 and Elvander 1988, 197–301 for arguments in favor of this policy.

73. See, e.g., Elvander 1980; Kjellberg 1983; Korpi and Shalev 1979; and Cameron 1984.

74. Interview with Meidner, 17 Dec. 1987.

75. See esp. Esping-Andersen 1985, and his contribution in the present volume.

Gullan Gidlund

4

From Popular Movement to Political Party: Development of the Social Democratic Labor Party Organization

The Social Democratic Labor Party has experienced the transition from an agrarian to an industrial society as well as the ongoing transition from an industrial to an information society. These revolving social changes confront political parties with diverse organizational prerequisites and challenges. The SAP was formed about a decade before the turn of the century, outside the established political groups and assemblies. Social democracy represented the emerging working class, and it demanded social justice and political power. For many it was the incarnation of a new and better society. The party has been in government for no less than half of its century-long existence; consequently, social democracy has attained a unique position of power in Swedish society and constitutes a central element in present-day politics.

TWO PHASES OF POLITICAL INCORPORATION

In existing representative democracies political parties have established a key role. Swedish popular government can justifiably be described as a "democracy through political parties." This governmental function means that each party, together with other parties, takes responsibility for political leadership and consequently possesses a clear orientation toward political decision-making on various levels in society.[1] Hence, through its governmental responsibilities a party becomes more or less incorporated in the political government of society—that is, in the state apparatus.

However, parties can also play another important role in democracy: that of being mass movements, which means that the parties are deeply rooted among members and voters. To function as a popular movement it is not sufficient merely to mobilize voters during an election; active participation from members and sympathizers between elections is also necessary. This requires the party to have an organization with a comprehensive program, decision-making capacity, economic resources, channels for information between the party executive and the base and between and among the various party levels, and effective modes of operation in order to mobilize members and voters.

The popular movement function is more or less accentuated in the Swedish parties. For the Social Democratic Labor Party, with its origins in popular movements (e.g., the labor movement and the cooperative movement), there is an ideal model characterized by widespread mass participation and a membership inspired with the desire to make great sacrifices for the party. This model has seldom been realized in any continuous sense; however, the popular movement ideal still serves as a prototype for the present-day, postmodern party.

In this chapter I shall try to respond to the following question: How has the Social Democratic Labor Party's incorporation in the political governing of society affected the party's internal organizational development? By organization I mean organizational structure, financing, and modes of performance. By political government I mean official activities and in general that authoritative decision making which applies to all citizens.

Two critical phases of this incorporation process will be examined. The first occurred during the initial decades when the party adapted itself to the new rules of parliamentary democracy. This phase culminated in the election of 1911—the first parliamentary election to implement the proportional voting system and in which all adult men were eligible to vote. Without taking sides in the controversy among scholars concerning precisely when the party chose the path of reform, it can be said that this path was embarked upon at least by that time. At the 1911 election the Social Democrats stepped into the election arena to acquire parliamentary power and a position of responsibility in Swedish society. The first part of this chapter will deal with the question of how the party organization developed in order to manage its required internal mobilization and cohesion, as well as its adaptation to new tasks such as election organization.

The second critical phase of incorporation began as recently as the mid-1960s. It was triggered by the decision in the Riksdag to introduce a national subsidy to political parties (1965).[2] According to the Social Democratic government, the basic motive behind this decision was that the political parties were considered of such importance to democracy that the state—which has the ultimate responsibility for the functioning of democracy—should ensure that their function was maintained. Through public financing, parties represented in political assemblies received economic compensation for those tasks they undertook related to governing Sweden. At this point, the Social Democratic Labor Party entered into the post-industrial era. In the second half of the chapter are discussed the organizational consequences of governmental responsibility for the Social Democratic Labor Party and the conditions this created for the popular movement function. This second phase has also witnessed significant changes in the socioeconomic structure and in the stability of the electorate.

The participation of Social Democrats in the election of 1911 cannot be viewed as merely a technical question without taking into consideration crucial attitudes toward societal change—reform or revolution. Neither can the position taken regarding public funding be treated as merely a technical question of subsidies. These issues involve fundamental principles concerning the view of the state and the parties' position in relation to the state apparatus and to the popular base.

THE POPULAR MOVEMENT AND ELECTION ORGANIZATION

Growth and Development

Seen from a theoretical perspective, the European labor parties around the turn of the century were generally mass parties. With such parties it is presumed that their concept of membership is well defined, that financing comes from membership fees and contributions from trade union organizations, and that there is a relatively centralized organization. According to the French scholar Maurice Duverger, the entrance of mass parties into the political arena entailed a democratization of party financing. Costs were distributed in the spirit of solidarity through small payments from a large number of members. This system could be compared with the elitist form of financing practiced in the opposite type of party, the "cadre" party, in which large donations from individuals, banks, and companies composed its economic basis.[3]

In the following section, the Social Democratic Labor Party's initial period will be dealt with. Three internally related aspects will be highlighted: first, the initial agitation and organizing phase, revealing the contours of a mass party with a strong popular base; second, the party–trade union link and early development tendencies in membership financing; and finally, the growth of the party as an election organization.

Agitation and Organizing

The most intensive period of Social Democratic agitating and organizing occurred between 1881 and 1911—from the first socialist speech in Sweden, which was given in Malmö by August Palm, to the first SAP election successes. In the party districts' chronicles, Palm's speech comprises something of a pivotal point of reference by which early or late agitation and organizing in the various parts of the country can be understood.[4] Printed socialist propaganda was not extensive and had a limited distribution, but socialist ideas were also spread by traveling craftsmen and journeymen, unskilled laborers, linemen along the new railways ("lineman socialism"), and the many workers who, because of unemployment or their socialist convictions, were compelled to have itinerant lives.

The initiative to call a conference for the purpose of forming a cohesive political party came from the tailor and agitator August Palm, who had just served one of his prison sentences for statements made in the socialist press. Party formation was accelerated by certain preparations on the part of the Liberals for the creation of some type of Swedish workers organization during the impending fourth workers meeting. The invitation—in the form of a manifesto—was published in the paper Social-Demokraten and was directed to all "socialist societies, workers' clubs, trade unions, [and] all of the associations of workers standing on the foundations of the class struggle."[5]

The conference was prepared by the Stockholm Social Democratic Association, with the journalist Hjalmar Branting, in the leadership, and was held in 1889 in Stockholm, with fifty delegates from sixty-nine organizations (trade union, political, and social) from fourteen different places throughout the country.

The first SAP conference voted in a decentralized organizational structure with three relatively autonomous districts—the northern/central, the western, and the southern. The division was a consequence of the fact that the labor movement was strongest in the largest cities—Stockholm, Gothenburg, and Malmö. The main task of each district was to direct local Social Democratic propaganda. The districts were composed of those organizations "formed on the basis of the class struggle." The highest level of decision making was to be the party conference, with delegates elected by local party branches. The party leadership during the early years was composed of seven appointed representatives whose task it was to implement conference decisions and represent the party, for example, through making political statements and handling contacts with Social Democratic parties abroad.[6] A more centralized alternative, with a party executive given leadership responsibilities and greater powers, won no acclaim in the party conference. Among the party founders there was a clear mistrust of authoritarian leadership, an attitude reflecting a certain ideological view but also caused by a power struggle, primarily between the central districts—Stockholm and Hjalmar Branting—and the southern, more radical segments of the workers movement—Skåne and Axel Danielsson.

Hence the hierarchical organizational structure characteristic of mass parties did not penetrate the Swedish Social Democratic Labor Party in the early years. It was not the German model that initially had an impact; affinities were rather with the Austrian labor movement's decentralized structure.[7] The structure of the SAP during its formative period was designed to strengthen mobilization at the expense of greater cohesion. But by 1894 the conference had already fortified the central party level and augmented cohesion through appointing a party executive (Partistyrelse) with decision-making responsibilities. The Stockholm members of this board formed an executive committee.[8] As the party executive expressed it in its first annual report, it had been reorganized into a "true, active executive."[9] Not until 1907 did the party formally acquire a party leader in the election of "the chief," Hjalmar Branting.[10] In his investigation of the party's first year, Hilding Nordström has stated that the period without authoritative leadership had certain negative consequences both for organizational development and for cohesion within the party. The seven appointed representatives primarily performed as representatives for their own districts and not for the party as a whole, and they lacked the power and thus the means to intervene.[11]

Despite this, the Social Democratic Labor Party and its executive rapidly developed into a unifying force for the various branches of the labor movement. In contrast, the British Labour party, for example, from the time it was formed in 1900 until 1918, was primarily an alliance of organizations that cooperated on the national level for the expressed purpose of promoting working-class representation in the lower house of Parliament.[12]

In 1898, the trade union branch of the labor movement formed its own central organization, the Confederation of Swedish Trade Unions, or *Landsorganisation* (LO). Quite logically, the separation of union and political leadership was followed by a buildup of the political base organization— *arbetarekommunen*, labor communes (local Social Democratic branches) all over the country. By the turn of the century there were approximately eighty labor communes, but after an intense period of agitation and organizing led by the party executive the numbers steadily rose. In 1911 the party executive reported 427 labor communes.[13] In this heavy growth phase, the division into three regional districts had become ineffective and was abolished by the party conference in 1900. Instead of in districts, party activities would be based in the labor communes, which would function as local political coordinators and be "directly subordinate to the party executive, the sole central leadership."

In conjunction with this change in organization, the party executive was expanded to twenty-three members, and a party secretary was also appointed.[14] The reform was controversial, however. In the south of Sweden, in Skåne, where organizational work had reached a certain maturity, the loss of the regional organization was felt in coordination efforts between organizations. It was in Skåne that the most vigorous demands for the reintroduction of districts occurred.[15]

Certain early labor communes or their predecessors were formed on the initiative of the most numerous socialist labor unions in places requiring union as well as political coordination. Several were in practice organizations for local union coordination, forerunners of LO sections or districts. Such was the case, for instance, in two small towns in the west of Sweden. The predecessor to Halmstad's labor commune was Halmstads Samverkande Fackföreningar (Halmstad's Coordinated Trade Unions), which was formed in 1895.[16] Mölndal's union of workers was formed and affiliated with the party; it existed for two years.[17] The vitality of some of the organizations was often fairly fragile: both union and political groups could disappear and arise again a few years later with new initiators and under new names.

Many labor communes were created by agitators who, on behalf of the party executive, traveled extensively around the country. During the early years the budget on the central level was dominated by costs incurred by agitation and propaganda.[18] The party executive's annual reports were filled with enthusiastic reports from agitators' travels, not least from the permanently employed agitators active during the most intense period of organizing. The basic desire—and the main task—of an agitator was to form a Social Democratic association after a meeting. Sometimes this happened, but sometimes a great deal of further work was needed.[19]

In the beginning, the labor communes carried out a score of activities using various modes of operation. In many cases they became centers of leadership during strikes and conflicts in the labor movement; such was the case with Sundsvall's labor commune in the north of Sweden during the early years.[20] The social and practical efforts by women to alleviate material suffering during strikes and industrial conflicts are occasionally mentioned in the historical records.

Political work was oriented toward studies, speeches, debates, distribution of printed matter, manifestations of various kinds, and election campaigning. This last item was slighted so long as voting rights virtually excluded workers from elections; the brunt of electioneering had to do with coordinating candidate ballots with the Liberals. In 1896 Hjalmar Branting had been elected to the Second Chamber on a Liberal ticket. In many places, the First of May events developed into a tradition of demonstrations in public.

Most of the labor communes were engaged in cultural activities: libraries were established, amateur theaters were created, lectures on authors and literary works were arranged. A large part of these cultural activities came to be incorporated in the Folkets Hus (People's Hall or Community Hall) and Folkets Park (People's Park or Community Park), organizations founded during the 1890s that quickly spread throughout the country. The Folkets Hus movement also enabled the agitators and later the newly formed labor communes to solve the difficult problem of finding venues. In many places where the labor movement was met with more or less open resistance from the church, police, and other authorities, people dared not rent out meeting halls for fear of reprisals.

Educational activities in the labor communes at the beginning of the century were dominated by subjects concerned with economy and political science. Not only Swedish conditions but also current economic and political events abroad were studied. An important development within the educational sphere was the formation in 1912 of the Arbetarnas Bildningsförbund, or ABF (Workers' Educational Association). The number of study circles, libraries, and lectures increased rapidly during the following years. At Brunnsviks *Folkhögskola* (adult education college or "Folk High School") an "experimental workshop" was conducted in which the study circle model and various pedagogical materials and methods were developed.[21]

The organizational work in the labor communes and SAP districts provided training and practical experience, necessary prerequisites for future representational duties on various levels in society. This internal training, in combination with the lecturing and study circles in labor communes and other associations in the labor movement, compensated many elected representatives for their lack of formal schooling.

Social traditions developed early on in most labor communes—picnics, parties, bazaars, and the like. Sometimes such festivities were arranged when a well-known member of the party executive came to visit, or sometimes to raise money. The old photographs of these occasions show happy if somewhat stiff-looking men, women, and children, all dressed up. These pictures contrast greatly with the grave portraits of men that otherwise dominate the party district records.

In the party districts' often well-written and engaging publications, women have no place during the first period of the party's history. This observation confirms previous knowledge, but at the same time it raises many questions. The historian Christina Carlsson, who has studied the view of women and policies concerning women in Swedish Social Democracy from 1889 to 1910, has recently criticized the lack of interest in research on the role of women in labor organizations. Organizational efforts and the formation of Social Democratic policy may have been led mainly by men, and therefore men's efforts have been the focus. If women have been noticed at all, it has been on men's terms.[22]

During its formative period, the labor movement acquired more and more of a mobilization structure. Within the course of a few years, the LO (1898), the socialist youth movement (1892), and the first Social Democratic women's organization, Stockholm's Public Women's Club (1892), were all formed. The Federation of Swedish Social Democratic Women was not created until 1920, but from 1907 onward, Social Democratic women's congresses were held regularly, and by 1907 there were more than eighty women's clubs throughout the country.[23] Later on, in 1928, another section was formed—the Swedish Association of Christian Social Democrats, Broderskapsrörelsen ("The Brotherhood Movement").

Expansion within the party, the need for planning continued agitation, and the development of election campaigns out in the party organizations renewed the need for a district organization. Only five years after the old regional structures were abolished, the party conference recommended new regional organizations.[24] District records from that time indicate that the need for coordination (particularly between labor communes) and for making agitation more effective was great. A few party districts were designated during the early years as simply "agitation districts." One of the tasks of the district was to reach areas where the party's presence was weak or nonexistent. In the Bohuslän region on the west coast the following strategy was decided on in 1907: "The actual agitation should mainly be carried on in those places where no organization exists or where it is weak. In those places where the labor movement has managed to attain some sort of stable ground, lectures on state and local government as well as national economy should be held."[25] In the district of Dalarna a plan for agitation was worked out, mainly aiming at "untouched territory."[26] The responsibility for agitation was gradually transferred to the district.[27] Finding suitable people for this proved to be difficult. There was also an economic problem: financing someone to be a full-time agitator in virtually inaccessible places for one or even several months. After requests from the districts, the party executive decided to provide support for the purpose, sometimes in the form of money, sometimes by sending one of the party's employed agitators to work for a few months. When the economy was at its worst, only printed propaganda was sent to the districts.

Collective Affiliation

At the turn of the century, the Social Democrats mainly came from the trade union movement. Early on there was a notion that reinforcing the organizational ties between unions and the political branches would strengthen the political movement: mass affiliation was seen as a prerequisite for political puissance. When separation became inevitable, mainly because of the difficulties involved with the SAP leading the struggles on the labor market as well as the campaign for voting rights, the connections between union and party were demonstrated in the decision in favor of obligatory affiliation of LO members to the SAP. At the first LO congress in 1898, when the LO was founded, twenty-four trade associations, thirteen independent unions, and nineteen local combined organizations were represented. The congress voted for obligatory affiliation, with 175 delegates for and 83 against.[28] According to the new statutes, an LO-affiliated labor union must "within at least three years after its entry into LO also become a member of the Social Democratic Labor Party; otherwise its affiliation with LO will be considered terminated."[29] The party's influence was also apparent in the ruling that two of the five members of the LO's executive should be appointed by the SAP.[30]

The party executive expressed satisfaction over the decision of the congress while denying that any real resistance to compulsory affiliation existed among the workers: "Nowhere has the so-called 'compulsory affiliation' to the party encountered any significant resistance among the workers themselves. As they enter into the ranks of the organization, the bands [of workers] will naturally and easily rally together under the red banners of socialism."[31] Despite this positive picture drawn by the party executive, opinion was actually divided about compulsory affiliation and the need for organizational cooperation between the unions and the SAP in general, especially within the trade union movement. In contrast to Hjalmar Branting, who spoke officially of "compulsion toward freedom," Axel Danielsson compared compulsory affiliation with the methods of the state church. Danielsson warned that the largest unions within the LO did not wish to be in the party, and he was proved right. The larger and most economically viable unions were indeed among those opposing compulsory affiliation and even, to a certain degree, cooperation with the SAP. It was feared that trade union organizing would be negatively affected by the connection.[32] The negative consequences of compulsory affiliation were clearly evident for the LO. In total, only thirteen trade union associations and two small individual unions had affiliated themselves with the LO by the middle of 1898. This meant that 60 percent of organized labor was not part of the newly formed central labor organization.[33]

For Branting, compulsory affiliation meant maximum cohesion within the labor movement. In a speech honoring the LO's first chair, Fredrik Sterky, Branting said that Sterky was the man who had the task of making the Swedish labor union movement "one" with Swedish Social Democracy and into a power "that will weigh even more than at present, on the political and social scales of society."[34] This was Branting's official vindication of the decision for compulsory affiliation. However, there is evidence indicating that, within a narrow circle of trusted friends, Branting expressed doubts about the decision's durability and defensibility. Instead, Branting would have recommended an introductory text in the LO's statutes declaring that the labor movement also had political duties.[35]

The strong reaction within the union movement led the LO congress of 1900 to abolish compulsory affiliation and replace it with the so-called voluntary collective affiliation, with the recommendation that all trade unions should be affiliated with the SAP. The LO congress of 1909 finally removed from the statutes the clause enjoining the LO to recommend that each union affiliate itself to its local SAP district or labor commune and thus to the party.[36] Thus, the question of collective affiliation was transferred to the hands of the local union organizations. At the 1908 SAP conference the forms of collective affiliation were discussed. This resulted in the decision to introduce the right of reservation, which gave each individual member of an affiliated union the right to remain outside the party.[37]

Membership Financing

The small subscriptions that were to finance the newly formed Social Democratic Labor Party were insufficient from the start. For several years the party executive tried to cover the costs of agitation through special levies and collections, even though the proceeds from the sales of printed propaganda were fairly large during the early years. The fact that the members of the party almost to a man were collectively affiliated rendered the income from membership fees vulnerable to economic recessions and strikes. Conflicts on the labor market caused temporary declines in LO membership, which had direct consequences for the party.[38]

At the time, there was clear resistance in party conferences to both levies and increases in the membership fees—set at five öre per member quarterly. Since 1894 part of the fees had been conveyed to the central party organization. Branting had to threaten conference delegates with an immediate collection for agitation purposes in 1897—a proposal that was immediately rejected. When the conference of 1900 in Malmö became intractable, Branting stated that the party executive would be "compelled to take into consideration how a prospective executive would be able to manage the party's affairs with the limited resources available as a consequence of the conference decision not to raise subscriptions." After a few small increases, the amount to the party central was doubled by the eleventh conference in 1920 to 40 öre per member per quarter, but only 20 öre for women and farm workers.

What is remarkable in this context is that it would be thirty-six years before the party raised the ordinary fees to the central level: not until 1956 were they raised to 60 öre, respectively 30 öre per member per quarter. Membership fees obviously did not follow the general development of prices and wages. According to the party leadership, one reason for the lag was that realistic margins for increases had already been utilized by party districts and labor communes. Also, membership was largely based on collective affiliation, and thus the subscription was included as a part of the union dues.

The system of differentiated fees (i.e., the regulation concerning exemptions for the sick, the unemployed, conscripts, and so on, and reductions for women and certain occupational groups) continually expanded. Although as of the 1940s the party leadership's policy was to have a single fee—equal for all—this reform was carried out in stages and not completed until 1968.[39]

After 1905, membership fees became the greatest source of income for the party central. However, this income became totally inadequate during election years. During the first real election year in 1911, the party's accounts reveal the income and cost profile that would continue to characterize its economy during the following decades: income from members' fees financed most of the expenses between election years (between 60 and 90 percent of costs), while election fund collections satisfied the special financial needs arising during election years. The peaks in the development of election costs have been strongly related to innovations in mass communication: from loudspeaker vehicles and sound films during the 1920s and 1930s to the mass distribution of propaganda material from the 1930s onward. It is propaganda that has required large economic commitments which can only marginally be replaced by the commitment of voluntary work by party members.

Election campaign fund-raising became more and more important for the SAP. It enabled the party to mobilize unions and the LO for the purpose of committing economic resources toward elections. Such contributions have of course been motivated by trust in the party's ability to realize the "collective goods" essential for the labor movement. According to Mancur Olson's theoretical perspective, union incentives for supporting the SAP have been rational, since as organizations they have possessed sufficiently large economic resources to influence the party's results in elections.[40] During the 1950s the trade unions subsidized about 90 percent of the election funds.

However, it is not through contributions to election campaign funding that the trade unions and the LO have made their greatest investments, but through being the real economic guarantors of the Social Democratic press. Already during the party's initial period, the press was considered one of the most important means in the political struggle. The newly formed party executive in 1894 was given the responsibility by the conference to make the press a top priority—to invest in written propaganda, start up a weekly, *Folkbladet*, and collect certain levies for that purpose.[41] This priority has continued and has been approved by party conferences. The treatment of the press issue within the SAP has been characterized by a century-long passion for the creation and maintenance of its own press. This is the conclusion that must be drawn after surveying the enormous sacrifices of time, money, and engagement made by the party on all levels to create, save, or reconstruct newspapers. This fervor of course was incited by the dominance of the bourgeois press, which during the early period of the labor movement directed heavy offensives against the movement. These experiences convinced the party of the necessity of starting its own newspapers. Even though confidence has been strong, the party's own economic resources for its press have been very limited; but on this critical point the trade union movement, with its greater funding resources, has been mobilized.

Election Campaign Organization

Like other Swedish parties, the SAP made an organizational adjustment to the new rules in the election system of 1910 so that the regional party organizations—the party districts—basically coincided with the new constituencies. Following an organizational inquiry, new districts were formed. In 1911 the SAP had twenty-two party districts; in counties with several constituencies, the districts were divided into wards.[42]

The years from 1906 to 1909 were fraught with difficult internal conflicts. The dispute with the anarchistic faction resulted in the suspension of its two main leaders, Hinke Bergegren and Carl Schröder. The general strike in 1909 entailed heavy setbacks for the LO and resulted in great losses in membership for the Social Democratic Labor Party as well, with tangible economic consequences. What finally reversed this negative trend was breaking into the electorate and mobilizing larger and larger groups of workers and members of the lower classes now eligible to vote through the suffrage reform of 1909. A certain amount of success could be noted already in the Riksdag elections in 1905, when the number of Social Democratic representatives in the Second Chamber increased from four to fifteen. This was also the year when the Social Democratic party group in the Riksdag was formed.

As in the Skåne district, everywhere in the country the word went out to mobilize party members for the parliamentary elections to the Second Chamber in 1911:

> Our sights must be focused ahead toward the coming elections. An intensive election campaign—all forces united—must be directed against the right-wing domination which is ruining the nation. With this year's election we stand on the threshold of a democratic parliamentarism which will create a society that will remove those barriers dividing people into classes, the oppressed and the oppressor. . . .[43]

In order to enter the electoral arena the party began to be trimmed into an election organization, an enterprise that the party executive, assisted by the districts, directed with a firm hand. In preparation for the 1911 elections, an ambitious survey was made by means of a questionnaire to the labor communes concerning local conditions and possibilities: "It was to ascertain activities and representation within various decision-making and corresponding local authorities."[44] In addition to information from previous elections, the chairs of the labor communes were to calculate election results in 1911 for their own constituencies as well as indicate whatever organized cooperation with the Liberals had occurred. Further, they were to examine whether local authority committees and assemblies were held at times and places that were convenient for the workers.[45]

At the election of 1911, the election organizations encompassed—in addition to district and constituency boards—an extensive network of representatives, especially in rural parishes, and committees in larger areas. In certain cities there was a system of neighborhood and block committees, and in Stockholm there were also ward committees.[46] The party district from Västmanland county proudly reported that its election organization "was without defect or blemish. Of the county's 69 parishes and 4 towns not one lacked election committees or representatives in the villages. The party has a strong, smooth and well-anchored election apparatus here."[47]

The district reports to the party executive indicate that the formation of the new election organization generally went quickly and effectively, especially in those districts where the labor movement already had strong ties. In northern Sweden, particularly in Västerbotten, electioneering went far less well. The party executive conceded "economic vulnerability, weak organizations and lack of community contact" as reasons for the poor election results in Västerbotten.[48] Election costs in the districts varied enormously. Gotland (a Swedish island in the Baltic) seemed to have the lowest costs—the whole campaign cost 150 kronor, money "brought in through [fundraising] parties and loans."[49] The highest costs were incurred by Stockholm—7,700 kronor; here meetings, parties, and sales of "election flowers" and the like were important sources of income. Other districts reported similar efforts, sometimes complemented by grants, collections, entrance fees for lectures, and levies. These reports describing the election organization, campaign work, economy, election results, and analysis provided the party executive and party workers all over the country with an excellent basis for planning and forming strategies for future elections.

"Distribution of literature," more or less systematic door-to-door canvassing, lectures, and public meetings were the most important election activities. Speeches and meetings were held by speakers allocated by the party executive or by candidates and local campaign workers. Nationwide tours were undertaken: the most famous, the "Red Car" tour, appeared to be very successful and is mentioned in many records. However, people also traveled around on cycles and on foot in order to reach as many as possible.[50]

Participation by party youth in the first major election campaign seems to have been extensive. John Lindgren has claimed that the considerable successes in the election of 1911 could be attributed to a great extent to the mobilization of SAP youth groups.[51] Herbert Tingsten pointed out that young people played an exceedingly prominent role within the SAP up to World War I because of the party's rapid growth. There were also a large number of young debaters during that period.[52]

After the election the Social Democratic group in the Riksdag increased markedly, containing no less than sixty-four representatives from the Second Chamber and twelve from the First Chamber. The election of 1911 entailed a test of strength for the party's capacity as an election campaign organization and its ability to attract voters. The first incorporation phase, in which it captured 28.5 percent of the electorate, constituted for the Social Democratic Labor Party the decisive step toward expanding its responsibility in political government on different levels of Swedish society.

After many years of reports from agitation tours and of forming organizations, from 1911 and onward over several years the party executive's records and the annals of district and labor communes are filled with enthusiastic reports of election campaigns and results. The march toward triumphant election statistics had begun.

THE POLITICAL LEADERSHIP

Altered Conditions

The introduction of public financing for political parties is strongly linked to structural changes toward a postindustrial society, in which the conditions for shaping opinion are altered.[53] From after World War II up to the 1970s, newspapers in Sweden underwent a process of concentration and monopoly formation, a process that was especially hard on many small bourgeois papers—the so-called "press death."

During the 1950s and 1960s, the LO and trade unions made considerable economic investments in the reorganized Social Democratic press, which was mainly financed by loans from unions. In addition, the unions bought' the newspapers *Aftonbladet* and *Stockholms-Tidningen* outright. However, in the end "press death" struck even *Stockholms-Tidningen*, which was laid to rest in 1966. The traditionally solid bond between the press and the party seemed to be on the verge of dissolution.

However, the altered circumstances in the media applied to other sectors besides the daily press. The mass media, particularly television, increasingly dominated and controlled political information. On the labor market, structural changes broke up old patterns. Within the service sector new groups developed, while both the old agricultural and the industrial sectors gradually diminished. For parties whose membership and voter bases resided primarily in the shrinking interest groups, future possibilities clearly lay in appealing to the new groups. Consequently, competition for voters stiffened, and the new struggle was carried on mainly in the mass media. Moreover, new forms of political participation arose parallel to parties and organizations—campaigns, action groups—which put the old established parties at a certain disadvantage because of their comparatively slow ways of working and hierarchical forms of decision making. Election campaigns and the administrative apparatus became increasingly expensive for the parties.

Against the background of the precarious situation of the press, the Social Democratic government appointed a Press Inquiry in 1963 to investigate the economic conditions of the press and consider special measures that could be taken by the state to maintain free opinion. Two years later the Inquiry proposed an annual state press subsidy of 25 million kronor to be paid out via the political parties. According to the members of the Inquiry, the parties were the obvious recipients of the funds because of the solid party ties to the Swedish daily press.[54]

The Press Inquiry's proposal was never implemented: when circulated for comment, it received very negative criticism, not least from the press itself. An alternative solution was offered by a representative from the Center party, namely to introduce a general party subsidy. This proposal satisfied both the Social Democrats' need for funds for their own closely associated press and the Center party's more existential needs for resources to carry out party activities. The LO, with its own interests firmly in mind, also approved the Center party alternative.

Public Financing

In 1965, with a wide majority consisting of Social Democrats, the Center party, and the Communist party, the Riksdag approved the introduction of a national subsidy to the political parties represented in the Riksdag. Twenty-three million *kronor* would be distributed proportionally according to the number of seats. The subsidy should be general, free of conditions or controls on its use. Predecision debates in the Riksdag and in the daily papers were intense and occasionally vituperous. The arguments were marked by fundamental differences regarding principles, but also by elements of party strategy that focused on determining which party would especially benefit from the subsidy.[55]

Of the public resources received by the SAP during the first year, 95 percent were awarded to the "A-press" (*Arbetarpress* or Labor press), the Social Democratic–aligned press. This percentage diminished gradually over the years, largely because of the introduction of a specific public press subsidy implemented in 1972, which meant that more public funds could be mobilized in supporting the A-press and especially the economically weak minor newspapers.

The national subsidy was never treated in party conferences, nor was it a discussion topic within the party. However, at the party conference in 1968 the fact that the national subsidy had become a press subsidy and was not filtered down through the party organization was openly criticized. Demands were also raised for enlarging the scope of public funding to cover local and regional levels. The Riksdag subsequently legislated a municipal and a county council subsidy in 1969, which gave local authorities and

counties the right to award funds to political parties on the local and regional levels. A conference statement by party secretary Sten Andersson in
1968 indicated that the government planned to introduce both subsidies for
the parties on the local and regional levels and a press subsidy, but that for
tactical reasons it was deemed prudent to be cautious.[56]

The SAP's basic attitude toward public financing has emanated from the
party's view of the political parties' significance for democracy and the
state's responsibility for ensuring that the parties fulfill their obligations.
The minister of justice, Herman Kling, expressed his own and his party's
views in 1965 as follows:

> The political parties are the primary actors in the continual societal
> debates which are a necessary prerequisite for democracy to main-
> tain a real content. Since the responsibility for the functioning of
> democracy lies ultimately with the state, the state cannot remain
> passive, neither vis-à-vis the impoverishment of the press debates
> nor in the face of political parties' financial difficulties.[57]

As in the proposition on municipal and county council subsidies four years
later, the overall aim was to reinforce the political parties' position in democracy: "Measures for the purpose of strengthening local democracy must
have their point of departure in the democratic system which we have
accepted in our country. This system is characterized by the influence of
our citizens being exercised through the political parties, and ultimately in
the general elections."[58] The emphasis on the resources as means to increase citizens' information about local authority questions and to augment
local information in election campaigns was so strong that the fact that it
was to be party subsidies became suppressed.[59]

The Social Democratic Labor Party has had a pragmatic as well as a
rationalistic view of party economy. Membership financing has not been
considered ideologically essential for the movement. Election fund-raising,
mainly from the union movement, gave the party early on a plutocratic
form of financing. When it became evident during the 1950s and 1960s that
membership financing and contributions from the unions could support
neither the increasingly costly election campaigns nor its own press, it was
concluded that even the party's economy must adapt to current conditions.
Thus it was clear that the position of Swedish Social Democracy in society
demanded a retrenchment of its economic resources or, as it was expressed
at the party conference of 1956, "the necessity of creating greater economic

resources to enable the party to expand its possibilities for carrying out effective and comprehensive activities, adapted to the times and the position occupied by Social Democracy in society today."[60] When the internal mobilization of economic resources failed, the SAP, through its political position, could mobilize public means for strengthening first of all its own but also other established parties' positions in Swedish democracy.

One of the prominent arguments for public financing in the mid-1960s was that it could enable the parties to relinquish funding from powerful financiers. What was referred to was primarily the economic support given to the Liberal party (Folkpartiet) and Conservative party (Moderata Samlingspartiet) from private industry, support that from a democratic point of view was unsatisfactory because it created dependent relations between the parties and their funders. Both parties from time to time had been criticized by the media and political opponents and so finally stopped accepting open and direct contributions from business. However, there is nothing to suggest that the SAP intended to alter its economic dependence upon the LO and the trade unions. At the conferences in 1967 and 1968 the party leader, Tage Erlander, accentuated the common interests shared between the party and the trade union movement, and the pleasure with which the party received its economic contributions.[61] It was essential to induce the trade union movement to continue economic support, despite the public appropriations, by asserting the unique position held by the unions.

Public financing now comprises the primary source of income for the SAP and for the other established parties. Above all, the two local government contributions, the municipal and county subsidies, have increased greatly, while new but still marginal forms of public contributions have been developed. From the start, there has been a tendency for local authorities with socialist majorities to provide more funding than those with bourgeois majorities.[62]

In an earlier research report on the budget strategies of regional party organizations, I have been able to show a clear difference between the SAP and the other parties. The income sources that the SAP reckons to be able to mobilize when in acute economic difficulties are union organizations, whereas other parties (the Conservatives, the Liberals, the Center party, the Communists, and the Christian Democrats) turn to individual voluntary contributors. The other very clear demarcation goes between parties that view the different forms of public funding as an important alternative and those that do not even mention them. To the SAP, increases in public subsidies are the second most important source of mobilization, while the Conservatives and the Christian Democrats do not even acknowledge these public sources as alternatives.[63] The principal differences among the parties regarding public financing still exist, and the SAP alone prefers income in large sums over the more time-consuming forms of fund-raising among individual members and sympathizers such as membership financing.

Collective Affiliation Reviewed

Criticism of collective affiliation has always existed primarily outside of but also within the labor movement. Since the mid-1930s the issue has been regularly taken up in the Riksdag; on several occasions the Riksdag has stated that collective affiliation should cease, and demands for legislation have increased.[64] The central argument has been that the phenomenon contravenes fundamental democratic principles in the Swedish form of government; each individual should have the right to determine his or her own party membership.

Over the years, the main argument promulgating collective affiliation has resided in the historically close connections between the SAP and the trade union movement. It has been claimed that collective affiliation is one of the organizational expressions of ideological accord. The links with the workers' struggles for rights of association at the turn of the century have also been emphasized. The defense of collective affiliation has often been tainted with bitterness toward the bourgeois opposition. The following extract from party secretary Bo Toresson's speech at the 1984 party conference illustrates typical lines of confrontation:

> Union-party cooperation is a thorn in the flesh of the bourgeoisie who know very well that the strength of the labor movement relies .on this cooperation. The bourgeois attacks are aimed at both the political content and the forms of cooperation. But it is actually uninteresting for our opponents how we organize ourselves—it is our cooperation as such they are out after. The attacks are politically motivated: the bourgeois want to weaken Social Democracy through breaking up our cooperation. It is as simple as that.[65]

Another line of defense has been to "inform" in order to obviate all misunderstanding concerning this form of association; and to make it clear that collective affiliation occurs in forms that do not involve compulsion for the individual. The main argument went as follows: members of union organizations are free to choose and are under no obligation according to statutes or directives from the LO, trade union, or party—it is a local question. The decision is preceded by a discussion; collective affiliation can be reviewed annually during budget negotiations or whenever anyone requests it, and when the decision on collective affiliation is made, it may be subject to reservation.

Before the conference in 1978, the SAP executive appointed a working group whose task was to survey the organizational cooperation between the party and the trade union movement, especially locally and regionally. At the conference the following clear points of departure were reported by the executive:

> It is ascertained beyond all doubt that collective affiliation has aug-
> mented the affiliated unions' political influence and this has been to
> the advantage of both members and society. It is also clearly evident
> that the future will demand ever stronger bonds between the party
> and the trade union movement. Hence, any eventual revision of the
> technical form of affiliation must be concerned to maintain the close
> ties between the political and the union branches of the labor move-
> ment.[66]

The new form of affiliation adopted by the 1987 party conference involved replacing collective affiliation of members with organizational affiliation. The union-party program of cooperation approved by the conference
contained the following important points of principle: a) that membership
in the SAP can only be founded upon individual affiliation (the transition
from collective to individual affiliation should have been carried out by 31
December 1990); b) that all union organizations—groups, clubs, sections,
branches, or their equivalents—should make decisions about organizational
affiliation to the party; c) that union organizations retain a basic mandate
upon their affiliation to labor communes, with rights of representation calculated according to the number of members in the union organization who
are individually affiliated with the party.[67] The last point reveals an important question, namely whether the unions will be able to obtain enough
representatives and retain influence in the labor communes even after
1990.

Economically, the new organizational affiliation entails a new system of
income for the party. In addition to the traditional membership fees, an
organization subscription has been introduced. Like the membership fees,

it has three parts: the labor commune, the party district, and finally the central party level each decide upon a sum for the member union organization.[68] It should be noted that the amount is based on the size of the union organization—that is, on the total number of its members—not on the number of individual members of the party.

The period of preparation for future union-party affiliation, inquiries, and in some places trials of the new affiliation form came to an abrupt end when in the autumn of 1986, at the point of voting on legislation concerning collective affiliation, the Communist party seemed prepared to vote with the bourgeois bloc. Just prior to the vote in the Riksdag, it was related at a press conference that the SAP executive had decided to propose a changeover to another form of affiliation at the 1987 party conference. This rapid turnabout seemed to have been an immediate reaction to the communists' moves and the impending risk of being forced into a change. The right of self-determination and self-initiated change has been stressed at recent conferences—for example, by party secretary Bo Toresson at the 1984 conference: "And finally! It is our common task to fight for our right to self-determination. No outside party, least of all the bourgeois parties, shall decide our internal affairs."[69]

Let us leave for a moment the political scene around the parliamentary decision in the autumn of 1986 and go backstage, where problems shaping up around collective affiliation were also in evidence. It had become increasingly clear that during the 1980s a critical point was reached when the disadvantages of this form of membership outweighed the advantages. In LO chair Stig Malm's words, it became "a millstone around the neck of the labor movement." Defending collective affiliation by stressing historical ties lost more and more ground. Criticism of collective affiliation during the 1980s was reinforced by anticollective trends promulgating individual free will, trends that placed especially the SAP at a disadvantage in the court of public opinion. With its central position in Swedish democracy, the party could not maintain a form of membership that was increasingly considered to be incompatible with fundamental democratic principles.

Even though collectively affiliated members comprised about 75 percent of the party membership, the economic incentives for collective affiliation have diminished. This is because of the present relatively limited economic importance of membership fees in relation to public economic support and the election contributions from unions. However, there is no doubt that collective affiliation has been exceedingly advantageous for the development of the SAP's membership and has contributed to the SAP's strength as a mass party. The absence of collective affiliation in Denmark is an important aspect of both the economic problems of Danish Social Democracy and the substantial decline in membership that occurred after World War II. According to the Swedish political scientist Nils Elvander, the Social Democrats in Denmark could not utilize the positive developments in the Danish LO membership during the same period.[70]

The Swedish model of collective affiliation, however, never acquired the totalitarian form of its English counterpart, in which economic dependence (over 80 percent) and the organizational connections between the trade union movement and Labour tied the party's hands. The question is whether this type of collective membership creates the myth of a mass party and, through high membership figures and large income, virtually obviates the incentives to build up a truly member-based popular party.[71]

One important explanation for the demise of collective affiliation in Sweden has been the gradual buildup of another local form of cooperation between the labor movement and the party: workplace organizations. This system of cells satisfies the need for long-term opinion formation, personal contacts, cooperation on both union and political bases—in other words, a structure of mobilization.[72]

One of the cornerstones in the workplace organization is the "s-representative," a party member who, according to the stated aims, shall be responsible for at most twenty-five co-workers. The recruitment of representatives and regular checks on how well this structure covers workplaces are the responsibility of mainly the union committees, which exist in every labor commune and party district. In the middle of the 1980s there were nearly 100,000 s-representatives, and the goal for 1990 was to double that number.

The other component in workplace organization is Social Democratic union clubs (consisting of LO members) and Social Democratic workplace associations consisting of members of the LO and/or white-collar unions. Union clubs arose primarily to create a political platform in union elections, but they have increasingly developed into politically active organizations. Workplace associations are more recent and are still being formed. In the mid-1980s there were 450 union clubs and associations, and the aim was to reach 1,000 by 1990.[73]

A New Type of Election Campaign
The work and the organization of political parties acquired new prerequisites through the development of mass communication, and greatly in-

creased transport facilities gave the parties new possibilities for mobilizing larger groups of citizens during elections.[74] Increasing proportions of parties' messages and public debates began to be communicated in the mass media: newspapers, radio, and, from the end of the 1950s, television. Swedish television offered only viewing time for organized debates between the parties; it did not "sell" time. However, after the first "television election" in Sweden in 1960, the leadership of the political parties carried on intense debates about media strategies, education, and adaptation to new media. A new period had commenced in which the ability of the mass media to direct public debates, focus interest on party leaders, and search after "scandals" was unavoidable. This new situation also improved the parties' opportunities to reach virtually the entire electorate at once. The effects of this on campaigns became marked on all levels in the Social Democratic Labor Party.

The role of the national party leadership was strengthened, especially at elections: planning for the increasingly important party leader debates and public question times on radio and TV became a leadership task. At the same time many of the traditional and almost ritual forms of organizational and election activities were carried on relatively unaffected. However, as early as 1960 representatives from certain districts reported that the labor communes requested fewer election meetings because of the debates in the mass media.[75] On certain occasions local election campaigning was coordinated with what occurred on radio or TV. Before the 1966 election labor communes were advised to arrange meetings for the evening the party chair was to be on the radio. His speech could then be understood as an appeal to party members, and after the meeting the formation of election and contact organizations could be discussed.[76] Another and much more common coordinated operation has been the distribution of leaflets at workplaces the day after the party leaders' debates on television.

Trimming election organizations is a fundamental part of election preparations. Within the SAP this has always involved intensive conferences, with summaries from representatives and other functionaries and election workers from all party levels including trade unions and closely associated mobilization structures. The development has been toward an increasingly rigorous network, with various phases in which activities and contributions from all party levels have been thoroughly stipulated. The increasingly strategic and detailed planning of election campaigns is not only related to adapting to and exploiting the mass media, but also to voter trends: diminished class and augmented opinion voting, less and less party identification, and more and more voters who decide in the final stage of the campaign.[77]

Party conferences occurring in the autumn before an election year preface the election campaigns. In this context it has been advantageous for the party to be able to manifest cohesion and signs of accord. Partly because of intensive monitoring by the press, radio, and TV, the conferences have developed into important arenas not only for the party's internal activities but also for the mobilization of voters.[78]

In election campaigns every party's ambition is to promote its vital issues. One method that has been tested in the SAP is to place different argumentation groups centrally in party headquarters with the task of monitoring and underlining essential issues in the election campaign.[79] Election campaigns have in practice always been a common concern of the trade union movement and the SAP, and this has been manifested in direct cooperation as well as in functional divisions of labor on the local, regional, and central levels. The centrally planned cooperation and coordinated activities in election campaigns have markedly increased, however, especially during the 1980s—an observation that holds even if one disregards the dramatic rise in the volume of election campaigns.[80] The increase in cooperation during election campaigns corresponds in time with work on the program of union and political cooperation, initiated in 1978 and presented and approved by the conferences during the 1980s—an organizational program strongly linked to the abolition of collective affiliation. Trimming the workplace organizations and the determination to expand political activity within trade unions became prominent goals from the end of the 1970s onward. Experiences of bourgeois election victories in 1976 and 1979 doubtless also increased the inclination toward mobilization within the trade union movement.

Bureaucracy and Professionalism Versus Internal Democracy

The amalgamation of municipalities during the 1960s and 1970s had direct consequences for political parties' organizational structures. The SAP drastically diminished the number of labor communes and in the beginning of the 1970s implemented a unified pattern of organization, with one labor commune and several Social Democratic associations in each municipality. By 1973 the party executive was able to state that the reform had been carried out in 220 of a national total (at the time) of 278 municipalities.[81]

The municipal and county council subsidies to the party provided sufficient economic prerequisites for expanding administrative capacities on both regional and local party levels. Administrative growth in organizations on these levels was rapid in all parties but particularly in the SAP during the first few years of the public subsidies, and expansion was greatest in the larger municipalities.[82] In a study from the end of the 1970s, it was stated that the SAP had the most developed administration of any party on the local level.[83]

Professionalization and administrative expansion on these levels had strong links with the expansion occurring on the municipal level, where public services were being enlarged. Professionalization and bureaucratization have also characterized the situation on the central party level, where, for example, information and investigation capacities of party headquarters have grown enormously from the mid-1960s onward—from occupying some ten employees to around eighty in just twenty years.[84]

The speed and the ability of the mass media to shape opinion and relate information have promoted new modes of operation on various party levels. This is particularly true for the central level. Information facilities for the press, radio, and TV have expanded, with press conferences and press releases becoming important elements. Over the years of SAP governments, the party has developed a tradition of going to the media via press conferences and presenting current political issues and important proposals that will be discussed in the Riksdag. During the 1970s a network of local information groups was formed in new labor communes, which were to monitor the national and local political situations. Through their representatives in workplace associations and through the mass media, the information groups were to lead as well as follow debates and attempt to acquire an understanding of information needs. The party executive's brief was to send material to these groups regularly in order to provide a basis for local information. The local (action) manifestos developed during this period were largely worked out by these new groups, with executive contributions in the way of political facts and arguments, layout, and textual suggestions. In addition, the groups worked with local newspapers, placing both articles and advertisements.[85] These activities relied upon the increased resources available to the party through municipal subsidies.

As in other parties, operations within the Social Democratic Labor Party have been marked by specialization and division of labor. This has meant, for instance, that working groups (permanent or temporary) have been set up on all party levels to monitor, investigate, or formulate programs within various policy or interorganizational sectors. In 1982 and 1983 the party had a comprehensive network of these special organs on the regional level—no less than fifty assorted groups could be identified.[86] New modes of operation often appear first on the central level (sometimes modeled after parliamentary forms) and are later adopted by lower-level party organizations.

The system of consultative surveys or meetings (*rådslag*), started in 1965, became a new form of cooperation between labor unions and the party. It quickly became established in labor movement and also existed in other organizations for several years. It was no happenstance that the consultative survey, in certain instances called the national survey (*storrådslag*), came to the fore in the 1960s, the decade of direct democracy and mass meetings. Other similar forms with strong mobilization capacities include large, centrally organized educational campaigns and prompt referrals for opinion to base organizations and closely associated support groups.

The aim of the first consultative survey in 1965 was "to engage party and trade union people in discussions on a broad front about future directions."[87] Its material, with centrally prepared questionnaires, was well planned. Before the first survey, some seventy meetings were held all over the country in conjunction with the party district and the FCO (Trades Council). A filmstrip was prepared, brochures were sent to households, and announcements were published in newspapers. Participants in this survey were reckoned by the party executive to number about 30,000; they were divided into 3,000 groups and were able to choose among five current political subject areas. During the meetings government ministers posed direct questions to the participants.

Such surveys and the practice of circulating reports or papers for comment (remits) have since been used for several political issues. During the 1960s economic policy (1967; 25,000 party members participating) and taxation policy (1969; 40,000 participants) were subjects for consultation. During the 1970s several surveys were held with fewer than 10,000 participants—on local democracy and social planning, for example—but there have also been larger surveys on energy (1974; 44,000 participants), the Wage-Earners' Funds (1978; 65,000 participants), and three workplace consultations concerning employment rights. Of the latter, the codetermination paper in 1975 attracted the most participation, with 125,000 people.[88]

Consultative surveys have sometimes had palpable effects on political decisions, particularly regarding issues of working life. Proposals have been sharpened on several points after a consultative survey and circulation for comment—for example, proposals concerning the health insurance reform, work environment legislation, employment security, and the codetermination law.[89]

It should be clear that consultative surveys and the circulation of papers for comment have mobilized large numbers of people in discussions of current political issues. Despite all efforts, it has been difficult to expand participation to include nonparty members and nonmembers of the LO. During the 1960s the proportion of nonmembers was 13 to 14 percent, but this figure decreased during the following decade.[90] The consultative surveys have also been criticized for being too controlled. In a motion to the conference in 1987 one labor commune expressed qualms about centrally initiated campaigns: "We ask ourselves if members of the executive really believe that campaigns are important or if it is simply the case that political activities should be directed from above, that the party executive wants to be involved and determine what will be discussed in the local party groups."[91] Consultative surveys can also have a legitimizing function, manifesting and confirming unity on already-decided issues. If the party positions on a current political question such as energy or the Wage-Earners' Funds are already fixed, the possibilities for open-ended consultative discussions become very limited because of the need for party cohesion.

Internal party mobilization and democracy can also be too time-consuming and in conflict with the overall goal of mobilizing voters at elections.[92] Educational activities have always emphasized the internal work of the party. Over the years a large number of traditional "party schools" and organization-oriented courses have been held. During recent decades centrally produced, large-scale educational campaigns have been introduced in conjunction with national elections or party conferences. The role of these campaigns has been to augment mobilization and bolster unity within the labor movement. The educational campaign "Your Election '70," for example, according to the party executive's report, attracted 64,340 participants; and in the campaign of 1972, "Solidarity for Security," over 4,000 study circles with more than 40,000 members participated.[93]

In addition to a stronger integration of union and political organizational activities, another development may be discerned, especially during the 1970s and 1980s: increasingly comprehensive and detailed central planning of activities in the base organizations. This can be observed in some of the areas where cooperation between the SAP and the LO has been intensified: election campaigns, the formation of workplace organizations, First of May demonstrations, educational and consultative survey work, and external information activities.

The modes of performance of party organizations have also been of interest to the conferences. At the 1978 conference an inquiry was launched into the party's internal activities (PIA). The inquiry presented its conclusions at the 1984 conference. In the report great weight was given to the role of Social Democratic base organizations, to the local associations and their influence in local government questions, and to the potential changes for the party that could arise from the new decentralization trends in the reorganization of the local government. According to the inquiry it was important that associations adopt local (action) manifestos.[94] At the conference in 1987 the party executive stated that many labor communes had conducted their own organizational investigations, and others were in the process of doing so. However, in other quarters it seemed as if this vital discussion of democracy had not even commenced.[95]

CONCLUSIONS

The Social Democratic Labor Party's incorporation into the government over the last one hundred years has greatly affected the party's internal organizational development. Its entry into the electoral arena in 1911 induced the mass movement party to create an effective election campaign organization, which required more economic resources than the original membership financing could provide. Mass membership, the necessary prerequisite for organizational strength and effectiveness, legitimized demands from large groups of workers for a political change in society. Through collective affiliation, the party acquired the attributes of a mass movement and, at the same time, the requisite economic resources.

Half a century later, during the second incorporation phase, which was distinguished by postindustrial development tendencies, the position of Swedish Social Democracy was the diametrical opposite. The welfare society that had been built up over decades through *folkhemmet* policies (i.e., creating a national society with the attributes of a domestic household or "home"), which involved heavy expansion of the public sector, was ideologically rooted in the idea of the "strong society." The state's sphere of responsibility tended to be expanded to include more and more of what was considered vital for reasons of justice and democracy. The state was no longer considered to be a repressive and threatening instrument in the service of the ruling class—a common view in radical circles around the turn of the century. Instead, the state was seen as an implement of democracy in the service of the good society. Considering the key role of political parties in democracy, it was deemed crucial that the state guarantee economic resources for the parties to be able to function and exercise democratic leadership.

In the construction and realization of the welfare society, organized interest groups, popular movements (union, cooperative), and the state developed a mutual dependency. The state needed such organizations' competence and also their legitimacy as popular movements. The organizations, for their part, needed the state in order to realize their goals and, gradually, also to finance significant portions of their activities from public funds. This meant that these organizations exerted a great deal of influence early on in the formulation of political problems, in the decision-making process, and in the implementation of political decisions.[96]

During the initial period of forming and organizing the SAP as a political party, party activities were an integrated part of a special life-style for the members. The labor communes were not only meeting places where political questions and events were discussed and dealt with; they were also forums for training and education in a broad spectrum of political, social, and economic questions. Cultural activities comprised a natural element in the labor communes' way of working and functioning during this initial period, which meant that lectures, parties, amateur theater, and libraries were considered important for the members' well-being. Social networks, fund-raising, and relief measures were developed for when members became ill or unemployed. In these party organizations—as in many other popular movements around the turn of the century—the growing working class was being socialized into collectivist, social engagement.

For the SAP as for other Western European labor parties that early on had such broad and all-encompassing activities for their members, several of these original functions dwindled away—later to cease altogether. What remains is the parties' exclusive role in the control and formation of public power.[97]

After a few years there occurred within the SAP a strong specialization of labor movement activities, in which, inter alia, cultural activities obtained their own special organizational sphere. In due course, labor movement culture became both commercialized and supported by public means. Education and training were taken over by the labor movement's own educational association (and gradually publicly subsidized) and by the public schools. The mass media acquired an increasingly evident role in political socialization. Relief work was successively taken over by the public social welfare system, and the social functions of party organizations gradually declined and gave way to political and organizational work.

The risk with such a development is that the impetus for membership and engagement in the party diminishes. The lack of social and cultural adhesion in party organizations weakens their identity and the links between the party and its membership.

Even though integration between the party and the state has gone far, the vision of the popular movement party still remains—sometimes with deep traces of nostalgia, sometimes with pointers to the future. This vision was expressed in the following way in a motion from the Stockholm labor commune at the 1987 party conference:

> The strength of popular movements—mass engagement and unity—must be resuscitated. It cannot be achieved in the same way as it was in the early days of the movement. . . . A new popular movement mobilization that springs from the new inequalities must be generated—a mobilization whose first prerequisite is the destruction of centralization and professionalization within the labor movement and in society. The labor movement must take upon itself the task of recreating a red web, a multiplicity of associations and other groups that join people together into a social network even in "new Sweden."[98]

Internal mobilization has been and still is a necessary precondition for the SAP's strength, not least among the electorate. The SAP has not been able to attain the high degree of mobilization that has characterized social democracy through party organization alone. Its mobilization has largely been considered a common cause for the party and the trade union movement. Collective affiliation finally became an embarrassment from a democratic point of view, but the new organizational forms of cooperation (especially organizational affiliation and workplace organizations) and increasingly shared activities have been adapted to the times and to party strategy. Through its solid incorporation into government, the SAP has the entire nation as its area of responsibility, a situation that indeed applies to a greater or lesser extent to all parties but that is accentuated with the SAP because of its long periods in government and its possession of political power.

NOTES

1. G. Gidlund and J. Gidlund 1985.
2. G. Gidlund 1983.

3. Duverger 1954.

4. Some fifty records and anniversary publications have been collected from SAP districts (some of them from local branches of the Social Democratic party), sources used in part for the historical sections of this chapter.

5. Lindgren 1934, 55–56.

6. *SAP Conference Minutes* 1889.

7. Nordström 1938.

8. *SAP Conference Minutes* 1894.

9. *SAP Annual Report* 1894/1895, 1.

10. Franzén 1985.

11. Nordström 1938.

12. Minkin 1978; McKenzie 1967.

13. *SAP Annual Report* 1911.

14. *SAP Conference Minutes* 1900.

15. Billing 1986.

16. *Halmstads arbetarekommun 90 år* (Halmstad's Labor Commune, 90 Years), 1985.

17. *Bohuslän's Social Democratic Party District over 50 Years* 1955.

18. G. Gidlund 1983.

19. B. Andersson 1977, esp. p. 25.

20. Olsson 1972.

21. Arbetarnas bildningsförbund (ABF), *Annual Report* 1912–1916.

22. C. Carlsson 1986.

23. C. Carlsson Wetterberg 1987, 11–16.

24. *SAP Conference Minutes* 1905. See Gröning (1988) for further information on the relations between the party executive and the districts.

25. *Bohuslän's Social Democratic Party District over 50 Years* 1955, 18.

26. Arndt Johansson 1955.

27. G. Gidlund 1983, 115–16 and 130.

28. Bäckström 1977, vol. 1.

29. *LO Congress Minutes* 1898, 11; Statute P. 1, pt. 7.

30. Ibid., P. 4, pt. 2, ceased in 1900; Hadenius 1976.

31. *SAP Annual Report* 1898, 5.

32. Hentilä 1979; Franzén 1985.

33. Bäckström 1977, vol. 1.

34. *Julfacklan* 1898, cited in Franzén 1985, 167.

35. Bäckström 1977, vol. 1.

36. *LO Congress Minutes* 1900, 1909.

37. *SAP Conference Minutes* 1908.

38. The section on membership financing is based on G. Gidlund 1983, 105–7.

39. See SAP 1968, "The Task of the 1964 Conference to Review the Entire System of Subscriptions," SAP statutes from 1968.

40. Olson 1965.

41. *SAP Conference Minutes* 1894; *Annual Report* 1894/1895.

42. *SAP Conference Minutes* 1905 and 1911.

43. Billing 1986, 126.

44. *SAP Annual Report* 1911, 27.

45. Form for election statistics, January 1911; *SAP Party Executive Archives*, F.XIIa:1b (1911–1924) (Labor Movement Archives).

46. *SAP Annual Report* 1911: "Election Campaign 1911," 150–80.

47. Ibid., 173.

48. Ibid., 175. Thus, the party executive views organizational lacunae as the main causes of poor election results. Cf. Frånberg (1983) and Ricknell (1971), who point to the radical "*norrlandsfrisinnet*" (Norrland liberalism) as a tough competitor to the SAP in the 1911 election.

49. *SAP Annual Report* 1911, 161–62.

50. Ibid., 160–80.

51. Lindgren 1950.

52. Tingsten 1941, vol. 1.

53. For information on the growth and development of public financing, see G. Gidlund 1983.

54. SOU 1965:22.

55. G. Gidlund 1983. On the debates in Parliament and in the newspapers, see pp. 185–87.

56. *SAP Conference Minutes* 1968.

57. Riksdagen, Upper House 1965:41:34.

58. Proposition 1969:126.

59. See also Riksdagen, Constitutional Committee 1963:36; G. Gidlund 1985.

60. *SAP Conference Minutes* 1956, 46.

61. *SAP Conference Minutes* 1967, 1968.

62. G. Gidlund 1983 and 1985.

63. G. Gidlund 1985.

64. Dahlgren and Silén 1986.

65. *SAP Conference Minutes* 1984, 181.

66. Sten Andersson at the 1978 conference, no. 9: *Guidelines: Democracy in Future Society*, 51–52.

67. SAP party executive's proposal to the 1987 conference, no. 9: *Guidelines: Democracy in Future Society*, 51–52.

68. Ibid.

69. *SAP Conference Minutes* 1984, 184. On the communist moves, see VPK, "Annual Report," in *Conference Annals: 70 Years, 1917–1987; VPK's 28th Conference in the Struggle for Socialism* 1987, 55–56.

70. Elvander 1980.

71. Crouch 1982.

72. SAP 1984a, 16.

73. Ibid.

74. Back 1972.

75. For example: *Västmanland's Party District—75 Years, Breakthrough, Formation, Development* 1981; *Halmstad's Labor Commune, 90 Years* 1985.

76. *SAP Annual Report* 1982.

77. See voter investigations, e.g., Holmberg and Gilljam 1987.

78. Pierre 1986.

79. *SAP Annual Report* 1982.

80. This is based on studies primarily of the party executive's annual reports and conference material.

81. *SAP Annual Report* 1973.

82. SOU 1975:18.

83. J. Gidlund and G. Gidlund 1981.

84. *SAP Annual Report* 1964 to 1986.

85. Ibid.

86. G. Gidlund 1985.

87. *SAP Annual Report* 1964, 29.

88. *Sap Annual Report* 1967–1978; S.-O. Hansson, "Rådslag under lupp" (review of Adrian Reinert's thesis), *Tiden* no. 2, 1988.

89. Reinert 1987; S.-O. Hansson 1988.

90. S.-O. Hansson 1988.

91. SAP Conference 1987, Motion no. 597.

92. *SAP Conference Minutes* 1981, 240.

93. *SAP Annual Report*, 1970 to 1972.

94. SAP 1984b.

95. SAP 1987, 12.

96. Eliassen 1981.

97. Panebianco 1988.

98. SAP Conference 1987, Motion no. 620.

On 19–22 April 1889, representatives of sixty-nine different organizations, most of them union organizations, gathered together for the Swedish Social Democratic Labor Party's inaugural conference. The building where they met, Tunnelgaten 12 (now Olof Palmes gata) in Stockholm (*above*) has been torn down. In order to underline the party's antiauthoritarian character, the conference did not elect a party leader but instead appointed eight representatives who were to coordinate party activities. One of the representatives was Hjalmar Branting (1860–1925) (*above left*), later party leader and Sweden's first Social Democratic prime minister (1920). Another representative was Fredrik Sterky (1860–1900) (*left*), who was chosen in 1898 to be the Swedish Trade Union Confederation's (LO) first chair. *Below*: Branting's draft minutes at a preparatory Social Democratic meeting on 4 April 1889. (All photos from the Labor Movement's Archives and Library, ARAB, Stockholm.)

The SAP was formed as an organization for everyone involved in the class struggle. The struggle against capital has remained a unifying theme at First of May demonstrations. *Above left*, 1949, banner text: "We Want Economic Democracy"; *below left*, 1967, center banner: "The People's Welfare Before Big Business." But practice has been characterized more by cooperation in order to achieve economic growth. *Above*, from a meeting at the prime minister's "Camp David," Harpsund, south of Stockholm, in November 1957. The meeting was attended by members of the government, the LO leadership, and representatives of the export industry (Prime Minister Tage Erlander, standing; *to his right*, LO Chair Arne Geijer). During the 1980s the opposition of capital took new forms. *Right*, in 1987 twenty thousand demonstrators gathered at a meeting arranged by the so-called 4 October Committee to protest the proposal for a collective capital formation to be controlled by wage earner organizations, the Wage-Earners' Investment Funds. Sign text: "Abolish Labor Unions. Individual ownership for *all*." (Photo: Sallstedts/Morgon-Tidningen; Hernried; Bo Holst/Morgon-Tidningen—all three ARAB; Sven-Erik Sjöberg, Pressens Bild.)

During the 1930s the struggle against unemployment became a primary concern for the Social Democratic Labor Party. The state's responsibility for employment was a fundamental point of the new economic policy. During the postwar period a great deal of the responsibility for employment was placed with the Labor Market Board, which through retraining programs, for example, tried to provide unemployed people with skills sought after by industry. *Above*: Unemployed workers at a closed-down building site in 1930. (Photo: Eric A. Lundquist.) *Left*: A woman (Berit Karlsson) had learned to be a welder at a labor market training course, part of a retraining scheme arranged by the state labor market authorities. She is now working in the metalworks ABE in Örnsköldsvik in northern Sweden. (Photo: Per Ågren.)

Housing policy illustrates the vision of the Social Democrats. The young construction worker on the Social Democratic Youth organization's poster of 1938 (*right*) concretely contributed to the new "People's Home." (Text: "We're Building The Country. Today and for the future. Sweden's Social Democratic Youth.") When the district of Augustenborg was being built in the southern Swedish town of Malmö in 1948, the farm laborer cottages, evidence of the old class society, were torn down (*above*). The happiness felt by the residents of new housing estates in their modern comforts has still not been quenched, not even by the social problems that have attended many of the suburbs built during the 1960s and 1970s.

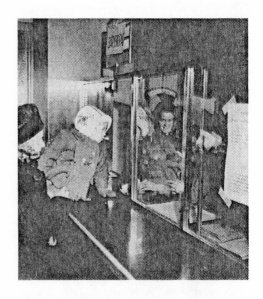

An important feature of twentieth-century Swedish social welfare has been the move from individual needs tests to a universal social policy. The old order is represented here by Stockholm's Child Care Bureau (*above left*) and by a picture showing the distribution of milk to poor children in Stockholm at the turn of the century (*below left*). In the new system no one had to explain himself or herself to strict authorities and social workers. As of January 1948, all mothers could get their child allowance at the post office (*above right*, picture taken in the Stockholm district of Hammarbyhöjden, 20 January 1948, the first day of the new system). Now school lunches provide all children, even "rich" children, with milk and food. The picture below, taken in the 1970s, is from Skärsätra School's cafeteria in Lidingö, outside Stockholm. (Photo right: Pressens Bild; other photos from the Nordic Museum in Stockholm.)

As a result of the 1938 and 1945 laws on vacations, all employees received the right to at least twelve days of paid vacation (at present it is twenty-seven days). Certain groups already had several days of leave written into their contracts. The picture above shows a young farm worker couple on their way home from vacation. They were met on the road by the writer Ivar Lo-Johansson and the photographer Gunnar Lundh. (Photo: Nordic Museum in Stockholm.) One of the major reforms of the postwar period was the introduction of the comprehensive school. In the internal discussions on school policy, two distinct approaches collided. One called for the fostering of an intellectual elite, regardless of social origins; the other aimed at giving everyone the same education and competence. Judging by its poster of 1948 (*right*), the Swedish Social Democratic Youth (SSU) would seem to support the first approach of fostering an intellectual elite based on "talent" rather than social origins (poster text: "Poor but talented—give him an equal chance"). In the background of the poster, a young man who has just passed the higher secondary school examination (*studentexamen*); in the foreground, and errand boy on his bicycle.

The conviction that Sweden should endeavor to serve peace has remained a cornerstone of Social Democratic foreign policy. In 1917 the chair of the Danish party, Thorvald Stauning (1878–1942, later prime minister for many years), Hjalmar Branting from Sweden, and Pieter J. Troelsta from Holland gathered international socialists at a conference in Stockholm in a vain attempt to put an end to World War I. *Above*: The Dutch-Scandinavian committee in Stockholm, May 1917. Branting and Troelsta are sitting at the far end of the table; Stauning, bearded, is nearest to the camera on the left. Nearest to the camera on the right is Gustav Möller (from 1924 to 1926 and 1932 to 1951 minister of social affairs). (Photo: Axel Malmström/ ARAB.)

On 26 April 1982, Olof Palme (1927–1986), then leader of the opposition, assembled the Nonallied Commission for Disarmament and Security (the Palme Commission) at a final meeting at the Grand Hotel in Saltsjöbaden outside of Stockholm (*above*). Palme is second from the left in the first row; Norway's prime minister, Gro Harlem Brundtland, is fourth from the left in the first row. The group includes many other well-known people, mostly politicians, from Eastern, Western, and neutral states. (Photo: Tommy Pedersen/Pressens Bild.)

The question of the role of defense in Sweden's security has been more contentious. The antidefense, antimilitaristic sentiments expressed in the election poster from 1914 (*far left*) dominated for a long time. (Text: "The Program of the Right means The People Under the Yoke of Militarism.") When World War II broke out, support for military defense was almost total. The party's election campaign in 1940 (*left*) reflected support for national unity and defense. Poster text reads: "Security for the home. Freedom for the country. Vote for the Labor Party."

"Our party has never been particularly interested in theoretical discussions." This pronouncement by Tage Erlander (1901–85; from 1946 to 1969 party chair and prime minister) was made at the 1956 party conference. It may be added that the theoretical debate that did occur was undogmatic and strongly oriented toward creating guidelines for practical political work. Nils Karleby (editor, 1892–1926), *above*, and Ernst Wigforss (1881–1977; from 1932 to 1949 finance minister), *left*, were very important in establishing the tenor of the debate. Karleby wrote *Socialism inför verkligheten* (Socialism Facing Reality) (1926), and Wigforss, *Socialism i vår tid* (Socialism in Our Time) (1952). (Photos: Hernried, both ARAB.) However, prior to the party split in 1917, there was a significant minority faction with stronger Marxist leanings. This faction dominated the Social Democratic Youth organization, and in March 1916, against the advice of the party executive, it arranged a large peace congress. When the congress manifesto was published in the youth organization paper *Stormklockan* ("Alarm Bell") it was interpreted as treasonable and was confiscated by the Justice Department. In the next edition, the text was removed, leaving an empty frame. (*Right*: Original examples in the National Archives, with the text of the manifesto.)

SOCIALDEMOKRATISKA UNGDOMSFÖRBUNDETS VECKOTIDNING.

LJUS ÖVER LANDET
DET ÄR DET VI VILJA

STORMKLOCKAN

27 Mars 1916.
9:e årg. N:o 14 B.
Socialistisk tidning.
Lösnummer 10 öre.

Ryssland i Sverge!

Hedén, Höglund och Oljelund häktade för landsförräderi.

Kämparna för Sverges fred i fängelse — krigshetsarna lämnas oantastade.

FRED TILL VARJE PRIS!

Manifest till Sverges arbetande folk.

SOCIALDEMOKRATISKA UNGDOMSFÖRBUNDETS VECKOTIDNING

LJUS ÖVER LANDET
DET ÄR DET VI VILJA

STORMKLOCKAN

25 Mars 1916.
9:e årg. N:o 14.
Socialistisk tidning.
Lösnummer 10 öre.

DEN STORA ARBETAREFREDSKONGRESSEN.

Samlande fredsparoller och enig stämning.

Helveteslarm i den reaktionära pressen.

Åtal mot Erik Hedén, Z. Höglund och Ivan Oljelund.

FRED TILL VARJE PRIS!

Manifest till Sverges arbetande folk.

Vår lösen är: Fred till varje pris!

ARBETAREFREDSKONGRESSEN I STOCKHOLM.

The practical methods for spreading the Social Democratic Labor Party's message have varied. In the 1911 election campaign, the "red car" raised a sensation. The picture (*far left, top*) shows it ready to start outside the Labor Library in Stockholm. In the front seat are two well-known radical Social Democrats, Z. Höglund and Karl Kilbom, who later became Communists only to return to the Social Democratic Labor Party. In 1927 the party tried to attract the attention of Stockholm residents with a boat (*far left, bottom*) and, in 1928, with a long line of cyclists (*left*). Banner text in boat reads: "Vote for the Social Democratic Labor Party." From 1932 onward the party election campaigns were largely successful. For forty consecutive years Sweden had a Social Democratic prime minister, so it is not surprising that the opposition tried to appeal to the voters' desire for change. The poster battle pictured above was waged during the 1965 election campaign. (Dagens Bild, detail—all from ARAB.) The first poster on the left is from the Liberal party. The text reads, "They can sit . . . Teach them to walk!" The ones who are to "walk" are the members of the coalition government, formed by the Social Democrats and the Agrarian party, represented on the poster by their party leaders, Tage Erlander and Gunnar Hedlund. The next poster gives the Social Democrats' response, "They want to sit . . . Let them stay! They are the best for the Swedish people," accompanied by pictures of the opposition leaders, Bertil Ohlin (Liberal) and Jarl Hjalmarsson (Conservative). The rest of the posters continue the "war" in words, even in rhyming couplets—a marked difference compared with present-day (1991) election posters with their blown-up pictures of party leaders and flat slogans.

UR FAMILJELIVET.
DET LIBERAL-SOCIALISTISKA ÄKTENSKAPET.

The Social Democrats' singular (by international standards) power position has depended to an extent on their willingness to cooperate. Through forming coalitions, the party has forestalled a concerted bourgeois front. The pictures on this page of three classic pairs illustrate this line in the party's political strategy: (*left*) the Liberal Nils Edén (1871–1945) and Hjalmar Branting in a tender reconciliation after forming a government in October 1917, with Edén as head of government (drawing by Ivar Starkenberg); (*above left*) Per Albin Hansson (1885–1946, prime minister 1932–46) and Agrarian party member Axel Pehrsson in Bramstorp (1883–1954, minister of agriculture 1936–45) after taking office in their respective ministries in September 1936 (Photo: *Dagens Nyheter*); (*above right*) Tage Erlander and the Agrarian/Center party leader Gunnar Hedlund (1900–1990, minister for home affairs 1951–57) confirming in October 1951 that, after protracted negotiations, a new red-green coalition would be formed. (Photo: a-bild/MT. All pictures ARAB.)

Villy Bergström

5

Party Program and Economic Policy: The Social Democrats in Government

The Swedish Social Democratic Labor Party (SAP) grew out of local socialist clubs and trade unions in response to the emerging capitalism of the late nineteenth century. The central party was formed in 1889. Until the Swedish Confederation of Trade Unions (LO) was created in 1898 the central SAP organization also served as the central trade union organization. Both branches of the Swedish labor movement were built up from below by the same people, as both party members and trade unionists.

Socialist ideas arrived in Sweden mainly from Germany. As the movement grew in Sweden it had no parliamentary representation because workers, lacking the requisite wealth and on subsistence wages, had no voting rights. However, by cooperating with the Liberal party the leader of the SAP, Hjalmar Branting, entered the Riksdag in 1897. In the wake of universal suffrage for men, introduced in 1911, the parliamentary group grew so large that the first Social Democratic government could be formed in 1920. The party split when a revolutionary faction left the SAP in 1917; the splinter group formed the basis for the Communist party.

To depict and analyze a century of Social Democratic economic policy would be an enormous task. Consequently I have limited myself to examining Social Democratic Labor Party programs and economic policy as a new government is formed. By this I mean the party's then-current program, decisions, and debates in party conferences as well as the economic policy presented in parliamentary motions in conjunction with forming a government. Within these perimeters, I shall focus upon a few important programs: the first Branting government and questions of nationalization; the new economic policy of 1932 and 1933; the Postwar Program; the party conference in 1956 and the subsequent government reshuffle; and the crisis policy of 1981.

How one should view the various party programs and their basic general principles is of course, an important question. I have taken them seriously as an expression of a desire to act when they are so concretely formulated that their objectives are very clear. In some cases the program is like a "root system in the mould of history," which helps the party to find a direction when inundated with the compromises of day-to-day politics. The program serves to unify the party and to keep it separate from other parties.[1] I have delimited "economic policy" to questions concerning the economic system—that is, to the large issues of ownership, planning, employment, and stabilization.

THE 1920s AS A POINT OF DEPARTURE

Eight years after its founding at the fourth party conference, the SAP adopted its own program; it had been preceded by programs approved by various Social Democratic groups, all of them heavily influenced by the German party. The same was true of the SAP's first program from 1897, which lasted until it was comprehensively revised in 1920. The 1920 program held until a new party program and the Postwar Program were adopted at the party conference in 1944.

Social Democracy in Power for the First Time

During the 1920s there were three Social Democratic governments, but what concerns us here is the party's policy while in government in light of the 1920 party program. When Hjalmar Branting opened the party conference in 1920 he asserted, "We know that the question of nationalization has become prominent throughout the world; people have demanded that with reference to social questions at least something of what Social Democracy has written on its banner should be carried out."[2] Rickard Sandler, who would lead the government when Hjalmar Branting died in 1925, was the party executive's speaker during the beginning of the program discussions. Sandler saw three stages in the development of the Swedish Social Democratic Labor Party. At the time of the first program in 1897 the SAP was a party of industrial workers, and this influenced the program. Its revision in 1911 had coincided with the beginnings of democracy, which in its turn had affected the new program. Sandler continued: "Likewise, we face a new era now: nationalization problems will henceforth dominate."[3] There is no doubt that nationalization was the pressing issue; and it was not merely a Swedish phenomenon, but one that occupied many other parties after the Russian revolution and the end of World War I.

The program itself was clear: it was a program for the nationalization of the Swedish economy, and in its basic principles, nothing else. The program begins with a grandiose social economic theory: "The main cause of those faults which disfigure present-day civilization is the private capitalistic mode of production which places rights of ownership in the hands of a minority, dooms the majority to propertylessness and dependence, and makes the opposition between workers and capitalists the determining characteristic of today's society."[4] Exploitation in all areas of society and rapid technical development accompanied by "an unnatural accumulation of wealth" on the one hand, and "enormous growth of the propertyless working class" on the other, are mentioned later on in the program. Also discussed are the randomness of capitalism and its inability to utilize fully the growing productive forces. Not even the highest form of capitalism, "trust formation," facilitates an extensive and efficient utilization of productive forces.

The program authors go on to discuss how these conditions have compelled the working class to organize in unions and cooperatives. Furthermore,

> this class struggle will not cease until society is so transformed that capitalist exploitation has totally ceased, the class society has fallen and mass poverty has been abolished.
>
> These things can only happen through the abolishment of private capitalist rights to ownership of the means of production, and the latter's coming under the control of society, and by replacing the present unplanned production of goods with a socialist production,

planned according to the real needs of society in order to increase the standards of welfare.[5]

The 1920 SAP program was unequivocal in its analysis and in its demands. However, no distinction was ever made between the question of ownership and how economic life is organized. The criticism leveled at capitalism in a Marxist-inspired analysis had to do with the distribution of income and wealth (exploitation), efficiency in the economic system (desultory production), and unemployment and misuse of capacity (full utilization of productive forces). The abolition of private ownership rights to the means of production was meant to facilitate a solution to all problems and to be clearly synonymous with the introduction of the planned economy.

From Words to Action

The first Social Democratic government, then, had a clear, unambiguous party program to act upon (it had seventeen other points, but the basic principles throughout were sufficiently clear). The government immediately got to work, setting up three inquiries into just those areas that the program concentrated upon, namely, "nationalization," "industrial democracy," and "trust control." In the terms of the program these inquiries concerned ownership, determination, and social utility. The Nationalization Committee is perhaps the most interesting, since the basic principles of the 1920 program are dominated by demands for nearly total nationalization of society's production apparatus. Both industrial democracy and trust control can be interpreted in "softer" terms as codetermination and competition legislation. The Nationalization Committee, however, would be dealing with the essence of capitalism—the right of private ownership.

The tone of the Branting government's directives to the Nationalization Committee is very different from that of the party program. Indeed, it can be said that the party program was totally repudiated, or at least the general principles (on the other hand, many of the seventeen points in the program were turned into practical politics). The government directives note the lack of the "general public's" influence over production; the owners of the means of production make the decisions without needing to take "sufficient consideration of society's, consumers' and employees' personal interests." There are no guarantees that either production as a whole will receive the most rational orientation possible or that profits within the various branches of industry will be used in the best and most defensible ways, socially or in terms of the national economy.

Such was the criticism in the directives, which went on to address themselves to state and municipal operation of areas such as communications, energy, and transport. Various forms of organization were discussed, such as the possibility of establishing "special social economic companies." Rigid forms of organization were to be avoided; what would be attempted was "to combine the advantages for the general public which could be achieved through providing the necessary space for *free initiative* while ensuring that the best for the whole is provided, which can never be achieved through individual acquisition."

The long introduction to the directives ends with the following, which seems utterly foreign to the thinking in the 1920 party program: "The lines of thought developed here have nothing to do with a schematic nationalization of total production; neither do the attitudes embraced by Swedish Social Democracy." The directives go on to advise the committee to explore areas in which nationalization might be practical and in what forms it should be applied. One condition is mentioned: "that production must not decrease during that transference into public ownership of the more important natural resources and larger means of production, which is palpably required by the interests of the nation."[6]

Undoubtedly Hjalmar Branting demonstrated great flexibility when he could be chair of the party whose basic principles were given the wording cited earlier while at the same time presiding over the government that issued these directives in the first tottering steps toward political implementation of the party's basic principles. Since the analysis and demands contained in these principles were so remarkably clear (but not necessarily either true or correct), the attitudes reflected in the directives quoted above seem difficult to understand. According to the party's basic principles the rights of private capital to ownership formed the basis of all misery and misfortune, and hence the demand for comprehensive nationalization and total societal control was nothing less than imperative.[7]

In the directives issued to the Committee on Industrial Democracy the necessity of a development within economic life parallel to that within the political is discussed: "namely, from an autocratic to a democratic rule." Reference is also made to the reservations expressed by the trade unions: "Industrial democracy may then be seen as a complement to the trade unions' efforts to safeguard their members' interests. However, through its organizational forms [industrial democracy] must also connect workers more closely to production, and create a new incentive to increase it in the interests of society as a whole."[8]

The committee carried out its work on industrial democracy rapidly. The result was a motion in the Riksdag in 1924 that proposed operation boards or committees for information and cooperation. Regarding the nationalization issue, it may be said that the same year it was highlighted in the party program as the primary objective of social democracy, it became buried in an inquiry lasting sixteen years. It reappeared at the party conference in 1932 when the party's own internal reappraisal also took place.

In fact the party seems not to have been so clearly unified on the issue of nationalization as the program and the conference debates would suggest. In another context I have shown that the party secretary Gustav Möller supported the party program, while Nils Karleby, a journalist who played an important role in the party discussion, argued in favor of another view. Ernst Wigforss, minister of finance from 1932 to 1949, occupied a middle position, stressing decentralization and the market economy within the framework of various forms of collective ownership.[9]

So much for the large, system-related problems regarding the program and practice during the first Social Democratic government. But how did the Social Democrats conduct their economic policy within the framework of capitalism? There were many demands referring to the economy in the seventeen points of the party manifesto—calls for direct progressive taxation in order to secure "social capital-formation," the eight-hour workday, unemployment insurance, and so on. No demands were raised for combating unemployment, either in terms of business cycles or as a permanent feature of 1920s capitalism.

The 1920s began with a serious crisis—falling prices, decreasing real wages, and widespread unemployment. The crisis of 1920–1921 was overcome more quickly than that of the 1930s, but, despite relatively rapid economic growth (in comparison with the 1930s) after 1921, high unemployment persisted throughout the whole period. The Social Democratic government had no independent economic policy on unemployment; it supported the conscious deflationary policy of 1920. In accord with the recommendations from a committee of finance experts, including among others the economist Gustav Cassel, the government formulated monetary goals intended to bring about a return to the gold standard of prewar parity. To achieve this, deflation, unemployment, falling prices and wages, and lower exchange rates for foreign currency (and revaluation of the krona) were required. The goals of the financial policy were budgetary. In a statement from the Brussels conference of 1920 that accompanied the 1921 financial plan, the following doctrine was formulated: "The nation that in its financial policy approves a budget shortage treads upon a downward slope which leads to ruin. To avoid this no sacrifice is too great."[10] Ernst Wigforss and others in the party were influenced by the well-known economist Knut Wicksell, who was closely associated with the labor movement. For the sake of justice, considering that fortunes had been undermined by inflation, Wicksell even proposed a return to 1914 price levels!

Behind this economic policy lay various considerations. One seemed to have been that real wages would be improved by the fall in prices at the same time as the government was safeguarding industrial competitive power. It was also apparently thought that only a return to the 1914 price levels was compatible with continued price stability and hence an even development of the business cycle.

PROGRAM AND GOVERNMENT POLICY AROUND 1932

With minor changes, the 1920 party program remained intact until 1944, when it was comprehensively revised. On economic policy, the 1920 program was, as has been mentioned, dominated by the demand for total nationalization and economic planning. In order to obtain an idea of the program behind the Social Democratic election victories in 1934, we should also look at the party motions in the Riksdag around 1930. However, the most important document in this context is the *Minutes* from the party conference held in March 1932, six months prior to elections to the Second Chamber of the Riksdag.

In 1928 the party had suffered a heavy defeat. From having attracted more than 41 percent of the votes in the 1924 election, the party received only 37 percent in 1928. According to party chair Per Albin Hansson, the 1928 election results were a consequence of the inheritance tax motion in the Riksdag of the same year. When one goes out to the voters it is necessary to "not only have an idea, a line, but also well-delineated proposals for the realization of the idea."[11]

The SAP soon recovered at the local elections of 1930, at which point the passivity in the stabilization policy had already been broken. The party had worked on motions for combating unemployment, both that which was considered permanent and that which arose in conjunction with the crisis.

We are now into one of the most "researched" phases of modern Swedish history. Landgren dates the swing to an active stabilization policy at 1930, and he bases this on the motions in the First Chamber as well as the parliamentary debates.[12] What is of interest here is not the origin of the ideas, but the program and the policy actually conducted. The party presented comprehensive, well-thought-out motions on the unemployment problem to the Riksdag, in which the main message was that the state should be given a totally different role than it had before in order to stabilize employment on a high level. In the motion from 1930 it was asserted that unemployment seemed to be permanent, not merely a phenomenon of the business cycle. Appeals were made to abolish emergency relief and instead to pledge the state to organize relief works for strictly market wages and employment conditions. A number of practical suggestions for state involvement were recommended.

The motion placed before the 1932 Riksdag was tantamount to a minor government report.[13] Over one hundred pages long, it contains analyses, calculations, and concrete proposals. About half of the text is devoted to the difficult situation of farmers. In contrast to the 1930 motion, which must have been composed during an intensive boom period in 1929 just before the advent of the international financial crisis, the 1932 motion dealt with unemployment and the effects of the crisis on households.

The demands from the 1930 motion were repeated: the Unemployment Commission should be abolished and unemployment combated by means of the state working through the open market—the normal conditions on the labor market should apply. The difficult situation in agricultural communities was analyzed in detail. A number of proposals for the amelioration of distress were presented, such as state support to farmers to help with interest payments. The motion contained a proposal for "public relief work" (the new term) for 30 million kronor and assistance to farmers for 24 million.

The motion contained a statement of political principle favoring a policy of general increase in demand in order to counter economic recession, a long-range policy for stimulating demand in order to reduce permanent unemployment, and a policy for agricultural support that would facilitate cooperation between the Agrarian party and the farmers' other interest organizations. In an article in *Tiden* (1932), Ernst Wigforss developed this strategy:

> Society continues to be transformed along Social Democratic lines.
> Large numbers of farmers, so far at least, have come closer to Social
> Democracy, and do not see their interests as incompatible with

those of the working class. This is why the discussion which is being conducted now, and which will assuredly continue, on Social Democratic guidelines for help for both workers and farmers, has a profound significance.[14]

The 1932 Party Conference

The motions discussed above—including those of 1932—existed when the party convened in March 1932. In the end, the conference replaced the nationalization program from 1920 with the course of action indicated in the two motions presented above.

In his opening speech, Per Albin Hansson presented the 1932 motion (I:109) as a fulfillment of the 1930 election program. He also said, "Not only wage-earners suffer under the flaws of the capitalist system, but also the agricultural class, which sees its security threatened; and even the middle class feels a growing uncertainty and longs for a radical change."[15] In a later speech on the current political situation, Per Albin Hansson returned to the 1932 motion in the Riksdag, which he said summarized, clarified, and made concrete the party's previous policy, making "a total picture of what we deem necessary and possible to carry out in order to combat unemployment. . . ."[16] Per Albin Hansson did not touch upon the question of nationalization, either in his introduction or in his statements about the political situation prior to the election, other than in general terms such as, "It is clearer than ever that only through society's controlling the productive forces can these forces be mastered and properly utilized for the fulfillment of the needs of the population. . . ."[17]

When the debate on nationalization finally got going, it became even more lengthy: it occupies over sixty-five pages in the conference minutes, without any contributions from the party chair. The points of departure for the debate were motions by Per Emil Brusewitz, Carl Lindhagen, and the Riseberga *arbetarekommun* (labor commune—local party branch). The Brusewitz motion, like that from Riseberga, demanded that the nationalization issue be highlighted in current policies. Brusewitz referred to the socialist workers conference in Vienna in 1931, during which the parties taking part were admonished to make the question of nationalization central to their crisis policies. The Riseberga group demanded a detailed ten-year plan for nationalization as a crisis measure. Carl Lindhagen's motion was vague and difficult to interpret, but he seemed to demand that the party program should be "carried over to current politics."

The party executive proposed a statement of principle on the nationalization issue. It was also proposed that a plan of action concerning this issue be drawn up by the executive when the Nationalization Committee's thoughts about the matter had been presented and examined.

On the basis of these motions and the party executive's proposals, a lengthy debate ensued. Rickard Sandler, the chair of the Nationalization Committee and the spokesman for the executive, said that Soviet Russia had been an inspiring example for those setting forth motions. However, what was taking place in Soviet Russia was not so much nationalization as "a gigantic experiment in industrialization" —and that under a party dictatorship. As long as a spark of feeling for the value of freedom still existed in Sweden, such a situation would be unthinkable. Sandler also stressed Sweden's international dependence, which set limits to a nationalization policy, as did "consideration of Swedish society's inner social structure." He claimed moreover that in large sections of Swedish economy "no typical private capitalist economy exists."[18]

Rickard Sandler had a certain inclination toward polemical—if not cynical—comments. Apropos of the International's recommendation to its member parties, he asserted: "With all due respect to the International, it must be said that it is easier to make a resolution on the moon concerning the nationalization which is to occur on earth, and it is easier to make a resolution in Vienna on the nationalization which is to take place in Sweden than it is to do it here."[19] Sandler wanted a resolution to be taken about principles, which would facilitate the drafting of certain guidelines—for example, that when the nationalization process is started, it should be carried out in the context of political, social, and economic democracy.[20]

Georg Branting, lawyer and son of Hjalmar Branting, responded to Sandler. "An economic catastrophe does not wait for statements from the Nationalization Committee," he said, and he recalled that the Socialist Labor International conference in Vienna in 1931 supported the exhortation to all member parties "to make the demand for nationalization central to their present policies."[21] Georg Branting's final demand was that when the statement of principle had been drawn up, the Draft Committee should take in point one of motion one, which concerned the resolution from the International—namely, that the demand for nationalization should occupy a central place in propaganda and information activities.

Bitter contributions were made, for example, by the old agitator Fabian Månsson, who dismissed the conference as immature and conservative.[22] Gustav Möller, soon to be minister of social affairs, referred back to the spirit of his long article in *Tiden* from 1918 about the social revolution and to Karleby's writings from the 1920s:[23]

> When I talk about nationalization today I mean every measure which involves progress in the extension of public ownership and of public control over individual ownership. I am thus not speaking of nationalization as a process to be suddenly carried out in each segment of our economy, or each branch of our industry. What I mean is that every step which extends public ownership, whether municipal or state, even including cooperatives, which I also consider a form of public ownership, every such step involves nationalization. And when these steps multiply, we can begin to achieve something that could be called a socialized society.

Möller concluded by saying that of course social democracy should work for nationalization. However, it was not to become a central point: "As long as the crisis goes on, the help measures as they are presented in our crisis aid motion, will by their very nature constitute the core of our program."[24]

Ernst Wigforss began by saying that the party executive had hoped the Nationalization Committee would have completed its work in time to provide the basis for a conference decision in 1932. By way of introduction and background, he also referred to social democracy's "Marxist orientation, which makes us view events, at least to a degree, as necessities determined by existing conditions. . . ." Wigforss said that a statement from the conference on the nationalization issue should be articulated accordingly, and referred to Per Albin Hansson's introductory remarks on the inheritance tax motion in 1928, that "everyone who reads it understands that . . . socialist intervention . . . is something that is to help people, even in the times in which we are living now." With this in mind, Wigforss argued, it was obvious that nationalization must be given priority.[25] However, he also said that making it concrete—the conference drawing up guidelines for an economic policy—was out of the question, and the party was still not clear about where it would intervene if it were in power.

Referring again to the 1928 conference motion on the inheritance tax, Wigforss insisted that "if we are to present any points they must be those with which people feel connected in their daily lives." Just such a connection was to be found in the 1932 party motion to the Riksdag.[26] Ernst Wigforss then offered a new perspective on the debate, saying that the Social

Democratic Labor Party has two roots, Marxism and economic liberalism. The socialist world view contains two lines of thought that do not necessarily coincide: the demand for nationalization and the demand for a planned economy. Nationalization is not necessarily the same as economic planning:

> We could take [the metal company] Boliden one year; we could set up a large shoe factory the second year; we could open a state-owned commercial bank the third; we could perhaps let the community take over the whole lumber industry the fourth year, etc. But please note that these measures would not take our economy out of the free market and its chaos. That we have a state-owned railway does not ensure our keeping the railway workers employed during a crisis.

Somewhat vaguely (in the minutes), Wigforss continued: "even socialists react to the idea of trying to intervene, [react] against the idea of trying to control the market." According to Wigforss, the planned economy should be pursued in parallel to nationalization.[27] He did not connect the party motion that had played a major role during the conference with a planned economy, but it is evident that he viewed the new economic policy as a step in the direction of the latter.[28]

After a long debate, the conference decided (in accordance with the party executive's proposal) to appoint a Draft Committee to formulate a statement on principles in the nationalization issue, in light of the economic crisis. Only 157 votes against 149 averted the acceptance of Georg Branting's demand that the conference, approving point one in motion one (the International's demand on its member parties), should refer this point to the Draft Committee for consideration.

Thus can large and dramatic changes of direction occur in a democracy: decades of debates are buried and new eras initiated by referrals—by a tiny majority—to a Draft Committee. The committee's statement involved a balancing act. Measures for nationalization were referred to as the party's greatest and most essential task, and references were made to the pursuit of socialized forms within business. However, these two powerfully formulated demands were surrounded by conditions and restrictions, so that the statement as a whole gave the party leadership free rein. The conference consented without debate.[29]

In Government

Social Democratic policy after the election victory in 1932 was well prepared. There was a settlement in the Riksdag with the Agrarian party based
on SAP motions, debates in the party conference, and various debate pam-
phlets. In 1933 a number of propositions were presented, based on the
party's preelection analyses and discussions. Propositions 209, 212, and 216
to the 1933 Riksdag had to do with combating the crisis and reducing the
suffering of the unemployed by reforming unemployment insurance, by
public works, and by various social and political measures. Other proposals, following ideas for support to farmers and the improvement of basic
pensions, were presented to the Riksdag during the following years.

As we know, there were intense political disputes about the budget and
unemployment policy in 1932 and 1933. The special construction that the
budget proposals were given in 1933 should be seen as a concession to
strident criticism from and great apprehension on the part of the opposition. The national budget was split into two separate entities—a heavily cut
"ordinary" budget and an "extraordinary" budget. The latter was accompanied by a plan for amortization. The organization of the budget was
based upon the economist Gunnar Myrdal's idea that the budget should be
balanced over a business cycle, not necessarily over an arbitrary period
such as a calendar year. Myrdal's norm meant that state wealth should be
maintained unaltered in the long term, which is the only rational interpretation of the demand for an annual balance. This budget policy has been
considered the first conscious implementation of Keynesian economic policy in the world.

Such a policy meant that state investments, which would be made sooner
or later, could be allowed to expand during a recession. Wages as well as
other employment conditions would be the same as elsewhere on the labor
market. From the budget year 1933–1934 such public relief work was financed with loans, even though they were not calculated to make profits.

The expansion of public relief work was significantly slowed down in
1933 and 1934 by a large-scale labor market conflict in the construction
industry. Subsequent historical research has indicated that the effects on
the Swedish economy of the financial measures taken were limited. Of
much greater importance was the more or less discretionary association of
the Swedish krona with the pound in 1931 when the pound was high. This
favored exports, which in turn became an expansive element in the economy.[30]

In contrast to the party's periods in government during the 1920s, Social

Democratic policies in the 1930s were consonant with the decisions made by the party conference. Party leadership went to battle at the 1932 conference—well prepared by assiduous investigations—for an active crisis policy, which relegated the party program of 1920 to the history of ideas. This program remained largely intact but had no effect in practice. The government could act, powerfully and assuredly: motives, arguments, and actions were in accord.

THE BROADENING OF POLICY:
THE 1944 PROGRAM REVISION
AND POSTWAR PROGRAM

In the introduction to "The Twenty-Seven Points" of the Swedish labor movement's Postwar Program, it is stated that the war economy had shown what possibilities existed for intensive production, in which, under public management, labor and capital were used in the best interests of society: "We need not endure unemployment and we can abolish poverty if the forces of production, which the war has demonstrated we possess, are used as fully in peacetime." Furthermore, the main objective should be "to coordinate economic activities with a planned economy so that the labor force and material resources are constantly utilized for effective production."[31]

Experiences of mass unemployment in the 1930s, the poverty that formed the background of those experiences, and the results of wartime economy explain much of the orientation in the party program revision of 1944 and the postwar manifesto. Nationalization as a central issue in the party's crisis policy had already been rejected in the 1932 party conference, and Wigforss especially had begun to assert "planned economy" over and above issues of ownership. The 1920 party program was ripe for a comprehensive formal revision; the real revisions had already been made by the 1932 party conference.

Program Revision
The clear and simple—but not necessarily correct—Marxist analysis of "the bourgeois society" was replaced by formulations that were less succinct, more discursive, and less categorical. The two printed pages of "General Principles" from 1920 were expanded to over five pages in 1944. They introduced the 1944 program, using expressions of which there are still

echoes in the 1989 program: "The goal of Social Democracy is to so transform the economic organization of bourgeois society that the rights of determination over production are placed in the hands of the people. . . ." This replaced the desire to "carry out the social liberation of the exploited classes . . ." of the 1920 program.[32]

It was primarily a question of a new choice of words in the introductory paragraph. However, the revision became more extensive where the program claimed that the mark of the bourgeois economy was not private individuals controlling property but the concentration of rights of ownership and the right to determine the use of capital. The new program presented a thorough argument concerning the concentration of ownership and power, whereas the old program's analysis was based on "exploitation." In both programs, insecurity, the "under-utilization of productive forces," and inequalities in the distribution of the results of production were criticized and condemned—even though the 1944 program acknowledged that the growth of national wealth has "led to a gradually improved livelihood, even for a broad majority of the population. . . ."[33]

What was new in the 1944 program was the emphasis on ideas of planned economy. The lack of "planning" was criticized in previous programs, but the concept played a larger and more independent role in the 1944 program, because "the lodestar for capitalist enterprise must be the possibility of accruing gains from capital and facilitating satisfactory profits for private individuals." The program maintained that in a changing economic climate, affected by technical, economic, social, and political forces, "this lodestar has been shown not to lead to the full employment required by society's best interests, or to a planned economy taking into account society's resources for the satisfaction of the needs of its citizens."[34]

The program discusses poverty in the midst of plenty, and unemployment coexisting with a shortage of the products of labor. Further, it says that

> this has made the working class more aware of its historical task of being the bearer of a new order of production which is not steered by single-minded and limited profit interests. It has widened the wage-earners' struggle for their own liberation, their class struggles against the possessors of power in the capitalist economy into a struggle for the working citizenry as a whole. This struggle is influenced by the class conflicts contained in bourgeois society, and also by the fundamental rights applying in this society.[35]

This last statement is a profession of belief in the constitutional state and democracy, but it is also a reformulation of the "mechanical" ideas of nationalization from the 1920s into a long-range demand for changes in the economic system. The meaning of this is evident in the following two paragraphs:

> Whether the economy is based on individual ownership rights or different forms of collective ownership, it must be organized into a planned economy if the labor-force and material resources are not to be wasted in unemployment or in insufficiently effective production. Such an organization can only come about under the leadership of society [meaning government, in this context] and with such an orientation that individual private profit interests and those of individual groups are generally subordinated to those goals commonly striven for.

Further,

> The influence of society [government] on productive forces, working people's share in ownership, planning in production and equality for all citizens are the guidelines for Social Democracy. They are guidelines for a socialist social order.[36]

The 1944 party program was a radical one in the sense that the demands expressed in it challenged the prevailing economic power relations and the distribution of income and wealth. It was comprehensive and concrete.

The Manifesto—The Party's Source of Inspiration During the Entire Postwar Period

The Swedish labor movement's Postwar Program contained a manifesto, a plan of action based upon the revised party program and consisting of twenty-seven points encompassing motives and demands. It can be interpreted in various ways. It is possible to read in it a liberal market economy, more or less the same as that which we have actually had and still have in Sweden; or the program could be said to indicate a planned economy, with strong elements of state ownership and state control over economic life. In fact, the pendulum has swung since the war. Sweden has had periods of state control (e.g., immediately after World War II). The state economic policy, which was ambitiously launched in conjunction with the extra party conference in 1967, is in line with the more "radical" interpretation. The profit-based crisis policy (with deregulation of mainly the capital market), which was in place after 1982, lies more in accord with the liberal interpretation. The bourgeoisie and the business community, however, interpreted the Postwar Program unequivocally, which gave rise to adamant political disputes and to what Per Albin Hansson, in a newspaper article, called OPE—opposition to the planned economy.

It would perhaps be well at this juncture to give a summary of the Postwar Program. The Social Democrats had won the battle over an active policy for stabilizing the economy. It was now time to raise the level of ambition in their economic policy. In the introduction to the twenty-seven points of the program, the following is stated:

> The main objective which remains is to coordinate economic activities into a planned economy so that the labor force and material resources are continually utilized for effective production. Such coordination should be carried out under the direction of society and so oriented that individual private interests are subordinated to those goals which are commonly striven for. These goals include every member of society having the opportunity for useful work. No employable man or woman should be without work against his or her will any longer than the time it takes to change from one job to another, or for education or retraining.[37]

To a great extent the program referred to an ambitious policy of full employment to which the party has since remained loyal and which, especially in recent years, it has managed to maintain despite the more unrestrained market philosophy that has come to pervade the rest of the world. However, the program also involved equitable distribution and economic democracy and was divided according to these three main areas.

Some of the points of the manifesto were controversial. For instance, in the section on full employment, point three was concerned with increasing employment under state leadership. A public coordination agency was demanded, which would ensure that capital was used in such a way that "the labor force and material means of production [are fully utilized] for useful tasks."

Point seventeen remained in the section on fair distribution and was headlined, "Equal living standards and reduction of class differences." It called for solidarity in wage policy and in social, economic, educational, and tax policies to be applied against the lack of equality that divides the people into separate classes.

In the third section on efficiency and democracy in economic life lay the most controversial points, an expansion of the 1930s policy. Point eighteen deals with the planning by society of investment activities, where the extension of a comprehensive state commercial banking enterprise is proposed. Insurance enterprises should be nationalized to win rationalization profits and increased control over the capital market. Investment activities should be led by a public cooperation agency.

Point eighteen together with point twenty-three would seem to be the most disputed. Under the latter, nationalization was demanded in areas where individual private enterprise led to bad management or to monopolies. In several industries companies were said to be split into too many units to be effective, while in others production was dominated by either one company or an amalgamation. In such cases, "the existing companies should be transferred to public ownership."

The points of the program were followed by explanatory texts. One of these contains the essence of the party's thinking on questions of system in the middle of the 1940s:

> To the degree that private enterprise succeeds in carrying out the given task—giving the masses as much of the benefits of life as is technically possible while fully and effectively utilizing the labor force and material means of production—it can in the future be allowed to function more or less as it did before the war. However, to the same degree that it does not carry out this task, it will be necessary for the agency of society [i.e., the government] to intervene with those planned economic measures which are deemed in each individual case to be most suitable. . . . [38]

This is a reflection of a pronounced pragmatism, which in part explains the swings in the SAP's practical politics in regard to economic life and which, when it applies to system questions, differentiates the SAP at least from communists and liberals, who view the economic system more stringently regarding principles.

Conference Debate

Georg Branting and Per Emil Brusewitz were members of the committee revising the party program. They had opposed the revision of the nationalization policy in the 1932 conference and now had reservations about the revision of the 1920s program. Their own proposal, presented in a motion to the conference, preserved most of the latter but expanded on it. Particularly retained was the position regarding private ownership rights—"the main cause of the failings inherent in our present civilization. . . ."[39] A long debate ensued between (among others) the authors of the motion and the main author of the revised program, Ernst Wigforss.

Although the debate was conducted by the same participants as in 1932—Georg Branting, Brusewitz, Wigforss, Möller, and Sandler—it now concerned itself less with factual questions than with a kind of semantics. The concept of "exploitation" was removed from the 1944 program, and "class struggle" was replaced by phrases concerning "the rights of determination over production in the hands of all the people" and "the liberation of the majority from dependence upon a capital-owning minority."

There are several details and a complete argument in Wigforss's presentation to the conference that shed light on the reasoning of the party leadership at that time. Wigforss clarified the distinction made in the 1932 debate between nationalization and the planned economy. He asserted that economic planning can be carried out to a significant extent without placing the rights to ownership in the hands of society: "It should be possible to lead production and keep it going by a number of other means than giving rights of ownership to society."[40]

Wigforss made a further distinction when he polemicized against the old Marxist idea of equating concentration of rights of ownership with concentration of power. Wigforss meant that the division of property was about as concentrated in 1944 as it had been fifty years earlier—about 50 percent of the wealth was owned by 2 percent of the population. In Wigforss's opinion this would not be important if it were not for the fact that economic power was concentrated in a small number of people—often a question of "self-controlled" companies. As long as the company management works in the interests of the owners, the management is the power, and it is "this concentration of power that, from a socialist viewpoint, is even more decisive than the concentration of ownership which is taking place."[41]

When the conference finally arrived at the point of casting votes, Sandler and Möller requested a delay. Georg Branting and Brusewitz had their own proposal—an extension of the 1920 program. Nevertheless, the conference approved the party executive's proposal for revision of the 1920 program.

What Became of the Program?

Assessment of the Social Democrats' policy after the dissolution of the wartime coalition government, which included all democratic (noncommunist)
parties, is made more difficult by the uncertain economic conditions prevailing between 1946 and 1953. After the war the exchange rates and international price relations were uncertain. In 1946 the value of the krona was
appreciated in connection with the export surplus and rising currency reserves. But in 1947 a large deficit in the balance of current payments arose,
and the foreign exchange reserves were drained. Expectations were for a
postwar depression like that which occurred after World War I.[42]

The regulations remaining from the war years did not come to be used
constructively in a planned economy for full employment and economic
efficiency, as had been anticipated in the 1944 Postwar Program. Rather,
the regulations remained as part of a crisis policy directed against a lack of
currency, threatened inflation, and exchange crises.[43] In 1949 Sweden
(along with Great Britain) devalued against the dollar. Then came the Korean crisis, which placed excess demands on raw material–based export
industries.

When one reads the Postwar Program now, forty years later, it seems
like a document that to a large extent staked out Social Democratic policies. Not everything succeeded, and some areas remained untouched for a
long time, but the program reads as remarkably modern and farsighted.

Let us first look at the program from a long-term perspective: economic
growth for increased real wages; solidaristic wage policy and income equality for farmers; security against unemployment, illness, and old age
through public insurance; protection for workers; equality in upbringing
and educational opportunities; and leveling of class differences—these are
some of the demands in the second section. We recognize these questions
as elements of practical politics, even though their implementation was not
immediate and, in certain cases, took decades—or indeed, is still waiting.

Other parts of the program have not been so important for practical politics. The first section is devoted to full employment, which has been the
ruling Social Democrats' most important issue, but the means to achieve it
have hardly entailed the coordination of business and industry under the
leadership of the state. A certain amount of industrial policy activity occurred twenty years after the 1944 manifesto when the current balance
deficit from 1965 was exposed. Among other things, these imbalances led
to an extra party conference in 1967 and the work of the "economic policy
committee," which showed that the ideas of 1944 persisted at the end of

the 1960s. However, even the economic policy commitments faded after a
few institutions such as the Investment Bank and the fourth ATP (Supplementary Pensions) Fund were established, in 1967 and 1973 respectively.
These institutions did not become the spearheads of renewal that had been
anticipated in the Postwar Program and in the program work with the new
economic policy at the end of the 1960s; neither did the Postwar Program's
first point concerning falling price levels with improved access to goods
become reality.[44]

However, ideas about effective employment exchange, retraining, occupational education and counseling, and support for the disabled have become reality. At the end of the 1950s labor market policy had become one
of the Swedish Social Democrats' most important action areas. Long-term
investments in housing and support for exports with state-supported credit
have been and still are vital policy issues.

The third section of the Postwar Program concerning efficiency and democracy in business and industry has had the least amount of influence on
policy. As has been mentioned, the program contains statements about societal planning of investment activities, foreign trade under public control,
and nationalization and support for publicly owned production. Other
points have played a larger role. Stabilization and rationalization of the
building industry, rationalization of agriculture, support for technical and
economic research, and the influence of workers over production are areas
that with varying intensity have occupied Social Democratic governments
during the postwar period. All this demonstrates that in the mid-1940s the
Social Democrats were capable of putting forth very constructive ideas, and
that their orientation at that time laid the foundations for several decades of
political work in certain areas.

Did the program then have immediate concrete effects? During the last
period of the coalition government the Social Democratic Labor Party gathered its strength for an assault on those areas in which the Postwar Program was the most controversial. A series of Social Democratic motions
before the Riksdag in 1945, the so-called Nationalization Motions, were
based on the Postwar Program's ideas on planned economy. A number of
inquiries on industrial rationalizations were set up, like the Myrdal Commission, established in 1944 by the coalition government with the official
title, "Commission for Economic Planning." This commission became an
economic center of power from which a long series of inquiries and proposals for economic policy issued. These were concerned with the anticipated postwar depression, investment activities, and trade policy, and they

included about fifteen industrial inquiries producing proposals for structural rationalizations and efficiency changes.[45]

This outburst of activity was in the end without result, presumably because the postwar depression failed to appear. Instead, there was a boom period with high demand, inflationary impulses, and a drain of foreign currency reserves in 1947. The election in 1948 did not go particularly well for the SAP; the communists lost a great deal, and the Liberal party (Folkpartiet) gained (−0.4 percent for the SAP and −4.0 percent for the communists; Folkpartiet more than doubled its votes from 1944).[46]

"OUR PARTY HAS NEVER BEEN ESPECIALLY INTERESTED IN THEORETICAL DISCUSSIONS"

From 1951 to 1957 the Social Democrats governed in coalition with the Agrarian party. The coalition was dissolved in 1957. The government split over the pension issue, but nothing of this was noted at the 1956 Social Democratic Labor Party conference.[47]

The Party Conference of 1956

The discussions that took place during the 1956 conference showed that something substantial had changed in Swedish society since the end of the war. Previous conferences in 1920, 1932, and 1944 were occupied with class consciousness, struggles against poverty, distress in large segments of the population, worry about mass unemployment, and uncertainty about the future. The atmosphere in 1956 was totally different: the conference was no longer the convening of a political movement from the underclass.

It is indicative that one of the texts presented to this conference was entitled "The Politics of Progress." Belief in science and research was widespread and was often reflected in party chair Tage Erlander's speeches and contributions to conference debates.[48] Another paper presented to the conference, "Program and Ideas," was little more than a compilation of conference motions concerning program issues and statements about these issues from the party Program Commission. Perhaps this is how it must be in coalition periods—everything was going so well. One recurring theme was that science promised a doubling of the standards of living in twenty years—indeed, every twenty years.[49] Tage Erlander formulated an idea that was fundamentally new in the mid-1950s in comparison with previous phases of party history: that the threat of recurring unemployment had been replaced by the security of a full-employment society:

> As long as employment was uncertain and income insecure, people had to occupy themselves with thinking about the day's problems. But if one has employment year after year, and a rising—albeit slowly—income, not only do their living standards rise, but also something happens inside them. They begin to plan for the future. It is not only a matter of managing food for the day and clothing, but also people can begin to plan their housing, for their own homes, for bringing up children—I have even heard that some people are thinking of getting themselves a car.[50]

Erlander continued, without irony but not without pride:

> The groups of people we represent are not the proletariat in the sense that they are without rights, oppressed and insecure as regards their existence and employment possibilities. A home of one's own, cars, life insurance, bonds, a savings account are no longer unknown quantities for a worker. Those we represent finally do not stand outside society; on the contrary, they have acquired a determining influence on society.[51]

He went on to describe how this new situation places extensive demands on society for education, research, housing, energy, and so on. In the future society must take on the responsibility for capital formation, but this must be accompanied by the people exercising more influence over its direction and extent and having democratic control over the new resources.[52]

Gunnar Sträng, the minister of finance, also went into this in his conference address on economic policy. He spoke of overbalancing the state budget as a way of increasing savings and capital formation, of surpluses in state industries, and of the formation of funds in connection with the question of pensions.[53]

That the party leadership was satisfied with what had been achieved since the end of the war seems evident from the above citations. However, sections of the conference were impatient. Hans Hagnell, an economist employed by the metal workers union, and Nils Kellgren, also an economist, had petitioned the party executive for a review of the party program for the 1956 conference. They thought that already-carried-out social reforms and the fact that full employment had been achieved gave the party new points of departure for its economic policy. The program from 1944 no longer covered modern issues. Even though gaps in the party program had been exposed to a degree by the labor movement's Postwar Program, Hagnell and Kellgren pointed out a number of areas that should be addressed in a modernized program: the forty-hour week, retirement pensions, long-term social planning, regional policy, and economic and industrial democracy, for example.

Hilding Johansson, a long-time member of the Riksdag, tabled a motion in the same agenda item as that indicated by Hagnell and Kellgren. According to Johansson, in the future, weight should be transferred from the elementary demands for security to problems of welfare and leisure. To a degree, problems concerning ownership rights and rights of determination acquired a new character.[54]

Motion 4 was written by Bo Elmgren from the village of Gusum. He demanded the dissolution of the coalition. The party needed a "break to recover" in order to renew the debate on ideas.[55] Tage Erlander, the party executive's speaker, began with Elmgren's motion, which he thought expressed the sentiments of many party members. However, according to Erlander, the party could not avoid governmental responsibility since it had a majority in the First Chamber. Governing on its own would risk "the party's decline if being in government could not be combined with the pursuit of a consistent government policy in those questions which are particularly urgent." However, like the Program Commission in its written statement to the conference, he concurred with the motion authors' demands for a revision of program principles and a new manifesto.

Thus the party executive responded to and accepted the criticism that in 1956 the party was still basing its activities on a twelve-year-old document. "The Politics of Progress" was a topical program, mainly oriented toward the next election and even more short-term than a manifesto. Yet in the conference debate Tage Erlander claimed that "perhaps never before has the party been required to take a stand on as radical a document as this one."[56]

The Program Text of 1956

It is difficult to understand Tage Erlander's evaluation of the program text, "The Politics of Progress." The text can be said to be radical in the sense that a profound social transformation is predicted as a result of science and technology, which would bring about multidimensional structural changes

in the economy, education, and the composition of the population and social classes. "The Politics of Progress" sings promises of growth, but it is
hardly radical in a political sense. It raises no far-reaching demands. It
challenges no privileges, except perhaps in the section on education, where
demands for more broadly based recruitment and the need for increased
resources for education are emphasized.

The theme of the document, which the party chair took up in one of his
conference speeches, is that improved living standards and increased welfare do not diminish the need for public commitment. On the contrary,
raising living standards augments the demands placed on society. People
want education for their children, medical care, and security in old age—
"the unsatisfied needs grow in strength."[57]

A couple of items in the text are worth noting. The idea was launched
that social policy acquires another orientation, lands on a higher level,
when poverty is relieved and full employment creates security and confidence. The task for social policy then becomes to create security for the
material level that has been attained. Social policy must be expanded in a
way typified by individual insurance agencies. Retirement pensions represented this new orientation: to guarantee the level of income attained when
one retires and extend that to the family after one dies.[58]

"The Politics of Progress" indicates the need for substantial resources in
education ("the large population of young people is a once-only opportunity
for society"),[59] housing, and research. The text ends with a discussion of the
socioeconomic balance problems.

It had previously been difficult to combine full employment with a
reasonably stable currency. These difficulties would now be even greater
since the demonstrated needs required a rising proportion of investment
from the total available resources. There would be less left over for rises
in real wages and consumption in the near future, because savings must
increase in order to do all the things necessary to preserve the socioeconomic balance. The need for large public savings is explicitly mentioned.

Compared with previous programs from 1920 and 1944, "The Politics of
Progress" is novel. The earlier programs tended to analyze the status quo
and then, from that analysis, call for changes. "The Politics of Progress" has
a dynamic element; it contains analyses of tendencies and directions of development, and it tries to predict what demands these will make on policy.
Policy becomes more a necessary adaptation than an independent force for
change.

Policy

It is remarkable that the dominant political issue at the end of the 1950s, retirement pensions, was only taken up in passing at the conference. Arvid Lövbom from the village of Boliden presented a motion that the Boliden party group took to the conference. The motion proposed that the so-called Åkesson committee's majority proposal for general retirement pensions be implemented "without delay." The proposal embraced those principles that came to characterize the ATP system (National Supplementary Pensions). Minister of Foreign Trade John "Kinna" (i.e., from the village of Kinna) Ericsson was the party executive's spokesman at the conference.

Ericsson has been credited by Tage Erlander for giving a speech for a limited circle of party and union members during negotiations at Harpsund in 1955 that swung Erlander and others over to favoring an obligatory pay-as-you-go system rather than a fully funded system. In its statement the party executive declared that it followed the work in the Ministry of Health and Social Services with "considerable impatience," and John "Kinna" Ericsson replied that "the government has not taken a stand on any particular proposal. All possibilities are thus open and it is our hope that a proposal shall be made, possibly by the next Riksdag—nothing can be ensured, but that is the goal."[60] That was all, and it is all the more remarkable since the party was clearly pondering the pension issue in 1955 and 1956. The leadership was uncertain how the problem should be solved and what support the party had for any of the alternatives. One would think that in such a situation the party, and particularly its highest decision-making organ, the conference, would discuss the matter and indicate guidelines for the party leadership.

The explanation for the "behind closed doors" treatment of the question is perhaps to be found in Tage Erlander's memoirs, where he says: "The parliamentary situation thus contributed to the necessity of handling the pension issue with care in the election campaign of 1956."[61] The election was held in September; the conference, in May. What was perhaps the most important postwar political issue was never taken up for serious debate during the conference that most closely preceded the party's definitive position. The final decisions were taken in the so-called inner circles.

The ATP (National Supplementary Pensions) reform was without doubt the most important political issue at the end of the 1950s. Otherwise, certain "strategic" alterations can be noted in government policies. The government's consolidated total budget rather than the current noncapital expenditures was in the center of the debate on fiscal policy, and the latter was considerably tightened up. The state budget's cash outcome swung by a couple of billion to a surplus of about half a million kronor at the beginning of the 1960s. A few percentage points of the rising public expenses were reallocated from consumption to investment. The VAT was introduced in 1960, which meant that consumption rather than investments would be held back during periods of excess demand.[62] The investment proportion of the GNP was raised.

All this was covered, if not in detail then in principle, in the 1956 party conference. The policies were described in principle both in "The Politics of Progress" and in Gunnar Sträng's speech on economic policy referred to earlier. However, the conference hardly discussed the marked commitment to labor market policy and the somewhat new orientation it acquired during the slump of 1958 and 1959. Labor market policy was no longer simply a policy against unemployment; in the future it would also attempt to relieve gaps in the labor force. Stimulating mobility was stressed more than it had been previously.[63]

Labor market policy has been one of the Swedish Social Democrats' most internationally remarked-upon commitments. The epoch-making expansion and revision of this policy was virtually ignored by the 1956 conference. However, as has been mentioned, labor market policy had been outlined in the Postwar Program.

FIGHTING THE CRISIS

Preparations for the 1982 election commenced for the Social Democrats in the spring of 1981 when an economic program, "The Future for Sweden: Measures to Guide Sweden Out of the Crisis," was drafted for presentation at the party conference the following autumn.

Sweden's economic problems had become serious. The manufacturing industry had been stagnant for almost a decade. Capital formation in manufacturing had been shrinking since 1976; indeed, capital *stocks* had shrunk, perhaps for the first time since the beginnings of industrialism a century before. The state's budget deficit leaned toward 90 billion krona, about 12 to 13 percent of GNP. This was an enormous figure, with a dynamic of its own that would make any government a victim of a national financial crisis. The deficit itself on this level *increased* the state budget deficit (everything else held constant) by 13 or 14 billion every year through interest on the increased debt that the deficit represented. There was a strong explosive force and consequently a great political risk in the dreadful condition of state finances.

The external balance was not much better off. In 1981 the deficit in current foreign transactions was 14 billion; in 1982 it would reach 22 billion, or about 4 percent of GNP. The Swedish state borrowed on the international capital market.

The Stablization Program

After the government reshuffle in 1957, when the Agrarian party's ministers left the coalition, the Social Democrats did not form a new government until 1982. (This explains the long interval in the chronology of our presentation.) During the intervening period the Social Democrats were in opposition for six years. One of the most controversial postwar questions had come up on the agenda through the Meidner group's investigation within the LO (Swedish Trade Union Confederation) of Wage-Earners' Investment Funds. The group's discussion drafts were presented in 1975. The question was discussed at the LO congress in 1976 and subsequently in various LO and SAP joint working groups. I will deal here with the fund issue as it appeared in conjunction with the election campaign of 1981 and before the formation of the government in 1987.

The party leadership must have had mixed feelings at the change of government in 1982. How should Sweden get out of the current crisis? Should measures be taken within the framework of the essential elements of postwar welfare—full employment, social security reforms, equitable living standards? "The Future for Sweden" deals with these questions.

"The Future for Sweden" is more of an analytic text than a traditional political program. Yet it is also very conventional, based on economic theory. The latter part of the program expands from stabilization policy arguments about the balance of resources to a number of economic policy proposals reminiscent of the labor movement's Postwar Program.

"The Future for Sweden" begins by analyzing structural problems in the manufacturing industries, the deficit in the state budget, the trade balance, inflation, and the employment situation. About employment it says:

> Thus it is worrying that in several places also in Sweden people have begun to view unemployment not as an unpleasant *result* of economic problems but as a method of *curing* them. This point of view can clearly never be accepted by the labor movement. Unemploy-

ment must never be seen as an aid to economic policy; on the contrary, it is the most important problem that economic policy has to solve.[64]

The employment issue leads into a discussion on the social and moral effects of the crisis. The program views both drug abuse and "the more and more palpable culture of violence" internationally as consequences of aggression in the wake of ever tougher living conditions. Social morals are also undermined by the fact that the crisis favors short-term speculation and not long-term productive work.[65]

In a central section the values behind the points of departure for the crisis policy are clarified. References are made to Ernst Wigforss's classic pamphlet from 1932, *Ha vi råd att arbeta?* (Can We Afford to Work?). The most important thing in fighting crises is to raise the level of activity while at the same time increasing capital formation within expanded limits: it is a matter of working and saving at the same time. The section also contains a further argument for a just distribution policy: the success of the crisis policy will depend on whether the distribution of responsibility and results is considered fair. Then follows a long defense of the public sector, which, it is asserted, has always been an important instrument in social democracy for realizing political goals. However, the program also strikes new tones: "The point of departure must be to protect those activities which are from social and/or egalitarian considerations the most urgent, regardless of whether this involves old or new commitments. Hence we cannot exclude the possibility that commitments already made might be cut back in order to make room for new ones which are deemed more pressing."[66]

In a later section a pivotal argument is conducted concerning the Social Democratic position on capitalism, which may be compared with a similar argument in the labor movement's Postwar Program. The argument is detailed and about a central issue in the party, and thus deserving of a long citation:

> As Social Democrats we think that society, i.e., all citizens, must have the right to determine the general conditions for enterprises, for example, norms for the protection of the environment and of workers. Society must also be able to influence those sections of business organizations which are vital to citizens' general demands on the economy, for example, a more equitable geographic distribution of jobs. Furthermore, citizens must be able to demand demo-

cratic control over capital formation and credit in order to ensure that accessible capital actually is used for productive investments.

Within these boundaries, which are decided by the citizens as a whole and which constitute overlapping demands on the economy, individual businesses must themselves decide the forms for their enterprises. For it is only in such a decentralized system that the company can rapidly transfer signals from consumers into production. It is only when the business or industry itself can make decisions that the employees are able to exert real influence over their work: if state agencies determine in even the smallest detail the activities of the enterprise, the employees will be denied influence.[67]

There are interesting comparisons to be made here with previous programs. Contrary to the ideas in 1920 about overproduction, wrong directions in production, and demands for state ownership and a planned economy, in 1980 decentralization was highlighted as a guarantee for obedience to citizens' demands on production, even though demands for the control of capital formation and the granting of credit harken back to old orientations. Industrial democracy, or codetermination, is even made dependent upon society being organized as a decentralized market economy.

We can also make comparisons with the conditional freedom of 1944. As long as the company or business is able to fully and effectively utilize productive forces, that is, according to the "needs" of the citizens, private enterprises can carry on as before. In "The Future for Sweden" the company in a decentralized market economy is presented as guaranteeing such efficiency—truly an enormous turnabout in thinking!

It is virtually impossible to comprehend the crisis program without understanding "devaluation for competitiveness," even though nothing like this could be intimated—much less developed—in the program. However, it is clear that the crisis group felt the entire successful Swedish postwar model—a powerful, internationally competitive Swedish manufacturing industry—was threatened. All agreed it was necessary to stimulate demand, but demand must come from abroad and from capital formation. Both these components should exact a favorable level of costs (high profits) and, in the future, lower cost increases than in the rest of the world.[68] The consequences of such a policy for distribution were worrying. Concentration of private power and wealth should not be allowed to increase: "Therefore one important prerequisite for a recovery policy is that Wage-Earners'

Funds are initiated and that injustices in the spread of taxation pressure are removed."[69]

The program authors claimed that both private and public consumption must be restrained. For state consumption, it was not a matter of reductions in absolute figures but rather growth lower than that of the GNP. It would hardly be possible to put state finances in order by raising taxes. For municipalities' expenses, it was thought that a 2 percent growth in consumption would be necessary to finance care for the aged and child care, the two areas that were explicitly excepted from the retrenchment policy.[70] Section five of the program was wholly devoted to fighting inflation. It contained influences from fairly new macroeconomic theory, which strongly asserts the role of expectation and trust, but it presumed close cooperation with union organizations and periodic administrative price control—the latter scarcely inspired by economic textbooks.

The crisis program contained, in addition to the macroeconomic proposals, a number of detailed ideas, mostly concerning economic policy: supply of raw materials, suggestions for new institutions such as the Swedish Market Council, public purchasing, energy provision, building, and exports.

The Party Conference of 1981
In the 1981 party conference there was a long debate on the crisis program, with about sixty contributions. In general, the program report was supported. Most of the contributions consisted of "testimonials" about the difficulties with employment and restraints in the contributors' regions or own industry. The conference debate confirmed a widespread crisis atmosphere throughout the country.

Ingvar Carlsson, who in 1982 would be a member of Olof Palme's new government and later prime minister, addressed the conference, warning that the party was perhaps locked into its "honorable past"—Ernst Wigforss and 1930s Keynesianism. According to Carlsson, the critical differences at present, which required a different course of action than that of 1933, were the existence of a huge deficit in the state budget and the fact that industry was too "weak" to utilize the effects of a generally expansive policy. In this he was absolutely correct.

The first contribution to the debate came from Bosse Ringholm, a leading politician in Stockholm. It was also one of the most important, referred to by many subsequent speakers. Ringholm sought a connection between the crisis program and the party program, especially regarding Social Democrats' view of economic democracy. He also wanted employment policy and the demand for full employment to be given more undivided attention. Ringholm received a great deal of support for the latter point, especially from many speakers.[71]

Many delegates discussed the public sector and expressed concern about what restraints on public spending—vis-à-vis the budget crisis—would mean for employment.[72] Nancy Eriksson, from the Social Democratic women's organization, had the following criticism, which remarkably enough no one else echoed: "I think that [we] use so many technical expressions. The program is not really much of a welcome for anyone coming into the party. But perhaps that is not what it is intended for; perhaps the program is only something for an elite to flaunt."[73] John-Olle Persson, from Stockholm and speaking for the party executive, defended the crisis group by saying that the program should be judged for what it was—a limited document. It was drawn up to provide solutions to the balance problem for the immediate future, neither more nor less. Ingvar Carlsson used roughly the same argument against Bosse Ringholm's demand that the crisis program should take up problems of economic and industrial democracy. However, Carlsson supported Ringholm's request for greater attention to employment. The conference decided to refer this question to the Draft Committee.

The Wage Fund Issue

During the one-hundred-year history of Swedish Social Democracy, the demand for "economic democracy" has numbered among the most controversial. The demand has always existed in the party programs and manifestos. The proposal for the Wage-Earners' Investment Funds makes general program formulations concrete, and thus it is not strange that the 1975 proposal was contentious.

When the economist Rudolf Meidner's group within the LO presented a proposal for Wage-Earners' Investment Funds, it was hardly anchored in the LO leadership, much less in that of the party. Meidner has claimed several times that he viewed his proposal as a subject for debate, nothing else. However, his proposal came to be approved by the LO national executive and presented at the LO congress in 1976. Meidner's was a far-reaching proposal, which through directed payouts based on company profits would more or less automatically transfer increasing amounts of large companies' own capital to the funds. The proposal applied mainly to big business, but the LO congress in 1976 amplified it by drawing a number of smaller companies into the system.

The party had been left behind. During the last half of the 1970s several joint working groups from the LO and the party worked on the fund issue, attempting to loosen up the original proposal. The party conference in 1981 was to form an opinion concerning a report commissioned by the 1978 party conference and produced by a joint LO and SAP working group; the report was also to be presented to the LO congress.

The proposal as submitted to the conference and the congress called for the Wage-Earners' Investment Funds to be built up through excess or surplus profits and by raising ATP charges. The funds would use their money to purchase shares in the companies. The idea was for there to be a fund in each district, with a board whose manner of election was left open to discussion.[74]

Kjell-Olof Feldt, the future minister of finance, was the party executive's speaker at the conference. He emphasized that, contrary to the claims of the opposition, the fund proposal was actually not a passing fancy on the part of a few bigwigs and theoreticians seeking more power. He presented four objectives for the establishment of the funds. They should facilitate solidarity in wage policy (profit sharing); they should counter the concentration of private power and wealth; they should reinforce the influence of employees in business and industry; and they should contribute toward increased savings and capital formation in Sweden (the payroll tax). Feldt underlined that the system would be decentralized, with many funds operating separately. One theme that often recurred was that the Wage-Earners' Funds would make it easier to restrain wage increases in order to strengthen competitive power in Swedish industry.

Feldt also said that one should listen to the criticism of economists, who expressed apprehensions about the funds placing their resources in doomed companies in order to save employment in various places. With clearly formulated demands the funds must be enjoined to make profits on their capital.[75]

Later, Feldt became less technical:

> The Wage-Earners' Funds are not just about money; they are also part and parcel of our efforts to create economic democracy. By that can be meant a great deal, but at bottom lies the dream of establishing the dignity of work, of erasing the old class boundaries in work-

ing life, of a system of production which is not only ruled by profit but also by people's need of secure and meaningful work.

He went on to say the following:

> A living democracy presumes engagement and participation on the part of many individuals. And not least, [it requires] the desire and the ability to take responsibility for common decisions. Thus we must arm ourselves with a certain amount of patience. It may be a matter of trial and error. In any case we need to discuss further how the democratic base of the Funds should be formed.[76]

Finally, Feldt appealed to the conference to allow the party leadership significant room to maneuver in formulating the final proposal together with the unions.[77]

The debate that followed was marked by support for the working group's proposal and bitterness about how virulent the opposition to the funds was. However, there were also critical comments. Stig Svensson from Skåne said that through Kjell-Olof Feldt the party executive had requested license to arbitrarily deal with the Fund issue.[78]

Peter Persson, also from Skåne, thought that the grass-roots organizations in the party had not had much to say about the new proposal, and that this had shattered the party's internal democracy.[79] The chair of the SSU (Social Democratic Youth), Jan Nygren, defended the party executive but wanted the conference to make the following statement: "Democratization of economic life is one of the decisive prerequisites for safeguarding Swedish industry and for ensuring full employment. Democracy and questions of influence should therefore be given a prominent role in the arguments around the Wage-Earners' Investment Funds."[80] There were also debates about individual links and the election procedure for the funds' boards. Hilding Johansson said that it would be unfortunate if there should be party politicizing in the general elections to the funds. In his opinion the whole thing concerned the expression of wage-earners' interests and nothing else.[81]

Party chair Olof Palme made a statement of principle in favor of the market economy and disclaimed administrative governance of economic life. However, he also indicated that the market economy could be combined with measures for increased equality and with democratizing influences.[82]

In his concluding speech Feldt suggested that the conference should make a special statement in accordance with Jan Nygren's proposal and that the issue should be referred to the Draft Committee. Otherwise, Feldt pleaded for an open decision in technical questions, and he warned that if the unions were to form the base for elections to the fund boards, the trade union movement would be placed in a double role. Feldt ended by saying, "Give us the guiding principles, give us the mandate to carry through the Wage-Earners' Funds, and we will get going."[83]

Kjell-Olof Feldt got what he wanted, but the conference finally made a statement in the spirit of Jan Nygren's proposal.[84]

Return to Power in 1982

There is a striking difference between the party's performance in 1956 and 1981. In 1981 there was a desire on the part of the executive to present to the conference the difficult problems that would be faced after the change of government. Well-prepared policy documents "Crisis Program" and "The Labor Movement and Wage-Earners' Funds" provided the bases for long debates.

Certain elements of policy from autumn 1982, especially devaluation, were naturally not discussed in the crisis program, even though it became the most important ingredient in the policy. Closely associated with the program were activation of public investment and the comprehensive ROT program (in English RRE, for rebuilding, renovation, and extending) for the building sector. The crisis program was called "The Policy of the Third Way." The "third way" involved combining savings and capital formation with increased work effort, as opposed to government cutbacks (the program of the Conservatives) and expanding governmental programs (the program of the Left). This SAP program lay behind a number of government proposals—1982/83:50, 1982/83:100, 1982/83:150, and 1983/84:40. The first step would be a cost adjustment, followed by a second step that should break cost trends and lower inflation.

The fund proposal was altered, and the result was five funds for the whole country instead of one in each district. The latter was deemed to risk "village politics," something that Feldt had warned against in his conference address.

The effect of government policy after 1982 was to vitalize especially the stock market but also the capital market in general. Private wealth increased greatly. The emphasis in the crisis program on a just distribution of burdens resulted in increased wealth taxes, raised inheritance and gift taxes, fewer deduction possibilities for savings in the form of stocks, and last but certainly not least the establishment in 1983 of the Wage-Earners' Investment Funds, the financing of which was based on "the distribution of excess/surplus profits" and a raising of payroll taxes in line with the conference proposal.

The first measures were singularly marginal in comparison with the dramatic rise of private fortunes that occurred in conjunction with the crisis policy. The same applies to the Wage-Earners' Funds, viewed in relation to the protracted "profit boom" in business and industry. The strident debates about the funds (which are still going on) are rather difficult to understand when one considers that at the turn of the year 1987/1988 Volvo's cash holdings would have been sufficient to purchase all five funds and the fourth AP fund all at once. Volvo's cash holdings were then over 20 billion kronor, which about corresponded to the assets in the five funds (under 10 billion) plus the fourth AP fund, the one pension fund that was allowed to invest in stocks. One private company (albeit the country's largest), which via cross-ownership controlled itself, controlled double the amount of *liquid* assets as those held by the Wage-Earners' Funds!

Hardly ever before in the party's history had private capitalism been so strengthened in so short a time as after 1982. It would also be difficult to find another period with such widespread redistribution of wealth for the benefit of wealthy private individuals as that of the 1980s.

WHAT IS SOCIALISM IN SOCIAL DEMOCRACY?

This overview of the SAP's programs and policies encompasses five changes of government, which could be seen to represent different phases or degrees of maturity in the party's history. First came the 1920s' rather derivative Marxist program, proclaiming that private ownership was the source of all evil. Consequently, the solution to all societal problems was simple: abolish private rights of ownership. However, the program provided no guidelines for the exercise of power in the 1920s.

At the end of the decade, the question of rights of ownership was ignored. When the parliamentary party embarked upon extensive inquiries, it was chastened by its failure in 1928 with a rather cautious inheritance tax motion in the Riksdag. Without theoretizing, the following questions were put: How are the living conditions for workers and farmers? And what can be done to relieve poverty? Concrete proposals in motions and, after the change of government, in propositions began to lay the foundations for the SAP's unique position in Swedish politics.

Then followed a maturation period during the 1940s, when the party's politics expanded to a breadth and level of ingeniousness that has never been surpassed. In fact, during the entire postwar period the party has used the Postwar Program for ideas.

In the fourth phase in the mid-1950s the party seemed to be "in tune with the times," which involved discovering lines of development and creating policies to support them. Debates about principles were correspondingly meager.

The fifth phase, finally, has become the old man's defense of his life's work. Ideas of welfare must be protected against a new liberalism, and policies of welfare against a new militant capitalism. Hence it is the defense of the party's historical achievements that dominates in this phase, not new ideas for the future.

There are at least two interpretations of what is happening now as the party marks its centennial. Perhaps we are witnessing a lull in the work on economic reform and in economic/political thinking—conditioned by external circumstances. But there may also be a change of emphasis in party policy, from promoting equality and the redistribution of and participation in economic benefits to the environment, ecology, and natural resources. The SAP has reached its unique position by orienting its policy toward the urgent, everyday problems of the large underprivileged groups in society. Perhaps now economic problems have been displaced?

The SAP's success began with practical politics building a bridge between workers and farmers in the 1930s and between workers and lower levels of white-collar workers through extensive social reforms involving health insurance, employment pensions, and education after the war. However, the classic front line of battle, work-capital, has been erected by one disputed issue without any successful bridge building—the Wage-Earners' Investment Funds.

Can this be the explanation for the savageness of the campaigns of business and industry, their unwillingness to compromise? The issue is, measured in economic terms, of little importance. Is it the knowledge of having pushed the SAP into a corner that keeps the battle going—that the SAP has forgotten the lesson from 1928? Or is it rather that business and industry have seen the funds as a confirmation that the SAP has "canceled" the implicit contract from the Saltsjöbaden Accords in 1938 concerning the division of tasks between the labor movement and industry? Actually, another pattern can be seen in the five phases, which somewhat alters the picture sketched above. The SAP began with a naive philosophy of nationalization that culminated in the party program of 1920. The political policy produced was very concrete: existing capital should be taken over; factories and natural resources should belong to society.

In the pragmatic phase two, the party dropped in practice the demand for nationalization of existing capital. Instead, a fifty-year nationalization of income flows was introduced. During the party's long period in government beginning in 1932, an ever-increasing share of income was transferred to society in order to be distributed in another way than it would have been under the aegis of market forces.

But this is not the whole story. From the beginning of the 1960s the nationalization of capital has returned in another form, first with the AP Funds and most recently with the Wage-Earners' Funds. The SAP is now prepared, via the nationalization of "finance capital," to create islands of collective ownership. This places lower demands on policy than the old "nationalization of factories." Ownership responsibilities (much less those of management) need not to be taken other than at a pace and to the degree to which preconditions exist in terms of competence and knowledge. Given this perspective, the implacability of business and industry is less incomprehensible.

In the end the question that finally arises is, What is socialism in social democracy? Is it at present only a matter of a weaker attachment to a liberal market economy than that of the bourgeois parties? A greater willingness to intervene in the play of market forces for the cause of redistribution? Is it simply that the SAP is not satisfied with a policy that aims at creating equal opportunities, but also tries to influence the outcome so that greater equality is established in all areas of society than would be the case through equal opportunities alone?

Let us look at some of the party's thinkers, Karleby, Sandler, and Wigforss—the three are sufficiently in accord to provide an answer. All three emphasize what is shared by liberalism and socialism. In their ultimate aims, liberalism and socialism are to a large extent in agreement, wrote Sandler in the Nationalization Committee. These aims are freedom, welfare, and the leveling of differences to the degree that this is compatible with continued progress.[85] Karleby agreed but also said that liberalism gave ownership rights their petit bourgeois artisan form, one that is not developed for that degree of large-scale activity demonstrated by modern production. Socialism has gone further to develop these ultimate aims under modern economic conditions.[86]

All three discuss freedom and "participation." In the Nationalization Inquiry Sandler wrote that freedom was an essential element of socialism: freedom to choose a job, freedom of movement, and being able to have "a position in general in the production process which in principle is not that of a tool, but which contains an aspect, adapted to the work in question, of freedom to shape [one's work]." According to Sandler, just this participation plays a very important role in the motives for nationalization. It can be questioned if this motive, "the altered position of working people within production," is not weightier than the striving for greater prosperity.[87]

Karleby was even more emphatic on this point. He was of the opinion that all the principal demands of social democracy can be combined in one point, namely, the working class's insistence on full participation in society, with no areas of exception.[88]

Wigforss treated these ideas clearly in his important *Tiden* article in 1949, which is worth citing directly:

> That security is a part of *freedom* should be as self-evident as the fact that it is not the whole of freedom, it does not automatically convey *independence, freedom of movement*, the possibilities of *active contributions and initiative*, which we associate with the word freedom. It is the employees' loss of these freedoms within large companies in modern industry which lies as much behind the socialist protests against capitalism as do demands for bread and security.

Surprisingly, later in the article he writes:

> It is the demand for freedom in the socialist pantheon of ideas that leads furthest in the direction of demands for collective ownership. Not necessarily a centralized collectivism, but something which is consistent with the idea of reuniting the workers with property.[89]

The idea lives on in the party—recall Kjell-Olof Feldt's address at the 1981 conference concerning the Wage-Earners' Funds, where he spoke of "re-establishing the dignity of work."

After the above overview of Social Democratic debates, it is clear that private ownership is not ascribed the same core position in social democracy as it is in liberalism. Liberalism strives for equalizing the distribution of property by seeking to spread savings and ownership among increasingly large groups and more and more social strata. Property provides security, influence, independence. Without denying the role of private ownership, social democracy attempts with other methods to liberate the citizenry for purposes of participation. Legislation can circumscribe the meaning of rights to private ownership; collectivization of ownership—by the state or municipality—and other forms of ownership such as cooperatives are such "other methods." Social democracy highlights no one form of ownership but instead works with different methods—legislation, taxation, collective ownership, and traditional nationalization—to promote in various ways the emancipation of all social classes. What is striking is, from the 1930s onward, its pragmatism and independence from any economic system—capricious and without principles, it may be claimed. Here is Karleby's conclusion:

> Herewith it is made clear, that the idea of the socialist society as a fixed organization is contrary in principle to the Social Democratic point of view. It is as easy to generally indicate the meaning of everyone's participation in society, which is the crux of Social Democratic demands, as it is difficult, if not impossible to concretely determine it. In fact it [the meaning] is dispersed in a series of concrete participations, conveyed in different ways, and varying with the times.[90]

In the end, perhaps what we have is a different comprehension of reality, in which case the Social Democratic view of the order of things would be: If everyone is to participate in society, then private initiative is not sufficient. Only through the collective may the exclusion of large groups be avoided.

NOTES

1. There is a great deal written about the development of ideas and practical politics during the period I am treating. I have worked fairly independently of this literature and concentrated on the original sources. However, there are a few important scholarly works that I would like to call to the reader's attention, works that delve deeper than is possible to do in a short paper on a long period. Tingsten (1941) and Lewin (1967) deal with the development of ideas. E. Lundberg (1953) and Unga (1976) focus upon economic policy. Rolf Eidem's book

Aktieägandet och demokratin (Stock Ownership and Democracy) should also be mentioned. It appeared in 1987, and hence its bibliography includes up-to-date references.

2. *SAP Conference Minutes* 1920, 3.

3. Ibid., 41–42.

4. *SAP Party Programme* 1920, "General Principles," 2d par.

5. Ibid., third and fourth paragraphs from the end.

6. See the directives to the Socialization Committee, reproduced in *SAP Report on Activities* 1920, 21–24.

7. An explanation for the obvious conflict between the program and the policy in 1920 can perhaps be found in what Tingsten calls Marx's large and small perspectives. See Tingsten 1941, 1:81–111.

8. See the directives to the committee on industrial democracy, reproduced in *SAP Report on Activities* 1920, 25–27.

9. V. Bergström 1984.

10. See the *Financial Plan*, app. 1, HRH proposition no. 1, 1921.

11. *SAP Conference Minutes* 1932, 363. Experiences from 1928 came to play a major role in the party's future actions. The election results are given in Elvander 1980, chap. 3.

12. See Landgren 1960, 60–62, and Motion 1:108 to the First Chamber of the Riksdag, 1930.

13. See Motion 1:109, 1932.

14. See Wigforss, 1932.

15. See *SAP Conference Minutes* 1932, 9.

16. Ibid., 368–69.

17. Ibid., 9.

18. Ibid., 424–27.

19. Ibid., 427 and 485.

20. Ibid., 430.

21. Ibid.

22. *SAP Conference Minutes* 1932, 2.

23. Cf. V. Bergström 1984.

24. See *SAP Conference Minutes* 1932, 448 and 451.

25. Ibid., 471.

26. Ibid.

27. Ibid., 474–75.

28. Cf. Wigforss's book from 1931, *Den ekonomiska krisen* (The Economic Crisis). The transition to a "planned economy ideology" is the subject of Leif Lewin's dissertation, "Planhushållningsdebatten" (The Debate on the Planned Economy) (1967).

29. See *SAP Conference Minutes* 1932, 513–14.

30. See V. Bergström 1969, and Jonung, 1977.

31. *The Labor Movement's Post-War Programme* 1944, 4.

32. *SAP Conference Minutes* 1944, 35.

33. Ibid., 36–37.

34. Ibid., 38.

35. Ibid., 39.

36. Ibid., 41–42.

37. *The Labor Movement's Post-War Programme* 1944, 4.

38. Ibid., 44–45.

39. Ibid., 45.

40. *SAP Conference Minutes* 1944, 62.

41. Ibid., 63.

42. Gunnar Myrdal warned of a postwar depression, but Wigforss was skeptical. See *SAP Conference Minutes* 1944, 68.

43. Fredriksson 1947, 35.

44. It is "Davidsson's norm" that is reflected here. Given contemporary experience, it is a strange idea—that increases in productivity should result in falling prices with constant nominal wages. Distribution policy was the motive force. However, in 1944 experience of falling prices alternating with periods of inflation lay close at hand. See Bentzel 1956.

45. See mainly the investigation concerning postwar economic planning, SOU 1944:57.

46. See Elvander 1980, chap. 5.

47. The quotation heading this section comes from Tage Erlander, who was the party executive's speaker on proposals and motions for the party program, a new manifesto, the coalition, etc. *SAP Conference Minutes* 1956, 267.

48. For example, see ibid., 270.

49. See Erlander's speech, ibid., 270.

50. Ibid., 269.

51. Ibid., 269–70.

52. Ibid., 271.

53. Ibid., 398.

54. Ibid., 258.

55. Ibid., 263–64.

56. Ibid., 271.

57. SAP 1956, 11.

58. Ibid., 34–35.

59. Ibid., 23.

60. See *SAP Conference Minutes* 1956, 336–37.

61. Erlander 1976, 139.

62. See V. Bergström 1969, 55 and 68.

63. Ibid., 75–76; also for references.

64. SAP 1981, 19.

65. Ibid., 19–20.

66. Ibid., 30.

67. Ibid., 41.

68. Ibid.

69. Ibid., 42.

70. Ibid., 53–54.

71. *SAP Conference Minutes* 1981, C, 8–9.

72. Ibid., 25 and 33.

73. Ibid., 42–43.

74. See *The Labor Movement and the Wage-Earners' Investment Funds* 1981.

75. *SAP Conference Minutes* 1981, C, 8–9.

76. Ibid., 12.

77. Ibid., 13.

78. Ibid., 15.

79. Ibid., 17.

80. Ibid., 20–21.

81. Ibid., 33–34.

82. Ibid., 40.

83. Ibid., 45.

84. Ibid., 160–62.

85. See for example Sandler in SOU 1936:7, 48.

86. V. Bergström (1984) treats this; see 447–49.
87. See Sandler in SOU, 1936:7, 39.
88. See V. Bergström (1984) for a survey of Karleby's writings.
89. See Wigforss 1949, 215.
90. See Karleby 1925.

Clas-Erik Odhner

6

Workers and Farmers Shape the Swedish Model: Social Democracy and Agricultural Policy

Any description of Swedish agricultural policy during the last one hundred years must be divided into two sections: one for the period before and one for the period after the 1930s. The issues that had to be confronted were totally different in the two periods. During the first the dominant question was how the Swedish nation, with a slowly growing industrial and urban economy, would be able to employ and support a rapidly growing population and how it would counteract emigration.

After the 1930s the issue was how the necessary restructuring in the economy should be carried out and how the redundant agricultural labor force should be transferred to more productive employment. A transition was necessary from a rapidly rationalizing agriculture, with diminishing labor requirements and increasing tendencies toward difficult-to-sell surplus production, to a rapidly growing industrial and service sector in great need of manpower. Moreover, this change had to be carried out with production preparedness intact (cf. page 187, note*) and with safeguards for social and cultural values in order to avoid social problems and conflicts.

Difficulties were increased by the fact that employment growth outside of agriculture was concentrated in certain expanding regions, which were largely the same as those with the best conditions for agricultural production. This created major problems for the vast areas of the country that had been cultivated and settled during the nineteenth century's heavy population pressure, when agriculture and the extraction of raw materials were the most important bases of the economy.

The two quintessential issues in agricultural policy prior to the 1930s were tariffs and land policy—that is, how much should food prices be raised in order to protect domestic production against cheap imports, and how should the cultivated or cultivable land be divided in order to provide as many as possible with income and employment. During the second period, the issues concerned how extensive agricultural production needed to be in relation to basic food requirements to ensure preparedness; how high price supports for agriculture needed to be to maintain such a level of production and give farmers, in relation to other groups, "equitable" incomes; and finally, how fast and in which way the rationalization of agricultural production should be implemented.

As always when there are such rapid changes in the actual issues, political opinion lagged greatly behind. For several decades after the 1930s, the political front went largely between those who were still trying to solve the problems of the previous period and those who wanted to tackle the new ones.

THE INTERNATIONAL BACKGROUND

A new era in agricultural policy began during the latter half of the nineteenth century when railways and steamboats connected centers of consumption in Europe with newly opened, fertile areas in distant parts of the world.

Since then, the international markets—apart from the war years and the odd occasion of simultaneous crop failure or monopolistic manipulations—have been characterized by surplus production and low prices. In due course access to virgin cultivation areas petered out; however, agrarian technology began to make possible increased yields from already cultivated land, with unchanged—or even numerically decreasing—livestock. The development of transport facilities intensified competition. Agricultural production increased in the old industrial countries as well, despite migration to urban occupations, because technical development was more rapid than the increase in consumption. The shortages during both world wars led to a considerable expansion of production in areas not involved in the wars; this did not diminish when production resumed in the war-torn areas.

However, the application of new techniques in countries with traditional agricultural structures was not unproblematic. Production costs remained higher than in the new production areas, and opposition to cheap imports intensified at the same time as the politically necessary protections resulted in price levels that held back sales. Great Britain solved this problem by opening its borders and allowing its own agriculture to atrophy. Denmark and Holland quickly changed over to livestock production before transport technology created competition from foreign producers in this market as well. However, most other countries erected border protections for their domestic production against cheap imports.

The diminishing farm population mainly succeeded in placing itself as a marginal group of voters between the conservative and socialist blocs, even though most farmers tended to be highly conservative, and it thus could usually get demands for economic protection satisfied. EC agricultural policies are a good contemporary example of this.

The export difficulties that import restrictions created for effective producers in countries with surpluses further depressed prices on the world market. To a significant degree, this market became a dumping ground into which excess production was shunted with various forms of subsidies so as not to squeeze prices on domestic markets.

The low prices on the world market have of course been glaringly obvious to consumers, and the Social Democratic and other socialist parties have been torn between the desire to give their large groups of supporters cheaper food, and the need to retain or obtain marginal voters from agricultural sectors in order to retain or obtain power. In many of the traditional industrial countries during the second half of the nineteenth century, small farmers movements or organizations began to appear with links to the labor movement, which made this political balancing act even more difficult.

FOOD TARIFFS AND SMALL-SCALE FARMING

During its first decades the Social Democratic Labor Party's attitudes toward agricultural issues were marked by tensions between Marxist theory and the realities that party leaders came in contact with; after 1896 as members of the Riksdag they had to deal with practical problems.[1]

One of the most important aspects of development at this time was the growing influence of farmers in the Riksdag. This made possible majority support for demands for protection against the import of cheap grain, a protection that mainly burdened those groups from whom the Social Democrats sought support. Another important consideration was the desire of the poor for land they could cultivate in order to relieve their pressing poverty—"land hunger." Tariffs and the land question—of which the question of Norrland (the northern two-thirds of the country) must be seen as a part—were the two issues that dominated agricultural policy until the crisis settlement of 1933.*

Agriculture in the First Party Program Discussions

From the first years of its existence until the 1897 party conference, the SAP seems to have viewed the 1886 program of the Stockholm Social Democratic Association as its party program.[2] The German Gotha Program was also directly relevant for the Swedish party.[3] The point of departure for agriculture as well as industry in SAP ideology was the conviction that technical development irrevocably leads to large-scale production and capitalist development, and equally irrevocably to concentration of ownership. Small farmers were said to be a "disappearing class in the middle" in capitalist society. In a socialist society this structure would have to be replaced by large-scale production by workers' cooperatives and by state ownership of the means of production, including land.

This was a theoretical Marxist point of departure, and one conveyed by the German party program. Herbert Tingsten has described how it was followed up, in speeches and in writing, during the 1880s when the agricultural population (two-thirds of the total, after all) was seen as "some sort of appendage to that society whose most prominent characteristic was the opposition between large-scale production and private ownership." The agricultural population was mainly thought of as an object of policy and a predetermined fate, and rarely in terms of groups whose active support and

---

*Cultivable land is scarce in Sweden, especially in the northern two-thirds of the country which mainly constitutes "Norrland." Accession to land, or "the land question," has therefore always played an important role in agricultural policy. In Norrland the timber companies acquired farmers' land and forests using rough methods, which incited a political reaction and gave rise to social legislation on land. This was known as "the question of Norrland." The own-your-own-home movement was a popular organization to create small farms by cultivating new land or splitting up big units.

participation could be won. During those first decades party leadership consisted of intellectuals and urban workers without any practical experience of the production sector that dominated the country's economy.[4]

During the 1880s and 1890s a discussion was carried on within the party and in the Social Democratic newspapers that illustrates the attempts to fit the realities of agriculture into the Marxist straitjacket; but many became aware of the tension between ideology and reality on this point.[5]

In a newspaper debate between Hjalmar Branting, at this time a leading politician in Stockholm, and Axel Danielsson, editor of the newspaper *Arbetet* in Malmö, in 1894 and 1895, there was obvious tension between the ideology of the former and the strategy of the latter. For Branting the dilemma was that something had to be done for the farmers to ameliorate the social effects of the process of concentration in agriculture, but the measures taken had to stop short of checking the process. Large-scale production was the only possible form in which to run efficient socialist agriculture, and it was easier to take over large-scale capitalist farming than to create large-scale farming under socialist rule.

Danielsson realized that it was simply necessary for the party to attract large sections of the agricultural population in order to reach a political majority that would ensure a socialist victory. In other words, the positive interest in agricultural questions was a result of the SAP deciding early on to try to gain a majority for a socialist program through universal suffrage. Branting and the other more ideologically inclined party leaders, however, remained stuck for a long time in this ideological dilemma.[6]

In the first real party program, adopted at the fourth conference in 1897, a political manifesto was incorporated into a revised statement of "general basic principles." These basic principles formed the guidelines for socialism, while the manifesto indicated what could be done within the framework of the existing society to improve the situation for neglected groups. In the former small farmers were described as a "disappearing antiquated social class." All means of production, including land, should be transformed into social property. The latter called for "the direct regulation of agricultural credit by the state. Legislation, with a guarantee that a rational agriculture is upheld, prevents the expropriation of small holdings without compensation or rights of use." Further, "judicial equality" was demanded between industrial workers and agricultural workers—for example, through the abolition of *legostadgan*, the old, very unfair law regulating agricultural employment.

A principal demand for free trade was expressed in the program, formulated as "the abolishment of all indirect taxes which chiefly weigh upon the productive classes." According to Simonson, however, the conference did not focus much attention on program writing.[7]

Resistance to Starvation Tariffs

During the last half of the 1880s an intense conflict over tariffs had raged in the Riksdag. The conflict was precipitated by the above-mentioned developments in transport, which meant rapid increases in supplies of cheap' imported grain. This led to a crisis in agriculture; the price of rye was halved between 1881 and 1887. The battle was won by the protectionists in the 1888 Riksdag.

The protectionist spirit was so strong in Sweden around the turn of the century that the tariff question never developed into a very comprehensive debate. Through the growing strength of the Liberals and Social Democrats in the Second Chamber, particularly after the suffrage reform in 1909 and the subsequent left-wing breakthrough in 1911, the tariff issue came back into focus during the years just prior to World War I. Since the Liberals at that time consisted largely of farmers, little of a free-trade tradition remained in the party. Thus the political play was very complicated.

The Social Democrats clearly perceived no disparity between their demands for abolishing food tariffs and their increasingly active engagement in small-scale farming and land questions. According to the 1908 party motion, tariffs only assisted "a few large land and mill owners." However, it became apparent that tariff revenues during the twenty-year development of the system had become such an important part of state finances that it was difficult to do away with them. For this reason, during committee discussions of the motion in 1908, Branting (now party chair) was forced to back away from demanding the abolition of grain tariffs, and instead requested a one-year suspension.

Furthermore, the abolition of food tariffs became more and more connected to industrial tariffs, in which the workers considered themselves to be directly interested. Consequently, the tariff issue became very contentious for the SAP. So that the party could clarify its position on this question, the party executive set up a three-man committee in December 1908 with the task of "carrying out a comprehensive investigation of the tariff question and related tax questions from a Social Democratic point of view."[8]

The committee became a minor scandal; it never delivered any usable results.[9] After this, attacks in tariff discussions became considerably milder.

The 1911 conference indeed added "above all, energetically combating tariffs" to the previous formulation against indirect taxes in the political program, but even though the parliamentary group doubled in size in 1912 as a result of voting rights reform, its increased influence was not felt in the tariff issue. The new group included ten farmers, which only added to the ambivalence. Further inquiries were proposed, as well as decreases in tariffs by a few kronor—which were achieved.[10]

The Land Question

It was in agricultural questions that the SAP had to make perhaps the most extensive ideological reassessments during the first three decades of its existence. The significance of these issues stretches far beyond agricultural policy per se, since the reevaluations entailed the first major entrance of reformism into the original Marxist ideology. This was true not only of Sweden: the Swedish debate was influenced by debates going on in other countries—especially Denmark, Germany, and England.

By 1910 this reevaluation was so extensive that, according to Gellerman, the Social Democrats took over the Liberals' role as the driving force behind the radical smallholding policy that the latter abandoned because of the growing influence of farmers in the party.[11] The reevaluation was henceforth to have a crucial importance for Social Democratic agricultural policy. We can identify influences from three different quarters leading to this 180-degree turnabout:

1. Contact with the actual living conditions and reactions of voters; emigration; and the strong support for the author and educator Karl-Erik Forsslund's and P. J. Rösiös's (often called "the apostle of farming") ideal small-scale farm (Storgården), conveyed to the party through inter alia its first farmer members of the Riksdag and later Branting's minister of agriculture, Sven Linders.
2. The romantic nationalistic currents of the 1890s, which had radical and conservative branches. The former was represented in the party mainly by the former Liberals Carl Lindhagen and Erik Palmstierna; the latter became the Conservative party's lodestar through Professor Nils Wohlin. The author Verner von Heidenstam, who was the chief representative of these national romantic currents, was one of the most assiduous speakers in Forsslund and Rösiös's youth movement.[12]
3. Foreign influences through "Georgism," German and English small farmer movements, and the Fabian Society's general evolutionary orien-

tation and agricultural program. As Björlin shows, the discussions abroad played a major role in the SAP's ideological development and were closely followed in the party press.[13]

An important element behind these influences, however, was a structural change in agricultural production, which has not previously been elucidated in this context. Through rising standards of living, demand for animal products increased in comparison with vegetable products—mainly grain and potatoes—during the decades prior to World War I. From 1876/1885 to 1906/1915 the proportion of animal product consumption in Sweden reckoned in calories rose from 24 percent to 33 percent. In 1930/1939 it was 44 percent.[14] This led to a change in production orientation. During the forty years from 1871/1875 to 1911/1915 grain production in Sweden rose by 45 percent and livestock production by 140 percent.

If one also reckons that the value added for animal products is five and one-half times higher than for grain, the value added of the former in 1871/1875 was approximately 40 percent higher than that of the latter, and in 1911/1915 it was about 130 percent higher. The rise was chiefly in milk products, which increased by 150 percent. At the turn of the century exports of butter accounted for 10 percent of the total Swedish export value. Within vegetable production sugar beet cultivation increased the most: from virtually nothing in 1871/1875 to about 900,000 tons in 1911/1915, at the same time as the sugar content of the beets was significantly raised through breeding.

With the technology of the time these expanding areas of production were well suited to small-scale farming. The new farming technology did not exclusively favor large operations: for instance, the separator, which had a breakthrough around the turn of the century, had a great impact on small-scale agriculture. From the start Branting and his party comrades should have seen agriculture as mainly a grain-producing occupation—it was after all around grain that the tariff battles were waged, and it was above all for grain production that large-scale farming was significant. However, Forsslund and Rösiös's small farmer movement was based to a great extent on the expanding production of animal products, in which small farmers were competitive. This was demonstrated by the development of family farming in Denmark. The shift in demand, so advantageous to small-scale (family) farming, supported the favorable public opinion toward small farmers, in Sweden and in other countries.

At this time the SAP was much too undeveloped to go its own ideological way. Lacking guidelines, particularly from the German party, the SAP remained passive in agricultural issues. However, for many new members of the party the lack of a positive agricultural program was inexplicable, especially since they could see (or experience firsthand) that the poor majority of farmers had in many ways the same problems as poor workers in cities and growing industrial communities.

The Question of Norrland and the
"Own-Your-Own-Home" Movement

Branting, then the lone representative for the SAP, was first confronted with concrete farming policy problems in the Riksdag through the "Norrland issue." This arose as a reaction against the timber companies' ruthless method of buying farms and adjacent forests from farmers who did not understand the forests' value.

Carl Lindhagen, who was then a Liberal, presented a motion to the Riksdag on this issue in 1901, which led to the establishment of the "Norrland Committee" in the same year. The committee presented its report in 1904; its most important proposal was to forbid companies from acquiring agricultural and forest land from private owners in Norrland forest. Land over and above the so-called auxiliary forest (the area considered necessary for the support of agriculture in the northern part of Sweden) was exempted. The committee's proposals, which were accepted by the Riksdag in 1906, became cornerstones of agricultural policy. The Norrland Committee also proposed special legislation to protect tenants on property owned by companies and other lumber interests. This became the point of departure for debates and legislation on "social tenancy," which are still current and through which the SAP has successfully safeguarded tenants' interests. Typically, Lindhagen expressed a divergent opinion in a reservation to the committee proposals. According to Prawitz, "for him, even more than for the majority of committee members, the social point of view was crucial. In contrast to the majority, he expressed this concern not in terms of advantages to the nation (the fatherland) but in support of individuals."[15]

Even before the Norrland Committee presented its proposals, the conservative government under Prime Minister Boström introduced a proposition concerning home ownership to the 1904 Riksdag. Toward the end of the nineteenth century, the "own-your-own-home" movement, under the influence of an increasing population and emigration, had grown into a real grass-roots movement led by Forsslund and Rösiö. The government bill promoting home ownership induced the four Social Democratic members of the Riksdag to present a motion that took up the issue of the form of tenure with state support for small-scale farmers. On land granted by the state the user should preferably have rights of use, not ownership. The state should not allow itself to be dispossessed of land, and the user should not need to borrow and pay interest on the large amounts of capital required for purchase. With this began the conflict over rights of use versus rights of ownership that for many years made it impossible to reach any agreement between the Social Democrats and the Liberals on the small-farm issue and, consequently, to achieve any concrete results.

Gellerman interprets the motion as the first clear expression of the party's turnaround in the land question.[16] Unfortunately, circumstances around the creation of the motion are unclear since no records were kept in the parliamentary group until it had expanded to thirteen members in 1906; however, it seems to have been mainly written by Anders Örne, a leading member of the cooperative movement. Simonson shows influences from the German Social Democratic theoretician Eduard David, who published a large work entitled *Sozialismus und Landwirtschaft* (Socialism and Agriculture) in 1903. He represented a tendency idealizing small-scale farming, diametrically opposite from that of the famous Austrian Marxist Karl Kautsky.[17]

The motion is clearly in support of small farming. However, its main aim would, seem to have been to delineate a socialist and cooperative alternative in the own-your-own-home movement in contrast to the Liberals' strong emphasis on the virtues of home ownership.

Yet debates over the following years clearly show that the party's ideological vanguard—Branting, the journalist C. N. Carleson, and the party secretary Carl Wickman, among others—still asserted the superiority (determined by evolution) of large-scale operations over small, even in agriculture. They viewed promoting ownership of one's own home more as a transitional activity within the framework of capitalism, which gave small farmers a possibility (through cooperation) of obtaining the advantages of large-scale operations. The idea that combined small-scale enthusiasts and large-scale ideologists was that of farmers' cooperatives—but no one asked the farmers if they liked the idea. However, until 1910 the SAP remained fairly passive in agricultural questions.

The Party Program of 1911

By 1911 the own-your-own-home debate had gained in political importance and had in part been melded together with the Norrland issue. The discussion came increasingly to be concentrated around the settlements in the vast swamps of Norrland intended to provide a livelihood inside the country for a growing population. This line was mainly pursued by romantic city-dwellers with very little knowledge of agriculture in general and still less of the conditions for it in Norrland. In 1906 Stockholm's Land Reform Association was formed, modeled after similar associations in England and Germany and led by the well-known economist Gustaf Cassel along with Carl Lindhagen, Erik Palmstierna, Yngve Larsson, and Sven Brisman. In 1909 and 1910 Lindhagen and Palmstierna left the Liberal party and became members of the SAP.

The voting rights reform of 1909, which was applied for the first time in the election of 1911, was especially reckoned to attract increased numbers of farming voters, so all parties tried to strengthen their agricultural profiles. For the party conference of 1911 the Social Democratic Labor Party executive appointed an agricultural committee, chaired by Lindhagen and with five farmers as members. Riksdag member and economic policy specialist Fredrik V. Thorsson and Palmstierna were also involved. Lindhagen set his stamp on the committee. He was not a Marxist; he described himself as a "humanist." According to Tingsten, Lindhagen based his ideas on "reported values which were said to be objective, not a historical interpretation with its associated predictions."[18]

Branting and others within the party executive were extremely critical of Lindhagen's proposals. The executive produced its own proposition for an agricultural program, which was presented in the conference. A special land committee set up by the conference was given the task of finding a compromise. It made certain minor changes and additions to the executive's proposal, which was adopted after a relatively uncontentious debate.[19]

The proposal added a twelfth point to the political program, one that was longer than all the other eleven combined. It begins with a statement of principle that is the core of the new policy. The statement still maintains continued social ownership of all land, but also says that the main part of the agricultural population is composed of "smaller farmers, crofters and farm workers" who, like wage earners, make up the exploited classes. Therefore, an agricultural policy should be pursued that favors these groups, helps them to make their production more efficient, and gives them security against the domination of companies and owners of estates. "Equally, society should take care that suitable land is held accessible on reasonable terms and in satisfactory forms for *all* who wish to devote their labor to the land" (my italics). Small farmers and farm workers should be able to acquire the advantages of large-scale farming through cooperative operations, and, as a last resort, it should be possible to expropriate larger properties when necessary to obtain the required land.[20]

The immediate consequence of the conference decision was, paradoxically, that for a long time the SAP's activities on the land question nearly ceased. In the election of 1911 the parliamentary group in the Second Chamber doubled in number, and ten farmers were among the newly elected. The growing influence of the farming community among the Liberals (in 1912 nearly 60 percent of their representatives in the Second Chamber were farmers) meant that they pursued a different line from that of the SAP. Even if the latter to a degree accepted land ownership rights, the conflict between that and rights of use still played a prominent role and would continue to do so until the 1920s.

A home ownership committee was set up in 1911. The results of its work were reported in 1914, but because of the outbreak of war its immediate significance was limited. However, the committee's report influenced the discussion after the war, as it claimed that small-scale farming was economically superior to large-scale operations with reference to intensive farming, especially of animal products. The core of this assertion was the conviction of the superiority of family farming, which came to have great importance for land policy after World War II.[21]

In the long term, however, the decision of 1911 must be awarded major significance. Land policy was taken out of the field of tension between ideology and strategy. Lindhagen definitely broke an ideological deadlock within the SAP, which the German party, for example, had not been able to do, and which, according to H. G. Lehmann, was the reason why it did not obtain a parliamentary majority before 1914.[22] The SAP's agricultural policy received, mainly through Lindhagen, an important injection of 1890s national romanticism, which softened the conflict of interests and helped to incorporate agriculture in the policy of consensus that since the 1930s has distinguished Swedish politics. Of utmost importance has always been the personal proximity of industrial workers to agriculture because of Sweden's late industrialization and because of the location of industries in small communities in rural areas.

FROM FOOD TARIFFS TO AGRICULTURAL REGULATION

During the years immediately after World War I discussions in the SAP and the parliamentary group were very much devoted to how the crisis measures that had been taken should be removed and how deflation, seen by everyone as mandatory after the inflation shock of 1919 and 1920, should be dealt with. A short-lived ideological debate arose, stimulated by the political upheavals occurring in the countries involved in the war.[23] The demands for nationalization were pacified by way of investigations made by the Nationalization Committee, which did not lead to any concrete proposals. Since 1911 agricultural policy had not occupied a central position in the ideological debates; the section dealing with agriculture in the political program was thoroughly revised at the 1920 and 1928 conferences, but changes in substance were limited. The point dealing with free trade was laconically formulated at the 1920 conference: "Free Trade: Foreign trade under the direction of the state."

The shifting tariffs on grain,* which were introduced in 1920 in exchange for supporting legislation for an eight-hour workday, were a pawn in the extensive negotiations with the Liberals, first in the Liberal–Social Democratic Edén government and then later when Branting sought support from the Liberals for his minority governments and later still when the prime minister of the subsequent nonpartisan government, Oscar von Sydow, sought support from the SAP in 1921.

Despite its principles of free trade, the SAP was forced in the Riksdag to accept the shifting tariffs. Even regulations for sugar became objects of intense attacks, but free trade supporters failed also here. The Liberals had developed into a strongly protectionist party. War experiences also gave rise for the first time to discussions about the need for production preparedness, which would come to be of great importance in agricultural policy after World War II.**

Toward Agricultural Regulations

After all these failures, interest in tariff questions faded, and between 1923 and 1928 they appear very rarely in the minutes of the party executive and the parliamentary group. Since the Social Democrats had entered the "government formation league," they were much more occupied by the purely political ups and downs accompanying the frequent changes of govern-

---

*Shifting or sliding tariffs were adjusted in response to changes in world market prices so that domestic prices could be kept unchanged.

**Sweden managed to stay outside the two world wars but was cut off from world markets and so had to feed itself. Because of crop failures on both occasions there was scarcity and rationing, more severe during the first than during the second war. These experiences generated a strong awareness in public opinion of the need for production preparedness in case of new cutoffs. Preparedness has become a key word in Swedish agricultural policy, one often exploited by farming interests.

ment—Sweden had eight different governments between 1920 and 1932. After deflation in 1921 and 1922, which hit all branches of the economy hard, agriculture had an if not altogether brilliant then at least an acceptable period up to the end of the 1920s. The need for protection against low import prices was not so acute.[24] Even so, farmers felt they were lagging behind the fairly strongly expanding industrial sector, a problem that became still more immediate after World War II.

During this time the issue of organizing agriculture played an active role in debates, and in due course in policy. Many who thought that farmers should organize themselves in the same way as workers viewed agricultural price regulations as a parallel to the workers' collective agreements. At the same time, industrial growth gathered speed. Relations between the two sectors gradually changed, and this affected (albeit in retrospect) the view of agriculture as the most important "resource reserve" or means of support in times of unemployment—at least within the political left inclined toward accepting economic changes.

Sven Linders was minister of agriculture in Branting's second and third governments, and Per Edvin Sköld was his under secretary in the last of these from 1924 to 1926. Sköld became the leading light in the SAP's agricultural policy for several decades, even though for long periods he had to devote his energies to other departments. He carried Lindhagen's ideas on, but whereas it is uncertain whether Lindhagen had ever held a dung fork, it is absolutely certain that Sköld had.

From the beginning Sköld was an ardent free trader. In an article in *Tiden* in 1926 he developed his view of agricultural policy.[25] He took up the idea from the 1911 own-your-own-home committee that small-scale farming as a form of production also had advantages economically over large-scale farming and thus that land policy was not merely a social issue. However, to make use of these advantages small farmers must organize themselves economically and professionally—examples from the growing trade union movement lay near at hand. According to Sköld the organization of Swedish agriculture lagged behind that in Denmark and Finland because of the farmers' lack of class consciousness. In other words, he wished to solve the problems of small farmers with the same means that were being effectively used for solving those of industrial workers. However, economic cooperation, which for the early ideologists mainly involved production cooperation in order to utilize the advantages offered by large-scale operation, now became purchase, processing, and marketing cooperation.

Sköld argued in favor of Sweden following the same lines as Denmark and Holland: concentration on livestock production, a development that had been halted in 1903 when the protectionists quashed the Boström government's proposal to abolish the prohibitive tariffs on corn (maize)—which in fact did not occur until 1910. Sköld did not believe that protection against the world market would be required. The absence of such protection meant that agricultural organizations would not need to come into conflict with consumer interests. This links up with the party's previous lines of thought on agricultural policy. Through agriculture making itself more efficient is created "the only solid foundation for attempts to provide new groups of people with bread and a livelihood by starting up new farms."[26] So far at least, there was no question of the state directing agricultural development. There were other interpretations of the goal of free trade within the SAP, represented by, for example, the cooperativist Anders Örne, who concurred with Professor Eli Heckscher's more orthodox standpoints.[27]

In 1928 a series of important organizational initiatives were taken by farmers to establish both professional and economic organizations, which led to the formation in 1929 of the RLF, the National Swedish Farmers' Union, and to a reorganization of Sweden's General Association of Farmers so that it could serve as the head organization for the producer cooperative movement.[28] The SAP's executive, in the wake of the "cossack" election of 1928, discussed participating in the organizing of farmers, but these discussions did not lead to any results.[29]*

In 1928 the first warning signals from the world market arrived. Sugar prices fell sharply during the autumn of that year; in 1929 grain prices followed suit. Meat prices had also been fluctuating for several years. Protection policies were dealt with by the right-wing government, which mainly represented large estate farmers, primarily in terms of a grain problem. After the war wheat cultivation had expanded at the expense of rye, but Swedish wheat was difficult to market because it was soft and had to be mixed with imported hard varieties to provide a flour that could be sold to bakers competitively with imported flour. Flour mills preferred to use only 40 percent Swedish wheat in their blends.

The falling grain prices were to the advantage of livestock producers, and

---

*The parliamentary elections of 1928 have been called the "cossack" elections because they were won by the conservatives after a very rough campaign. Their main argument, shrewdly combining the old fear of Russians with the new fear of communists, was that Russian cossacks would be allowed to ravage the land and rape the women if the Social Democrats came to power.

opinion among farmers was divided. The SAP supported small farmers in their resistance to raised grain tariffs. However, livestock production expanded greatly because of improved profitability both in Sweden and in other countries. When rising unemployment simultaneously limited demand for more expensive foodstuffs the world market prices for these products also fell, primarily butter prices.

Already in the summer of 1928, following motions by a Social Democratic member of the Riksdag, O. E. Sjölander, and some right-wing members, the departing Ekman government set up an inquiry on the economic situation in agriculture with the brief of suggesting measures for improvement. The SAP's representative in this inquiry was Nils Adler, a farmer from Skåne and close associate of Sköld. The inquiry produced proposals that became the core of future agriculture regulations.

In the Riksdag of 1930 the Lindman government was forced by growing rural opinion to submit proposals for support of grain cultivation through raised tariffs, milling obligations,* and even certain supports for livestock production as well as for efforts to organize within agriculture. This was done after great internal malaise. The proposals were worked on by a specially appointed committee, and they initiated lengthy debates. This was the beginning of the modern agricultural regulation system.

Support for farming and the social land questions were intensively discussed in both the SAP's executive and the parliament group at the end of 1929 and during the 1930 Riksdag. Also discussed was the question of in some way forming a government with the Liberals. One idea was that agriculture should be assisted by reducing industrial tariffs rather than by raising agricultural ones.

The agricultural crisis deepened, however, and world market prices for livestock plummeted, affecting smaller farmers. At a discussion about the tariff inquiry in the party executive in November 1931, the future minister of finance Ernst Wigforss said: "Up to now we Social Democrats have said no to all help to farmers which would involve any considerable costs. This policy can no longer be justified." Sköld, however, stated that "there can be no question of any permanent support. If the present crisis does not abate, agriculture must adapt to the prevailing conditions." Party chair Per Albin Hansson concluded: "It makes sense that the distress of the farmers should be combined with that of the industrial workers."[30]

---

*"Milling obligations" implied that by law the mills had to use a determined minimum share of Swedish wheat in flour production.

The Crisis Settlement of 1933

After the election victory of 1932, in the introduction to his speech to the party executive Per Albin Hansson said that "there is a clear mandate from the people for an *anti-protectionist* policy" (my italics). Later on he said, "We also have the important trade policy questions where there is a majority for free trade." However, Hansson also did not exclude the possibility of a state foreign trade monopoly. The proposals for the government program included the following points concerning agricultural policy: (a) continued state support to indebted farmers; (b) retained milk regulation pending further experience; (c) retained grain regulation, with consumers' interests monitored; (d) continued regulation of sugar, with the interests of consumers and workers monitored; and (e) the commencement of inquiries concerning agriculture agreed upon by the Riksdag. In addition, in a special point it was stated that the farm worker question was to be examined.

Per Albin Hansson further claimed that agreement prevailed with the Liberal party over trade and agricultural policy, but cooperation in government was prevented partly by differing opinions about financial questions in the crisis policy and partly by the fact that the Liberals were inept negotiators in the present situation. The SAP executive voted twenty-two to five in favor of forming a government. Sköld was one of the five against.[31]

The financing of the crisis policy—unemployment policy and agricultural supports—became the hardest nut for the new government to crack in the Riksdag of 1933. Deficit financing (borrowing) to combat crises was at the time an utterly unknown idea, and the conservative parties had the most remarkable notions about what sorts of catastrophes, especially inflation, would be brought about by such a financial policy. Economic experts—with a few notable exceptions within what would later be called the "Stockholm School"—shared these fears, as did banking people, including the head of the National Bank of Sweden, Ivar Rooth.

After extended discussions the Agrarian party proved to be the only party sufficiently pragmatic to accept these ideas. As late as after the election in September of the previous year, cooperation with the Liberals was the only alternative that seemed worth discussing; party consultations during the Riksdag seemed to have been commenced with this in mind.

The crisis settlement has been thoroughly described by several authors, both contemporary and present-day. Wigforss's *Memoirs* are among the most important references. Gunnar Hellström has discussed them thoroughly, emphasizing agriculture policy.[32] Together with Per Albin Hansson, Wigforss and Sköld seem to have been the most important advocates.

Early on during the Riksdag they signaled that the government was willing to compromise, especially on agricultural issues. Together with the whole party, they were forced into the process that led to an agreement to abandon several central ideological principles, particularly free trade.

This was motivated by the crisis having changed character. Because of countries' uncoordinated protection measures, relations on the world markets had lost contact with the actual conditions of production to the degree that world market prices could no longer be accepted as norms for domestic price and structural adjustments. Obstacles for Swedish exports had consequently become so difficult to overcome, that imports had to be checked to preserve the balance in foreign trade. Sköld made these statements in the Riksdag as early as February.[33] Wigforss developed the consequences in a memo for negotiations, which he later related in his memoirs. He claimed that Sweden could be forced to orient its policy toward a greater degree of self-sufficiency and forgo profits from international trade if the obstacles to Swedish exports persisted.[34]

The ideas of economic planning, which had been a complement to the doctrine of nationalization and later became a substitute for it, may have made it more palatable for Sköld and Wigforss to abandon free trade when they could declare that market mechanisms were not functioning properly. What Leif Lewin says about the unemployment program's politically stimulating effects through being concrete and anchored in reality can probably also be applied to agriculture regulation.[35]

FAMILY FARMING

Land policy between the wars was mainly characterized by the slow processing of the consequences of industrial expansion and the increased possibilities of earning a living outside of farming, as well as by diminishing population growth. During World War I the own-your-own-home inquiry, was put on ice until 1919 when the Edén government, in which the SAP participated, proposed that activity be expanded. It was decided that the own-your-own-home projects should be supported by advantageous loans, and that those people who created their own new homes and reclaimed land should have priority. This orientation toward land reclamation was bolstered when the deflation crisis in the early 1920s "brought about a new interest in making land available for as many as possible."[36] In 1927 a fund was established for the strengthening of "incomplete farms" through land reclamation. The settlement inquiries resulted in a trial project in 1917 and from 1925 onward in a special organization with its own funding provisions in the northernmost provinces. The results of these endeavors were a disappointment to all enthusiasts.[37]

In the beginning of 1918 the parliament group and party executive had decided in favor of Nils Adler's proposal to draft a concrete program for the land question.[38] However, nothing seems to have been produced. The same year, the Edén government set up a Land Commission that was once again to address the whole land issue. Members of the commission included both Lindhagen, who was now a left-wing socialist, and Nils Wohlin of the Agrarian party. The commission's proposal involved an expansion of the 1906 law prohibiting companies from acquiring farms in Norrland to encompass the entire country, including even forest lands beyond the auxiliary forests. The law was also to apply to individual speculators or "jobbers." Thus, the proposal anticipated the laws on land acquisition that would be passed after World War II. The commission also proposed a law against neglect of farm land.

Both Lindhagen and Wohlin submitted long, personal statements on principles to the commission. Lindhagen pursued his idealistic "land for all" program, against the commercializing of land ownership. Wohlin followed a completely opposite line: he wanted a numerically limited but well-situated farmer class with farms sufficiently large to operate rationally. This was in and of itself a reasonable objective, which gradually became accepted after World War II, but the motives behind it were partly nationalistic and racist, advancing sentiments that appeared later in Nazi Germany.

Lindhagen's increasingly utopian land program gradually led him into conflict with the more realistic Sköld. At the 1932 SAP conference Sköld replied to a motion from Lindhagen by saying that it would not be reasonable to create new farms when the great majority of the nation's farmers "are in economic misery without parallel in history."[39] However, this should not be taken to mean that Sköld was against Lindhagen's program: his objections referred only to the prevailing situation. Addressing the party executive in the autumn of 1935, Sköld said that "our major thrust should henceforth be in the social land issue now when general agricultural policy is less pressing. . . . We must concentrate our efforts on the creation of new farms. In one generation 50,000 small farms for workers and 20,000 leaseholds should be created. Specially pertinent is to pursue sensible set-

tlements in Norrland and also to increase the acreage of incomplete farms."
According to Sköld, the nationalization of land would be a means of preventing speculation, "but our people are not ready [for this]."[40]

This was a very ambitious program compared with the rather limited achievements of previous activities. In response to Lindhagen's motion at the 1932 conference, Sköld said: "with reference to obtaining land for our citizens, it must be said that up to now very little has been able to be done."[41] The conference made very positive statements concerning the land question.

Since Sköld formed the SAP's agriculture policy for more than a quarter of a century, his views are important. He had a strong personal engagement in agriculture. His point of departure seemed to be the family farm, that is, a farm sufficiently large to sustain and employ a family. However, like Lindhagen, Sköld seems for quite a long time to have been of the opinion that as many as possible should be given the opportunity to be farmers, and that for that reason the size of farms must be limited. Rather late, he saw the shift in the goals of family farming—from providing a livelihood for a family to effectively utilizing its labor force—that was brought about by the successful employment policy implemented after World War II.

AGRICULTURAL CALCULATIONS AND INCOME EQUALITY

Price Policy in the 1930s

As of 1932 the SAP also had long-term responsibility for agricultural policies. During the periods of coalition governments with Agrarian party ministers of agriculture, Sköld, besides being head of first the department of trade and then of defense, functioned as a powerful shadow agricultural minister. A description of the SAP's agricultural policy during this period is therefore less a description of debates and programs than of an implemented policy.

Until animal products, especially butter, began to be affected by the 1930s farming crisis, the Social Democrats were free to simultaneously advocate free trade and small-scale farming. The question of tariff protection basically related to grain and sugar, which were mostly produced by big farmers. The conditions of farm workers had mainly comprised the social element in protection policies, and it was possible to remain rather unresponsive to the farmers' somewhat vague demands for a "more just" or "solidaristic" tariff protection. In his speech to the party executive after the election victory of 1932, Per Albin Hansson continued to stress free trade.

However, through the crisis settlement with the Agrarian party the government also received responsibility for the income of small farmers—through border protection, price regulations, and subsidies. To start with the objective was simple: to avoid a catastrophe. When the situation on the world market stabilized and improved somewhat in the mid-1930s, it was thought that, although that goal had been achieved, the situation had not improved enough to warrant lifting protective measures. Goals for prices were formulated in percentages of average levels for 1925–1929, and they were raised successively from 75 to 100 percent.

The difficulties of continuing support policies without more precise distribution policy objectives were obvious, however. Both internal and external criticism—from consumers (consumer cooperatives, so partly internal)—was sharp. It was asserted that many farmers who received support through the system lived much better than the industrial workers who provided the support. The differences between regions and between farms of different sizes and efficiency created familiar problems regarding justice and equity.

The first analysis and criticism of the system of regulation, which was gradually developed after the parliamentary decision in 1930 and the crisis settlement of 1933, was made on behalf of the KF (the Swedish Cooperative Union and Wholesale Society) by Mauritz Bonow in 1935. Anders Örne, as always opposed to all forms of tariff protection for both agriculture and industry, was heavily engaged in consumer cooperatives and influenced the KF's attitudes toward economic questions. Bonow concluded that the price rises up to that time were considered legitimate by consumers; prices had not yet exceeded 75 percent of the average levels of 1925–1929. Even so, for low-income earners the price rises, especially the duty on margarine, were felt.[42]

A few years later the economist Gunnar Myrdal published a pamphlet, *Jordbrukspolitiken under omläggning* (The Changes in Agricultural Policy), which also took up the effects of price regulations on income distribution. Myrdal represented a new view of agriculture as part of an industry undergoing continuous technical and economic changes. According to this view, agricultural policy should focus on adapting to this development. He was the first to articulate rationally the problems arising from state control over farmers' incomes.

At the price level that was required to provide reasonable livelihoods for the vast majority of farmers, the large productive farms were stimulated into producing a surplus that had to be exported abroad, often at a considerable loss. At the same time there were large groups in society that continually could afford neither quantitatively nor qualitatively adequate food. It should be possible to find a system whereby those within the country who needed it could have access to the surplus.[13] Myrdal thus anticipated the discussion on high price policy versus low price policy that became a central theme in agricultural policy during the postwar years.

At the outbreak of World War II in 1939, the problems became, as in 1914, the reverse: what mattered was to avoid repeating the jobbing and shortages of World War I. Prices had to be adjusted to stimulate production without the consumers being excessively affected.

The newly formed Food Commission, in negotiations with farmers' organizations, produced a calculation of agriculture cost increases compared with a base period, 1935–1937, which included the labor provided reckoned according to the wage rates of farm workers. The aim of this was to keep price rises within these limits. Through a relatively faster increase in negotiated farm workers' wages, the entire farming industry improved its revenues; the improvements were justified by the role played by agriculture in sustaining the population in the new situation.

This estimate, generally referred to as the Agricultural Cost Estimates, came to play a dominant role in price policy, not only during the war but also thereafter. It was not replaced by another system until 1956 and was normatively described in terms of "justice for farming," which created strong and occasionally troublesome political ties.

Because of better food administration and larger production capacity in Swedish agriculture, food supplies were managed during World War II without any serious shortages, despite very low harvests during the first years of the war. The not so remote experience of the support received by farmers during the previous crisis might have contributed to increasing solidarity on their side. Experiences from two world wars had established in Swedish opinion a strong awareness of the need for food supply preparedness in case of renewed blockades (cf. page 187, note **). This became a very important card in the agricultural policy game, which during the "cold war" period was rapidly exploited by agricultural interests.

The Postwar Program

The most important postwar policy document is the labor movement's Postwar Program, prepared during the final years of the war. In the program the goals and the two means of postwar agricultural policy were set. Under point ten there are the following statements: "Equal income for equal performance, both in comparisons between farms and with other industries," and "working farmers must be given a position equal to those of other groups of workers." Pending a rationalization of agriculture, "special support measures should be undertaken for farmers of incomplete farms in order to ensure them a reasonable livelihood."* Striving for equality not only applies to monetary income: standards for the rural population regarding housing, domestic fixtures and fittings, labor-saving equipment for housework, social and cultural services, and education should be raised to the rising levels enjoyed by urban dwellers.

The goal of income equality should be achieved by two means:**

1. "State support for agriculture will continue to be necessary to raise and maintain living standards for the large neglected groups within agriculture." This general price support should aim at making rationally run family farms fully profitable.
2. Incomplete farms should be transformed into complete family farms "through consolidating, supplementing or other means. . . . Part of the support should be in the form of loans and subsidies for such equipment as will make production more efficient."[44]

It should be underlined that the focus of the program was on rational family farming; the goals were not yet tied to any particular acreage size.

The need to make concrete these general guidelines for price adjustments and rationalization entailed the setting up of a new inquiry, the Agricultural Committee (JK) of 1942. Under the influence of the 1930s problem with surpluses—which were expected to return after the war—land policy increasingly tended to turn into a rationalization policy from the previous

---

*"Incomplete farms" were farms with too little land for a farmer's family to earn a living on it by conventional farming. The concept became increasingly important in the policy shift from "providing a living" to "efficient use of the labor force."

**Income equality has been the key concept of agricultural policy since World War II. It first implied that farmers on family farms should be able to earn as much from farming as a worker in industry earns from his or her employment. Later it referred to a farmer on a basic farm (and subsequently a model farm), compared to a worker in manufacturing.

policy of land reclamation and establishment of new farms—even though this was still not a generally held position. The older view of agriculture as the most basic staple industry, the only truly secure and reliable one through all vicissitudes, still had a strong following in all political parties. And this view gained support when the Commission for Postwar Planning (the so-called Myrdal Commission) predicted worldwide employment problems after the war. Sköld himself advanced this position at the SAP conference in 1952.[45] With Sweden's heavy dependency on the rest of the world, full employment would be difficult to realize.

In its proposals the Agricultural Committee combined price policy and rationalization policy (land policy) through proposing—in line with the Postwar Program—that prices be adjusted so that farmers on rational units (family farms) would receive an income equivalent to that received for comparable work in other industries. Farmers *presently* on incomplete farms would receive a cash payment, which would stop when they gave up farming. Structural policy should aim at combining and supplementing small farms so that they could become rational, and in this way external rationalization could be one of the means of achieving the goals of income policy. However, internal rationalization was equally important and should also be supported.[46]

This was Sköld's basic idea for family farming, which had already been expressed in his *Tiden* article in 1926.[47] It was understandable that the Agricultural Committee strongly stressed the need for being prepared for emergencies, but it also asserted that production must be kept within definite limits to realize the income goal. These objectives could easily be thwarted by difficult-to-sell surpluses, so the committee stated that the goal for production should be 92 percent of what was required for total self-sufficiency.

Rationalization should aim at creating—when possible—"model farms" (20 to 30 hectares of arable land), that is, family farming one size above basic farm units (10 to 20 hectares of arable land).[48] The latter were to remain the basis for price setting for the foreseeable future. Rationality was clearly conceived mainly as a question of being able to use machinery and, consequently, as a question of the area of cultivated land. Model and larger-scale farms were too few to become the basis for price setting.

The Agricultural Committee discussed high- and low-level price schemes: the former meant that all support issued from higher prices; the latter, that world market prices were allowed to prevail within the country, and support was paid as direct subsidies. The committee chose the high price scheme even though, in consideration of the proposed producer subsidies for milk, it was called a middle price scheme. Despite marked interest in the low price scheme on the part of consumers (with motives similar to those once expressed by Myrdal), the high price alternative remained until 1973, when a middle price scheme was established with food subsidies.

The Agricultural Committee also proposed a new extensive organization under the auspices of the Board of Agriculture—the Farming Committees—that would direct rationalization, and means were proposed for loans and subsidies to farmers undertaking rationalization.

The more modern view of agricultural policy, which was expressed by Myrdal in 1938, was confirmed by the economists Erik Lundberg and Ingvar Svennilson in a special statement. From the beginning this statement was more comprehensive than it appears to be in the final report since, during the verification of the report, parts of it were incorporated into the committee's main declaration—although clearly without affecting the latter's conclusions and proposals. Gunnar Sträng from the Farm Workers Trade Unions and several other important representatives of the LO were members of the committee. The SAP was represented exclusively by farmers.

The Agricultural Committee's proposals were presented in 1946, but their main elements had been discussed before in the party executive as well as in the parliamentary group.[49] The proposals were met by a storm of criticism from agricultural organizations that considered them too far-reaching on both rationalization and limits on production. In a review of the report, I raised the opposite question: whether the goal of "model farms" was sufficiently far-reaching considering the fact that external rationalization should be a long-term activity.[50]

As minister of agriculture in 1947 Sköld shaped the proposition based on the committee's proposals. On three crucial points he deviated from them. He thought it unnecessary—even unsuitable—to stipulate any fixed guidelines for the extent of agricultural production yet. He also thought that external rationalization should be entirely limited to creating basic farms, and the following year he proceeded to propose a new land acquisition law that de facto blocked the creation of larger farms. Finally, Sköld reshaped the proposed cash subsidies to *present* farmers on incomplete farms into a means-tested producer subsidy for milk that was tied to the farm. The Riksdag rejected means testing, and thus the Agricultural Committee's idea that the subsidies should be constructed so as to exert pressure for external rationalization was lost.

Sköld's and the government's motives for obliging farming opinion on these important points cannot be read in any minutes or other records. In his proposition Sköld explained the reduction of rationalization goals by stating that model farms would become dependent upon an employed work force that was much too difficult to procure. With continued technical development, however, this should have been a transitory problem. External rationalization is a very long-term project, and both model and even larger farms soon became single-family enterprises.

Explanations should be sought among political factors. Sköld and several others in the government felt that it might be necessary to resuscitate their 1930s cooperation with the Agrarian party. Criticism of the government from the right wing and the Liberals had been exceedingly rancorous at the end of 1946 and the beginning of 1947. In his diary entries for 17 January 1947 relating negotiations with the Agrarian party, Sköld wrote:

> I stressed how very important it was that the decisions in agricultural questions were not met by mistrust on the part of the farmers. . . . My other line was that through these negotiations to maintain contact with B.-F.[51] in order to retain the possibility of reasoning with them—without at the same time having the whole opposition gathered together.[52]

This interpretation is also supported by Prime Minister Tage Erlander's notes from 14 May 1947: "In this situation we can preserve our freedom of movement if we smash the bourgeois front. The farmers are willing." However, this strategy collapsed, this time on the farm price negotiations. Erlander's notes reveal not only a certain amount of desperation concerning the problem of inflation, but also Sköld's intensive efforts to find solutions.[53]

The Expanding Role of Organizations

Destruction during World War II was much more extensive than during the first, and it took much longer for normal relations on the world market to be restored. In 1950 the Food Commission was replaced by a "peace organization," the National Agricultural Board (JN). The fairly wide range of interests represented on the former was replaced in the latter by a clearer and more limited party representation: two farming and two consumer representatives (the LO and the KF). This had one effect that was probably not anticipated: through its limited membership the Agricultural

Board became better able to negotiate than the Food Commission had been with so many special interests represented. When the parties on the Agricultural Board had reached a price agreement on the basis of the Agricultural Cost Estimates, it was very difficult for the government and the Riksdag to change it, at least in any significant way—and they never did.

This meant that initiatives in questions of agricultural policy as regarding consumers were transferred to organizations within the labor movement— the LO and the consumers' KF. These organizations were quite independent but at the same time close to the party. Debates on agricultural policy in the party executive and the parliament group during the next few years became more and more infrequent and rather frustrated. Complaints were raised over the Agricultural Cost Estimates, which many thought unreasonable, and over their links to farm workers' wages. However, in the end nothing much could be done about the agreements concluded by the negotiating parties. Contributing to the complaints and general dissatisfaction was the fact that miscalculations by the Agricultural Board were subsequently discovered, in some cases involving significant sums, which drew great attention from the press. However, even at party conferences agricultural issues played a subordinate role.

In discussions concerning political collaboration with the Agrarian party in the autumns of 1948 and 1951 agricultural issues became prominent. In 1948 the Agrarian party withdrew, but in 1951 an agreement was reached. The international situation was tense (the Korean crisis), and food supply preparedness was considered vital. Discussions revolved around prices and subsidies (margarine duties, etc.), and most judged that the coalition would be paid for by higher prices, higher than would otherwise be allowed. Yet Sköld claimed that price regulations in the current situation would protect consumers: "I do not think that the Agrarian Party can get more out of collaboration than we have to concede because of our general obligations." Concerning structural rationalization, Erlander said the agreement meant that it would be implemented "at the quickest pace permitted by state finances."[54]

Collaboration, however, was not without hitches. Late in the winter of 1952 when negotiations between the Agricultural Board and the farmers were sluggish, the new agriculture minister, Sam Norup, unconstitutionally stepped in and, sitting down with his farming colleagues, reached a price agreement that, among other things, included a retroactive slaughter premium for pigs that gave rise to a great many jokes in the press. However, Norup's way of dealing with this situation provoked strong reactions from consumer representatives. Sköld admitted at the party conference of the same year that "at this year's agriculture negotiations things occurred which should never have happened. . . ."[55]

In 1953 the Cooperative Union (KF), the LO, and the TCO (Swedish Confederation of Professional Employees) formed the Consumer Committee for Agricultural Policy, which was to be an organ for consumer consultations, information, and coordination. During the 1950s this committee was fairly active and important.

The parliamentary decision of 1947 called for price setting to aim at income equality between farmers on basic farms and employees with comparable work within other industries. But very little was said about how this goal should be implemented. The transition to more normal supply conditions was still seen to be far off. In 1952 an inquiry was set up to clarify how the 1947 decision should be put into practice. The inquiry was conducted by representatives of the parties concerned and in close conjunction with the Board of Agriculture. This group presented its proposals in the autumn of 1954. As a comparative income group outside of agriculture, the members of the inquiry chose industrial workers in the region with the lowest cost of living. On the basis of their calculations, the inquiry was able to state that farmers on basic farms had reached income equity.

The conclusion of the inquiry led to a bill in 1955, which was to be written by Norup, in consultation of course with the entire government, and in particular with Sköld. After agreement had been reached concerning guidelines, however, Norup revised and adjusted to the extent that the content of the proofs sent to the other ministers was considerably different from what had been agreed upon. But Sköld here truly lived up to his role as "shadow agricultural minister" (he was actually finance minister). His copy of the proofs is preserved, with seventeen temperamental comments. The bill was finally altered so that it followed what had originally been agreed upon.[56]

The following year, 1956, the Agricultural Board negotiated with the farmers on the implementation of the system thus agreed upon, which was based on median prices and upper and lower price limits as well as fixed import duties as long as domestic prices lay within these limits. Negotiations were protracted and complicated, occasionally involving the government, but in the end a three-year price agreement was reached that would replace the yearly, politically unwieldy rounds of negotiations.

In 1957, through vigorous interventions, consumer organizations stopped one of the Agrarian party's most cherished projects—the proposal to complete, on very favorable terms, incomplete farms with forest lands, primarily from state-owned domains. The LO's comments concerning the inquiry's proposal concluded with the following: "The results of the inquiry can be summarily characterized as unsuitable proposals, based on faulty conclusions drawn from unrealistic assumptions. LO finds it impossible that a so badly anchored investigation should provide the basis for any measures whatsoever, not to speak of measures which can have such far-reaching consequences for the Swedish economy."[57]

The Six-Year Agreement

The role of consumer organizations (the LO's and the Cooperative Union's) in farm policy culminated a few years later. The Agrarian party had broken away from the coalition, Gösta Netzén was agriculture minister, and Sköld was a very active member of the Agricultural Committee in the Riksdag. In the beginning of 1959, when the three-year agreement from 1956 was to be replaced, calculations revealed that an income gap had again arisen between industrial workers and farmers on basic and model farms. This gap was so large that even negotiators representing farmers realized it could not be closed through price increases. The leader of their negotiation delegation was Gösta Liedberg, a large-scale farmer and right-winger who was not a member of the Agrarian party—a fact that seems to have been important for the negotiation results.

Negotiators representing the consumers were aware that the goal of income parity for basic farms was in the long run untenable considering the increasingly rapid rises in industrial productivity, which made possible real wage rises of 4 to 5 percent annually. The possibilities for rationalization of basic and model farms were limited when production growth for these farms was estimated at only about 2 percent per year.

After having knocked their heads against insoluble problems in various rounds, the negotiators concluded that the income differences should be resolved gradually over a six-year period (amortized). In return, the income equality goal should be shifted from basic farm units to model farm units. This change of aims, which had been declared by the Riksdag, was naturally an item that the negotiators had no authority to agree upon. On the other hand, under the prevailing circumstances this decision was a necessary one, and one the political authorities were incapable of making. The government was happy with the agreement, but the Riksdag accepted it with reservations.

The Riksdag and the Agriculture Committee tried to return the initiative to political authorities by requesting a new agriculture inquiry from the government. Thus the Agriculture Inquiry of 1960 was commenced, in which organizations' representatives again acquired a strong position. The Inquiry went on during the six-year agreement and reported in 1966. In 1963 a consumer delegation, headed by a provincial governor, was appointed to be a party in price negotiations.

The Central Problem

The central problem with the objectives of postwar agricultural policy, decided in 1947, became increasingly obvious over time. Income equality with industrial workers was to be awarded to farmers whose farms were too small to be able to keep up with the hectic industrial production and productivity growth. The latter was reckoned as over 4 percent annually during the 1950s and over 8 percent per year during the 1960s, while a special study for the 1960 Agriculture Inquiry showed that for staple agriculture growth was only 2 percent. From 1950 to 1965 the share of the GNP covered by agricultural production diminished from 8 to 4 percent. In addition, the processing stage, which accounted for an increasing proportion of consumer food bills, also had a weak productivity development.[58] The goals of distribution policy were thus much too static.

Farmers used the need for preparedness as an argument to mask efforts to retain as many farmers as possible in agriculture and as many acres as possible under the plow. But the static income goal led to such high prices that high-capacity enterprises were tempted into a production increase, which created hard-to-sell surpluses.

Opinions within the SAP were not monolithic. There were many older Social Democrats who stayed committed to the agriculture policy established by Lindhagen in 1911 and modernized by Sköld in 1947. The old guard in the SAP thought it more important that as many as possible receive a fair livelihood through farming than that the labor force engaged in agriculture, like its counterpart in other industries, be utilized as effectively as possible for the benefit of the *whole* population. The production and structural policy goals were also far too static in the context of the enormously rapid postwar development.

It was unavoidable that, emotionally, people could not keep up with the rapid changes demanded by technical and organizational development. All industrial countries struggled with the same problem. Many understood that the country that could quickly adapt to these changes would gain great economic advantages, but no one had the political strength to bring this about. Farmers, with or without their own political parties, were critical marginal voters everywhere.

Structural Imbalances

The main significance of the agreement in 1959 to shift income policy goals was that it broke the political adherence to the 1947 agricultural policy, which had already become antiquated. In 1947 it was not possible to foresee the rapid development that would occur within other industries after the war, and the effects the need for labor would have on agriculture. As has already been mentioned, the Myrdal Commission had reckoned with the risk of employment problems. On the other hand, the formal structural rationalizations under the aegis of the provincial farming committees went much more slowly than expected—statistics show a slow reduction in the number of incomplete farms and a small rise in basic farms, but hardly any increase in model farms. At the same time there was a rapid movement of labor away from agriculture.

However, those who moved did not wish to sell their land; they, and those who stayed on but changed occupations, leased out their land to neighbors or worked it themselves extensively, as part-time farmers, and without livestock. The steady increase in the number of tractors eased transport and thereby made possible short-term, uncontrolled leasing, often with only verbal contracts. Longer-term contracts by law involved the landowners in various kinds of obligations. This led to a fairly unplanned, unstable, and irrational cultivation structure. According to the Agricultural Committee's calculations, three-quarters of land completion up to the beginning of the 1960s occurred through leasing and only one-quarter through land acquisition. The reasons for this were the restrictive acquisition legislation and the reluctance of absent owners to part with their land when their incomes in their new occupations were good enough so that they were not forced to sell. The old farm had both an emotional and a security value.

The distortion of the rationalization drive resulting from the all too static structural policy can be tellingly illustrated by the Agricultural Committee's calculations of the returns on different production inputs. From the end of the 1930s to the end of the 1950s inputs of machines, fodder, and fertilizer tripled, while those of labor diminished by 25 percent. At the end of the period returns from increased inputs of labor and machines were less than half of what was invested—that is, there were considerable losses—while increased investments in farm land and animals gave a profit three and five times above the investments, respectively. All this clearly indicates overmechanization, too little acreage, and buildings of too small a size in the individual enterprises.[59]

AGRICULTURE—ALSO A BRANCH OF INDUSTRY

The most important result of the Agricultural Committee's inquiry would seem to be that it applied a modern economic view to agriculture. Its proposals aimed *to facilitate the adaptation of agriculture* to economic development instead of what was in many respects attempted before, namely, *to shield it from pressures to adapt.* The new orientation meant that society did not protect industries or enterprises from the consequences of long-term structural change (protection from temporary difficulties might, on the other hand, be justified in order to prevent destruction of capital). People, however, could be protected, helped, and supported through the necessary process of adaptation. The committee also asserted that the income goals of agriculture and the labor movement's policy of wage solidarity, often considered counterparts, were in fact very different. The latter puts pressure on the enterprise's economy and thereby compels structural change, while the former guarantees profitability and thereby tends to be structurally conservative.

Since production surpluses became a growing problem for agricultural policy during the 1970s and 1980s, it is interesting to note that the Agricultural Committee thought that the push for self-sufficiency could be reduced considerably without jeopardizing supply preparedness; what should be striven for was a production that, with a normal harvest, would satisfy 80 percent of the population's calorie requirements. This reduction was reckoned to have been achieved toward the end of the 1970s.

With an actual degree of self-sufficiency of 95 percent and strong tendencies toward increasing production, it was necessary according to the committee to observe great caution in using price setting to attain income goals. Tendencies toward rising production were caused by rapid technical development and by the fact that the structural situation made increasing production the easiest way for farmers to increase their incomes. Possibilities for cost rationalization were extremely limited on all small farms. The committee suggested that this be compensated for with increased support for adjustments both within and outside of agriculture. But proposals for incentives and support for adjustments have always met acrimonious resistance from agricultural organizations.

The Agricultural Committee did not see any reason for setting an upper acreage limit for rationalization. The family farm was still to provide the norm, but such farms came to look very different from those that had originally been discussed.

The New Agricultural Policy

While the Agricultural Committee was conducting its inquiry, the SAP appointed its own agricultural policy group in 1963, chaired by the agriculture minister, Eric Holmqvist. The group drafted an agricultural program, the New Agricultural Policy, which was approved by the party executive and presented in March 1966 together with the committee's work. The SAP program largely concurred with the committee's proposals, and on those points where the inquiry was not unanimous the SAP agreed with the consumer representatives.

The committee's proposals and the SAP program were met by extremely harsh criticism from agricultural organizations. In the local elections in 1966 the SAP had its worst showing since the war, especially in rural areas. In the postelection analyses carried out by the party executive and the parliamentary group, agricultural policy was not deemed very important for the election failures.[60] However, in the opinion of many the program was too consumer-oriented—experience shows that being pro-consumer gives few political returns—and too little emphasis was placed on the advantages for farmers in the new policy. The 1966 election results show that agriculture still had a strong hold on Swedish opinion, despite the fact that only a small percentage of the population was directly employed in it.

The 1966 election losses prompted self-examination within the SAP and concentration on a more thought-out and consistent industrial policy. This became the main theme of the extra party conference in 1967, in which agricultural policy was seen as part of this industrial policy: the same conditions and demands would be placed on agriculture as on all other branches of the economy. Preparedness for blockades was no longer exclusively an agricultural problem; through increasing international economic ties there were many socially necessary enterprises that were dependent upon foreign supply at the same time as agriculture also became increasingly dependent upon imported means of production, not least on fuel.

Agriculture in European Integration

At about the same time, questions concerning European integration became prominent. In the Common Market, agricultural policy (CAP) together with the coal and steel industries were from the beginning the most important economic issues, while agriculture was totally excluded from discussions in the EFTA.

For its agricultural policy the EEC chose a system of regulations that to a great extent copied the Swedish system—despite expressed warnings. The agricultural population should, according to the Treaty of Rome, be ensured of a just or reasonable living standard, to be achieved partly through price supports and partly through rationalization of production. I myself indicated in 1962 that the critical question for Swedish agriculture with reference to links with the EEC was what price levels would prevail.[61] This assessment is still relevant.

When the party executive discussed EEC issues in September 1961, Erlander underlined that upon joining there would be no question of conducting a national agricultural policy. However, he also indicated that the prerequisites for carrying on farming in Sweden "within certain areas" would probably be reasonable, perhaps even favorable. In a report given to the parliamentary group in December 1967, the conclusion was that the only problem was price levels, which at that time were higher in Sweden. The form or organization of the CAP presented no problems.

THE THIRD PHASE OF AGRICULTURAL POLICY

Industrial expansion in Sweden during the 1960s exceeded that of the 1950s. Industrial wages rose on average 9 percent annually, and productivity by over 8 percent. This made it even more difficult for agriculture to keep pace in income development. When a decision in 1967 abolished all size limits in rationalization, the number of farms diminished rapidly. The number of milk producers dropped by one-fourth in three years. This led to increased production of cereals and pork, resulting in large surpluses. At the same time production techniques were developed that made farming even more dependent upon imported fertilizers and insect controls. The degree of self-sufficiency in cereals went from just about level in 1961/1963 to double what was required in 1971/1973. Surpluses in butter and pork also grew in the early 1970s, and this resulted in large export losses.[62]

In consideration of these rapid changes, another agricultural inquiry was begun in 1972. In light of the general agricultural policy goals decided on in the 1967 Riksdag, the inquiry was to examine questions such as the extent of production, the system of price regulation, and the form of rationalization supports. This inquiry reported its findings shortly after the change of government in September 1976. Its results could be described as a survey of agricultural policy; the inquiry proposed no changes in goals or fundamental guidelines. Under the influence of a certain scarcity of food-stuffs on world markets in the beginning of the 1970s, with sharply rising prices and the anxiety felt in these markets because of the oil crisis, the need for supply preparedness was strongly stressed in the conservative government's agricultural program of 1977. Also stressed was the need to provide poor countries with food. Svante Lundqvist, the SAP's shadow agricultural minister, generally agreed with the government's position but claimed that the conservative government wished to create polarizations in agricultural policy through formulations indicating that producer interests should take precedence over those of the consumers.[63]

World market scarcity, however, proved to be caused largely by speculation, and the problem of surpluses returned with a vengeance during the 1980s. When the checks on rationalization were abolished in 1967, the technical developments in agriculture already referred to got a second wind. This led to large surpluses, but in the long run the most significant aspects of development were its environmental effects—both in terms of actual content of foreign substances in products and the spread of such substances in the environment. Environmental effects had already necessitated certain specific measures—for instance, against disinfectants with a high quicksilver content and against DDT—but from the end of the 1970s onward there was more of a general reaction to the environmental effects of agriculture. This reaction provoked an investigation of food production in 1983.

With the 1980s agricultural policy seems to have entered an entirely new phase. Raw material production is now a small branch of industry; processing and the distribution of raw materials are much larger. However, agriculture is now a major issue because of its effects on the environment and because of its role vis-à-vis European integration. About these questions it is still too early to write history; they are in brutal collision with a public opinion still bound to the past and its values but also intensely worried about new developments. The dimensions of the problems and the political difficulties faced in trying to cope with them guarantee that agricultural policy will continue to have a pivotal position in the SAP. Berndt Ahlqvist has put it in a nutshell:

> To produce grain which we do not need and which causes the national economy great economic losses, we stuff the land with nitrogen. This nitrogen then leaks out into the sea and contributes to

poisonous algae proliferating over huge areas, causing ecological catastrophes of a hitherto unknown extent.

This is about nothing less than state-subsidized madness.[61]

NOTES

1. Seppo Hentilä points out that the German SPD's *Erfurtprogram* in agriculture was not a "Marxist" interpretation of Marx and Engels but was based on Kautsky's economic determinism. Referring to Marx's criticism of the Gotha Programme, Hentilä claims that the program was positive toward small farmers as members of the oppressed proletariat. Hentilä 1979, 209.

2. Branting, 1:196–98.

3. Tingsten 1941, 1:142.

4. However, at SAP conferences individual voices were raised reminding the conference of the importance of the agricultural population. As early as during the constitutional conference in 1889 members of Hedared's Social Democratic Association and Ystad's Workers' Club asked: "In what way should the workers on the land best be organized?" At the 1891 conference Norberg's mine workers' union, represented by Hjalmar Branting, asserted that "the party must broaden its work in organizing Sweden's miners and agricultural workers." *SAP Conference Minutes* 1889 and 1891.

5. Björlin 1974, 76–78. Björlin claims that Branting was disappointed by the fact that, because of Kautsky's dominance, the German Breslau conference gave no lead in this dilemma; it rejected the "revisionist" proposals that had been drawn up by a special agricultural committee.

6. Simonson (1985) especially stresses the importance of the issue of universal suffrage and its associated strategies for the SAP's attitudes toward agricultural policy around the turn of the century.

7. Ibid., 179.

8. *SAP Executive Minutes*, 6 Dec. 1908.

9. Ibid., 1909 and 1910.

10. Gellerman 1958, 202–4. Gellerman states that "one finds a shift in the motivation of the motion and indications of pressures which suggest that the party was forced to abandon its attacks on food tariffs. . . . The ideal of free trade envisioned by various Social Democratic representatives glided further and further away from realistic policy."

11. Ibid., 166.

12. Ibid., 64.

13. Björlin 1974, 74–76.

14. J. Juréen, Unpublished calculations for the 1942 Agricultural Committee, table 10:4, p. 197 (National Archives).

15. Prawitz 1951, 39.

16. Gellerman 1958, 157–58.

17. Simonson 1985, 184.

18. Tingsten 1941, 1:215. According to Björlin (1974), Lindhagen entered the workers' party "not because his view of society was socialist, but because the policies he embraced had the greatest chances of being heard in the Social Democratic arena."

19. *SAP Conference Minutes* 1911.

20. The 1911 conference decision has been variously interpreted. Tingsten claims that

"ideologically, the Social Democrats ceased to perform as a workers' party in the sense they claimed to be." Like Tingsten, Gellerman refers to a victory for Lindhagen but also claims that his contributions to the land question "did not cause land policy to deviate from those guidelines that had previously been drawn up in the party manifesto, which distinguishes itself from the previous years' by being much more active." Björlin states that "non-Marxist ideas began to be more deeply entrenched in Social Democracy," a set of ideas that to a certain extent can be traced back to Lindhagen personally and his activities in parliament. In direct contrast to this, Hentilä (in accord with Simonson) claims that the 1911 conference brought the SAP closer to Marxism. This claim is based on Hentilä's view that the SAP's former position on the land issue was "Kautskyist" and not Marxist, and that Marx in fact saw small farmers as allies of the proletariat. At the same time Hentilä also claims that Lindhagen's and Palmstierna's membership in the party was more "a sign that SAP was prepared to accept contributions from the radical bourgeois reform programme."

21. Prawitz 1951, 72–73.

22. Hans Georg Lehmann, *Die Agrarfrage in der Theorie und Praxis der deutschen und internationalen Sozialdemokratie* (Tübingen, 1970). In Simonson 1985, 261.

23. Tingsten 1941, 1:304–5.

24. Hellström 1976, 150.

25. Sköld 1926a.

26. Ibid., 225.

27. Hellström 1976, 176.

28. Ibid., 159–61, 167.

29. *SAP Executive Minutes* 15 Nov. 1928.

30. Ibid., 20 and 21 Nov. 1929.

31. Ibid., 1932.

32. Hellström 1976, 484–86.

33. Riksdagen, *Minutes of the Second Chamber*, 1933:14.

34. Wigforss, *Minnen* (Memoirs), vol. 3, 1954, 37–39.

35. Lewin 1967, 78–79.

36. Prawitz 1951, 73; Sköld 1926b, 148.

37. Prawitz 1951, 65–67; Sköld 1926b, 148.

38. *SAP Executive Minutes* 21 and 22 Apr. 1918.

39. *SAP Conference Minutes* 1932, 104.

40. *SAP Executive Minutes*, 29 Oct. 1935.

41. *SAP Conference Minutes* 1932, 104.

42. Bonow 1935, 247–48.

43. G. Myrdal 1938, 121–23.

44. *The Labor Movement's Post-War Programme* 1944, 15, 24–25.

45. *SAP Conference Minutes* 1952, 328.

46. For a complete discussion of this, see, e.g., Odhner 1953 and Nordlander 1946.

47. Sköld 1926a.

48. There is some difference of opinion as to what the Agricultural Committee actually proposed for the external rationalization. On the one hand it is said that in principle it should be confined to the farms "below the level of basic farm units" (SOU 1946:42, p. 51), while on the other (p. 153) the committee in principle advises that, when a choice is possible, priority be given to creating "model farms."

49. *SAP Executive Minutes* 9 Dec. 1945 and the Social Democratic parliamentary group's *Minutes* 1 June 1944 (Labor Movement Archives).

50. Odhner 1946, 499.

51. Abbreviation of *Bondeförbundet*, the name of the Agrarian party.

52. Sköld's notes in Jonasson 1976, 140.

53. Erlander 1973, 313–14.

54. *SAP Executive Minutes* 26 Sept. 1951.

55. *SAP Conference Minutes* 1951, 332.

56. These papers are in the collections of the present author.

57. LO *Annual Report* 1957, 252–53.

58. Edgren, Faxén, and Odhner 1970, 256–57.

59. Odhner 1966, 25–27.

60. *SAP Executive Minutes* 1 Oct. 1966 and the Social Democratic Parliamentary Group *Minutes* 11 Oct. 1966.

61. Odhner 1962, 62.

62. Hedlund and Lundahl 1985, 119.

63. Riksdagen, *Minutes from the Second Chamber*, 1977:54.

64. B. Ahlqvist in *Östra Småland*, 28 May 1988.

Ann-Sofie Ohlander

7

The Invisible Child?
The Struggle over
Social Democratic
Family Policy

A CONFLICT WITHIN THE LABOR MOVEMENT

In 1900 a new Workers' Protection Act was passed in Sweden. One of its paragraphs particularly concerned women with children and may be considered as the first instance of legislated family policy in Sweden: "As regards work in the industrial occupations, a woman who has had a child may not be employed during the first four weeks after the birth, unless it is confirmed by a medical certificate that she can without harm begin to work earlier."[1] Women employed in factories were thus not allowed to work for four weeks after giving birth. The law was meant to take consideration of the woman's and infant's need for rest, and to allow the mother to nurse her baby. However, there was no economic compensation for this compulsory leave, so it became an infringement upon the welfare of the woman and her child. Indeed, the presence of a male breadwinner was tacitly assumed; but in practice many women supported their families alone, and in those cases where both the man and woman worked, the woman's income was often essential for the family's meager existence.

It would take no less than thirty years to redress this anomaly. The regulations on mandatory leave after the birth of a child remained—the time was even extended to six weeks in 1912. However, a law covering maternity insurance, which gave the mother economic support during this time, was not passed until 1931.

The history of maternity benefits is not only interesting per se as an important family policy measure; it also illustrates a fundamental (and still existent) problem in Swedish and Social Democratic family policy. The formation of a law giving postnatal maternity leave without economic compensation is indicative of a particular social mechanism of oppression that seems to be a continually recurring element in family policy. At the turn of the century it was considered essential that mothers be given time to nurse and look after their babies in order to reduce infant mortality—hence the regulations in the Workers' Protection Act. However, at the time there was also a current of opinion condemning women as morally responsible for infant deaths. Through information and supervision these mothers were to learn to nurse their babies and care for them in a more hygienic way. Thus, often in practice—as in the legislation under discussion—the almost insurmountable difficulties many mothers faced in supporting and looking after their children were ignored. Mothers were at once seen as responsible and dependent: they were given the responsibility for the welfare of their children, while being economically and legally dependent and unfairly treated in a way that made it difficult to bear that responsibility.

Women were exposed to a profoundly contradictory definition. They were compelled to contain, and in some way in their own private lives to resolve, a basically social conflict, and one that ultimately stemmed from a denial of parenthood, care, and upbringing as *socially* existent, a denial of reproduction—or in other words, of the foundation for the continued existence of society.

To be at once powerless and held responsible for what one has no power over is most assuredly a common social mechanism of oppression. Only when this conflict is released, "externalized" from its bearers, and becomes visible—social in a real sense—can it be resolved. It is part and parcel of such a conflict that it is often unacknowledged, and it can therefore be difficult to perceive in a historical context or to verify in historical sources.

The conflict between parenthood and earning a living, which mainly takes place in women's (mothers') lives according to the view presented here, is the fundamental point of departure for an analysis of Swedish and

Social Democratic family policy in the twentieth century. This conflict not only occurs *between* political parties but also *within* them—in the present case, in the Social Democratic Labor Party. To put it simply, the conflict may be seen as a struggle, primarily on the part of women, to politicize and make visible this whole socially suppressed side of reality.

A POLICY OF MOTHERHOOD OR OF FAMILY

The Concept of Family Policy

Family policy is a generally accepted and commonly used expression, and it may seem a bit surprising that in the present context, it is fairly new in the Swedish language. According to the Advisory Council for Swedish Terminology and Usage the term was first used in its modern sense in 1948 in an article in the newspaper *Morgonbladet*.[2]

During earlier periods *family policy* was basically equivalent to two different terms. One was *maternal policy*, which was used from the beginning of the twentieth century onward. Later, during the 1930s, *population policy* became the relevant term for much of what is presently encompassed by family policy. Population policy went out of fashion after World War II when the content and consequences of the term in Nazi Germany were revealed.

When the term *family policy* began to be used, it was partly a way to avoid using the word *population*, but it also expressed a view that not only the woman/mother but also the man/father could be considered as a more direct participant in the care of the family and of children. In official contexts the term appeared in the 1950s. In 1965 it was used to designate an inquiry, the Family Policy Committee, which was appointed by the Social Democratic government with Ulla Lindström, minister of the Department for Social Affairs, as chair. The term first appeared in a Social Democratic Labor Party program in 1960, in which an "active family policy" was one of the program points.[3]

The second chapter of the Family Policy Committee's report dealt with "Society's Support for Families," and the subtitles contained the basic elements of this support: universal child allowance, housing allowance, study aid, allowance advances, household loans to newly married couples, tax reliefs, services to families with children such as nurseries and babysitters, and protective legislation mainly in connection with the institution of child welfare officers.[4] This list constitutes a de facto definition of family policy, to which must be added policies having to do with pregnancy, birth, and postnatal leave, regulations on working hours for parents of small children, and the like.

I have chosen preliminarily to use the Family Policy Committee's definition and to complement my discussion by taking up questions concerning pregnancy, birth, and infant care for historical analysis. However, with such an analysis it is important to recall that the Swedish family has undergone enormous changes over the past century, judicial as well as practical.

The Changing Swedish Family

During the eighteenth century, marriage was the normal condition for all members of the Swedish population. At the same time, average life expectancy was low, about thirty-five years; many became widows or widowers, and the rate of remarriage was high. In the nineteenth century, the unmarried members of the population increased in number, and large groups remained unmarried for the duration of their lives. Among women born during the 1870s, one-fourth never married.[5]

During the twentieth century, the marriage rate increased again and the average marriage age decreased; to be married was again the general life pattern. During the 1960s a marked rise in common-law marriages occurred—a kind of privatization of marriage. The approbation of society was no longer necessary to form a family, and correspondingly society's interest in controlling family formation diminished.

Divorce was very unusual in Sweden during the nineteenth century, and the relevant laws were also very restrictive. Despite this, at the end of the century there was a slight increase in divorces, and after new, more liberal marriage laws were passed in 1915 the number of divorces rose sharply. This rise continued steadily and was further accentuated after the even greater liberalization of marriage laws in 1970.

During the nineteenth century fertility was very high, but many infants died during their first year of life—in 1900 as many as one-tenth. However, there followed a marked decrease in infant mortality in Sweden, and by the 1930s levels were among the lowest in the world. Toward the end of the nineteenth century a new significant change in the family pattern took place: birth control began to be practiced. Around the turn of the century, families had an average of four children, but in the 1930s the number had dropped to two children or less. Even today in Sweden, one or two children per family is common.

However, the use of birth control was met with stiff resistance, especially from conservative groups. As a consequence of this, a law was passed in 1910 that forbade information on and sales of contraceptives; it lasted until 1938. Abortion legislation also ought to be mentioned in this context. Very stringent and restrictive laws governing abortion were in force until 1938; a real liberalization of abortion legislation did not occur until 1974.

Children born out of wedlock and their mothers found themselves in a very difficult social situation. They were penalized in various ways by society at large and in their immediate environment, and the sanctions did not cease until well into the twentieth century. Mortality among children born out of wedlock was also for a long time much higher than among children born within a marriage. Important improvements in the condition of the former and their mothers came in 1905 when children were granted inheritance rights from their mothers, and in 1917 when the mothers received state support in their efforts to obtain maintenance from the fathers and the child welfare officer institution was created to safeguard the interests of mother and child.

Widows with children were also burdened with the sole responsibility for their families, as were wives of men who for various reasons could not work or who had abandoned their families. In an investigation from the turn of the century in Stockholm, it was calculated that about one-third of all families in the city consisted of mothers alone with their children. If the focus had been exclusively on the lower social strata, the figure would certainly be even higher.

Marriage and family patterns were not the same throughout the whole population. As early as the nineteenth century, among the poorer, propertyless groups in the countryside and in the cities, men and women lived together without being married; it was common for people to be expecting or to have children before marriage. The authorities often had little success trying to get these relationships legalized. In this regard, there was a clear difference between upper- and middle-class patterns, which contained tight internal controls over marriage and premarital cohabitation, and the working-class pattern in which social control and middle-class conventions were less powerful. These differences were maintained into the 1930s. Investigating that period, I have found it reasonable to interpret these differences as indications of working-class nonconformity with the ruling class in society—indeed, perhaps a protest against official and conventional forms of cohabitation.[6]

Early Social Democratic Family Policy

In the earliest Social Democratic Labor Party programs there were only a few points that fall under what could be defined as family policy. One was point twelve of the municipal program from 1900 concerning "the establishment of municipal and school kitchens for the provision of good and nutritious food at the cheapest prices; the introduction of free meals for school children upon the request of their parents. . . ." This point recurred in the 1901 and 1905 slightly revised versions of the 1897 program, with the addition that holiday camps should be started for city children who were frail or ailing. Demands for school doctors, free medicine, and arrangements for sports, play, and physical training were added in 1908.

These early points still involve family policy interests in only a limited sense. However, the corresponding point in the 1911 program was significantly expanded:

> For the protection and care of women and the new generation, maternity hospitals and homes for mothers prior to and after delivery will be established. Local authority bureaus for the safeguarding of the mothers' and children's rights. When required, support will be given to assist mothers to nurse their children themselves. Compulsory medical care for all children during the first years of their lives. Through publicly provided infant clinics, nurseries and mandatory feeding of undernourished children, local authorities are to monitor the health of the growing members of families. Provision of camps in the countryside for frail children. Expansion of the powers of child-care and fostering authorities.

This was a total program, which in contrast to previous efforts concentrated on central family policy elements such as maternity and infant care, nursing, medical care, and the difficult circumstances of foster children. Only mothers were mentioned, albeit with a certain patriarchal tone—"care and protection"; the point concerned maternity policy, not family policy.

What were the sources of this program point? Without doubt, one important background element was a motion that the local party branch (*arbetarekommun*) in Malmö contributed to the 1905 party conference. The motion originated with the Malmö Social Democratic women's discussion club and called for measures to help unmarried, abandoned, and destitute mothers. In the debate at the party conference Elma Danielsson and Anna Sterky, who was in charge of the Women's Trade Union (existing from 1902 to 1909), claimed that a man who abandoned a woman carrying his child should be equated with a strikebreaker who betrays his comrades. They were supported by F. V. Thorsson, member of the Second Chamber of the Riksdag.[7] Here the women took the initiative. And it was among the Social Democratic women's groups that maternal policy demands were made—in other party political contexts, women were conspicuous by their absence.

At about the same time, Social Democratic women began to organize their activities on a national level.[8] Formally, the National Federation of Social Democratic Women came into being in 1920 when it was clear that Swedish women would obtain the right to vote and to be represented in the Riksdag the following year. Women's organizations also arose in the Liberal and Conservative parties. However, in practice the Social Democratic women's federation had been active for a long time in local women's clubs and nationwide women's conferences.

At the first of these conferences, which was held in 1907, four motions were presented concerning the improvement of the situation for single mothers. Three of the motions applied only to unmarried mothers and their children. The doctor Alma Sundqvist, who also worked energetically against prostitution, gave an introductory speech in which she proposed comprehensive measures to legally and economically ease the circumstances of these mothers.[9]

The Social Democratic women focused their demands on precisely that point in which the conflict between women's double burdens of care and breadwinning was most obvious—the issue of unmarried mothers. It is worth noting too that they expressed themselves without any moralizing overtones, except in references to the fathers who abandoned their children. The legal and social situation of unwed mothers and their children was at that time still ridden with injustices and prejudices. In his study of the policies of poor relief agencies toward single mothers in Gävle in 1910, Jan Gröndahl has pointed out that widows with small children were treated significantly better than unmarried mothers and their children. The children of the latter were often forcibly separated from their mothers.[10]

The Social Democratic women's support for unwed mothers also had another side—a radical view of marriage. Christina Carlsson, who has analyzed an earlier Swedish Social Democratic view of women and relevant policies in her doctoral dissertation, claims that the motions of 1907 ultimately made motherhood viable outside of marriage.[11] This was to be achieved in two ways: making fathers assume their responsibilities, and promoting state intervention. The Social Democratic Women's conference in 1907 also adopted a resolution demanding that women be awarded the right to take the oath in paternity suits; that the state provide a child support allowance, graduated according to the incomes of both parents; and that mother and child be able to obtain support through public means—and not poor relief—when the father did not fulfill his obligations.

Some conference participants went even further: for instance, Ruth Gustafsson (later one of the first female Social Democratic members of the Riksdag) made an appeal for "free marriages." According to an article in *Morgonbris* in 1908, "marriages of conscience" ought to be pursued in order to avoid the humiliating marriage laws that placed the married woman under the guardianship of the man. It is worth recalling that a married woman was still legally a minor until 1920. However, according to Christina Carlsson, it is difficult to know how established such a radical view was among Social Democratic women in general.[12]

Maternity insurance was on the agenda at the 1907 SAP women's conference. The women had tried to find a male speaker on this issue, but failed. Ruth Gustafsson made a general address: "It is not charity we should be promoting but rights for all, and we should be working on reforms that will give our children the possibility of living sound and happy lives."[13] Once the voting rights proposal was accepted, women would be able to sit on local councils and from there work further with these questions. A motion on maternity insurance was adopted without debate by the conference.

In 1908 the question of maternity insurance came up in the Riksdag—did the Social Democratic women's initiative perhaps exert influence? Yet the physician and social politician Edvard Wavrinsky's motion in the Riksdag was criticized for being too limited by a writer in *Morgonbris*. The anonymous writer asserted that men's and women's liberation rested upon economic independence, which ought to be realized through public provisions. A general maternal insurance was called for, independent of civil status, occupation, or social class and awarded until the children were able to support themselves. According to the writer, to give birth to, care for, and bring up children was as much employment as were the paid occupations.[14]

This is a radical point of view, which attempts to expose and politicize that conflict between support and care that I initially claimed was fundamental for a historical understanding of family policy as a whole. Such a point of view was very far from that held by the members of the parliamentary committee that in 1911 presented an extremely narrow proposal for maternal insurance. Even though the proposal was approved by the Riksdag in 1912, it was quickly annulled by the Law Council, which rejected it as unconstitutional. As mentioned earlier, not until 1931 was a law on maternal insurance finally passed.[15]

Efforts to attain independence for women/mothers and demands for family support from fathers are recurring themes in Social Democratic women's political activities. In 1910 the Social Democratic Women's Club in Norrköping presented a motion at the second International Social Democratic Women's conference, which uncompromisingly articulated demands for labor parties to show solidarity with women and "stamp all men who have abandoned the mothers of their children as pure and simple traitors." However, the motion was not even considered at the conference. An article in *Socialdemokraten* dismissed the proposal as absurd.[16]

According to Christina Carlsson, in questions relating to single, unwed mothers, conflicts with the men within the party were particularly evident. Carlsson also states that the Social Democratic women's views on motherhood and marriage were far more radical than those of women in the bourgeois women's movement. However, the Social Democratic women had difficulties getting the attention of their male colleagues, even if there were exceptions.[17]

The Social Democratic women's demands for justice and support for single mothers were repeated at the women's conferences in 1908, 1911, and 1914.[18] For example, in 1908 the "foster child industry" came up for discussion. To oppose this industry, it was demanded that mothers should have the opportunity to care for their own children, and in particular that single mothers should receive a child care allowance through the maternal insurance benefit; that the children's fathers should fulfill their obligations; and that homes for single mothers and their children as well as nurseries and crèches should be created.[19]

Noted with approval in the annual reports from conference period 1917–1919 was the new legislation from 1917 that improved the legal standing of unwed mothers and their children. Noted as well were the new, more liberal marriage laws passed in 1915.[20]

Social Democratic politicians also returned to the maternal insurance issue several times, even if there were no results until 1931 (and those under a Liberal government). In 1914 the Social Democrats Erik Palmstierna and Gustaf Steffen presented motions on maternal insurance to both chambers of the Riksdag.[21] The authors called for better care of women in confinement and newborn children. In due course the motions were handed over to the "maternal insurance experts" in 1926. Kerstin Hesselgren (chosen by both Social Democrats and Liberals) and Agda Östlund (Social Democrat) placed a motion on maternal aid in the Riksdag in 1924. Later Kerstin Hesselgren became chairman of the 1926 committee on maternal insurance; the work of this committee gradually led to the law of 1931. In the interim, SAP member Signe Vessman, among others, had also presented a motion on the issue in 1928.[22]

Not surprisingly, the first Social Democratic women in the Riksdag engaged themselves in the maternal insurance issue. They had the backing of the National Federation of Social Democratic Women in the Riksdag. However, the party as a whole devoted little attention to the subject. In 1928 the Municipal Program was revised, and the former point six became point seven, abridged as follows:

> Compulsory medical care for infants. Instruction in child care. Children's health centers, homes for unwed mothers with infants; summer camps and nurseries and crèches to be set up. Support for needy mothers during nursing.

In the debates in the Social Democratic parliamentary group, questions concerning maternity benefits and family policy in general were conspicuous by their absence. The social insurance question was defined in the parliamentary group in 1926 to include sickness, accident, and unemployment benefits. In 1928 Gustav Möller opened in the parliamentary group with "the social insurance questions—unemployment, sickness and basic pension." Great attention was paid to the question of unemployment. Maternity policy was first mentioned in the minutes of June 1930, where it was noted that the proposal for maternity insurance was basically in accordance with the committee proposal.[23]

Perhaps the weight given by the party to unemployment issues during the 1920s and 1930s could be contrasted with that given to maternal benefit issues, questions involving women and children. It may be a way of analyzing to what extent Social Democratic politics were primarily politics for men—Social Democratic women did not have the numbers to assert themselves in the party, nor were they able to be successful in those issues they considered important.

The statements of family policy given in the 1928 party program remained for a long time unrevised in the Municipal Program. However, in the main program manifesto of 1944 family policy cropped up as point thirteen:

Support for the creation of families and households. Society guarantees good and spacious housing at reasonable prices for families with children. Measures which ease work in the home and child care and upbringing. Social measures for reducing the burden of supporting children.

However, the program item in fact arrived rather belatedly, since the 1930s marked the breakthrough of Social Democratic family policy—albeit not designated in terms of maternal benefits, but rather in terms of population policy.

FAMILY POLICY AS POPULATION POLICY

As already mentioned, population policy appeared in political debates as early as the turn of the century. However, the arguments scarcely met with approval from the Social Democratic party. Gunnar and Alva Myrdal's complete volte-face and the way the issue came to mark the earlier question of maternity insurance were quite new, creating confusion and sometimes indignation among those who had formerly stood for a Social Democratic point of view. However, some approved: Social Affairs Minister Gustav Möller viewed the arguments concerning population policy as tactical, as providing a way of getting the bourgeois parties to accept pressing social reforms.[24]

Crisis in the Population Question
The Social Democratic women obviously felt taken unawares when Alva and Gunnar Myrdal, in their book *Kris i befolkningsfrågan* (1934; Nation and Family, 1941), at a single stroke gave the old, typical women's issues a new legitimacy and a new guise.

This can be illustrated by the abortion issue. In 1935 a committee appointed by the minister of justice presented a proposal on abortion legislation that acknowledged social grounds for abortion. The proposal was approved by the National Federation of Social Democratic Women, but when made public it was met by a storm of protest. The Myrdals' ideas about population were pitted against the proposal. "Those who most eagerly fought for a humanizing of the law on abortion, which the Social Democratic women had always done, now appeared as less responsible vis-à-vis questions of fertility," writes Hulda Flood, historian of the Social Democratic women's movement.[25]

A new abortion law was passed in 1938. It included no social grounds for abortion, clearly a result of a round of consultation in which the 1935 Population Commission had categorically reproved social reasons as grounds for abortion. It was felt that such an extension of the legislation would increase the number of abortions and hinder the quantitative goals of the pronatalist population policy.[26] The 1935 Population Commission advocated several other family policy measures, even if most of the proposals in the commission's report and eighteen other papers were rejected.

In 1937 housing loans were established with the quantitative aim of encouraging earlier marriages, thereby extending the fertile period of married women and attaining higher birthrates. One finds both quantitative and qualitative population arguments behind the 1937 law on maternal aid for new mothers in particular need of help. The measure was so overwhelmingly utilized that the originally allocated sums were exceeded many times over. Poverty among Swedish mothers had clearly escaped the notice of politicians. Another law came into existence that also provided a relatively modest allowance to more or less all women who had children. The decision to build residential blocks for large families in difficult economic circumstances was part of this package. In 1938 an important law was passed forbidding employers from dismissing women employees on grounds of pregnancy, and in the same year the 1910 law against the sale of contraceptives was abolished—the principle of voluntary parenthood would now prevail.[27]

New Family Policy Measures

Thus, population considerations motivated the focus on family policy ideas and measures during the 1930s. The same political lines were continued in the Population Inquiry set up in 1941. The main result of the inquiry was the introduction of universal child allowances in 1948.[28]

From the perspective of population policy the individual is seen as a means rather than an end, and therein lies a profound conundrum for every democratic society. However, it is obvious that many Social Democrats did not share the Myrdals' policy views but concurred with Gustav Möller that population policy should be used as a tactic to carry out social reforms. The same tactical motivations behind accepting population policy ideas were also held by the Norwegian *Arbeiderpartiet* at this time.[29]

What did the views of population policy mean for those to whom it most applied—women and children? I have earlier referred to the negative responses from the National Federation of Social Democratic Women to the effects of the "population question" on abortion laws. Another negative effect pointed out by historian Louise Drangel was that the maternity benefits of 1931 disappeared with the advent of maternal aid. This meant that new mothers working outside the home no longer received an allowance during postnatal maternity leave.[30]

However, the policy also held significant improvements for women and children—that married women could no longer be dismissed because of pregnancy was one such positive measure. It was also very important that maternal aid, maternity insurance, and, later, the child allowance were paid to the *mothers*. In this respect, the Scandinavian countries and England seem to be unique; in other European countries family benefits normally went to the father, or took the form of tax deductions from the father's income. The sociologist Helga Hernes has asserted that this aspect of Scandinavian family policy contained an emancipating factor for women, who through receiving these benefits were able to have a real, if limited, influence over the family's economy.[31] In a conference on maternal aid in 1939 it was also pointed out that, particularly in the countryside, for married women to be responsible for money was altogether novel.[32]

For the Social Democratic women, the fact that women received these allowances directly was an important factor in their support for benefits instead of reduced taxes. In a statement to the Ministry of Social Affairs concerning the 1954 Family Inquiry report, it was said that

> in the opinion poll carried out in the Federation, the social and psychological value of paying the allowance directly to the mother has been particularly emphasized. Raising standards of living through some form of deduction for children and a consequent tax reduction for families cannot be considered an equivalent contribution toward the support of the children.[33]

Children were still the woman's responsibility: no assumption of responsibility on the part of the man/husband was to be expected. Financial support paid to women was thus only logical. The problem of women's sole responsibility for children and simultaneous economic powerlessness was the same as at the turn of the century—still unchanged and unresolved.

The Social Democratic women's mixed feelings about population policy concerns for fertility in the 1930s and 1940s recurred, this time sharply articulated. In conjunction with the appointment of the Population Inquiry in 1941, the Federation of Social Democratic Women circulated a questionnaire about the population issue among their members.[34] Among other things, the federation wanted to know whether this issue required "an altered attitude toward life," a new view of children and the family.

Of the local groups that replied to this question, 13 were positive but no less than 135 were negative, with the recurring argument that such a view was undemocratic. The responses contain expressive denunciations: "No dictatorship, no children by order"; "We cannot agree that people should have children as a duty to society"; "As Social Democrats we cannot agree to the new ways of life indicated. . . . Society cannot be an end in itself, and its members must live a humane and worthy life. . . . We still claim that the individual is primary and society, secondary"; "We believe that a woman should decide herself whether to have children. She should have interests and tasks in society other than simply functioning as a machine for the procreation of children"; "An attitude toward life which causes people to disregard their own welfare in favor of fulfilling their duties to society can never be accepted by Social Democratic women. We shall decide ourselves whether we will have children, and if so, how many." In these utterances the Social Democratic women were very consciously safeguarding central democratic values, and were presumably more conscious in this regard than many of their contemporary male party colleagues.

THE RISE OF THE MODERN FAMILY POLICY

The next revision of the Social Democratic party program occurred at the party's twenty-first conference in 1960. Point twenty-five included the following:

> Active family policy. A society more favorable to children.
> Support for families with children.
> Support for parents in the task of bringing up children.
> Family counseling and sexual information.
> Housewives' work load diminished through rationalizing housework.[35]

Again, the change in the program may be seen as an afterthought. It is worth noting that rationalization—not increased participation on the part of men—was seen as the solution for easing women's work in the home. It would be awhile before the notion of practical contributions from men toward domestic and parental responsibilities made itself felt in politics.

However, the demand for increased social commitments to single-parent families entailed a breakthrough in the party program for a question that had occupied Social Democratic women since the creation of the party— the situation of single mothers and their children. This question was revisited during the 1950s, and it is significant that, in conjunction with their work in the 1954 Family Inquiry, the Social Democratic women especially emphasized the importance of improving the situation for single mothers and their children.

The Family Inquiry in 1954 was initiated by a female Social Democratic minister, Ulla Lindström, and in her own record of the inquiry's investigations she stated:

> Single mothers clearly constitute the proletariat which at present lies at the bottom of Swedish society. When *one* person cares for and supports her child, the burden consumes her strength and impoverishes her economy. The courts demand a much too small maintenance from the fathers, the wage market treats women as "coolies." It is a severely reduced standard on which children of single mothers must live.[36]

The Family Inquiry devoted a special report to single mothers, *Support for Single-Parent Families.*[37] The Federation of Social Democratic Women made the following remarks in their submission to the inquiry: "Effective social measures of various kinds to ease the burdens of single mothers are one of the most urgent tasks just now. . . . [The] Federation stresses the urgent need . . . to improve social support for the neglected group which single mothers comprise in Welfare Sweden."[38]

The situation of single mothers demonstrated that the burden of the social conflict between reproduction and production was still being borne by women—by mothers—unaltered from the turn of the century. The German historian Gisela Bock has also pointed out that during the twentieth century European women have been in a more exposed position than men socially and economically, and that this vulnerability is shared by the children.[39] During the 1950s married women in Sweden ran the risk of poverty despite raised standards of living. This hazard was implied by Ulla Lindström when she presented the Family Inquiry's report to the Social Democratic parliamentary group in March 1956. She pointed out "that the first child often gives rise to the greatest changes in a family's way of life. For instance, the mother has to stop working. . . ."[40] The woman then takes the economic risks, and this is made even more palpable if she later becomes single. Yet practical parental responsibilities for men were not a real option, not even for a feminist like Ulla Lindström.

In the parliamentary group Ulla Lindström also underlined single mothers' need for expanded social institutions such as day nurseries. In an investigation of the withdrawal of women from the labor market during the twentieth century, the Swedish professor of women's history Gunhild Kyle has shown that the expansion of day nurseries and child care institutions that actually occurred was largely steered by labor market interest in the female labor force, not by the needs of women and children.[41]

In the 1950s there was an expansion of family policy reforms, most probably connected with an improved economy. In 1955 all mothers received maternity allowances of at least 270 kronor. This benefit reduced the area of maternal aid, which was abolished in 1963 and replaced by an augmented maternal allowance of up to 1,080 kronor. The universal child allowance, initially 260 kronor, has been gradually raised, but it is not pegged to the cost of living index.

Housing policy also contained elements important for families. In 1935 the Social Housing Commission proposed—in the true spirit of population policy—that special accommodations be built for large families in impoverished circumstances ("large families" were those containing three or more children). On the basis of this proposal, the decision was made to build large family blocks, particularly in cities and counties dominated by Social Democrats.

In 1946–1948 this form of housing support was abolished and replaced by a family housing allowance to low-income families. In 1969 this was replaced by a rent allowance for families with children. Other items under family policy are preschools and schools, school health provisions, free school meals, and the like—reforms that began in the 1950s.

What role, then, did the women in the party play in the reforms of family policy? First, it must be said that their numbers in the party have remained low. In 1930 women comprised a mere 14 percent of the membership; in 1985, only 36 percent. Nineteen percent of the women in the party in 1930 were also members of the federation. That figure rose to 34 percent in 1955, but dropped again to 10 percent in 1985.

According to Gunnel Karlsson, who has written on the history of the

Federation of Social Democratic Women, both women and the federation have had perennial difficulties in asserting themselves and attaining any real influence in the party. It took a long time for women to obtain any substantial representation in the party leadership, which expected loyalty from the women but often responded negatively to political initiatives taken by female members.[42] However, Karlsson claims—and this is also confirmed by my own investigations into family policy—that the Federation of Social Democratic Women in fact often comprised something of the party's avant-garde. That it remained so in questions concerning improvements in women's and children's rights is obvious.

Also in other contexts the women's federation worked independently. Their independence was especially noticeable in the 1950s when the women opposed the party line in the nuclear arms issue. As indicated inter alia by Karl Molin in the present volume, their contributions on this issue were crucial to Sweden's decision not to become a nuclear nation.[43] During the 1940s as well, the Federation of Social Democratic Women resolutely safeguarded central democratic values, a position illustrated in my analysis of its views of population policy at that time.

When women gradually began to enter the party leadership and obtain posts in Social Democratic governments, social and family policy issues became more prominent. However, Gunnel Karlsson's assessment of the whole is that a large number of the Social Democratic reforms in practice benefited primarily the party's male voters. Yet I would claim that not least in questions of family policy, the last few decades have indicated a rising female radicalism in party policy, perhaps particularly during the period when the SAP was in opposition from 1976 to 1984.[44]

WHAT IS SPECIFICALLY SOCIAL DEMOCRATIC IN SWEDEN'S FAMILY POLICY?

In the foregoing I have discussed family policy in terms of its relation to the real situation of women and children in society, and in terms of the actions of the National Federation of Social Democratic Women. It is quite clear that the rights of women and children did not occupy a prominent position in Social Democratic politics for a long time, and that it has been very difficult for women to succeed with their demands for improving their own and their children's circumstances. Thus family policy has been very largely a question of *male* policy (often an absence of policy), or a question of a policy concerning women that has been construed in men's terms.[45] However, in this context a discussion of the specifically *Social Democratic* elements in family policy is pertinent: how were family policy proposals and solutions within the SAP affected by Social Democratic ideology and practice?

One major ingredient in Social Democratic family policy from the start was the effort to abolish inhumane poor relief institutions, to erase the detestable and humiliating "pauper's stamp" on those receiving help. "It is not charity that we should be promoting, but rights for all, and we should be working on reforms which will give our children the possibility of living sound and happy lives," said Ruth Gustafsson in 1908.

Efforts to erase the pauper's stamp were reflected in the 1930s population policy. Maternal aid, for which women in particular need were eligible, was not administered by the municipality's poor relief board but by the child welfare board, precisely in order to avoid contact with poor relief agencies. The residential blocks for large families engendered a categorization that lowered the status of the buildings and their residents. This was one of the reasons why they were abolished and replaced with housing allowances for needy families, regardless of where they lived. Extending the child allowance to *all* children without means testing was also a way to avoid the labeling of "charity cases," to create rights for individuals and obligations for society.[46]

Social Democratic ideology was also manifested in credit and financing programs. Household loans to newly married couples, initiated in 1937 to promote early marriages, were administered by the National Bank of Sweden, an institution that normally did not deal with loans to private persons. This meant that individuals did not have to apply to private commercial banks. The state loans for the building of residential blocks for large families were primarily granted to housing cooperatives or public housing companies such as the Association of Tenants' Savings and Building Societies (HSB).[47]

The forms of support to families also reflected Social Democratic thinking. I have already presented the arguments of the Federation of Social Democratic Women against tax deductions as aids to families—that such deductions from the man's taxes would not directly benefit the children, whereas an allowance paid to the mother would. However, there is another reason why tax deductions were rejected: they would not benefit the poorest, those worst off, those who did not have any appreciable income to deduct from.

Differences in opinion between the Social Democrats and the bourgeois parties remain, discernible in parliamentary motions and the bourgeois parties' minority reports in family policy inquiries. Political differences also exist regarding forms of child care, where the Social Democrats prefer collective, publicly supported day nurseries and preschools while the Center party and the Conservatives have promulgated care allowances for family members who stay at home to care for their children.

FROM MATERNAL ALLOWANCE TO PARENTAL INSURANCE

From the 1950s onward there was a succession of family policy inquiries. I have already mentioned the one in 1954; in 1961 the Social Policy Committee presented its report *Support for Mothers*, which provided the basis for the new maternal allowance. In 1962 Ulla Lindström set up the so-called Family Working Group, whose brief was "to delineate and analyze problems associated with public services for families with children."[48] The working group proposed a care allowance, but the question of infant care and supervision was still considered exclusively a woman's province.

In 1965 Ulla Lindström appointed a Family Policy Committee that produced several reports. The 1967 report, *Child Allowance and Family Supplement*, continued to refer only to the maternal allowance and maternity insurance. However, in the report from 1972, *Support for Families*, parental insurance was proposed.[49] Finally it became conceivable for the man to care for infants and obtain leave from his work in conjunction with the birth of his child.

Historically, this is an exceedingly significant change. The conflict between reproduction and production has been made tangible, not only as a problem and a responsibility for women, but also as a conflict of responsibilities for men. It is still too early to tell whether such exposure of the fundamental conflict arising in a society that does not recognize the central role of reproduction will lead to corresponding social changes.

What lay behind this change? In general, there are several factors that can explain why male acceptance of the responsibility of child care occurred at the beginning of the 1970s. One factor is that the activities of the new women's movement began to show results. Another is that the massive flood of women to the labor market revealed their conflict-ridden position between reproduction and production.

Among the political parties during the postwar period, it was the Liberal party that first and most radically addressed issues of sexual equality and family policy. Eva Moberg was in the forefront, and her ideas on equality—also within the family—gradually formed the basis of parental insurance. Louise Drangel, who has dealt with the history of the Liberal party with reference to sexual equality, indicates that the Liberals led in this issue: the other parties simply followed along. She also concludes that, in their struggle for equality in practice, the Social Democratic women had more in common with women in the Liberal party than with men in their own. The Social Democrats not only rejected the bourgeois parties' proposal for a care allowance in order to give priority to the expansion of day nurseries; Social Democratic men were also either negative to or wary of proposals from their own women's group for a compulsory division of parental leave and for the introduction of the six-hour workday. The compulsory division of parental leave was in fact included in party demands from 1976 to 1979 but disappeared when the SAP returned to power in 1982.[50] In the work of the Family Policy Committee, changes can be read not only in the printed report from 1972, but also in a stenciled report from 1969 on equality between women and men regarding national health insurance.

Equality between women and men in working life and at home is included, albeit as a rather weakly formulated political goal, in the Social Democratic Labor Party program from 1960. In the program it is pointed out that there continues to be "a stubborn resistance to justice for women in working life. Neither have women at home fully received their part of social advances." The goal has "expanded into a struggle for equal treatment of all citizens, regardless of whether they are men or women."[51]

A working group with representatives from the party and the LO presented a report entitled *Equality* to the Social Democratic Labor Party conference in 1969. The report took up the relation between women and men in the family and asserted that not just the mother but also the father needed contact with their infant child. The authors further claimed that, since it has become more common for parents to share the care and upbringing of children, it follows that the right to a leave of absence at the birth of a child should be shared between the parents.[52] In 1969 the LO's council for family questions presented a report, *The Trade Union Movement and Family Policy*, to the secretariat. The report declared that there must be two roles, one in work and one in the family, and that these roles should be filled to an equal degree by women and men.[53]

In conjunction with their congress in September 1972, the National Federation of Social Democratic Women published a program pamphlet, *The Family and the Future: A Socialist Policy for the Family*, which called for a far-reaching social responsibility for child care and supervision from an early age. However, also underlined was the demand for parental insurance, enabling the mother and the father to share leave at the birth of a child.

At the 1975 party conference guidelines for a child and family policy program were confirmed. These included a significant expansion of public child care, successive increases in the child allowance, higher housing allowances, better housing opportunities, and possibilities for parents to follow their child's development, as well as special parent education.[54] On the basis of these guidelines, a child and family policy group was started within the party in 1976. The group authored a program that was approved at the 1978 party conference: *The Labor Movement and Family Policy: A Child and Family Policy Program*. The program included a demand for an extension of the parental leave period and a reduction of the workday for parents of small children (the latter had been expressed earlier the same year in a pamphlet from the National Federation of Social Democratic Women, *The Six-Hour Working Day*).[55]

In the 1978 family policy program the goal of equality within the family was clearly expressed:

> Only through a policy which aims at equality between all people can equality between the sexes be realized. . . . The adult family members' economic independence must be anchored in working life, and therefore the universal right to work is a prerequisite for equality between women and men. Lack of opportunities for employment affect women hardest. . . . Gaps in child care provided by society block women's opportunities for paid employment and education. The traditional pattern of sex roles discriminates against women and hinders men from participating in their child's development and care. Formally, men and women have equal rights, but in practice there remains much to do. Women in the worst situations are most affected by these gaps [in provision]. Consequently, reforms must be primarily directed towards those women living in the most difficult circumstances. . . . Equality between women and men must be realized in the home, at work and in society in order to create a society favorable to children.[56]

In this document a great deal of the conflict between production and reproduction has risen to the surface and been recognized. Much of the argument is familiar from the first Social Democratic women's concerted political demands at the turn of the century—for instance, mention of the
vulnerability, the *risks* run by women because they commonly have less
well paid work and less education than men. One should also note the new
insight that traditional sex role patterns prevent men from participating in
their children's development and upbringing. A social role encompasses
not only behavior but also experience—in this context, a fundamental social experience that many men lack. The conclusion of the 1978 statement
is clear: it is the children who suffer most from gaps in equality between
the sexes.

Quantitatively, Swedish family policy differs greatly from that of other
European countries and, above all, the United States, where the right to
paid leave at childbirth is both limited and short in duration. But qualitatively the differences are even greater. Swedish legislation is probably
unique in giving to and requiring from fathers the same rights and responsibilities for small children as the mothers have.

At present, Swedish birthrates are among the highest in Europe. Could
this be a result not only of the good opportunities for parenthood provided
by Swedish family policy, but also of the fact that the decision to have a
child might be facilitated when responsibility is divided between both parents?

In the Social Democratic Labor Party program from 1975 point twenty-
four contains a comprehensive family policy program, but it is hardly as
radical as that of 1978. The crucial point in the party program is the third,
dealing with equality, which ends by calling for "the same rights and the
same responsibilities for men and women in the family, in working life and
in society."[57]

However, how close these goals are to being realized in practical politics
is open to discussion. In the 1988 election campaign, the National Federation of Social Democratic Women's demand for a shorter workday was refused in favor of the LO's demand for a statutory six-week holiday. As
usual, the federation formulated its demand with the women and children's
(and fathers') best interests in mind; and as happened so often before, it
was forced to give way to a demand that benefits adult men in full-time
work.

Behind the demand for equality between women and men in the family
lies concern for the essence of the continuity of human society—reproduc-

tion. Beyond the realization of equality between women and men in the family and in work perhaps also lies the insight that a society that denies its essence becomes a society in conflict with itself, a society in which the weakest and at the same time the most important members, the children, have to bear the burden of that conflict—to the detriment of future society.

During the whole history of the SAP the National Federation of Social Democratic Women and its forerunners have continually tried to highlight this conflict, make it tangible, and politicize it, often with paltry assistance from the party. In the future, will the efforts of Social Democratic women still be decisive for Social Democratic family policy and thus also for social justice and balance in this crucial issue?

NOTES

1. SFS 1900:75.
2. Information to the author in 1987 from the Advisory Council for Swedish Terminology and Usage, Stockholm.
3. *SAP Municipal Programme* 1964 (cf. party programme edition in 1964), 19.
4. SOU 1972:34 (Family Support).
5. S. Carlsson 1977. Cf. Kälvemark (Ohlander) 1983.
6. Kälvemark (Ohlander) 1980, 137.
7. C. Carlsson 1986, 266.
8. C. Carlsson 1986.
9. Ibid., 266 and 270.
10. Gröndahl 1986.
11. C. Carlsson 1986, 266–68.
12. Ibid., 268–69. *Morgonbris* (Morning Breeze) is a Social Democratic Women's Federation paper, first published in 1908 by labor movement women.
13. Negotiations at the first Swedish Social Democratic Women's Conference in Stockholm, 2–6 August 1908. *Minutes*, 59.
14. In C. Carlsson 1986, 268.
15. SFS 1912:339; SOU 1929:28, 23–25; SFS 1931:281.
16. Y. Hirdman 1983, 24–26. See also C. Carlsson 1986, 269.
17. C. Carlsson 1986, 276.
18. Flood 1960, 108–10.
19. Ibid., 109.
20. Ibid., 126.
21. Motion to the First Chamber of the Riksdag 1914:80 and to Second Chamber 1914:168.
22. Motion to First Chamber 1924:202 and to Second Chamber 1924:327; SOU 1929:28.
23. Social Democratic Parliamentary Group, *Minutes*, 5 June 1930 (Labor Movement Archives).
24. See Hatje 1974, 31.

25. Flood 1960, 193.
26. Kälvemark (Ohlander) 1980, 86–87.
27. Ibid., 55–57.
28. Hatje 1974, 102–4. See also Elmér 1975, 102.
29. Nielsen 1979.
30. Drangel 1984.
31. Hernes 1986.
32. Kälvemark (Ohlander) 1980, 95–96.
33. *SSKF* (National Federation of Social Democratic Women in Sweden) *Annual Report* 1956, 35.
34. Ibid., 1941, 42–44.
35. *SAP Party Programme* 1960 (1964 edition), 19.
36. Lindström 1969, 42.
37. SOU 1956:47.
38. *SSKF Annual Report* 1956, 57–58.
39. G. Bock, *Women's Right and Women's Welfare: Maternity and Visions of Gender in Social Policies and Social Movements: Europe 1880s–1940s* (Florence: European University Institute, 1986, Stencil).
40. Social Democratic Parliamentary Group *Minutes* 6 March 1956.
41. Kyle 1979.
42. Karlsson 1990.
43. Karlsson 1990; K. Molin in the present volume.
44. See also Karlsson 1990.
45. Cf. Qvist 1977.
46. Hatje 1974; Kälvemark (Ohlander) 1980.
47. Kälvemark (Ohlander) 1980.
48. SOU 1961:38; SOU 1964:36, 2.
49. SOU 1967:52; SOU 1972:34, 30–32 and 248–50.
50. Drangel 1984.
51. *SAP Party Programme* 1960, 5.
52. Cf. SOU 1972:34, 178.
53. Ibid.
54. SAP 1978b.
55. SSKF 1974 (1978 edition).
56. SAP 1978a, 10–11.
57. *SAP Party Programme* 1975 (with changes from the 1984 party conference included), 30.

Thord Strömberg   8

The Politicization of the Housing Market: The Social Democrats and the Housing Question

A SOCIAL DEMOCRATIC "SUCCESS STORY"

The clearest watershed in the history of Swedish housing policy appeared in the years just after World War II, when the local authorities began to be seriously used as political instruments. The working class, previously having to rely on charity or self-help, was now able to push through political decisions that shielded segments of the housing market from private speculation. The formal foundation of this development was laid in the Riksdag in 1946, when the local authorities were advised to create "public" housing companies to produce and manage rental housing.

In international comparisons, postwar Swedish housing policy has been considered a "success story." According to a euphonic chorus of scholars, Sweden has managed to raze slums and provide the whole population with housing of the highest international standards. Everyone also seems to agree that the Social Democratic Labor Party has played a key role in this story, even if interpretations of its basic message vary.

One common interpretation is that the Swedish Social Democrats have succeeded in socializing the housing market (i.e., consumption) even though the means of production are still mainly in private hands. According to this view, a group of interests called "the coalition of popular movements" has had the initiative in housing policy since the early 1930s. This coalition has been led by the Social Democratic Labor Party and includes the tenants' movement (the Tenants' Association, HGF), construction workers' unions, and the cooperative housing movement. In sharp opposition to this group has been the "business coalition," containing representatives for private interests in the housing market and supported by the bourgeois parties.[1]

Another view with a totally different emphasis is based upon the so-called historical compromise between labor and capital, which developed during the 1930s and which provided the preconditions for the "Swedish model." Representatives from the working class and large capital together should ensure the regulation of the housing market to prevent land speculators and profiteering landlords from sabotaging rational housing arrangements. Private capital should not be bound up in unproductive investments. Good inexpensive housing should be built in places where industry generally had good prospects.[2]

In the background lurks the classic conundrum: is the linchpin of society consumption or production—Weber or Marx? In the present context there is no reason to get involved in this discussion; suffice it to say that both perspectives contain the necessary prerequisites for the housing policy that has actually developed. The organization of and links between various interests are vital components in any analysis of power. At the same time, it is clear that representatives for organized interests cannot act outside of the structural boundaries that capitalism in its various stages of development sets for political action. Such analyses are necessary but hardly sufficient to understand why Swedish housing policy in particular should develop into an international "success story."

The general wave of radicalization that swept over Western Europe at the end of World War II included an increased social responsibility for people's housing. However, it is worth noting that among the five Western European countries that still carried on an active housing policy in the middle of the 1960s, Sweden alone committed resources on a large scale to general support for public rental housing. The most common alternative was to augment support for self-help organizations—housing cooperatives.[3] This was the case in Norway, for example, where leftist groups within the Social Democratic Labor Party that had advocated public rental housing were defeated by representatives for cooperative solutions. In Denmark the issue of concentrating on public rental housing or cooperative housing divided the Social Democrats into a left and a right wing.[4]

The decision to concentrate on public rental housing is obviously an important ingredient in the "success story." The decision was formally taken in the Riksdag in 1946, but in reality the issue is far more complicated. A formal decision is only the final link in a long process beginning with the idea and continuing through implementation. Furthermore, it is by no means self-evident that the decision in question will be implemented. Despite the parliamentary decision on support for the building of public housing, it was in fact the politicians in the hundreds of counties and municipalities who had the final say. Thus, interest should not be focused only on the national level. However, since important aspects of local housing policy are taken up elsewhere in this anthology, I will devote my remarks principally to the question of how Sweden's postwar public housing policy developed. What is the history of the politicization of the housing market, seen from the vantage point of central party organs? Where should the boundaries be drawn? What should the tools be? In my conclusion, however, I do discuss the question of the municipal realities that best favored the implementation of a centrally formulated housing policy.

A PARADISE FOR WOLVES AND JACKALS

In the nonregulated capitalist system that prevailed in Sweden during the second half of the nineteenth century, the housing market in cities was "a paradise for wolves and jackals."[5] In the countryside and small industrial communities, where the patriarchal pattern had not yet been corroded by the market economy, housing was tied to employment well into the twentieth century. In the new industrial urban areas the separation between the spheres of production and reproduction went much faster. The first wave of migrating industrial workers normally had to crowd in as tenants in the old craft-workers' quarters. Cattle sheds and warehouses, brewing houses and bakery huts were elevated to dwellings for the rapidly growing class of industrial workers.[6]

The social misery issuing from these overcrowded and unhygienic conditions should have stimulated residential building, especially when the tenants' purchasing power rose during the last decades of the century. However, the interplay between production and reproduction functioned badly. Credit markets for industry and housing construction had totally different business cycles. Boom periods for trade and industry attracted workers to the cities, but since the owners of capital had better alternatives for investments then, little new housing was built. Capital for large-scale housing construction was available only during industrial recessions when large capitalists basically functioned as private bankers for self-appointed builders who, without their own capital, constructed miserable workers barracks in the hope of earning profits from rents. Many went bankrupt when the economy made an upswing and interest rates were raised. Residential building came to a standstill, and overcrowding increased.[7]

Abundance and scarcity existed side by side, and philanthropically inclined people had no difficulties finding objects for their charity. "In the dark and dank, and in dirty rags a wretched race is growing up here," wrote the Gothenburg Committee on Pauperism in 1865. This committee, which had been initiated by a liberal politician and publicist, worked out a comprehensive program for a municipal, socially oriented housing policy. Fifteen years earlier, the city of Gothenburg had actually built a number of houses "for the working class," so one would have thought the program had good prospects. However, the City Council rejected the proposal, arguing that housing construction was a task for individual enterprise. This was in fact a more or less undisputed doctrine; the Committee on Pauperism and its predecessors must be viewed as exceptions to this rule.[8] Sympathy should be channeled into private charity.

HOUSING POLICY: A MAKESHIFT SOLUTION

The latter half of the nineteenth century was the epoch of urban fires in Swedish history. In the overpopulated inner-city quarters fires could easily spread from open hearths to clusters of wooden houses. The situation forced the state into a cautious intervention in the liberal order: a building ordinance was established in 1874, with demands for planned construction. "The efficacious organization of cities depends greatly upon their builders' good will and their Councils' solicitude. However, legislation should not be ineffective," according to the minister in charge.[9]

It soon became evident that the building ordinance was a far too feeble instrument for those politicians who wanted to oppose the landowners. The first real attack on the inviolability of private ownership rights arrived in the form of the 1907 City Planning Act. The municipalities were now formally able to prevent unplanned building. However, any real breakthrough was thwarted because the municipalities' right to purchase land was limited by stiff compensation rules.[10]

Many of the period's debaters saw rising prices for land as the basic cause of the disparities on the housing market. On this point Marxists could be in accord with conservative economists. As early as 1807 Napoleon had introduced a tax on "unearned land increment," and in several quarters in America and Europe at the end of the century economists discussed various solutions to the problem.[11]

Politically, a measure had to be found that did not challenge too obviously the sanctity of the right to private ownership. In Sweden the response became the Institution of Site Leasehold Rights. The 1907 law on "users' rights to real property" determined that in the future local authorities should be able to rent out their land. The contracts could include detailed regulations on how the sites should be used, and by means of recurrent rent rises the "unearned land increment" could be returned to the local authority. But the rule that rent alterations could not be made in intervals of fewer than twenty-six years and the banks' reluctance to give loans to property on leaseholds rendered the Institution of Site Leasehold Rights in practice a very blunt instrument in the struggle against speculating landowners.[12]

Politicization

Neither the city planning law nor the Institution of Site Leasehold Rights had been created for primarily social reasons; nor was the 1904 parliamentary decision to grant favorable loans to workers of "lesser means" wishing to build their own homes. The decision was made mainly to try to hinder massive emigration and safeguard access to the agricultural labor force.[13]

However, the view that the housing question was first and foremost a social problem for city and state to deal with began to be articulated during the first decades of the twentieth century by a vocal segment of opinion. The Central Union for Social Work (CSA), which was formed in 1903, played a role in the development of Swedish social policy similar to that of older associations like the Fabian Society in England and the Verein für Sozialpolitik in Germany. However, in contrast to these predecessors the CSA proclaimed itself a politically neutral organization. Even if its leadership was in practice dominated by liberal-minded politicians and white-collar workers, the label of political neutrality soon came to stamp the CSA in people's minds as a semiofficial state agency. It was able to find channels into central management, the Riksdag, and the cabinet. In this way the CSA came to sponsor two central organs for housing policy: the Swedish Town Federation (1907) and the National Social Welfare Board (1912).[14]

At the time of World War I, the idea still prevailed that, if society were to take responsibility for housing problems at all, the responsibility should fall on the local level. Housing policy was viewed as a subdivision of social (public) welfare, or poor relief. Consequently the Swedish Town Federation rapidly became a central body in all housing policy discussions. Starting in 1916 the federation organized a series of housing conferences in which local authority experiences were recast into guidelines for the future. By 1917 regular advice to municipalities was in such demand that a permanent housing council was established. This later became a powerful advisory body in the process of state reforms.[15]

The first important task of the National Social Welfare Board, together with the state-appointed Housing Commission, was a national housing survey. The results, presented in 1914, were alarming: more than every third family lived in "overpopulated flats" (according to the norm, more than two people per room, kitchen included), and rent levels were very high. Overcrowding was most widespread in small industrial communities, where it was common for workers' families to live together in one room with a stove. In the larger cities, families normally lived in flats with one room and kitchen, but there the rents were higher. Also, the curves describing the development of rents were steeper than others.[16]

The Housing Commission concluded that Swedes generally lived worse and more expensively than people in other industrialized countries in Europe—and the situation looked to be degenerating. In the industrial boom that had been going on since 1910, capital shifted from building enterprises to industry even though demand for housing in industrial localities was increasing. As an effect of the outbreak of war, interest rates and building material costs shot up, which aggravated the situation—especially in those places where war-related industries attracted labor.[17]

The situation provoked a wave of housing proposals and reforms, which must be regarded primarily as crisis measures pending "normal times." A law on mediation in rent disputes was adopted in 1916 and complemented a year later by a law on rent increases. This did not mean that rent levels were frozen; the law merely aimed at preventing rents from being raised by leaps and bounds. The goal was to gradually adapt rents to the stabilized price levels that were expected after the war. By international standards, these interventions in the market were very slight: the mediation boards were not given the right—as in England and Norway—to pronounce binding judgments, and rent regulation was abolished earlier in Sweden than in other comparable countries.[18]

In 1917 the Riksdag confirmed the details of the crisis program. The decision on rent regulation was supplemented by stipulations concerning subsidies to major building companies. Those building small flats in densely populated areas could reckon on a state and municipal subsidy covering one-third of the building costs. The state stood for two-thirds of the amount, and the local authorities, in addition to their direct subsidy—which could consist of sites free of charge—would be responsible for administration and control.[19]

Thus for the first time the state assumed economic responsibility for housing provision at the same time as the principle of free price formation on the housing market was abandoned. The right to market-level profits was no longer self-evident. Moreover, the state and local authorities would encourage those builders who did not aim at maximizing profits. This category comprised a fairly motley group: state, municipal, half-municipal, cooperative, and "public." The last-mentioned entity was defined in the 1914 survey as that housing production which "is not aimed at profits but has instead other social goals."

The measures taken by the Riksdag in 1917 had rapid effects. The decline in private residential building, which in 1917 was at only about 35 percent of the figures from 1913, was not halted but was somewhat compensated for by local authority initiatives. The emergency housing that then came into being was plain and drab (in some places, "to the everlasting delight of vermin"), but there were also indications that in many cases the local authorities assumed greater responsibility for housing provision than the Riksdag had stipulated.[20]

However, during the next two years, when the Riksdag—in reaction to continuing price rises in building materials, less migration to cities, and the tendency toward lower birthrates—reduced subsidies, the local authority initiatives were throttled. Furthermore, the war was over, and the threat of immediate revolution had proved empty. In such circumstances, the housing policy of 1917, described as "an extraordinary, temporary crisis relief measure" in the 1918 housing proposals, could be reviewed.[21] It was the task of the first Social Democratic government to adopt a position on this question.

In the Social Democratic local authority program from 1911 building site speculation was referred to as the main housing problem: "Municipal land policy aims at stopping [the use] of land as a trade commodity, which, considering its monopolistic character on every level of capitalistic society, has brought about pernicious social consequences." Therefore, local authorities should "acquire ownership rights" to attractive building sites and then utilize the Institution for Leasehold Rights or some other form of usufructuary right when the sites are made available for building. To the degree that local authorities had the financial means, they themselves should assume the role of builders, and "in such cases consideration should be taken to the housing needs of those of little means." Management of local authority buildings could be carried out "in conjunction with cooperative enterprises."[22] Aside from a minor revision in 1928, this program applied until 1944.

In the discussions on conditions for continued coalition with the Liberals after the universal voting rights reform was carried out, the Social Democratic executive and parliamentary group were forced to clarify their view of future housing policy. How should the prerequisites be created for the local authorities to approach the goals presented in the party program? What should the role of the state be? How useful was the cooperative housing movement to Social Democratic housing policy?

In the autumn of 1919, before commencing negotiations with the Liberals, the party executive discussed a draft for a program in which housing questions occupied a very prominent place. Local authorities were designated as primary actors but were expected to provide only 20 percent of the necessary capital. The state ought to contribute 75 percent, and the builders themselves were to provide the rest. The state and local authorities' contributions were to be financed mainly by a tax on rent rises. The establishment of cooperative housing companies would be promoted through "special privileges," but it was up to the local authorities to ensure that the cooperatively managed dwellings did not become objects of speculation.[23]

In the program that finally provided the basis for negotiations with the Liberals, the details of the proposal had been edited out. Housing still occupied a central position, but now it was in terms of housing production being municipal or cooperative in character, and the state and local authorities awarding "very significant sums" to relieve the acute housing shortage. Judging by the response of the Liberals, these were not very contentious points. Negotiations in fact failed, but the failure was not due to dissension over housing policy.[24]

The Social Democratic minority government that took office in the spring of 1920 thus presented a well-prepared, well-grounded housing policy proposition. However, it was exposed to fairly rough treatment in the Riksdag. The parliamentary majority vetoed the idea of taxing rent increases and reduced the size of the funding, partly on the grounds that the new working hours law would open up new possibilities for people to build their own homes. The building workers' strike then going on was deemed to give extra weight to the argument. However, also relevant was the fact that few questioned the hypothesis that home ownership made for the best family housing. To this end, loans for the acquisition of individual homes became very favorable.

Depoliticization

Inflation reached its peak in 1920; during the following two years, prices plummeted. It became cheaper to build, and rising unemployment caused demands on housing markets in densely populated areas to diminish. The Social Welfare Board, which drafted housing policy questions, did not interpret this as an effect of a transitory economic depression, but considered that "those previously employed in trade and industry could not in future, to the same extent as before, retain their jobs—even after normal conditions on the labor market return." Migration from the cities and lower birthrates were envisioned—and, as a result, less need for family housing.[25]

The decision to gradually abolish subsidized housing construction and rent regulation must be seen against this background. Although it was a bourgeois government that wielded the ax in 1923, and even though Social Democratic members of the Riksdag tried to restrain the pace, it is clear that the Social Democrats viewed the politicization of the housing market as an emergency measure. Just before the decision to do away with rent regulation, the party executive received many letters and resolutions from members who, in common with the Social Democratic Women's Federation paper, *Morgonbris*, feared a "rent catastrophe" when the market, released from all restraints, started to set housing prices. The system of lodgers, which had led to the "dissolution of morals," would become increasingly widespread. "It is not only the very poor who are dreading the first of October."[26] The issue was then politically very sensitive, and despite opposition from inter alia the party's former finance minister, F. V. Thorsson, the parliament group decided to attempt to get the proposal remitted to the appropriate committee in order to extend rent regulation for those who were expected to be hit hardest—tenants in small flats in the big cities.[27]

The decision to gradually suspend state rent regulations was approved—

by one vote. This decision placed Sweden in a unique position among European countries. Sweden was now not only the country with the worst housing standards and highest rents but also the first to depoliticize the housing market. Why did the Social Democratic Labor Party not act more resolutely in the circumstances?

It is obvious that there was still a lack of structural prerequisites for realizing the ideas about the politicization of the housing market that had been expressed in the party's local authority policy program. In the first place, the party was in the minority in the Riksdag and in almost all counties and municipalities. Second, the Local Government Act prevented local authorities from devoting themselves to questions other than those able to be defined as "concerns of common order and economy." Thus they could not simply be used as tools of Social Democratic interests. And finally, housing cooperatives were not yet ready to shoulder their awarded role. To all this could be added a few more internal problems.

The party executive's proposal for a division of roles between the state, the local authority, and cooperatives did not have support in the party membership. It actually bordered on an ideological dividing line in party debates in the 1920s, where the dominating state socialist perspective competed with a more syndicalist-inclined alternative in which cooperative self-management—and also cooperative production of housing—was central. Guild-socialist and Austro-Marxist ideas were put forth by such prominent party members as Ernst Wigforss, Arthur Engberg, and Gustav Möller— all of them future members of the government.[28] The structural obstacles to a new order on the housing market meant that the various currents of opinion did not have to rise in the public arena during the 1920s. The latent conflicts hardly favored a gathering of Social Democratic forces in housing policy, however. In addition, party leadership had to pay attention to political forces on the left, who saw in the budding tenants' movement an excellent platform for "popular front politics."

The war was "midwife" to the tenants' associations. Organizing began in earnest when the rent increase law was adopted in 1917 and consolidated when the law was annulled in 1923. At first the main goal of the associations was to ensure that the law was followed, then that it was retained, and finally to lessen the effects of releasing the "wolves and jackals." On the initiative of the left-wing socialist and professor Gunnar Bergman in Lund, a federation of tenants' associations was formed in 1923, which represented eight cities and over 5,000 members. Very soon it became evident that the federation contained two factions. The first, dominated by the socialist and communist left-wing and with its center in Gothenburg, wanted to make the National Tenants' Association into a "nonpartisan" protest organization against private landlords—a "people's front." The second, under the influence of the architect Sven Wallander and other pioneers of housing cooperatives in Stockholm, saw the tenants' movement as a base for the HSB (Association of Tenants' Savings and Building Societies), whose national organization was founded in 1924. With support from the HSB tenants would be able to help themselves. Conflicts between the two factions paralyzed the national association during the whole of the 1920s and delayed its entry into the Social Democratic–controlled "coalition of popular movements." Doors opened first in the 1930s after individual associations had accepted organizational cooperation with the national HSB.[29]

Thus, various obstacles were raised—both within and outside of the labor movement—against a radical politicization of the housing market. On the other hand, as demonstrated in the parliamentary debates on housing financing, total retreat was hardly possible: flagrant housing needs were all too obvious, and examples of state and local authorities assuming responsibility were too fresh.

When the Social Democrats were returned to government in the autumn of 1924, Minister of Social Affairs Gustav Möller appointed an inquiry that was to produce a proposal on how "secondary credit" should be arranged in the future. State loans should become a permanent element in housing policy, according to Möller. The inquiry, which presented its conclusions in February 1925, stated that private builders were not interested in building residential buildings for the "classes of lesser means." In the proposition Möller seized upon this and underlined the great social significance of housing issues. State loans from a "housing loan reserve fund" should be transferred from "tenement blocks" to owner-occupied dwellings and cooperative building firms. In addition to the expected social gains, the goal of reducing building costs could be reached because residents could contribute their own labor. The social affairs minister also thought that the division of responsibility between the state and local authorities should be retained, as housing must continue to be considered a local concern. The local authorities should continue to be agents for the loans, guarantee repayment, and contribute building sites. Members of the inquiry—and Möller—proposed, however, an interesting alteration: loans should not be made to local authority companies.[30]

The proposal for an expanded and permanent state loan fund was vetoed by the bourgeois majority in the Riksdag, but Möller and other leading

Social Democrats warned that the issue would arise again. The Liberal cooperative-supporter and CSA veteran Gerard H. von Koch also argued for a permanent solution "as soon as circumstances allow."[31]

When the Social Democratic contributions to the parliamentary debates are analyzed, several fundamental aspects of the party's view of the housing question during the 1920s appear. There was never any real discussion of comprehensive politicization of the housing market. Limits for state and local authority commitments should be drawn on the basis of the social problems associated with inadequate housing. There seems to have been total agreement that the private building firms and the private sources of credit had in the past disregarded the needs of the population with "less means." Too few cheap apartments had been built; and so in normal times, the state should ensure that the production of housing had a social orientation. However, no plans for regular local authority or state housing production were launched. The best solution, according to Gustav Möller, was home ownership, which would engender "different care and consideration of home and family on the part of those building their own homes."[32]

The proposal to ensure the granting of credit for small flats and homes was hardly revolutionary, especially since it had support deep within the Liberal ranks. Neither did the idea of pursuing social policy with the aid of public or cooperative housing firms bear a special Social Democratic stamp; already during the war the idea had been formulated by civil servants and liberally minded politicians on the Social Welfare Board and the housing council of the Town Federation. In other words, it may be claimed that at the end of the 1920s the Social Democrats still lacked an independent and radical alternative to market-controlled housing provision.

HOUSING POLICY: A CRISIS SOLUTION

Under the pressure of the major unemployment crisis at the beginning of the 1930s, some of the structural obstacles blocking the politicization of the housing market began to crumble. Through the settlement with the Agrarian party in 1933, the Social Democrats obtained a majority for their policies in the Riksdag. In the tenants' movement, the line favoring housing cooperatives had emerged victorious. With the aim of coordinating their membership recruitment, the national Tenants' Association and the HSB organized a common annual general meeting in Örebro in 1931. Assisted by a tenants' movement now dominated by Social Democrats, the HSB was able to establish itself as a full member of the "coalition of popular movements," while the local authorities were prevented from expressly conducting policies favoring particular interests.

Housing construction occupied a central position in the 1933 crisis settlement, mainly because housing production could employ comparatively many people—wages accounted for about half of the total production costs, and building materials were almost exclusively produced within the country. Of the 75 million kronor designated for labor market measures in the 1933 budget proposals, 20 million were designated for housing construction. The money mainly went toward the renovation of unsanitary dwellings in rural areas. A building workers' strike somewhat hindered the utilization of loans for housing construction in the cities. Yet the meager results must also be seen as an effect of the still prevalent view that supports should not jeopardize market solutions: the state should intervene only in situations when private initiatives could not be expected. The fact that, despite this, urban housing production from 1933 to 1935 doubled in comparison with the previous two years was primarily due to the significant decline in interest rates following upon a downturn in industrial trends.[33]

Without doubt, in terms of the future the most important housing policy measure taken by the Social Democratic government in 1933 was the appointment of the Social Housing Commission. This commission continued for fourteen years and played an exceedingly dominant role in the formation of housing policy until the late 1960s. Its secretary was Alf Johansson, an economist with a background in the so-called Stockholm School and consequently in accord with the ideas that formed the basis for Social Democratic crisis policy. In other words, he was not at all averse to the idea of using housing policy as a means for regulating the business cycle. This became an underlying assumption in the housing policy formulated by the commission.

To the social dimension of housing policy had now been added a fundamental economic one. Despite this, the way toward a politicized housing market could be embarked upon under fairly calm political circumstances since measures could be adapted to a problem area about which all the political parties were united—namely, population. Both the decision about housing support for "large families with small means" in densely populated areas (1935) and the decision in favor of increased commitment to the building of single-family houses in rural areas (1938) were motivated by the expectation that they would encourage higher birthrates. Conditions for support for "large families with small means" and for subsidies for building homes for the elderly (1939) were that the dwellings held to a minimum standard regarding space, that the aim of the builders was not primarily to make profits, and that the builders worked under the supervision of the local authority. The local authorities were expected to provide building sites and administrative resources and to guarantee payment of rents. The latter condition appeared in order to prevent local authorities from loading their poor relief costs onto the state.[34]

After a lengthy puberty, the HSB had attained sufficient maturity in the beginning of the 1930s to become an instrument of housing policy. In 1925 the HSB's national association had been recognized as a mediation agency for state housing loans. Three years later it was able to comment upon legislative proposals for housing credit and new rules for tenant-owners' cooperative societies; when executive member Sven Wallander was invited to sit on the Social Housing Commission, the process was complete. At the same time an organizational breakthrough occurred. During the first half of the 1930s HSB associations started up in nearly all the larger towns and cities. The number of member associations increased from eight in 1929 to forty-nine in 1935. According to the HSB's annals 1933 was the great breakthrough year. The HSB's national association was not slow to exploit the situation. As soon as the decision in favor of support for "large families of lesser means" was final, local politicians were visited by HSB representatives who, with standard floor plans in hand, sold their services.[35] So it is not strange that those local authorities wishing to take advantage of the state housing subsidy almost without exception chose to cooperate with the HSB.

For the HSB as an organization, housing measures in the 1930s meant space for growth. However, even more important was that the HSB could enter into the "coalition of popular movements" forming in Social Democratic–governed cities and counties. The HSB became the tool of Social Democratic housing policy locally as well as centrally. But for the housing market as a whole the policy interventions of the 1930s had only marginal significance. The vast majority seeking housing were still being referred to the private housing market, which during the latter half of the decade made large profits on low interest rates, increased buying power, and continued migration to industrial workplaces in densely populated areas. For the Social Democratic Labor Party, housing policy was still only a means that could be used to correct undesired effects of the market economy.

PLANNED ECONOMY WITH RESERVATION RIGHTS

Then came the outbreak of World War II in autumn 1939. Interest rates increased in response to credit shortages that quickly arose when resources were transferred to defense. Access to building materials and labor became uncertain. Finally, when it was feared that general anxiety about the future would dampen demand for new housing, building virtually ceased altogether.[36]

This time the national politicians acted fast. Using the preparations laid by the Social Housing Commission, the Riksdag decided on subsidies for housing production in January 1940. When this proved not to have the desired effects, new measures were taken entailing increased support, but also a gradual sharpening of political control. In the spring of 1942, the Riksdag decided upon a loan and subsidy system that on the one hand guaranteed builders returns on invested capital while on the other placing a definite ceiling on profits by freezing rents at 1942 levels. Accompanied by labor and material regulations, this system spread resources among building, defense, and energy supply; and via a quota system for densely populated areas, local authorities were advised annually how many dwellings could be built. Public housing companies, including cooperatives, received loans and subsidies up to 95 percent of the actual building costs, while private builders had to provide 10 percent of their own capital. Local authorities were expected to subsidize half the site costs. As during World War I, they were exhorted to "initiate measures for the furthering of housing provision" through, for example, ensuring that half or wholly municipal housing firms received the same economic advantages as housing cooperatives.[37]

These decisions were taken at a time of general labor shortages when both net migration to urban areas and family formation were on the rise, which increased the housing shortages that had quickly arisen. The aim of the political intervention on the market was not to reestablish prewar levels of housing construction. War industries required limitations on civilian investments, but the politicians thought that there was a proper margin for bargaining in the housing sector. A total stop, on the other hand, would threaten to destroy the production apparatus and create critical unemployment among building workers. In addition, a socially devastating housing shortage could be anticipated in the long term.[38] After the bottom was reached in 1941, production figures went up, attaining "normal" levels in 1945.

The Program

It can be claimed that, culturally, Sweden was a German colony well into the 1930s; but in the following decades, partly because of the war, leaders of public opinion began to be inspired by Anglo-Saxon countries. This was very much the case regarding housing, where the English Labour government's attempts at controlling development were of particular interest.[39]

Demands for more social involvement in housing were clearly articulated in both the Social Democrats' and tenants' movement's postwar programs. Goals included abolishing the housing shortage and raising housing standards. These goals were not determined by social considerations only, according to the program authors; also for labor market reasons, the state and local authorities should concentrate efforts on a high and even level of housing production. This point was particularly important just then, when a severe postwar depression was anticipated. The state should guarantee credit with low interest rates, but the local authorities were given the initiative to establish building and real estate companies. In addition, building land should be made "public" and awarded leasehold rights (this latter provision was especially stressed in the tenants' movement program).[40]

The prerequisite for realizing these goals was a series of good years immediately after the war. In the Riksdag as well as in most of the large municipalities, the Social Democratic Labor Party had acquired a political majority. At about this time, the American sociologist and cultural historian Lewis Mumford's powerful plea for collective solutions, *The Culture of Cities* (1938), had begun to exert considerable influence on leading architects and social planners. In "Planned Social Building," a paper attached to the Social Housing Commission's first report in 1945, Mumford's most eloquent Swedish disciple, Uno Åhrén, transformed his ideas into practical recommendations.[41] In general, the proposals made by the Social Housing Commission were in tune with the socialistic spirit of the times. Links between the commission and the labor movement's Postwar Program were close, as Gärd Folkesdotter has pointed out: "Some of the same people were involved with both. The choice of words and formulations are often very similar."[42]

However, the political spectrum of the parliamentary parties was broad. Farthest to the left, the communists pressed demands for nationalizing the building industry and for obligatory municipal housing exchanges. At the opposite end, the right wing argued for the abolition of building and rent regulations.[43] Among the Social Democrats many influential members shared the communists' view that rapidly rising building costs issued from an increasingly monopolistic building industry. However, many also believed the solution lay in competition, not in nationalization. In a motion to the Riksdag in 1944, four prominent members proposed that the state encourage cooperative production of building materials.[44] But the main Social Democratic opinion leaned to the right, even on this proposal. The state should promote rationalization and research in building techniques but otherwise let the market steer production, according to Gustav Möller in a debate in the Riksdag. Treatment of the inquiry resulting from the radical motion shows that Möller's views were shared by the majority of powerful Social Democrats.[45] However, in the end, all rallied around the Social Democratic "minimum program": in future, multifamily dwellings should be managed by public or local authority companies. The question was only what was meant by "public or local authority" in this context.

Local Authority or Cooperative?

The system of loans and subsidies built up during the early 1940s favored "public" and self-built housing. Pressed by relatively worse credit conditions and by rent regulation, private builders tried to creep in under the mantle of "public" through forming private tenant-owner housing associations. Builders could build while transferring the less profitable management responsibility to those tenants able to obtain investment capital. In the municipalities, where unemployment among building workers was coupled with a rapidly growing housing shortage, people happily endorsed the generous definition that a couple of Social Democratic members of the Riksdag tried to promulgate: "Every company that in a sensible way serves the public is a public company, regardless of what category it belongs to."[46] However, the concept soon came to be narrowed down.

The Social Housing Commission's first report was presented at the end of 1945. Its provisions were very broad:

> A housing policy program must be formed so that in the best possible way it satisfies different concerns: [1] that of social housing—to assist in raising housing standards; [2] that of the labor market—to contribute to stablizing employment; [3] that of the population—to generate better conditions for creating and developing families, and to help spread the costs of child care, etc.

Thus, in the future apartments should be built large enough so that at most two people would have to share a room (not including kitchen). Considering the then-extant housing stock, this would mean that production of the common one-room flat should cease altogether. Quantitative goals were high—above the previous record from 1939 by one thousand units over a fifteen-year period. Yet the greatest challenge was most likely the promise of comparatively low rents: for a newly built one-bedroom flat, the rent should not exceed 20 percent of the average industrial wage. [47]

One condition for attaining the cost goals was the restraint of private profit interests in the management of rented accommodation. This could be temporarily accomplished through rent controls, but in the long run the solution lay in an increasing share of rented accommodation coming into public ownership. "Public" presumed local authority involvement, but no precise rules for how this involvement should be shaped were stipulated by the commission. "The commission assumes that in the near future, several types of public housing companies will appear, with varying origins and degrees of local government involvement." The commission advised, however, that the most reasonable model for the future was that practiced in the management of housing for large families. What is more, tenant-owner housing associations—as in the early 1940s—should receive the same credit advantages as the public managers of rental housing. [48] Thus the Social Housing Commission proposed that cooperative forms should play a leading role in future housing policy. However, in the proposition to the 1946 Riksdag Gustav Möller indicated that builders should be divided into three categories: public housing companies should receive state aid up to 100 percent of costs; cooperatives, 95 percent; and private firms, 85 percent. The Riksdag adopted the proposal. [49] What had happened?

The decision in favor of the proposal clearly involved a step to the left. Primarily public rental housing should be produced, not cooperatively owned dwellings. For the initiated, this turn of events was not totally unexpected. Headed by Sven Wallander, the HSB had at this point succeeded in acquiring a very strong position in the Social Democratic Labor Party. On housing policy, the argument in favor of cooperative solutions reached far outside already committed circles. In propaganda, developments in Norway were used as frightening examples of how things could go if politicians unreservedly took upon themselves the responsibility for housing provision. In Norway, the state had been encouraging local authorities to form public housing companies since World War I, with the result that questions of evictions and rent increases had landed in open political debate. Consequently, in the mid-1930s it was decided to work indirectly—cooperative housing companies received extensive economic support, and capital investments (deposits) were subsidized. Sven Wallander commented that "under certain circumstances, it can be rather a relief for local authorities to be able to blame someone else."[50] However, in leading Social Democratic circles the argument for an open politicization was clearly more weighty.

For a start, the HSB was no longer alone in the field. Out of the unemployment crisis in the building trade at the beginning of World War II arose a new housing cooperative organization anchored in the labor movement: Svenska Riksbyggen, the Cooperative Building Organization of the Swedish Trade Unions. It was started in Gothenburg in 1940 and supported by the Building and Woodworkers Union and the Bricklayers Union. Uno Åhrén became head of the Riksbyggen in 1942 and immediately set to work on a long-term strategy for the enterprise, advising that it should concentrate on helping local authorities with their housing planning. In the 1930s Åhrén had publicly advocated economic planning as a social ideal, and in his opinion, the need for planning production and consumption of residential housing was especially great just then in the 1940s. He predicted that in order to arrange the payment of loans in the future, the state would place demands on the local authorities to that end. He did not try to refute the opinion that cooperation with local authorities under such circumstances would give the Riksbyggen a central social role.[51]

So now there were two cooperative organizations aspiring to leadership in housing in the labor movement. Since they were also based in different sections of the movement, the risk of splits within the "Coalition of Popular Movements" was obvious. In this context the local authorities were more neutral agents.

The other and probably decisive argument against giving cooperative housing associations the same credit and subsidy conditions as public companies had been clearly expressed in the commission's report: the market had a surfeit of owner-occupied cooperative dwellings. During World War II the local authorities almost without exception had chosen to continue along the path laid out by the housing policy reforms of the 1930s. The recommendation to "initiate measures for the furthering of housing provision" was only half-heeded. Very few wholly or partly public housing companies were formed; instead, the formation of cooperative housing associations was encouraged through local authority contributions toward deposits.[52]

The consequences were not long in coming. In 1943 the Riksbyggen's newly formed local section in Örebro complained that "clientele with purchasing power are beginning to thin out while unlimited numbers of potential purchasers without [ready cash for] deposits are registering."[53] In this situation a purely Norwegian type of solution was naturally difficult to defend—"measures for the furthering of housing provision" must be directed toward the rental market.

Planned Economy on the Local Level

The municipalities and local authorities were now earmarked as the most important instruments in Social Democratic housing policy. But instruments must be sharpened to function effectively; and most important for this purpose was to change the rules governing jurisdiction, which ever since the start of local authorities in 1862 had forbidden them to deal with anything other than "concerns of common order and economy." The local authorities had later in practice transgressed their legal powers, but in several instances controversial local authority decisions had been canceled on the basis of these rules. Under such conditions, a socially oriented local housing policy had few prospects of succeeding. Hence in 1946 the government initiated a change of laws, and two years later the Riksdag voted to expand local authorities' area of jurisdiction. It now became legally possible for them to also make decisions that would favor selected groups of residents.[54]

One of the basic ideas behind the series of housing policy reforms that the Social Democrats pushed through the Riksdag between 1946 and 1948 was, as has been implied, that future production of housing should be planned. For municipalities and local authorities this meant that clear plans for building in general, and residential building in particular, were required and that they had access to a tool for powerful legal pressure—"planning monopoly." An inquiry on the revision of city planning laws had already been started in 1941, and its proposal, presented at the end of the war, was based on the old idea that the landowner who was prevented from building on his land for reasons of city planning should be compensated. The Riksdag had to wait almost two years for a motion on the matter, and by then the proposition had acquired a totally different character: "In order that land may be used for conurbations, it is presumed that it is proved suitable for the purpose in accordance with the law governing planning."[55] Densely populated municipalities should in principle be able to determine what should be built where, and when. Since already during the war the local authorities were given the task of functioning as mediators for state housing loans, in practice they could also pick and choose among prospective builders.

The Social Democratic parliamentary majority thus equipped the local authorities with well-honed planning tools. Would they use them? The answer to that was far from self-evident. The Social Housing Commission had the idea that the state could force the local authorities to act: in the proposal for the law on housing provision, it says that the local authorities should be enjoined to form public housing companies. But many authoritative consultative bodies, headed by the Town Federation, rejected the idea of force. Local authorities' right to self-determination, they maintained, must not be infringed upon. The bourgeois parties in the Riksdag concurred with the criticism, and, since the opposition was joined by the odd Social Democrat, the proposal was rejected.[56] The decision about who should build what would in the future be made by local politicians who could choose to be actively involved in the market, or to be passive. What did they choose?

THE LOCAL REALITY

At the end of 1978 the national organization of public housing companies, SABO, had 242 members. These members, representing about 90 percent of all public housing companies in Sweden, became the subjects of a comprehensive investigation, one aim of which was to identify the features of the local authorities that promoted commitments to public housing management. Among the many variables included in the statistical model of analysis, two were particularly illuminating. First, it was obvious that residential building under public auspices was first started in densely populated urban local authorities in which public housing companies were given (comparatively speaking) a good deal of leverage in the distribution of housing quotas and credit. The second statistically reliable observation was that localities with a large percentage of Social Democratic and communist voters had a greater proportion of public rental housing than other localities.[57]

However, exceptions to these and other less well articulated rules were many. Göran Lindberg, who conducted the investigation, admitted surprise that the "percent explained" was so low. He believes that unique traditions and power constellations, which could not be reduced to statistical variables, could contribute to explaining the deviations.[58] A great deal suggests that he is right. From his figures one can conclude, for instance, that expansive localities with strong housing-cooperative traditions tried to cope with housing provision primarily by encouraging the production of cooperatively owned flats.[59] So what was the local political culture that best favored the development of public housing?

Örebro has been referred to as the municipality in which Social Democratic housing policy has been most clearly expressed.[60] One of the characteristic signs of this is the large proportion of public rental units in Örebro's housing stock. This profile has not been raised at the expense of private builders—in comparison with those in other heavily populated, urban-dominated, and Social Democratic–run local authorities, housing cooperatives in Örebro have had to take a back seat. The main explanation for this development is that housing cooperatives had a weak position within the "Coalition of Popular Movements," which during the years just after the war made the decisions about residential building in Örebro.

In localities where during the interwar period the Social Democratic Labor Party leadership's exhortations had been followed, housing cooperatives had flourished. This was not the case in Örebro—which meant that neither the HSB nor the Riksbyggen were successful in recruiting influential local politicians to their camp when the signals for a new housing policy began to be heard. In the local Social Democratic Labor Party and in the Örebro City Council, party leadership openly declared that housing cooperatives "do not build for our people."[61]

The Stiftelsen Hyresbostäder, the Rental Housing Trust in Örebro, formed in the autumn of 1946, got off to a flying start. The new builders built on a totally new scale: the first project, Rosta, contained thirteen hundred flats—the equivalent of more than two years' worth of the "quota allocation." In practice, the state allocation of credit and subsidies created a ceiling for production in the municipalities, which provoked the private builders in Örebro to ask, with good reason, "Should the local authorities take the whole quota and begin to build themselves?"[62]

Apprehensions were soon proved to be exaggerated. The Rosta project was spread over five years, with the rationale that by spreading it out room would be left for other builders, and contracts went to some of the town's larger building firms. In the beginning of the 1950s the new pattern of distribution was stablized. The Rental Housing Trust directed the building of large rental estates on the town's periphery. Progressive architects and social planners were given opportunities to show what they could do, and new residents were given access to good and inexpensive housing. Private builders were referred to the town's commercial center, where rent regulations did not apply; and in competition with the trade union–owned BPA, the private builders continued to make money on construction carried out under the aegis of the public housing trust. The previous vociferous political disputes concerning questions of the Rental Housing Trust's role on the market were toned down.[63] The important dividing line went instead right through the "Coalition of Popular Movements."

In Örebro the premises for "coalition negotiations" were given. Neither the HSB nor the Riksbyggen could mobilize sufficient political resources when disputes arose concerning the distribution of building quotas. However, the Rental Housing Trust could, and it quickly entered into an almost symbiotic relationship with the Social Democratic local council leadership. In the 1950s and 1960s the chair of the council finance department was also director of the trust. For him and his closest colleagues, the issue was perfectly clear very early on: it was not their people who were standing in line for HSB and Riksbyggen cooperative apartments. This observation was confirmed when the state introduced the "ceiling on loans" in 1955, which meant that the required cash deposit went over the previously normal 5 percent of the building costs.[64]

The Rental Housing Trust in Örebro thus became a rapidly growing "fledgling" that seriously threatened to shove its coalition brothers out of the nest. What is more, this municipal trust also took over decision-making rights in housing policy questions from the local council and finance department. And this was the case not only in Örebro. The judicial rules that surrounded trusts, foundations, and stock companies came to function as protective shields behind which important housing policy decisions could be made. For example, in Örebro the trust managed all important land deals without any involvement from the directly elected bodies. This meant that the municipal planning monopoly in practice was conducted by the trust's board, which did not hesitate to make use of it more or less openly.[65] During the 1960s the trust's role in local policy expanded. The Housing Exchange, of which the trust's director was chair, introduced a priority system that was used to promote recruitment of desirable labor and also as an instrument in social policy.[66]

In short, the "model city," Örebro, has been characterized by a heavily politicized housing market. The politics have been conducted by a very small group of Social Democrats who, with the tacit approval of their party cohorts, have been able to act behind a protective bureaucracy. Decisions have been made with alacrity, and the risk of paralyzing public disputes over details in issues of housing policy has been minimized.

"THE PEOPLE'S HOME"

The cost goals formulated by the Social Housing Commission were achieved in the mid-1950s. Low, regulated rents in combination with continued intensive urbanization created growing housing demands, which later became an increasingly heavy political burden on the government party. Under pressure from the 1964 Social Democratic Labor Party Conference, the parliamentary majority decided to take the bull by the horns: in one decade one million dwellings should be built. This was done, with the result that the housing stock grew by about 3 percent per year. At the end of the period Sweden was said to have achieved the highest housing standard in the world measured in terms of space and equipment. It was

Figure 1.   Population and Housing Stock, 1945–1975

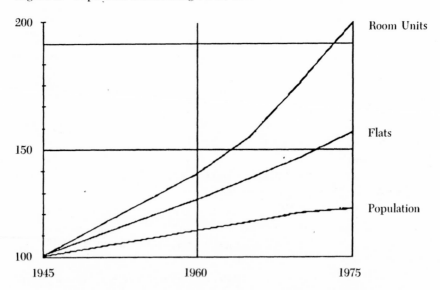

Source: R. Johansson and B. Karlberg, *Bostadspolitiken* (Housing Policy) (Helsingborg, 1979), p. 40.

"an incredible performance," according to one of the researchers referred to at the beginning of this chapter.[67]

The "success story" culminated in the Million Dwellings Program, which was carried out in close cooperation between state and local levels and in accord with the by now traditional division of responsibility. The local authorities were responsible for planning, and in their capacity as chief of the largest builders—the public companies—they were also responsible for production being oriented to long series. The state was responsible for long-term credit, which was to be awarded primarily to large-scale public housing projects. Through the national system of building norms for residential housing, building on an industrial scale would be promoted.[68]

The large scale and the industrialized construction were important prerequisites for the "success story," but they were also vulnerable to the venom of critics. Demands for technical rationality led to uniformity and lack of identity. According to researchers and social critics, life in suburban areas was characterized by passivity, isolation, and alienation and their concomitant social problems.[69] When the suburban Skärholmen Shopping Center outside Stockholm was opened in 1968 as an early tribute to Social Democratic housing policy, a cultural affairs journalist on the liberal *Dagens Nyheter* wrote that "even in the midst of all the hullabaloo, it was clear to many that what they were opening was a '70s slum."[70]

Even so, it was a very Swedish slum. The housing policy that resulted in the opening of Skärholmen's center among other things distinguished itself from the international pattern in two ways. First, the quality was remarkably high. "Before we begin to complain about what is wrong, [let it be said that] we Swedes have a luxurious standard of housing in comparison with most other countries," asserted one of the most eager Swedish critics in the mid-1970s.[71] Second, no special group was singled out as the object of public care. The state was to take responsibility for the construction of the "people's home." In the new constitution that was adopted in 1974, all Swedish citizens were guaranteed not only the right to work and education, but also to housing. Even if the municipal housing companies were awarded comparatively better lending terms, all forms of housing ownership and tenure have been incorporated in the housing policy sphere. According to the Social Housing Commission, state financing of housing construction should comprise "the obvious basis for future housing policy."[72] In Figure 2, where Finland illustrates a more "normal" housing policy from the Western European point of view, it is evident that such has been the case: more

Figure 2. The proportion of completed flats (%) with state loans in Sweden and Finland, 1950–1985.

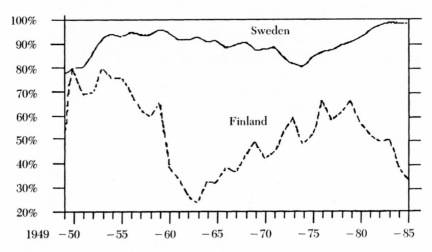

Source: Niva 1989, 112.

than 90 percent of all housing produced in Sweden from 1946 to 1985 involved state loans.

State assistance with the financing of housing construction was naturally a very important means to achieve the ambitious housing policy goals. First and foremost, state assistance helped to maintain high and comparatively steady production. Furthermore, state loans have been associated with detailed quality norms since the mid-1950s, and the building entrepreneurs who did not follow these norms simply did not receive state loans. This meant in practice that all new housing met a very high standard and that the proportion of private luxurious building was limited.

Later, lending regulations aiming at limiting profits on the production side were developed. To a Swedish observer who has watched building costs skyrocket and noted the advancement of building companies through the clearance and rebuilding of inner-city areas, it would seem reasonable to consider such efforts to restrict profits as having failed.[73] However, by international standards Swedish housing policy appears to have been fairly successful in its attempts to restrain building costs. Local authorities in Sweden have obtained better control over sites suitable for building than has been the case in other comparable countries; and with altered lending regulations, the state has tried since the mid-1970s to stimulate competition in production, according to the researchers who have investigated this issue.[74]

Housing policy aimed at regulating conditions for the production of dwellings, but few obstacles blocked profitable resales. In the case of housing cooperatives, the system of regulations has actually been liberalized since World War II. Since the 1920s the individual cooperative housing association has been considered the owner of the dwellings, which at least formally entailed a guarantee that "individual profit" would not occur in that housing stock. However, since 1969 a member of a housing cooperative has been able to put his or her dwelling up for sale on the open market. The economic differences between private and cooperative ownership have thus been largely erased. A similar tendency may be noted regarding private rental apartments. Various types of rent regulations have prevented property owners from charging maximum rents, but here also more market-oriented regulations were introduced at the end of the 1960s. Moreover, in practice private landlords have always been allowed to pick and choose their tenants.[75] In fact, only in rental housing managed by local authority companies (public housing) has "the entire population been given access to sound, spacious, well-planned and efficiently equipped dwellings of good quality at reasonable cost."[76] Since the mid-1970s about 20 percent of the residential housing stock has consisted of such dwellings.

Since the beginning of the 1970s, economic and political support for state and local authority production and management of rental housing has sharply decreased in Western Europe. The most attractive buildings have been sold to private owners or changed into cooperative associations. In many places, perhaps most clearly in Great Britain, the local authority-owned rental units are now beginning to be considered ghettos, where only

Table 1.   Tenure of Housing Stock 1945–1990 (percentages).

	1945	1960	1970	1975	1980	1985	1990
State, municipal, etc.	5	4	4	4	4	2	1
Public housing companies	2	9	17	20	20	21	21
Cooperative	4	11	14	14	14	16	18
Privately rented	51	40	30	23	21	20	20
Owner-occupied	38	36	35	39	41	40 (99)	40
Total	100	100	100	100	100	100	100

Source: Swedish official statistics.

the very poor and socially outcast people live.[77] With the breakdown of the communist regimes in Eastern Europe, the housing market of the planned economy seemed to have received its political coup de grace.[78]

In Sweden these tendencies are comparatively weak. The tax reform launched by the Social Democratic minority government in the autumn of 1989 did presume heavy cuts in the general support for housing construction, but this did not mean in principle any real changes of direction. Although in the early 1980s several local authority housing companies had started to sell some of their housing stock—normally to the HSB or the Riksbyggen—after the parliamentary decision in 1986 prohibiting buyers from taking over the favorable state loans, interest in such purchases tangibly dropped. A few years later, a law was introduced that made it difficult for the local authority housing companies who were so tempted to sell their rental units.[79] The clear message was that public housing was not to be squandered. Hence the most fundamental idea behind postwar housing policy could be defended despite an otherwise very clear tendency toward privatization in other social areas that were also subject to Social Democratic "economic planning." Why? There are at least two answers to this question.

First, public housing has never seriously threatened the development of the capitalist economy in Sweden. On the contrary: the political intervention in the housing market has been basically of the same nature as investments in education and communications—they have comprised elements in the formation of an infrastructure aimed at supporting industrial development. Residential housing has been built at the right time, in the right place, and at a price industrial workers have been able to pay. This has helped to dampen expressions of the bourgeois parties' aversion to regulating the market. When it also became apparent that the Postwar Program's threat to socialize the housing market and state or local authority competition within the building industry had not been implemented, the "coalition of business and industry" lost its primary objective.[80] The political resistance to public housing was therefore never especially strong.

Second, the organizations that have been the bearers of public housing have become, as a consequence of the relative size of the sector, powerful elements of the political establishment on the state and local levels. In addition, many leading Social Democrats, especially on the local level, have been involved in the management of the local authority housing companies, or they have been associated with the tenants' associations, which have mainly recruited their members from among local authority housing company tenants. This particular part of the "coalition of popular movements" forms a power structure of corporatist implementation in the local authorities—and naturally functions also as a shield against attack.[81]

What of the people behind the protective barriers? Are they prepared to defend their form of housing against attacks? In the long run, the answer to this question will probably decide the future of the housing policy model that the Social Democrats developed after the war.

There is hardly any doubt what the answer would have been if the same question had been asked at the end of the 1960s. In the "model city" of Örebro, the Social Democratic leadership considered the residents in the first housing areas as "their people." They had been selected from a long list of housing applicants, and the demands for orderliness were clearly expressed. Those who managed to pass through the eye of the needle landed in "the people's home," in which the city's leading Social Democrat, Harald Aronsson, had the role of family father. The households with a death in the family or a serious illness could expect a visit from him. If a tenant landed in a temporary economic crisis, Aronsson could apply for financial assistance from one or another fund; if the problem was of a more fundamental nature, the family received help to move to a cheaper flat.[82] With reference to the chapter in the present volume by Billings et al., it may be said that Örebro lay somewhere between Vienna and Malmö. In the case of Örebro, it was neither a socialist challenge to the city's bourgeoisie nor an attempt to implant a self-help strategy in the working class; instead it was a question of well-meaning, patriarchal care. It was not difficult for the residents in the local authority housing areas to identify their benefactors—the Social Democrats were the givers of all good gifts.

If the question were to be posed now at the beginning of the 1990s, the answer would be far from self-evident. Ever since local authority rental housing began to be used as a means of social policy, the rental contract has ceased to be proof of orderliness. A vote for social housing is consequently no longer so obviously a vote for social security and group membership. Furthermore, and perhaps most important, the family father has left the "people's home" and has been succeeded by professional representatives of housing market organizations. It is no longer sufficient to take one's problems to some easily identifiable political benefactor. The benefactors' replacements, the permanently elected ombudsmen in the county tenants' association and various employees of the local authority housing companies or social service agencies are considered more as alien bureaucrats than as fathers in "the people's home."[83]

Housing policy again risks being depoliticized, but now not primarily as a result of bourgeois politicians pushing for a "free" housing market. To a large extent the real rights of decision over public housing have instead been transferred from the open political arena to a closed boardroom where the housing policy organizations that were devised over decades of Social Democratic rule now live their own lives. The Swedish housing policy model may be able to cope with threats from political opponents, but it should watch out for its friends.

NOTES

1. On the "coalitions," see Headey (1978), 13–15 and chap. 9; Gustavsson (1980), 180–81; Esping-Andersen (1980), 541–42; Zetterberg (1978), 5–6.

2. *Housing, States and Localities* 1985, especially chap. 3; *Bostad och kapital* (Housing and Capital), 1974, chaps. 4 and 5.

3. Donnison 1967, 97–106, and Esping-Andersen 1980, 9 and 459. The five countries mentioned by Donnison are Sweden, France, Holland, Norway, and West Germany.

4. Gulbrandsen 1982, 288–93; Tufte 1975, 27–29.

5. Andrae 1984, 101; also 1977.

6. Paulsson, part 1, 1972, 491–95.

7. Hammerström 1979, 34–35; cf. Andrae 1984, 107.

8. Alf Johansson 1962, 512–18.

9. Sandahl 1983, 23.

10. Wannfors 1962, 214–18.

11. Fürst 1958, 13–15. The idea of "unearned land increment" stemmed from Ricardo and Mill and was politically interpreted by Henry George, whose program was advocated by the conservative Swedish economist and politician Gustav Cassel, among others. Cf. Nuder 1971, 38–41, and B. Holmström 1988, 8–10.

12. Leasehold Rights, SOU 1980:49, 35–47; Strömberg 1984, 32–35.

13. Sandahl 1983, 29–30. The "own-your-own-home" movement had a clear nationalistic foundation and received great support from the "extreme conservatives at the turn of the century." See Torstendahl 1969, 37.

14. Lindeberg 1983, 7–17; Social Housing Commission, *Final Report*, SOU 1945:63, part 1, 13–15; B. Holmström 1988, 6. The Social Democratic element on the CSA's board hardly contributed any nuances to the picture of a liberal pressure group. Erik Palmstierna had a background in the liberal camp, and Otto Järte would come to make advances to the right.

15. Back 1980, 2 and 8–9.

16. SOU 1945:63, 15 and 19; Back 1980, 4–19, and Alf Johansson 1962, 555–57. Back and Johansson point out that after the rent regulation law was abolished in 1923, the International Employment Bureau in Geneva was able to state that, among the countries investigated, the relation of rent to living costs had developed most unfavorably in Sweden.

17. Alf Johansson 1962, 532; SOU 1945:63, 25.

18. Except for Holland, where rent regulations were abolished the same year as they were in Sweden. Back (1980) has a detailed account of the treatment in parliament of housing

proposals in the period 1916–1925. See also SOU 1945:63, 25–42, and Alf Johansson 1962, 532–66.

19. Sandahl 1983, 33–34.
20. SOU 1945:63, 30; Alf Johansson 1962, 537.
21. SOU 1945:63, 30–35.
22. Program citations in Lindhagen 1972, 175–76.
23. Back 1980, 46–48. Back points out that municipalities were also selected to be the main actors in housing policy in the party program of 1920. Cf. Gerdner 1946, 94–157.
24. Gerdner 1946, 62–157.
25. Alf Johansson 1962, 551–53.
26. *Morgonbris*, no. 5, 1923 (published by the National Federation of Social Democratic Women, Stockholm).
27. Social Democratic Parliament Group *Minutes*, 27 Feb. 1923 (Labor Movement Archives) Stockholm.
28. Review by Lars Olsson of Christer Lundh's thesis, *Debatten om industriell demokrati 1919–1924*, in *Arkiv för studier i arbetarrörelsens historia*, no. 38, 1987. Cf. Back (1980), 47, who argues in a polemic against Gerdner that recommendations for housing cooperatives hardly cropped up wholly unmediated in party discussions in 1919–1920 and hence were not a reflection of the dawning interest in guild socialism. The cooperative currents ran deeper and wider than that, according to Back. Conflict arose in a short debate during the party executive's discussion about continuing collaboration with the Liberals on 26 May 1919 when Harald Åkerberg said: "Does Möller think that the party should bring the operation of the state to its knees? There are divided opinions whether it should be a state or cooperative operation." Neither Möller nor Branting, however, wanted to admit that such a dispute existed.
29. Hultén 1973, 32–39, 43–48, and 82–84.
30. Proposition 1925:202 and app. A.
31. Riksdagen, *Minutes of the First Chamber* 1925:38.
32. Riksdagen, *Minutes of the Second Chamber* 1925:41. Cf. Back 1980, 50–62.
33. SOU 1945:63, 71–78.
34. Ibid., 71–132. The Myrdals' book *Kris i befolkningsfrågan* (Nation and Family [1941]) was published in 1934. As Ann-Sofie Ohlander points out elsewhere in this anthology, Gustav Möller used population policy arguments for tactical purposes: through talking about threats to the Swedish race he was able to get the bourgeois parliamentary majority to go along with social reforms. On the effects of population policy, see Kälvemark (Ohlander) 1980.
35. Gustafson 1974, 48–51.
36. SOU 1945:63, 174–75.
37. Ibid., 195–201. The proposals were presented in SOU 1939:4 and 1942:3. All emanated from the Social Housing Commission.
38. SOU 1945:63, 175–77; Erlander 1973, 153–55.
39. Articles by Per Holm, Arne S. Lundberg, and Göran Sidenbladh in *Plan*, no. 4, 1977.
40. *Labor Movement's Post-War Programme* 1944, 23–24 and 98. Cf. National Tenants' Association 1945. See also Hatje 1978, 65–68.
41. Uno Åhrén wrote an enthusiastic review of *The Culture of Cities* in *Byggmästaren*, no. 20, 1942. Åhrén's contribution to the Social Housing Commission is in SOU 1945:63, 581–640. For Mumford's significance in the Swedish debate on social planning, see, e.g., S. Sahlgren in *Plan*, no. 4, 1977.
42. Folkesdotter 1981, 74.
43. Hatje 1978, 58–62.
44. Riksdagen, *Minutes of the Second Chamber*, Motion, 1944:421. The proposal was rooted in the labor movement's Postwar Program.

45. Riksdagen, *Minutes of the First Chamber* 1946:43, 124; Hatje 1978, 93–99. The inquiry was not over until 1957. The "left-wing falange" included the various organizations of building workers, while Alf Johansson was one of many who had doubts. Ann-Katrin Hatje, who has studied reference material concerning housing policy inquiries during the 1940s and 1950s, believes there to have been a general division in the Social Democratic party: the "popular movement" group's proposals were more left-wing than those of the group of civil servants who had the ear of the government (pp. 114–15).

46. Strömberg 1984, 44; Hatje 1978, 89 (quote).

47. SOU 1945:63, 349 (quote), 351–69 and 435.

48. Ibid., 537.

49. Proposition 1946:279; First Chamber 1947:34; Second Chamber 1947:34.

50. Nestor 1979, 114–16; Gulbrandsen 1980, 303 and 305; and *Minutes* from the Housing Policy Conference in Stockholm, 8 Jan. 1948 (Department of Social Affairs, nonexecutive documents, Jan.–Feb. 1948 in the National Archives).

51. Rudberg 1981, 159–60.

52. SOU 1945:63, 543–44.

53. Strömberg 1984, 48.

54. H. Johansson 1966, 39–40.

55. Sidenbladh in *Plan*, no. 4, 1977, 199, where influences from Attlee's Labour government are pointed out.

56. Hatje 1978, 73–75.

57. Lindberg 1982, 131–23. Lindberg makes the important reservation that the explanations presented are only so "in a statistical sense." As he points out, causal explanations cannot be achieved with statistical methods (p. 49).

58. Ibid., 130–31.

59. Ibid., 132.

60. See, e.g., a survey article by Eva Eriksson in *Arkitektur*, no. 6, 1979.

61. Strömberg 1984, 42–63 and 118.

62. Ibid., 51.

63. Ibid., 52–55.

64. Ibid., 59–63. Cf. Gustafson 1974, 63–64. Gustafson points out that the heavy increase in deposit amounts—up to 15 percent of the building costs—caused a social restructuring in the HSB's membership.

65. Egerö 1979, 98–102; Strömberg 1984, 62–63. It has been shown that in practice the municipal planning monopoly could function as an efficient planning means only when the local authorities, or the municipal housing trusts themselves, owned a large part of the land suitable for building. "When the builders own the land, the local authorities are powerless." (Uno Åhrén, interviewed in *Arkitekttidningen*, no. 15, 1979).

66. Egerö 1979, 116–25; Strömberg, *Mönsterstaden: Mark och bostadspolitik i efterkrigstidens Örebro* (The Model City: Land and Housing Policy in Postwar Örebro), 1989, 21–23.

67. Headey 1978, 82 (quote); Pierre 1986, 221. Pierre points out that this conference decision was unusually categorical. The contents of the parliamentary decision are in Proposition 1965:1, app. 13; Proposition 1966:1, app. 13; and 1967:100. One of the greatest supporters of the program was the SSU (Social Democratic Youth), whose chair was Ingvar Carlsson. Cf. L. Holm 1987.

68. Sandahl 1983, chap. 5.

69. In their first chapter Franzén and Sandstedt (1981) summarize the criticism against the Million Dwellings Program's suburbs.

70. Cited in *Arkitektur*, no. 11, 1968, under the headline "Presskoncentrat" ("Press Summaries").

71. *Herta* no. 2/76. Interview with Ulf Brunfelter, the Building Committee of Private Commerce and Industry.

72. SOU 1945:63, 500. A departure from this principle was made during the period from 1967 to 1974, when the general interest subsidies were canceled. However, in conjunction with the review of housing policy carried out in 1974, a general interest subsidy was reinstated with the expressed intention of treating all forms of tenure equally (Niva 1989, 285).

73. See, e.g., Thomas Hall, "Bygga på åttiotalet: en fråga om kohandel?" in *Dagens Nyheter*, 5 Sept. 1989.

74. Dickens et al. 1985, 110–14; Niva 1989, 310–20; Esping-Andersen 1980, 8 and chap. 10.

75. Sandberg and Ståhl 1976, 17; Gustafson 1974, 63–64.

76. Proposition 100/1967, 172. Cf. Proposition 150/1974, 348.

77. Elander 1991, 29.

78. European Network for Housing Research *Newsletter*, Jan. 1991; National Swedish Institute for Building Research.

79. Elander 1991, 29.

80. Danermark et al. 1985, 24–25.

81. Lundqvist 1988, 172.

82. Strömberg 1989, 24.

83. Jacobson 1991.

Peter Billing,
Lars Olsson, and
Mikael Stigendal

9

"Malmö—Our Town":
Local Politics in Social Democracy

We are sitting in the Hotel Stockholm in Malmö on 6 November 1881, listening to a bearded master tailor: "Gentlemen! It is no disgrace to be a socialist. Know that [to be] a socialist means to improve society, and what can be better than to help improve that society which is rotten, that society founded on lies and consisting of injustice. . . . In the unions of workers lies the germ of new ideas which in time will rule the world."[1]

The words are August Palm's,[2] and they come from Sweden's first socialist speech, *Hvad vilja socialisterna?* (What Do Socialists Want?). The speech was described in the newspapers as "rather confused," and many listeners were seen to smirk at the "foreign words and swearing."[3] But when the workers associations proliferated into a nationwide labor movement, the jeering died down. In honor of Master Palm's centenary in 1949, the Social Democratic editor Rickard Lindström recalled events in Malmö during the 1880s and 1890s: "if like various religions, the labor movement would designate certain places as holy, Malmö should certainly be one, socialism's Mecca or Jerusalem or whatever, for here occurred a miracle of creation."[4]

IT ALL BEGAN IN MALMÖ*

The country's first union of workers, the Swedish Workers Association, was formed in Malmö (1882), as was the first socialist women's association, the National Association of Women Workers (1888). Axel Danielsson, author of the party's first program, lived and worked in Malmö during the latter part of his life.[5] The Swedish labor movement erected its first Folkets Hus and created its first Folkets Park (People's or Community Hall and People's Park) in Malmö. In due course the town's sons and daughters were elected to important positions in both the government and the Riksdag. In the Malmö City Council the Social Democrats retained the confidence of the voters for sixty-seven years. The choice of Malmö, "our town," to represent a successful local social democracy is not difficult to justify.[6]

When the Social Democrats won their first election to the Malmö City Council in 1919, the working class all over Europe was striving for socialism. However, the advent of democracy in Central, Western, and Northern Europe did not result in any genuine Social Democratic government in the 1920s. Instead, opportunities for socialist politics arose in the large industrial towns and cities. All eyes were focused on Vienna, where the labor movement carried out a "social experiment," a reformist alternative to the Russian revolution, between the fall of the monarchy in 1918 and the victory of fascism in 1934. Along with the Swedish Social Democrats' economic crisis policy during the 1930s, the "Austro-Marxist" cultural and social policy in Vienna is usually referred to as an example of successful Social Democratic policy during the interwar period.

In Malmö the party was not ravaged by fascism, but neither were the dreams of a "socialist city" realized. The election failure of 1985 and the perspective of a century provoke questions concerning the prerequisites for

*Malmö is situated in Skåne (Scania), the southernmost province of Sweden, across the Sound (Öresund) from Copenhagen. Malmö has been the third largest city in Sweden since the turn of the century. In 1989 it had a population of 230,000; its location in a prosperous agrarian region with wealthy capitalists and cheap labor as well as its proximity to the continent, which has facilitated both commerce and access to modern ideas, laid the foundations for the political success of Social Democracy in Malmö. [The early success on the local level was soon followed by a considerable influence on a national level, both in government and in the Riksdag. As a consequence the Social Democrats from Malmö were assigned a crucial role in the shaping of Social Democratic policies. Accordingly, when the opportunities for local initiatives were hampered by restrictions, e.g. in housing construction, the Social Democrats in Malmö found themselves in a more privileged position compared to their counterparts in (most) other Swedish cities.]

local Social Democratic politics, their orientation, and their limitations, to which we will address ourselves. We hope to sharpen the outline of developments in Malmö by making comparisons with those in Vienna. Through using pairs of contrasts—working class–petite bourgeoisie, men–women, labor–capital, self-help strategy–municipal socialism, and the neighborhood community–"dis-community"—we shall try to show how a system developed. In the shadows of the system social forces were gathering, forces that began to proliferate when the system became undermined.

THE NEIGHBORHOOD COMMUNITY

In depictions of the fledgling labor movement, poverty and oppression are normally emphasized. The sense of community that arises when people live close to each other has been noted less often. Having one's work, living quarters, shops, and like-minded people as well as different generations all in close proximity promoted a sense of belonging, and together they formed what can be called a neighborhood community, which undoubtedly facilitated political mobilization.[7]

Between People and Class
Neighborhood communities were above all dominated by the working class, and in particular by women. Men primarily shared long workdays together and the good opportunities offered thereby for discussions. Many women participated in the community of the workplace, but they also met in shops, in the courtyards while hanging out the laundry, on the landings, and when there was no more sugar, flour, or coffee in the larder. The neighbor woman kept an eye on the children and took care of them when their mother got a bit of work. In Malmö many women were wage earners in their own home, working in the home industries. In the factories, where about 45 percent of the workers were women, women most often had inferior jobs (e.g., in the textile mills) and were therefore forced to submit to foremen or superior skilled workers, who were men. In a city like Malmö, with entrenched poverty and a great many menial female jobs, men and male culture early on formed enclaves of authority in working life while having only nominal responsibility for the neighborhood community as a whole.[8]

The city of Malmö.

© Malmö stadsbyggnadskontor (*Source*: Malmö Municipal Planning Office)

Parts of Malmö Mentioned in Chapter 9 (most names come from former farms or villages):

Augustenborg (August/a: name; borg = castle)	E 5
Ellstorp (Ell from Elna; torp = village or crofter's holding; named after Elna Perstorp, 1898)	
Hamnen (= the harbor)	E 2
Holma (home = islet)	D–E 1
Innerstaden (downtown)	C 5
Kirseberg [Kirse [dialect.]: cherry; berg = mountain/hill)	C–D 2–3
Lindängen (lind = linden/lime tree; äng = meadow)	F 2
Lugnet (= the quiet place)	D–E 6
Möllevången (dialect: windmill field; vången: idiom for rotation farming)	D 3
Rosengård (= rose garden)	D 3–4
Sorgenfri (= without trouble)	F 4
Stadion (= stadium)	D–E 3
Triangeln (= triangle)	C 4
	D 3

The neighborhood communities in the growing industrial cities also contained members of the lower middle class: for example, shoemakers, shopkeepers, fishmongers, and barbers/hairdressers. Mutual dependence and shared poverty normally put the working class and the "proletarian" petite bourgeoisie on good relations. Some working-class families also conducted various sorts of "small business" alongside their ordinary work. Tailors could stretch their wages by making suits in their free time. Casual workers, like stevedores or building workers, could change into some sort of small businessmen when there was less work. The links between small business activities and the working class were often formed by women. Wives would go out to the country and exchange old clothes for chickens, eggs, and pork; others sold vegetables in the square. In these respects, the two classes entered into each other's daily lives. With their shops and beer halls as meeting places, the lower middle class multiplied the possibilities for shared existence. The daily life of the neighborhood community revolved around working-class women and men and the petite bourgeoisie—their working times, mealtimes, opening times, washing times, and sleeping times.

Malmö's labor movement grew out of such ties and the close proximity between the working class and the lower middle class. In the quarter of Kirseberg, however, rampant poverty, closeness to the countryside, and lack of factories resulted in impotent class feelings and paralyzed political struggles. In the Möllevången district, on the other hand, there were plenty of factories to create a breeding ground for working-class consciousness, and shopkeepers were defied by workers who started their own consumer cooperatives, Seger and Solidar (Victory and Solidarity). The interdependence of the working class and the petite bourgeoisie was weakened when wages stretched far enough for workers to pay with cash in the shops. In Folkets Park, Folkets Hus, and the ABF (Arbetarnas Bildningsförbund, the Workers' Educational Association) the working class created its own culture. However, the throng of factories, tenement houses, and the typical Möllevång neighborhood square arose after 1905; so during its first decade, the SAP was not affected by the social character of either Kirseberg or Möllevången.

In fact, perhaps the typical Social Democratic neighborhood community was to be found between Kirseberg and the newly built Möllevången. Perhaps the Malmö party was most influenced by the relations between the working class and the "proletarian" lower middle class that prevailed in the districts of Lugnet and Östra Förstaden toward the end of the nineteenth century, where the close proximity of these classes neither paralyzed nor incited conflict but instead generated a successful political force.

The SAP's election successes occurred when the party understood that it should utilize this political force through directing its efforts toward ordinary people in general instead of narrowly focusing on class. The Social Democratic movement in Malmö, probably earlier than elsewhere, positioned itself politically between "class and the people," and by doing so the party achieved a correlation between its political orientation and the popular voter base of neighborhood communities.[9]

The same year the SAP came to power in Malmö (1919), its counterpart in Vienna took up residence in the town hall. The Social Democrats in Vienna, however, were influenced much more by the working class per se than by ordinary people in the broad sense of the term.

Red Vienna

With the peace treaties of 1918, Austria lost its old multinational empire's large industrial centers and agricultural resources in the East. Industries were now concentrated in Vienna. The capital's large working class and strong labor movement were confronted with a countryside dominated by the agrarian petite bourgeoisie and the Christian-Social party.[10] A national coalition government had been formed when the empire broke down in order to ensure a bourgeois democracy. When the wave of revolutions in Central Europe began to ebb and the ruling class in Vienna started to recover, the crisis-based coalition became unviable. It was dissolved, and the Christian-Social party formed a government with its headquarters in Vienna. Supported by the Catholic church, it relentlessly attacked the Social Democratic opposition.

Thus the opportunities for Social Democratic reform policies arose on the local level in Vienna. When the first local general election occurred in 1919, the Social Democrats won overwhelmingly. The newly elected mayor, Jakob Reumann, set the tone immediately: "The social revolution must follow upon the political. When society takes over the means of production, important tasks fall to the State's largest municipality. [We] shall commence the great work of making the municipality master of the land [and] obtain for all residents suitable homes."[11]

The prerequisites for local authority intervention were substantially improved by the constitutional changes of 1922, when Vienna was made into a state. This enabled the Social Democrats to enact both legislation and taxation without being threatened by interference from the national government. An ambitious housing program was initiated in Vienna, and from 1920 to 1933 over fifty-eight thousand flats were built in the Wiener Höfe. Residential buildings were equipped with social amenities such as children's nurseries, collective washing facilities, medical and dental services, libraries, and social service advice bureaus.

The housing program was part of what we will term a *municipal socialist* strategy. The Social Democrats in Vienna intended to go beyond the existing framework of society in a socialist direction and did not hesitate to challenge openly the city's bourgeoisie. In order to satisfy working-class interests to as great an extent as possible and to hold rent levels down, building was financed by special, socially equitable taxes that were earmarked for the purpose. In fact the entire housing project was financed through taxes on the upper class—for example, taxes on superfluous rooms in residences, on vehicles, on entertainment, on dogs, on servants, and on expensive restaurants.

It was also part of this municipal socialist strategy to encourage socialist culture and socialist ideals. A large number of Social Democratic associations or societies were formed so that people could participate in the socialist process. Remarkably, many women participated in these groups in Wiener Höfe—93 percent, according to an inquiry from 1931. Great weight was also given to educating children in working-class culture, not least through the workers' association Kinderfreunde and its school for training socialist educators.

To symbolize political goals, the blocks in Wiener Höfe were named after leading figures in both the domestic and the international labor movement, but also after prominent bourgeois radicals: Friedrich Engels-Hof, Liebknecht-Hof, Jean Jaurès-Hof, George Washington-Hof, Goethe-Hof, etc. Most symbolic of them all, however, was the Karl Marx-Hof's kilometer-long building, broken only by a viaduct-like portal in the middle through which about forty thousand people passed on Sunday mornings on their way to soccer matches at Hohe Warte Stadium.

The Social Democrats in Vienna created a novel neighborhood community through which political struggles ran like a red thread. However, in comparison with its counterparts in Malmö, Wiener Höfe lacked a similar close connection between the working class and the lower middle class. To Vienna's large lower middle class (40 percent of the population before the war), municipal socialism was a direct threat. Even the coalition government's reforms—the eight-hour workday, paid holidays, collective contract agreements, and workers' councils in factories—which were adopted through Social Democratic initiatives, engendered discord and faction since the reforms did not take petit bourgeois interests into account. And indeed, the lower middle class was hit hardest by the economic crisis of 1923, with its soaring inflation. The successes of the Social Democrats' municipal socialism in Vienna widened the boundaries between the petite bourgeoisie and class-conscious workers, and this opposition laid the foundations for fascism in the Austrian lower middle class.

The majority of workers supported the Social Democrats in elections. In 1919 the party received 54 percent of the votes in Vienna; in 1927, 60 percent; and in 1932, 59 percent. However, only the working class in Wiener Höfe was prepared to defend its party at any price, and possibly there was some degree of alienation between politically conscious workers in Wiener Höfe and the working class in the older neighborhood communities. At the beginning of the 1930s, the majority of the working class still lived in close proximity to the petite bourgeoisie in the old working-class quarters within Wiener Höfe. In February 1934, after four days of class warfare concentrated in Wiener Höfe, the municipal socialists had to lay down their arms. Supported by the lower middle class, the fascists put an end to the experiment with socialist neighborhood communities in Vienna.

FROM CONFRONTATION TO MUTUAL UNDERSTANDING

Industrial Empire and Traditions

In contrast to their party comrades in Vienna, the growing Social Democratic movement in Malmö was faced with powerful and well-organized capitalists, whose power derived from several centuries of capital accumulation and traditions. The majority of Malmö's large companies, headed by the textile factories and Kockum's Mekaniska Verkstad, inter alia an important shipbuilding company, composed a network of dependence and control. Toward the end of the nineteenth century, Skåne's Enskilda Bank, at the time the largest commercial bank in Sweden, placed itself in the center, like a spider in a web. The board of this bank determined the future of Malmö's economy.[12]

These same powerful capitalists, sitting in the city council, created the best possible conditions for industrial capitalism. This concentration of economic, political, and ideological executive power reached a peak during the decades around the turn of the century, when the city's undisputed patriarch, Carl Herslow, was chair of both the city council and Skåne's Enskilda Bank. As chief editor, managing director, and chair of the board of *Sydsvenska Dagbladet*, the leading bourgeois newspaper, Herslow also had control over the written word.

The leaders of the labor movement must have been forced to think carefully, confronted as they were with such formidable bourgeois resources. In Malmö the road to socialism seemed much more difficult than in Vienna, where industrial capitalism had developed under the aegis of empire and where the bourgeois class's access to independent power resources was limited. When the empire collapsed, the bourgeois class subordinated and bound to it was also weakened. In Malmö, a well-integrated and strong bourgeois class repelled the workers' strikes and demonstrations with force. Defiance of bourgeois order was severely punished, and Axel Danielsson's own periods in prison led to a change of political course. The dreams of a revolution "early in the morning" were replaced by a daily struggle for the right to vote "on Social Democratic bargaining territory."[13] Danielsson's newly awakened insights attracted the particular attention of a skilled worker with roots in the peasant class: Nils Persson.

The Social Democrat Nils Persson

Nils Persson was born in 1865 to relatively well-off farmers in Östra Wemmerlöv, a small village in Skåne.[14] Books interested him early in life, and he was said to have read the Bible through twice. In 1884 he became an apprentice bricklayer in Malmö and four years later became a journeyman. He joined the Malmö Bricklayers Association, one of the first modern trade associations. Alongside union work, he completed his education to become a master bricklayer in the Technical Evening School in Malmö and at a school in Copenhagen. In 1892 he was elected chair of the trade association and two years later entrusted with the leadership of the newly formed Swedish Bricklayers Union. Persson represented the union for thirty years as secretary and treasurer as well as chair—executive meetings were held in the Perssons' living room.

In 1892 Nils Persson married Mathilda Isberg, whom he met through union activities. She was a leader in the Malmö women's discussion club, a forerunner to the SAP women's movement, and she joined the party in 1889, the year it was formed. The women's club often complained of the men's lack of interest in organizing women. Axel Danielsson enjoined the women to restrain their own demands in the interest of the entire working

class, that is, the men.[15] The very words "women's movement" made the
blood rise among many men; contributions from women were requested
only during strikes, a fact recalled by Martha Larsson: "Then the local party
group would send us female members out to bolster the morale of the
strikers' wives: we organized coffee klatches, encouraged visiting and told
them what a great thing they were helping to fight for."[16]

When several leading women in Malmö, such as Elma Sundqvist (Danielsson), Martha Larsson, Maria Osberg (Wessel), and Mathilda Isberg
(Persson), married prominent men in the party, Malmö's burgeoning
women's movement was weakened. For Mathilda Persson, marriage meant
that she found herself managing the ongoing affairs of the Bricklayers
Union (for instance, correspondence, circulars, and payments) since Nils
Persson was often in Stockholm.

Nils Persson was named chair of the Social Democratic newspaper *Arbetet* and participated in the formation of a cooperative association of bakeries
and the consumer association PAN. When Danielsson died in 1899, he was
succeeded by Persson as the party's first candidate for both the local council and the Riksdag. In 1901 Persson was elected to the city council, and
the following year he occupied one of the party's four seats in the Riksdag.

Persson made it clear early on that politically he advocated negotiation
and mutual understanding. During a speaking tour in 1903, his speeches
were admired, even in the right-wing press: "His speech was given in a
most moderate tone. No harsh language was used. He did not see a 'scoun-
drel' in every employer, [and] the views he presented were in most cases
such that under certain conditions, they could be accepted by anyone."[17]
Persson's confidence in negotiation and in the state, however, lacked Danielsson's critical wariness. Under Persson's leadership the Malmö labor
movement's underpinnings in the Marxist tenets propounded by Danielsson were weakened. Instead, Persson's invocations of state intervention
revealed glimpses of the professional friend of the temperance movement
with rural origins. Persson was thus instrumental in placing the labor
movement "between class and state."[18]

As a living link between the petit bourgeois and the working class, Persson often revealed tendencies toward social liberalism. Possibly more than
anyone else in the Social Democratic group in the Riksdag he was on good
terms with the Liberals. Liberal parliamentary representatives often concurred with Persson's statements, and he did not oppose the Liberal government's proposal in 1906 for legislated state mediation in labor market
disputes.[19] In the same year he made a statement dismissing narrow, class-

oriented politics: "A happy future development in our country chiefly requires that the *entire population* feels an affinity with the country and its institutions."[20]

Together with Nils Persson, such leading party members in Malmö as August "Kabbarparn" Nilsson and Värner Rydén endeavored to follow Danielsson's change of course. Nilsson took over the editorship of *Arbetet* after Danielsson and sat on the city council with Persson in 1901. Rydén was a teacher in the Malmö elementary schools and was voted into the Riksdag at the same time as Nilsson in 1905. Together with Nilsson and Rydén, Persson belonged to the right wing of the party's parliament group.[21]

The Dawn of Mutual Understanding

In the spring of 1889, the workers at the Skånska Cement factory in Lomma, outside of Malmö, formed a workers' club. Over four hundred workers rapidly organized themselves. The factory management, led by its director, R. F. Berg, perceived the workers' club as a threat and responded with comprehensive reprisals. Although the conflict ended in victory for the factory management, it gave Berg food for thought. In the newspaper *Arbetet* Axel Danielsson harshly attacked Berg, calling him "cement-hearted." "Another such victory and the cement company is lost," predicted Danielsson.[22]

In time, Berg came to the same conclusion. When the workers at the cement factory in Limhamn formed a labor union nine years later, he met them with a different attitude. Later, Berg became one of the country's most ardent advocates of mutual agreement. In 1906 he was instrumental in guiding the SAF (Swedish Employers Confederation) toward the negotiation table:[23] "It has cost me—to renounce many prejudices and many old axioms, to exchange many old ideas for new, to cease being a benevolent patriarch and instead feel pleased when people can help themselves."[24]

In Malmö Berg was a member of the city council, where his efforts were shared by leading bourgeois factions. Kockum's director, Hjalmar Wessberg, signed one of the country's first collective agreements in 1897. Carl Herslow himself early on stressed the importance of political accord.[25] They were ready to shake hands—but not with just anyone. The urgent need to improve the living conditions of a large majority of people was not to be allowed to jeopardize society's economic prerequisites. Clad in the attire of socially responsible liberalism, the leaders of Malmö's bourgeoisie advanced to meet their counterparts on the other side. Led by Nils Persson, Malmö's labor movement reached out and took the proffered hand of this powerful group.

When the Social Democrats won the local election of 1919, political accord was well prepared for. Nils Persson, the new leader of the council,
succeeding the right-wing capitalist Ernst Wehtje, Sr., recalled in his
maiden speech the importance of mutual agreement: "Even though the
election has gone along party lines, I am nonetheless convinced that . . .
we should be able to agree on one thing—to devote all efforts to our town,
for the benefit of its inhabitants."[26] Persson's speech lacked the socialist
fervor expressed by his counterpart in Vienna, Jakob Reumann, at the
same time.

Only two years later, this mutual understanding was put to the test. In
the question of reimbursement for emergency relief work, Nils Persson and
six other leading Social Democratic council members reached a compromise with the Conservative party. This provoked protests from the council's majority of Social Democrats and from party members. The editor of
Arbetet, Arthur Engberg, was also critical. At a stormy meeting in Folkets
Park, during which someone spat in Nils Persson's face, all seven were
forced to resign from the city council. However, both Social Democratic
and bourgeois members of the council refused to accept their resignations,
so they were withdrawn.[27]

This event gives a measure of how well anchored the commitment to
accord was in the parties' leadership. Despite a grueling internal debate
and appeals for unity from the local SAP chair, Olof Andersson, the seven
decided not to submit to the will of the majority.[28] The bourgeois parties
were faced with the possibility of seriously deepening the splits in the labor
movement and discrediting its leadership by accepting the resignations.
Instead, they chose to safeguard accord. Their positions were reviewed in
the leading bourgeois organ, *Sydsvenska Dagbladet*: "As regards those individuals now obliged to resign, we must admit—albeit as political opponents—that they represent the best of what the Social Democratic Labor
Party has to offer in terms of experience—independence and competence.
Should their resignations be decisive, it will not only be a loss for the
party, but also a very great loss for the whole community."[29]

The Strategy of the Arbetarekommun[30]

The local party's early orientation toward political accord issued out of the
confrontation with a powerful bourgeoisie that would not allow itself to be
disregarded. In contrast to Vienna,[31] municipal laws harnessed Malmö Social Democrats to a fairly cautious reform policy. The regulation concerning
a qualified majority had been incorporated into the municipal laws in 1862,
and it was not repealed until the 1940s. It stipulated that a two-thirds ma-

jority was required for decisions regarding, for example, "the purchase of such property wherein purchase does not impinge upon the carrying out of approved city plans or the parceling out of land" and "the granting of funds for new purposes or needs."[32] The regulation concerning a qualified majority substantially circumscribed political democracy in the local council.

The orientation toward political accord was linked to a strategy that can hardly be called socialist. Rather, the Social Democratic leadership in Malmö was guided by a strategy we will term the *strategy of self-help*, which advocated market-oriented self-help (e.g., cooperative home ownership or cooperative associations) more than local authority control. The idea of self-help originally derived from Axel Danielsson, who became "the first Swedish Social Democrat to give consumer cooperation an ideological motive."[33] For Danielsson, self-help was part and parcel of socialist strategy, and in the pamphlet *Social självhjälp* (Social Self-Help) from 1898, he based cooperation on Marxist social analysis. Danielsson wished to use cooperation "to transform the bourgeois society's economic organization. . . . All forms of cooperation are, of course, . . . a direct enemy of capitalism."[34]

Danielsson's advocacy of cooperative self-help released a strong ideological current within Malmö's labor movement and, in our judgment, should be counted as his most permanent legacy. After his death in 1899, however, such intervention to transform the economic organization of society was deferred to a distant future. Under the influence of leading Social Democrats such as Nils Persson and Emil Olsson, self-help initiatives were successively adapted to the market economy, and the party confined itself to improving the living conditions of the population within the framework of capitalism. This "self-help strategy" can be characterized as social-liberal reformism in contrast to the type of socialist reformism pursued by, for example, the local Austro-Marxists.[35]

With dampened socialist ambitions, self-help was implemented within the framework of accord as an independent strategy. Without immediately encroaching upon the capitalists' power, cooperation managed to satisfy demands from the working class to struggle collectively for better living conditions; moreover, the owners of capital found no reason to combat measures that would ensure their access to a labor force. Under the aegis of mutual agreement, Malmö City Council approved in 1922 a bipartisan motion from the Social Democrat Johan Nilsson and the Conservative manager of a large woolen mill, August Schmitz, to establish a large owner-occupied housing association.[36]

In the strategy of self-help both "the Fighter with burning feelings and

courage" from 1910 and Möllevången from the 1920s were formed into a
bulwark that the bourgeoisie did not find overly challenging.[37] However, in
the neighborhood communities this self-help strategy also caused the first
split between the working class and the petite bourgeoisie when competition intensified between private and cooperative food shops.

CHANGES IN THE NEIGHBORHOOD COMMUNITIES

The Self-Help Strategy

With a good deal of pain and anguish, Malmö was transformed from a
middle-sized trading town to one of the country's major industrial cities.
Between 1890 and 1920 the population increased from 48,000 to over
114,000. Many new arrivals faced uncertain employment and miserable
housing conditions. During the period of skyrocketing prices, unemployment, and housing shortages during World War I, the problems became
acute. In order to give all its inhabitants a roof over their heads, the municipality was forced to set up emergency housing in the damp prison cells of
the old fortress of Malmöhus, in quarters belonging to the Swedish tobacco
monopoly, in the run-down water tower in the district of Kirseberg, and
elsewhere.[38]

In the mid-1920s in the district of Sorgenfri (the name means "without
trouble"), a number of barracks for housing the poor and large workers'
families were erected. This was conceived as an emergency measure, but
the municipality did not tear down what the locals called "the Hollyvood
barracks" until the 1960s: "Hollyvood, the realm of the poor—here live the
very poorest people in Malmö . . . people who have been evicted, who
have happened to get sick, the unemployed, the divorced, the old, or those
who in one way or another have landed by the wayside."[39]

In light of the neighborhood communities' great need for change, the
measures implemented by the city after the Social Democrats came to
power in 1919 seem at first glance rather modest. Municipal socialist efforts
were made, but to a limited extent. No particular increase in municipal
housing or land acquisition, for example, occurred during the first fifteen
years of Social Democratic rule. In addition to the period of inflation and
the qualified majority rule, the parliamentary decision to retrench loans
and the abolition of rent regulations in 1923 set palpable limits on the city's
range of action. However, the city's modest efforts may primarily be ex-

plained by the self-help strategy and its strong hold on the party. After the death of Nils Persson in 1927, the managing director of the consumer cooperative Solidar, Emil Olsson, was elected the new Social Democratic chair of the council, and the city government began to lean toward what can be called political assistance to market-oriented self-help.[40]

Backed by the city, market-oriented self-help flourished during the 1920s and 1930s. The building of owner-occupied cooperative homes increased enormously from 1911 to 1935, when seventeen owner-occupied housing areas were completed in Malmö and its suburbs. Between 1920 and 1940 over seven thousand cooperatively owned flats were built containing popular modern amenities such as bathtubs, laundry rooms, refrigerators, and central heating. During the same period housing cooperatives increased their share of the total multifamily housing stock from about 2 percent to 18 percent. The consumer cooperatives Solidar and Seger welcomed a stream of new members, and everywhere in Malmö many new shops were opened. In 1926 the two cooperatives merged, and by 1930, with 13,000 members (every tenth inhabitant) and 172 shops, Solidar was the country's second largest consumer cooperative association.[41]

Thus, in contrast to their comrades in Vienna, the Social Democratic leadership in the Malmö city government took on no comprehensive responsibility for the transformation of their immediate surroundings. Instead, the party's successes must be measured by the expansion of self-help. However, self-help was not suitable for everyone. The real underclass in neighborhood communities was generally not embraced by the changes brought about by self-help. The unemployed, the elderly, the sick, unskilled laborers, and the large families from the Sorgenfri barracks could neither afford the deposits required for cooperative housing nor pay cash in cooperative shops.

Neither were the doubly employed women in these communities included in the self-help strategy. Among the fifty-seven board members of Solidar in 1925, only four were women, all of them "wives."[42] Rather, the expansion of the strategy was connected with the decline of the women's movement; the local SAP executive contained no women for thirty years, from 1912 to 1942. The city's large lower working class composed of women thus wielded no political influence, and consequently their vital experience of human relations was not taken advantage of.

The strategy of self-help was primarily directed toward the upper strata of the working class—conscientious workers, likely married, who represented an ideal within the labor movement in the early twentieth century.

In particular, self-help attracted healthy, steady, capable, and industrious men, generally with a bit saved on the side. One of the more prominent of these men was Hugo Åberg.[43]

A Cooperative Entrepreneur

Hugo Åberg was born in 1905 in Malmö.[44] His father worked as a lineman on the railroad, and Åberg followed in his father's footsteps. The strong hands required of a brakeman were an advantage when Åberg went to practice boxing on free evenings. Along with the working-class sport of boxing, Åberg learned early on to play the accordion, the musical instrument of ordinary working people. At the age of fourteen he earned his first money playing for a dance. Åberg did not stay long with the railroad, but instead set out for the countryside to look for work. He was employed as a young, "kid" farmhand and had the task of breaking in young horses.

However, Åberg quite soon returned to Malmö, where he landed in the beginning of the bitter 1930s. On one occasion he was designated the town's poorest man by a clothing shop and was given a free suit. Åberg straightaway became a member of the SAP and, being unemployed, engaged himself in the association of unemployed persons, where he was given the task of doling out benefits. In due course Åberg was employed as an assistant on a construction site, and he devoted his free time to studying the science of building materials in order to retain employment. When he was only twenty-seven he borrowed money from the bank to build a house; when the house was finished, he sold it and made a small profit. Åberg continued to build single-family houses, and his profits increased. News of his effective building techniques spread.

Perhaps because of his party membership, Åberg soon came into contact with the Hyresgästernas Bostadsproduktion HB (Tenants' Housing Production Company) in the latter half of the 1930s. He offered to build cooperative housing for the HB on the allotment area, Ellstorp, which he had bought from the city with the industrial capitalist Ernst Wehtje as creditor.[45] The HB was so satisfied with the finished product—high-rise blocks—that Åberg was made managing director, and he remained committed to cooperative housing until 1958. Alongside his engagement in cooperatives, he acquired a considerable fortune in harness racing and private building projects. His crowning glory was the Kronprinsen (Crown Prince), the country's highest residential block; he died a few years later, in 1969, as "the country's richest Social Democrat."[46]

Hugo Åberg exemplifies the sort of person who could utilize the self-help strategy; his career also illustrates how the labor movement's contacts with large capital interests developed. Among the letters commemorating Åberg's sixtieth birthday in 1965 was one from Ernst Wehtje, Jr.: "We met for the first time over thirty years ago in company with my seventy-year-old father. . . . You then laid the foundations for a trust that later stretched far and wide. . . . We are proud to have such a builder among us, a master of planning and executing ideas in tune with the times—and for posterity."[47]

Ernst Wehtje, head of Sweden's most powerful finance family in the 1950s and 1960s after the Wallenbergs, was the capitalist patriarch of Malmö. From his own companies, Skånska Cement and Skånska Cementgjuteriet (Skånska Cement Foundry), he dominated a sphere of interests that encompassed most of the city's large businesses.[48] He doubtless offered both Åberg and the HB credit, favorable prices, and reliable deliveries.[49] Through Åberg, Wehtje's capital interests also wielded increasing influence over the transformation of neighborhood communities.

The Municipal Socialists

Malmö's rapid growth, its troublesome unemployment, and its chronic housing shortages exposed the lacunae in the self-help strategy. The SAP's success in the parliamentary election of 1932 and its attainment of a qualified majority in the city council elections of 1934 (retained until 1946) created favorable conditions for local authority intervention. Aided by more generous housing loan regulations and the parliamentary decision in 1935 on support for large families, a social housing policy was formed in Malmö. Between 1937 and 1942, through the Solgård Foundation, the city built over two hundred flats for large families. With the building of special pensioners flats and the introduction of a family allowance for housing and a municipal rent allowance, Malmö in the 1940s pioneered social housing policy in certain respects.[50]

With the rise of social housing policy appeared a new faction in the party whose most prominent representative was Axel E. Svensson, chair of the third section of the city Finance Department (later the Real Estate Committee) and member of the party's Council of Representatives. His criticism of the housing cooperatives' orientation toward the upper strata of the working class and the HB's close associations with capital were warmly received among those wishing to increase local government responsibility for shaping the neighborhood community. The local socialist faction was well anchored in Malmö's LO section, Fackföreningarnas Centralorganisation, or FCO (Labor Unions' Central Organization, i.e., the Trades Council) of which Svensson was chair. At this time the FCO was dominated by representatives of men's groups, whose interests the cooperative movement was largely unable to satisfy.[51] On Svensson's initiative, FCO representatives adopted a resolution in 1945 advocating social development in a socialist direction.[52]

In addition to the FCO, the socialist faction was supported by building workers and their construction company, Malmö Byggnadsgille (the Malmö Building Workers Guild). Union support was probably motivated more by dissatisfaction with cooperative housing under the HSB (the National Association of Tenants' Savings and Building Societies) than by local socialist conviction. When Malmö construction workers formed a local association of the trade union movement's own housing company, Svenska Riksbyggen, in 1944, they turned against the HSB: "If we could draw most of its work away from HSB it would be fine as that company has blocked building workers' wages and their interests. . . ."[53]

The growth of a municipal socialist faction within the party was further promoted by internal oppositions within the housing cooperative movement. Strained relations between the Malmö Hyresgästförening (Tenants' Association), formed in 1932, and the HSB led the Tenants' Association to build its own cooperative housing. This went well, and in 1938 the HB (Hyresgästernas Bostadsproduktion, the Tenants' Housing Production Company) was formed, with Arnold Sönnerdahl as chair of the board and (as of 1940) with Hugo Åberg as managing director.[54]

The arrival of two tenants' building societies in Malmö caused the national HSB great problems, but an attempt to merge them failed. The national association was not pleased about the HB's extensive building projects and about its installing Hugo Åberg as head of production without putting the position out to tender. Threatened by expulsion from the national organization, the HB was forced to halt Åberg's private building projects in 1940. The association's attempts to merge the HB and the HSB finally succeeded in 1943; the composition of the new HSB board was largely identical to that of the old HB.[55]

The radical upswing at the end of the war bolstered the efforts of the municipal socialist faction; in the labor movement's Postwar Program and the Social Housing Commission the faction obtained its ideological manifestos. Among the most important elements in the municipal socialists' strategy were leasehold rights and the municipal housing company, MKB. In 1945, on the municipal socialists' initiative, the city council decided upon leasehold rights as a general principle for land and site policy. Municipal property was no longer sold, but leased for a period of fifty or seventy-five years against an annual charge. The city's possibilities for control over building of not only residential accommodation but also industrial areas increased substantially.[56]

The Social Housing Commission's proposal for municipal housing companies fell on sympathetic ears in Malmö. In September 1945 the Social Democrats' Council of Representatives motioned on the issue: "For large groups of low wage earners, housing standards can only be raised if the city takes over control of both production and management of rental housing. For this purpose, a special organ is needed, possibly in the form of a company, to plan and finance building, and if deemed suitable, produce residential housing and manage rental property."[57]

In the city council debate on the Malmö Kommunala Bostadsbolag, or MKB (Malmö Municipal Housing Company), the Conservatives made a frontal attack on the proposal. In their submission they asserted that the proposal aimed at "a total nationalization of the housing market in the city. Such a development . . . is contrary to our basic attitudes concerning the manner of human coexistence in the economic sphere."[58] From the Social Democrats' bench, the proposal was defended by Axel E. Svensson, backed by inter alia Nils E. Lindberg, who in his contribution underlined the local socialist spirit of the motion: "Private economic interests ought to be disconnected from property, and the building materials industry should be nationalized. . . . many categories of people in our society, such as large families, pensioners and single people, will not obtain decent housing at decent rents until the city itself builds it."[59]

The Conservatives' vociferous protests were of little avail: backed by a qualified majority, the SAP drove the proposal through the council. The confrontation also showed that the issue of municipal housing companies fell far outside the boundaries of mutual political understanding.

Augustenborg

In 1948 the Malmö Municipal Housing Company started to build its first residential area, Augustenborg, in the southeastern part of the city.[60] The project was finished four years later and provided about six thousand eager tenants with sixteen hundred light and spacious apartments. It must have felt wonderful to finally be able to sink into the warm water of one's own bath! Children no longer needed to be crowded into the kitchen, and summer evenings could be spent on the balcony. In contrast to the dark and narrow world of the old back courtyards, Augustenborg's fluid boundaries and winding roads gave an impression of space and freedom. It probably fulfilled the dreams of many: "On Sunday morning the sun beamed through the window and I thought I had arrived in heaven."[61]

Poverty, darkness, and misery were built away, but at the same time people lost some of the old community meeting places and contact points. The closeness between production and reproduction disappeared when workplaces and dwellings were located in different parts of the city. The yards were utilized primarily by the children, and stairways were cleaned by employed staff. The area's motley blend of people from different backgrounds likely engendered a certain amount of insecurity; doors no longer stood ajar. When the children had their own rooms, the parents could invite friends home instead of meeting neighbors on the landing. Proximity to small shops did not change much, but in the absence of busy roads children were sent to shop. Shopowners normally did not live in the district and no longer so naturally melded into the community. The ties between the petite bourgeoisie and the working class were weakened, but not broken.

The old meeting places were deliberately replaced by recreation centers. The owner supplied carpenter's benches, looms, table tennis equipment, crafts workshops, bridge tables, and the like in the many cellar premises on the estate. The equipment was disposed of by recreation associations formed by the tenants, and the associations even organized soccer games between local teams as well as midsummer festivities. However, generally the recreation rooms were used on weekends, and thus they only partially replaced the old social meeting places like the outhouse, streetcorners, and gateways or doorways.[62]

Augustenborg was pervaded by municipal socialist goal consciousness. The area was designed by Svenska Riksbyggen in conjunction with the chief of city planning, Gunnar Lindman, and it was largely built by Malmö Byggnadsgille. In accordance with Axel E. Svensson's expressed wishes, and under the leadership of the MKB's director, Sture Nyström, the area seemed to be remarkably permeated by the ideas encompassed by the Social Housing Commission. One of the members of the commission, Uno Åhrén, was also chief architect at Svenska Riksbyggen at the time.[63] Inspired by the Anglo-American discussion on the so-called neighborhood units, Åhrén and his sympathizers aimed at "supporting the formation of a democratic type of human being, in whom freedom and independence were combined with social responsibility."[64] Neighborhood units were designed to create a "we" feeling and counteract totalitarian political ideals.[65]

Like their counterparts in Vienna, Malmö's municipal socialists openly challenged the city bourgeoisie. The differences between Vienna and Malmö are otherwise obvious: Malmö's municipal socialism lacked the breadth, the multiplicity, and also the restrictions of its Viennese counterpart. No new "socialist culture" was proclaimed in Malmö; Augustenborg was not built only for politically conscious workers (as was, for example, Karl Marx-Hof) but for people in general.

The Return of the Cooperative Entrepreneurs

Augustenborg appeared during a period when cooperative housing ventures had to be content with standing in the shadows of public housing. Through its representative on the board of the MKB, Erik Svenning, the HSB tried in vain to obtain management of the area's buildings. The director of the MKB, Sture Nyström, viewed all division of responsibility as risky, and determined that "the company should have total control over employment and work assignments."[66]

The disputes between the municipal socialists and proponents of cooperatives culminated in 1949–1951. In a letter to the minister of social affairs, Gustav Möller, in the autumn of 1949, Axel E. Svensson reported that the HSB in Malmö had padded its costs for some properties. The report prompted Möller to convene a meeting in which Svensson, HSB representatives Erik Svenning and Algot Nilsson, and others participated. To Möller's question concerning proposed measures, Svensson replied that it was possible "to allow the whole thing to depend on whether guarantees were made that in the future nothing similar would ever happen again."[67] At the local SAP executive meeting when the issue was discussed, the HSB was occasionally severely criticized. The treasurer, Erik Forsberg, "finally asked whether HSB took into consideration the low wage earners whom it had let swallow the hook."[68]

Agreements between the HSB and large companies, however, gradually undermined the position of the municipal socialists. In 1956 the HSB closed a cooperative agreement with Byggmästarnas Gemensamma Byggnadsbolag, or BGB (roughly, the Building Contractors' Common Building Company), in which Skånska Cementgjuteriet dominated. In 1952 the HSB and Skånska Cementaktiebolaget combined to form the real estate company Kjellhus.[69] An agreement affecting employees and flats in various places in Malmö, and effective from 1946 onward, was also drawn up between the HSB and Kockums. To relieve labor and housing shortages after the war, Kockums advanced deposits to those employees wishing to live in

HSB flats, thereby attracting many supporters of cooperatives among metal workers. Prominent representatives of the Metal Workers Union (e.g., Erik Ek and Carl Ljungbeck) were elected to both the FCO's leadership and the HSB's representatives' council during the 1950s. In this way the organizations were conjoined, and in 1956 the FCO chair, typographer Thure Jacobsson, was elected chair of the HSB.[70]

In 1949 the city council approved a motion from the HSB on the establishment of a loan fund for people who did not possess sufficient capital for deposits on cooperative flats. In protest against the election of HSB ombudsman Algot Nilsson to the Finance Department's third section, Axel E. Svensson resigned as its chair in 1949 and thus also as a member in the party's Council of Representatives. He was succeeded by Erik Svenning. One result of these events was that the HSB retained an influence in the third section of the Finance Department, which would be significant for the future.[71]

In conjunction with the city council group's discussion of the distribution of the building quota for 1952, Axel E. Svensson, in his capacity as newly appointed managing director for Svenska Riksbyggen, made a proposition directed against the HSB and Hugo Åberg in particular: it aimed at increasing not only Riksbyggen's and Byggnadgillet's but also the MKB's portion of the building quota. The proposal had no effect upon the distribution of the quota, but it did provoke intense discussions within the Council of Representatives on the party representation in the MKB and their links to various building contractors. The discussion was concluded when both Erik Svenning of the HSB and Axel E. Svensson of Svenska Riksbyggen left the company board in 1953. The following year, Svensson left Malmö to take a seat in the Riksdag; with him out of the picture, the fate of municipal socialism was finally sealed.[72]

THE SYSTEM

Mutual Agreement and the Self-Help Strategy
The return of the cooperative entrepreneurs entailed that agreement between the labor movement and the owners of capital was expanded and intensified. A kind of division of responsibility between the city and industry was developed. The city supplied the best possible infrastructure of streets, water, drainage, electricity, sidings, and harbors for industrial pro-

duction. Capitalists accumulated capital through carrying on industrial production and not through property speculation. Under the unifying force of mutual understanding arose a system of ideas, contact networks, executive power, planning, and regulating that resulted in constantly increasing real wages, profits, and tax revenues. The pattern undoubtedly existed in other parts of Sweden as well, but in our view it prospered more in Malmö than in most other places.[73]

The system flourished during the 1950s and most of the 1960s. Kockums reported the highest annual figure for launched tonnage in the world. The MAB and MYA enterprise was described at its centenary in 1956 as "the largest and most comprehensive textile company in the Nordic countries." Malmö Strumpfabrik (Stocking Factory) was known as "leading in northern Europe." Unemployment was held down to insignificant levels, and dissatisfied workers could change jobs without much difficulty. Malmö rewarded its inhabitants by charging the country's lowest tax; it also had the country's lowest rents. Malmö's city library was chosen by UNESCO as an international model library.[74]

The system was administered by the Social Democrats, who maintained the confidence of the majority of voters. The party also succeeded in mobilizing the largest voter participation in elections in the country.[75] In 1949 after Emil Olsson, the municipality was led by S. A. Johansson, chair of the Commercial Employees Union. As possibly the system's most natural administrator, he unified the party while at the same time attracting the total confidence of the bourgeoisie.[76] In contrast to attitudes toward later municipal patriarchs, against Johansson not even the city's most right-wing newspaper could find grounds for complaint: "His moderate and expert leadership in Council debates in combination with sympathetic conduct has created respect for him as a person as well as for his fundamental knowledge about municipal concerns."[77]

As a sort of correlative to mutual political understanding, the party and the labor movement in Malmö came even more than before under the influence of the strategy of self-help. The municipal socialists' MKB was gradually deprived of its autonomy and often passed over in the distribution of attractive new building sites.[78] Even attitudes toward leasehold rights were questioned, as the following statement from S. A. Johansson at a discussion in the party council group in 1959 reveals: "Leasehold rights are a fundamental principle, but it is not prudent to be rigidly bound as regards economic development. However, leasehold rights are the issue which above all reflects our fundamental socialist attitudes."[79] The massive expansion of the public sector in the 1950s and 1960s was not an integral part of goal-conscious municipal socialist strategy. Health care, social services, and schools were not devoted to the creation of a "socialist human being," as they were in Vienna; neither most likely were they engaged in fostering a "democratic human being," as in Augustenborg.

The HSB's dominant position in Malmö lacked equivalents elsewhere in the country. In both Stockholm and Gothenburg, cooperative owner-occupied housing comprised about 15 percent of the total housing stock in 1965—equivalent to the national average—while in Malmö the corresponding figure was almost 30 percent.[80] The HSB's managing director, Oscar Stenberg, was elected to succeed S. A. Johansson as chair of the city council in 1962. During Stenberg's period in power, however, the reverse side of the system was revealed. The question of in whose name the city could be designated "ours" was highlighted when the housing area of Rosengård came into existence.

Rosengård

Rapid growth and urban migration in the 1950s and 1960s placed demands on the municipality for new housing; in 1965 there were 30,000 people on the housing waiting list. Malmö's finances, however, also permitted slum clearance. Under the Social Democratic government–initiated Million Dwellings Program, the housing project Rosengård (Rose Garden) was built on the eastern edge of the city. Planning for Rosengård began in the mid-1950s, but it was not ready to receive its twenty-thousand-odd tenants until the end of the 1960s. Overcrowded, damp, and drafty accommodations were replaced with ones built to modern standards, and doubtless many new residents of Rosengård also found the warm water of their own baths wonderful to sink into.[81]

Along with the Malmö Municipal Housing Company, MKB, the privately owned BGB and the cooperatively owned HSB were the designated building contractors, and the area was divided into three approximately equal parts. The planning was given over to the building contractors after the municipality had ruled on the necessary limits. This deviated from the ideas and ambitions behind Augustenborg—the city having comprehensive influence—and, consequently, social housing considerations were largely absent. Instead, Rosengård was greatly pervaded by capital interests. Architecturally stereotyped buildings, simple floor plans, and straight angles were chosen to give the highest possible economic dividends. Not even the MKB's own section of the estate departed from this pattern.

Rosengård seems to exemplify a very advanced stage in the mutual agreement between the labor movement and large companies, in which priority was given to ensuring access to the labor force during years of expansion. This agreement was regulated in, for example, the General Planning Committee, which was responsible for long-term planning and on which seven out of nine members represented building contractors and their associated interests. Of the municipal Building Committee's seven members, four represented building company interests, and the committee was presided over by the chair of the city council, the HSB's Oscar Stenberg.

Wholly in line with the good contacts between cooperatives and big business, the Wehtje family took advantage of its capital interests in the building of Rosengård. Cement, concrete, and other building materials were mainly obtained from the Skånska Cement enterprises. Among the businesses most engaged in the project were Skånska Cementgjuteriet and Skandinaviska Banken, where Wehtje was chair. The Wehtje family also had considerable influence over the decision-making process through the BGB, Skånska Cementgjuteriet, and Skåne's Chamber of Commerce. The mutual agreement reached between the labor movement and large capital owners also contributed to maintaining lower rents than in other large cities.[82] In addition, buildings were rapidly and (presumably) smoothly produced. However, the neighborhood community was definitely lost, and in many ways came to be replaced by a remote or estranged community, what we shall call the "dis-community."[83]

The Spread of the "Dis-Community"

In other places in Sweden as well, close neighborhood communities were transformed into "dis-communities," where people became estranged from each other and social relations were difficult. In Malmö this development was hastened by the strong position of mutual agreement, but we would also argue that the absence of women in the planning and decision-making process contributed to the rapid spread of "dis-communities." When Rosengård was being built there was not one woman on either the General Planning Committee or the Council Building Committee. A woman retained the right to express opinions only in her role as housewife; both the MKB and the HSB set up women's committees that demanded rationalization of housework.[84]

However, women in their capacity as central figures in neighborhood communities or as the lower working class in working life lacked any influence to stop the spread of the "dis-community." In the network of human relations in neighborhood communities women often developed social qualities that the men lacked. And since women were more or less excluded from political influence, their experience of close human relations was never acknowledged. Of more than thirty Social Democrats on the city council, fewer than five were women during the halcyon days of the system in the 1950s and 1960s. Women's issues were considered administrative problems and subordinated to labor market policies.[85]

Rosengård not only illustrates an advanced mutual accord between labor and capital but also pivotal relations between the upper and lower strata of wage earners and hence also between men and women. Gender segregation within Malmö's industrial structure from the early days of the labor movement has remained during the twentieth century. Traditional female industries such as textiles and food, underpaid and heavy, employed respectively 21 percent and 11 percent of the city's total industrial work force in 1960.[86] In the same year 50 percent of all women between twenty and sixty-four years of age were in paid employment.[87]

Since the strategy of self-help primarily suited an upper strata of better paid, capable, industrious, healthy, and reliable wage earners, it favored men. Thus labor market privileges were re-created in the party, and the return of cooperative leaders reinforced gender segregation and male culture. Worst affected were groups of immigrant women in the 1960s and 1970s, who also lacked the "right" language and the "right" culture.

Neither did the petite bourgeoisie fit into the system, and consequently Rosengård provided no space whatsoever for small business enterprises. Despite the fact that the population of Rosengård was about equal to the size of a small city, there were no small businesses and shops in the area. Instead, a large shopping center was built. Large-scale replaced small-scale. For Rosengård residents the nearest shop could be up to 800 meters away, and there were no cafés, restaurants, or pubs in the district. The petite bourgeoisie was totally left out of the system.

The system also engendered social vulnerability. Areas like Rosengård lacked social contact points or meeting places. The residents' different backgrounds, nationalities, religions, languages, and dialects also hindered the feeling of belonging to a community. A social and political rootlessness was established, and not even the most modern washing machines, window insulation, or television could remedy it. Only shared working life—albeit one dissolving in division of labor, time studies, and piecework—could meanwhile protect people from being almost wholly isolated.[88]

THE SYSTEM OUT OF BALANCE

In the 1970s one of the system's two pillars of support gave way.[89] Stiffening international competition exposed an obsolete industrial structure. The crisis actually began in the 1960s when several of Malmö's old textile industries were forced to close. In 1972, the patriarch of capitalists, Ernst Wehtje, died, and power over the several remaining central industrial firms moved to other parts of the country. Even the web of capitalist economic, political, and ideological power began to crumble during the 1960s and 1970s.

The system's other pillar, the labor movement, was put into an awkward situation. With the weakening of the capitalists' position, one of the century's greatest obstacles to municipal socialism was removed. Malmö's Social Democrats, however, lacked the ideological tools, and municipal socialism was never an issue. In line with the entrenchment of self-help strategy in the party, the Social Democratic municipal leadership chose instead to try to reestablish the system. Hence Malmö was one of the few local authorities to employ an economic consultant in the mid-1970s. Later, more and more committees and collaborative organs were formed in order to check industrial decline. The harbor was expanded, and a research center was opened. In conjunction with expanded municipal initiatives and a correlated demand for efficiency, municipal and party power became concentrated in a few individuals.

Even so, the number of workplaces within the manufacturing industry was halved during the 1960s and 1970s. Large workplaces with their time-honored camaraderie disappeared. The average number of employees in each workplace within the manufacturing industries dropped from eighty-three in the beginning of the 1950s to eighteen in 1984. It is true that the number of municipal employees more than doubled during the 1960s and 1970s, but continuity and the sense of belonging were obstructed by constant temporary and part-time employment conditions. The groups of people with a total lack of connection to working life—ordinary and premature pensioners, young people, and the unemployed—increased drastically during the 1970s and 1980s. Working life, with its opportunities for social and political stimulation became more and more peripheral to the city's pulsing daily life.

In the years prior to the election in 1985, social rootlessness infested various parts of the city. Margins shrank for many in the wake of unemployment and retraining schemes. The consequences of this displacement included unparalleled use of tranquilizers, comparatively many abortions, and rising crime statistics. Unsurprisingly, the "dis-community's" estranged housing estates like Rosengård, Lindängen, and Holma were among the worst affected, and they were centers of fairly widespread loneliness. The development of the "dis-community," with its wide spaces between people and its remoteness from politicians and political decisions, prepared the ground for a new political force.

The change of government in the municipal elections of 1985 was decided by the unexpected success of a novel political party. The supporters of the Skåne party were primarily people on the margins of the system; on the party's local radio station many lonely and rootless people made themselves heard. Also, people whose experience of the system was framed not by welfare but by oppression, control, and entangled bureaucracy contacted the party's self-appointed "folk tribunal." The local radio re-created some of the neighborhood community's qualities by facilitating lively discussions for people who normally were not listened to. During thousands of broadcasting hours the party leader, Carl P. Herslow, interpreted and reformulated spontaneous expressions of dissatisfaction into political demands.

Herslow himself was a direct descendent of the city's powerful turn-of-the-century patriarch with the same name. Over several years Herslow developed contacts with petit bourgeois circles in Skåne. In 1979 the Skåne party was formed with the purpose of opposing the system's regulations, power concentration, and social safeguards and promoting small business and a free market economy. Herslow may be viewed as one of the country's first and most consistent neoliberals. Support from only small businessmen was not sufficient for election victories in 1979 or 1982; but with the local radio broadcasts in 1983, in which political discussion was mixed with record requests and greetings from the public, Herslow was able to broaden his support. Around the party core of small businessmen gathered people who for one reason or another were able to unite in their criticism of the system and its central political administrators, the Social Democrats.

Discontent was particularly directed toward Nils Yngvesson, Social Democratic chair of the council executive and in a class by himself when it came to sitting on various committees. At a time when conditions in the lives of many Malmö inhabitants were deteriorating, the municipal leadership offered signals of uninterrupted welfare by building a new city hall, stock exchange, concert house, golf course, and luxury hotel in the city district of Triangeln.

The concentration of power within the city and the party, the distance between those in power and those without, turned receptiveness into what many must have perceived as deafness. The local authority leadership's inability to handle the discontent can also be explained in terms of the local Social Democratic Labor Party's weak links among women. When the textile industry collapsed in the 1960s and 1970s and about six thousand jobs disappeared in the course of some twenty years, many women became employed in the city's public sector. In the election of 1985, women comprised 74 percent of the city's public employees, yet women still did not possess political influence equivalent to their numbers. The number of female Social Democratic Council members did increase to nine (out of a total of thirty-two representatives) before the election of 1985; but women's experience of human relations, now from public sector areas such as health care, was still not utilized. Thus, budget cuts from the beginning of the 1980s were made among wage earners to whom the municipal leadership traditionally lacked channels of communication. Politicians without insight into the conditions of the caring professions created stress and insecurity that employees in these professions lacked the political influence to prevent.[90]

After the Election Victory in 1988

In the local elections of 1988 the Social Democrats were returned to power in Malmö, despite the inclusion of increased local taxes in their program. The voters clearly still placed a great deal of confidence in the party, which seemed better equipped for new commitments, especially vis-à-vis environmental issues, than it was before. However, no one escapes his or her own history. Malmö's enfeebled economy, profound social problems, and conflicts of interest confronted the election winners with enormous difficulties. Moreover, the bourgeois local government between 1985 and 1988 privatized large amounts of property in Malmö and replaced leaseholds with private ownership. Even parts of the MKB were privatized, and in the summer of 1988 the entire housing area of Lindängen was sold to a private Stockholm company. Thus, not only was every attempt at traditional municipal socialism undermined, but also local political independence.

Now, the building of Triangeln (currently known as Skåne's Manhattan) is being completed, with a Sheraton Hotel in its center. Among the entrepreneurs involved is the labor movement–linked Svenska Riksbyggen. Contrary to Axel Danielsson's original ideas and also to ideologist Anders Öhrne's classic definition of market-oriented cooperative self-help from

1919, the present director of Riksbyggen, Ralf Hultberg (also chair of the board of the newspaper *Arbetet*), propounds profit as an end in itself, even for popular movement enterprises.[91] On an information board at Triangeln, the labor movement's own insurance company, Folksam, which financed the project, proclaims: "We build on a belief in the future!" Among the city's *flâneurs*, who saw the working-class quarter of Lugnet's old neighborhood irretrievably obliterated a few blocks away when the last two houses were razed in June 1988, the question has arisen: Whose belief in the future is referred to?

What are the repercussions of the cooperative movement's profit orientation on Malmö's heavily committed social democracy? Will it lead to widening the gaps between the weak and strong groups of wage earners? Can the demands especially from women in the often underpaid and overworked public sector be satisfied while at the same time the party expands its responsibilities for a capitalist market economy? Is it at all possible to recreate and augment the human qualities of the neighborhood community in a "dis-community" that does not safeguard vital experiences of human relations but instead revolves around economic interests?

NOTES

1. A. Palm 1981, 101, 111.
2. August Palm was born in Fåraback, outside of Malmö, in 1849. As an itinerant journeyman tailor in Germany and Denmark during the 1870s, he came in contact with socialism. In 1881 Palm returned to Malmö, where he gave the first socialist speech in Sweden. In 1885 he moved to Stockholm, where, among other things, he helped start the newspaper *Social-Demokraten*. With his unconventional agitation methods, Palm quickly fell out with people in the party's moderate and intellectual circles, among them Hjalmar Branting, who forced him off the paper. Palm died in 1922 and is considered a pioneer of socialism in Sweden.
3. Billing 1986, 41.
4. *Arbetet* (Malmö), 8 Feb. 1949.
5. Axel Danielsson was born in a village in Värmland in 1863. After studying, partly in Uppsala, he worked as a fiction writer in Stockholm. In 1885 he was engaged by Palm as co-editor of the *Social-Demokraten*. At Palm's request Danielsson moved to Malmö in 1887 and immediately started the newspaper *Arbetet*. Until his early death in 1899, Danielsson was the Social Democrats' foremost journalist and publicist. He was well versed in the socialist classics and translated many into Swedish. Under the influence of the German Social Democrats' Erfurt Program, Danielsson authored the SAP's first party program in 1897.
6. The expression "our town" began to be used by Malmö's local Social Democrats in their election paper during the 1930s.
7. This presentation is based on descriptions of various neighborhoods in Malmö during

the decades around the turn of the century in Blomquist 1985; Greiff and Larsson 1978; Gräv där du står-cirkel (Dig Where You Stand study circle), Kockums 1986; "Nagelapan" 1984; Thagaard 1985; and interviews with the following old Malmö residents: Ella Björklund, Stig Larsson, and Friden Johansson.

8. C. Carlsson 1986, 32ff.; C. Carlsson Wetterberg 1987, 13; Liljeström and Dahlström 1981, 140ff.

9. Fryklund and Peterson 1983.

10. This section is based on *Austro-Marxism* 1978; Engelmann 1966; Kanitz 1974; Kulemann 1979; A. Pelinka 1977; Rabinbach 1983; Weihsmann 1985; Wulz 1979.

11. Wulz 1979, 209.

12. See Peterson, Stigendal, and Fryklund 1988, 21ff.

13. Alsterdal 1963, 290, 293.

14. The following on Nils and Mathilda Persson is based largely on interviews with their son, Ture Persson, and on material in his possession. See Holmqvist 1983, 207ff.

15. C. Carlsson Wetterberg 1987, 11, 13.

16. *Memorial Publications 1901–1926*, Malmö Arbetarekommun 1925, 16.

17. *Borås Tidning* 1903 and *Gotlänningen* 19 Aug. 1903.

18. See Olofsson 1979.

19. Westerståhl 1945, 117, 293–95.

20. *Sydsvenske män* (Southern Swedish Men), 1906, 58.

21. In a letter to Fredrik Ström in 1909, Kata Dalström, the Social Democratic woman agitator, described Persson and Rydén as representing "the greyest shade of social democracy." (Dalström 1987, 337). Around 1920 both Nilsson and Rydén were relieved of their political duties for a time: Nilsson because of his statements on the railway workers' wage demands, Rydén for indulging in shady speculation.

22. Uhlén 1949, 75–78. R. F. Berg's altered view of the labor movement is described by Gustav Möller, who worked as Berg's private secretary from 1901 to 1906. See Möller 1971, 131ff.; Jönsson and Lindblom 1987, 61ff.

23. Schiller 1967, 35, 68.

24. Uhlén 1949, 154; Bresky, Schermann, and Schmid 1981, 34.

25. On Wessberg, see Stråth 1982, 78–81. On Herslow, see Lindskog 1948, 48, and Bringmark 1962, 146.

26. *Arbetet* 5 Apr. 1919.

27. Malmö Arbetarekommun, Council group *Minutes* 19 Oct. 1921, par. 3; 16 Nov. 1921, par. 1; and 26 Nov. 1921, par. 1–2; Malmö Arbetarekommun, Executive *Minutes* 4 Nov. 1921, par. 5, and *Minutes* of meeting 14 Nov. 1921, par. 3 (Labor Movement Archive in Malmö). See also Uhlén 1949, 471–73.

28. Malmö Arbetarekommun, SAP Council of Representatives *Minutes* 11 Nov. 1921 par. 1; and 9 Nov. 1921, par. 2.

29. SDS 16 Nov. 1921.

30. Labor Commune—local Social Democratic party branch.

31. Telegram in the possession of Ture Persson.

32. *Sweden's Municipal Code*, par. 18, pt. 4; and par. 41. Published by P. E. Sköld, Stockholm, 1927. See also Norrlid 1983.

33. Alsterdal 1963, 345.

34. Quoted in ibid., 1963, 247 and 351.

35. For a review of the differences between socioliberal reformism and reformist socialism, see Olofsson 1979, 31.

36. The Rostorp Association's Twentieth Anniversary publication, 1943, 11–12; Kristenson 1975, 131–33.

37. Lines from one of the Swedish labor movement's most famous songs, "Arbetets söner" (Sons of Work), with text by Henrik Menander.

38. Bjurling 1956, 198ff.; *Bostaden Malmö* (Malmö Housing), 1983, 18–19.

39. M. Andersson 1979, 39.

40. Statistical information has been obtained from the *Malmö Municipal Yearbook* 1920–1935.

41. Kristenson 1975, 121–23; Malmö Arbetarekommun election publication *Vi och vår stad* (We and Our City), 1942, 20; *Bostaden Malmö* 1983, 21; *HSB 1925–1950*, 1950, 36–38. By 1940 Malmö had the largest proportion of cooperative flats in the country; Elldin 1957. See also Ruin 1960.

42. Figures from Johan Larsson's collection (Labor Movement Archive in Malmö).

43. Ambjörnsson 1984, 471ff.; C. Carlsson 1986, 51ff. On the firm links between housing cooperatives and the upper strata of the working class and also the middle class, see Gustafson 1974, 60.

44. The following presentation is based on articles in *Aftonbladet* 18 Nov. 1969, *Arbetet* 10 Feb. 1972, *Expressen* 9 Nov. 1968, and *SDS* 12 Apr. 1964 and on information obtained from Erik Adamsson, Mary Andersson, and Axel E. Svensson.

45. Malmö City Council, Borough Finance Department, Third Section, *Minutes* 1936, no. 573; and 1937, no. 619; Malmö City Council *Minutes* 1937, no. 44 (Malmö City Archives).

46. *Aftonbladet* 18 Nov. 1969.

47. Letter published in *En bit Malmö* (A Bit of Malmö), 1965.

48. Peterson, Stigendal, and Fryklund 1988.

49. In addition, Wehtje occupied a leading position in Skandinaviska Banken, the bank used by the HB and later by the HSB; *HSB 1925–1950*, 1950, 82.

50. Alf Johansson 1962, 573–75; *Final Report of the Social Housing Commission*, pt. 1, SOU 1945:63, 75–78 and 86–88; Malmö Arbetarekommun election publication, *Vi och vår stad* (We and Our Town), 1942, 20–21; Malmö Arbetarekommun, *Annual Report of the City Council* 1944, 3 and 1947. For a discussion of housing for large families, see Kälvemark (Ohlander) 1980.

51. Between 1943 and 1948 the FCO's board comprised union representatives of brick-layers, railway workers, food, leather, transport, and metal workers as well as municipal workers. The Malmö FCO was formed in 1913, but included no women representatives until 1956.

52. Uhlén 1949, 533.

53. Malmö Building Union's coordinated locals, *Minutes* of the 11 Apr. 1944 meeting. The union had run Malmö Byggnadsgille since 1925, and serious collaboration had never been established with the HSB. The disputes between the union and the HSB should also be seen in light of opposing ideologies, consumer cooperation vs. guild socialism; see Lundh 1987, chap. 11.

54. *MHF 1932–1942*, 1942, 31, 47, 81, and 133–35; *HSB 1925–1950*, 1950, 45–46, 52, and 58–60.

55. Gustafson 1974, 137–39.

56. Malmö Arbetarekommun, *Annual Report of the Council of Representatives* 1943, 2; 1945, 4; Malmö Arbetarekommun, *Municipal Action Programme* 1947. For a discussion of leasehold rights as an instrument of planning, see Strömberg 1984, 32–35.

57. Malmö City Council *Minutes* 1946, app. 182, 1–2; SOU 1945:63, 525ff.

58. Malmö City Council *Minutes* 1946, app. 182, 5–11.

59. Malmö City Council *Minutes* 1946, no. 5.

60. The following section is based on interviews with Augustenborg dwellers Elvy and Sture Sörensson, Jan-Inge Jönsson, and the MKB's director from 1947 to 1975, Sture Nyström, as

well as the MKB memorial publication, *Malmö—vår stad* (Malmö—Our Town) (1956); Nyström and Månsson 1960; *Vi bygger och bor på Augustenborg* (We Build and Live in Augustenborg), 1950; Pfannenstill 1953; L. Holm 1958; MKB's Executive *Minutes* (MKB Archive, Malmö).

61. Elvy Sörensson, who has lived in Augustenborg since her family moved there in 1951.

62. Recreational activities in Augustenborg were unique in Sweden and attracted great notice. Interview with Sture Nyström and Erik Adamsson, who initiated these activities.

63. According to Sture Nyström, Lindman was very close to Åhrén. For a discussion of the Anglo-American debate on city planning and neighborhood units and their importance for especially Uno Åhrén, see Elander 1978, chap. 3; Rudberg 1981 and 1982.

64. SOU 1945:63, 614.

65. Rudberg 1976.

66. MKB Executive *Minutes* 30 Sept. 1948, app. 70; 25 Nov. 1948, app. 88; 9 Feb. 1949, app. 38; 8 June 1949, app. 55; 13 Sept. 1949, app. 64.

67. Malmö Arbetarekommun, Executive *Minutes* 17 Dec. 1949, no. 184 and app. 139.

68. Ibid., 13 Jan. 1950. That the dispute was a delicate issue for the party is revealed in council chair Eric Holmqvist's statement that "the meeting should not be discussed outside, as it could be taken as a pretext for making a political affair out of the criticism against HSB to an even greater extent than it has been already."

69. HSB Malmö, *Annual Report* 1944, 8–10; 1945, 5; 1952, 6.

70. Ibid., 1946, 9; interviews with Stig Malmström, ombudsman in the Commercial Employees Union, and Lillemor Carlsson.

71. *HSB 1925–1950*, 1950, 72. Malmö Arbetarekommun, Executive *Minutes* 17 Dec. 1949, app. 139.

72. City Council SAP Group *Minutes* 19 Sept. 1951, par. 9, app. 9, and 20 May 1952.

73. Peterson, Stigendal, and Fryklund 1988, chap. 1.

74. Malmö Arbetarekommun, Council of Representatives *Annual Report* 1958 and 1959; Bringmark 1962, 151ff.

75. Korpi 1981.

76. Interview with S. A. Johansson's son, Bengt Johansson.

77. SDS 12 May 1952, from Elsy and Gösta Möller's clipping collection.

78. According to information derived from Sture Nyström and Anna-Greta Skantz. In addition to Malmö, Örebro was the city originally held up as a model regarding municipal housing production. However, while the MKB's share of housing stock in 1965 was only 14 percent, the comparable figure in Örebro was 31 percent. See Strömberg 1984, 112.

79. Malmö Arbetarekommun, City Council Group *Minutes* 21 Jan. 1959, par. 5; see also 17 Nov. 1959, par. 4. From 1945 to 1985 municipal land increased from 25 to 50 percent, and land put in leasehold from 3 to 15 percent; calculations from the *Malmö Yearbook* 1945; City of Malmö, *Annual Report of Municipal Administration*, Property Management, 1962–1985.

80. See *The Population and Housing Census* 1965, pt. 5, table A1.

81. The following is based on Flemström and Ronnby 1972 and the MKB's annual reports and anniversary publications.

82. Flemström and Ronnby 1972, 156.

83. We are indebted to Bernt Eriksson for suggesting the concept of the "dis-community."

84. Interview with Anna-Greta Skantz, among other things chair of the Social Democratic District for Women in Skåne from 1960 to 1983 and member of the HSB's and the MKB's women's committees.

85. Anna-Greta Skantz and Hilma Osbeck.

86. SOS Industri 1960.

87. Malmö, *Statistical Yearbook 1971*, table 4.

88. On the effects of the welfare society on social relations, see Liljeström and Dahlström 1981, 323ff. See also the English historian Eric Hobsbawm's "The Labour Movement and the City" (*New Left Review*, no. 166, 1987), in which he discusses the dissolution of the neighborhood community and the consequences of this for the labor movement's possibilities of political and union mobilization.

89. See Peterson, Stigendal, and Fryklund 1988.

90. Interview with Lena Rubin, ombudswoman for the women's group in Malmö. Rubin claims that women's representation is worse in southern Sweden than in other parts of the country. Cf. the state inquiry on female representation, "Varannan damernas" (roughly, Every Other Lady), SOU 1987:19.

91. Presentation of Hultberg's book, *Vänstern och vinsterna* (The Left and Profits), in *Arbetet* 12 Feb. 1987.

10

Bo Lindensjö

From Liberal Common School
to State Primary School:
A Main Line in Social Democratic
Educational Policy

During the 1950s and 1960s Swedish education received a great deal of international attention. Why? Was it because Swedish Social Democracy demonstrated how a traditional educational system could be dismantled and replaced with a system of mass education without subverting the political and economic system? Or was it because of the systematic, almost scientific character of the reform? The planning, which has been closely examined by Dahllöf, commenced with the lower levels of education and "culminated" in the advanced, a process that took twenty-five years.[1]

Was this international interest simply a side effect of interest in the Swedish welfare state as such, or was it due to the Social Democratic reforms' particular ability to optimize—in the spirit of the welfare state—both egalitarianism and efficiency?

According to the American political scientist Arnold Heidenheimer, who has made international comparisons, the educational reforms carried out under the aegis of Swedish Social Democracy are unique in that they attempt to achieve the political goal of social leveling and efficiency—adapting schools and the labor market to each other.[2]

A LONG HISTORICAL PROCESS

Heidenheimer has spotted important elements in the Social Democratic reforms, not least the striking and singular blend of unequivocal political and social egalitarian aims and technocratic efficiency. According to Heidenheimer, the success of the reforms derived from the fact that the party was able to mobilize both "the leaders of class-conscious workers and the technocrats in the growth-conscious bureaucracy."[3] His postulation rather overestimates the role of the leaders of class-conscious workers and underestimates that played by elementary school teachers. Another problem with Heidenheimer's presentation is its finality: it gives the impression that the Social Democratic school reforms were consistently developed during the 1940s and that over the following decades they were once and for all perfected.

Hence, taking advantage of recent research on the growth of compulsory education, I would point out that Social Democratic school policy is not simply the result of various political decisions made during the 1940s and their implementation during the following two decades. It is the result of a long historical process, marked by battle and strife—not only with the bourgeois parties and the established corps of teachers within higher education, but even with factions within the party itself.[4] Above all, I would show that Social Democratic educational policy is not a finished product, not a final achievement—and this lack of finality is clearer at present than ever before. I will conclude my presentation with a discussion of the goals of school reform and main tendencies in present-day development.

Social Democrats, Liberals, and the School

When Swedish Social Democracy began to take shape during the 1880s, education was not a central issue. It is true, as the historian Gunnar Richardson has shown, that local Social Democratic groups did often demand free, common, secular, obligatory state schools in their programs. And indeed, political agitation could contain points of view on education and demands for schools. Higher secondary schools were attacked for "fostering class, estate, and wealth" and elementary schools for being "a public convenience in the service of the priesthood of the state church in order to keep the masses in obeisance."[5]

However, these are rather dubious expressions of genuine interest in educational questions. Why were state schools sought after? Was it to liberate the school from dependence on priests and parsimonious local authorities, or was it that consistency demanded that "the state itself create the means for fulfilling one of the duties imposed by the state"?[6] Existing sources provide no answers. According to Richardson, it is doubtful whether these programs, which essentially were translations of Danish or German originals, can shed any light on whether Swedish Social Democrats at that time possessed any sort of well-thought-out views on education.

Occasionally, socialist Sunday schools were formed to "attempt to spread socialism among future generations" and to convey the sort of general knowledge that was neglected in elementary schools.[7]

However, these schools were meant to complement elementary schools, not replace them. And even though people attacked "the tyranny of the catechism," they also admitted that working-class children needed instruction and that elementary school provided training in useful skills such as reading, writing, and arithmetic. In accordance with orthodox Marxist interpretations, and perhaps even more in light of their own experience, people seemed not to give much weight to educational issues. In any case, these issues were far less vital than the distribution of welfare, universal suffrage, and the length of the workday.

Yet the issue of education was on the general political agenda. In conjunction with the municipal reform of 1862, which strengthened the independence of the local authorities, and the representation reform of 1866, which abolished the Riksdag of the Estates, Liberals like S. A. Hedin had argued for increased popular education. However, these reforms had no effects on compulsory education. The agrarian class, whose position was strengthened by the reforms, created special folk high schools for its youth. With universal suffrage at hand in the 1880s, radical Liberals claimed that more and even better popular education was needed. Their standpoints were sometimes seen as manipulative: class-conscious Liberals for reasons of vile self-interest wanting to "educate away" working-class socialism. However, more often it was a case of the Liberals trying to scare the Conservatives in power with the consequences of neglecting popular education.

One way of achieving educational goals was to found workers' associations after the German model, the so-called Workers' Institutes. They began as sickness and burial funds but increasingly offered educational activities, mainly lectures. These lectures were intended to prepare workers to participate in various social activities and to promote egalitarian and friendly relations between classes. These institutes could appropriately be compared with the farmers' folk high schools. However, one can concur with Tomas Englund's questioning whether workers actually comprised a majority in the institutes and whether the latter in fact extended much beyond the skilled "workers' aristocracy," who sometimes seemed to have used their education to distance themselves from the working class.[8]

The Elementary School

The other Liberal alternative had to do with remodeling the school system. At several of the five workers' meetings organized during the 1870s and 1880s by the Liberal workers' association movement, the school issue was discussed.[9] At that time the school system comprised consistently organized parallel systems. Wealthy children went to special private schools, while workers' and farmers' children went to elementary schools. The education of a small number of privileged children cost the state nearly as much as that of the far more numerous poor children. The Liberals began to assert that it was the elementary school, the school of the popular majority, that the state should support. They demanded improved education, free of charge, with a common public school as the base.

According to the elementary school teacher and Liberal Fridtjuv Berg, who participated in the third workers' meeting, the elementary school should not be a "paupers' school, a caste institution," but a common school for children of all classes. Although Berg gave pedagogical reasons for his proposal, and although, as Richardson points out, his motivations issued from liberal individualistic principles,[10] there is no doubt that, like the educational policy of the Social Democrats over the next one hundred years, Berg placed high value on equality between classes.

Berg believed that if all children went to the same school, at least for a time, the class differences between them could be bridged. The desire for good teaching also argued for a common basic school: unless the children of the upper classes attended elementary school, they would not be interested in its quality. Later on, Social Democrats often reiterated Berg's points when arguing for general instead of selective political solutions.

When the Social Democratic Labor Party was formed in 1889, no party program was adopted. Inspired by the German Gotha Program, the Social Democrats demanded universal and equal suffrage and an eight-hour workday. The first program was adopted at the fourth party conference in 1897. The program was based upon the German Erfurt Program and demanded state control over the important means of production.[11] Religion was declared to be a private matter. The school should be separated from the church and made into "a common, culturally fulfilling, school for all citizens." Åke Isling, one of the leading scholars in this area, interprets this formulation to mean that the Social Democrats aligned themselves with the Liberal basic school program,[12] and over the coming decades the party would work in conjunction with the Liberals toward realizing a basic school. It is worth noting that on one occasion Berg participated in a May Day demonstration and that in 1886 Hjalmar Branting proposed Berg as a candidate in a by-election to the Second Chamber.

Social Democratic interest in school issues began to grow, even though the party largely continued to leave the practical work on these issues to cultural radicals, Liberal politicians, and, not least, the corps of elementary school teachers. However, the Social Democratic and Liberal principle of basic schools met with stiff conservative resistance. In 1894 a certain connection between the elementary school and grammar school had been established, which led to a decision to make entry requirements to grammar school correspond to the elementary school's third year. From the vantage point of the basic school, this was positive in the sense that the elementary school's three years could now provide a basis for the grammar school. However, it was a modest success since the well-off and well-educated could choose to qualify their children for grammar school in other ways than through the elementary school.

As minister of education in both of Karl Staaff's Liberal governments in 1905–1909 and 1911–1914, Fridtjuv Berg was able to promulgate a more liberal cultural policy. In 1906 he put through a controversial spelling reform, meant to create consonance between the spoken and written word. In 1909 a step was taken toward the basic school through the decision to establish local authority intermediate schools, that is, the four-year lower secondary school, which provided an extension of the six-year elementary school in areas without grammar schools. Berg even attempted to improve the status of elementary school teachers by raising demands on prospective teachers and extending their training time.

The Social Democratic Educational Offensive

After the voting rights reforms at the beginning of this century had given increased power to the Liberals and Social Democrats, and after they had formed a coalition government in 1917, the Social Democrats—who had been given the Ministry of Education—had greater possibilities of transforming the school system. Värner Rydén (like Berg, an elementary school teacher) was given this task. When Berg died in 1916, Rydén became the most active advocate of a basic school. He set up a special investigation, the

Schools Commission of 1918, devoted to giving children better educational possibilities and to creating a more unified school organization. One expressed aim was to promote equality—not only between social classes, but also between the sexes: girls' education should be attended to "to the same extent as boys'."[13]

Rydén received full support for his efforts from the 1920 party conference. The radical party program from that conference, which demanded nationalization, progressive wealth taxation, and sharper inheritance tax regulations, also underlined the importance of a common elementary school as a basis for the education of the citizenry.[14]

The Schools Commission presented its report in 1922. The division between "pauper schools" and "fine schools" was criticized. The four-year municipal intermediate school, introduced in 1909, demonstrated that a common six-year school functioned well. Consequently, according to the report, there was no reason to separate grammar school children from elementary school children after the third year. The commission proposed a universal, common six-year elementary school, and also proposed that state support for parallel school forms cease and that the elementary school be linked to higher education through a four-year lower secondary school and a three-year upper secondary school (gymnasium).[15] These far-reaching ideas did not survive confrontation with the political realities of the 1920s, a decade stamped by minority parliaments in which Social Democratic, Liberal, and Conservative governments succeeded each other. Formal comments on the proposals were deeply split: bodies or agencies with links to elementary schools were positive; those associated with higher education, negative. That the conservative press went against the proposals was no surprise either.

Although less radical than Fridtjuv Berg's classic liberal program, the commission's proposals were also attacked by the liberal press and Liberal politicians. Splits within the Liberal party over the question of prohibition in 1923 could have played a part. Urban Liberal groups were associated with grammar school and university traditions, while rural Liberals often firmly supported Berg's program. However, at this point it was the Social Democrats who committed themselves not only to the commission's proposals but also to the basic school program itself.

Parliamentary instability did not make the adoption of the proposals easier; changing minority governments had their effect on the proposals. When the time finally came to formulate government propositions from the commission's proposals, there was little left of the original program. A Liberal education minister in C. G. Ekman's minority government and former elementary schoolteacher and school inspector, John Almkvist, authored the proposition. The idea of a six-year elementary school as a universal basic school was abandoned, and a double link between the elementary school and grammar school was proposed—after the third and sixth years of elementary school.

For most Social Democrats the proposition was unacceptable. Even though the party was not totally united behind the school issue, the Social Democrats felt themselves to be the only reliable source of parliamentary support for the principle of a basic school. A party motion demanded that the Schools Commission's initial proposals be implemented. A Schools Committee was formed to settle the issue under the leadership of Värner Rydén. He achieved a compromise with the Agrarian party. The double transition point between the elementary school and grammar school had to be retained, but the first was delayed from the third to the fourth year of elementary school (the second, after the sixth year, was kept). These decisions also involved girls' schools becoming nationalized and many grammar schools becoming coeducational.[16]

As Åke Isling has pointed out regarding the basic school program, this was a "meager compromise," certainly in comparison with the commission's initial proposals.[17] Parallel education was consolidated and legitimized. In a motion signed by the leading Social Democrats Rickard Sandler and Ernst Wigforss, among others, the Social Democrat, popular educator, Good Templar, and teachers' college lecturer Oscar Olsson demanded the creation of a comprehensive school.[18] The common six-year basic school should be followed by a three-year intermediate school; and these should have a common organization, be divided into a practical and a theoretical study line, and include a certain amount of shared content in general subjects. In contrast to the party motion, special attention was not paid to poor, bright students; emphasis was on improved education for all.

The Absence of Reforms

In 1932 the Social Democrats commenced a long period in government—at times in coalition with the Agrarian party. The times of balancing-act parliamentarianism were over. One would have expected education to be given priority, especially since a party motion in 1927 had vowed to activate the basic school question at the first suitable opportunity. However, as has been indicated, the parliamentary group was not united. According to Bo Rothstein, members' views varied to a certain degree according to class and educational background.[19] Advocates of popular education included Rickard Sandler and Oscar Olsson; Värner Rydén and Josef Weijne supported elementary schools; and Arthur Engberg and Olof Olsson worked on behalf of grammar schools and higher education. When Engberg was appointed minister of education with responsibility for schools in 1932, it meant that the higher education faction was strengthened.

Despite the promise contained in the 1927 party motion, Engberg did not bring up the question of the basic school program. Instead, he pursued the policy of supporting different forms of education on their own terms. The elementary school was given more weight by the decision in 1936 to add an extra year; the extension was motivated by the argument that a democratized society increasingly needed well-educated citizens. However, because of the great variation in local authorities' economies, a twelve-year transition period was granted. According to Åke Isling, who has assessed it in terms of the idea of a basic comprehensive school, this decision to add a seventh year to elementary school only reinforced and legitimized the system of parallel schools.[20]

This is not to say that democracy and equality in education were considered unimportant. Democratizing grammar schools and promoting equality between social classes were major elements in the party's educational policy. However, it was thought that these aims were best achieved through removing the economic and social barriers hindering studious children of the working and agrarian classes from pursuing higher education. It was a kind of elitist egalitarianism; individuals were considered to have different degrees of talent at birth. Innate differences were equally distributed throughout the classes. Equality consisted of providing the most intelligent or talented, regardless of origins, the same opportunities for higher education. The grammar school was increasingly considered to be an elite school for those with the greatest aptitude for studies.

Arthur Engberg's period as minister of education has sometimes been considered as almost totally lacking in any efforts toward educational reform. He did set up an industrial education inquiry to increase and reorganize occupational education—within the context of combating unemployment. However, there is good reason to believe that the inquiry was initiated by Gustav Möller, minister of social affairs, and not by Engberg.[21] In the spirit of the new humanism, Engberg's gymnasium reforms were primarily intended to promote the importance of culture in the school. This entailed strengthening the position of classical languages in the classics (Latin) track and of history and Swedish-language subjects in the science track.[22] Through to an extent replacing grammar school teachers' representation in Cathedral Chapters with ministers, he also contributed to augmenting the church's influence in the school system, which was directly contrary to the then prevailing views. In 1938 Engberg also successfully induced the Riksdag to reject a Liberal party motion for public inspection of the educational system, which he believed would only complicate the adoption of necessary measures in various areas of education. In his memoirs, Tage Erlander depicted Engberg's school policy as "the absence of reforms."[23]

Why was Engberg's policy domain during the 1930s so wholly bereft of reforms? Why were the party's albeit modest successes during the 1920s not continued further "in new reform initiatives or political planning"?[24] Åke Isling underlines the atmosphere of crisis in the 1930s: enormous unemployment and a stagnating economy. Under these circumstances, the Social Democrats gave priority to acute economic and social problems instead of trying to secure the basic school program. Isling notes that some of the old "orthodox" Marxist views returned; for example, there was the idea that the "belly" should take priority over the "brain"—the latter could be dealt with when the former was taken care of. The party concentrated its innovative and offensive powers on economic and social policy.[25]

Gunnar Richardson stresses the anxiety about the academic labor market. A common, universal education in the form of a comprehensive school would risk attracting too many to theoretical courses of study. The question was not so much whether they would manage such studies, but rather whether there would be any work for them afterward.[26] The highly educated unemployed, it was feared, might allow themselves to be recruited to authoritarian movements. Engberg was not moved by these arguments to limit admission to universities, but among Social Democrats they definitely generated a certain amount of doubt about the basic comprehensive school program.

Another argument against the program was that it was politically controversial. Not only was it attacked by conservative and liberal politicians and a powerful bourgeois press; it was also dubious whether the program was supported by the agrarian and working classes, whom it was intended to benefit.[27] In addition, as has been mentioned, there was a certain not insignificant amount of disagreement over the question in the Social Democratic parliamentary group and within the organized labor movement as well.

Among the views on popular education within the labor movement was the notion that democratizing the grammar school, in the sense of socially broadening its recruitment, might run counter to democratizing society at large. If the grammar school, which gave its pupils an upper-class upbring-ing, were to recruit pupils from the working class, the working class would risk being deprived of its talent. For this reason, certain quarters of the labor movement were not all that keen to correct the injustices that the "class gap" between the elementary school and the grammar school caused. For example, one of the most famous persons in earlier Swedish adult edu-cational activities, Gunnar Hirdman, asserted that there were "injustices," but they were at least "useful injustices" for the working class.[28] In an ex-tension of this discussion, there was talk of founding a special "folk" univer-sity, where those who had shown aptitude for study through popular edu-cation but who were not allowed to study at a university would be able to continue their educations.

THE BEGINNING OF A NEW DEVELOPMENT

Elementary School Teachers' or Grammar School Teachers' Policy

When World War II broke out, the coalition government of Social Demo-crats and the Agrarian party was replaced by one also including the Liberal and Conservative parties. Regarding education, this involved an important change: the Conservative leader, Professor Gösta Bagge, replaced Arthur Engberg as minister of education. Right from the start, the new minister seems to have been of the opinion that problems of education had been allowed to accumulate for far too long without anything being done. The problems seemed to him so manifold that he chose to set up a public in-quiry, the Schools Commission of 1940, which was to investigate a number of problems involving the relationship between elementary schools and secondary schools. It is important to examine this inquiry, as it not only helped to activate a Social Democratic discussion of education but also to produce alternatives, around which future discussions would revolve.

According to Bagge, the problems of the various educational subdivisions were so interconnected that it was no longer possible to resolve them indi-vidually. For example, the question of uneven social and regional recruit-ment to higher education, which resuscitated the issue of links between elementary schools and grammar schools, was brought up. However, Bagge lacked any sort of plan on this question, so he thought it necessary to investigate "the entire educational system, from preschools to universi-ties."[29] This was to be carried out by a committee composed exclusively of specialists.

In the First Chamber of the Riksdag, the initiative was opposed by Arthur Engberg, who may very well have felt himself personally criticized. Earlier, in 1938, Engberg had rejected a similar idea contained in a Liberal party motion calling for a total overview of the school system, and now again he opposed the desire to solve the problems of education "in one blow." Instead, he promulgated the strategy that characterized his own administration—gradually to dispose of those "obstacles and barriers of an economic nature."[30] He also questioned the inquiry's one-sided composition of experts and suggested that, if there must be such an inquiry, it should include politicians.

That the government was a coalition government possibly excluded such a political composition. The investigation was organized into two groups, each representing one of the school forms, elementary and grammar. Bagge himself was chair, and he hoped by the nonpartisan composition of the inquiry to avoid conflicts and to reach agreed-upon solutions. However, this was not to be the case, for politics intruded in the shape of a conflict of interests between representatives of elementary schools and grammar schools.

To sort out at what age students should be "differentiated" in light of differences in aptitudes, the inquiry turned to available scientific expertise, namely, the four professors of pedagogics and psychopedagogics. They were requested to respond to questions about when school should be started, when it should be divided into different levels of difficulty, and when it should be concluded. Three of the experts stated that at the age of eleven children's abstract abilities are sufficiently developed to be able to determine their aptitude for higher studies with some degree of certainty, and they proposed separating students at that age. The fourth expert, who was particularly interested in practical aptitudes, found that these developed a few years later and therefore proposed a somewhat later age.[31] The former view won the approval of the grammar school section; the latter, that of the elementary school.

School Debate Despite Political Party Truce

The parties had agreed on a truce during the war and consequently did not take an active part in the school debate, which was instead conducted by popular movements and by individuals within and to an extent outside of the labor movement, and by involved teachers' organizations. The discussion partly consisted of criticism of the existing school system. The school was said to preserve and reinforce inequalities in society. Critics asserted that it was now necessary to change the school so that social injustices between classes, between rural and urban areas, and between girls and boys could be eliminated. The content and working forms of education must also be changed and adapted to modern society.

Among many others in the labor movement, the social politician Alva Myrdal worked for the reform of the schools. She made particular references to American education, underscoring the paradox that the strongly capitalist and competitive American society created a more egalitarian and democratic school system than the Swedish.[32] The new school should offer more freedom and greater respect for children's different personalities. This did not mean that pupils must be sorted into different school forms; it could be achieved through individualizing instruction within the classroom.

However, many influential Social Democratic educationalists represented other points of view—in the spirit of Arthur Engberg. They defended splitting up the school system into elementary schools and grammar schools. They criticized the existing situation only to the degree that they questioned whether in fact only the most gifted students were being recruited to the grammar schools.

In an article in *Tiden*, Stellan Arvidson, scientist and "ideologist" in school matters, raised the question of what constituted a Social Democratic educational policy. In reply to his own question, he stated that, strictly speaking, it was to ensure that students receive just that education which best suited them. Only aptitude for studies and not the family's social position should determine a student's choice of studies. Only a small proportion of students can manage the lower secondary school with ease, he argued, and even fewer can handle the upper secondary work. Democracy and equality in education entail sifting out the gifted for advanced studies, regardless of social background. Those persons concerned about only the development of the elementary school represented an undemocratic policy, which would involve higher studies being reserved for wealthy children regardless of whether they were gifted.[33] Ragnar Edenman, later minister of education and culture ("*ecklesiastikminister*"), was also actively engaged in the issue of broader recruitment to higher studies and called for selection for admission to grammar school and an expanded stipend system to give greater opportunities to talented working-class children.

The Party Begins to Be Engaged

In 1944 the labor movement drafted its postwar program, the so-called Twenty-Seven-Point Program. This social and economic program, which had been created in collaboration with various labor movement organizations, also contained several points on education. Equality was central: the most important task of the school was to provide equal education for "all young people, regardless of parents' incomes and place of abode."[34]

According to the program, class differences were re-created primarily because children from poor backgrounds had difficulties getting access to an education. Consequently, a nine-to-ten-year comprehensive school should eventually be created, to provide good civic and humanitarian education. This was vital, not only in order to create equality, but also to expand and improve recruitment to the most important posts in society. Current selection for such posts was more or less confined to children of the urban upper and middle classes.

At the party conference the same year (which has been closely examined by Richardson), Per Nyström, radical Social Democrat and social politician, presented a motion concerning schools. He claimed that political democratization had not been followed by educational—that is, democratization of the school. The party executive commented on the motion and admitted that the party lacked an up-to-date school program.[35] The conference adopted a new party program that disregarded the Postwar Program's demand for a comprehensive school. Instead, what was known as the "grammar school line" was recommended, with elementary school as the basic school and a "just" selection to higher studies. The conference, however, instructed the party executive to appoint a special committee to draft a school program. The committee would contain representatives from various "factions," namely, comprehensive school supporters such as Alva Myrdal and Oscar Olsson and grammar school advocates like Ivan Pauli. It was clear that the party was now willing to commit itself to education in a way quite different from that of the 1930s.

The committee was deeply divided on the issue of streaming—that is, separating students by abilities. Those promulgating the grammar school wanted early streaming, believing that intellectually homogeneous classes were essential to good instruction. Gifted students would not come into their own as well in the fifth and sixth year of elementary school as they would in lower secondary. In response, the advocates of comprehensive schools asserted that early grouping of children involves disadvantages, especially for working-class children. Thus, selection should be made as late as possible. In the end, Alva Myrdal attempted to mediate with the attitude that this was not a question of political principles but a psychological cum pedagogical issue, a scientific question. In this she used a method of dealing with educational policy disputes that would come to be very common: referring questions on which there was no agreement to scientific judgment.

The committee did not finish its work, and Richardson confirms that it remained very split.[36] However, a first draft of a labor movement school program was written, which included a demand for a nine-year universal school. The draft also contained a statement to the effect that "the question of streaming into different lines or according to a certain grouping during the later school years is to be decided after the immediate commencement of a large-scale trial." The draft seems never to have been submitted to the party or any other labor movement organization; but as we shall see, it came to be used in another way.

THE COMPREHENSIVE SCHOOL

The Party Makes a Decision

As a consequence of the end of World War II, the coalition government resigned in July 1945. It was succeeded by a wholly Social Democratic government, with Per Albin Hansson as prime minister. Tage Erlander was appointed minister of education, possibly because he lacked a background in educational policy and therefore was not associated with any faction. In the following year he appointed a new committee, the Schools Commission of 1946, despite the fact that the already-existing inquiry was not finished. The members of the commission were political appointees. Many came directly from the SAP's school committee—for example, Josef Weijne and Alva Myrdal. Erlander himself was chair, and Stellan Arvidson was appointed as one of the secretaries.

A frequently mentioned explanation for the Social Democratic government's decision to form a new inquiry is the deep discord prevailing in the old one.[37] Although the inquiry had managed to agree on a great deal— eight-year compulsory school attendance, mixed-ability primary school, a streamed upper level—total disagreement prevailed in questions of the timing of the streaming. The majority in the inquiry, who were associated with grammar schools, demanded selection after four years and wanted to retain the five-year lower secondary school. The minority, with ties to the elementary school, thought that a true basic school required at least six years of common school attendance; only after that should streaming be implemented. It should be noted, however, that neither was there much unanimity within the Social Democratic Labor Party. The party contained factions with very different views of school: a grammar school faction wanting to create equality between social classes through augmenting the stipend system and recruiting gifted children from the working and agricultural classes; an elementary school faction wishing to expand the elementary school into a comprehensive school—viewing the mere division into different types of schools as unegalitarian and undemocratic.

Perhaps, as Sixten Marklund suggests, the combination of fear of unemployment at the end of the war, the pressure to give youths employment, the need to coordinate school with other social areas, and the rising birthrate—all more or less technical questions not treated by the existing inquiry—necessitated appointing the new commission.[38] In retrospect, however, Erlander judged the effort as clearly political: it was motivated by the notion of the school as "a class society in miniature."[39] It is worth noting that although the school inquiry could not even agree on a six-year "basic school," the School Commission was to examine whether a basic school principle could be applied to a nine-year compulsory school.

In 1948 the commission presented its ideas on a nine-year compulsory comprehensive school.[40] The commission did not accept the inquiry's argument in favor of early streaming, which was thought to acknowledge only theoretically gifted children—practical talents show themselves later than theoretical ones. If children had to select lines of study too early, they ran the risk of disregarding practical education on faulty grounds. Equality would be encouraged partly through the improvement of educational opportunities for unfairly treated groups, and partly through practical and theoretical education being given equally high status. Clearly, the recently divided Social Democrats managed to agree, and even the party's former grammar school faction agreed to the comprehensive school. What is remarkable is that Arthur Engberg supported the comprehensive school proposal and that Stellan Arvidson was its most important architect.

The commission proposed a nine-year comprehensive school, with eight common years and one differentiated: a three-year primary level, three-year intermediate, and three-year upper level, taught by primary and elementary school teachers and academically trained upper-level teachers. During the seventh and eighth years, specific interests could be satisfied through free optional courses. Within the classroom, teachers could differentiate by means of "individualizing" their instruction. Passive classroom pedagogics should, if not be replaced by, then be complemented by active methods. In principle, all school forms for the different age groups were to be combined into one, even though later compromises were made approving both lower secondary schools with practical subjects and girls' schools.

Reception of the proposal, in the press as well as among consultative bodies, was extremely divided, albeit along lines that could hardly have been surprising.[41] Once again, authorities and organizations with ties to the elementary school were very positive, while those associated with grammar schools and other institutions of higher education were equally negative.

Just prior to the parliamentary discussion of the proposal (which has been thoroughly analyzed by Marklund), the situation was as follows:[12] within the SAP the proposal was well anchored, and it was also accepted by the communists. The Conservatives approved only the nine-year obligatory attendance—everything else should be decided by the outcome of a trial period. According to the Conservatives, the comprehensive school should not replace the grammar school, and they opposed late streaming. The Liberals accepted the principle of the comprehensive school and nine-year compulsory attendance but also opposed late streaming. The Agrarian party was split, and among other things wanted the possibility of making the last two years voluntary.

"A Political Nebula"

In the special school committee, which was formed for the purpose of reaching a compromise, the Social Democrats made an interesting concession. They agreed that the comprehensive school should be implemented "to the degree that the intended trial proves its suitability" as a replacement for a number of school forms. That the municipal girls' school and practically oriented intermediate school were not mentioned constituted another concession. The decision in favor of nine-year compulsory attendance was unanimous. However, what was meant by the statement that the comprehensive school should be implemented to the degree that the trial proved its suitability? Was it a question of when or how the comprehensive school should be established? Or would it be established only if all were unanimously in favor?

The Social Democrats interpreted the decision to mean that the compulsory school would be established, but that the trial would determine *how*. The Conservatives' interpretation assumed that the trial would determine *whether* the comprehensive school would be established at all. Also on the issue of streaming, the Social Democrats made a concession regarding what role the trial would play as a basis for a decision. It was decided that an inquiry "at the end of the decade" would evaluate the results. This decision was, in Richardson's words, "a political nebula."[43]

The following year, the subject of the trial came up in parliamentary discussions. Comparisons of knowledge levels and proficiency among the school forms indicated that comprehensive school pupils actually knew less and performed less well than those in lower secondary schools.[44] Against this background, Conservative party representatives asserted that "fairly certain conclusions" could be drawn: the attempt demonstrated that it was not justifiable to replace existing school forms with the comprehensive school. Advocates of the comprehensive school, however, argued that differences in types of pupils, teacher categories, methods, and the like rendered it impossible to come to such a conclusion. In conjunction with this discussion, the Riksdag's Standing Appropriations Committee stated in 1956 that the trial should result in a nine-year mixed-ability compulsory school.[45]

In 1957 it was decided that a special school working party would evaluate the trial comprehensive school and suggest how the compulsory school should be organized and connected to other forms of education. This task was to be completed in time for a decision to be taken in the 1962 Riksdag. Ragnar Edenman became chair of the working group, and Jonas Orring its first secretary. Other members included politicians, parents, and representatives of employers, employees, and educational bodies. Once again scientific expertise was called upon to inform the group about current research in the question of streaming. The working party wished to know if and when general talent and special talent could be distinguished. The results were hardly able to provide guidelines in the question of timing; on the other hand, they did indicate significant "intraindividual" differences, that is, that individuals were frequently more gifted in certain areas or respects and less gifted in others.[46]

That the comprehensive school would be established was now clear; the question was how. Would there be early or late streaming? Organizational or pedagogic? Selective or free options? Social Democratic opinion preferred as little organizational differentiation and as much pedagogical individualization as possible. Eight common years and one streamed year were called for. The party was supported by the Agrarian party and the communists, although the latter wanted even less differentiation. The Liberals wanted a comprehensive school with built-in lower secondary, practical lower secondary, and girls' schools, and streaming after six years. The Conservatives, finally, opposed the comprehensive school's exclusion of other parallel school forms such as lower secondary and girls' schools.

The working group managed to achieve a compromise: wholly unified school attendance for the first six years, followed by the possibility of options during the seventh and eight years and choice of subject lines in the ninth year.[17] However, the problem of other types of schools (for example, practical lower secondary and girls' schools) had to be solved. Two-year supplementary lines after the basic nine years, the so-called continuation schools, were proposed. Later, the Conservative representative resigned but submitted a statement for consideration in which he claimed that the promised comparisons of competence between the different schools had not been made, and consequently there was no basis upon which to form an opinion. When the proposal was circulated for examination, the old conflicts were renewed. However, only various academic bodies and the National Union of Teachers were totally negative. The differences between the academic teachers and elementary school teachers surfaced again, for the elementary teachers were strongly in favor of the proposal.

In order to deal with the government's proposal for the 1962 Riksdag a special school committee was set up—like the one in 1950. The chair of the committee was the Social Democrat Emil Näsström, and its secretary was Jonas Orring. Decisions could be made under the aegis of unanimity concerning the main lines of the reform. A new, compulsory, comprehensive "basic" school was to be successively introduced over the whole country. The "base" school was now established, and the entire parallel school system on the compulsory level had been abolished. Through the 1969 revision of the curriculum, which removed the option of choosing among the various course lines, uniformity became even greater. Students and parents in consultation with the school were in principle free to choose levels of difficulty in certain subjects.

The last "hurdle" of the comprehensive school reform, a uniform training of all teachers regardless of year, remained. With such a training program, the old gap between teachers' college–trained primary and elementary school teachers and the academically educated grammar school teachers would finally disappear. A uniform comprehensive school teachers' education was investigated during the last half of the 1970s. An overlapping training program, with specializations in languages, natural sciences, or social sciences and oriented toward the first to seventh or the fourth to ninth years also exists at present, despite stubborn opposition from *Folkpartiet* (the Liberals) and *Moderata Samlingspartiet* (the Conservatives), who have claimed that the quality of teaching in the upper forms was threatened by the introduction of the program. Under the influence of both this criticism and that from upper-form teachers, the Social Democratic minister of education, Bengt Göransson, rejected the National Board of Education's proposal for a single, uniform, compulsory school teaching post—to the exasperation of the nonacademic teachers' organizations. To accept ten differently specialized positions in order to ensure "competent teaching" meant, according to the critics, retaining class differences in the teaching corps and complicating the development of the nine-year compulsory school.

A DEMOCRATIC SCHOOL

The overriding aim of SAP educational policy has been "to democratize the Swedish school system."[48] The expression "a democratic school" was used with particular intensity by the 1946 Schools Commission—understandably, in light of the just concluded war. Yet both before this and afterward, the term has arisen in Social Democratic debates. A democratic school did not then mean a school in which decisions were taken in a formally democratic way, but a school that satisfied the demands of a democratic society.

Perhaps the expression is best understood as a summary designation, a slogan for the new school's ambitions. A democratic school provides educational opportunities "for all"; it fosters democratic values and puts them into practice; it promotes student activities in decision making and teaching by giving all students the same material and manifold opportunities for group work and discussions. A democratic school is adapted to the modern, "progressive" society's multifarious political, social, and economic needs.

Equality

The observation has often been made that goals of organizations are seldom stable over time, seldom unambiguous or even internally compatible. Nevertheless, *social* equality has been a constant aim of Social Democratic educational policy—which is not to say that the goal of equality has been clearly formulated or compatible with the other aims of the party in the educational system. However, as long as the party has had an educational policy, the goal of equality has occupied a special position (at least rhetorically). During recent decades, however, the question of equality between men and women has somewhat overtaken the question of equality between social classes.

In principle, equality has often denoted "real" similarities in social conditions between classes, groups, and individuals. The educational system has been conceived of as a tool for "abolishing differences in individuals' social and economic conditions in the sense that they are stamped by the social class structure."[49] If, like the early Social Democrats and (to some degree) sections of the 1930s SAP, one accepts this striving for equality in terms of results but does not see the school as especially suitable for attaining these ends, there are no grounds for giving special priority to the school system.

This attitude allowed for another view of education and equality that was often advocated by the party's academic wing, and which might be called elitist. Aptitude was seen as inborn and, after a certain age, measurable. It was thought to be equally distributed among the social classes, although external economic and social conditions made it difficult for working- and agrarian-class talents to make a mark within the educational system. On these grounds many of the party's politicians involved in educational issues during the 1930s and 1940s considered equality in education as a question of recruiting the most gifted individuals, regardless of social background, to grammar schools and advanced studies. They wanted stricter weeding out among middle-class groups and increased study subsidies for gifted students from the working and agrarian classes. Their intention with this was to promote "fairness" or equality in starting opportunities for everyone with the same capabilities. Nothing less than high aptitude should determine whether to continue on to selective grammar schools and advanced studies.

Later on, this view met with strong criticism, for instance, in association with the Schools Commission. Even if pupils were different from each other in aptitude, personality, and ability, it was both undemocratic and inegalitarian to group them into different classes and schools on such premises. Despite their differences, they should be kept together in the same classes and schools as long as possible. Pedagogically motivated streaming could be accomplished by means of individualization within the framework of the class. Olof Palme reiterated this criticism as recently as 1968 during the preparation of the university reform: the ideology contending that "everyone should be given the same chance after the starting gun, in the belief that everyone starts in the same place"[50] uses education to defend against dividing people into different pigeonholes and stables.

Instead, education could be used to create equality. During the attempts at the comprehensive school reform, another view of equality could be observed in the party: namely, compensation. Study aptitude was seen as a result of both inheritance and environment. Students could be helped or hindered by their social conditions, but at no point could this be definitely measured and used to justify streaming. The greatest possible mixture of ability was to be desired, especially for the sake of the less gifted, as it would give them the best chance of developing. The school itself was to compensate for socially inherited disadvantages. This compensatory view of education received ideological support at the end of the 1960s from the minister of education, Ingvar Carlsson, who declared that the nation was giving the best education to those most suited for it. "Tomorrow it will be the worst off who will be given that chance."[51]

In the long run, the Swedish pursuit of equal rights in education has been a compromise between two contrasting approaches: giving the best education, on the one hand, to the best students, and, on the other hand, to the most needy students. Taking account of both individual differences and interests and the diverse needs of the labor market, it became necessary, despite all, gradually to give students different kinds of education. The basic problem was actually that the various choices of education were linked with status. Equality is largely a question of how groups and institutions in society evaluate different types of education and occupations, and thus it is a matter of changing the evaluations. The state itself is an important distributor of status and prestige, and consequently one way to encourage equality would be to ensure that at least the state and the educational authorities did not consider one type of education as "worth more than any other."[52]

To achieve equality and equal opportunities in education, the party has devoted efforts toward the greatest possible amalgamation of all students; the eradication of status differences between the theoretical and the practical, and between women and men, for example, by abolishing *examina*—leading, prestigious names in education; and the delay of definitive choices by, for instance, giving all comprehensive school pupils, regardless of levels of difficulty in the chosen courses, the same assessment for all gymnasium (upper secondary, for students sixteen to nineteen years old) lines.

Regarding equal opportunities between men and women, progress in the comprehensive school can be described as a "success story." The proportion of female upper-form teachers has increased and continues to do so. Girls choose theoretical subjects more often than do boys; girls receive higher marks than boys, both in the nine-year compulsory school and the gymnasium, when comparing performance levels in standardized achievement tests and standardized national tests.[53] All this is in accordance with criteria that would be uninteresting if all types of education were in fact equally "refined."

In general, empirical observation indicates that class differentiations have to a great extent been re-created in the new school, and the possibility exists that the growing proportion of female upper-form teachers may be more of an expression of the sinking status of the teaching professions than of educational policy successes. Even though girls' industriousness is rewarded with honors in school, in comparison with boys on the same level they are awarded more subordinate positions outside, in the workplace.

According to Lena Johansson, neither are status differences between types of education so easily erased by means of educational policy decisions. Politically, they are presented as a kind of "prejudice," even though the politicians and authorities making such assertions ambivalently seem to share such "prejudices" themselves: if every kind of education was as "fine" as the next, it would not matter in the least who chose what. However, perhaps it is not a matter of "prejudices"; perhaps individuals who wish to have independent and well-paid work simply behave rationally when they choose theoretical studies. Perhaps it is not the "evaluations" that need changing, but society's structure of rewards—for example, "wages, working conditions and bonuses connected to jobs which the various lines of education lead to."[54]

I am not altogether certain that Johansson's line of reasoning holds. Indeed, a great deal suggests that the status associated with certain kinds of education and occupations has in fact decreased, initially just because of the political decision to offer education to a greater number of people. Very likely this is only the first step in a process in which wages, working conditions, and benefits will also come to be changed. This seems to be the case with both traditional theoretical gymnasium and university studies leading to, for example, teaching and social work occupations, which have lost status.[55] This is not to say that on the whole status differences between types of education and occupations have been eliminated. Status boundaries have been moved to occupations and kinds of education that have been able to retain their exclusivity, primarily because of restrictions and professional monopolies.[56] Certain status differences have been erased, while others remain. A wholly different question, of course, is whether it is desirable that, in an unequal "status society," it is precisely those teaching our children who are losing status.

Freedom of Choice

To a high degree school policy has also been intended to bolster students' possibilities of developing their individual capabilities and interests through free choices. One basic idea behind previous school reforms has been that all individuals have the right to an education that corresponds to their aptitudes and interests. The Schools Commission, and the Social Democratic debates that preceded it, expressed the idea that children's different personal prerequisites should be noted, respected, and taken as points of departure in individualizing classroom instruction. This freedom of choice has not only been expressed in individualized teaching and free optional courses in the compulsory school; it also informs the attempts to organize the entire educational system so that "dead ends" can be avoided—in other words, to give all students the possibility of changing their minds both during and after school attendance.

The individualistic educational policy of encouraging students' freedom of choice inside and outside of school has without doubt been a dilemma for Social Democrats. On the one hand, freedom of choice has seemed more attractive to the party: it has made it possible for all students to choose theoretical studies if they so wish and not risk being excluded as they were in the old lower secondary school—a freedom of choice for social leveling. On the other hand, there is much to suggest that free choice contributes more toward maintaining and re-creating existing class differences in society. The party also seems to have gradually acquired a more instrumental view of freedom of choice; it has a utility value if it contributes to leveling and makes space for compromises with the bourgeois parties—but it has little intrinsic value.

The Needs of Society

One particular problem with freedom of choice is the uncertainty of whether the students' educational decisions will actually be in accord with society's needs and demands for educated people. It is obvious that the educational reforms of past decades have in fact been far less dictated by the desire to satisfy individual demands for education than by society's needs for well-educated citizens. The Schools Commission predicted a "significant popular psychological resistance" to extending obligatory school attendance.[57] That societal needs have played a considerable role in educational policy is of course particularly clear regarding demands for an educated work force. In a certain sense, decision-makers have always tried to shape education to respond to labor market needs.

In the discussion of Social Democratic educational policy in the 1930s, I did not exclude the possibility that the "absence" of a comprehensive school reform could have been due to concern that such a school would attract more students to theoretical courses than would be required to sat-

isfy labor market needs for a theoretically trained work force. It is also clear
that one important factor behind the Social Democratic desire to expand
the school system at the end of the war was worry about the employment of
large groups of young people at a time when economic stagnation was predicted.

However, the desire to adapt the educational system to the needs of the
labor market subsequently came to far exceed such purely reactive ambitions. One important motive behind the school reform was doubtless to
identify and recruit working- and agrarian-class talents, the so-called gifted
reserves, to supply the increasing need for qualified labor. However, the
school's social and economic task was not thought to be limited to the indirect, to sifting out the qualified work force required by the labor market.
Through qualifying individuals for jobs that increased the material welfare
of society, agencies of education could also directly play a major role in the
process of national economic growth.

Flexibility and Efficiency

As a consequence of the school's important social and economic task as well
as the increasing pressures on state finances, efficiency came to have an
expanding role in school planning. Even so, I think it must be interpreted
as an expression of the expanding dominance of an educational bureaucracy
when, in the mid-1960s, the aims of flexibility and efficiency were no
longer seen merely as natural marginal stipulations for educational activities, but were given the rank of all-embracing educational policy goals.[58]
The school system began to be considered essentially complete. However,
it had to be equipped in such a way that when the students' or society's
economic demands for education changed, the system could react by itself.
The school then must fulfill high demands for efficiency in the sense of
effectively learning to use scarce resources.

Quality

One important theme in educational policy has to do with the quality or
standards of teaching. It is my impression that very different standpoints
can be distinguished in the party, even if they are not very easy to pin
down: no one expressly advocates lowering standards or reducing quality.
However, I still think it possible to detect diverging views, if somewhat
indirectly, in discussions of the school's goals.

Conflicts over the quality of education rarely arise in a parallel-organized school system. It is normally taken for granted that the quality of, for example, elementary school teaching is quite different from that of the grammar school. If the former is considered mainly to consist of effectively instructing the majority of students in reading, writing, and arithmetic as well as good behavior, the latter is intended to prepare a minority of specially selected students for qualified studies in, for example, science or classical languages. The problem becomes more pointed, however, when a general compulsory school is combined with a selective entry school. Quality is often brought to the fore in the issue of consequences for that education which is thought to "correspond" to the selective entry school.

Within Swedish Social Democracy, a couple of main lines can be discerned in the question of quality. According to the Social Democratic "grammar school line," the grammar schools' quality was evident in students' putative ability to manage advanced studies. Quality was promoted by, among other things, the students being selected to continue on to grammar school on grounds of demonstrated aptitudes. This was prepared earlier by a certain amount of selection through successive examinations, or "thinning out." During the trial period such views were also evident in the acceptance of the "comparison frenzy," when, in order to accept the reform, it was demanded in principle that the new experimental school's students should perform as well as the old lower secondary school's.

Against such attitudes it was argued—in association with the debates preceding the Schools Commission—that the new school should not be evaluated only in terms of criteria for the old lower secondary school. The new school had to fulfill many new goals that were never on the agenda for the lower secondary school. Thus the concept of quality had to encompass not only theoretical knowledge and aptitude for higher studies, but also democratic attitudes, equality, personal development, and preparation for working life. These goals were to be acknowledged when judging the school's "quality."

Ever since the attempt to create a uniform school commenced, quality has appeared as the new school's Achilles' heel. Bourgeois politicians, grammar school teachers, and others involved in education debates have more or less permanently questioned whether the quality of education in the new school has really measured up, whether it has equipped the students with firm knowledge in important nontheoretical and theoretical subjects.

STRATEGIES OF POLITICAL STEERING

I would like to conclude by attempting a short discussion of a few factors that may have influenced the political strategies the Social Democrats have tested in education during various stages: namely, the party's trust in scientific knowledge and its vision of party-political unity. The following is meant to outline these strategies:

	Trust in Science	
	Low	High
Party-political unity High	1	3
Low	4	2

The Small Steps Strategy

When trust in science as a basis for decision making has been low but party-political unity has tended to be high, an incremental, cautious, step-by-step strategy has characterized the party. Wavering knowledge entailed uncertainty about the effects of eventual measures; and consequently only small steps were taken, which, if necessary, could be retracted (1). Political unity meant that no significant active political influence needed to be exercised in education.

Arthur Engberg's school policy during the 1930s, when agreement prevailed among the parties (albeit not yet within the labor movement), is an example of this cautious strategy, which was notably not typical of other sectors. Compare the great anxiety over eventual effects of the introduction of the comprehensive school with, for instance, the active social and labor policy, in which the party believed it had the support of authoritative economic theory. Neither comprehensive goals nor an orientation to long-term action determined educational policy; it was characterized by many small measures, which were indeed sometimes repealed. The strategy of small steps and circumscribed political influence perhaps contributed to the avoidance of mistakes; but it also led, as we have seen, to hiding controversial questions, and to confining political discussion to prepared compromise alternatives.

Political Consensus Strategy

From the end of the war, a growing reliance on research as a basis for decision making, in educational questions and elsewhere, can be detected among Social Democrats. Since then, the party has entrusted research with providing bases for decisions and evaluations. More major decisions have been preceded by thorough inquiries that have included significant research contributions. An example of this is the treatment of streaming—how and when schoolchildren should be sorted into groups according to differences in study aptitudes.[59]

At that time the party also began to test its school policy and soon found itself in a situation of party-political discord. The combination of reliance on research and dissension led to a "political strategy of consensus" (2), active efforts to bolster unity in a broadly based support for a particular policy. The role of administration was expanded. From essentially devoting itself to implementing regulations, administration became more and more involved in producing compromise alternatives and creating institutional arrangements in which disputes could be discussed and settled. Principal decisions appeared to be open, almost indecisive, or in any case marked by the desire not to be rushed. Formulating specific goals was to be avoided in favor of a more general active orientation that was compatible with different results.

Especially contentious political questions, in which unanimity could not be achieved, were declared scientific and handed over to research and experiment for determination. However, it is clear that the Social Democrats in fact often used research and experiment to address wholly different questions than merely the gathering of knowledge: political manipulation—for example, to "depoliticize" issues, or to delay decisions about which there was political discord, or to foster "pragmatism," as when the experiment with the comprehensive school was expanded during the 1950s in order to satisfy growing demands for education. It is also clear that in the long term, the party did not allow itself to be hindered by undesirable research results.

Increasingly, consensus—the attempt to reach a broad agreement over party lines—came, perhaps even primarily, to apply to the large, organized "public interests." This gave the party special opportunities to "mobilize counter interests," to create a "social front" against adversely affected groups, especially grammar school and university teachers. Support from the politically and professionally well organized elementary school teacher corps, which expected rewards in the form of the satisfaction of many professional interests, was important. One possible weakness in the strategy was that potential opponents, especially the Conservatives, sometimes refused to show their colors clearly and only gradually demonstrated their lack of loyalty to the policy—perhaps because it became evident that the Social Democrats almost always accepted compromise as a launching point for more far-reaching efforts.

Technocratization

Social Democratic educational policy has been strongly influenced by a centralist point of view. The party has seldom doubted the value of deciding and regulating school organization, resources, and content on a high central level. The pivotal features of this centralization have been thorough investigation and planning, "major" national reform decisions, centrally initiated and bureaucratically controlled reform implementation, and a comprehensive packet of regulations to "control" the field.

This strategy was considered to benefit implementation of the political goals of education. Centralization involves important decisions being made in proximity to the political institutions of government and parliament. There is hardly any doubt that strong centralization, from the point of view of efficiency, was an advantage when preparing and implementing the reforms, since it set up a central vantage point to provide an overview, coordination, and overall evaluation. Centralization also meant that the decisions and compromises that were reached did not need to be repeated on local levels.

When unanimity concerning the school issue, especially during the 1960s, began to seem definite and the party increasingly put its trust in scholarly or scientific products as foundations for decision making, Social Democratic methods of controlling schools and education began to assume pure technocratic characteristics (3). Political accord and belief in scholarly references made it natural to "professionalize" planning and to reduce political influences. The central administration also had the responsibility for long-term planning for the schools, which further strengthened its position. Moreover, as we have seen, this professionalization was expressed in the fact that the demand for efficiency in education was ranked above overall goals for the school system. It was also demonstrated in the postcomprehensive school reform curriculum—in the ambition to express both the aims of the curriculum and evaluations of student performance in behavioral science terms.

Goal Orientation

Technocratic rule, however, entailed overestimating *both* the value of scholarly, expert knowledge as a foundation upon which to make decisions and political unity. When technocratization did not appear to promote goal attainment or efficiency, and when it also initiated political conflicts, Social Democratic educational policy landed in a new situation (4).

The new situation has been characterized by less trust in scholarly bases for decisions and less unanimity regarding educational policy and has provoked a new, very defensive Social Democratic strategy. The strong position of the central administration of education has been questioned. Demands for "participation" (i.e., local participation by various involved groups) have arisen. The traditional Social Democratic doctrine—that the national political leadership, on the basis of the greatest possible agreement and after consultations with organized interests, should determine educational goals, content, and organization—is on the retreat.

The new strategy is usually presented in terms of decentralization, deregulation, and local independence or goal setting.[60] The national political leadership has the responsibility of formulating the overall goals of education, but a great deal of independence regarding means is given to local authorities, who are also accountable to the local political leadership (which can of course be of another party than that of the government). The national leadership is forced to "rule" within a vague legal framework, abstract goal formulations, and by attempts at persuasion and so on. The position of the central education administration is profoundly unclear. It seems to be striving to seize the role of determining whether national goals are achieved. The intention is that this goal-steering strategy should not adversely affect such large-scale projects as a comprehensive school system and an equal opportunity education. It will be an interesting task for research to determine whether this in fact holds true.

NOTES

1. Dahllöf 1967 and 1971.
2. Heidenheimer, Heclo, and Adams 1983, 44–46; Heidenheimer 1978, 1. Note, however, that the emphasis in these complex aims has been variously distributed at different stages. If egalitarian aspects have dominated in the basic nine-year education, efficiency considerations have dominated at the gymnasium, college, and university levels.
3. Heidenheimer 1978, 3.

4. Isling (1974 and 1984) deservedly underlines the battle aspects. His "partisanship" for a certain policy, however, tempts him into assuming that the school should, and was predetermined to, develop in a particular way. One risk of choosing categories of analysis among partisan standpoints in the political process is that one is also tempted to choose heroes and villains. Cf. Richardson (1983, 38), who views the presentation of the 1940s school policy as "a struggle for and against a democratic school system" as one of the "new myths."

5. Richardson 1963, 288–90.

6. Ibid., 291.

7. Ibid., 305.

8. Englund 1986b.

9. Ibid., 90–92; Richardson 1963, 273–75.

10. Richardson 1963, 277; also Englund 1986b, 90–92.

11. SAP Party Programme 1897; Conference Minutes 1897.

12. Isling 1984, 155.

13. Herrström 1966, 200.

14. SAP Conference Minutes 1920.

15. Herrström 1966, 44–46.

16. S. Carlsson 1980, 546; Herrström 1966, 283–85.

17. Isling 1984, 167.

18. Herrström 1966, 200.

19. Rothstein 1986, 134.

20. Isling 1974, 64–66.

21. Rothstein 1986, 131; Isling 1984, 217.

22. Gustavsson 1988, 166.

23. Erlander 1973, 234.

24. Rothstein 1986, 134.

25. Isling 1984, 208.

26. Richardson 1978, 25. Cf. Murray (1988), who claims that politics can simply be construed as a "deviation" from theoretical studies.

27. Isling 1974, 55–57.

28. G. Hirdman 1938, 14. Isling (1984, 225) points out similar points of view within the Agrarian party, which feared that increased educational opportunities would attract young people away from rural communities and farms.

29. SOU 1944:20, 25.

30. Riksdagen, First Chamber, 17 Jan. 1941; cf. Richardson 1978, 62, and Isling 1984, 252.

31. For a thoroughgoing presentation of this question, see Marklund 1985.

32. A. Myrdal and G. Myrdal 1941. For a more basic survey of this debate, see Englund 1986b, 2:321–23.

33. Arvidson 1941.

34. The Labor Movement's Post-War Programme 1944, 18.

35. See Richardson 1978, 226.

36. Ibid., 250–52.

37. Isling 1984, 265.

38. Marklund 1980, 108–10.

39. Erlander 1973, 233.

40. SOU 1948:27.

41. Marklund 1980, 108–10.

42. Ibid., 156–58.

43. Richardson 1967; see also Marklund 1980, 213.

44. Marklund 1982.

45. Riksdagen, Standing Committee of Supply SU 1965:154.

46. According to Härnqvist (1987), these results influenced the working party regarding "the proposal that alternative courses in the seventh and eighth years could be chosen separately from each other and not as a package of easy and difficult courses respectively . . ." (p. 25); cf. also Marklund 1985.

47. Marklund 1983, 57.

48. SOU 1948:27, 1.

49. Rothstein 1986, 92.

50. O. Palme, Speech held in Linköping, 11 Mar. 1970. Citation from Per Stjernquist's statement in U68 main report, SOU 1973:2, 654.

51. Quoted from OECD 1970.

52. OECD 1967.

53. Emanuelsson and Fischbein 1986.

54. L. Johansson 1970.

55. See Ginner (1987, 50), who argues for the possibility that this actually was a conscious strategy in sections of the party.

56. It is fascinating to contemplate the consequences in terms of status for, e.g., the medical profession if one chose to play nurses off against doctors in the same way that elementary school teachers and grammar school teachers have been played off against each other. Nurses could have undergone a rapid, intensive training to be doctors and been allowed to substitute as doctors, etc.

57. SOU 1948:27, 47. Cf. also Englund (1986a), literature that presents the state's need for civic education as an important driving force.

58. OECD 1967, 49. For a discussion of this, see Lindensjö 1981, 37.

59. For a discussion of the role of research in educational policy, see Husén 1987 and 1988.

60. For various discussions of this, see Ramström 1988; Wallin 1988; and Lindensjö and Lundgren 1986.

r
Alf W. Johansson and
Torbjörn Norman

11

Sweden's Security and World Peace: Social Democracy and Foreign Policy

SOCIALISM AND INTERNATIONALISM

"The working men have no country. We cannot take from them what they have not got." These words from the *Communist Manifesto* (1848) have been of immeasurable importance for the socialist view of the nation, its foreign policy, and defense. For the rising working class, the power of the state belonged to the capitalists and the ruling classes. Its military might was not only directed toward asserting national sovereignty but also against the "internal" threat—the emancipation of the proletariat. Its foreign policy was incompatible with the people's desire for peace, and was conducted by princes with allegedly divine authority, irresponsible cabinet politicians, and secretive diplomats. Against the almighty state and its symbols of supremacy stood the International of the working class, with its red flag. Only after the working class had accomplished its historical work of liberation would world peace be feasible. The *Communist Manifesto* was very clear: "When class conflicts cease, so also will hostile relations between nations."[1]

Along with a merciless critique of the existing system and confirmations of proletarian internationalism, it is not surprising to find in the early labor movement examples of indifference to the state and its foreign policy. This attitude, in association with utopian ideas, may explain how a left-wing socialist like Carl Lindhagen in 1914 could propose an "unarmed Nordic neutrality"—an absurdity in international law—and how Otto Grimlund, who shared Lindhagen's opinions, could publicly assert at the beginning of World War I that although unarmed neutrality might lead to "invasion, a beachhead, annexation for a time by one of the warring sides," it nevertheless would be "the greatest guarantee for peace and national independence." Even if foreign policy opinion formation within the SAP has not been subjected to systematic study, it can be maintained that the instances referred to here reflect a marked minority opinion.[2]

Surveying a century of SAP foreign policy, it seems quite natural to connect it with a number of leading figures, beginning with Hjalmar Branting. In contrast to defense issues, foreign policy did not play a prominent role in debates at SAP conferences, executive meetings, and parliamentary group sessions until the 1960s. With the Social Democrats in government, the constitutional structures themselves direct the focus to personalities; as in no other sphere of government, foreign policy has been conducted by ministers (ministerstyre)—although this is in principle at variance with the Swedish constitution.

The Social Democratic leader Hjalmar Branting rejected the Communist Manifesto's statement about workers lacking a country: "In my view this statement is not correct, for to the Swedish native land no one has a better or more natural right than all Swedish people, who by their labors have created this country. . . ."[3] Later Branting found support for his views in Jean Jaurès's L'Armée nouvelle from 1910 (actually a proposal for army organization for the French House of Deputies): "A little internationalism leads away from the mother country, a great deal leads back to it again. . . . A little patriotism leads away from the International, but a great deal leads back to it again." A translation into Swedish of a few fundamental chapters of Jaurès's work was made by Hjalmar Branting and his son Georg and published in 1916 as a rebuke to the antidefense left-wing of the party.[4]

With Branting, as generally within the Social Democratic movement, foreign policy appears in two dimensions: the security dimension, with the native nation-state as the basis for ideas, and the ideological/declaratory dimension, with the world community forming the basis of its ideals. The latter dimension, often carped at by the political opposition as revealing a lack of national consciousness or ideological arrogance, is an integral part of social democracy: the key concept here is, in Branting's words, solidarity, "the pivotal force in the modern workers' world . . . first created by shared misery but then raised and expanded into the propelling moral force for nothing less than a whole new society."[5]

A natural forum for the ideological/declaratory dimension of foreign policy was the Second International, one of whose major concerns was peace and in whose congresses Branting participated from 1891 onward. As has been stressed by several scholars, the International's program for peace had two sides. A curative program—securing peace through the removal of the capitalist system—was paralleled by a preventive program, which to a great extent concurred with bourgeois pacifism.[6] At the Stuttgart Conference in 1907, in which ideas about peace provoked intense argument, Branting successfully took up the cudgels for international arbitration, a prominent idea within the bourgeois peace movement which Branting otherwise sharply criticized for being naive and utopian. At the pacifist congress in Stockholm in 1910 Branting emphasized that a strong power behind the instruments of peace was mandatory, a power like that represented by the international working class through its International. Proof of the strength of socialism seemed evident in the International's extraordinary meeting in Basel in 1912, called because of the threatening situation in the Balkans. Branting shared the optimism about peace that suffused workers' groups after the conflict had been localized and seemingly settled. That this was an illusion grew clear two years later when the International became one of the first victims of the exploding conflict between national forces and great power alliances.

Branting's attitude toward Swedish foreign policy prior to World War I is closely connected to his attitude toward questions of democracy and defense. In foreign policy his views often corresponded markedly with those of the Liberals or the Liberal left wing: for instance, in the assertion of Swedish and Nordic neutrality, in the struggle against the constitutional right of the monarchy to determine war or peace, in the question of the dissolution of the union of Sweden and Norway, and in 1908 when Russia attempted to disregard the prohibition against fortifying the Åland Islands laid down in the Treaty of Paris in 1856. For the entire Left, czarist Russia was the stronghold of reaction and the greatest threat to Sweden's peace. The Russification of Finland was condemned, and, together with the Liberals, Branting made a strong personal contribution toward asserting rights of asylum for political refugees from the czarist realm.

During World War I Branting was one of the most prominent champions of Swedish neutrality. His desire for domestic truce, criticized by the party's left wing, also contained a warning against being enticed by Germany into an alliance (*Kisatelegrammet* 2 August 1914). After assuming a wait-and-see attitude during the initial stage of the war, Branting freely expressed his sympathies with the entente and thereby was able to develop in a remarkably free way the ideological/declaratory dimension of his foreign policy. His successor during World War II would, however, find himself in a very different, and hard-pressed, situation.

Activism also had to be fought within the SAP's own ranks: in 1915 three of the party's most outstanding young intellectuals who advocated alliance with Germany were expelled. Long-standing controversies over defense issues as well as disagreements over parliamentary democracy and the incipient peace were the reasons why the party Left was expelled in 1917.

In the same year, the SAP formed a coalition government with the Liberals. For social democracy in government, the security dimension of foreign policy would henceforth be mandatory. The coalition's first (and successfully carried out) task was finding a solution to the trade policy controversies with the entente powers. Under the influence of an unexpectedly rapid end to the war and upheavals in Europe, political democracy was carried to victory in Sweden in 1918.

During the latter period of the war, spokesmen for the wholly Swedish-speaking Åland Islands approached the Swedish government requesting to be allowed to return to their former mother country. The request, based on an undisputed referendum in the islands, was received positively by the Liberal–Social Democratic government, who saw a possibility of once and for all solving a century-old security problem and supporting the principle of self-determination, promulgated by President Wilson and warmly defended by Hjalmar Branting. The government's position provoked intense ire in Finland—as did the sending of marine forces to the Åland Islands during the Finnish civil war, not least among Finno-Swedes—and led to a protracted crisis in Finnish-Swedish relations. The Swedish attempt to get the question on the agenda at the peace conference in Paris came to nothing; it was finally referred to the League of Nations.[7]

BETWEEN THE WORLD WARS

The League of Nations
At the end of World War I in 1918 Sweden's security situation was exceedingly favorable. The threat from Russia seemed to be removed for the foreseeable future. Finland and Poland had recovered their national indepen-

dence, and the three albeit fragile Baltic republics together formed a barrier against the disintegrating Russian empire. Germany had ceased to be
either a threat or, in the eyes of many, a possible ally. In this situation,
Sweden was invited to join the League of Nations, created by the victorious powers and written into the Peace of Versailles.

Making a decision about the league was fraught with political controversy. Sweden faced a historic choice: membership obliged participation in
sanctions and was thereby incompatible with Sweden's time-honored tradition of neutrality. Against membership arose the traditionally pro-German
Right—who regarded the League as the guarantor of Versailles—the
Agrarians, and also the Left Socialists, who viewed the new peace organization as an imperialist conspiracy against the nascent Soviet state. After dramatic parliamentary debates, entry was finally secured by the Social Democrats, led by Branting, and the Liberals. Entry into the League of Nations
was, according to the Social Democratic leader, "a duty toward all of mankind"; in the new times that were dawning it was necessary "to relinquish
our time-honored neutrality, which has entailed letting the world go its
own way while we see to it that we stay out of conflicts to the degree that
this has been possible and permitted by the belligerent powers." The ideological and security aspects of Branting's foreign policy here underwent a
symbiosis.[8]

Hjalmar Branting's high regard for the League of Nations was anchored
in his view of democracy and socialist ideology. Against Lenin's program
for the expansion of the war between the great powers into an international
revolutionary process as the ultimate means to achieve world peace, Branting hailed the efforts of Western democracies to replace the fragmentary
international law, whose powerlessness had been exposed in 1914, with an
international rule of law. "Democracy is Peace"—that was how Branting
formulated his theory of peace in the autumn of 1917, a theory that has
proved valid. Two years earlier he had unequivocally supported a system of
collective sanctions, ultimately military, against aggressors.[9]

In Woodrow Wilson's draft for the League of Nations' Covenant the International's preventive program for international arbitration, disarmament, and open diplomacy was resurrected. Branting praised the American
president as "a historical pathbreaker for the working class" who would
carry on and consolidate his work.[10] Both leaders were inspired by the theory of natural rights as embodied by the great constitutional documents of
the late eighteenth century: the American Declaration of Independence
and the U.S. Constitution, the French Revolutionary Constitution, and the
Declaration of Human and Civic Rights. It is also evident that Branting,

who throughout the war had tried to unite the fragmented socialist forces into one International, envisaged the League of Nations, being the future seat of Social Democratic democracies, as in fact a new International, infinitely more powerful than the old one and indeed a useful counter to the communist Third International—the Comintern.

From 1920 until his death in 1925 Hjalmar Branting formed three Social Democratic minority governments; in the second, he was both prime minister and foreign minister. As leader of the Swedish delegation to the assembly of the League of Nations and, from 1922, Swedish representative in the council of the League of Nations, he occupied an often delicate national representative position, which in conjunction with the unstable parliamentary situation at home clearly circumscribed his political freedom of action as well as the ideological/declaratory dimension in his League of Nations policies. Branting and the Swedish delegation's tactics in the Åland Islands question aroused conservative criticism, as did his efforts in 1923 to bring the Ruhr crisis and the question of reparations before the league council: according to the opposition his policies favored French interests. Branting's attempt in 1924 to find arguments for Swedish disarmament policies in the Geneva Protocol also met with right-wing opposition; league policies, however, played a remarkably minor role in the Swedish decision to disarm in 1925. Branting's dramatic assertion of the league's competence in the Corfu crisis of 1923 was greatly praised in all circles, even though the public was not told that Prime Minister Ernst Trygger had made him refrain from any steps that might have brought about sanction proceedings against Mussolini's Italy. The Åland Islands issue was settled in 1921 by the council of the League of Nations; sovereignty was awarded to Finland, the people of the Åland Islands were granted extensive powers of self-government, and to satisfy Swedish security demands the islands were made neutral.

Östen Undén had been working with Branting on league policies since 1921. During his period as foreign minister from 1924 to 1926, Undén became famous for his offer to withdraw Sweden's council mandate during the so-called council crisis in 1926 in order to ensure Germany a permanent council seat without expanding council membership, which he had long opposed. His gesture came to be interpreted as an expression of altruism, true to the spirit of the league, and was later approved by the government. In fact, the gesture was an expedient to get out of a diplomatic quagmire: by vetoing the expansion of the council during the dramatic and unforeseen development in Geneva, Sweden appeared to be threatening the relaxation of tension brought about in Locarno. In contrast to Branting's, Östen Undén's league policy concentrated on international law and, in particular, on the development of arbitration: Undén was one of the driving forces behind the so-called General Act of 1928, a comprehensive international arbitration treaty to which individual countries could subscribe or join with various kinds of reservations.

At the beginning of the 1930s flaws in the central functions of the league became increasingly obvious. Confronted with the various ominous manifestations of dictatorships, the concept of international solidarity seemed more and more hollow, and on the commencement of the Abyssinian war collective security seemed an illusion. For Sweden and its Scandinavian neighbors, neutrality was once again an option.

On 30 August 1935 Undén, reserved and factual as always, addressed students in Uppsala on the prospects for the League of Nations. However, the preserved manuscript contains phrases omitted from his speech that attest to his bitterness and deep feelings. He stated that neutrality had been revived because of the "bankruptcy of the idea of solidarity and organization." "This fact must perhaps be accepted with resignation, but the apostles of neutrality will never be heralded as the liberators of mankind."[11] In light of this admission, Östen Undén's subsequent high estimate of Swedish neutrality appears in somewhat paradoxical relief.

The Threat of Fascism

The Nazi takeover of Germany confronted Swedish Social Democracy with a new threat and new problems.[12] The primary task was to prevent the fomenting of Swedish fascist groups as a consequence of developments on the continent. When in April 1933 the SAP executive discussed what measures could be taken to prevent the rise of a strong Swedish fascist movement, several speakers contended that the best remedy was a strong and decisive Social Democratic policy.

"A positive program for crisis issues is essential in the struggle against fascism," asserted Gustav Möller, minister of social affairs in the new government.[13] The political settlement with the Agrarian party in May 1933 (the so-called "horse trading") demonstrated the Social Democrats' determination to acquire the parliamentary prerequisites for the effective execution of power, even at the price of diluting their ideological principles.

Hitler in power meant a concerted attack on the fundamental principles that had guided Swedish Social Democracy during the 1920s: collective security and disarmament. Already in October 1933 Germany announced its withdrawal from the League of Nations and simultaneously withdrew from the international disarmament conference. In March 1935 Germany openly proclaimed its intention to rearm. The new international tensions and doubts about the league's peacekeeping ability forced the Social Democrats into reexamining their position on disarmament. At the 1932 conference those opposed to continued unilateral Swedish disarmament had asserted their argument only with difficulty. When the next conference took place four years later, the issue was not whether to rearm, but how much rearmament would cost.

The sharp conflicts between the European labor movement and fascism created problems for the Social Democrats as a ruling party in the sense that they had to avoid having their foreign policy taken as a militant policy dictated by party ideology. The party leadership had to preserve national unity on foreign policy, while at the same time not colliding with opinion within the party and the trade union movement through ostensible passivity. It is revealing that when the Swedish trade union movement, on the initiative of the international confederation of trade unions, called for a boycott of German goods in September 1933, Foreign Minister Rickard Sandler took exception to the idea in a speech. At a meeting of the LO and the party in November of the same year Sandler strongly criticized the boycott, saying that such measures could go counter to their own aims and lead to consolidating the German people behind the Nazi regime.[14]

The boycott appeal rapidly faded away. When the question was debated in the Riksdag the following year, the Social Democratic party leadership's attitude was very defensive. It clearly wanted to avoid getting on the wrong side of bourgeois opinion regarding policy toward Germany. Sandler argued that external pressure could not bring about a change of regime in Germany. At the SSU (Social Democratic Youth) conference in 1934 he claimed that it was essential to differentiate between "domestic policy problems and international imperatives." The possibilities for peaceful coexistence with states that were objectionable on ideological grounds should not be made more difficult. The Social Democrats had understood this in relation to the Soviet Union, and the same now applied to Nazi Germany.[15] This was a straightforward declaration that state interests alone would determine foreign policy. In one of his first speeches as foreign minister Sandler had stated that one of the foremost tasks of foreign policy was to promote trade interests.[16] Not least from this point of view was it important to check the formation of antifascist opinion: after Great Britain, Germany was Sweden's largest trading partner.

The powerful wave of antifascism that arose in Sweden during the Abyssinian war in 1935 and 1936, however, did not pose much of a problem for the government since Swedish opinion across the political spectrum unanimously condemned the Italian aggression.[17] The question of Spain in the summer of 1936 was another matter. The SAP's leader, Per Albin Hansson, who had assumed the role of leader of the parliamentary opposition for a few months, declared on 1 July that there could be no question of restraining expressions of sympathy for Spanish democracy. This openness, however, would soon be abandoned. In early August the LO contributed 50,000 kronor to the international solidarity fund for Spain and called for additional fund-raising within the trade union movement.[18] This produced a fierce reaction from the bourgeois press, where attitudes toward the government forces in Spain were chilly—if not openly hostile (and consequently favorable to the insurgents). This situation clearly risked polarizing opinion between the labor movement and the bourgeoisie. However, in mid-August Per Albin Hansson underlined that, despite the engagement of the labor movement, he was not about to allow the issue of Spain to become a point of contention between social democracy and the bourgeoisie. What Social Democrats personally felt was one thing, he explained, "a country's official position, as conveyed by its government, another."[19]

Coalition with the Agrarian party after the election of 1936 also forced the Social Democratic party leadership to maintain a certain distance from labor movement opinion on Spain, but at the same time the Social Democrats had to prevent the communists, with their open engagement in the issue, from strengthening their influence under the guise of popular front politics. This dilemma was resolved by the Social Democratic leadership remaining in the background while the trade union movement and the International became the visible representatives for Social Democratic opinion in the Spanish question. That this would create certain tensions between the LO and the party was inevitable. While the Social Democrats as ruling party adhered to the policy of nonintervention (to which Sweden agreed in July 1936 under the so-called Bramstorp summer government), which in reality meant declining to help the government forces in the Spanish conflict, Swedish Social Democratic representatives signed the International's resolutions in which this policy was condemned.

Party Secretary Anders Nilsson has written that party leaders experienced the situation as "uncomfortable" and "embarrassing."[20] Many members also opposed the party's stance, which they thought was much too cautious. The party leadership defended itself with the argument that the nonintervention policy was a peace policy, intended to prevent the civil war in Spain from developing into an international conflict. As international tensions increased and the line of neutrality became more pronounced, the possibilities for the type of double-edged profile that characterized the party's position on Spain diminished. The Social Democratic leadership was compelled to more actively dampen antifascist opinion. In October 1938 a circular signed by the prime minister and the foreign minister was sent to selected newspapers. In the letter, the press was admonished to observe restraint lest Sweden's policy of neutrality be undermined.[21] Neutrality also compelled separation from the revived 1923 Socialist Labor International, in which there was anyhow little engagement on the part of Swedish Social Democrats. Already in 1934 Sandler had stated—without regret—that the International played an "insignificant role."[22]

The intensifying political situation abroad in 1938 increased the discord between the International's declared antifascism and the Swedish party's neutral position. This discord was highlighted when in March 1938 two Social Democratic representatives signed a resolution from the International in which League of Nations members were exhorted to "halt Italy's and Germany's aggression."[23] This was directly counter to the official Swedish line. At the subsequent meetings of the International, the Swedish party firmly declared that it was not prepared to sign any resolutions not in accord with Sweden's official neutrality.[24]

Sandler and the Nordic Policy

Rickard Sandler, a complicated, elusive figure, was foreign minister in both of Per Albin Hansson's governments during the 1930s. His contributions have been predominantly judged as negative. He has been depicted as a naive proponent of disarmament during a time characterized by the fascist nations' ruthless rearmament, as a Nordic politician inclined to have illusions, but also as an adventurous power politician. All these descriptions contain a kernel of truth, but there also was a pragmatic, almost cynical element in his attitudes toward international questions.

Even if, to begin with, Sandler attached great hopes to both the League of Nations and to international efforts for disarmament, the Swedish policy remained cautious, almost noncommittal. Maintenance of collective security was seen as a shared responsibility, which in reality meant that Sweden made its own position dependent upon that of the other nations, particularly Great Britain.

Sandler hoped that the league's position in international politics would be reinforced, but a return to neutrality was an option he kept open. He saw no absolute opposition between the policy of solidarity in the league and neutrality; hence Sweden retained the right to "once again take the neutral way" if need be, if collective security did not function.[25] The league's lack of universality and doubts about the efficacy of the sanction policy necessitated this option. Sandler thought its lack of universality was the league's greatest weakness, but in the beginning of his period as foreign minister he entertained hopes that it would be overcome. When in 1934 he described the entry of the Soviet Union into the league as a "historic event," it was obviously because he perceived it as a step in the right direction. At this point Sandler seems to have still believed that Germany's notice of withdrawal could be rescinded and that the United States would eventually approach the league.[26]

The crisis in Abyssinia in 1935 and 1936 demonstrated that Great Britain and France were prepared to go along with the league only to the degree that it coincided with their own national interests. The great powers would rather sacrifice a small member state than allow a break with Italy. For the small nations of Europe this was a major blow, but it also revealed how illusory was the belief that the interests of great powers and small nations could always be made to correspond.

The palpable fragility of collective security forced the small nations to question whether membership in the league did not create risks more than provide security. Through the league small nations risked being drawn into great power conflicts, which was the reason why in July 1936 Sweden and several other small countries declared their independent positions regarding the sanction paragraph. At the same time, neutrality was emphasized more and more.

The retreat into straightforward neutrality was not carried out unopposed within Swedish Social Democracy. There were Social Democrats, including Ernst Wigforss, who wanted commitment to collective security, despite the risks of being tied up with great power interests.[27] According to these Social Democrats, to the degree that the major powers in the League of Nations stood for a policy aimed at curtailing the expansion of the fascist states, that policy represented a supranational interest. However, the Western powers' capitulation to Hitler in Munich in September 1938 shattered all such hopes.

In April the same year the Nordic countries had issued common neutrality regulations. This disengagement from the league was primarily due to the breakdown of collective security, but it was also connected to the altered political situation in the Baltic region stemming from the naval agreement between Germany and Britain in June 1935. This agreement exposed the Baltic to German and Soviet power struggles; continued commitment to collective security under the circumstances—in which the Soviet Union professed to be an eager supporter of the league and collective security—could press Sweden toward the Soviet Union, something that the Swedish foreign affairs leaders wished to avoid.[28]

For all that, however, Sandler was not prepared to ally himself with those who wanted Sweden to go the whole way and resign from the League of Nations. The international situation might still improve, and consequently all ties to the league should not be cut.

The Nordic line in Swedish foreign policy, which appeared at the same time as the neutrality line after 1936 and which in certain respects was directly connected with it, can to an extent be seen as a continuation of the cooperation among the Nordic countries within the league. However, it was also a continuation of the cooperation, resumed at the beginning of the 1930s, between the Nordic Social Democratic parties and the trade union federations in the Nordic labor movement's coordinating committee.[29]

This committee became a forum for the Nordic parties to discuss domestic policy issues along with foreign policy and to synchronize policy toward the Socialist International.

In the public discussions in Sweden at this time there was an increased interest in Nordic questions and the common Nordic heritage. For Sandler this interest offered an opportunity to escape the impotence of "absolute" neutrality. A pure isolationist neutrality was not only ideologically humiliating; it was also unsatisfactory in terms of security. The involvement of a Nordic neighbor in war would constitute such a threat to Sweden that it was paramount to make a concerted effort to strengthen the whole Nordic region's neutral position.[30]

From the start, Sandler clearly understood that the prerequisites for a Nordic defense alliance did not exist. The Nordic defense preparations that Sandler discussed did not refer to a common defense of the borders of the Nordic countries, but only to a coordination of defense forces in areas that were, from the perspective of security, particularly exposed. Sandler thought that such coordination would strengthen the Nordic nations' chances of staying out of a war between the great powers. He mentioned three areas as potential objects for coordination: the Åland Islands, the Scandinavian Arctic, and Öresund (the Sound). In fact, the Åland Islands were the only area where coordinated defense measures were tested. One important motive behind this policy, which was initiated in 1938, was to counter the distrust expressed by the Soviet Union toward Finland on several occasions, and to bolster Finland's possibilities of remaining neutral.

In retrospect, it is evident that the Swedish policy scarcely contributed toward increasing the Soviet Union's trust in Finland's desire for neutrality. Sandler's policy seems rather to have bolstered the Finnish leadership's determination not to respond to the secret proposals from the Soviet Union in 1938 and 1939 that were aimed at reinforcing Soviet military positions in the region around the Finnish gulf. From this point of view Sandler's Nordic policy seems almost tragic, since it created false hopes in Finland and clouded the Finnish leaders' perception of how exposed Finland's position was. Sweden's willingness to take security risks on behalf of Finland was also very limited. In his loyalty to Finland, Sandler represented a special line within Swedish Social Democracy, a line that actually had most of its support among conservatives. Only by presenting the policy as limited and conducted with the approval of the great powers was he able to carry opinion. When it was evident that the Soviet Union had objections to the Swedish-Finnish plans on renewed militarization of the Åland Islands, Sweden quickly withdrew (June 1939). From the Swedish perspective, the entire raison d'être of the policy was lost if the action only impaired Sweden's relations with the Soviet Union.[31]

However, Sandler wanted Sweden to carry out the planned measures— even against the Soviet Union's expressed wishes. He regarded Soviet policy as opportunistic but basically peaceful, and this determined his belief that in the end the Soviet Union would approve the Swedish-Finnish plans for the Åland Islands. These notions also influenced his view that decisive behavior toward the Soviet Union was the best policy. Sandler considered the Moscow Pact of August 1939 to be a confirmation of the opportunism of Soviet policy. Thus when he proposed to the government on 3 October 1939 that Sweden should give Finland "a guarantee in the nature of a defensive alliance," he did so in the conviction that decisiveness on the part of Sweden and Finland would make the Soviet Union give up attempts to advance its position at Finland's expense.[32] However, the coalition government was not prepared to follow Sandler into hazards of such power politics—caution clearly ruled the majority within the government. Yet as long as Sandler remained foreign minister, Swedish foreign policy retained elements of activism, which led to intensive disputes—for instance, Finance Minister Ernst Wigforss strongly opposed Sandler's management of foreign policy. The Soviet Union's attack on Finland on 30 November put an abrupt end to all Sandler's notions of the Soviet Union as "actually, a powerful peace factor."[33] On 2 December 1939 he resigned.

SOCIAL DEMOCRACY AND THE COALITION GOVERNMENT'S FOREIGN POLICY

The coalition government in charge of Sweden's destiny during World War II contained a dominating Social Democratic element. The choice of a nonpolitical expert as foreign minister, the diplomat Christian Günther, emphasized that foreign policy was to be considered a shared responsibility. Prime Minister Per Albin Hansson, in a speech on the first day of the war, had set out his foreign policy program: keeping Sweden out of war while preserving national unity, a program to which he was unswervingly loyal for the entire duration of the war.[34] And indeed, more than anyone else, the prime minister set his stamp upon Swedish foreign policy during the war.

Per Albin Hansson's attitude toward foreign policy issues could be characterized as *lillsvensk* ("Little" Swedish): a passive, wait-and-see attitude, aimed at avoiding complications and without ambition either to improve Sweden's security or to prevent or guard against potential threats through foreign policy initiatives. The ideological/declaratory element was reduced to a minimum: security policy as the art of survival was quintessential. The war was perceived as a temporary disturbance in the building of the welfare state; it therefore had to be waited out. Undoubtedly, this passivity accorded well with the country's situation after June 1940: Sweden was surrounded by German-controlled territory, and it was obvious that the scope for an active foreign policy had become exceedingly limited. During the second half of 1940 there seemed once again to be possibilities of bolstering Finland's neutral position through an active policy. Yet even if Per Albin Hansson agreed to initiate preliminary discussions with Finland, he was very skeptical about the entire project, and he announced its failure at the beginning of 1941 without noticeable regret.

The policy toward Finland during the first years of the war was a subject of contention between the Social Democrats and the Conservatives, whose leader, Gösta Bagge represented more of an expansive *storsvensk* ("Great" Swedish), historically motivated line. During the Winter War between Finland and the Soviet Union, Sweden made no declaration of neutrality:

Sweden's position was defined as nonbelligerent. This was facilitated by the fact that the Soviet Union did not regard the conflict with Finland as a war. However, no clash between the Conservatives and the other parties in the coalition government occurred. The government was pressed into cohesion by fears that too deep an engagement on Finland's behalf would draw Sweden into the war between Germany and the Western powers. However, Sweden gave Finland extensive humanitarian, material, and economic assistance.

The government also permitted the establishment of a voluntary force but firmly rejected demands for military intervention with regular Swedish troops. The Swedish people were deeply engaged in Finland. The antidictatorship opinion against "Nazi-bolshevism," which arose after the Moscow Pact and which found an outlet in Ture Nerman's paper *Trots Allt!* (Despite All), comprised a potential seedbed of activism, within the Social Democratic party as elsewhere. However, Per Albin Hansson did not seem overly worried that this faction would attract any sizable support, not even during the so-called February crisis in 1940 when for a few days activist opinion lambasted the prime minister. On the contrary, the attacks activated Social Democratic opinion in support of his commitment to maintaining peace. For Per Albin Hansson's position as national leader and guarantor of peace in Sweden, the importance of his clear affirmation of nonintervention during the Winter War can hardly be overestimated.

After June 1940 Germany had gained a near hegemony in the Scandinavian region. The balance of power was toppled both in the east (the Moscow Pact) and in the west (the defeat of France). The preconditions for a strict Swedish policy of neutrality had radically deteriorated: a certain amount of adjustment from the Swedish side appeared unavoidable. On 18 June 1940 the Swedish government assented to a German demand to be allowed to transport soldiers on leave to and from Norway on Swedish trains. The Swedish policy toward Germany from 1940 to 1941 has sometimes been characterized as a policy of concession; however, the term is much too unequivocal to encompass the nature of Swedish-German relations. The Germans reckoned that German victories would bring a latent pro-German opinion into the open. The Swedes wished to avoid provoking the Germans while at the same time underlining that relations with Germany were to be kept within the framework of Sweden's declared neutrality.

What was perhaps most feared during the summer of 1940 were direct German demands for a *Neuordnung* in Sweden. Clearly, Per Albin Hansson had such demands in mind when, during a conversation with the Conservative leader Bagge in September 1940, he explained that he wanted "to maintain neutrality and peace, but could imagine future conditions that might necessitate Sweden's risking war."[35] There was no open debate on a "New Order" at this time, although it is evident that the issue was discussed internally, even in Social Democratic circles. The question that had to be posed was whether Nazi Germany's power required a revision of Sweden's previously wholly dismissive attitudes. One person who obviously entertained such thoughts was Allan Vougt, chief editor for the newspaper *Arbetet* and Social Democratic group leader in the Second Chamber. After a trip to Denmark in July 1940, he asked whether it was not time for Swedish Social Democrats, possibly in cooperation with their Danish and Norwegian counterparts, to embark upon a new course regarding Germany. Vougt's suggestion was not colored by any Nazi sympathies, but rather by pragmatic considerations. What he seemed to have in mind was to counteract a certain defeatist atmosphere within the labor movement, which entailed the belief that all would be lost if Germany won the war.

However, Vougt won no sympathy for his views. The question of relations with Germany was discussed in the beginning of August 1940 by the party's executive committee and the LO leadership. According to Hansson's somewhat cryptic diary entry, they agreed "to hold firm and try to pilot our way through, keeping our independence intact vis-à-vis the unknown."[36] The idea of trying to obtain a relaxation of tension in relations with Germany through an ideological opening toward the Nazi regime was rejected.

Another solution to the problems that the altered power relations in Europe posed for the Swedish Social Democrats was suggested by Defense Minister Sköld in December 1941 at a Social Democratic executive meeting. After positing that one had to expect Germany to retain a dominant power position in Europe for a long time to come, Sköld asked if his party should not withdraw from government in order to "keep itself intact during an eventual period of German influence."[37] What Sköld wanted to suggest was that if the Germans won in the east, the concessions demanded of Sweden would be so enormous that the Social Democrats could never be enjoined to accept them. In such circumstances, it could be prudent for the party to step down voluntarily. Like Vougt, Sköld received no support for his views. That Per Albin Hansson dismissed Sköld's proposition is obvious: Hansson would have considered voluntarily handing over the government to politicians more sympathetic to Germany as perfidious. Since after the

1940 election the Social Democrats had majorities in both chambers, giving up power would have also caused a breakdown of the parliamentary system.

Relations with Germany were brought to a head at the outbreak of the war with Russia in June 1941. The demands made by the Germans—for instance, to transport an armed division from Norway to Finland—clearly transgressed the bounds of neutrality. A crisis threatened that could shatter the coalition. The decision-making process was complicated from the start when the head of state, Gustav V, declared that he thought the German demand should be accepted, and that he was even prepared to reconsider his constitutional position if it was not. This declaration from the king put those wishing to refuse the German demand at an initial disadvantage. The strongest opposition came from within Social Democratic ranks; but an attempt to coerce a refusal would have certainly destroyed the coalition government, which the prime minister wanted to avoid doing at all costs. Because of the king's threat, and in the situation arising from the new German-Soviet war, a purely Social Democratic government was untenable from the standpoint of security; it would have assumed the character of a ministry openly hostile to Germany. On the other hand, a more apolitical "monarchical ministry," like that of Hammarskjöld's in 1914, could not be expected to exert any forceful opposition against Germany.

The stand taken by the Social Democratic ministers in government discussions was also influenced by the apprehension that consent to the Germans would initiate a new pro-Finnish and anti-Bolshevik foreign policy. After a difficult decision-making process, the government acceded to the most important German demands; but since it was also clearly stated that transit permission was conceived of as a once-only concession, a limit to concessions was drawn. When at the end of July the Germans returned with a new request for transit permission, it was immediately denied. Even if consent to the Germans was felt to be humiliating, the so-called midsummer crisis of 1941 cannot be seen solely as a failure of Swedish Social Democracy. Through their forcefully articulated opposition, the Social Democrats contributed to stabilizing opinion and setting limits to concessions. At the end of the summer of 1941 the Germans observed that the Swedish consent in June had not initiated any new positive policy toward Germany. During the autumn of 1941 Germany raised sharp complaints against Sweden, but by the spring of 1942 the Germans clearly seemed to accept Swedish neutrality. During the rest of the war, the central German goal regarding Sweden was to preserve access to Swedish iron ore exports.

Thus the Swedish policy toward Germany retained its character of negative adjustment to shifts in power relations. It may be noted that there were voices, even within the government, arguing for a policy more positively prepared to meet Germany halfway, but these factions (except during midsummer 1941) never managed to set their stamp on politics in any decisive way. To have prevented that was probably the Social Democrats' most important contribution during the war.

During the last years of the war Sweden was exposed to increasing pressure from the Western powers, especially on reducing Swedish trade with Germany. There were forces among the Social Democrats calling for a more open attitude toward the allied powers and a more resolute attitude toward Germany. However, Per Albin Hansson consistently dismissed every form of what he called "reprisal policy" toward Germany. The final years of the war contained the same policy of negative adjustment to the power positions as had marked the previous years.

For the Social Democrats, World War II became a demonstration of the value of a Swedish policy of neutrality. Even if in terms of international law the coalition government did not succeed in maintaining a wholly uncontentious line, its neutral policy created a basis for preserving national unity and functioned as a shield against undesired foreign policy engagement and ties. Toward the end of the war, it was clearly evident—perhaps clearest with Defense Minister Sköld—that for the Social Democrats neutrality was not only perceived as a means of keeping Sweden out of the war, but also as an instrument for safeguarding the Swedish welfare system in the future. The emotional ties with neutrality that the experiences of the war created within the Social Democratic movement became without doubt the most important foreign policy legacy from that period.

THE POSTWAR PERIOD

Sweden, the United Nations, and East-West Bloc Divisions

At the end of World War II Sweden was not in the favorable strategic situation that had prevailed immediately after 1918. In the east, the Soviet Union ruled over an area stretching from the Finnish Gulf to Lübeck, and it had incorporated the Baltic republics. Finland had rescued its national independence but was still within the Soviet sphere of interest. Norway and Denmark emerged severely weakened from the German occupation.

In the final stages of the war Sweden possessed significant military strength. A disarmament policy along the 1920 Social Democratic lines was not viable because of renewed international tensions immediately after the war. The successfully asserted neutrality was highly regarded. However, despite this and in contrast to 1920, there was no widespread opinion suggesting that Sweden dismiss all forms of foreign policy collaboration. The bitter conflicts in 1920 over Sweden's entry into the League of Nations were not repeated when the question was raised concerning Swedish membership in the United Nations, the new international organization for peace that the allied powers—including the United States, which had remained outside of the league—had decided to establish. Sweden's geopolitical position as well as its Scandinavian neighbors' positive attitudes toward the new organization simplified the decision. At the same time, the high expectations for future world peace, which not least the Social Democrats had attached to the League of Nations, were lacking. When the United Nations commenced its operations, the conflicts between the former allied powers had deepened and the division of the world into two blocs was under way.

Formally, membership in the United Nations was no more compatible with neutrality in a traditional sense than membership in the league had been. However, in a conflict between two nations in which the U.N. Security Council had chosen not to intervene, other U.N. members could remain neutral. Sanctions, economic as well as military, required the consent of a qualified majority in the Security Council, including the permanent members: a veto from any one of the latter would consequently paralyze any action. Should an armed conflict break out between the great powers in the Security Council, "neutrality would be revived," according to the expressive formulation in one of the official statements solicited from the Swedish government. Under such circumstances, the international organization would of course be dissolved.[38]

In the Social Democratic government led by Per Albin Hansson that succeeded the coalition government in 1945, Östen Undén was appointed foreign minister. In his early comments on the United Nations may be traced both criticism of the formation of the charter (the veto clause) and preparedness to sacrifice the putative proviso of neutrality: "Relinquishing neutrality is a logical consequence of entry into an organization which rests upon obligations of solidarity among its member states."[39]

However, his hopes for an exemplary organization would soon be shattered. When in October 1945 the government declared its intention to apply for membership in the United Nations, objections were raised on grounds of the international political situation: if the United Nations, "contrary to expectation," was split into two great power blocs, Sweden must assert its right to keep clear of such formations.[40] Under these conditions, Sweden entered into the United Nations in November 1946. However, the issue of neutrality required further clarification. In a statement in February 1948 the government underlined its repudiation of totalitarian regimes, while also—almost ten years before the Soviet leader Khrushchev launched the theory of peaceful coexistence—asserting the principle that "nations with widely different political, religious, economic or social views and institutions could live peacefully side by side."[41] In a party executive meeting in spring 1948, on the threshold of negotiations on a Nordic defense alliance, Undén posited that neutrality was compatible with U.N. membership: "The Charter has . . . legalized the policy of neutrality."[42]

Clearly, Undén presumed that opposition between the great powers in the Security Council and a consequent utilization of the veto would be permanent; regional agreements for the maintenance of peace and security were in fact not incompatible with the U.N. system. It also deserves to be emphasized that the veto right in reality meant that Sweden would be without U.N. assistance in the event of aggression from its nearest great power neighbor.

Like those of the League of Nations, the goals of the United Nations very largely concur with the goals of social democracy: peace, freedom, international justice, respect for human rights, social progress. As the SAP programs in 1920 and 1944 hailed "a democratically organized union of nations," the 1960 program called for "active participation in the United Nations" and "respect for the principles of the U.N. Charter." The latter program also included the foreign policy goal of preserving national peace and independence through "a firm policy of neutrality," buttressed by a positive attitude toward defense. At the same time, the program declared that Sweden would participate in "efforts to ensure world peace and to achieve international disarmament." The program item on "international policing powers" (included in 1920 and 1944) was removed in 1960: clearly the idea of an international police in an international community governed by the rule of law had been referred to the realm of unattainable utopias.

Östen Undén served as foreign minister from 1945 to 1962. Through his long career as Social Democratic statesman, League of Nations delegate, and law scholar he acquired unique experience and an international reputation. As a person he seemed to all appearances reserved, stiff, and rather chilly. Although his foreign policy speeches, which could expand into lectures on international law, were anything but fiery or exciting, they were convincing through sheer weight of fact and were sometimes tinged with the speaker's aptitude for irony and sarcasm. Östen Undén became a contentious figure in public opinion; but within his own ranks—in the government, even during the coalition with the Agrarian party from 1951 to 1957—his authority was solid, and without any doubt during his period in office he shaped all the essentials of Swedish foreign policy. Under his supervision, after the collapse of the idea of a Nordic alliance, Swedish foreign policy was stamped by what became the classic doctrine: "Nonalignment (vis-à-vis great power blocs) during times of peace is predicated upon neutrality in war." A prerequisite for this doctrine is, paradoxically enough, that the United Nations cannot function according to its ideals: in a world community with solidarity rather than a balance of power as guiding principle, neutrality would be by definition an anomaly.

Swedish neutrality under Östen Undén also came to influence the SAP's attitudes toward the Socialist International, which was reestablished after the war. On occasion tensions arose similar to those experienced by the party during the 1930s. During the Korean War the party's representative participated in the International's condemnation of the war, from which the government felt obliged to dissociate itself. On other occasions the SAP came into conflict with those member parties who for ideological and security reasons were in favor of NATO.[43]

During the period just after the war Sweden tried to maintain a balance between the antagonistic power blocs that were being formed. This was expressed in both the wide-ranging credit and trade agreements with the Soviet Union in 1946 and participation in the Marshall Plan in 1948. Undén's attempts to establish correct and constructive relations with the Soviet Union and hence to remove Soviet distrust of its noncommunist neighbors was, however, only partially successful: border violations, espionage, the Raoul Wallenberg affair, and the shooting down of a Swedish plane during a reconnaissance mission over the Baltic in 1952 all increased tensions. The Swedish government did not mince words when criticizing the Prague coup in 1948, the crushing of the Hungarian uprising in 1956, and the suppression of the "Prague Spring" in 1968. However, despite all this the government and particularly its foreign minister had to bear heavy conservative criticism for being excessively pro-Soviet. Undén was castigated for the extradition in 1945 and 1946 of Balts who had fought under German command; only much later did it become known that he disliked the decision but declined to jeopardize the position of the government.

Östen Undén and the Swedish government were often accused of indifference to the integrative forces in Europe. Even so, Sweden entered the Council of Europe, formed in 1949, and the following year became a contractual member of GATT. However, Sweden did not join the EEC, as its supranational goals were deemed incompatible with neutrality. Despite the differing orientations in their security policies, an extensive integration of the Nordic countries has occurred, partly through the Nordic Council; defense questions, however, fall outside of the council's brief.

One main theme in Östen Undén's foreign policy was that Sweden should follow an independent, objectively charted course between East and West without ties, superfluous censures, or professions of sympathy. He claimed that for his own party, this was ideologically natural: "both bourgeois capitalism and communism" were alien to social democracy; foreign policy connections should not be allowed "to be influenced or defined, by the economic and political regimes prevailing in other countries." This statement suggests that since it represented a third way between capitalism and communism, the Social Democratic Labor Party—more than the other Swedish political parties—should be able to maintain a nonpartisan position between the growing great power blocs. By Undén's criteria, true neutrality was thus totally incompatible with, for example, the "Western-oriented nonaligned position" advocated by the Liberal leader, Bertil Ohlin. Undén's assertion of the idea that ideological values should not determine relations to other states parallels Sandler's speech to the Social Democratic Youth conference in 1934.[44]

Undén's views were stamped by bourgeois circles as crude homespun philosophy and criticized for their alleged negligence in the observance of democracy. Undén's sharpest critic was Herbert Tingsten, *Dagens Nyheter*'s chief editor and the most prominent spokesman for Swedish membership in NATO. In time the realpolitik substance in Tingsten's polemic faded and began to be replaced by something resembling a personal vendetta.

Undén dismissed the criticism, sometimes in the guise of an editorial writer in the Social Democratic press. According to an important government statement in May 1950, Sweden would not be able to significantly affect the balance of power through association with either bloc; however, even internationally it could be valuable "if we endeavored to gradually form a type of society that encompassed both political and economic democracy, a society which through its structure would perform as a genuine political democracy, with a capacity for real social justice."[45] In this way,

Sweden could stand as a model for a peaceful world. The view that the world inexorably tended toward being split between a capitalist and a communist bloc must be countered, and such a view would lose its credibility were the political democracies capable of implementing the welfare state "as we in Sweden are attempting to do." Such a development would even influence the communist world, which had so far not managed to combine socialist economy with political liberty. The message in this text is central and exacting: peace may be secured if other democracies followed the Swedish welfare state model, which would simultaneously exert a democratizing influence on the communist world. It is an extension of Hjalmar Branting's theory of peace from World War I—"Democracy is Peace"—and a quintessential principle underpinning the Swedish doctrine of neutrality. The declaration was completed by a condemnation of all dictatorships and a profession of "ideological kinship with Western democracy."[46]

The Nordic Defense Alliance

During the last years of World War II Sweden conducted a rather tentative debate on future security policy. Several prominent Social Democrats were positively inclined toward a Nordic defense alliance. Östen Undén was also leaning toward Nordic cooperation within the framework of a new collective security organization. He presumed that any future sanction obligations for the Nordic states would be confined to their own region, and consequently that cooperation in defense would contribute toward limiting the Nordic countries' engagement with the rest of the world. Undén's views were markedly different from those appearing in the debate in Norway, where the discussion was more wide-ranging and conducted from a broader international perspective, and where resistance to the idea of a future Norwegian isolationism was very clear. The Norwegian Social Democrats viewed future Norwegian security policy in terms of efforts toward European and international integration. Thus already during the war, Norwegian and Swedish views of future security policy diverged.[47]

However, in 1948 the Swedish government initiated negotiations with Norway and Denmark on a Scandinavian defense alliance.[48] The immediate background to this activation of Swedish foreign policy was the rising international tension caused by the communist coup in Czechoslovakia in February 1948; rumors of a new Soviet thrust against Finland and Norway were also circulating. At about the same time, Europe took the initial steps toward an Atlantic defense alliance. The Swedish government at this point also received information indicating that Norway was on its way into the sphere of Western powers, and so it had reason to fear not only that Norway and Denmark would orient themselves toward the Western power bloc, but also that Swedish opinion would tend in the same direction. Thus, it cannot be overlooked that one important motive behind Undén's initiative for Scandinavian defense alliance negotiations was to prevent Swedish opinion from sliding further toward the West. In accepting the idea of a Scandinavian defense alliance, the bourgeois parties (who were most open to a Western orientation) also had to accept a policy of non-aligned neutrality and a rejection of Swedish participation in the North Atlantic Treaty Organization.

At the initial discussions between Undén and Norwegian politicians in May 1948 the Swedish foreign minister made it very clear that cooperation could only be carried out under the aegis of neutrality. The Norwegians then made it clear that they were interested in Scandinavian cooperation regarding security per se, but not on the basis of neutrality. The negotiations could have broken off then and there, but the parties had an interest in their continuance: the Norwegian foreign policy leadership wished to convince a group within the Norwegian Arbeiderpartiet (Labor party) that a Scandinavian defense alliance was not a realistic security policy alternative; the Swedish foreign policy leadership wished to stabilize opinion around continuing the policy of neutrality. Hence, from the start the real prerequisites for agreement between the Swedish and Norwegian points of view were limited. How convinced the parties became during the negotiations of the possibilities of influencing each other is hard to say.

At the end of 1948 Norway and Denmark received word that they would shortly be asked whether they were willing to participate in negotiations on an Atlantic pact. This accelerated the decision-making process. The negotiations conducted between the Scandinavian government leaders in Karlstad on 5 and 6 January 1949, in Copenhagen between 22 and 24 January, and in Oslo at the end of the month came to nothing, however. Even if Sweden was prepared to compromise somewhat concerning the possibilities of American arms deliveries, there was a fundamental dividing line separating the Swedish and Norwegian points of view throughout. The Norwegians were inclined toward an alliance that would contribute to the West's deterrent capabilities, while the Swedes intended an alliance that would be able to keep the Scandinavian area out of a war between the major powers. The Norwegians pursued a line of solidarity with the West, which the Swedish foreign affairs leadership was not willing to accept.

The Swedish Social Democrats' attitude toward the negotiations was a mixture of engagement and skepticism. Prime Minister Erlander pursued the issue by referring to the fact that Nordic cooperation was included in the 1944 party program. Regarding security, the motive was to reduce the risk of an isolated Soviet attack on Sweden; but there was also an element of propitiation, difficult to pin down, toward Sweden's Scandinavian neighbors for shortcomings in Swedish wartime policy. Undén's engagement in the issue was palpably less than Erlander's, but with his long experience of foreign policy he understood that the sharpening of international tensions in the late winter of 1948 necessitated some form of Swedish initiative. Even negotiations that give no results can often be valuable—as legitimation, alibi, or excuse, or as a way to conduct policy through a critical phase.[49]

Östen Undén and Neutrality

Östen Undén's achievements as a U.N. politician were punctuated by strict observance of the organization's charter as well as respect for the sanctity of international agreements and conventions—he had manifested the same convictions in the League of Nations. At the same time, developments meant that the politics of ideas had to give way to pragmatism. When the Korean War broke out in 1950 Sweden provided humanitarian support to the U.N. actions against the aggressor; but it rejected the Security Council's recommendation (made in the absence of the Soviet Union) of military aid and refused to label China as an aggressor to avoid expanding the conflict into a direct confrontation between the great powers. The same pragmatic considerations lay behind Sweden's voting for the "Cooperation for Peace" resolution in 1950 (which in the event of a deadlock enables the Security Council to give the General Assembly, with a qualified majority, the authority to recommend sanctions against the party violating the peace), while simultaneously underlining its intentions of staying out of all conflicts between the leading powers in the Security Council. By virtue of its neutrality policy, Sweden has been particularly suitable for U.N. peacekeeping operations; more than fifty thousand Swedes have been so engaged. Not unexpectedly, discussions of the role of the United Nations were especially lively during Dag Hammarskjöld's remarkable period as secretary general (1953–1961). Sweden was a member of the Security Council in 1957 and 1958, and during the U.N.'s operations in the Congo fifteen hundred Swedes participated in military actions. The relationship between Undén and Hammarskjöld—former government colleagues—was primarily trusting. It is known that Undén even considered Hammarskjöld a suitable successor to the post of foreign minister.

In the autumn of 1961, in his most noted appearance in the United Nations, Undén proposed a "non-atom club" of states presumed to demand a universal test-ban treaty and to refuse to manufacture nuclear arms as well as receive them in their own territory. The Undén plan was approved by the General Assembly—the Eastern states in favor against the West's opposition. The plan was never implemented internationally; but it put a stop to the Swedish nuclear arms disputes. A test-ban treaty, supported by the great powers, was initiated in 1963, and this was followed by the treaty prohibiting the spread of nuclear weapons in 1968.   .

During his long period in office, Östen Undén came to personify Swedish neutrality. While his conservative critics preferred to describe Sweden's position as *nonaligned*—thus asserting that Sweden's foreign policy alternatives in a crisis situation remained open—Undén emphasized in the mid-1950s that the term was inadequate because it did not "express a determination to conduct a neutral policy in the event of war." The correct term for Sweden's position in peacetime was *neutral,* and consequently it should be made crystal clear that in the event of war the country was determined to remain outside all conflicts.[50]

Swedish neutrality, however, is not synonymous with having neutral views. Undén realized that a credible foreign policy required restraint in the expression of opinion. In the autumn of 1959 he refused the pronouncedly anti-Soviet right-wing leader, Jarl Hjalmarson, a place in the U.N. delegation of that year. In the Riksdag, Prime Minister Erlander developed the Undénesque formulation that "intemperate attacks by influential politicians on other states' policies obstruct the policy of neutrality which we officially adhere to." If "[we] constantly and ardently" took the side of one party, "we would lose all prospects for working for peaceful coexistence and reconciliation."[51] Undén further underlined this argument in one of his last speeches, entitled "Realism and Idealism in Foreign Policy" (July 1962), which was at once a warning and a testament.[52] A few years later, Östen Undén's reserve would be exchanged for Olof Palme's fervor.

A NEW INTERNATIONALISM

Östen Undén was succeeded as foreign minister by Torsten Nilsson, who occupied the post until 1971. He was followed by the Social Democratic foreign ministers Krister Wickman, Sven Andersson, Lennart Bodström, and Sten Andersson. In 1969 Tage Erlander resigned as prime minister and was succeeded by Olof Palme. Like Branting, Sandler, and Per Albin Hansson, Olof Palme set his stamp on Swedish foreign policy; everything suggests that he was largely his own foreign minister.

With Olof Palme a new generation acceded to the SAP leadership. He was born in 1927; the gap in years from Östen Undén (b. 1886), Tage Erlander (b. 1901), and Torsten Nilsson (b. 1905) is striking. With his passionate temperament, fervent engagement, and exceptional rhetorical gifts, Olof Palme became the spokesman for young generations who, in reaction to the isolation of World War II and the petrified postwar relations between the major world powers, wanted to raze walls and open borders to signal a new internationalism and solidarity between peoples.

Östen Undén's period as foreign minister after World War II was that of the Cold War nuclear threat, with the United States and the Soviet Union heading two hostile military blocs whose line of confrontation went right through Europe. At the same time a new chapter of world history could be discerned in the breakup of colonial empires. The liberation of the third world became a prime motive in Olof Palme's internationalism, accompanied by insights into such new global threats as the population explosion, diminishing natural resources, and environmental destruction.

In Europe Willy Brandt's Eastern policy and recognition of the sovereignty of the two German states led to stability and the easing of tension. When the final document from the Helsinki Conference on Security and Cooperation in Europe was signed in 1975, Palme described it as "the closest we can come, thirty years after the end of the Second World War, to a formal peace treaty."[53] Olof Palme's international activities attest to how he saw the axis of world politics turn from east-west to north-south. This perspective is also imprinted in the SAP's program from 1975: under the heading "All People's Freedom, the Whole World's Peace" (a quote from Carl Lindhagen), it is declared that a peaceful world presumes self-determination for every nation and that through cooperation among peoples a new and just economic world order will be attained.

In a speech to the Broderskapsrörelsen (Swedish Association of Christian Social Democrats) in July 1965, with the Vietnam War in the background, Palme raised a subject that would repeatedly return in his political speeches. He maintained that nationalism in Asia and Africa had an enormous explosive force that was nourished by "the old idea of the equal value of mankind, regardless of race and skin color . . . largely the French Revolution's old slogans of freedom, equality and brotherhood," the slogans that once ignited the young labor movement in Europe. The fundamental

values of social democracy made it a duty to be on the side of the oppressed. The liberation of the new states was inexorable and irresistible:
"we must live *with* it and perhaps also *for* it." Palme returned to this
theme, for example, in a conversation with the French journalist, Serge
Richard: "In Africa, in Asia, freedom, equality and brotherhood are not
empty words"; they express revolt against privileges as they once had for
European revolutionaries; it was the task of socialism to make common
cause with the oppressed. In his above-mentioned speech to the Christian
Social Democrats, Palme elaborated that while the industrialized world experienced class divisions, ruinous technological development, and the destruction of its environment, the efforts of the third world could be a source
of inspiration, for here was "a new and meaningful idealism, chances that
seem to have been wasted in other places in the world."[51]

As Branting and Undén had done, Palme condemned both capitalism
and communism—neither could guarantee freedom, equality, and justice.
"The great task of democratic socialism," he urged in a speech in Finland in
August 1974, "is to rally people around an alternative to capitalism and
communism." The same fundamental idea recurs in Palme's correspondence with Willy Brandt and Bruno Kreisky in 1974.[55]

As a neutral state without a colonial past or political ambitions, Sweden
had a special mission: to spread the message of international solidarity with
the liberation struggles in the third world. Swedish neutrality was not isolationist; "our policy of neutrality is an active one." Moreover, Sweden had
its own interest in supporting the third world: "From a security perspective, this policy also provides support for the right of all small countries—
including Sweden—to form their own futures without foreign intervention."[56] This future should be democratic. As it was for Branting, democracy
was for Palme the supreme principle: "For us, democracy is the core of
socialism." Human dignity was synonymous with political freedoms, the
right to work and health, education, social security, the right and opportunity to shape the future together with others. The quote is taken from
Palme's address to the SAP conference in 1975.[57] The driving force behind
Palme's internationalism was, as it was with Branting, the immortal ideas of
freedom, equality, brotherhood—natural rights rather than Marxism.

All this serves as the background to Olof Palme's assiduous work in the
United Nations; in the Socialist International, revitalized by Willy Brandt;
in the Palme Commission, which in 1982 united statesmen from East and
West and presented a program for common security and disarmament; and
in the Brandt Commission, which sought a north-south dialogue and a solu-

tion to international development questions through the Five-Continent Initiative. Remarkable here are Palme's attempts to bridge power structures and ideological deadlocks through a worldwide network of personal contacts, and his desire in the name of common goals to find more rapid channels and smoother organizational forms for international cooperation, even outside the United Nations.

Within the United Nations and its organs, Sweden has followed Undén's line on disarmament (to which significant contributions have been made by a number of Social Democratic women such as Alva Myrdal, Inga Thorsson, and Maj Britt Theorin). With roots in Undén's and Urho Kekkonen's ideas, plans for a nuclear-free zone in Scandinavia have been pursued by Palme and his successors. In the United Nations (Sweden's membership in the Security Council was renewed in 1975–1976) Sweden has been a persistent spokesman for human rights and the formation of norms for international law; here a direct line of descent can be drawn from Branting and Undén in the League of Nations. Following a Swedish initiative, the United Nations called its first conference on the environment in Stockholm in 1972. The Secretary General appointed Palme mediator in the war between Iraq and Iran, which started in 1980. Palme visited these countries five times in what was likely the most difficult international commission a Swedish Social Democratic statesman had ever undertaken.

In its basic document (Proposition 100/1962), Swedish foreign aid policy was expressly designated as a part of Swedish foreign policy. In general, foreign aid—both within and outside of the United Nations—entails an enormous broadening of and a new form for Swedish foreign policy and, from a wider perspective, Swedish security policy. Earlier than any other state, Sweden achieved its goal for foreign aid: 1 percent of GNP (in 1987/1988, about 10 billion kronor).

Swedish criticism of South Africa's apartheid system, articulated by Östen Undén and pursued intensively by Olof Palme and his successors, is reflected in the fact that more than 40 percent of bilateral aid has gone to South African front-line states. Special legislation in 1987 prohibited all trade with South Africa and Namibia; this was the first time Sweden adopted economic sanctions without being compelled to by the U.N. Security Council, and it consciously contravened a fundamental principle in the GATT treaty. The decision, which was described as a once-only measure and motivated by the particularly abominable conditions in South Africa, is primarily significant as a departure from the Undén line in U.N. policy.[58]

Olof Palme became world famous for his vehement criticism of the

United States' involvement in the Vietnam War, while, at the same time, his actions provoked a feud in Sweden. In 1968 the opposition demanded his resignation as prime minister, and the Conservative leader, Gösta Bohman, castigated Palme as Undén had done with Jarl Hjalmarson in 1959. When, on 23 December 1972, Palme compared the American bomb offensive to the worst atrocities committed by twentieth-century dictatorships, a difficult, protracted crisis arose in American-Swedish relations. Diplomatic contacts were reduced to a low level. The United States refused a Swedish ambassador *agrément*—a unique indication of displeasure in Swedish-American relations. Palme's message to President Nixon on 24 December 1972 has been interpreted as a retreat; in fact, it accused the United States of violating the foundations of its constitution and traditions of freedom, and thereby the fundamental principles of democracy:

> Many times in the past people all over the world have looked to the United States for moral authority and leadership in the fight for peace and in the protection of fundamental human values. Personally I am deeply indebted for the inspiration that American ideals of democracy have given me. The Vietnam War, as it has developed, has just because of this created sorrow and disappointment, feelings that I know to be shared by millions of people in Sweden and in other countries. Such reactions are particularly strong among young people and involve the risk that they will lose faith in democracy and democratic values.[59]

In his interview with Serge Richard, Palme underlined that the Vietnam War was not only directed against national liberation, but it was also a violation of the most noble traditions of the American people.

As a consequence of his stance in the Vietnam conflict (which had no counterpart in other neutral governments), Palme was accused by the Swedish opposition not only of disregarding Swedish security interests but also of pursuing "a domestic foreign policy."[60] That his actions were tactically designed to win over militant opinion on Vietnam is probably indisputable, but Palme's own strong personal engagement in the issue cannot be doubted. To a great extent he represented a new type of statesman who, through the development of mass media and communications, is directly confronted with foreign events that older generations of state leaders only would have learned about belatedly through diplomatic reports.

Under Östen Undén the security and ideological/declaratory dimensions of Social Democratic foreign policy had been balanced, the latter basically limited to the framework of U.N. membership. Under Olof Palme the latter expanded to unprecedented dimensions, while the former was more or less dogmatized. Swedish neutrality and nonalignment was affirmed in increasingly clear-cut formulations. Thus when the Social Democrats returned to government in 1982 after six years in opposition, they declared that there should be neither expectations nor apprehensions that Sweden "even under strong external pressure" would relinquish its neutrality. Later on, this declaration became even more emphatic: "our declared intention [is] to refuse to abandon the policy of neutrality, even under powerful external pressure, [and] never to become an outpost for any military alliance" (Olof Palme, 12 December 1985). Because there was so clearly no question of alliances, to the rest of the world Sweden has become a de facto permanent neutral power, despite the fact that Swedish neutrality is neither guaranteed nor written into the constitution or state treaties, and its content is independently defined.[61]

For many observers from both East and West, Olof Palme's active foreign policy seemed incompatible with the traditional type of neutral policy. It could also be ambiguous whether and to what degree Palme's personal engagement in different contexts bound the Swedish government: a number of "scandals" from Palme's later years may be explained by this.

The security policy pattern that was formed in the Nordic countries after the failure of the defense alliance negotiations in 1948 and 1949 has been consolidated and shown to be stable—"the Nordic balance" is the phrase used. It presumes a nonaligned, relatively well-armed Sweden between Finland on the one side and Denmark and Norway on the other, connected to NATO through an "attenuated" membership that in peacetime requires no stationing of nuclear weapons or allied troops on Scandinavian soil.

Since the beginning of the 1980s, Sweden's territorial waters have been violated by foreign submarines. Whether or not the violation of Swedish sovereignty in peacetime can be shown to be continual and systematic, it seems reasonable to conclude that one or more powers have been testing the fundamental thesis of Swedish foreign policy: nonalignment in peace, neutrality in war. Under these circumstances, the security policy and ideological/declaratory dimensions of Social Democratic foreign policy may appear less credible and applicable; consequently, the "Nordic balance" could be in peril. At the SAP conference in 1975, Defense Minister Sven Andersson underlined that the prerequisites for an active foreign policy by

Social Democratic standards are domestic stability and a safeguarded security situation "in our part of the world."[62]

Neutrality presupposes defense. "Our party does not advocate unilateral Swedish disarmament," proclaimed Olof Palme at the 1981 party conference.[63] However, Swedish defense spending has been reduced since the beginning of the 1970s: its proportion of the GNP over the last twenty years has decreased from 5 percent to 2.8 percent; the defense slice of the state budget has been cut from almost 20 percent to 8 percent. In the long run, this development could lead to a reexamination of one of the integrative cornerstones of Swedish Social Democratic security policy—compulsory military service. A more far-reaching reduction in defense could even jeopardize the principle of defending the entire Swedish territory, hitherto championed by the Social Democrats. At the same time, the situation has been complicated by new international threats that can only be met by global cooperation: environmental destruction, energy crises, the population explosion, and international terrorism.

In neutrality there is an intrinsic element of isolation, whose opposite is integration. The most important integration question for Sweden in the 1990s is its position regarding the EC (European Community). The Social Democratic government has rejected membership on the grounds of concern for Swedish neutrality; however, concern for the future of the Swedish welfare model in an integrated Europe would also seem to be a crucial consideration. For a nation like Sweden, dependent upon exports, this entails far-reaching trade and foreign policy problems.

Neutrality, which none of the Swedish political parties is likely to dispute, has increasingly appeared as the natural foreign policy of the Swedish welfare state. It has acquired an aura of being self-evident and unassailable, and has become an important element in the exercise of political power in the sense that the consensus reached concerning the goals of foreign policy has had an integrative effect on the political system. At the same time it may be argued that the Swedish doctrine of neutrality has tended to be a means of political ostracism. The application of foreign policy doctrine has been regarded as a Social Democratic privilege, and any alteration of this would involve a threat to the doctrine's credibility.

When democracy was established in Sweden, conservatives depicted the labor movement as a threat to the nation because of its putative inability to govern. At present it is claimed that its long period in government has entitled it to be termed a "Social Democratic security policy hegemony."[64] This is an expression of Social Democratic self-assertion and self-perception, but it is equally a conclusion that is not wholly lacking in historical justification when one reviews Social Democratic foreign policy. The content of the ideological/declaratory dimension of Swedish Social Democratic foreign policy has undoubtedly been increasingly affirmed by other parties. Its security-motivated neutrality can be linked with Hjalmar Branting's formula, expressed in his May Day speech in 1895: "Solidarity internationally applied means brotherhood among nations."[65]

The revolutionary events in Eastern Europe and the breakup of the Soviet Union, which have occurred since this chapter was written, have prompted us to provide a brief review of Swedish foreign and security policies since 1989. Sweden has landed in a situation reminiscent of that prevailing after World War I. Finland has attained a more markedly independent position, and the Baltic States have achieved a precarious freedom. The policy of nonalignment and neutrality are no longer self-evident.

With the easing of bipolar tensions, integration efforts in Europe have achieved a new dynamic. It is increasingly obvious that the division of Europe into two free-trade blocs—the EC and the EFTA (European Free Trade Alliance)—can be only a transitional solution. Hence, in 1991 the Social Democratic government declared its intention to apply for Swedish membership in the EC. The same line has been followed by the nonsocialist government, which succeeded the Social Democrats in the autumn of 1991.

Against the background of the end of the Cold War, the previous near consensus about the value and inevitability of Swedish neutrality has collapsed. Political commentators and historians have critically examined postwar Social Democratic foreign policy, accusing it of being too benevolently palliative to the Soviet Union, too critical of the United States, and lacking subtlety in its evaluations of certain third world regimes. The Social Democrats have also been accused of unjustifiably presenting Swedish foreign policy as a moral exemplar for a free world.

The new nonsocialist government has departed significantly from previous policy on several points since coming to power in 1991. It has curtailed Sweden's extensive engagement in various third world countries, choosing instead to concentrate foreign policy in Europe and in those nations in Sweden's geographical sphere, particularly the Baltic States.

Meanwhile, a reevaluation by the Social Democrats of the value and applicability of neutrality under the new circumstances has been unavoidable. It is difficult to assess the current points of view because of the fluctuating character of the situation. In any case, the dogmatic line for neutrality seems to belong to a bygone era.

NOTES

1. Marx and Engels in *The Revolutions of 1848* (Harmondsworth: Penguin, 1973), 84; Hjalmar Branting's afterword to the Communist Manifesto, in *Tal och skrifter* (Speeches and Writings), 1:283–85.
2. Riksdagen, Second Chamber, Motion 1914B:202; *Stormklockan* 12 Sept. 1914.
3. Branting, *Tal och skrifter*, 5:63.
4. Jaurès 1916, 149–50.
5. Branting, *Tal och skrifter*, 9:314.
6. M. Grass 1975, 11–13.
7. T. Norman 1985, 15–17.
8. Second Chamber 1920, no. 18, p. 32; no. 23, p. 40.
9. T. Norman 1986.
10. Branting, *Tal och skrifter*, 9:314.
11. The Östen Undén Collection, L108:1:50 (Royal Library, Stockholm).
12. On Swedish Social Democracy and fascism, see A. W. Johansson 1987, 91–102.
13. *SAP Executive Minutes* 23 Apr. 1933 (Labor Movement Archives, Stockholm).
14. On the boycott, see Nordström 1972, 53–55; Anders Nilsson, "På Per Albins tid" (On the Times of Per Albin), Memoirs, 147–48 (in Anders Nilsson's Archive, Labor Movement Archives, Stockholm).
15. *SSU Conference Minutes* 1934, 93.
16. Speech in Gothenburg 29 Oct. 1933, in Sandler 1934, 5–7.
17. Tingsten 1944, 254–57; Adamson 1987, 99–101.
18. Nordström 1972, 169–70; Lundvik 1980.
19. *Social-Demokraten* 15 Aug. 1936.
20. Anders Nilsson (see n. 14), 199.
21. A. W. Johansson 1988, 25–26.
22. *SSU Conference Minutes* 1934, 92.
23. Tingsten 1944, 292.
24. A. W. Johansson 1988, 23; Anders Nilsson's Archive, vol. 19: Draft of instructions for delegates to the International.
25. Sandler 1934, 82.
26. *SSU Conference Minutes* 1934, 89; Sandler 1934, 84.
27. Wigforss, *Minnen* (Memoirs), vol. 3 (1954), 127.
28. Lönnroth 1959, 147–48.
29. Blidberg 1984.
30. Sandler 1939, 96–97.
31. Carlgren 1977.
32. Westman 1981, 20.
33. Sandler's words on what he thought the role of the Soviet Union was in the budget debates of 17 Jan. 1940 in the First Chamber, 1940:3, 33–35; see also A. W. Johansson 1973, 120–31.
34. For this section in general, see A. W. Johansson 1988.

35. Gösta Bagge's Diary, 16 Sept. 1940 (National Archives, Stockholm).

36. Per Albin Hansson's Diary, 5 Aug. 1940 (Labor Movement Archives, Stockholm).

37. *SAP Executive Minutes* 21 Dec. 1941.

38. *Comments on the U.N. Charter*, drawn up by the Royal Foreign Ministry, Stockholm, 1946 (document published by same), 50.

39. Undén 1945, 11; Y. Möller 1986, 235.

40. Andrén and Landqvist 1965, 95.

41. Ibid., 101.

42. *SAP Executive Minutes* 6 Apr. 1948.

43. Misgeld 1984, and also 1985, 197–213.

44. Y. Möller 1986, 298.

45. *Foreign Policy Issues 1950/1951*, draft 1952, 12–13.

46. Ibid., 36.

47. Blidberg 1987; Östen Undén in *Svensk ordning och nyordning* (Swedish Order and New Order), 1943, 157–59.

48. Y. Möller 1986, 317–19. See also Nils Andrén's fine review of Möller in *Fred och säkerhet* (Peace and Security), 1986–1987, 224–26 (published by the Foreign Policy Institute, Stockholm, 1988); Erlander 1973, 362–64; Ohlin, vol. 2.

49. On the domestic policy factor, see Karl Molin's "Neutralitetens dolda kris 1948–1949" (The Hidden Crisis of Neutrality, 1948–1949), Paper given at the Foreign Policy Institute Conference "Socialdemokratin och svensk utrikespolitik från Branting till Palme" (Social Democracy and Foreign Policy from Branting to Palme), 18–19 May 1988, published in *Socialdemokratin och svensk utrikespolitik* (Social Democracy and Foreign Policy), 1990, 74–86.

50. *Foreign Policy Issues 1957* (published 1958), 27–28.

51. *Foreign Policy Issues 1959*, (1960), 36.

52. *Foreign Policy Issues 1962* (1963), 30–32.

53. *Foreign Policy Issues 1976* (1977), 8.

54. *Foreign Policy Issues 1965* (1966), 42–44; O. Palme 1978, 17. Olof Palme's foreign policy has been sketched by Pierre Schori; see Schori 1986, 162–64.

55. *Foreign Policy Issues 1974* (1975), 43; Brandt, Kreisky, and Palme 1975, 96.

56. SAP Conference, 1984, *Motions*, vol. 1, 49.

57. *SAP Conference Minutes* 1975, vol. 1, 95, 97.

58. Riksdagen, Foreign Policy Committee, 1987/1988:20.

59. *Foreign Policy Issues 1972* (1973), 187 (citation from English original).

60. Bohman 1970.

61. A. W. Johansson and T. Norman 1986, 39.

62. *SAP Conference Minutes* 1975, vol. 2, 405.

63. *SAP Conference Minutes* 1981, vol. A, 57.

64. Pierre Schori, AiC Europe Seminarium in Stockholm, 30 Jan. 1988; see Schori 1988.

65. Branting, *Tal och skrifter*, 5:78.

Karl Molin

12

Party Disputes and Party Responsibility: A Study of the Social Democratic Defense Debate

DISCIPLINE AND DISCUSSION AS PARTY PROBLEMS

One of the main tasks of a political party is to bring people with similar values and interests together for the purpose of common political action. In accordance with the maxim "union is strength," they generate a force that they would lack were they alone or divided. A party is also an organization for forming opinion on questions about society. Through open debate and intellectual vitality it reaches clarity and depth in its opinions, while its political guidelines are continually tested and developed under the impressions of new experience.

In a functioning party, then, there must be both cohesion and open debate. Therein lies a problem: if demands for cohesion go too far, the party loses its power to develop ideas that flow from an unrestricted formation of opinion. This brings on the threat of a despotic leadership and the ideological petrification that Robert Michels described in detail in his 1911 account of the German Social Democratic movement.

The need for coordination and discipline is, as Maurice Duverger has pointed out, partly dependent on the party's size. The amiable domestic anarchy that can characterize a liberal party with a few thousand members cannot be achieved in a mass formation without causing insufferable chaos. Duverger considers that mass parties have consequently tended toward authoritarian conformity not just in administrative practices but also in internal debate and political moves. While his most glaring examples are not taken from social democratic parties, he evidently believes that even they have been distinguished by a considerable degree of internal discipline.

If scholars have pointed out the dangers that lie in excessive discipline, leading politicians have often pointed in the opposite direction: that excessively free internal conditions cause a party to lose its power of action. Having a mandate from the electorate, the party must be able to move from words to action if it is to fulfill it. This requires that goals be formulated, and opponents and putative political allies faced, by a united party. If a party cannot gather its strength it will inevitably fail its supporters and its public duty.

If one accepts this tension between unity and internal freedom as permanent and unavoidable in the physiognomy of a democratic party, then one must try to follow more closely how it has been handled on different occasions, and to determine which considerations have lain behind the priorities that have been chosen and which forces in the party have been opposed to one another. Such an attempt is undertaken in what follows.

Our investigation concentrates on three situations when the SAP was in crisis with respect to its inner cohesion: the developments before the 1917 party conference, when an internal crisis led to a split in the party; the settlement within the party before the 1932 election; and finally, the great conflict during the late 1950s over arming Swedish forces with nuclear weapons.

The core issue in each of these contentious situations was exactly the same, namely, defense. Ever since compulsory military service was introduced in 1901, defense has had a unique ability to excite storms of political feelings. Debates over it have been characterized by the links between questions about the meaning and justification of defensive capacities, and attitudes toward national solidarity. Against the conservative view that defense obligations were unconditional for all, the radicals asserted that a country that was indifferent to the demands of the impoverished majority could not count on popular support for its defense efforts. On one level, conflicts have always concerned the nature and extent of the individual's duty to the nation; similarly, the internal conflicts of the Social Democratic movement have always involved the question of the party's duty to the nation.

THE PARTY SPLIT OF 1917

The Formation of a Left-Wing Opposition
In January 1915 when Zeth Höglund, chair of the Social Democratic Youth Organization and leader of the party's radical faction, came into the parliamentary group, the conflict between the right and left wings of the Social Democratic Labor Party, which had been a fact of the internal life of the party for almost a decade, entered a decisive stage. The party that had been formed in 1889 had aimed at being, in an open, antiauthoritarian spirit, a gathering place for all who wanted to work for the good of industrial and agricultural workers. Side by side at its first conferences, parliamentarians and revolutionaries had learned how to formulate programs and resolutions that gave each other latitude. Even the violently inclined anarchists, led by Hinke Bergegren, could remain part of the party, admittedly exposed to hostile conference resolutions in 1891 and 1905 but not actually expelled until 1908.

This antiauthoritarian attitude was underlined by the formal structure of the party. Its leadership comprised seven appointed representatives who represented different groups in the party. They seldom arranged meetings and had no contact with districts or local associations. The party had no authorized spokesman. At its third conference in 1894 a party executive was elected, however, and in 1897, eight years after the party had been founded, the first party program was adopted. A party leader was formally elected in 1907.

This internal freedom, which the pioneers of the party had seen as its hallmark, became a growing problem when the possibilities approached of playing an important role in national politics. In 1910 the party's parliamentary group comprised thirty-five members, and as the electorate in the next election was to include all adult males no one doubted that there would be a great advance for the Social Democratic movement. Whether the party would have the inner strength to take advantage of the advance, however, was an open question.

The problem was nowhere more evident than in the issue of defense.

The positive but economical attitude to defense of the party leader, Hjalmar Branting, and his foremost supporter, F. V. Thorsson, contrasted with variously expressed attitudes hostile to defense. Some said that the country was not worth defending; others, that violence was legitimate only as a means of liberating the working class. Still others were opposed to all forms of violence. A vigorous objection to defense was found in the Danish slogan "Hvad kan det nytte?" ("Of what use is it?"), which claimed that military force could never realistically protect a small nation.

The tug-of-war between these different attitudes was reflected in conference debates on the defense item in the party program. The 1905 conference exhibited a certain positive attitude by preceding the slogan "Struggle against militarism" with the words "A people's defense system." At the 1908 conference a majority agreed to remove this, amending the slogan to "Struggle against militarism. Successive reductions of military burdens leading to disarmament." There were also formulations on arbitration agreements and international cooperation against war that could be interpreted to imply that political and judicial peace guarantees should be established before commencing disarmament. On these grounds Branting and others in favor of defense could accept the change, but no one denied that it indicated a move toward the left.

After the 1908 conference the question was whether this inclination to the left was to be reflected in the policies of the parliamentary group. The party's youth group, led by Z. Höglund, claimed that the parliamentary group was treating the conference decision nonchalantly and carried on an intensive campaign in their weekly, *Stormklockan* (Alarm Bell), against the "degrading compromises" of the party leadership. At the youth conference in October 1909 Höglund stated that the group's position was a scandal, and the conference demanded that the party's representatives uphold the disarmament line and refuse all allocations of funds to the existing defense establishment.[1]

The left wing could regard the major speech by a sympathizer, Värner Rydén, in the 1910 Riksdag as a measure of success for its efforts. Although he affirmed that every nation had a right to live its own life undisturbed by others, he still argued in favor of disarmament on the grounds that Sweden could not defend itself against a great power. A majority of the parliamentary group agreed with the contents of the speech, and the party executive agreed to publish it as a pamphlet. In the eyes of the party leadership the situation was threatening and called for a response.

The Return of the Right Wing of the Party

The party leadership answered the arguments that were hostile to defense by stating that disarmament must depend on the growing popular support for the Social Democratic movement and on the development of international law. This reply was developed primarily in the party's motion to the 1911 Riksdag, which could be read as cautious but unambiguous criticism of Rydén's speech the year before.

The motion had been drafted by Erik Palmstierna, a former Liberal, with the help of F. V. Thorsson and Otto Järte, the editor of *Social-Demokraten*. It argued in favor of "neutrality defense" that, in the event of war internationally, would safeguard Swedish frontiers without assuming the unrealistic task of repelling an isolated attack by a great power. In concrete terms the motion embodied a plan to reduce the defense burden from 80 million kronor to 60 million and to limit the length of service for conscripts. The reduction was considered justified by the size of the military apparatus being too large even for its limited duties.

That the parliamentary group supported this motion signified a success for those in favor of defense, which immediately incited the left wing to new attacks. When the party executive met in January 1911 it had to consider a motion from the Stockholm labor commune (*arbetarekommun*) calling for "the complete abolition of military force" to be adopted as part of the party's program. Those in favor of the motion now demanded that, regardless of the consequences, the party's position on defense should be made quite clear. For their part, Branting and Thorsson let it be known that, should the party executive accept the motion of the radicals, they would resign. As a result, they won a clear majority for their resistance to disarmament.[2]

In the party conference a few months later, Branting and Thorsson repeated their threats of resignation and could thus defeat the opposition by a comfortable margin, but those hostile to defense were still able to demonstrate their strength. Some fifteen delegates put forward a draft resolution declaring that disarmament, "in principle essential, is what all must devote their best efforts to achieving," while successive reductions of military burdens was the path that "at present" could most suitably be followed. Scarcely incompatible with the earlier decision, this formulation became a rallying point for those who wanted a stronger emphasis on the eventual goal of disarmament. The resolution, later associated with the name of Ivar Vennerström, was adopted by a 72-to-59 majority.

According to the opposition a majority of the conference delegates was basically in favor of the disarmament line, but the party leadership's threat of resignation induced some delegates to support the leadership and the old formulations in the party program.[3]

Despite the Vennerström resolution the 1911 conference gave the party leadership the upper hand, a position that was to be further strengthened that autumn. Since the election that year to the Second Chamber—the first according to the new electoral law—resulted in advances for the Social Democrats and losses for the Conservatives, the Liberals, having a majority, formed a government on their own, with Karl Staaff as prime minister. Under his leadership a far-reaching left-wing collaboration was established with the Social Democrats, markedly enhancing the prestige of the party leadership.

In the area of defense policy, this cooperation involved the Social Democrats in a parliamentary inquiry charged with showing how funds could be saved and greater efficiency achieved within the defense organization. The work was divided among four commissions, and, in addition to Branting and Thorsson, Värner Rydén and Adolf Christiernson were appointed to represent the Social Democrats. While the two newcomers were known to be moderately hostile to defense, what they would experience would soon cause them to change their tune.

Between Patriotism and Liberalism

While the commissions were at work, the question of defense was at the center of debate as never before. What aroused interest was not the parliamentary inquiry but the patriotic campaign commenced primarily by Sven Hedin, the famous explorer and traveler, and Manfred Björkquist, initiator of a patriotic, Christian students' movement. Hedin began writing his pamphlet *Ett Varningsord* (A Word of Warning) a few days after Staaff had appointed the defense savings commission, and from 25 January 1912 more than a million copies of this unfeignedly demagogic pamphlet were spread throughout the country. Together with Björkquist's national fund-raising for an additional armed cruiser, this was the overture for a nationalistic campaign in favor of the strongest possible defense and against "socialists, anti-militarists, pacifist sheep and other types of eager disarmers."[4]

The defense inquiries were pursued in the shadow of this patriotic campaign; and what leaked out of them was sensational, at least in part. Rydén, who had said earlier that Swedish defense was pointless, now said the question should be seen in the perspective of a general European conflict.

Should Russia take the offensive, most of the Russian forces would not be engaged in the vicinity of Sweden; thus, defending Sweden would no longer be militarily impossible. Rydén became a proponent of a Swedish defense.

What happened to Christiernson, once a nihilist over defense, raised even more left-wing hackles. While engaged on the commission on the length of service for conscripts, he became transformed. Together with the representative of the Conservatives he argued in favor of the maximum length, thus outdoing both the Liberals and his own party leader, who was in favor of defense.[5]

The left faction remained passive during the start of this period of growing enthusiasm for defense, although it did take the remarkable step (in organizational terms) of forming Socialdemokratiska Vänsterföreningen, the Social Democratic Left Association, to ensure greater firmness in its efforts to fight against evasiveness in the party's policy and to restore respect for "the clear principles of socialism, its straight paths and lofty goals."[6] Branting considered that "a reserved attitude" toward the new organization was best, as did the party executive, which was content to declare that "the union of special tendencies" risked splitting the party. Instead, members should work in unity to advance the Social Democratic popular movement. In consequence of this statement those members of the party executive who had initially joined the new association decided to leave it. The 1914 conference approved the party executive's explanation, and the association, which had anyway existed rather obscurely, was dissolved.[7]

The general political tendency toward the right during these years of premonition of war between the great powers unavoidably favored the right wing of the party and the party leadership. After Staaff's major speech in the naval center of Karlskrona on 21 December 1913, in which he abandoned most of his plans for achieving monetary savings, those in favor of successive disarmament became hopelessly isolated. At the 1914 conference the right wing tried to advance its position, proposing that the Vennerström resolution should be annulled and that the program point on defense should be altered to indicate that Swedish disarmament would unambiguously depend on international guarantees of peace. The party leadership was forced, however, to state that the attitude of the conference was ambivalent and hard to determine. By a small majority it decided not to alter the program and by a large majority to preserve the Vennerström resolution unchanged. On the other hand, it endorsed continued cooperation with the Liberals, whose approval of defense had recently become much more marked.[8] Within the Social Democratic Labor Party defense sympathies had perhaps increased under the influence of defense propaganda and the conversion of its representatives in the commissions of inquiry, but the party leadership could not obtain any clear indication on this point. The opposition still had a firm grip on the opinion of active party members.

The struggle that now ensued within the Social Democratic movement concerned in essence not merely the party's future but that of the nation. This was clear to those who perceived that the Social Democrats represented a majority of the working class, which, as a consequence of the process of democratization, would acquire increasing influence over the future composition of the Riksdag. Among liberal Swedes were many who both saw the significance of this and felt they ought to try to influence it.

A leading example of this sort of responsible liberal was Erik Palmstierna, who, before applying for membership in the Stockholm labor commune in the summer of 1910, had been a member of Frisinnade Klubben (the Liberal Club), Centralförbundet för Socialt Arbete (the Central Union for Social Work), and the parliamentary group of the Liberal party. In his memoirs he wrote that he wished to support Branting's attempt to foster the working class and induce "the feeling of a sense of responsibility for the land of its birth." To the rage of the *Stormklocke* faction Palmstierna's career advanced rapidly, so that he became one of the party's foremost representatives in the Riksdag. It was he who initiated the major motion on defense in 1911, which he described as a "concrete pile driven into a swamp."[9] He and other Liberal "infiltrators" were neither the only nor the most important of the members of this great didactic mission; its central figure was in fact the leader of the Liberal party, Karl Staaff. His goal was to incorporate the working class into the community of the nation by striving against tendencies within the labor movement toward a dissolution of society and by encouraging far-reaching social reforms for the good of the great majority of the population.

The Liberals' policy on defense was a part of this national integrative policy. In a letter that dealt with the defense commissions, Staaff wrote that it was one of the most important tasks of Liberals "to try to induce the main part of the Socialists to recommend an effective defense." He went on to write that it would be necessary "to turn the Socialist paladins toward loyal, national, parliamentary work and to urge them to share the *responsibility* for what is done in matters of state."[10]

The didactic ambition behind the defense inquiries seems also to have been generally known in the Riksdag. The Conservative Hugo Hamilton noted on several occasions in his diary how people spoke of "the fostering influence of the defense commissions." For his part, he did not believe that this missionary work by the Liberals would do any good.[11]

Neither did the Conservatives share the Liberal belief that a positive policy on defense would be supported by political democratization and social reforms. From the point of view of the Social Democratic movement it was of central importance that the Liberals were the dominating political force during the years in which the movement was preparing itself for a leading political role. It was also a condition that was to be of decisive importance for the party's internal struggles.

The Settlement

By the time the Riksdag met in January 1915 the political scene had changed dramatically. After the farmers' march in February 1914—a demonstration for national defense and royal power—and the king's palace courtyard speech to the participants in this demonstration the nationalist forces had seized the initiative. Staaff's government had been replaced by the conservatively inclined government of civil servants led by Hjalmar Hammarskjöld. The Conservatives had made electoral gains at the expense of the Liberals, and in the Second Chamber the Social Democrats had become the largest party. The government had presented the 1914 defense estimates, which included a large increase in defense appropriations. After the outbreak of war in August 1914 the German Social Democrats had decided to approve credit for equipping the army. Hopes that international socialism might check militarism had come to naught.

This confronted the leadership of the Swedish Social Democratic movement with two fundamental political truths. The first was that being in favor of defense was an absolute precondition for parliamentary success; the second, that the Social Democratic movement now bore the main responsibility for the country's continued democratization. This being so, it was undoubtedly problematic to be confronted by a parliamentary group of party members who were radically inclined, hostile to defense, and always ready to take the political offensive.

In many political quarters, Höglund's entry into the Riksdag was awaited with relish; and indeed in February, when the government's defense bill was under consideration, he managed to embarrass the party leadership by arranging a demonstrative vote against the 1914 army organization. The party conference the previous autumn had decided to refrain from any attempt to abandon the army plan, but this did not prevent the internal opposition from exposing the split in the party.[12]

As a direct consequence of the actions of the opponents within the party, the parliamentary group changed its internal rules of order to require the approval of the group as a whole for any initiative in the form of a motion, question, or reser.ation on any point of larger political or tactical importance. No member of the group might make any statement or vote against any decision that the group deemed to be binding.[13] Once the party's decision-making bodies had made up their minds, open expressions of dissenting opinion must cease—such was the fundamental demand for loyalty asserted by the new regulations of the party leadership. Although they remained in force until 1923, the disciplinary regulations were never used; but this did not of itself lessen tension within the parliamentary group. On the contrary, the regulations came to symbolize the repression that the majority was held to exercise.[14]

An alternative means of forcibly uniting opposed wills might be to acknowledge the split without necessarily denying important common interests. In 1912 the Left Association had implied an acceptance of factions within the party framework, and in April 1916 the same thought reappeared in a proposal from the opposition to the parliamentary group on a "voluntary division" between the two tendencies. The group's appointed representatives rejected the proposal, and thereafter the opposition felt free to pursue its own goals in the Riksdag.[15]

In April 1916 the minority was forced off the board of *Social-Demokraten* but started its own paper, *Politiken*, by way of riposte; its first issue appeared the same month. Differences had been further underlined in March, when the Social Democratic Youths' Peace Conference was convened to deal with "the position of the working class in the event of an outbreak of war." In the view of a majority of the party, the real purpose of the conference was not to strengthen the workers' peace efforts but to undermine the position of the leadership of the Social Democratic movement.[16] After this, all that was really left was to pick up the pieces and polish the arguments to be deployed in the settlement that would now have to take place at the next conference.

So when the tenth party conference met on 12 February 1917, a statement by the party executive in effect required the youth movement at its next conference to withdraw earlier criticism of the party's parliamentary group for having abandoned the party program, to undertake not to conduct "a special policy" at the next election, and to work loyally in accordance with the decisions reached by the party and its branches. The statement was addressed to the "leading men" of the youth organization, who would be deemed to have placed themselves outside the party if these conditions were not satisfactorily met. The opponents were thus faced with a choice between, on the one hand, admitting their errors and promising loyalty and, on the other, "to have placed themselves outside the party." The conference approved the statement by a vote of 136 to 42.

The close association between the internal dissensions and the defense question was demonstrated when the conference dealt with a resolution about the motivation of the party program's point on defense. The resolution declared that the party stood for the right of nations to self-determination and was prepared to defend its country against an aggressor. It thus held that a point of view based on a principle of "defense nihilism" must definitely be rejected. The resolution was accepted, also by a vote of 136 to 42.[17]

Seven days after the conference had ended, on 27 February 1917, *Politiken* published a manifesto and announced a meeting at which a new party would be formally constituted. The next day the opponents registered their withdrawal from the Social Democratic parliamentary group. Thenceforth, sixteen former Social Democratic members of the Riksdag represented Sveriges Socialdemokratiska Vänsterparti (Social Democratic Left Party of Sweden).[18]

Discipline and National Integration

During the period leading up to the party split of 1917, the party's own rules of order were accommodated to the demands placed on a party that wished to play a leading parliamentary role. To achieve influence in the Riksdag, the SAP had to unite around a national policy in cooperation with the Liberals and thus had to accept military defense. The developments during this second decade of the twentieth century caused the Social Democratic movement to become an integrated part of the political system. To make this possible, the party leadership had been obliged to make credible the claim that progressive reforms could be achieved by parliamentary means. That it could do this is closely related to the existence of a politically important, democratic, and reform-minded liberalism.

Clearly it was crucial that Swedish politics not be dominated by an irreconcilably antidemocratic, royalist conservatism but by the liberalism represented by Karl Staaff, which wished to bring the working class into responsible participation in the democratic process. The credibility of the radical image of Sweden as a fortified workhouse declined once it became clear that, in weighty matters, the Social Democrats had powerful allies. The opposition within the party lost ground.

Judging from membership numbers, the strategy of the party leadership succeeded. Internal statistics for 1917 show that although party districts in Norrbotten and Västmanland lost large numbers of members, there was a net gain of almost ten thousand members for the country as a whole. At first, the electoral response to the split was less positive for the mother party. In the 1917 parliamentary elections the Left Socialists won 8.1 percent of all votes, or 20.6 percent of the vote for socialist parties. In the 1920 elections, however, their share of socialist votes dropped. In 1921, when the franchise was first extended to women, the Left Socialists again won 8.1 percent of all votes; during the rest of the 1920s, they never won more than 14.7 percent of working-class votes. The parties to the left of the Social Democrats (the Left Socialists and the communists) were never of more than marginal importance.

In Germany, where liberalism was more or less powerless and the bourgeois parties were dominated by a nationalistic conservatism that disliked reform, things were clearly different. The German Social Democratic Labor Party split in 1917, with the result that first an independent social democratic party and then a communist party became its dangerous rivals. In 1920 the independent party won just over 43 percent—and the main party just 52 percent—of the votes cast for socialists. During the rest of the 1920s the communists were the stronger challenger, winning a share of socialist votes that varied between 26 percent and 35 percent.[19]

In Norway, to take an example nearer at hand, where no grounds for cooperation between the Arbeiderpartiet (DNA) and the liberal Venstre existed from the turn of the century until the early 1930s, a movement for reform was even more suppressed. A syndicalistic left opposition grew steadily in influence, and by 1918 it took over the party. In Denmark, by contrast, the parliamentary cooperation between the Social Democratic movement and the liberal Radikale Venstre that had existed since 1905 reached its fulfillment in 1916, when the two parties formed a coalition government. This well-integrated Social Democratic movement had no problem with opposition on its left, and the left-socialist breakout, which occurred here as well, won no more than 1 percent of the socialist vote. These comparisons seem to confirm that in Sweden the existence of an influential, reform-minded liberalism contributed to causing the split in the Social Democratic Labor Party to turn out well for its reformist leadership.

FROM THE "COSSACK" ELECTION TO THE CRISIS SETTLEMENT

A New Opponent

Once the left-wing opposition had departed to form its own organization, life in the party was undeniably calmer. Branting's and Thorsson's leadership was unanimous and undisputed. An internal split no longer marred the party's chances of playing a leading political role and of commencing societal reforms. However, an obstacle did exist in the parliamentary situation.

In the first election under the new democratic franchise the Social Democrats' share of the vote (almost 30 percent) made them the largest party, but they had neither a majority nor any natural partner for a coalition since there was now no chance of cooperation with the left. The situation was frustrating. On the principle of advocating parliamentary democracy, the party could not refuse the responsibilities of government—but these were largely meaningless from a practical political point of view since any genuinely Social Democratic proposal would be at once voted down. Between 1920 and 1926, the three Social Democratic governments that took office revealed their nature principally in the commissions of inquiry into industrial democracy and nationalization that they set up. The disarmament embarked on during the Sandler administration was, in origin and direction, more liberal than social democratic.[20]

After the third Social Democratic government resigned in June 1926, the party became internally more turbulent. Branting and Thorsson had died, Per Albin Hansson was the acting party leader, a new generation occupied the leading positions in the party, and conditions for the exercise of authority were uncertain. In January 1926, against Hansson's wishes, the party executive decided on an organizational association with the Höglund party—that is, the section of the breakaway group that did not follow the Comintern line. Having had second thoughts, this section now promised all that its mother party demanded and guaranteed that it would stay loyally in line.[21]

The position of the new party leader was not very strong. In the executive he soon had two almost permanent opponents, of whom one was Höglund; the other, Arthur Engberg, chief editor of the *Social-Demokraten,* the newspaper traditionally regarded as the party's principal organ, consistently refused to publish what his party leader wrote. In 1928 Höglund won election over Hansson as chair of the Stockholm labor commune. At the party conference that year, where Per Albin Hansson was formally elected party leader, there had been a move to launch the candidacy of Ernst Wigforss to draw off support from Hansson. Wigforss refused to allow this, and Hansson was elected "unanimously and with acclamation." In his brief speech of acceptance, he said he believed in the future loyalty of "the opposition that is in fact present here."[22]

During its years in opposition from 1926 to 1932, debate over defense contributed greatly to the party's radicalization. After the 1925 decision on the reduction of armaments, Hansson tried to compromise with the bourgeois left to remove the defense question from the front line of national politics. Many in the party, disappointed by what they regarded as a tame decision, tried to keep it there.

Motions to the 1928 conference demanded an energetic policy on disarmament and the adoption of "total and immediate national disarmament" as the formal goal of the party. Hansson emphasized the party-political aspects of the matter: public opinion was not ready for total disarmament, and should the party indulge in demonstrative politics it would only undermine its position. The focus of compromise was to be moved to the right. The motion to change the party program was rejected without a vote; it was replaced by a statement exhorting the party to strive toward a reexamination of "the efficiency of our military defense."[23]

Tactical considerations did not hinder Hansson from showing a radical profile. On the question of defense he gave the impression of favoring unilateral disarmament in principle; in the discussions of the party's 1928 election manifesto he successfully pressed for the inclusion of wide-ranging formulations on nationalization and the leveling of wealth.[24] On the threshold of the 1928 election campaign the party lacked both concentrated inner power and clear and realistic goals, and its leader seemed to waver in his view of where it was going.

Election Defeat and the Policy of the Folkhemmet[25]

The 1928 election, known as the "Cossack" election (see page 189n), was a serious blow to the Social Democrats, who lost fourteen seats and just over 4 percent of the electorate. Analyses of the results held that the foremost cause was the party's radical tone, manifested in its well-known motion on inheritance taxes and its election cooperation with the communists.[26] One of the disturbing factors in the election results was that the Social Democrats did not gain from the much greater participation by the electorate. The belief that the party would find among workers an immense reserve of voting strength showed itself to be "decisively erroneous," according to the party executive's analysis. In fact, some two hundred thousand workers had voted bourgeois: the politically dormant working class had fallen victim to bourgeois demagoguery.[27]

Without tracing Hansson's responses to the 1928 election in detail, one may observe that he was seeking new political lines that would lead the party out of its difficulties. In September 1929 he gave a full presentation of those ideas that, in his opinion, the party ought to follow.

In two programmatic articles, "The Concept of Class Struggle" and "People and Class," Per Albin Hansson argued that the core of Social Democratic politics is not the class struggle but an interest in society as a whole. In his view, the party's central thesis is the idea of society as a product of the interplay of special interests of equal legitimacy. Democracy would be realized in the course of this interplay, and the forward march of socialism would repress personal and group egotism. Key words in the Social Democratic movement should be *people* and *cooperation,* rather than class and the class struggle. He presented "the people's party line," which strongly emphasized the value of a national community; and his positive attitude to defense in principle is wholly consistent with this.[28]

Hansson's ideology of community was expressed in part polemically, clearly a challenge to several other leading party members. Even though adherence to undiluted, textbook socialism and consequently to the class struggle was in decline, there were still many who felt these new signs indicated ideological impoverishment and the loss of political teeth.

The sort of disputes that existed in the party in the early 1930s showed up clearly in the debate that followed the fatal shooting of a number of demonstrating workers in Ådalen (a sawmill community in northern Sweden) in May 1931. Many in the party saw this as an expression of unprovoked class violence. At some twenty meetings of workers in various parts of the country, the military personnel who were summoned and the employers were accused of perpetrating this crime. Hansson, however, tried to find a standpoint that afforded mediation, and he pointed out that some of those who had urged on the demonstrations were also responsible.

The ideological nature of the differences was perhaps most clearly visible in the responses to the judicial aspects of the matter. In his comments, Wigforss advanced the theory of different appreciations of legality: the bourgeois had one, the labor movement another. The principle of freedom of work, which the bourgeois affirmed with the help of the law, was not more absolute or holy than the morality of solidarity embraced by the workers. Against this, Hansson emphatically claimed that offenses against existing law must always be condemned; he called Wigforss's explanations "quasi-philosophical exegeses."[29]

These differences were further sharpened in the preparations for the 1932 conference. Some ten of the motions received that autumn by the party executive took up conditions on the *Social-Demokraten*, criticizing its political tendencies and objecting to the party chair's lack of influence over the party's principal organ of public opinion. Other motions, among them some from the labor communes of Stockholm and Gothenberg, demanded that the party intensify its work for unilateral Swedish disarmament and inscribe this into the party's program. That widely differing groups existed within the party and were gathering strength before the conference was quite clear.

A further expression of mobilization by factions was the nationwide collection for Arthur Engberg and the *Social-Demokraten* launched by the Stockholm labor commune and the Fackliga Centralorganisation (FCO), the Trades Council. The bourgeois papers took this as proof that the old Höglund faction, having risen again, was preparing a show of strength at the conference. The labor movement papers, which were faithful to Hansson, were of the same opinion and sounded the alarm of a new 1917.

The Settlement

The turning point in the struggle came when the party executive met in mid-November 1931 to deal with conference motions. Hansson recapitulated his criticism of Engberg and the Stockholm faction and demanded better discipline. He also made it clear that a positive response to the motions on disarmament would make his position untenable; his opponents replied by demanding collective leadership and more frequent conferences.

Positions seemed to be deadlocked when Wigforss—highly regarded by members of the radical opposition, who evidently considered him one of their own—pointed out that while the left-wing line might well come to be that of the party as a whole, nothing of any value could be done as long as the party squandered its ability to act. He thought Engberg ought to understand that and accept the limitations on personal freedom of action that responsibility for the party involved.

Wigforss's words on party responsibility seem to have broken the logjam. Many speakers returned to them, with the result that Hansson and Engberg were together charged with formulating the executive's reply to the controversial motions. And so they did: a joint Hansson-Engberg line emerged from the four days of meetings. The leadership agreed not to take over the *Social-Demokraten*, but its columns would be open to the party leader; and the party would postpone a decision on defense until the 1930 Defense Commission had reported. Among those who supported this line was the former faction leader, Zeth Höglund. The remaining small opposition group was represented by party members in good standing, whom no one could suspect of aspiring to the leadership.[30]

The work of pacification was completed at the 1932 conference, which unanimously accepted the statement on the party press once those most directly involved had assured the conference that they would now cooperate for the good of the party.[31] This spirit of agreement also marked the debate on defense.

On examining the factual arguments put forward in the course of the long, very thorough debate on defense, it can be claimed that they constitute probably the strongest manifestation of support for total unilateral disarmament that has ever occurred in Swedish politics. Of some thirty speakers, more than two-thirds supported various demands for radical disarmament. Of those who spoke in favor of the party executive's motion only Möller had anything positive to say about military defense. Hansson explained that his point of view would be determined by the work of the Defense Commission. The final vote gave victory to the party executive, by 243 against 165; but many had previously explained that there was in fact an overwhelming majority for disarmament, so the party executive prevailed only out of respect for unity in the party.[32]

The respect paid by the conference to demands for unity should be understood as respect for the gravity of the country's parliamentary and economic crisis, and for the seriousness of the Social Democratic leadership, not least Hansson, in its intention that the party should now assume the leading position in Swedish politics.

The events that were to follow the 1932 conference are the stuff of general Swedish history: the SAP published a new program for that year's election, in which it reaped great success. Once in office, the party won parliamentary support for its plan to resolve the economic crisis. Thus ending the country's political paralysis, it was able to initiate a period of intensive social reform that won the approval of the electorate in successive elections. The united party had at last indisputably taken over the leading role in Swedish politics.[33]

Competence in Government and Party Responsibility

In important respects, the debate within the party after the 1928 election can be seen as a direct continuation of the one that had preceded the resolution of the crisis of 1917. Well-known problems of principle recurred: the demand for room for an opposition contrasted with the need for discipline, and an unwillingness to accept the responsibilities of office without unrestricted opportunities to pursue undiluted policies contrasted with the need to accept responsibility for the development of parliamentary democracy.

While the problems of principle were the same, the role of the Social Democrats in the development of national politics was different. During the second decade of the century, the party had attracted the well-meaning, didactic interest of the Liberals, who intended to engage the party in responsible work within the framework of national democracy—the paladins of socialism were to be enrolled in the Home Guard. By the beginning of the 1930s, the Social Democratic movement was an integral part of the national community that actively took on responsibility for political democracy and social peace.

Developments during the 1930s brought about a fundamental change in Swedish politics under the leadership of the Social Democratic Labor Party. The party that had been doubtful and unsure of itself, fearing office because it did not know what to do with it, raised the standing of democracy by its deliberate, thought-out policy and took an undisputed leading position in the political life of its country. Its inner consolidation during the early 1930s was a necessary precondition for these advances.

The unity achieved within the party did not entail holding fast to an agreed line through controversial issues: no such guideline was formulated for either defense or nationalization questions—the previous ambiguities persisted. Instead, all factions agreed to defer consideration of these two outstanding points of dispute for the time being. The motivation behind this truce was the weight of responsibility that rested on the party and its leadership in the difficult situation the country and its political system were in. Hansson explained often and emphatically that the Social Democrats had to work toward a more sensible parliamentary system and a more stable government, and this was also his argument for his party's acceptance of office after its victory in the 1932 election.[34]

In short, responsibility for the country and for democracy was intimately linked with responsibility for the party. As Hansson explained, the greater the responsibility resting on the party, the greater its need for internal cohesion. It had no time for internal squabbles, nor could it risk being suspected by its opponents of being unable to stick to the policies set out in its program and decided at its conferences.[35]

These developments within the Swedish party were paralleled elsewhere in Scandinavia. In 1933–1934 the once so radical Norwegian Arbeiderpartiet put forward a crisis program that marked a sudden departure from a policy of dogmatic class struggle to one of active reforms. In 1935 the party accepted for the first time the national symbols of flag, anthem, and a national day. Since the mid-1920s in Denmark the Social Democratic movement, led by Thorvald Stauning, had been developing into an undogmatic party of reform that appealed to the population as a whole, to the middle class not less than to the workers: its program to meet the crisis and its settlement with the farmers in May 1935 were natural extensions of its continued deradicalization.

The development of the Swedish party seems most like that of the Danish, and the question is whether one may reasonably say that inner consolidation, assumption of national responsibility, and elevation of democracy to a position of overriding ideology in both countries can be associated to an abandonment of socialist ideals. Perhaps in anticipation of this question, Hansson said on more than one occasion that this must not happen. He told the 1932 conference that "less than ever have we reason to doubt our socialist ideas and their victorious power," and he went on to call for continued agitation in accordance with the old lines.

Ernst Wigforss also refused to view the crisis program and the policy of consensus as the start of deradicalization. Rather, he maintained that concrete policies should be allowed constantly to create new points of departure for information about and debate on long-term goals. In his view, this was needed not just to open the eyes of the broad masses but to create clarity and unity within the party itself.[36]

What the pacification efforts of 1930 meant for the party's policy was unclear at the time, and still is. One can at least say that the intention of its leading architects was not to turn the movement into a general welfare party but rather to move it toward socialism through a dialectical process, in which what was done in practice was to be followed by debate until agreement was reached on what to do next. In this way, a transformation of society could be achieved with the support not just of a unified Social

Democratic movement but of an overwhelming majority of the population as a whole.

THE DEBATE OVER NUCLEAR WEAPONS

The Defense Dispute in a New Form
The party-political differences over defense declined as the strife within the Social Democratic movement abated. In March 1938, a few days after the German invasion of Austria, a largely unanimous Riksdag decided on an additional allocation of 70 million kronor for defense improvements. This ushered in a thirty-year period of party-political unity over defense, which ended in 1968.

Unity over this rearmament did not entail identical perceptions of the situation. Within the Social Democratic parliamentary group two clearly differing views arose: one claiming that the strong defensive capacity built up before and during World War II should be a permanent postwar feature, the other maintaining that defense organization should be flexible, able to adapt to changes in the realities of foreign policy.[37]

Near the end of the war the proponents of flexibility sensed better times in the offing. In various contexts they protested against the gloomy view of the future reflected in the long-term plans that were being urged. For their part, those in favor of defense wanted to set out the lines for the future before experience from the war faded; they issued warnings of the "destructive forces" that would be released as soon as the war between the great powers had ended. Even so, the theoreticians' demand for flexibility was nearly realized in the spring of 1948, when the 1945 Defense Committee put forward a proposal for retrenchment. The communist coup in Prague intervened, and the high wartime level of expenditure remained in force.

In the mid-1950s signs were hopeful again. During Khrushchev's first years, the "thaw" began in the Soviet Union, and the new regime showed its peaceful intentions by proposing international disarmament and cutting its own armed forces by 1.2 million. In July 1954 a cease-fire was achieved in Indochina, and the following summer the leaders of the great powers met in Geneva for conciliatory talks.

To the Swedish prime minister the situation seemed quite bright. On 13

September 1955 in a survey of the political situation, Tage Erlander said that it was necessary to make the utmost use of present opportunities.[38] What he had perhaps not considered was that the tendencies toward a decline in tension would revive demands for Swedish disarmament—which did in fact happen. A debate on "neopacifism" flared up in the mid-1950s.

In these circumstances some leading Swedish military figures began to talk of arming the forces with nuclear weapons. In the autumn of 1954, the commander-in-chief considered that a public inquiry should be charged with making clear how these weapons could be incorporated into Swedish defense capacities. The question began to be discussed seriously within the government in autumn 1955, and it was then that opposition within the party woke up.

The Social Democratic Women Take a Stand

The party leadership was first informed that the leaders of the Federation of Social Democratic Women were decidedly against arming the Swedish forces with nuclear weapons on 30 November 1955, when the federation's executive presented their views to Tage Erlander. Some days earlier, Ulla Lindström, a minister without portfolio, had taken part in a discussion at the home of Inga Thorsson (F. V. Thorsson's daughter-in-law) and had spoken of a government meeting held on 23 November in which the question of nuclear weapons had been discussed for the first time. Most participants had indicated either a positive or a wait-and-see attitude. This news prompted the executive of the Women's Federation to take action.

On 17 December the federation, now joined by the party's women members of the Riksdag, once again presented its views to Erlander, who had been joined by the minister of defense, Torsten Nilsson. The two ministers promised that nothing would happen in the matter until it had been discussed in the parliamentary group.

The leadership of the federation would later claim that on this occasion it clearly expressed its views on the political treatment of the question of nuclear weapons. The essence of the women's position was that the question should not be regarded as a "party issue," meaning that, without regard to the views of the leadership, individual members of the party should be free to express their own opinions. According to the federation, at the meeting with Erlander and Nilsson all had agreed on this point.[39]

This demand for unrestricted debate showed its explosive force when, on 21 February, the party executive met to discuss the question of nuclear weapons. For some time at this meeting, only the first speaker, Foreign Minister Östen Undén, took exception to the thought of a Swedish atom bomb. The former defense minister, Sköld, showed himself to be clearly in favor. Had Erlander been obliged to make up his mind without delay, he would have been in favor, and Defense Minister Nilsson seemed to share this view. While others were doubtful, most agreed that no position should be taken publicly for the time being since neither technical nor international aspects were clear.

This prohibition on further debate was, as Inga Thorsson pointed out, contrary to the view of the Women's Federation. She explained that the federation had said no to nuclear weapons and intended to maintain that view even if the party chose to reserve judgment. She set out the moral grounds for the federation's attitude: that living generations bore a responsibility not just for the country and the party but for coming generations: "Our sense of self-preservation concerns mankind as a whole."

Excepting Undén, all other speakers objected to Thorsson's declaration and appealed to her to try to see the matter calmly and not to cause dissension in the party. Sköld inserted a threat: until now, those who thought as he did had said nothing; but should the federation continue its agitation they would feel obliged to counter this "impossible propaganda."

By his statements, party executive member Ragnar Lassinantti revealed how difficult it was for the men in the party leadership to imagine that the Women's Federation could pursue such a serious opposition. "I believe," he said in a conciliatory manner, "that in this, as in so many other critical situations, the women will choose to follow the men." Eventually, Erlander stated that all members of the executive who had spoken had affirmed that the party should not take a position, meaning that "we should not make any binding statement."[40] With this, it became clear that the federation's view of how the question should be dealt with could not be reconciled with that of the leadership. Nor did federation members individually refrain from demonstrating their views. At the federation's 1956 conference a motion from the Stockholm district called for a statement against Swedish nuclear weapons. The executive responded with such a statement, which was accepted unanimously by conference. In her speech, Inga Thorsson again emphasized the decisive weight of the moral aspects of the issue.[41]

The women's declaration did not give rise to any real debate within the party.[42] But it was nonetheless evident that the federation consistently rejected the party executive's demand for discipline and silence.

The Prohibition on Debate Questioned

The party leadership's qualms about the prospect of an internal debate on nuclear weapons were linked to the general political situation. After the 1956 election, which was not disturbed by any debate on nuclear weapons, there was a need to gather strength. The party had lost four seats, and the leadership felt that it had to win the support of white-collar workers to retain its dominant political position.[43] This was the situation in which the proposal on general and obligatory supplementary pensions was worked out: it would solve the last remaining problem of security for blue-collar workers and even offer support to the large number of white-collar workers who were not covered by private pension arrangements.

The lull in the debate on defense that the leadership wanted within the party spread to the other parties as a consequence of the agreement over the issue among the four large parties in February 1958. It provided for a relatively costly framework for defense but also for a rise in taxes that would leave something left over for other purposes. The question of nuclear weapons would be put off, although research on protection but not design was permitted. In this way the defense question was resolved with the greatest possible consensus, which enabled the parties to devote themselves undisturbed to the coming strife over pensions.[44]

The significance of the settlement became evident when two elections were held—a general election in June and a local government election in October—without the nuclear arms issue playing any important role.[45] In other contexts, however, the debate could not be hindered. In the Riksdag the opponents of nuclear weapons showed their strength in the spring of 1958 by tabling a motion with forty-five signatories, which explained, inter alia, that the signatories accepted the postponement agreed upon by the parties and even the research into protection but reserved their right to work openly against nuclear weapons in the Swedish defense forces.

In the parliamentary debate that eventually followed the election, the Social Democrats split into two groups. Inga Thorsson warned that opposition to nuclear weapons was considerable in the Social Democratic parliamentary group, even though no one intended demonstrating this by putting the matter to a vote. The new defense minister, Sven Andersson, acknowledged that one reason for the postponement was "the fact that everyone knows"—namely, the deep division of opinion.[46]

The correctness of this appraisal was confirmed by a comment on the defense agreement by Gunnel Olsson, the leader of studies in the Women's Federation. She affirmed that if the party as a whole voted in favor of nuclear weapons, the Social Democratic women would oppose this regardless of the damage it might do to the party. Were the bomb accepted, the women "would revolt."[47]

In the face of this promise, the party leadership could only hope that the position taken up by the Women's Federation would remain isolated within the party. At the meeting in November 1956 they had received soothing assurances from the chair of the Social Democratic Youth, Bertil Löfberg, who had asserted that the youth of the party favored a positive policy on defense and that the organization supported the postponement. However, at the Social Democratic Youth Conference in the spring of 1958, much suggested that the desired isolation had not materialized, and that the Women's Federation had strongly impressed the young people of the party.[48]

The Youth Conference was dominated by a long debate on defense, in response to motions demanding the reduction of Swedish defense and a formal statement against Swedish nuclear weapons. Among those who spoke, the nuclear opponents were clearly in the majority, many referring to the Women's Federation for moral support. Some criticized the efforts of the party leadership to stifle every little "youthful debater" and claimed the right to follow their consciences in reaching an opinion.

In addressing the motions, the executive had said that no opinion should be expressed until circumstances had become clearer. In a long speech the chair argued along the lines of Erlander and the party executive: should an opinion now be voiced, this would inexorably cause dissension within the youth organization, the party, and the country, to the detriment of foreign and defense policies. This youthful statesmanship won little applause from the delegates.

The situation was saved by a speech by Olof Palme, containing a new suggestion for a statement. Palme also favored postponement but supported it with a more thorough argument anchored in international developments; he also expressed respect for the arguments against nuclear weapons that had been voiced during the conference. Supported by the chair, Löfberg, Palme's proposal won a narrow majority when finally put to the vote.[49]

The Youth Conference revealed a growing opposition to nuclear weapons and the postponement desired by the party leadership. The debate could not be stopped. In late November 1958 it flared up in the Riksdag after a question by Inga Thorsson; it continued in the 1959 debate on the budget, and it became intense when the two chambers of the Riksdag debated motions from the bourgeois parties demanding nuclear arms in the Swedish defense forces. Sköld made good his threat to attack the "impossible propaganda" of the Women's Federation publicly; he did so in company with six other writers in *Svenska Atomvapen?* (Swedish Nuclear Weapons?), which laid out the political, strategic, and technical preconditions for equipping the Swedish forces with nuclear arms. Shortly afterward Thorsson edited and published *Nej! till svenska atomvapen* (No! to Swedish Nuclear Weapons), which included a contribution from her and from Wigforss and Sandler, among others.[50]

The critical discussions on the subject from the internal point of view of the party were to be conducted in a study group announced by the party leadership during the Youth Conference. The study group formally began its work in November 1958.[51]

The Settlement

The study group, which had eighteen members representing various shades of opinion as well as ancillary organizations, was led by Erlander and entered the final stages of its work in the autumn of 1959. Folkpartiet, as the Liberal party was now called, had set up its own inquiry, and there was concern over which would report first. For the Social Democrats it was important to be ready before delegates to the 1960 conference were chosen. In Erlander's view, the party would suffer were the election to be marked by disputes over nuclear weapons.

The study group produced a report, of which a preliminary version was presented to the party executive on 11 November 1959. Its conclusion was that "in present circumstances, overwhelming arguments militate against a decision to manufacture Swedish nuclear weapons." A definite decision could be made in the mid-1960s, since not until then would their manufacture be feasible. In the meantime, research could be conducted within the framework of the 1958 agreement that, in the group's opinion, would permit a certain extension of research into protection; it recommended that the government issue a directive to that effect.[52]

These recommendations were very similar to the parties' decision in February 1958 to postpone development, which had been generally accepted within the Social Democratic Labor Party. The statement that manufacture was not viable at present was an item of news that doubtless affected public opinion, but in substance it was of little import since Sweden still lacked nuclear production capacity. The extension of research on protection lay within the framework of retaining freedom of action that had been at the core of the previous agreement.

Although the group had reached conclusions that generally followed an already accepted line, it had been able to retain its unity only with great difficulty. Its problem had been that both sides wanted to advance their positions. Supporters of nuclear weapons had scarcely anticipated a positive answer but had hoped for a postponement combined with preparations that would pave the way for a decision to proceed.[53] Opponents wanted a binding decision against Swedish nuclear weapons.

The possibilities of reaching an acceptable compromise were affected by two important considerations, one of which was the ever-present desire to keep the question of defense outside party-political conflict. Although the great pensions struggle was over, this treatment of defense was still of central importance, perhaps even something of a national duty obliging the group to reach conclusions that would gain support not only within the Social Democratic movement but also in the bourgeois parties. Because they—especially the Conservatives—contained strong advocates of nuclear weapons, this ambition to preserve the peace significantly supported Sköld and his allies in the party.

The second important factor was the attitude of the Social Democratic women toward the demand for party discipline. In a letter written during the summer of 1959 the Women's Federation executive had reminded the party executive that the women felt the question of nuclear weapons to be one of conscience, about which individuals must come to their own conclusions independently of any decision by a majority of the executive or parliamentary group. Adherents on both sides should remain free to debate the question openly.[54] Many in the study group evidently had trouble accepting the idea that the women had arbitrarily granted themselves dispensation from the demand for discipline. During the group's meetings that summer and autumn distrust was rampant, leading to offensive exchanges and abruptly concluded sessions.

In the end, the result was a victory for the women's demand for unconfined debate, although this was apparent not from the report but rather from Inga Thorsson's public statements. The report, she said, was not an expression of agreement over the issue, and when her federation confirmed its no to nuclear weapons in March 1960 she could make it known that the, proponents of this line had received "clear guarantees" that the free debate would be allowed to continue—such guarantees had been a precondition for accepting the decision on postponement.

Despite this, the report by the study group was a clear political success. On 14 December the SAP executive decided unanimously to accede to its lines of thought and opinions. The reception of the report in the press was generally good, and the Liberals and the Center party accepted its main lines of argument. The Conservatives, who accepted postponement but still demanded research into design, were isolated. During the spring of 1960, the conferences of the Women's Federation and the party each approved the report without difficulty.

The report of the study group had won the party leadership what it most needed, namely, time. Under the aegis of the postponement, consensus grew during the ensuing years. Eighteen months after the report had been published, the news spread that Sköld had changed his mind and now thought that no move toward Swedish nuclear weapons was justified; other leading party figures soon followed him.[55] In 1968, when the government clearly expressed the same view, it met no political opposition worth the name. This development during the years after the great dispute makes the story of the nuclear weapons debate nourishing food for thought: it was in fact the undisciplined opposition that turned out to have been right from the start.

Oppositional Views on Unity

There are distinct similarities between the view of the party's problems that Per Albin Hansson put forward in 1931 and 1932 and that which Erlander followed during the last half of the 1950s. During each period international tension relaxed briefly, which stimulated the party's latent dislike of defense expenditure and fondness for visions of disarmament. Each leader had to survive severe defeats in the struggle for seats in the Riksdag, and each had to find a policy that could broaden electoral support. Each worked in accordance with a strategy centered on the concepts of fitness for office and party responsibility.

For Erlander as for Hansson, the ability to take and hold office was closely linked to splits between the bourgeois parties. The Social Democrats, not having a majority in the Riksdag, needed to concentrate on questions over which their opponents disagreed and to avoid all others. Defense was among the latter, and it was important not to disturb the party truce that had been initiated in 1938 and consolidated during the war. Under the aegis of this truce, defense costs could rise while the Social Democrats exploited their opponents' disagreements over other questions.

The highly visible element of national responsibility in Hansson's view of office reappeared among the party leadership in the 1950s. To a high degree, Erlander shared Hansson's judgment that minority governments posed dangers for Swedish parliamentary democracy. He gave greater weight to the party's responsibility for national security than had his predecessors in the early 1930s. He emphasized, as did two defense ministers, Torsten Nilsson and Sven Andersson, that a searing party-political debate on the defense question would be a national calamity.[56]

To Erlander the concept of party responsibility meant what it had meant to Hansson and Wigforss during the internal settlement in 1931 and 1932: directing efforts toward areas where unity of purpose was evident, deflecting them from others where no unity could be reached.[57]

Opinions were divided between the party leadership and the opponents of nuclear weapons over what might be demanded in the name of party responsibility and internal discipline. The Women's Federation was often admonished for damaging the party by refusing to fall into line.[58] The women's often energetic defensive arguments included emphasis on the general point that free debate was a prerequisite for a vital political movement. Inga Thorsson claimed that the real danger lay in the fear of freely expressed opinion: "When the day comes that complaints are stilled, demands no longer raised, and the party's various organizations silent, then the party will have lost something that we cannot afford to lose."[59]

In asserting the party's need for a free exchange of opinions in order to preserve its vitality, the members of the Women's Federation had adopted a party point of view. Important as this might have been, they reached the heart of the dispute only when they had altered this perspective. In the women's opinion, when the demand for unity was regarded from the point of view of individual members, its bounds were seen to stop short of "matters of conscience." Beyond these bounds, individuals must be free to express their views regardless of whether they diverge from those of the party leadership. The question of Swedish nuclear weapons was just such a "matter of conscience." In the summer of 1959 the Social Democratic women published their objections to the views of some of their male comrades who, being unwilling to accept the women's arguments, wanted to deem the matter a "party question"—that is, an issue over which party leadership was entitled, after debate, to demand members' loyalty to the decision taken.

This criticism was fundamental: against party responsibility, the Women's Federation pitted the conscience of the individual; against national security, the future of mankind. Not general criticism of the leadership and its politics, this differed from criticism by earlier opponents, followers of Höglund and Engberg. The significance of this difference emerges if one makes a comparison with contemporaneous events in Norway.

In the early 1950s an organized leftist opposition had emerged within the Norwegian Social Democrats (DNA) opposing not only the party's policy over NATO but also its alleged neglect of socialist goals in its program. Conflicts sharpened in 1957 and 1958, when the opposition protested against NATO plans to station nuclear weapons in Norway and West Germany. As a result, the leader of the left wing was expelled from the party in 1961, and a new party, *Sosialistisk Folkeparti*, was formed.[60]

The Swedish party might have split over nuclear weapons, but limiting the dispute to a single question made it easier to skirt this danger: once the matter in dispute was resolved, no further subject of controversy replaced it. Even so, many in the party were aggravated by the women's lack of consideration in putting their consciences before their responsibility to the party that had achieved so much. Ten years later, perhaps equally many believed that a measure of well-considered relentlessness might be just what a party needs.

RESPONSIBILITY AND FACTION

The question of how the Social Democratic Labor Party balanced the demand for solidarity in joint action and a free formation of opinion can in general be answered quite simply: up to World War I, the party's view of differences of opinion was extremely tolerant. Advocates of unprovoked violence were expelled, but in other respects differences of opinion—philosophical, ideological, and those regarding practical politics—clashed unrestrained. The leadership had to answer criticism, not silence it. During the war, when the responsibilities of office were approaching, demands for solidarity and respect for decisions were sharpened. The principle of free debate before and solidarity after a decision was codified into the "discipline regulations" of the parliamentary group in 1915.

Although these rules of order remained only briefly in force, the principle lived on. After a period of internal friction in the late 1920s the regulations were confirmed through Hansson's resolution with his critics in 1931 and 1932. Concessions in minor matters in order to gain overall strength and thereby effectiveness and fitness for office were accepted as necessities. This was further developed in Erlander's time, when a united party was a precondition for the strong government that was vital for the nation as a whole. The image of the parliamentary paralysis of the 1920s served to illustrate the frightening consequences of faction.

That these discipline regulations became generally accepted has naturally influenced the conditions for the political debate and the conflict of opinion necessary to preserve the party's vitality. To what extent has it been feasible to maintain a point of view at odds with that of the leadership? To answer so complex a question in full would require a more extensive investigation, but two central aspects are evident. One is the importance of organization for the effectiveness of opposition; the other, the link between internal discipline and the integration of the labor movement with the nation.

The maxim that unity gives strength applies as much to opposition within a party as to the party itself. This is not to say that the substance of an argument is without value, only that it is not a sufficient condition for success. Altering the party line requires the weight generated by organization—many party members saying the same thing, and an even greater number thinking it.

Even though it felt less favored than the party leadership, the Höglund faction marshaled considerable resources in this respect, which explains in part why the struggle between the two went on so long. The leadership had to campaign intensively against its opponents before it felt strong enough to gather a majority of conference votes to expel them.

The importance of organizational support for the Höglund opposition appears when it is compared with the ideologically related opposition conducted by Arthur Engberg. Judging from the debate at the 1932 conference, a majority of delegates supported his isolated line on disarmament; but as Engberg was not attached to any firm group, Hansson could reach a personal agreement with him and his sympathizers in the executive before the conference. This split the opposition, and sufficient conference delegates could be brought over to the "right" side.

Of the three opposition movements discussed here, Tage Erlander met the best organized and most determined over the question of nuclear weapons. From time to time the Social Democratic women put their organization at the disposal of a nationwide campaign against nuclear weapons, and before the 1960 conference there were grounds for believing that the opposition had grown into a dominant force within the party. Unlike Hansson, Erlander had no chance of splitting the opposition by reaching an accommodation with its leading proponents. Inga Thorsson was not only an individual who could mold opinion but the voice of a united organization. The party leadership found it expedient to avoid having a conference and conference elections taken up by the question of nuclear weapons. This naturally strengthened its opponents' position on the internal study group that ultimately devised the formula of postponement which paved the way for the victory of the opposition.

On all these occasions the discipline rule was invoked, although the possibility of expulsion, its only possible sanction, was always limited because it could not be resorted to like a rule of law, always applied to a certain crime. Instead, it is a political instrument for use according to circumstances: a well-organized opposition cannot be expelled without risk of devastating the mother party. If the opposition cannot be forced back in public opinion before the decisive stroke, a truce must be reached. An opponent like Engberg, whose support among conference delegates was probably as strong as Höglund's or the Women's Federation's, could not mobilize any organized support and so could relatively easily be impounded and disciplined. Obviously, a prerequisite for political weight also *within* a party is a high degree of organization.

The possibility of an opposition developing within the party framework has evidently very much depended on the sort of political pressure that can be brought to bear against it. This acquired a wholly new character once the SAP leadership decided systematically to emphasize its responsibility for the political development of the country, a decision that achieved its breakthrough in the 1932 election campaign. With the Social Democratic movement then beginning to grow into a party in symbiosis with the state, internal opposition appeared in a new light. On becoming responsible for the well-being of the country, the labor movement increased its demands for discipline not just in politics but also in working life. During the 1930s the trade union movement improved its position vis-à-vis the employers' organizations while also more sharply requiring its members to observe the terms of the agreements it had reached. Once notorious for its strikes, Sweden became admired for the tranquillity of its labor market.

Per Albin Hansson's 1930s overwhelmingly demonstrated the political power that could be generated from cohesion and party responsibility. In 1946 Erlander could step into a historical inheritance with the seemingly unequivocal rule that if splits lead to political stagnation, cohesion leads to reforms and progress. During his years as leader the conception of the party and state as a symbiosis was further developed, and the idea that the party's and the nation's interests were in extensive agreement became widespread.[61]

Once the Social Democrats were not only incorporated into the national community of values but also had become a guarantee for its continued existence, offenses against the party's internal cohesion were imbued with a new gravity. They posed a challenge both to the party and to the nation, and it is possible that within the party an ideal was formed that gave the wisdom of statesmanship more weight than independent thinking about the future.

There were situations, however, in which the party's symbiosis with the state could stimulate party members to engage more fiercely in its internal debates, because all knew that the crucial struggles took place not between political parties but within the Social Democratic Labor Party. One such struggle had been over nuclear weapons: once the debate had started both sides were dominated by Social Democrats, and its ultimate resolution, which was to be decisive for the government and the Riksdag, was worked out within the confines of a Social Democratic study group. For the Federation of Social Democratic Women, one may reasonably suppose that this reinforced its fighting spirit.

Even if the pressure for unity becomes strong in a party in symbiosis with the state, opposing tendencies do exist. However, more than "tendencies" are likely to be required in order to refute Robert Michels's comment from 1911 that "the top leadership always represents the past rather than the future."[62] An almost continuous war of opinion may be needed to preserve the party's vitality and renewal, and in practice the choice lies between accepting this and losing the political initiative to opponents.

NOTES

1. Lindbom 1952, 138–43.
2. Höglund 1928, 500–501; *SAP Executive Minutes* 12–15 Jan. 1911 (Labor Movement Archives).
3. Tingsten 1967 (1947) 2:165–66; Lindbom 1952, 161–162; Höglund 1928, 501–2.
4. Stenkvist 1987, 247–49.
5. Östberg 1990, 217–36.
6. Lindbom 1952, 169.
7. Höglund 1928, 515–17; Lindbom 1952, 168–69.
8. Tingsten 1967, 2:170–71.
9. Palmstierna 1951, 148–50.

10. Östberg 1990, 258; Staaff 1918, 2:160–63, 181, 206–7; Kihlberg 1963, 296.

11. Hamilton 1955, 183, 199, 220.

12. Edenman 1946, 206–7, 209–11.

13. Ibid., 216–17.

14. Ibid., 226.

15. Ibid., 231–35.

16. For the views of the party leadership, see G. Möller and Hansson 1916, 95, 107; Höglund 1929, 91–108, 236.

17. SAP Conference Minutes 1917, 36, 38, 45, 54; Höglund 1917, 145.

18. Edenman 1946, 239.

19. Berghahn 1982, 284.

20. On minority parliamentary politics, see Nyman 1947, 1–16.

21. SAP Executive Minutes 15 Nov. 1925, par. 11; 11 Jan. 1926, par. 4; Gröning 1988, 159–60.

22. For examples of disputes in which Hansson had to give way, see the Executive Minutes of 15 Nov. 1925, par. 11, 11 Jan. 1926, par. 4, and Spring 1928, over minister socialism. Evidence of disputes may be found in Wigforss 1980, vol. 8 (Minnen, vol. 2), 256, 261–62; SAP Conference Minutes 1928, 261–62. Disputes within the SAP in 1928–1932 have been described and analyzed in a thesis by Bengt Schüllerqvist (Department of History, Uppsala University), to whom I am indebted for permission to make use of his work.

23. Tingsten 1967 (1941), 2:204–8.

24. Ibid., 206; Schüllerqvist 1988, 8 n. 1.

25. I.e., the "People's Home."

26. SAP Annual Report 1928, 73–78.

27. Ibid., 43; also Wigforss 1980, vol. 8 (Minnen, vol. 2), 280.

28. SAP Annual Report 1928, 7–10.

29. For Wigforss's comments, see his "Historisk materialism och klasskamp" (Historical Materialism and Class Struggle), Wigforss 1980, 1:58–60; see also vol. 8 (Minnen), 285–86; Schüllerqvist 1988, 23–25.

30. Schüllerqvist 1988, 41; see also SAP Conference Minutes 1936, 496, 507, 508.

31. SAP Conference Minutes 1936, 495–510.

32. Ibid., 237–345; Tingsten 1967 (1941), 2:215–21.

33. For the program, see SAP Annual Report 1932; for the role of defense, see Wigforss 1980, vol. 2 (Minnen, vol. 2), 371.

34. Nyman 1947, 56–59, 135. See also, for example, SAP Conference Minutes 1932, 306.

35. Nyman 1947, 9–10; SAP Conference Minutes 1932, 289 (Wigforss), 338 (Hansson); see also Wigforss 1980, vol. 8 (Minnen, vol. 2), 371.

36. SAP Conference Minutes 1932, 8–9, 35, 469–70.

37. K. Molin 1974, 89–98.

38. Sydow 1978, 51. A recent Ph.D. thesis (Nilsson Hoadley, 1989) on the Federation of Swedish Social Democratic Women and the issue of nuclear weapons gave rise to a debate participated in by inter alia Inga Thorsson (Tiden 1990:1, 30–34). The view of the role of the Women's Federation presented in this chapter is close to that of Inga Thorsson.

39. Sydow 1978, 51; Lindström 1969, 67; Rudling 1975, 20 and 80 (interview with Inga Thorsson); letter to the party executive from the executive of the Women's Federation (SSKF), 30 June 1959, appendixes to the Minutes of the executive of the federation for 31 Aug. 1959 and 9 Oct. 1959 (Labor Movement Archives). The letter is mentioned in Sydow 1978, 358–59.

40. SAP Executive Minutes, 21 Feb. 1959, par. 9; see also Sydow 1978, 62–66; Erlander 1973, 86–88; Y. Möller, 1986, 466–68; Lindström 1969, 97–98.

41. National Federation of Social Democratic Women, *Conference Minutes* 1956, 146–50, 176.

42. But see the exchanges between Lassinantti and Thorsson at the 1956 party conference, *Conference Minutes* 97 (Lassinantti), 547 (Thorsson).

43. *SAP Executive Minutes*, 25 Sept. 1956. See also Lindström 1969, 107–8. On Erlander's position after the election, see Ruin 1986, 48–49, 66; see also Geijer 1969, 68–70.

44. Erlander 1973, 90–91.

45. For a view of the role of the question of nuclear weapons in the campaigns, see Ahlmark 1965, 26, and Sydow 1978, 206.

46. Ahlmark 1965, 16–18; Sydow 1978, 207–8 (also 468–69 n. 4); H. Lundberg 1988, 217; Y. Möller 1986, 474.

47. National Federation of Swedish Social Democratic Women, *Annual Report* 1958; Rudling 1975, 38.

48. *SAP Executive Minutes* 21 Feb. 1956, comments by Sträng and Löfberg.

49. SSU (Social Democratic Youth), *Conference Minutes* 1958, 247 (Löfberg); for references to the Women's Federation, see 236 (Rune Johansson), 258 (Sune Jönsson), and 259 (Näslund); for criticism of the party leadership, 254 (Elmgren); for Palme's speech, Löfberg's support, and the final vote, 281–82, 287.

50. *Svenska atomvapen?* (1959) and *Nej! till svenska atomvapen* (1959).

51. The announcement about the study group came during the Youth Conference on 24–28 Aug. 1958. Yngve Möller has described how he had first suggested a study group at a conference with the editors of the Social Democratic press on 3 June (Y. Möller 1986, 474–75). In mid-August, a similar idea, which arose during the annual conference of the Brotherhood Movement, was expressed in a letter to the party executive; it suggested that a general committee be appointed to study the question of nuclear weapons. See H. Lundberg 1988, 217.

52. SAP 1960, 113, 117.

53. Sydow 1978, 354.

54. Executive of the National Federation of Social Democratic Women to the party executive, 30 June 1959, appendix to the Women's Federation Executive *Minutes* (see 31 Aug. and 9 Oct. 1959).

55. Y. Möller 1986, 482.

56. SAP 1960, 113–17. For a general discussion of Erlander's feelings on the identity of interest between the party and the nation, see Ruin 1986, 206.

57. Erlander 1973, 86, 91; Sydow 1978, 360.

58. Rudling 1975, 82 (interview with Inga Thorsson).

59. *SAP Conference Minutes* 1956, 547.

60. Elvander 1980, 193–200.

61. Ruin 1986, 206.

62. Michels 1983, 90–91 (1st ed. published in German in 1911).

Tim Tilton

13

The Role of Ideology in Social Democratic Politics

Five central themes in Swedish Social Democratic ideology deserve special attention: integrative democracy, society as the "people's home," the compatibility of equality and economic efficiency, social control of the market economy, and the "strong society" as a precondition for increased individual freedom of choice. I do not claim that these themes are the only unique features of Swedish Social Democracy or that comparable themes do not exist in other Social Democratic movements. I claim only that together these elements give Swedish Social Democracy a distinctive and persistent character despite changes in the party's social base and in its views about appropriate measures for the nationalization of production. Furthermore, these ideological themes constitute an essential component of any satisfactory explanation of Swedish economic and social policy.

FIVE CENTRAL THEMES

The first central notion of Swedish Social Democracy may be termed *integrative democracy*. Swedish Social Democrats rapidly recognized democratic decision making as the ultimate standard of legitimacy, superior to "imperatives" of materialist development or to anarchist activity. This choice ruled out both proletarian dictatorship and terrorism. It focused the party's efforts on the attainment of political democracy as its first overriding objective. The party never seriously entertained the Leninist idea of an elitist revolutionary cadre. Political democracy, however, was not enough. From its origins Swedish Social Democracy has been committed to creating a state in which first industrial workers and then employees in general participated on equal terms in the organization and governance of society. The democratic ideal ought to infuse not only political life, but social and economic organization as well. Thus from Per Albin Hansson through Tage Erlander and Olof Palme to the present, party leaders have spoken of a three-stage development through political democracy to social and economic democracy as well.

The content of this slogan can be gleaned from the writings of Nils Karleby, who emphasized participation as the central element of Social Democratic transformation. Karleby saw "the working class's full participation in society" as "the goal of Social Democratic efforts"; this goal would be achieved when labor was "an equal partner in the development of the methods, form, and content of social life and no area of social life was excepted from being considered and ordered from the viewpoint of social utility (*ändamålsenligheten*)."[1] It was the task of social democracy to complete the prematurely halted work of the liberal bourgeoisie in extending human freedom.

The most compelling formulation of this ideal, however, appears in a little-known essay, "Some Viewpoints on the Nationalization Question," that Gustav Steffen wrote for the Nationalization Committee in 1920.[2] Steffen, a professor of sociology whom Branting had persuaded to accept a seat in the Riksdag, regarded "deproletarianization" as the central objective of social democracy. For Marx, he argued, the concept of the proletarian was fundamental. The concepts of surplus value, capital, and exploitation were secondary; accumulation, concentration, crisis, and catastrophe, tertiary. Marx's overriding concern was to humanize the worker. The worker lacked political power, economic resources, and material security. These disadvantages rendered him passive and inactive. A raw material used by others, the proletarian lacked property and the opportunity to direct his work. Capitalism foreclosed for him not only income from capital, but also participation in and responsibility for the organization of economic activity. For Steffen the absence of freedom, participation, and responsibility was the central problem of proletarianization: if the worker grew prosperous but lacked political and economic power, he remained a proletarian.

The solution lay in schooling and organizing workers to assume political and economic power. Steffen envisaged nationalization less as a transfer of property rights than a "summarization of the methods for his [the worker's] liberation from the economic and social immaturity of the proletarian condition."[3] The point of nationalization was to integrate workers into the economic life of society. Labor could achieve this integration only by casting aside its passivity and schooling itself to assume positions of responsibility within the process of production. Political democracy, Steffen argued, created a political situation that allowed this transition to proceed along nonrevolutionary lines.

Steffen's conception, like those of the major Social Democratic spokesmen, envisions democracy not as class rule by the poor or by workers but as the rule of all. A strong preference for consensual democracy underlies the actions of Social Democratic leaders. Branting sought a broad alliance with the Liberals in order to introduce universal suffrage. Then in the tumult of 1918 he confined his program to gains that reflected a broad consensus. Per Albin Hansson sought broad agreement not just during the national coalition government of the war years, but before and after it. Erlander and Palme regularly sought coalitions with one or more of the nonsocialist parties. Even Wigforss, arguably the most controversial of Social Democratic spokesmen, urged cross-class cooperation in his Bourse Society speech of 1938.[4]

This emphasis upon integration, full participation, and consensus leads naturally to a second central notion, the *folkhemmet*, the conception of society and state as the "people's home." Per Albin Hansson's classic formulation of this ideal merits repetition:

> The basis of the home is togetherness and common feeling. The good home does not recognize anyone as privileged or misfavored; it knows no special favorites and no stepchildren. There no one looks down upon anyone else, there no one tries to gain advantage at another's expense, and the stronger do not suppress and plunder the weaker. In the good home equality, consideration, cooperation,

and helpfulness prevail. Applied to the great people's and citizens' home this would mean the breaking down of all the social and economic barriers that now divide citizens into privileged and misfavored, into rulers and dependents, into rich and poor, the glutted and the destitute, the plunderers and the plundered.[5]

Solidarity and equality of consideration characterize the good home; there consensus is the objective and democratic persuasion the method of governance.

The force of this ideal lies not only in its intrinsic appeal, but also in its contrast to the partriarchal ideals of the traditional Swedish mill towns (*bruk*). In many of the small rural settlements where much of the nation's industrial development originated, a kind of predemocratic welfare state emerged. In Gustavsberg, for example, the owner's expensive estate stood prominently above the neat houses of the white-collar personnel and the ordered ranks of the workers' company-built dwellings. The owner provided health care and a variety of other welfare benefits—until the workers had the temerity to organize a union, at which point the firm terminated benefits. In contrast to this patriarchal, class-stratified social provision, the ideal of the people's home postulated a community where members could claim equal rights to universally provided services and where social provision derived not from aristocratic largesse but from democratic decisions.

The greater equalization produced by universal social policy, progressive taxation, solidaristic wage policy, and movement toward sexual equality need not constitute an impediment to efficient production, Swedish Social Democrats have consistently argued. Indeed, the third great theme of the movement's ideology is the compatibility, even complementarity, of socioeconomic equality and economic efficiency. The distinctiveness of this position can be seen by contrasting the titles and themes of two books. The late Arthur Okun gave his book *Equality and Efficiency* the subtitle *The Big Trade-Off*, and contended that efforts to establish a highly egalitarian society must result in significant losses of productive efficiency.[6] On the other hand, the authors of *Den produktiva rättvisan* (Productive Justice)[7] argued powerfully for the greater efficiency of an egalitarian, full-employment society. Since social science has done little to resolve this issue, one must adopt the more modest objective of understanding how Swedish Social Democrats have argued their case.

Preventive social policy, Gunnar and Alva Myrdal maintained, requires equality and promotes efficiency. If children are to be desired, born, and reared to be productive adults, society must invest in their welfare and that of their families. Expenditures on their education and health should be seen not as burdens upon production, but as investments in human capital. Society's greatest asset is its human resources, which must not be squandered or allowed to atrophy. This appreciation of the role of social policy in the production of the labor force can sound callous, mechanical, and calculated, but it represents a commitment to realizing the potential of each individual. Similarly, the Myrdals' progressive emphasis upon the rights of women cites the economic benefits of enlisting the talents of women in all spheres of society. This notion of maximizing the use of society's human resources has penetrated deeply into Swedish society: leading Swedish executives (still mostly men) promote their own Swedish model of doing business based on the full development of the skills of employees.[8]

LO, the Swedish Trade Union Confederation (Landsorganisationen i Sverige), as early as its 1941 report *The Trade Union Movement and Industry*, presented the first of a series of arguments for the benefits of equality in promoting longer-term growth and efficiency.[9] Increased productivity and the rationalization of production were essential if Sweden was to enjoy higher standards of living, the LO committee agreed; but if the benefits of economic progress flowed disproportionately to capital, workers would resist modernization, disrupt production through strikes, and reduce efficiency because of lower morale and effort. Using an approach that more American and especially British businesses might well have heeded, the LO stressed that the restructuring of the economy, far from being simply a matter of financial calculation, required an essentially political compact with labor—labor's cooperation in modernization in exchange for full employment, more egalitarian distribution, and a larger share in management decisions.

The LO has also couched its case for solidaristic wage policy in terms of efficiency as well as equity. Over time, the trade union economists Gösta Rehn and Rudolf Meidner demonstrated, the operation of a more egalitarian wage structure would pressure the economy's least efficient firms to improve productivity or go under. Meanwhile, the most efficient firms, by paying somewhat lower wages than they could afford, would accumulate "extra profits" for reinvestment in their enterprises. The system thus created a bias toward enhanced productivity. Under such a system of equal pay for equal work, profits more nearly approximated a measure of a firm's efficiency rather than a measure of its bargaining power vis-à-vis workers.

During the late 1970s and the 1980s some interesting shifts in the Social

Democratic commitment to equality and efficiency occurred. On the right, Kjell-Olof Feldt (in 1982 the minister of finance), the party economist Klas Eklund, and others have criticized the progressivity of the Swedish tax system as debilitating in its effects and have instituted measures to reduce marginal rates of taxation to 50 percent, an action that of course reduces the progressivity of the tax system and its impact upon upper-income recipients. Feldt and his advisers have also emphasized the need to restore the profitability of Swedish firms and to limit wage increases. Neither of these measures, it need hardly be said, has proved popular with the LO.

On the left, the trade union economists Per-Olof Edin and Anna Hedborg have argued for a reevaluation of efficiency, one that places less emphasis upon profits as a measure of efficiency and more upon employee welfare, particularly the welfare that comes from increased control over and satisfaction in one's work.[10] While maintaining that "there is no decisive contradiction between the democratization of working life and the renewal and greater efficiency of the economy,"[11] Edin and Hedborg clearly regard growth and the pursuit of maximal productive efficiency as less dominant objectives than hitherto. They speak of the decreasing marginal utility of growth and emphasize employee welfare, treating the achievement of profit as a constraint rather than the fundamental objective. In making their case for an economy based on Wage-Earners' Funds, they set up "the new assignment—to establish an organization of labor that can give scope for much greater portions of human capacity and well-roundedness (all-sidighet)."[12] The goal of efficiency as they reinterpret it focuses inward on the satisfactions and capacities of employees rather than outward on the production of goods and services.

The stark poverty that characterized Sweden well into the twentieth century compelled Swedish Social Democrats to consider how to increase production and not merely how to distribute the results. For decades many believed—insofar as they thought about the specific structures of a socialist society—that socializing the means of production, by which they customarily understood nationalizing industry, transportation, and finance, was the remedy to all the problems of capitalist production. Gradually, however, the sobering impact of political difficulties and economic examples forced a revision. The movement came to a position favoring a socially controlled market economy rather than nationalization of productive enterprise. In this view (the fourth central theme of Swedish Social Democracy), social control of the economy takes precedence over questions of formal ownership. Nationalization becomes a possible instrument for Social Democratic purposes, but not a necessary or even a preferred one. Periodically, as in the immediate post–World War II period or during the wage-earner debate of the 1970s and 1980s, the socialist aspiration for public ownership revives, but increasingly proposals envision public ownership in the form of independent corporations, cooperatives, or employee-owned businesses rather than state corporations. Why did this transition to a more diffuse notion of socializing the economy by subjecting it to public control occur, and what is its content?

The origins of this transition lie in the party's early shift on agricultural issues. In Germany Kautsky's *Die Agrarfrage* (1895) had asserted the necessity of agrarian concentration, the proletarianization of small farmers, and an eventual large-scale public agriculture. Consequently, social democracy had little to offer small farmers and largely restricted its appeal to working-class voters. This approach remained the dominant outlook within German Social Democracy until 1927. In Sweden, however, the party adopted a new agricultural program in 1911 (much like that recommended by German revisionists such as Eduard David). It envisioned the continued viability of small farming. As early as 1907 Branting had written that Marx's predictions of an inevitable concentration of agricultural units had proven invalid. Cooperatives, he argued, could provide the advantages of large-scale production while keeping the worker united with his means of production.[13] The 1911 program encapsulated two crucial decisions for Swedish Social Democracy. First, the party would not limit its appeals to the industrial working class, but would seek the support of "little people" and workers in general. Second, socialism did not necessarily require government ownership of the means of production; producer cooperatives composed of small-scale owner-operators could be an acceptable form of economic organization.[14]

Because the party treated agriculture and industry as distinctly separate categories, the 1911 program made little immediate impact on thinking about the organization of industry. It was primarily the impact of the electoral defeats in 1920 and 1928 and secondarily the influence of liberal economic theory and of problems in obtaining union support for nationalization of industry that spurred a rethinking of the movement's views on industrial organization. Under the influence of Karleby and Sandler, the party tacitly shifted to a conception of a socialized market economy, in which markets functioned under socially controlled conditions.

This social control had four facets. First, as Karleby emphasized, the labor movement had to move to equalize the background conditions under which markets operated. Markets responded to demand and supply; the distribution of income and property shaped the nature of demand and supply. If incomes were highly skewed in their distribution, markets for luxury goods might displace the provision of more essential items. By shifting the distribution of incomes and property in a more egalitarian direction through solidaristic wage policy, progressive taxation, and social welfare policy, Social Democrats could enlist markets to fulfill essential human needs. This strategy focused not on abolishing or on heavily regulating markets, but on restructuring the background conditions that determined what resources' people brought to the market.

A second strategy, "framework legislation," aimed at a more fundamental reorganization of markets themselves. For the economy as a whole there were policies to make some of the critical assumptions underlying the liberal model of perfect competition—perfect information and no transportation costs, for instance—more nearly true. Government undertook to supply thorough information about job vacancies and job-seekers and to subsidize the costs of labor mobility so that they fell upon society as a whole rather than upon the individual worker. For specific industries like housing and agriculture, the government established standards of production, subsidized loans, and various special incentives to encourage production and the reorganization of industry.

In its most ambitious form this sort of framework planning verged on economic planning. The Swedish word *planhushållning*, like the English term *planning*, is extraordinarily ambiguous. It can mean—and has meant —anything from the application of monetary and fiscal policy to the reorganization of specific industries to the coordination of the economy as a whole. "Planning" entered the Swedish Social Democratic debate in a serious way in the 1920s in the work of the Nationalization Committee and then in the writings and speeches of Ernst Wigforss. The party's general skepticism about governmental competence following the experience of rationing during World War I and then the force of the Soviet example produced a general disillusionment with any sort of detailed economic planning. When Wigforss recommended *planhushållning* in 1930 and the years immediately following, he was advocating the equivalent of Keynesian countercylical policy, with governmental pressure for more efficient organization of production and more equitable distribution.

With the revival of the economy, seemingly because of Wigforss's policies, "planning" gained popularity and the Social Democrats began to entertain more ambitious hopes. As Wigforss reports in his memoirs, there was little clarity about precisely how to proceed, but he spoke of the possibility of "planning of both public and private investments" and of the planned nationalization and concentration of certain industries.[15] The Social Democrats proposed negotiations with industry to explore a cooperative execution of this program. This initiative Wigforss characterized as a "reformist utopia." "Society would transform itself, assume more and more socialist traits with the willing cooperation of the capitalist entrepreneurs themselves!"[16] These discussions terminated with the outbreak of the war, but the increasing and often successful public penetration of the economy during the war years revived Social Democratic aspirations at war's end. The new thrust for a bolder implentation of "planning" found embodiment in *The Postwar Program of Swedish Labor* and in Commerce Minister Gunnar Myrdal's call for a radical restructuring of various industries under governmental direction.

The great debate over economic planning leading up to the 1948 election, together with the economic difficulties of the immediate postwar years, quashed Social Democratic zeal. Under the new slogan of "industrial policy," similar aspirations reappeared in the late 1960s only to sag again after the Social Democrats regained office in 1982. The general conclusion must be that the idea of thoroughgoing economic planning has led a precarious and suspect existence within Swedish Social Democracy—with the exception of two areas, agriculture and housing, in which it has thrived in a somewhat looser form that recognizes consumers and producers as independent economic agents and regulates the framework within which they act. Neither market nor plan per se, but planned markets—that is the Swedish third way in economic planning. The classic formulation of a publicly structured framework for market activities still belongs to Per Albin Hansson. In discussing the dividing line between social democracy and its nonsocialist opponents, he stressed bourgeois blindness to the possibility of a socialized market economy: "In this confinement by the dogma of the saving grace of free enterprise alone the bourgeois parties dare not conceive a combination where freedom for private initiative is framed or curbed by social control."[17]

The fourth form of social control proceeds from the notion of property as a bundle of rights. In its classic formulations by Nils Karleby and Gunnar Adler-Karlsson this concept emphasizes the divisibility of property rights. Property does not consist of an indivisible amalgam of rights, a "natural" right, which must be held either publicly or privately (and thus transferred en bloc from private to public hands in an single dramatic action). Rather, property involves a multiplicity of rights that can be divided up and placed in a variety of different hands—public, private, or mixed. Under this way of conceiving property, nationalization can be a gradual process, a paring away of capitalist prerogatives until they are fully absorbed by "the public" or fully subjected to social control.

Under this approach, dubbed "functional socialism" by Adler-Karlsson, private enterprise is slowly hedged about and infiltrated with a series of measures that steer its operations toward public objectives. The range of such measures is broad and varied—the eight-hour day, industrial accident legislation, zoning laws, environmental restrictions, collective bargaining legislation, and a host of other measures. In Sweden, unlike the United States, one seldom hears the complaint that business captures regulatory agencies for its own objectives. (Such criticisms are not nonexistent, however: in 1987 critics accused the government of abetting Bofors in its illegal weapons exports and of permitting industry to pollute the environment with an enormous number of dangerous chemicals.) The more customary criticism is that the strategy of gradually socializing property rights reaches an eventual impasse when the incursions of society touch the fundamental core of property rights (usually undefined). In this view property is not an onion to be peeled away completely, but rather an artichoke: once the peeling is done, a firm, resistant center remains.[18] Only a successfully thorough erosion of property rights could resolve this issue definitively, but in the meantime one can observe that the gradualist strategy has the substantial merit of leaving future possibilities open and not foreclosing further advances.

Swedish Social Democracy has recognized the value of markets. The precise conditions under which these markets are to operate, and in particular the role of private enterprise in the economy, have been highly ambiguous and prone to fluctuation with the political climate. In 1938 Wigforss said that it was incorrect to think of "a specific form of economic organization as the one proper or suitable form under all conditions," an observation that cut against public as well as private enterprise.[19] In the same speech he stated that the government "must recognize the need to maintain favorable conditions for private enterprise in all those areas where it is not immediately ready to replace this private enterprise with some form of public activity."[20] Similarly, in appraising the party's postwar program, Tage Erlander stressed its lack of dogmatism: "The demand for nationalization had been pushed into the background. Now the slogan was: let private industry under social control take care of what it can take care of. Society will not intervene other than when it is found to be necessary."[21]

Just what Social Democrats might interpret "society" regarding as "necessary," however, has fluctuated widely. It is precisely the ambiguity of these formulations that makes it wrong for Tingsten to have concluded that Swedish Social Democracy had abandoned its socialist heritage. Patently, both the Postwar Program and the Wage-Earners' Funds proposals envisioned a substantial nationalization of private industry. It is more nearly correct to conclude that the variety and ambiguity of the Swedish Social Democratic tradition on the issue of property ownership and social control allow the party to shift its position with changes in the political climate. In more radical periods, demands for some form of public ownership resurface; in conservative eras the party becomes the steward of a socially controlled private market economy. The overall trend, slow as it may be, is clearly toward an increase of the power of labor relative to capital.[22]

Clearly the conception of a socially controlled market economy rejects the idea that the growth of the public sector necessarily imperils individual liberties. On the contrary, Swedish Social Democracy—this is the fifth major theme of its ideology—has contended that a proper expansion of the public sector extends freedom of choice. Tage Erlander, the most consistent and self-conscious advocate of this position, insisted that "it is a mistake to believe that people's freedom is diminished because they decide to carry out collectively what they are incapable of doing individually."[23] Erlander never tired of citing the increased security and freedom that modern social policy created for common people. Health insurance freed them from the high costs of medical care and their attendant anxieties; pensions, from the risk of an impoverished old age; housing policy, from the squalor and potential for illness found in slum conditions; full employment policy, from the risk of unemployment. Professor Gösta Rehn similarly stressed social democracy's role as a movement for freedom. The labor market policies associated with his name expand job opportunities for individual workers. His arguments for greater choice in the use of pension rights rest on the same principle—that the public sector can increase individuals' freedom and opportunities.

This fifth principle rests on two further convictions. The first is that the government effectively represents society's wishes—that government is democratic. The presumption here is that rulers act on behalf of citizens' interests, not (as in some narrow versions of public choice theory) strictly in their own interests. The second conviction is that taxes do not abuse citizens' freedom but instead allow them to pay for public services. Taxation in this view represents less an act of coercion than simply a way of paying a price for public services. Gunnar Sträng, the legendary minister of finance under Erlander and Palme, is widely credited with having persuaded the public of the need for higher taxes, particularly the turnover tax.

The Social Democratic regime in office after 1982 has retreated somewhat from this position. And it has deregulated portions of the financial world and dealings in foreign currencies. It has effectively privatized certain public sector economic activities. It has lowered marginal tax rates. And it has gradually allowed itself to consider whether public provision of such services as day care and health care must be organized as public monopolies.

The five central themes of Social Democratic ideology are not separate strands, but parts of a coherent pattern. The drive for integrative democracy means that all citizens are to be embraced in the national community, the *folkhem*, to be treated there with equal consideration and to enjoy fully the freedoms of citizenship. These freedoms cannot be limited to the political sphere. Because private capital resists the extension of public welfare provisions and the democratic organization of economic life, the government must intervene to maximize prosperity and democracy. It is impossible to determine dogmatically just what the proper bounds of this intervention should be, but it must rest on a firm democratic basis (and thus is likely to be gradualist and nonviolent in its implementation). It should recognize the value of socially controlled markets as one instrument of social coordination. Underlying this pattern is a commitment to rational competence, to scientific standards, and to optimism about the human capacity to reduce random chance in human life.

This central vision does not exhaust the riches of the Swedish Social Democratic tradition, nor is it without its own internal tensions. As in virtually all lively socialist traditions the impetus toward state control competes with decentralizing syndicalist impulses. Erlander's commitment to the "strong society" confronts impulses for local and neighborhood control, a conflict that can also be expressed as a tension between the quest for just and uniform national standards and the desire for local determination and variation. The classic tensions of modern Social Democratic parties—public ownership versus social control of industry, the pursuit of traditional industrial working-class interests versus employee interests—also find expression in Sweden.

Much of the debate over the nature of Swedish Social Democracy has focused on its evolution as well as its contemporary character. In light of the competing claims advanced by Tingsten and Lewin, what can one say about the historical development of Swedish Social Democracy? In particular, does it represent a (rational, in Tingsten's view) abandonment of the party's socialist heritage?

The answer to this question should be clear. There is a fundamental consistency in the five central themes of Swedish Social Democratic ideology. Each is implicit and most are explicit as early as Branting's writings and speeches. The *values* of Social Democracy—full participation, integrative democracy, solidarity, equality, efficiency, freedom, and security—have steadily oriented the movement's actions. Together they constitute an ideal broader and more complex than Lewin's "social democratic conception of freedom."

The *interests* that the party represents have expanded from the traditional working class to include first small farmers and rural workers and then white-collar personnel. Tingsten's thesis emphasizes most of all, however, the *view of social evolution* and the *means* of social democracy. The notion that early Swedish Social Democracy widely endorsed a "catastrophe" theory envisioning the crisis, collapse, and socialist reconstruction of capitalist society is, I believe, just wrong. At least as prominent in the early party is a vision of *democratic* evolution, of the labor movement forming unions to extract concessions from capital and gaining universal suffrage to win elections and implement its aims. Unless one takes this view it is difficult to explain the party's commitment to parliamentarianism at its Norrköping conference in 1891 and those distinctive phrases in the first official party program (1897) citing capitalism's generation of a labor opposition that will overcome it. The commitment to parliamentarianism and democracy has always been overriding.

The development of the Social Democratic position on means has been more complex. Until 1918 very little consideration was given to questions of economic and particularly industrial organization. The notion of nationalization was invoked, but more as a ritual formula than as a concrete policy suggestion; its content remained unspecified. At the close of World War I the Swedish Social Democrats along with their Scandinavian sister parties adopted nationalization and industrial democracy as their central program points. The combination of practical problems in determining the specific institutional structures and policies for making good on these slogans and political difficulties in obtaining an effective majority blocked the implementation of these objectives, leaving the Social Democrats in the embarrassing position of endorsing liberal monetary policy in day-to-day questions. Wigforss's efforts in the late 1920s to make inheritance and wealth taxes the centerpiece of Social Democratic strategy proved politically unpopular. Not until the early 1930s, when the Social Democrats enunciated their economic crisis policy and added to it Möller's developing social welfare programs, did the movement find a politically effective strategy.

The success of the modest welfare statist strategy of the 1930s has widely been viewed as a reason for the Social Democrats' abandonment of the notion of nationalization. There can be little doubt that substantial portions of the Social Democratic movement have indeed rejected nationalization at least as a timely and feasible option and perhaps even as a desirable option; Tage Erlander, Olof Palme, and Kjell-Olof Feldt have shown little enthusiasm for the extension of public ownership in private industry. Another substantial portion of the labor movement, however, has not abandoned nationalization as an objective, and from time to time its ideas prevail. In the 1930s the state extended its ownership of railroads and iron ore, and Wigforss proposed national coffee and gasoline monopolies. The Postwar Program advocated social planning of investment, social control of foreign trade, and support to cooperative or socialized production where private enterprise engendered inefficiency (*misshushållning*) or monopoly. Party conferences in the postwar period have often endorsed the nationalization of banking, insurance, and pharmaceuticals. Finally, in the mid-1970s the Meidner plan projected a scheme for the gradual nationalization in union hands of the bulk of Swedish industry.

If Swedish Social Democracy's values have remained relatively constant, its critique of liberal capitalist society has evolved as economic and political circumstances have changed. Swedish Social Democracy has been remarkably averse to utopianizing. Wigforss's provisional utopia, itself largely contentless, represents the high-water mark of such speculation. On the whole the movement's ideologists have focused on the abuses of liberal capitalist society and sought to remedy them. Committed to democratic means as well as ends, they have sought allies in order to form a majority for their reformist projects. In the process they have gradually deemphasized the replacement of "capitalism" by "socialism" and instead tried to reshape liberal market society so that all individuals possess the capacities and the resources to make free choices within this system.

IDEOLOGY SHAPES POLICY

Has ideology made a difference in the nature of policy? Much contemporary literature on the welfare state downplays or negates the role of ideology and ideas in the formation of policy. Influential studies treat the development of the welfare state as a functional adaptation to modern industrial society,[24] a reflection of labor's power within civil society,[25] or a result of state capacity.[26] These studies tacitly assume the presence of the will and the intellectual knowledge to develop social policy and then fail to appreciate significant national variations in the structure, coverage, financing, and benefits of specific programs. In the first part of this chapter I sketched the importance of ideology in political life; I now want to illustrate some important ideological influences on policy, choosing areas where Swedish social and economic policy displays distinctive features.

Full employment is central to the Swedish conception of the welfare state. Over decades the party and the unions have drummed home the main arguments for full employment. It is critical to a person's welfare and sense of belonging. It is more productive than simply paying unemployment compensation. It increases the bargaining power of employees. It generates tax revenues rather than requiring their expenditure. Ever since the 1930s, when the Social Democrats succeeded in reviving an economy in the throes of depression, high employment has been an important policy objective, one increasingly accepted by other parties. Unemployment (defined at an unusually low level by international standards) became as delicate a political issue in Sweden as inflation in Germany. This broadly shared commitment to full employment is in itself an important factor in explaining the persistence of full employment, as Göran Therborn, an analyst customarily skeptical of idealistic explanations, has shown.[27]

Universal social policy is a second critical pillar of the Swedish welfare state. There was no particular reason why Swedish social policy should have been universal rather than worker-based as in Germany, or confessionally linked as in the Netherlands, or remarkably segmented as in France or Italy. One has to acknowledge the impact of Branting's commitment to universalism in 1913 and of Möller's commitment to the classless treatment of citizens within the welfare state. Universalism as an ideology continues to shape policy. It underlies arguments for resisting means-testing in the current period of retrenchment, for expanding day care, and for replacing the means-tested housing allowance with larger (universal) family allowances.

A number of nations display some form of *industrial democracy*, but Sweden is remarkable for the comprehensiveness of its program. Industrial democracy extends across all industries and the public sector, not just particular branches of industry. It embodies potentially all facets of employer-employee relations—from safety, job security, wages, work organization, even the business plans of the firm. It extends from the shop floor to the boardroom. The unions' original reluctance to accept coresponsibility for the direction of the firm and their gradual acceptance of the principles of industrial democracy illustrate the importance of the ideological underpinnings of this policy.

Solidaristic wage policy is hardly the automatic policy of labor unions. From Gompers's "More" to Lenin's castigation of "economism," the assumption has been that unions existed to extract the highest possible wage. In the most highly productive industries (those capable of paying the most generous wages), such a policy is in the workers' clear material interest. Yet the Metal Workers' Union, one of the best-paid groups in Swedish labor, has traditionally been the major exponent of solidaristic wages. The pursuit of this policy by the LO and the TCO has succeeded in narrowing differentials within their respective ranks, an outcome not easily explained without the force of ideology.

Active labor market policy in its various facets occupies a larger share of GNP in Sweden than in other OECD countries. The origins of active labor market policy lie less in clear ideological directives than in wartime exigencies, but the expansion of these policies in later decades stems in large part from the acceptance of the Rehn-Meidner model and from the emergence of labor market policy as a distinctive policy sphere. If one compares British or American policy discussions, one is struck by the absence of a organizing conception (or institutional structure) similar to the Swedish one. It is little wonder, then, that both countries lack the coherent approach of the Swedish system.

Collective capital formation contains the potential for extensions of public ownership; consequently, it is open to cries of "socialism" and usually proves highly controversial in most OECD countries. In the United States, for example, the Republicans attacked the buildup of Social Security funds in the late 1930s and seem prepared to attack the present developing surplus. In Sweden, after considerable controversy, a substantial measure of collective capital formation has become accepted practice. The budget surpluses called for by the Rehn-Meidner model were relatively noncontroversial compared to the funded system established for the supplementary pension scheme in 1958. There the debate focused specifically on the propriety of such a large accumulation of funds in public hands. The continuing controversy over the Wage-Earners' Funds has obscured both the fact of their formation and the dedication of other profits taxes to "renewal funds" and to funds for the improvement of the work environment. Again it is hard to imagine the development of public capital building without the support of Social Democratic ideology.

The list of examples could easily be extended. *Women's issues* are hardly resolved in Sweden, but women are more active participants in the wage force at higher levels of pay than elsewhere in the world. Day care facilitates their entry into the labor force.[28] Parental leave insurance recognizes both the equal obligations of parents in child-rearing and a public obligation to provide financial support for parenting in earliest childhood. The availability of birth control, abortion, and frank sexual education similarly is hard to imagine without the efforts of Alva Myrdal and her co-workers. Sweden's policy for the handicapped aims at reintegration to an unusual degree. Housing policy fosters public and cooperative building. The school system rests on an ideology of democracy and cooperation. The health care system is universal.

Immigration policy is in many ways an ideal example to illustrate the force of ideology in shaping a distinctive Swedish policy. unlike Continental models, Swedish policy treats foreign workers as immigrants (*invandrare*), not as guest workers (*Gastarbeiter*). The goal is to integrate them into Swedish life by making language instruction available for free, making social services available on equal terms, gradually extending voting rights, and publicly condemning racial incidents. Above all, foreign workers are not viewed as expendable labor power to be sent home in periods of economic contraction. This inclusive, integrationist approach flows naturally from Social Democratic values; it has not been entirely successful, but it demonstrates a marked improvement over Continental efforts.

SOCIAL DEMOCRATIC HEGEMONY

The success of these various policies has profound political consequences; it solidifies Social Democratic hegemony or, as Frank Castles has called it, "the Social Democratic image of society." Hegemony refers not so much to tenure in political office as to dominance in the sphere of values and culture. Sometimes this dominance manifests itself in electoral results—as in the 1960 and 1985 elections, which were virtual referenda on, respectively, the supplementary pension scheme and the welfare state in general. Even more telling, however, are periods when the party falls from power and policies do not change markedly—and if they do, the new policies result in electoral defeat for their proponents. This interpretation fits the period of bourgeois rule from 1976 to 1982. For four years social policy continued as before; when in 1980 the bourgeois government attempted to curtail the welfare state, it triggered a general lockout and a strike and spiraled down to electoral defeat. It is conceivable but premature to suggest that the 1980s mark the end of fifty years of Social Democratic hegemony. Safer is the conclusion that the period of Social Democratic ideology not only shaped public policies but citizens' conceptions of their country, its values, and their own personal commitments—in short, their personal identities.

To maintain a consistent record of radical reform, one that transforms society and individual citizens, a party must wield ideological as well as policy tools. As Diane Sainsbury (1980) has neatly demonstrated, ideology functions during elections to mobilize traditional supporters, to legitimate past and future policy, and to recruit new voters. The most telling impact of ideology, however, comes when it infiltrates opponents' thinking, first dividing them and thus facilitating reform, and eventually penetrating and reordering their outlook. Examples of this phenomenon abound in the history of twentieth-century Sweden, beginning with the conversion of the leaders of export industries to democracy by the end of World War I. In the late 1930s, Wigforss reported, many Social Democrats thought in terms of a "reformist utopia" in part because they saw how "social policy measures and forms of organization that earlier had been declared irreconcilable with the necessary conditions of existence for bourgeois society gradually became accepted." Finally, one saw in the 1985 election the remarkable spectacle of the Conservatives laying claim to the uncorrupted legacy of Per Albin Hansson and the *folkhemmet*. The diverse functions of ideology—to guide policy, to transform institutional procedures, to legitimate action, and to attract voters—gradually fuse in their ability to transform the most recalcitrant and the most decisive element of society, the human beings who compose it.

NOTES

1. Karleby 1976 (1926), 87.
2. Steffen 1920.
3. Ibid., 6.
4. Wigforss 1980, vol. 3; cf. chap. 6.
5. Hannson 1982, 227.

6. Okun 1975.
7. *Den produktiva rättvisan* (Landsorganisationen i Sverige, 1984).
8. Arbete och värdighet 1985.
9. Landsorganisationen i Sverige 1941.
10. Edin and Hedborg 1980, 54.
11. Ibid., 55.
12. Ibid., 54.
13. Branting 1929, 2:323.
14. On the 1911 program and its importance, see Simonson (1985) whom I follow closely.
15. Wigforss, 1980, vol. 9 (*Minnen*, vol. 3), 121.
16. Ibid., 122.
17. Hansson 1935, 205.
18. Abrahamson and Broström 1979.
19. Wigforss 1980, 3:310.
20. Ibid., 3:297.
21. Erlander 1973, 281.
22. For a somewhat different interpretation, see Steinmo (1988).
23. Erlander 1954, 21.
24. Kerr 1960; Wilensky 1975.
25. Korpi 1978; Stephens 1979; Castles 1978.
26. Skocpol 1980.
27. Therborn 1986.
28. Ruggie 1984.

Klas Åmark

Afterword:
Swedish Social Democracy
on a Historical Threshold

There are thresholds in time. When one steps over a time
threshold it is like entering a room where one has never
been.
—Ivar Lo-Johansson, *Tröskeln: Memoarer från 30-talet*
                (The Threshold: Memoirs from the Thirties)

THE PARTY IN A CRISIS OF CONFIDENCE

When the Social Democratic Labor Party celebrated its centenary in April
1989, it seemed that its unique position of power was intact. Soon after,
however, signals began to appear indicating otherwise. What happened?
Why has Swedish Social Democracy been deserted by the electorate, and
its faithful supporters rendered passive? Why has the party repeatedly got-
ten into public disputes with the Confederation of Trade Unions (LO)? Is it
a matter of temporary discord, or a fundamental and long-term crisis that
will have repercussions far into the future?

The crisis of confidence was most clearly demonstrated by opinion polls,
which gave a fairly consistent picture of potential electoral support for the
Social Democrats. In the spring of 1989 voter support dropped from the 43
percent held by the party in the 1988 election to 38 percent. One year
later, in spring 1990, support sank to a record low of about 32 percent.[1]
The foremost winners in the public opinion polls were the Moderata samlingspartiet (Conservative party) and the small Kristdemokratiska samhällspartiet (Christian Democratic Social party). The latter had no seats in

the Riksdag but for the first time passed with a good margin the magic 4 percent line, which qualifies a party for parliamentary representation in Sweden.

The election in September 1991 was the worst for the SAP since 1928: the party received only 37.6 percent of the votes, a fall of 5.6 percentage points since 1988. In Swedish terms, it was a major election failure; however, since the party's place in the opinion polls had been much lower for a long time prior to the election, the election campaign itself was considered quite a victory for the party and its leader, Ingvar Carlsson. The SAP also suffered losses in the concurrent municipal and county elections—especially in the larger cities.

The parties in the middle of the political spectrum—the Center party and the Liberals (the Folkpartiet)—also incurred losses in the election, as did the Left party. The Green party lost all its seats in the Riksdag. In this election with so many losers, the right-wing parties became the winners. The Conservative party (Moderata samlingspartiet), standing for economic liberalism, became clearly the largest bourgeois party, and its leader, Carl Bildt, the new prime minister—the first Conservative prime minister in Sweden since the 1920s. The Christian Democratic party, conservative in values, obtained seats in the Riksdag by a wide margin. The totally new populistic party of small business, Ny Demokrati (New Democracy), also entered the Riksdag.

Tendencies that have long been perceived in Swedish voting behavior have been reinforced. Among these tendencies may be mentioned mistrust of the established parties, especially of those responsible for implementing government policies; increasing numbers of blank votes; more and more last-minute voters; and a particularly great sensitivity to current opinion among youths and in the big cities. The Social Democrats lost ground especially in the three largest cities, Stockholm, Gothenburg, and Malmö. All three cities elected bourgeois majorities. The election was thus not only a great defeat for the SAP, but it also meant a marked destabilization of one of the Western world's most stable parliamentary systems. Both luck and skill deserted the Social Democrats.

My thesis is that the party's long-term power base was severely disrupted around 1990. Among the structural changes behind this disruption were internationalization and the growth of a strong new middle class. These changes in turn affected the ability of Social Democrats to enter into class alliances successfully. Likewise, the Social Democrats altered the content of their policies so that they no longer stood for what Göran Therborn in this volume has called "class politics" (see Chapter 1). The universal social policy, the significance of which has been indicated by Gösta Esping-Andersen (see Chapter 2), has been questioned by the Social Democrats themselves. The Swedish variant of a Keynesian policy of balancing business cycles was put aside after the election victory in 1982 and replaced by a supply-side policy that created disputes between the government and the working class and between the party and the LO. The Social Democratic movement no longer represented the conviction pointed to by Tim Tilton (see Chapter 13), namely, that equality and economic efficiency could be combined. Equality was sacrificed on the altar of economic growth.

At the beginning of the 1990s, and under the pressure of sinking figures in opinion polls, the Social Democrats were forced to develop a new economic policy that followed upon the results of the "policy of the third way." Consequently, they had to make decisions on a number of momentous questions that had been deferred for several years, partly because of the party's lack of unity and uncertainty about their solutions.

THE ECONOMY AND TAXES

The economic crisis of the mid-1970s led to substantial budget deficits (peaking in fiscal year 1983/1984) and rising unemployment, which even at its most extensive (3.5 percent) was low by international standards. By 1988 the budget was balanced, and registered unemployment was just over 1 percent. The major problems issuing from the economic crisis and the periods of bourgeois government from 1976 to 1982 had thus been solved.

The most important goals of the policy of the "third way" had been attained. The government was now free to tackle new problems. A shift was particularly noticeable in Finance Minister Kjell-Olof Feldt's last budget in January 1990.[2] Inflation was presented as the greatest threat to Swedish welfare and to a just distribution of wealth and income. Inflation also threatened to undermine the competitive power of Swedish industry on international markets. Substantial devaluations at the beginning of the 1980s had given the Swedish export industry palpable advantages over its international competitors. The devaluations, however, had not been used to lower prices and augment exports, but mainly to improve the industry's profit margins. Toward the end of the decade the advantages derived from devaluating the krona had been largely used up. Competitive power and market shares became key words in the economic and political debate, and the complications of the supply-side policy for the labor movement became increasingly evident.

Sweden's allegedly weak economic growth was cited as a pivotal problem. The notion of feeble economic growth was a dogma particularly among bourgeois economists and politicians, but it was a concern shared by the finance minister. Yet, as the sociologist Walter Korpi has shown, this notion rests on flimsy foundations: in comparison with the richest OECD countries Swedish growth is not notably low.[3]

The deficit in the balance of payments at the end of the 1980s was a new problem, further aggravated by the fact that the government and the National Bank of Sweden gradually discontinued currency controls. They were totally abolished in 1989. This increased the risk of sudden currency outflows when actors in the currency market mistrusted the government's economic policy, a scenario that would require rapid intervention by the government. Precisely this occurred in autumn 1990.

A major tax reform—"the tax reform of the century," according to Social Democratic rhetoric—was presented as a panacea for the ailing economy. At its conference in 1987 the party had drawn up guidelines for a major tax reform that would reduce marginal taxes, broaden the tax base, and limit deductions. Taxation of various kinds of income and benefits was to be as uniform as possible. These proposed changes in the tax code meant that the Social Democrats, in effect, would no longer be using tax policy to redistribute income.

Several large committees were formed to present investigations on which decisions would be based. How comprehensive the reform would be, however, was not made clear.[4] The committees' reports were presented in several thick volumes in the summer of 1989.[5] The following autumn the Social Democrats and the Folkpartiet (Liberal party) agreed upon the main elements of "the tax reform of the century."

The main proposal contained several important fundamental principles.[6] Most wage earners were to pay the same local taxes as earlier—about 30 percent. A national income tax of 20 percent would be levied on taxpayers with the highest incomes—approximately 10 percent of taxpayers—resulting in the marginal tax of 50 percent the Liberals had demanded in the election campaign of 1988. The major difference, therefore, concerned the national taxes. Most high-income wage earners had previously paid a national tax of up to 45 percent of their income. The calculated cost of the tax reform was approximately 65–70 billion kronor.

The tax reform was to be financed in several different ways. A uniform tax of 30 percent on capital income was introduced, and deductions were radically reduced. These measures were intended to intensify taxation on capital while diminishing opportunities for tax avoidance and tax evasion. The value-added tax (*moms*) would be extended to several areas not previously covered. A significant part of the tax reform would be financed through increased housing costs. The reform also included a large number of detailed and complicated regulations that were meant to simplify the complex Swedish tax system.

When a reduction of marginal taxes is financed by a raised value-added tax and increases in the cost of housing, high-income earners inevitably will be favored at the expense of low-income earners. This effect had indeed been noted in the objections to the Liberals' tax policy during the election campaign of 1988, and it contributed to that party's poor election results. From autumn 1989 the objections were also leveled at the Social Democrats. The changes in capital taxation, however, should have the opposite effect, favoring low-income earners; but there has been a remarkable silence in the public debate about that part of the tax reform, even from the Social Democrats.

For those claiming that state involvement in the economy leads to faults in the system, agricultural policy has long provided a good example. Since the crisis of the 1930s state intervention in the agricultural economy has been considerable. By means of a complicated system of negotiation, agrarian interest organizations have been able to exert substantial influence over state expenditures on agriculture.

Consequently, deregulation of agriculture has recently been considered one of the most important measures for increasing the market features in the Swedish economy and for facilitating adaptation to the EC (European Community). The Riksdag ruled on the issue in June 1990, approving a certain degree of deregulation in setting the prices of some agricultural products. According to the government, deregulation in agriculture is essential for reducing food prices in Sweden.[7]

Whether this is indeed true is still being debated, but in the summer of 1991 food prices actually dropped slightly. Border protection continues, pending GATT negotiations on a general termination of international restrictions on agricultural commerce. The government made proposals on this in spring 1991.[8]

Sweden's relationship with the EC is one of the most important issues in current Swedish politics. Sweden has long been one of the leading members of EFTA (European Free Trade Association), which has been negotiating with the EC about closer cooperation. This aspect has been fairly uncontentious; whether Sweden should be a full member of the Common Market is another matter.

One of the most crucial obstacles to membership has been Swedish neutrality. To an initiated observer, however, it became apparent at the party conference in autumn 1990 that the party leadership was prepared to recommend full EC membership in a few years' time. In conjunction with the currency crisis arising in the autumn of 1990, the Social Democrats publicly announced that they would prepare for application for full membership in the EC, with the proviso of retained Swedish neutrality.[9] This turnabout was supported by the bourgeois parties, and in December 1990 the Riksdag authorized the government to apply for membership.[10] Only representatives of the Vänsterpartiet (Left party, former communists) and the Miljöpartiet (Green party) protested.

The Social Democrats' change of attitude toward this issue was a great surprise to the general public. Many statements from leading Social Democrats had given the voters reason to believe that the party did not want—or at least was doubtful about—membership in the EC. But leading party members apparently had changed their minds some time earlier and deliberately waited for a suitable occasion before declaring openly an opinion they knew was controversial within their own party. The SAP continued this new offensive in its 1991 election platform, outlining a vision of a future Social Democratic EC.[11] The decision of the Social Democrats to seek membership in the EC was directly affected by the great changes in Eastern Europe. The relaxation of Cold War tensions meant that Swedish membership no longer clearly placed Sweden in one of the two great power blocs.

THE SAP AND THE LO

With the substantial growth of the public sector, Social Democratic politicians have assumed an increasingly important role as employers. Meanwhile, they continue to represent the workers' political interests. After 1982 the conflict between these two roles became more marked: in official party documents the party favored solidaristic wage policy, but in reality party support has been less clear-cut.

The State Employers Administration also accepted the SAF (Swedish Employers Confederation) wage philosophy: that wages are a tool for management and shall be used to encourage individual commitment and to solve market-conditioned recruitment problems. This requires, among other things, major changes in the wage structure and in relations between individual and group wages.[12]

It is not possible to carry out such changes and at the same time hold wage levels down. Employers, and especially the state, find themselves in a dilemma, the extent of which they have not fully grasped. Different wage policy goals intersect and are difficult to implement simultaneously. The burden of responsibility for wage increases in Sweden (which are continually higher than increases in productivity) lies therefore not only with wage-earner organizations, but very much with employers and with the Social Democrats, who have been the largest employers in the country by virtue of their political power over the state, local, and county authorities.

Sweden's high inflation is often referred to by leading politicians and economists as the cause of the much too high wage rises. According to Social Democratic wage policy, checking wage increases is an absolute necessity for successful economic development. This has been proclaimed so often and so forcefully by finance ministers that it has lost credibility among wage earners and the general public. Since 1982 the government has tried to influence wage negotiations in various ways without taking the full step of devising a state income policy, so the effects of government involvement have been limited.[13]

The government continued to follow the supply-side policy embarked upon after the 1982 election. This policy requires restraints when the economy is on the decline, and it has created new tensions between the party and the LO. In the supplement to the budget in spring 1989 a raised value-added tax was proposed as a central restraint measure—immediately after parties on the labor market had signed two-year contracts.[14] The proposal met with emphatic protests from the LO and was not supported by the Riksdag.[15]

The problem had not been solved by spring 1990. Wage drifts were extensive, and they rendered the 1989 wage contracts almost worthless. Moreover, certain groups of government employees, especially teachers and the police, had received huge raises. Drastic measures to hinder continued compensation disputes among wage earners seemed necessary when discussions between the government and labor market parties came to naught.

In February 1990 the government presented a remarkable proposal, for which it managed to obtain the LO's support.[16] The proposal called for a total wage freeze during 1990 and 1991, price and rent freezes, a freeze on stock dividends, and a freeze on local authority taxes. The most sensational aspect of the proposal, however, was a total ban on strikes coupled with heavily increased strike penalties. The proposal was presented while bank employees were out on strike and local authority employees were on the verge of open conflict.

The government thought that it had the support of LO leadership. But when LO members and the public turned out to be against the proposal, the LO's leader, Stig Malm, was forced to retreat and make apologies to his membership. Neither was there support for the controversial proposal in the Riksdag, and the SAP had to back down, proposing that obligatory industrial peace be replaced by obligatory mediation.[17] This modification, however, was no help. The crisis package failed in the Riksdag, and the government fell, resigning because the bourgeois parties refused on principle to approve a proposal for a strike ban that had attracted the support of many LO union chairs.[18]

Nevertheless, the bourgeois parties were not prepared to form a government or to call a new election. Ingvar Carlsson returned as prime minister but with a new finance minister: Feldt was succeeded by Allan Larsson, former general director of the National Labor Market Board. The change in ministers did not have much effect on economic policy.

The acute crisis was resolved with a new crisis package that the government negotiated with the Liberals. It contained a temporary hike in the value-added tax and certain cuts in the social insurance system.[19] The electorate's judgment on the crisis package was severe: support for the Social Democrats fell to approximately 32 percent of those indicating a party preference, and it remained at that low level for another year.

In autumn 1990 a new public dispute broke out between the party and the LO. Stig Malm, chair of the LO, published a very harsh criticism of the government's economic policy, attacking both its tax policy and its acute crisis policy. He even asserted that the economic crisis was not serious enough to warrant the drastic measures that so affected LO members.

This time Malm received a good deal of support from his membership, but the reaction from the party leadership and the parliamentary group was harsh. At quickly arranged meetings attended by the party's executive committee (of which Malm was a member), the chairs of LO unions, and the parliamentary group, Malm was compelled to apologize to the finance minister and members of the Riksdag for his personal attack. This public confrontation in all likelihood had been preceded by a long internal debate between the LO and SAP leadership in which LO leaders criticized the SAP's economic policy for favoring high-income groups to the detriment of LO members. The acute crisis within the Social Democratic movement was resolved in a characteristic way: a common working group was formed for the purpose of preparing the platform for the parliamentary elections in 1991.

The SAP election platform, presented in January 1991,[20] suggests a party leading with its left foot. Traditional Social Democratic goals are invoked in order to assure party members and voters that the party is what it used to be. Thus, full employment is hailed as the priority, over and above fighting inflation. The platform also defends policy over and against the market, that is, the possibility of creating both economic growth and just distribution through state regulation and control of the economy. To this extent the platform is a traditional one. But the party must be more open than it has been in the past when choosing the means to attain its ends.

THE PUBLIC SECTOR

One issue in Swedish politics that has been both central and diffuse is the restructuring of the public sector. Debureaucratization, decentralization, and efficiency were important goals for Social Democracts during the 1980s, but success in reform has been limited.[21] The debate on the "system faults" in Swedish society has continued indefatigably, and the demands by bourgeois parties for cuts, privatization, and greater efficiency in the public sector have been made with unmitigated force.[22]

Educational policy has been important in Sweden and for the Social Democrats since 1945. Despite great investments, economic and political, many problems in education have only increased. The schools have also become a symbol for rigid and inept bureaucracy—inefficient and showing diminishing "productivity." Economists declare that costs per student have increased instead of decreased. In the debates on education, economic and pedagogical arguments are mixed together.

One of the problems often identified in school management is that many teachers are state employees, whereas other areas of responsibility lie with the local authorities. Education Minister Göran Persson (who was sometimes pointed to as Ingvar Carlsson's crown prince) was directed in 1989 to transfer the responsibility for teachers' salaries to the local authorities as part of the decentralization of the public sector. At the same time, he was supposed to address the heated issue of teachers' wages and hours. Teachers' pay, especially that of comprehensive school teachers, had over several decades dropped so low in relation to other wage levels that problems with teacher recruitment were becoming acute.

The academically educated teachers organized in the SACO (Swedish Confederation of Professional Associations) went on strike to protest the reforms and the leveling of wages within the teaching corps. With the support of the Left party, however, the government's reforms were approved by the Riksdag, to take effect in 1991.[23] The state as employer, represented by the State Administration for Collective Bargaining,[24] also agreed to an exceptionally high wage rise in order to relieve recruitment problems and to facilitate carrying out the reform, despite all the finance minister's words of warning in his budget.

SOCIAL POLICY

In the debate on the effects and desirability of state intervention in the economy and social life, social transfers play a major role. The public sector's portion of the GNP dropped from about 67 percent at the beginning of the 1980s to about 60 percent in 1990. A considerable portion of the total resources of society nonetheless passes through the public sector, and about half of that portion consists of social transfers through the system of social insurance. Should there be a system shift in the Swedish economy, something drastic will have to be done about the universal social insurance policy.

The two largest segments of this system are health insurance and pensions. It is part and parcel of traditional Social Democratic policy to defend the system of social insurance against bourgeois attacks and to safeguard a universal social policy. However, even within the Social Democratic movement changes in the system have been discussed; and in fact, decisions made around 1990 altered several aspects of the system.

Toward the end of the 1980s, after wage contract insurance was combined with state insurance, health insurance benefits rose to almost 100 percent of most people's income from work. That is, when a worker was sick, he or she could usually collect benefits equivalent to his or her salary. Even Social Democrats increasingly accepted the idea that such a level was too high if people were to be encouraged to work as much as possible. In addition, serious problems with early pensions and rehabilitation of the chronically ill and those with occupational injuries arose. During 1990 the Social Democrats investigated various ways of attacking these problems. In conjunction with the acute economic crisis in the autumn of 1990, when the state should have been retrenching the economy, a reduction in the level of compensation for the first three months of sick leave was proposed.[25]

The Social Democrats have long defended the universal retirement pensions that had given the party such political success during the 1960s. But in the 1991/1992 budget proposal, Finance Minister Allan Larsson let it be known that he was willing to contemplate a change in the pension system, making it more individual and encouraging more individual saving[26]—that is, moving in the direction advocated by the bourgeois parties.

Within family policy and related areas, major choices also have had to be made. In preparation for the election campaign of 1988, the LO's leadership persuaded the party that a sixth week of vacation was more important than the reduction of working hours demanded especially by the National Federation of Social Democratic Women. The party also promised to extend the right of parents to remain at home to care for children from twelve to fifteen months, with state parental insurance benefits. This pledge, however, was withdrawn in the crisis package presented in spring 1990.[27]

ENVIRONMENTAL POLICY AND ECONOMIC GROWTH

After the 1979 nuclear accident at Three Mile Island in the United States, there was a referendum in Sweden on nuclear energy. It was not a matter of merely saying yes or no; the voters were faced with three quite ambiguous proposals. None clearly won approval, but the proposal for rapid dismantling failed to gain a majority. The Social Democratic and Liberal line called for retaining already existing nuclear power plants in Sweden and those being built, but dismantling them gradually—a process to begin in 1995 and to be completed by 2010.[28]

Doubts about this position have been growing. Industry and representatives of certain LO unions have claimed that nuclear power is needed for the energy-intensive production sector and that other energy sources are still too dangerous for the environment—in spite of the Chernobyl accident, fallout from which also hit Sweden. In early 1991 the Social Democrats came to an agreement with the Liberal party and the antinuclear Center party (the former Agrarian party) that entailed modifying the previous decision to begin winding down nuclear power facilities in 1995; but 2010 remained as the end date for the Social Democrats and the Center party.

An excellent example of the way in which policies on the environment have given way to those on economic growth is the proposed Öresund Bridge. Sweden (and Norway) lacks land connections with the European continent (apart from the connection to Finland, in the north). The proposal to build a bridge over the sound (Öresund) between Sweden and Denmark was part of the plan to expand and improve the road system from Norway and Sweden to Europe and the EC. Environmentalists protested this one-sided commitment to road traffic and motor vehicles at the expense of collective or rail transport. The SAP conference in autumn 1990 approved the proposal to build a bridge with both road and rail facilities, but a large minority objected and proposed a rail tunnel instead.[29] In both of these central environmental issues, environmentalists within the party have had to give way to forces favoring growth.

THE BREAKDOWN OF CLASS POLITICS

Despite the difficulties confronting the Social Democratic movement in the 1990s, there are some grounds for optimism, at least in the short term. The tax reform improved the financial condition of many wage earners. The party leadership demonstrated firmness by making decisions on a number of vital issues. The first election platform of the 1990s showed that the Social Democrats, after a period of vacillation and internal conflicts, had returned to policies built on traditional Social Democratic values. All this argues for a recovery for the party.

However, other factors seem to indicate that the party's crisis is deeper and more long-lasting. One of the major causes of the crisis lies in Social Democratic welfare policy. Methods must be found that enable the expanded welfare state to reform itself and to raise the quality of its welfare—in health care, social services, education, and elsewhere. Without continual qualitative development and more economically effective administration, there are two very real dangers: that growth in the whole economy will stagnate, and that citizens' confidence in the welfare state and in politics as a means of steering it will be undermined.

Those who argue that the SAP should return to its traditional policies are therefore wrong, strategically. The present large problems in the public sector cannot be solved by traditional Social Democratic politics. The reverses experienced by the Social Democratic movement are ultimately connected with the failure of traditional forces to find methods for renewal. Simply maintaining the old politics is no solution for either the Social Democratic Labor Party or the welfare state. The Social Democrats face similar dilemmas in other areas, perhaps most obviously in environmental issues. After the election in 1988 the Social Democrats demonstrated clearly that, when push comes to shove, they would choose growth over the environment. This choice alienates environmentalists from the party.

It has been claimed that since about 1982 the Social Democratic movement has chosen a new political line, a right-wing position promoting economic growth over welfare and equitable distribution policies. For this reason the party has lost many of its left-wing voters and activists. This assertion has been supported by voter studies.[30]

The aim of the party leadership seems to have been to gain support among the large middle groups of white-collar workers and well-paid workers (most SAP politicians themselves belong to these groups). It was thought that low-paid workers would remain loyal to the party in the absence of any political alternatives. This policy was already in force during the pension dispute in the 1950s, and it was successful then. But by 1990 the tactic failed to function. More and more SAP voters and activists opted for passivity rather than having to defend to their co-workers, friends, and neighbors what they deemed their leadership's right-wing politics—for instance, in the tax issue. There was, apparently, some threshold of disgrace for ordinary members that the party unwittingly overstepped in 1989–1990. Yet many of these voters seemed to return to the SAP just before the election. It is too early to say whether this was due to the attractions of Social Democratic policies or to fears of having as prime minister the Conservative party leader, Carl Bildt.

But why has the party not attracted new voters and sympathizers on the right to compensate for the losses on the left? There are two factors at work here. First, the SAP's new policies have been carried out in collaboration with the Liberals and/or the Center party. Why should supporters of these two parties switch over to the SAP when their own parties are working in collaboration with it? Second, Social Democratic dominance in the domestic ideological debate has been undermined. The political field has been stretched to the right, and this has been accompanied by an increased understanding of the advantages of the market and the benefits of privatization. These changes, frankly, have occurred more rapidly than SAP policy development. The political distance between the Conservative party's neoliberal economic policy and the Social Democratic position is in fact greater in 1991 than it was in 1982. The election results also showed a comprehensive swing to the right within the Swedish electorate. It was therefore in the climate of public debate that the greatest changes occurred during the second half of the 1980s. In the public arena the Social Democratic movement has lost much of the dominance it had held since the 1930s.

However, the fall of the communist regimes in Eastern Europe does not herald the demise of social democracy in Sweden, despite assertions to the contrary by certain Swedish commentators. The Swedish social system is totally different from anything in Eastern Europe, and Sweden faces problems distinct from those faced by Eastern European countries. That being said, the fall of the communist regimes has contributed toward changing the ideological climate. Trust in state regulation of the market economy has, for example, been weakened—even within the Swedish left.

Thus, from 1988 to 1991 the Social Democrats made decisions on a number of important questions, and in several instances these decisions indicated a change of direction. Some of the decisions were prepared in the party conferences of 1987 and 1990, but others came as surprises, at least to the general public and to many ordinary party members. This is particularly true both for the move regarding the EC and for the final composition of the tax reform, with its low state tax. At the same time a certain ambivalence and ambiguity existed in Social Democratic policies on several important issues, and this has made it difficult for both voters and ordinary party members to perceive long-term political aims. There are reasons for recalling the words of Prime Minister Tage Erlander after the election failures of 1966: "The most damaging statement made about us during the entire election campaign was Hedlund's [the Center party leader] . . . that one did not recognize the Social Democrats."[31]

Ambiguity and changes of direction have contributed to the widespread conception that the party has abandoned traditional Social Democratic politics. From a scientific point of view this is a complicated assertion that is difficult to analyze. Social democracy has a rich legacy of ideas; it embraces a liberal social tradition, which was especially prominent around 1960, and a radical tradition, which informed policy during the first half of the 1970s. Some of the problems voters may have in recognizing the party are likely dependent upon a normal pattern of swings—in 1990 from left to right— within the framework of previous Social Democratic politics. In other respects, though, recent Social Democratic political behavior clearly suggests a change in relation to the party's one-hundred-year-old traditions.

The idea that equality and efficiency can be made to harmonize, which was so important when welfare policies were developed and expanded in the 1950s and 1960s, was seemingly abandoned in the early 1980s. Likewise, the ambition to steer the economy with the assistance of politics has been markedly reduced, especially in comparison with the high-flying plans of the 1970s. Full membership in the EC does not mesh with what the party has been asserting publicly since the 1950s. The leadership has acted as though increased inequality is necessary in order to raise economic efficiency, in both the economy and the public sector. Groups with reasons to feel especially threatened by these new attitudes include low-wage earners and women in the public sector.

At the beginning of the 1980s the party leadership chose to put their trust in liberal economists and their supply-side policy instead of in Social Democratic economists and their own "model" —a counterpart of the Rhen model of the 1950s. It may be argued that a supply-side policy can never be Social Democratic; but as long as the only alternative is a Swedish version of conventional balancing of the business cycles, the argument is hardly credible. New ideas for shaping a Social Democratic macroeconomic policy are lacking.

THE "STEEL CAGE" OF STRUCTURES—OR THE VICTORY OF THE MIDDLE CLASSES?

There are other, more complicated reasons why the SAP has failed to assert a traditional Social Democratic profile in the 1980s and the beginning of the 1990s. New structures have forced the Social Democratic movement to alter its policies, and they have obstructed the possibilities of steering the country by political means. Most important in this context is internationalization. Sweden has an open economy with a large export industry. This means that the rules governing the Swedish economy must conform successively to those applying in the major competitor countries, not least

. those in the EC. Consequently, Sweden must adapt to conditions in other countries, regardless of whether the Swedish people want to or whether Sweden becomes a member of the Common Market. The prerequisites for an independent Swedish stance, a unique Swedish model, are thus much weaker than they were before. The abolition of currency regulation meant that Sweden could no longer make any greater demands on capital than ' were made in other countries. The costs for a specific Swedish environmental or regional policy would thereafter have to be shifted onto other production factors, not least the labor force.[32]

However, there is also a more limited, domestic structural change that has particularly affected the Social Democrats and their relations with the LO and other parties on the labor market. The ideal of industrial peace and compromise associated with the Swedish model is no longer viable. New white-collar groups have made themselves heard in the struggle over contracts, and they show little social responsibility. They are not as close to the SAP as is the LO, and they enter into labor disputes only when it serves their purpose to do so. By international standards they are well organized in unions. At the same time, union organizations for white-collar workers are less centralized than the LO, and they no longer accept the LO's hegemony over wage policy. Many white-collar workers demand that wage policy solidarity be abandoned and replaced by individual wage contracts that reward competence and education. The workers within the LO still outnumber white-collar workers by more than two to one, but the TCO (Swedish Confederation of Professional Employees) negotiates for about the same total wage sum as the LO because TCO members have much higher wages than LO members. So the TCO is much more important for the Swedish economy than its membership numbers show.

Now, when the Swedish model is undergoing great changes—possibly even leading to its ultimate disintegration[33]—the question arises: Who will abolish it? The Swedish model must be seen as a result of conscious choices and not determined by socioeconomic development; that is, it should be seen as a kind of informal contract between different interests and parties in Swedish society. It rests on a compromise between the strongest and best-organized reformist labor movement in the world and the strongest and best-organized capital sector. The weak and poorly organized middle groups in society have had to pay the price for this balance of power. The long-term social changes that are now solidifying have, therefore, strengthened the middle groups considerably. White-collar workers have become a large social group, well organized in unions; but they lack both a common ideology that can meld them together and a centralized leadership that can guarantee compromises with the other blocs. For the SAP, white-collar groups are difficult to handle as coalition partners in a power struggle.

These middle strata often do not accept the dominance of the labor movement in, for example, wage policy and distribution questions. They demand a new type of wage differentiation and distribution policy that would give the well-educated, competent, and industrious worker individual opportunities for economic rewards.

Although the effects of the major redistributions occurring in Sweden since the mid-1970s (resulting from the state budget deficit, devaluations, inflation, and the large increase in the value of stocks and property) have not yet created a wealthy and well-situated upper-middle class, the tendency exists and will become more and more important in Swedish politics. The increasing prosperity of many middle-class households creates a market for the privatization of health and social services and education that has not previously existed in Sweden. With the new parliamentary party, the Ny Demokrati (New Democracy), Sweden has obtained a typical Scandinavian party of dissent and also a political representative for many dissatisfied small-business people who are tightly wedged between organized capitalism and the Social Democratic state. The Ny Demokrati seems as well to have brought together antiforeigner sentiments amongst the population. The economic policy of the "third way" has contributed to the formation of new social actors who threaten the dominance of the Social Democratic Labor Party and, ultimately, the existence of Social Democratic society itself.

NOTES

1. Monthly opinion polls published by SIFO (Swedish Institute of Public Opinion Research) in *Svenska Dagbladet* and other newspapers, by TEMO in *Dagens Nyheter* and elsewhere, and less often by the Statistiska Centralbyrån (Central Bureau of Statistics), which interviews many more people than do the other agencies.

2. Proposition no. 100, 1989/1990, app. 1 (also published as *Government Budget Proposal 1989/90*, Ministry of Finance, 1989). See also Proposition no. 150, 1989/1990 (*Revised Budget*).

3. See articles in the journal *Ekonomisk debatt* (Economic Debate), nos, 5, 6, 7, and 8, 1990.

4. *SAP Conference Minutes* 1987; SOU 1989:33, 34, 35, 38.

5. SOU 1989:33, 34, 35, 38. The guidelines for the tax reform were approved by the party executive on 22 Nov. 1988.

6. Proposition nos. 50 and 110, 1989/1990.

7. Proposition no. 146, 1989/1990; Agricultural Committee Report 1989/1990, no. 25.

8. Proposition no. 87, 1990/1991, p. 14.

9. *SAP Conference Minutes* 1990; government paper no. 50, 1990/1991.

10. Foreign Policy Committee Report no. 8, 1990/1991: *Sweden and West European Integration,* 22 Nov. 1990.

11. SAP Political Platform, adopted by the party executive and LO executive 24 Jan. 1991, *Facts and Background; Sweden in a New Europe; Political Report* no. 2, 1991.

12. See Sjölund 1987, 1989.

13. See, e.g., government budget proposals 1986/1987–1990/1991, and Ahlén 1989.

14. Proposition no. 150, 1988/1989 *(Revised Budget).*

15. Finance Committee Report no. 30, 1988/1989.

16. Government Proposition no. 95, 1988/1989.

17. Motion no. 2, 1989/1990 Labor Market Committee (L. Ulander et al.).

18. Finance Committee Report no. 20, 1989/1990.

19. Proposition no. 114, 1989/1990; Finance Committee Report no. 10, Riksdag Papers nos. 204, 205.

20. Political platform adopted by the SAP's party executive and the LO's secretariat on Jan. 24, 1991 (see also the election manifesto adopted by the party executive, 16 Aug. 1991).

21. An account of goals and ambitions may be found in the government proposition no. 100, 1990/1991, app. 2, *Development of the Public Sector* (Ministry for Civil Service Affairs). See also Proposition no. 14, 1990/1991, *Responsibility for Service and Care of the Elderly and Disabled.* . . .

22. See, e.g., Olsson 1990.

23. Government Proposition no. 41, 1989/1990; Education Committee Report no. 9, 1989/1990; and Riksdag Paper no. 58, 1989/1990. See also Proposition no. 18, 1990/1991, and no. 4, 1988/1989.

24. This institution negotiates for the state with all state employees.

25. Government Paper no. 51, 1990/1991.

26. Budget Proposal 1991/1992.

27. Proposition no. 114, 1989/1990; Finance Committee Report no. 20, 1989/1990; Riksdag Papers nos. 204, 205.

28. See, e.g., Larsson 1986; Holmberg and Asp 1984.

29. *SAP Conference Minutes* 1990.

30. Walter Korpi in *Aftonbladet,* 16 Jan. 1991.

31. Cited by Therborn in the present volume, p. 26.

32. See *Demokrati och makt i Sverige* (Democracy and Power in Sweden), the main report from Maktutredningen (Power Inquiry), SOU 1990:44, chaps. 10 and 11; *Makt och internationalisering,* 1990.

33. An opinion put forth by the Power Inquiry in its final report; cf. chap. 11.

Appendix

Governments, 1888–1991

Prime ministers

6 Feb. 1888–12 Oct. 1889	D. A. Gillis Bildt
12 Oct. 1889–10 July 1891	Gustaf Åkerhielm
10 July 1891–12 Sept. 1900	Erik Gustaf Boström
12 Sept. 1900–5 July 1902	Fredrik F. von Otter
5 July 1902–13 Apr. 1905	Erik Gustaf Boström II
13 Apr. 1905–2 Aug. 1905	Johan O. Ramstedt
2 Aug. 1905–7 Nov. 1905	Christian Lundeberg

Governments

7 Nov. 1905–29 May 1906	Liberal (Karl Staaff)
29 May 1906–7 Oct. 1911	Conservative (Arvid Lindman)
7 Oct. 1911–17 Feb. 1914	Liberal (Karl Staaff)
17 Feb. 1914–30 Mar. 1917	Conservative (caretaker government) (Hjalmar Hammarskjöld)
30 Mar. 1917–19 Oct. 1917	Conservative (Carl Swartz)
19 Oct. 1917–10 Mar. 1920 [a]	Liberal–Social Democratic coalition (Nils Edén)
10 Mar. 1920–27 Oct. 1920	Social Democratic (Hjalmar Branting)
27 Oct. 1920–13 Oct. 1921	Stopgap government (Louis De Geer the younger; Oscar von Sydow)
13 Oct. 1921–19 Apr. 1923	Social Democratic (Hjalmar Branting)
19 Apr. 1923–18 Oct. 1924	Conservative (Ernst Trygger)
18 Oct. 1924–7 June 1926	Social Democratic (Hjalmar Branting, d. 24 Feb. 1925; Rickard Sandler)
7 June 1926–2 Oct. 1928	Coalition government: *Frisinnade* (libertarians/freethinkers) [b]–Liberal (Carl Gustaf Ekman)

2 Oct. 1928–7 June 1930	Conservative (Arvid Lindman)
7 June 1930–24 Sept. 1932	*Frisinnade* (Carl Gustaf Ekman; Felix Hamrin)
24 Sept. 1932–19 June 1936	Social Democratic (Per Albin Hansson)
19 June 1936–28 Sept. 1936	Agrarian (Axel Pehrsson-Bramstorp)
28 Sept. 1936–13 Dec. 1939	Social Democratic–Agrarian coalition (Per Albin Hansson)
13 Dec. 1939–31 July 1945	Four-party coalition: Social Democratic–Conservative–Liberal–Agrarian (Per Albin Hansson)
31 July 1945–1 Oct. 1951	Social Democratic (Per Albin Hansson, d. 6 Oct. 1946; Tage Erlander)
1 Oct. 1951–31 Oct. 1957	Social Democratic–Agrarian coalition (Tage Erlander)
31 Oct. 1957–8 Oct. 1976	Social Democratic (Tage Erlander to 14 Oct. 1969; Olof Palme)
8 Oct. 1976–18 Oct. 1978	Three-party coalition: *Centerpartiet* (Center, formerly Agrarian)–*Moderata samlingspartiet* (Conservative)–*Folkpartiet* (Liberal) (Thorbjörn Fälldin)
18 Oct. 1978–12 Oct. 1979	*Folkpartiet* (Liberal) (Ola Ullsten)
12 Oct. 1979–22 May 1981	Three-party coalition: *Centerpartiet* (Center)–*Moderata samlingspartiet* (Conservative)–*Folkpartiet* (Liberal) (Thorbjörn Fälldin)
22 May 1981–8 Oct. 1982	Coalition: *Centerpartiet* (Center)–*Folkpartiet* (Liberal) (Thorbjörn Fälldin)
8 Oct. 1982–1 Oct. 1991	Social Democratic (Olof Palme, d. 28 Feb. 1986; Ingvar Carlsson)
1 Oct. 1991–	Four-party coalition: *Moderata samlingspartiet* (Conservative)–*Folkpartiet* (Liberal)–*Centerpartiet* (Center)–*Kristdemokratiska samhällspartiet* (Christian Democratic) (Carl Bildt)

Notes: The party-political orientation of the governments is indicated after 1905 (Karl Staaff, Liberal). As a rule, the governments up to that date were nonpartisan, appointed by the crown, and hence lacked clear party-political profiles. For these governments only the prime ministers' names are given.

[a] The Liberal–Social Democratic government of Nils Edén and Hjalmar Branting, formed in 1917, is usually referred to as the first parliamentary government in Sweden.

[b] The name *Frisinnade* refers to the party's connections with religious groups and assemblies that are independent of the Swedish state church.

	Swedish Social Democratic Labor Party Membership 1889–1991	
Year	No. of Members	Population (December 31)
1889	3,194	
1890	6,922	4,774,409
1900	44,100	5,136,441
1905	67,325	
1906	101,929	
1907	133,388	
1908	112,693	
1909	60,813	
1910	55,248	5,522,403
1914	84,410	
1915	85,937	
1916	105,275	
1917	114,450	
1918	129,432	
1920	143,090	5,904,489
1930	227,017	6,142,191
1940	487,257	6,371,432
1950	722,073	7,041,829
1960	801,068	7,497,967
1970	890,070	8,081,229
1974	1,001,406	(The number of members exceeds one million.)
1980	1,205,252	8,317,937
1983	1,233,166	(The party's highest membership figure.)
1986	1,207,383	
1987	1,163,555	
1988	1,116,218	
1989	1,014,565	
1990	838,822	8,590,630
1991	259,077	

Sources: Social Democrats, Verksamhetsberättelser (Annual Reports), 1989, 1990, 1991; Historisk statistik för Sverige I (Historical Statistics for Sweden I), 1955; Statistisk årsbok (Statistical Yearbook).

Note: The number of members is given per decade. Particular years characterized by marked membership fluctuations are also given (the years before and after the strike in 1909; during World War I; and at the end of the 1980s; see chap. 4). The decline in membership after 1988 may be explained by the fact that collective affiliation (i.e., collective membership in the party of local trade union organizations) had been abolished. For purposes of comparison population figures for the whole country are given per decade.

SOCIAL DEMOCRATIC LABOR PARTY LEADERS, 1907–1991

HJALMAR BRANTING (1860–1925) became the leading figure of the Social Democratic Labor Party soon after its formation in 1989. He was the party's first conference-elected chair in 1907. Branting was the first Social Democrat to be elected to the Riksdag in 1896. He was finance minister from 1917 to 1918, prime minister in the first Social Democratic government in 1920, and prime minister from 1921 to 1923 and from 1924 until his death in 1925. He was succeeded as prime minister (but not as party leader) by his partymate Rickard Sandler (1884–1964).

PER ALBIN HANSSON (1885–1946) was chosen party chairman by the party conference in 1928 (deputy party leader in 1925). He was elected to the Riksdag in 1918 and served as defense minister in 1920, 1921–1923, and 1924–1926. He formed the Social Democratic government in 1932 and was prime minister until his death in 1946.

TAGE ERLANDER (1901–85) succeeded Per Albin Hansson as party chair and prime minister in 1946. He was elected to the Riksdag in 1932, was minister without portfolio (i.e., junior minister without his own department) from 1944 to 1945, and was minister of education from 1945 to 1946. He resigned as party chair and prime minister in 1969.

OLOF PALME (1927–86) succeeded Tage Erlander as party chair and prime minister in 1969. He was elected to the Riksdag in 1958 and served as minister without portfolio from 1963 to 1965, minister of communication from 1965 to 1967, and minister of education from 1967 to 1969. He was prime minister from 1969 to 1976 and again from 1982 until his death in 1986.

INGVAR CARLSSON (b. 1934) succeeded Olof Palme as party chair and prime minister in 1986 and continued in these posts until 1991. He is still party chair. He was elected to the Riksdag in 1965 and served as minister of education from 1969 to 1973 and as minister of housing from 1973 to 1976. He was deputy prime minister from 1982 to 1986.

ELECTION RESULTS, 1911–1991: VOTER PARTICIPATION AND RELATIVE DISTRIBUTION OF BALLOTS

Elections 1911–1930								
Second Chamber Riksdag (SR), and Municipal (Mu)								
Year	Election	Voter Participation	M	C	Fp	S	VPK	Other
1911[a]	SR	57.0	31.2	—	40.2	28.5	—	0.1
1914 Apr.[b]	SR	69.9	37.7	—	32.2	30.1	—	0.0
1914 Sept.[c]	SR	66.2	36.5	0.2	26.9	36.4	—	0.0
1917	SR	65.8	24.7	8.5	27.6	39.2	—	0.0
1919	Mu	63.3	24.9	13.2	25.4	36.3	—	0.2
1920[d]	SR	55.3	27.9	14.2	21.8	36.1	—	0.0
1921[e]	SR	54.2	25.8	11.1	19.1	39.4	4.6	0.0
1922	Mu	38.2	31.8	11.9	17.1	34.7	4.5	0.0
1924	SR	53.0	26.1	10.8	16.9	41.1	5.1	0.0
1926	Mu	49.8	28.9	11.7	16.1	39.0	4.1	0.2
1928	SR	67.4	29.4	11.2	15.9	37.0	6.4	0.1
1930	Mu	58.2	28.4	12.5	13.5	41.4	4.0	0.2

Elections 1932–1950								
Second Chamber Riksdag (SR), and Municipal (Mu)								
Year	Election	Voter Participation	M	C	Fp	S	VPK	Other
1932	SR	67.6	23.5	14.1	11.7	41.7	8.3	0.7
1934	Mu	63.6	24.2	13.3	12.5	42.1	6.8	1.1
1936	SR	74.5	17.6	14.3	12.9	45.9	7.7	1.6
1938	Mu	66.0	17.8	12.6	12.2	50.4	5.7	1.3
1940	SR	70.3	18.0	12.0	12.0	53.8	4.2	0.0
1942	Mu	66.9	17.6	13.2	12.4	50.3	5.9	0.6
1944	SR	71.9	15.9	13.6	12.9	46.7	10.5	0.7
1946	Mu	72.0	14.9	13.6	15.6	44.4	11.2	0.3
1948	SR	82.7	12.3	12.4	22.8	46.1	6.3	0.1
1950	Mu	80.5	12.3	12.3	21.7	48.6	4.9	0.2

Elections 1952–1968
Second Chamber Riksdag (SR), and Municipal (Mu)

Year	Election	Voter Participation	M	C	Fp	KDS[f]	S	VPK	Other
1952	SR	79.1	14.4	10.7	24.4	—	46.1	4.3	0.1
1954	Mu	79.1	15.7	10.3	21.7	—	47.4	4.8	0.1
1956	SR	79.8	17.1	9.4	23.8	—	44.6	5.0	0.1
1958[g]	SR	77.4	19.5	12.7	18.2	—	46.2	3.4	0.0
1958[h]	Mu	79.2	20.4	13.1	15.6	—	46.8	4.0	0.1
1960	SR	85.9	16.5	13.6	17.5	—	47.8	4.5	0.1
1962	Mu	81.0	15.5	13.1	17.1	—	50.5	3.8	0.0
1964	SR	83.9	13.7	13.2	17.0	1.8	47.3	5.2	1.8
1966	Mu	82.8	14.7	13.7	16.7	1.8	42.4	6.4	3.6
1968	SR	89.3	12.9	15.7	14.3	1.5	50.1	3.0	4.1

Elections 1970–1985
Riksdag (R) and County/Municipal (C/Mu)

Year	Election	Voter Participation	M	C	Fp	KDS	mp[i]	S	VPK	Other
1970	R	88.3	11.5	19.9	16.2	1.8	—	45.3	4.8	2.3
1970	C/Mu	88.1	11.7	19.5	16.2	1.8	—	45.6	4.4	2.6
1973	R	90.8	14.3	25.1	9.4	1.8	—	43.6	5.3	2.3
1973	C/Mu	90.5	13.9	23.7	10.4	2.1	—	43.2	5.1	3.7
1976	R	91.8	15.6	24.1	11.1	1.4	—	42.7	4.8	1.7
1976	C/Mu	90.4	15.1	22.1	11.3	1.8	—	43.0	4.9	3.6
1979	R	90.7	20.3	18.1	10.6	1.4	—	43.2	5.6	2.1
1979	C/Mu	89.0	18.6	17.7	10.4	2.1	—	43.0	5.8	2.4
1982	R	91.4	23.6	15.5	5.9	1.9	1.7	45.6	5.6	3.8
1982	C/Mu	89.6	21.7	15.3	6.0	2.4	1.6	45.5	5.4	2.1
1985	R	89.9	21.3	12.4[j]	14.2	—[j]	1.5	44.7	5.4	0.5
1985	C/Mu	87.8	20.6	11.9	12.4	2.0	2.5	42.6	5.3	2.8

Elections 1988 and 1991
Riksdag (R), County (C) and Municipal (Mu)

Year	Election	Voter Participation	NYD[k]	M	C	Fp[l]	KDS	mp	S	VPK[m]	Other
1988	R	86.0	—	18.3	11.3	12.2	2.9	5.5	43.2	5.8	0.7
1988	C	84.2	—	17.9	12.4	12.3	3.1	4.8	43.7	5.3	0.6
1988	Mu	84.0	—	18.1	12.5	11.3	2.8	5.6	41.6	5.5	2.6
1991	R	86.7	6.7	21.9	8.5	9.1	7.1	3.4	37.6	4.5	1.2
1991	C	83.8	0.7	23.2	11.0	10.8	7.0	3.1	38.3	4.8	1.0
1991	Mu	84.0	3.4	22.2	11.2	9.6	5.8	3.6	36.6	4.8	2.9

Sources: SOS Allmänna valen (National Election); *Statistisk årsbok* (Statistical Year-book); Stig Hadenius, Björn Molin, and Hans Wieslander, *Sverige efter 1900: En modern politisk historia* (Sweden After 1900: A Modern Political History) (Stockholm, 1991).

Notes:

General note: The Conservative party (M) changed its name in 1969 from *Höger-partiet* to *Moderata samlingspartiet.* The Agrarian party (C) changed its name in 1957 from *Bondeförbundet* to *Centerpartiet.* Through the amalgamation of *Frisin-nade landsförening* and the Liberal party (*Sveriges liberala parti*) in 1934 *Folkpar-tiet* (Fp) was formed. The Communists (VPK) changed their party name in 1967 to *Vänsterpartiet Kommunisterna.*

Note on tables since 1970: Since the reform of the constitution in 1969, the Riksdag has been a single-chamber body. Riksdag and local (municipal and county) elections are held on the same day. To qualify for a seat in the Riksdag a party must receive at least 4 percent of the national votes, or 12 percent in at least one district. As of 1976, non-Swedish citizens resident in Sweden at least three years, have the right to participate in municipal and county elections. Non-Swedish citizens comprise approximately 4 percent of all those entitled to vote. But their voting participation rate is about 30 percent lower than that of Swedish citizens. This is a partial expla-nation for the differences between the numbers voting in the national and the mu-nicipal/county elections.

[a]The first election after the 1907 voting rights reform.

[b]Staaff's Liberal government stepped down after the Farmers' March and the "courtyard coup" in February 1914 and was succeeded by Hammarskjöld's Conser-vative government. This was followed by a new election.

[c]Ordinary election.

[d]The Left Socialists obtain 8.1 percent of the votes in the 1917 election and 6.4 percent in the 1920 election.

[e]The election in 1921 was the first with true universal suffrage, that is, the first election in which women had the right to vote.

[f]A new party: *Kristen demokratisk samling* (Christian Democratic Coalition party; in 1990, *Kristdemokratiska samhällspartiet*—Party for a Christian Democratic Soci-ety).

[g]Extra election called because of the ATP (pensions) issue.

[h]Ordinary municipal election.

[i]A new party: *Miljöpartiet* (mp; "Environment party"—Green party).

[j]Election collaboration between *Centerpartiet* and KDS, *Kristen Demokratisk Samling* (Christian Democratic Coalition Party) under the party name *Centern.*

[k]*Ny Demokrati* (NYD; New Democracy party) was formed in the spring of 1991.

[l]*Folkpartiet* (Fp; "People's party") changed its name in 1990 to *Folkpartiet libera-lerna* ("People's party—The Liberals"). Referred to in this book as the Liberal party.

[m]*Vänsterpartiet Kommunisterna* (VPK; Left party—Communists) changed their party name in 1990 to *Vänsterpartiet* (V; Left party).

Compiled by Marie Hedström

Bibliography

The bibliography contains only works referred to in the notes. References to Official State Inquiries (*Statens offentliga utredningar*) are listed under their Swedish abbreviation, SOU. For the corporate bodies LO, SAF, SAP, and SSKF cited in the notes, see Landsorganisationen i Sverige (Swedish Confederation of Trade Unions), Svenska arbetsgivareföreningen (Swedish Employers' Confederation), Sveriges socialdemokratiska arbetareparti (Swedish Social Democratic Labor Party), and Sveriges socialdemokratiska kvinnoförbund (National Federation of Social Democratic Women in Sweden), respectively.

Works are cited under the first author or corporate body; works with more than three authors or corporate bodies are cited by title, not by editor.

The international section also includes some of the most important titles published since 1988 but not referred to in the notes. Cf. *Foreign language literature on the Nordic labour movements.* Edited by Marianne Bagge Hansen and Gerd Callesen. Copenhagen: Arbejderbevægelsens Bibliotek og Arkiv, 1992.

When complete publication data is given in the bibliography for works cited, note references are shortened. References to stenciled papers, collections and archives, and other source material are listed only in the notes.

TITLES IN ENGLISH, GERMAN, AND SPANISH

Adamson, Carol Alice. *Sweden and the Ethiopian crises, 1934–1938.* Unpublished diss., University of Wisconsin, Madison, 1987.

Adler-Karlsson, Gunnar. *Functional socialism: A Swedish theory for democratic socialization.* Stockholm, 1969.

Adler-Karlsson, Gunnar. *Reclaiming the Canadian economy: A Swedish approach through functional socialism.* Toronto, 1970.

Ahlén, Kristina. Swedish collective bargaining under pressure: Inter-union rivalry and incomes policy. *Industrial Relations,* 1989, no. 3.

Alapuro, Risto. *State and revolution in Finland.* Berkeley, 1988.

Alford, Robert R. Class voting in the Anglo-American political systems. In *Party systems and voter alignments: Cross-national perspectives.* Edited by Seymour M. Lipset and Stein Rokkan. New York, 1967.

Austro-Marxism. Translated and edited by Tom Bottomore and Patrick Goode; with an introduction by Tom Bottomore. Oxford, 1978.

Baldwin, Peter. *The politics of social solidarity: Class bases of the European welfare state 1875–1975*. Cambridge, 1990.

Berghahn, Volker R. *Modern Germany: Society, economy and politics in the twentieth century*. Cambridge, 1982.

Blidberg, Kersti. *Just good friends: Nordic social democracy and security policy, 1945–50*. Oslo, 1987.

Bok, Sissela. *Alva Myrdal: A daughter's memoir*. Reading, Mass., 1991.

Brandt, Willy, Bruno Kreisky, and Olof Palme. *Briefe und Gespräche 1972 bis 1975*. Cologne, 1975.

Cameron, D. Social democracy, corporatism, labour quiescence and the representation of economic interest in advanced capitalist society. In *Order and conflict in contemporary capitalism: Studies in the political economy of Western European nations*. Edited by John H. Goldthorpe. Oxford, 1984.

Carlson, Allan C. *The Swedish experiment in family politics: The Myrdals and the interwar population crisis*. New Brunswick, N.J., 1990.

Castles, Francis G. *The social democratic image of society: A study of the achievements and origins of Scandinavian social democracy in comparative perspective*. London, 1978.

Collins, Randall. *Weberian sociological theory*. Cambridge, 1986.

Crouch, Colin. The peculiar relationship: The party and the unions. In *The politics of the labour party*. Edited by Dennis Kavanagh. London, 1982.

Democracia, desarrollo y equidad: La experiencia de Suecia: Reflexiones para latinoamericanos. Edited by José Goñi. Caracas, 1990.

Dignity at work: A book dedicated to Pehr G. Gyllenhammar. Edited by Bo Ekman. Stockholm, 1985.

Donnison, David V. *The government of housing*. Harmondsworth, 1967.

Duverger, Maurice. *Political parties: Their organization and activity in the modern state*. London, 1954.

Einhorn, Eric S., and John Logue. *Modern welfare states: Politics and policies in social democratic Scandinavia*. New York, 1989.

Elander, Ingemar. Good dwellings for all: The case of social rented housing in Sweden. *Housing Studies*, 1991, no. 1.

Electoral behavior: A comparative handbook. Edited by Richard Rose. New York, 1974.

Electoral change in advanced industrial democracies: Realignment or dealignment? Edited by Russel J. Dalton, Scott C. Flanagan, and Paul Allen Beck. Princeton, N.J., 1984.

Electoral participation. Edited by Richard Rose. London, 1980.

Eliassen, Kjell A. Organizations and pressure groups. In *Nordic democracy: Ideas, issues, and institutions in politics, economy, education, social and cultural affairs of Denmark, Finland, Iceland, Norway, and Sweden*. Edited by Erik Allardt et al. Copenhagen, 1981.

Emanuelsson, Ingemar, and Siv Fischbein. Vive la différence? A study on sex and schooling. *Scandinavian Journal of Educational Research*, 1986, no. 2.

Engelmann, Frederick C. Austria: The pooling of opposition. In *Political oppositions in Western democracies*. Edited by Robert A. Dahl. New Haven, Conn., 1966.

Englund, Tomas. *Curriculum as a political problem: Changing educational conceptions, with special reference to citizenship education*. Lund, 1986. (1986a)

Esping-Andersen, Gøsta. *Social class, social democracy and state policy: Party policy and party decomposition in Denmark and Sweden*. Copenhagen, 1980.

Esping-Andersen, Gøsta. *Politics against markets: The social democratic road to power*. Princeton, N.J., 1985.

Esping-Andersen, Gøsta. *The three worlds of welfare capitalism*. Princeton, N.J., 1990.

Europäische Arbeiterbewegungen im 19. Jahrhundert: Deutschland, Österreich, England und Frankreich im Vergleich. With contributions by John Breuilly et al. Edited by Jürgen Kocka. Göttingen, 1983.

The foreign policies of West European socialist parties. Edited by Werner J. Feld. New York, 1978.

Gidlund, Gullan. Conclusions: The nature of public financing in the Nordic states. In *The public purse and political parties*. Edited by Matti Wiberg. Helsinki, 1991.

Gidlund, Gullan. Public investments in Swedish democracy: Gambling with gains and losses. In *The public purse and political parties*. Edited by Matti Wiberg. Helsinki, 1991.

Grass, Günter. *Aus dem Tagebuch einer Schnecke: Roman*. Darmstadt, 1972.

Grass, Martin. *Friedensaktivität und Neutralität: Die skandinavische Sozialdemokratie und die neutrale Zusammenarbeit im Krieg, August 1914 bis Februar 1917*. Bonn and Bad Godesberg, 1975.

Gustavsson, Sverker. Housing, building and planning. In *Politics as rational action: Essays in public choice and policy analysis*. Edited by Leif Lewin and Evert Vedung. Dordrecht, 1980.

Hadenius, Stig. *Swedish politics during the twentieth century*, 2d rev. ed. Stockholm, 1988.

Hamilton, Malcolm B. *Democratic socialism in Britain and Sweden*. Basingstoke, 1989.

Hammarström, Ingrid. Urban growth and building fluctuations: Stockholm, 1860–1920. In *Growth and transformation of the modern city: The Stockholm conference, September 1978, University of Stockholm*. Edited by Ingrid Hammarström and Thomas Hall. Stockholm, 1979.

Headey, Bruce W. *Housing policy in the developed economy: The United Kingdom, Sweden and the United States*. London, 1978.

Heclo, Hugh, and Henrik Madsen. *Policy and politics in Sweden: Principled pragmatism*. Philadelphia, 1987.

Hedström, Peter, and Stein Ringen. *Age and income in contemporary society: A research note*. Stockholm, 1987.

Heidenheimer, Arnold J. *Major reforms of the Swedish education system: 1950–1975*. Washington, D.C., 1978.

Heidenheimer, Arnold J., Hugh Heclo, and Carolyn Teich Adams. *Comparative public policy: The politics of social choice in Europe and America*. New York, 1975.

Heidenheimer, Arnold J., Hugh Heclo, and Carolyn Teich Adams. *Comparative public policy: The politics of social choice in Europe and America*, 2d ed. New York, 1983.

Hernes, Helga Maria. Die zweigeteilte Sozialpolitik: Eine Polemik. In *Wie männlich ist die Wissenschaft?* Edited by Karin Hausen and Helga Nowotny. Frankfurt am Main, 1986.

Housing, states and localities. Contributions by Peter Dickens et al. London, 1985.

ILO (International Labour Office). *International survey of social services*, 2 vols. Geneva, 1933–36.

Kälvemark, Ann-Sofie. *More children of better quality? Aspects on Swedish population policy in the 1930's*. Uppsala, 1980.

Kanitz, Otto Felix. *Das proletarische Kind in der bürgerlichen Gesellschaft; Kämpfer der Zukunft: Für eine sozialistische Erziehung,* new ed. Edited by Lutz von Werder. Frankfurt am Main, 1974.
Korpi, Walter. *The working class in welfare capitalism: Work, unions and politics in Sweden.* London, 1978. (1978b)
Korpi, Walter. *The democratic class struggle.* London, 1983.
Korpi, Walter, and Michael Shalev. Strikes, industrial relations and class conflict in capitalist societies. *British Journal of Sociology,* 1979, no. 2.
Kuhnle, Stein. The beginnings of the Nordic welfare states: Similarities and differences. *Acta sociologica,* 1978, supplement (*The Nordic welfare states*).
Kulemann, Peter. *Am Beispiel des Austromarxismus: Sozialdemokratische Arbeiterbewegung in Österreich von Hainfeld bis zur Dollfuss-Diktatur.* Hamburg, 1979.
Labor market reforms in Sweden: Facts and employee views. Contributions by Allan Larsson et al. Stockholm, 1979.
Lewis, Jane. *The politics of motherhood: Child and maternal welfare in England, 1900–1939.* London, 1980.
Lindblom, Paul. Ernst Wigforss. In *Klassiker des Sozialismus.* Vol. 2, *Von Jaurès bis Marcuse.* Edited by Walter Euchner. Munich, 1991.
Lundqvist, Lennart. Corporatist implementation and legitimacy: The case of privatization in Swedish public housing. In *Housing Studies,* 1988.
Mackie, Thomas T., and Richard Rose. *The international almanac of electoral history,* 2d ed. London, 1982.
Martin, Andrew. Is democratic control of capitalist economies possible? In: *Stress and contradiction in modern capitalism: Public policy and the theory of the state.* Edited by Leon N. Lindberg. Lexington, Mass., 1975.
Martin, Andrew. The dynamics of change in a Keynesian political economy: The Swedish case and its implications. In *State and economy in contemporary capitalism.* Edited by Colin Crouch. London, 1979.
Martin, Andrew. Economic stagnation and social stalemate in Sweden. In United States Congress, Joint Economic Committee. *Monetary policy, selective credit policy, and industrial policy in France, Britain, West Germany, and Sweden.* Washington, D.C., 1981.
Martin, Andrew. Trade unions in Sweden: Strategic responses to change and crisis. In *Unions and economic crisis: Britain, West Germany and Sweden.* Contributions by Peter Gourevitch et al. London, 1984.
Marx, Karl, and Friedrich Engels. *Werke.* Berlin, 1957–68.
McKenzie, Robert. *British political parties: The distribution of power within the conservative and labour parties,* 2d ed. London, 1967.
Meidner, Rudolf. *Employee investment funds.* London, 1978.
Meidner, Rudolf, and Anna Hedborg. *Modell Schweden: Erfahrungen einer Wohlfahrtsgesellschaft.* Frankfurt am Main, 1984.
Michanek, Ernst. *For and against the welfare state: Swedish experiences.* Lecture given in Berlin, October 1963. Stockholm, 1964.
Milner, Henry. *Sweden: Social democracy in practice.* Oxford, 1989.
Minkin, Lewis. *The labour party conference.* London, 1978.
Misgeld, Klaus. *Sozialdemokratie und Aussenpolitik in Schweden: Sozialistische Internationale, Europapolitik und die Deutschlandfrage, 1945–1955.* Frankfurt am Main, 1984.
Misgeld, Klaus. As the Iron Curtain descended: The coordination committee of the Nordic labour movement and the socialist International between Potsdam and Geneva (1945–1955). *Scandinavian Journal of History,* 1988, no. 1.

Möller, Gustav. The unemployment policy. *Annals of the American Academy of Political and Social Science*, vol. 197, 1938 (*Social problems and policies in Sweden*, edited by Bertil Ohlin).

Myrdal, Alva, and Gunnar Myrdal. *Nation and family.* New York, 1941.

Nordström, Byron John. *Swedish labor and foreign policy, 1933–1939.* Ann Arbor, Mich., 1972.

OECD (Organization for Economic Co-operation and Development). *Educational policy and planning: Sweden.* Paris, 1967.

OECD. *Policies on educational growth.* Paris, 1970.

OECD. *Social expenditure, 1960–1990: Problems of growth and control.* Paris, 1985.

OECD. *Historical statistics, 1960–1985.* Paris, 1987.

Okun, Arthur. *Equality and efficiency: The big trade-off.* Washington, D.C., 1975.

Olson, Mancur. *The logic of collective action: Public goods and the theory of groups.* Cambridge, Mass., 1965.

Olsson, Sven E. *Social policy and welfare state in Sweden.* Lund, 1990.

Panebianco, Angelo. *Political parties: Organization and power.* Cambridge, 1988.

Party systems in Denmark, Austria, Switzerland, the Netherlands, and Belgium. Edited by Hans Daalder. London, 1987.

Pelinka, Anton. Kommunalpolitik als Gegenmacht: Das "rote" Wien als Beispiel gesellschaftsverändernder Reformpolitik. In *Kommunalpolitik und Sozialdemokratie.* Edited by Karl-Heinz Nassmacher. Bonn, 1977.

Pelinka, Peter, and E. Woller. Die SPÖ und die Jugend: Partei der Jugend? In *Roter Anstoss: Der "Österreichische Weg": Sozialistische Beiträge.* Edited by Josef Hindels and Peter Pelinka. Vienna, 1980.

Pontusson, Jonas. *Public pension funds and the politics of capital formation in Sweden.* Stockholm, 1984.

Pontusson, Jonas. Labor, corporatism, and industrial policy: The Swedish case in comparative perspectives. *Comparative Politics*, 1991, no. 2.

Przeworski, Adam. *Capitalism and social democracy.* Cambridge, 1985.

Przeworski, Adam, and John Sprague. *Paper stones: A history of electoral socialism.* Chicago, 1986.

Rabinbach, Anson. *The crisis of Austrian socialism: From Red Vienna to civil war.* Chicago, 1983.

Rein, M. *Women in the social welfare labor market.* Berlin, 1985.

Reinert, Adrian. *Wege aus politischer Apathie? Organisierte Formen gesellschaftspolitischer Aktivierung als Problem der Sozialdemokratie in Schweden und der Bundesrepublik Deutschland.* Frankfurt am Main, 1988.

The Riksdag: A history of the Swedish parliament. Edited by Michael F. Metcalf. New York, 1987.

Rose, Richard, and Guy Peters. *Can government go bankrupt?* New York, 1978.

Rothstein, Bo. Corporatism and reformism: The social democratic institutionalization of class conflict. *Acta sociologica*, 1987: no. 3/4.

Rothstein, Bo. *Marxism and institutional analysis: Working class strength and welfare state development: The Swedish case.* Uppsala, 1989.

Rothstein, Bo. Institutional analysis and working class strength: The Swedish case. *Politics and Society*, 1990, no. 3.

Rothstein, Bo. State structure and variations in corporatism: The Swedish case. *Scandinavian Political Studies*, 1991, no. 2.

Ruggie, Mary. *The state and working women: A comparative study of Britain and Sweden.* Princeton, N.J., 1955.

Ruin, Olof. *Tage Erlander: Serving the welfare state, 1946–1969.* Pittsburgh, 1990.
Sainsbury, Diane. *Swedish social democratic ideology and electoral politics, 1944–1948: A study of the functions of party ideology.* Stockholm, 1980.
Särlvik, Bo. Recent electoral trends in Sweden. In *Scandinavia at the polls: Recent political trends in Denmark, Norway, and Sweden.* Edited by Karl H. Cerny. Washington, D.C., 1977.
Scase, Richard. *Social democracy in capitalist society: Working-class politics in Britain and Sweden.* London, 1977.
Shaw, Eric. *Discipline and discord in the labour party: The politics of managerial control in the labour party, 1951–1987.* Manchester, 1988.
Shorter, Edward, and Charles Tilly. *Strikes in France, 1830–1968.* London, 1974.
Simonson, Birger. Sweden. In *The formation of labour movements, 1870–1914,* vol. 1. Edited by Marcel van der Linden and Jürgen Rojahn. Leiden, 1990.
Smeeding, Timothy. Patterns of income and poverty. In *The vulnerable.* Edited by John L. Palmer, Timothy Smeeding, and Barbara Boyle Torrey. Washington, D.C., 1988.
State, economy, and society in Western Europe, 1815–1975: A data handbook in two volumes. Contributions by Peter Flora et al. Frankfurt, 1983–87.
Steinmo, Sven. Social democracy vs. socialism: Goal adaption in Social Democratic Sweden. *Politics and Society,* 1988, no. 4.
Stephens, John D. *The transition from capitalism to socialism.* London, 1979.
A success story? Housing policy in three Swedish communes. By Berth Danermark et al. Örebro, 1985.
Sully, Melanie A. The socialist party of Austria. In *Social democratic parties in Western Europe.* Edited by William E. Paterson and Alastair H. Thomas. London, 1977.
Sweden before and after social democracy: A first overview. By Göran Therborn et al. *Acta sociologica,* 1978, supplement (*The Nordic welfare states*).
Swenson, Peter. *Fair shares: Unions, pay, and politics in Sweden and West Germany.* London, 1989.
Swenson, Peter. Labor and the limits of the welfare state: The politics of interclass conflict and cross-class alliances in Sweden and West Germany. *Comparative Politics,* 1991, no. 4.
Therborn, Göran. Electoral campaigns as indicators of ideological power. In *Rethinking ideology: A Marxist debate.* Edited by Sakari Hänninen and Leena Paldán. Berlin, 1983.
Therborn, Göran. Class analysis: History and defence. In *The sociology of structure and action.* London, 1986. (1986a)
Therborn, Göran. The working class and the welfare state: A historical-analytical overview and a little Swedish monograph. In *Det nordiska i den nordiska arbetarrörelsen.* Femte nordiska konferensen för forskning i arbetarrörelsens historia, Tammerfors, den 23–27 augusti 1983. Edited by Pauli Kettunen. Helsinki, 1986. (1986c)
Tilton, Timothy A. Why don't the Swedish social democrats nationalize industry? *Scandinavian Studies,* 1987, no. 2.
Tilton, Timothy A. *The political theory of Swedish social democracy: Through the welfare state to socialism.* Oxford, 1990.
Tingsten, Herbert. Stability and vitality in Swedish democracy. *Political Quarterly* (London), 1955, no. 2.
Tingsten, Herbert. *The Swedish social democrats: Their ideological development.* Totowa, N.J., 1973.

Towards a democratic rationality: Making the case for Swedish labour. Edited by John Fry. Aldershot, 1986.

Webber, D. Combating or acquiescing in unemployment? Economic crisis management in Sweden and West Germany. *West European Politics*, 1983, no. 1.

Weihsmann, Helmut. *Das rote Wien: Sozialdemokratische Architektur und Kommunalpolitik, 1919–1934.* Vienna, 1985.

Westeuropas Parteiensystem im Wandel. Edited by Landeszentrale für politische Bildung Baden-Württemberg. Stuttgart, 1983.

Wilensky, Harold L. *The "new corporatism," centralization, and the welfare state.* London, 1976.

Wirtschaftsdemokratie: Ihr Wesen, Weg und Ziel. Edited by (the order of) the Allgemeiner Deutscher Gewerkschaftsbund by Fritz Naphtali. Berlin, 1928.

Working-class formation: Nineteenth-century patterns in Western Europe and the United States. Edited by Ira Katznelson and Aristide R. Zolberg. Princeton, N.J., 1986.

TITLES IN SCANDINAVIAN LANGUAGES

[Swedish Å {õa} = Aa]

Abrahamsson, Bengt, and Anders Broström. *Om arbetets rätt: Vägar till ekonomisk demokrati.* Stockholm, 1980.

Ahlmark, Per. *Den svenska atomvapendebatten.* Med ett appendix av Hans-Åke Dhejne. Stockholm, 1965.

Alsterdal, Alvar. *Brandsyn i samhället: Axel Danielsson 1863–1899.* Malmö, 1963.

Åmark, Klas. Från kaos till ordning: Forskning på 80–talet. *Arbetarhistoria*, 1984, no. 3/4.

Åmark, Klas. *Facklig makt och fackligt medlemskap: De svenska fackförbundens medlemsutveckling 1890–1940.* Lund, 1986.

Ambjörnsson, Ronny. Logen 880 Skärgårdsblomman. In *Den dolda historien: 27 uppsatser om vårt okända förflutna.* Redaktörer Ronny Ambjörnsson och David Gaunt. Stockholm, 1984.

Andersson, Birger. *Arbetarrörelsen i Skaraborg: Socialdemokratiska partidistriktet 50 år.* Tidaholm, 1977.

Andersson, Dan. *Vad säger marknaden om solidarisk lönepolitik?* Stockholm, 1987.

Andersson, Mary. *Sorgenfri: Dokumentärroman.* Stockholm, 1979.

Andersson, Rolf, and Rudolf Meidner. *Arbetsmarknadspolitik och stabilisering.* Stockholm, 1973.

Andersson, Sten. Arbetsfreden, arbetarrörelsen och minoritetsparlamentarismen 1923–1928. Stockholm, 1987. Stencil.

Andersson, Sten. *Mellan Åkarp och Saltsjöbaden: En studie av arbetsfredsfrågan i minoritetsparlamentarismens Sverige.* Stockholm, 1990.

Andersson, Sven. *På Per Albins tid.* Stockholm, 1980.

Andrae, Carl Göran. Proletära organisationsformer 1917: Militärdemonstrationerna och arbetarkommittén. *Arkiv för studier i arbetarrörelsens historia*, 1975, no. 7/8.

Andrae, Carl Göran. Från borgargård till hyreshus. In *Årsbok. Kungl. humanistiska vetenskaps-samfundet i Uppsala, 1975/1976.* 1977.

Andrae, Carl Göran. Att veta sin plats: Människorna, husen och den sociala miljön i Uppsala mot 1800–talets slut. In *Städer i utveckling: Tolv studier kring stadsförändringar tillägnade Ingrid Hammarström.* Edited by Thomas Hall. Stockholm, 1984.

Andrén, Nils, and Åke Landqvist. *Svensk utrikespolitik efter 1945.* Stockholm, 1965.

Arbetareförsäkringskomitén. *Arbetareförsäkringskomiténs betänkande.* Stockholm, 1888–89. 3 bd i 12 vol. [Bd] 1: *Utlåtande och förslag,* vol. 3, *Ålderdomsförsäkring,* 1889. [Bd] 2: *Öfversigt af lagstiftningen rörande arbetareförsäkring i åtskilliga främmande länder,* 1888.

Arbetarrörelsen och löntagarfonderna: Rapport från en arbetsgrupp inom LO och socialdemokraterna. Stockholm, 1981.

Arbetarrörelsens efterkrigsprogram: De 27 punkterna med motivering. Har utarbetats av representanter för arbetarrörelsens olika huvudorganisationer. Socialdemokratiska arbetarpartiet et al. Stockholm, 1944. Ny tr., 1945, 1946.

Arvidson, Stellan. Demokrati och realskolebildning. *Tiden,* 1941, no. 10.

Åsard, Erik. *LO och löntagarfondsfrågan: En studie i facklig politik och strategi.* Stockholm, 1978.

Åsard, Erik. *Kampen om löntagarfonderna: Fondutredningen från samtal till sammanbrott.* Stockholm, 1985.

Askling, Lena. Så vanns väljarna: Pensionerna och fonderna avgjorde? *Tiden,* 1982, no. 7.

Back, Pär-Erik. *Det svenska partiväsendet.* 3d, rev. uppl. Stockholm, 1972.

Back, Pär-Erik. *Bostadsbyggande och bostadshyra i svensk politik 1916–1925.* Gävle, 1980.

Bäckström, Knut. *Arbetarrörelsen i Sverige,* 2 vols. Ny utg. Av författaren bearbetad och förkortad, 2d uppl. Stockholm, 1977. Vol. 1, *Den svenska arbetarrörelsens uppkomst och förening med socialismen.*

Bentzel, Ragnar. Produktivitetsproblem i den penning och lönepolitiska diskussionen i vårt land. *Ekonomisk tidskrift,* 1956, no. 4.

Bergman, Åke. *Den nya given: Artiklar och reportage om arbetet.* Stockholm, 1986.

Bergström, Hans. *Rivstart? Om övergången från opposition till regering.* Stockholm, 1987.

Bergström, Villy. *Den ekonomiska politiken i Sverige och dess verkningar.* Stockholm, 1969.

Bergström, Villy. Arvet från tjugotalet präglar dagens politik. *Tiden,* 1984, no. 8.

Billing, Peter. *Människovärdet vi fordra tillbaka: Arbetarklassens formering och det socialdemokratiska arbetarepartiets framväxt och utveckling i Skåne fram till 1911: Minnesskrift.* Utgiven av Skånes socialdemokratiska partidistrikt 1905–1985. Malmö, 1986.

En bit Malmö: Tillägnad Hugo Åberg på 60–årsdagen 11 maj 1965. Edited by Hans E Arwastsson et al. Malmö, 1965.

Björk, Kaj. Vårt parti och andras. *Tiden,* 1949, no. 4.

Björlin, Lars. Jordfrågan i svensk arbetarrörelse 1890–1920: En översikt. *Arbetarrörelsens årsbok,* 1974.

Bjurling, Oscar. *Stadens fattiga: En studie över fattigdom och fattigvård i Malmö.* Lund, 1956.

Blidberg, Kersti. *Splittrad gemenskap: Kontakter och samarbete inom nordisk socialdemokratisk arbetarrörelse 1931–1945.* Stockholm, 1984.

Blomquist, Elsie. *Möllevången i våra hjärtan: En berättelse i ord och bild.* Malmö, 1985.

Bohman, Gösta. *Inrikes utrikespolitik: Det handlar om Vietnam.* Stockholm, 1970.

Bohusläns socialdemokratiska partidistrikt under 50 år, 1905–1955. Redigerad av Gunnar Gustafsson. Uddevalla, 1955.

Bonow, Mauritz. *Staten och jordbrukskrisen.* Stockholm, 1935.

Bostad och kapital: En studie av svensk bostadspolitik. Kenneth Boberg et al. Stockholm, 1974.

Bostaden Malmö: En utställning om boendet under 1900–talet: Jubileumsutställning: Bostadsförmedlingen i Malmö 1913–1983, Kommendanthuset, Malmö museum. Margareta Hartman, Anne-Lis Winberg, and Ulf Bjelkare. Malmö, 1983.

Branting, Hjalmar. Ett modernt socialförsäkringsförslag. *Tiden.* 1908, provhäfte no. 1.

Branting, Hjalmar. *Tal och skrifter i urval,* 11 vols. Redaktion Z. Höglund et al. Stockholm, 1926–30.

Bresky, Tomas, Jan Scherman, and Ingemar Schmid. *Med SAF vid rodret: Granskning av en kamporganisation.* Stockholm, 1981.

Bringmark, Gösta. *Från dagaträl till medborgare: Malmö stadsfullmäktige 100 år: En krönika i ord och bild om stadens utveckling 1863–1962.* Malmö, 1962.

Bröder, låtom oss enas! En krönika i ord och bild om Bondeförbundet i svensk politik under fyra årtionden. Edited by Gustaf Jonnergård. Stockholm, 1950.

Carlgren, Wilhelm M. *Varken—eller: Reflexioner kring Sveriges Ålandspolitik 1938–1939.* Stockholm, 1977.

Carlsson, Christina. *Kvinnosyn och kvinnopolitik: En studie av svensk socialdemokrati 1880–1910.* Lund, 1986.

Carlsson, Sten. *Fröknar, mamseller, jungfrur och pigor: Ogifta kvinnor i det svenska ståndssamhället.* Uppsala, 1977.

Carlsson, Sten. *Svensk historia: Tiden efter 1718.* Stockholm, 1980. Vol. 2 of Carlsson, Sten, and Jerker Rosén. *Svensk historia,* 2 vols. 4th uppl. 1978–80.

Carlsson Wetterberg, Christina. "-ingen kvinnofråga existerar-": Kvinnoorganiseringen inom den tidiga arbetarrörelsen. *Arbetarhistoria,* 1987, no. 4/1988, no. 1.

Casparsson, Ragnar. *LO: Bakgrund, utveckling, verksamhet.* Stockholm, 1966. (1966a)

Casparsson, Ragnar. *Saltsjöbadsavtalet i historisk belysning.* Stockholm, 1966. (1966b)

Dahlgren, Magnus, and Ulf Silén. Kollektivanslutningen. Umeå, 1986. Stencil.

Dahlgren, Stefan. Sociologin i planeringen. *Plan,* 1977, no. 4.

Dahllöf, Urban. *Skoldifferentiering och undervisningsförlopp: Komparativa mål- och processanalyser av skolsystem 1.* Ny uppl. Stockholm, 1967.

Dahllöf, Urban. *Svensk utbildningsplanering under 25 år: Argument, beslutsunderlag och modeller för utvärdering.* Lund, 1971.

Dalström, Kata. *Brev till Hjalmar Branting och Fredrik Ström.* Inledning och kommentarer Rut Berggren. Lund, 1987.

De Geer, Hans. *SAF i förhandlingar: Svenska arbetsgivareföreningen och dess förhandlingsrelationer till LO och tjänstemannaorganisationerna 1930–1970.* Stockholm, 1986.

Drangel, Louise. Folkpartiet och jämställdhetsfrågan. In *Liberal ideologi och politik 1934–1984.* Stockholm, 1984.

Dybdahl, Vagn. *Industrialisering og folkestyre 1849–1939.* 3d opl. Copenhagen, 1978.

Edenman, Ragnar. *Socialdemokratiska riksdagsgruppen 1903–1920: En studie i den svenska riksdagens partiväsen.* Uppsala, 1946.

Edgren, Gösta, Karl-Olof Faxén, and Clas-Erik Odhner. *Lönebildning och samhällsekonomi*. Utgiven av SAF, LO, TCO. Stockholm, 1970.

Edin, Per-Olof, and Anna Hedborg. *Det nya uppdraget*. Stockholm, 1980.

Egerö, Bertil. *En mönsterstad granskas: Bostadsplanering i Örebro 1945–75*. Stockholm, 1979.

Eidem, Rolf. *Aktieägandet och demokratin: Ägarfrågan från brukssamhälle till kompetenskapitalism*. Stockholm, 1987.

Eklund, Per. *Rätten i klasskampen: En studie i rättens funktioner*. Stockholm, 1974.

Elander, Ingemar. *Det nödvändiga och det önskvärda: En studie av socialdemokratisk ideologi och regionalpolitik 1940–72*. Stockholm, 1978.

Elldin, Harald. *Kooperativa Föreningen Solidar: 50 år i samverkan*. Malmö, 1957.

Elmér, Åke. *Folkpensioneringen i Sverige med särskild hänsyn till ålderspensioneringen*. Lund, 1960.

Elmér, Åke. *Från Fattigsverige till välfärdsstaten: Sociala förhållanden och socialpolitik i Sverige under nittonhundratalet*. 6th rev. och utök. uppl. Stockholm, 1975.

Elmér, Åke. *Svensk socialpolitik*. 12th uppl. Lund, 1978.

Elvander, Nils. *Skandinavisk arbetarrörelse*. Stockholm, 1980.

Elvander, Nils. *Den svenska modellen: Löneförhandlingar och inkomstpolitik 1982–1986*. Stockholm, 1988.

Englund, Tomas. *Samhällsorientering och medborgarfostran i svensk skola under 1900–talet*, 2 vols. Uppsala, 1986. (1986b)

Ericson, Hans-Olof. *Vanmakt och styrka: Studier av arbetarrörelsens tillkomst och förutsättningar i Jönköping, Huskvarna och Norrahammar 1880–1909*. Lund, 1987.

Erixon, Lennart. Den svenska modellen i motgång: En analys av dess effekter och förändrade förutsättningar under perioden 1974–1984. *Nordisk tidskrift för politisk ekonomi*, 1984, no. 15/16.

Erlander, Tage. Samarbete och strid i efterkrigspolitiken. *Tiden*, 1958, no. 6.

Erlander, Tage. *Tage Erlander*, 6 vols. Stockholm, 1972–82.

Feldt, Kjell-Olof. *Samtal med Feldt: Berndt Ahlqvist och Lars Engqvist intervjuar finansministern*. Stockholm, 1984.

Feldt, Kjell-Olof. *Den tredje vägen: En politik för Sverige*. Stockholm, 1985.

Flemström, Carin, and Alf Ronnby. *Fallet Rosengård: En studie i svensk planerings- och bostadspolitik*. Stockholm, 1972.

Flood, Hulda. *Den socialdemokratiska kvinnorörelsen i Sverige*. Ny, utökad uppl. Stockholm, 1960.

Folkesdotter, Gärd. *"Störtas skall det gamla snart i ljuset": Bostadssociala utredningens syn på äldre bebyggelse*. Gävle, 1981.

Föreningen Rostorps jubileumsskrift: Rostorps Egnahem 20 år. Rostorp, 1943.

Frånberg, Per. *Umeåsystemet: En studie i alternativ nykterhetspolitik 1915–1945*. Umeå, 1983.

Franzén, Mats. *Grannskap och stadsplanering: Om stat och byggande i efterkrigstidens Sverige och Finland*. Stockholm, 1989.

Franzén, Nils-Olof. *Hjalmar Branting och hans tid: En biografi*. Stockholm, 1985.

Fredriksson, Karl. Efterkrigsprogrammet förverkligas. In *Vår politik: Dagsfrågor och idéfrågor i socialdemokratisk politik*. Utgiven av Sveriges socialdemokratiska arbetareparti. Stockholm, 1947.

Fryklund, Björn, and Tomas Peterson. Klass och folklighet. *Sociologisk forskning*, 1983, no. 2.

Fryklund, Björn, and Tomas Peterson. Högervågens folkliga appell. *Zenit*, 1985, no. 4.

Furåker, Bengt. *Stat och arbetsmarknad: Studier i svensk rörlighetspolitik*. Lund, 1976.

Fürst, Per-Erik. *Indragning av "oförtjänt" värdestegring*. Stockholm, 1958.

Fürth, Thomas. *De arbetslösa och 1930-talskrisen: En kollektivbiografi över hjälpsökande arbetslösa i Stockholm 1928–1936*. Stockholm, 1979.

Geijer, Arne. Fackföreningsrörelsen och det socialdemokratiska partiet. In *Idéerna som drivkraft: En vänbok till Tage Erlander*. Edited by Leif Andersson. Stockholm, 1969.

Geijer, Lennart, and Folke Schmidt. *Arbetsgivare och fackföreningsledare i domarsäte: En studie i rättsbildningen på arbetsmarknaden*. Stockholm, 1958.

Gellerman, Olle. *Staten och jordbruket 1867–1918*. Stockholm, 1958.

Genombrott, uppbyggnad, utveckling: Västmanlands socialdemokratiska partidistrikt 75 år, 1906–1981. Västerås, 1981.

Gerdner, Gunnar. *Det svenska regeringsproblemet 1917–1920: Från majoritetskoalition till minoritetsparlamentarism*. Uppsala, 1946.

Gerdner, Gunnar. Ministären Edén och författningsrevisionen. In *Kring demokratins genombrott i Sverige*. Redigerad av Stig Hadenius. Stockholm, 1966.

Gidlund, Gullan M. *Partistöd*. Lund, 1983.

Gidlund, Gullan M. *Det kommunala partistödet: En studie av kommunernas och landstingens stöd till de politiska partierna*. Utgiven av 1983 års demokratiberedning. Stockholm, 1985. (1985a)

Gidlund, Gullan M., and Janerik Gidlund. Partiernas liv och folkstyrelsens villkor. In: *Makten från folket: 12 uppsatser om folkstyrelsen*. Stockholm, 1985. (1985b)

Gidlund, Janerik, and Gullan Gidlund. *Ty riket är ditt och makten: De politiska partiernas roll i svenska kommuner*. Stockholm, 1981.

Ginner, Thomas. *Den bildade arbetaren: Debatten om teknik, samhälle och bildning inom Arbetarnas bildningsförbund 1945–1970*. Linköping, 1987.

Gräv där du står-cirkel (Kockums). *"Kockumsknogaren."* Redigerad av Karin Salomonsson. Malmö, 1986.

Greiff, Mats, and Hans Larsson. *Lugnet: En stadsdel i Malmö, dess tillblivelse och utveckling från 1863 till 1915*. Lund, 1978. Stencil.

Gröndahl, Jan. Fattigvården och de ensamstående mödrarna i Gävle omkring 1910. Uppsala, 1986. Stencil.

Gröning, Lotta. *Vägen till makten: SAP:s organisation och dess betydelse för den politiska verksamheten 1900–1933*. Uppsala, 1988.

Gulbrandsen, Lars. *Fra marked til administrasjon? Boligmarked og Boligpolitikk i Oslo i det tjuende århundre*. Dissertation, Oslo University, published 1982.

Gustafson, Lars. *HSB under femtio år: En organisationsstudie*. Stockholm, 1974.

Gustafsson, Siv, and Petra Lantz. *Arbete och löner: Ekonomiska teorier och fakta kring skillnader mellan kvinnor och män*. Stockholm, 1985.

Gustavsson, Bernt. Socialism och bildning: Artur Engbergs ideologi. In *Ideologi och institution: Om forskning och högre utbildning 1880–2000*. Sven-Eric Liedman and Lennart Olausson, eds. Stockholm, 1988.

Hadenius, Axel. *Facklig organisationsutveckling: En studie av Landsorganisationen i Sverige*. Stockholm, 1976.

Hadenius, Stig; Björn Molin; and Hans Wieslander: *Sverige efter 1900. En modern politisk historia*. 12th, bearb. uppl. Stockholm, 1991.

Halmstads arbetarekommun 90 år, 1985: Minnesskrift. Halmstad, 1985.

Hamilton, Hugo. *Dagböcker*, 2 vols. Utgivna av Gunnar Gerdner. Stockholm, 1955–56.

Hammarström, Olle. 1970-talets reformarbete i arbetslivet. In *1970-talets reformer i arbetslivet: En antologi om den nya arbetsrättslagstiftningen*. Stockholm, 1982.

Hansson, Per Albin. *Demokratisk samverkan eller nationell splittring?* Stockholm, 1934. (1934a)

Hansson, Per Albin. *Den stora krisuppgörelsen: En väg ut ur krisen*. Stockholm, 1934. (1934b)

Hansson, Per Albin. *Demokrati: Tal och uppsatser*. Stockholm, 1935.

Hansson, Per Albin. *Koalitionspolitiken: Utgångspunkter, principer, program*. Stockholm, 1938. (1938a)

Hansson, Per Albin. *Oppositionen och koalitionen*. Stockholm, 1938. (1938b)

Hansson, Per Albin. *Från Fram till folkhemmet: Per Albin Hansson som tidningsman och talare*. Urval och inledning Anna Lisa Berkling. Solna, 1982.

Härnqvist, Kjell. En SOU-forskares hågkomster. *Forskning om utbildning*, 1987, no. 1.

Hatje, Ann-Katrin. *Befolkningsfrågan och välfärden: Debatten om familjepolitik och nativitetsökning under 1930- och 1940-talen*. Stockholm, 1974.

Hatje, Ann-Katrin. Bostadspolitik på förändrade villkor: En studie om den statliga bostadspolitikens mål och medel under 1940- och 1950-talen. Stockholm, 1978. Stencil.

Hedlund, Stefan, and Mats Lundahl. *Beredskap eller protektionism? En studie av beredskapsmålet i svensk jordbrukspolitik*. Malmö, 1985.

Hellström, Gunnar. *Jordbrukspolitik i industrisamhället: Med tyngdpunkt på 1920- och 30-talen*. Stockholm, 1976.

Hentilä, Seppo. *Den svenska arbetarklassen och reformismens genombrott inom SAP före 1914: Arbetarklassens ställning, strategi och ideologi*. Helsingfors, 1979.

Herrström, Gunnar. *1927 års skolreform: En studie i svensk skolpolitik 1918–1927*. Stockholm, 1966.

Hirdman, Gunnar. *Kulturell demokrati*. Stockholm, 1938.

Hirdman, Yvonne. Den socialistiska hemmafrun: Den socialdemokratiska kvinnorörelsen och hemarbetet 1890–1939. In *Vi kan, vi behövs! Kvinnorna går samman i egna föreningar*. Brita Åkerman m fl. Stockholm, 1983.

Hobsbawm, Eric. Arbetarrörelsen och storstaden. *Arkiv för studier i arbetarrörelsens historia*, 1988, no. 39.

Höglund, Zeth. *Hjalmar Branting och hans livsgärning*, 2 vols. Stockholm, 1928–29. Vol. 1, *Hövdingen*, 1928. Vol. 2, *Statsmannen*, 1929.

Höglund, Zeth. *Minnen i fackelsken*, 3 vols. Stockholm, 1951–56.

Holm, Lennart. Ett bostadsområde blir äldre. *Byggforum*, 1958, nos. 7 and 8.

Holm, Lennart. Miljonprogrammet då och nu. *Arkitektur*, 1987, no. 7.

Holm, Per. Det långa perspektivet: Om planeringsproblem och planeringsideologier då och nu och sedan. *Plan*, 1977, no. 4.

Holmberg, Sören. *Svenska väljare*. Stockholm, 1981.

Holmberg, Sören. *Väljare i förändring*. Stockholm, 1984.

Holmberg, Sören, and Kent Asp. *Kampen om kärnkraften: En bok om väljare, massmedier och folkomröstningen 1980*. Stockholm, 1984.

Holmberg, Sören, and Mikael Gilljam. *Väljare och val i Sverige*. Stockholm, 1987.

Holmqvist, Eric. *Från ståthållare till skomakare: Skånska riksdagsmän på 1800-talet*. Stockholm, 1983.

Holmström, Barry. *Rätten till markvärdestegringen: Förslag och åtgärder under 1900-talet.* Stockholm, 1988.

HSB 1925–50. Edited by Arnold Sönnerdahl and Got Sjölander. Malmö, 1950.

Hultén, Gösta. *Kris i hyresfrågan.* Stockholm, 1973.

Husén, Torsten. *Jämlikhet genom utbildning? Perspektiv på utbildningsreformerna.* Stockholm, 1977.

Husén, Torsten. Utbildningsforskning i Sverige: Ett 30-årigt perspektiv. *Forskning om utbildning,* 1987, no. 1.

Husén, Torsten. *Skolreformerna och forskningen: Psykologisk pedagogik under pionjäråren.* Stockholm, 1988.

Hydén, Håkan. *Rättens samhälleliga funktioner.* Lund, 1978.

Hyresgästernas riksförbund. *Utrota bostadsnöden: Hyresgäströrelsens bostadspolitiska efterkrigsprogram.* Stockholm, 1945.

Isling, Åke. *Vägen till en demokratisk skola: Skolpolitik och skolreformer i Sverige från 1880- till 1970-talet.* Stockholm, 1974.

Isling, Åke. *Kampen för och mot en demokratisk skola,* 2 vols. Stockholm, 1980–1988. Vol. 1, *Samhällsstruktur och skolorganisation.* 2d uppl., 1984.

Jacobsen, Tord. *Välviljans förtryck: En fallstudie av allmännyttig bostadspolitik.* Lund, 1991.

Jaurès, Jean. *Arbetarne, fosterlandet och armén: Tre kapitel ur "L'armée nouvelle."* Stockholm, 1916.

Johansson, Alf. Bostadspolitiken. In *Hundra år under kommunalförfattningarna 1862–1962: En minnesskrift.* Utgiven av Svenska landskommunernas förbund, Svenska landstingsförbundet, Svenska stadsförbundet. Stockholm, 1962.

Johansson, Alf W. *Finlands sak: Svensk politik och opinion under vinterkriget 1939–1940.* Stockholm, 1973.

Johansson, Alf W. Den svenska socialdemokratin och fascismen på trettiotalet: Några reflexioner. In *Utrikespolitik och historia: Studier tillägnade Wilhelm M. Carlgren den 6 maj 1987.* Edited by Mats Bergquist, Alf W. Johansson, and Krister Wahlbäck. Stockholm, 1987.

Johansson, Alf W. *Per Albin och kriget: Samlingsregeringen och utrikespolitiken under andra världskriget.* 2d tr. Stockholm, 1988.

Johansson, Alf W., and Torbjörn Norman. Den svenska neutralitetspolitiken i historiskt perspektiv. In *Neutralitet och försvar: perspektiv på svensk säkerhetspolitik 1809–1985.* Edited by Bo Hugemark. Stockholm, 1986.

Johansson, Arndt. *Arbetarrörelsen i Dalarna.* Utgiven till Dalarnas socialdemokratiska partidistrikts 50-årsjubileum 1955. Falun, 1955.

Johansson, Bernt, and Lars Borgnäs. *Bostäder och boendeförhållanden i Sverige 1945–1960.* Stockholm, 1968.

Johansson, Hilding. *Folkrörelserna.* Stockholm, 1954.

Johansson, Hilding. Den kommunala verksamhetens expansion. In *Kommunerna i förvandling.* Edited by Gunnar Wallin, Hans G. Andersson, and Nils Andrén. Stockholm, 1966.

Johansson, Lena. *Utbildning: Resonerande del: Utkast till kapitel 7 i betänkande om svenska folkets levnadsförhållanden att avgivas av Låginkomstutredningen.* Stockholm, 1970.

Johansson, Ralph, and Björn Karlberg. *Bostadspolitiken.* Helsingborg, 1979.

Jonasson, Gustaf. *Per Edvin Sköld 1946–1951.* Under medverkan av Lars Sköld. Uppsala, 1976. (S. 134–93: Per Edvin Skölds anteckningar 1946–1951).

Jonasson, Gustaf. *I väntan på uppbrott? Bondeförbundet/Centerpartiet i regeringskoalitionens slutskede 1956–1957.* Uppsala, 1981.

Jönsson, Nine Christine, and Paul Lindblom. *Politik och kärlek: En bok om Gustav Möller och Else Kleen*. Stockholm, 1987.

Jonung, Lars. Knut Wicksells prisstabiliseringsnorm och penningpolitiken på 1930-talet. In *Ekonomisk debatt och ekonomisk politik: Nationalekonomiska föreningen 100 år*. Utgiven av Jan Herin and Lars Werin. Stockholm, 1977.

Kälvemark, Ann-Sofie. Kommer familjen att överleva? Historiska aspekter på äktenskap och familj i det svenska samhället. In *Den utsatta familjen: Liv, arbete och samlevnad i olika nordiska miljöer under de senaste tvåhundra åren: En antologi från Familjehistoriska projektet vid Historiska institutionen, Uppsala universitet*. Edited by Hans Norman. Stockholm, 1983.

Kampmann, Viggo. *Økonomisk demokrati: Et forslag til lovfæstet udbyttedeling mellem arbejde og kapital*. Copenhagen, 1970.

Karleby, Nils. Socialdemokratisk samhällssyn. *Tiden*, 1925, no. 1.

Karleby, Nils. *Socialismen inför verkligheten: Studier över socialdemokratisk åskådning och nutidspolitik*. Ny utg. Stockholm, 1976.

Karlsson, Gunnel. *Manssamhället till behag? 17 år som kvinnoförbundets ordförande, Lisa Mattson*. Stockholm, 1990.

Kihlberg, Leif. *Karl Staaff*, 2 vols. Stockholm, 1962–63. Vol. 2, *Regeringschef, oppositionsledare: 1905–1915*, 1963.

Kjeldstadli, Knut. "Arbeider, bonde, våre hære-": Arbeiderpartiet og bøndene 1930–1939. *Tidsskrift for arbeiderbevegelsens historie*, 1978, no. 2.

Kjellberg, Anders. *Facklig organisering i tolv länder*. Lund, 1983.

Klockare, Sigurd. *Svenska revolutionen 1917–1918*. Stockholm, 1967.

Korpi, Walter. *Arbetarklassen i välfärdskapitalismen: Arbete, fackförening och politik i Sverige*. Stockholm, 1978. (1978a)

Korpi, Walter. *Den demokratiska klasskampen: Svensk politik i jämförande perspektiv*. Stockholm, 1981.

Kristenson, Hjördis. Det egna hemmet. In *Bygga skånska städer: Aspekter på stadsarkitektur efter 1850*. Edited by Ragnar Gustafson. Malmö, 1975.

Kupferberg, Feiwel. Byggnadsarbetarstrejken 1933–34. *Arkiv för studier i arbetarrörelsens historia*, 1972, no. 2.

Kyle, Gunhild. *Gästarbeterska i manssamhället: Studier om industriarbetande kvinnors villkor i Sverige*. Stockholm, 1979.

Landgren, Karl-Gustav. *Den "nya ekonomien" i Sverige: J. M. Keynes, E. Wigforss, B. Ohlin och utvecklingen 1927–39*. Stockholm, 1960.

Landsorganisationen i Sverige. 15-mannakommittén. *Fackföreningsrörelsen och näringslivet*. Stockholm, 1941. (LO 1941)

Landsorganisationen i Sverige. Organisationskommittén. *Fackföreningsrörelsen och den fulla sysselsättningen: Betänkande och förslag från Landsorganisationens organisationskommitté*. Stockholm, 1951. (LO 1951)

Landsorganisationen i Sverige. Kongress (16th, 1961, Stockholm). *Samordnad näringspolitik*. Stockholm, 1961. (LO 1961)

Landsorganisationen i Sverige. Kongress (17th, 1966, Stockholm). *Fackföreningsrörelsen och den tekniska utvecklingen: Rapport från en arbetsgrupp till 1966 års LO-kongress*. Stockholm, 1966. (LO 1966)

Landsorganisationen i Sverige. Kongress (18th, 1971, Stockholm). *Demokrati i företagen: Rapport till LO-kongressen 1971*. Stockholm, 1971. (LO 1971a)

Landsorganisationen i Sverige. Lönepolitiska kommittén. *Låglön och välfärd: Rapport till LO:s lönepolitiska kommitté inför LO-kongressen 1971*. Stockholm, 1971. (LO 1971b)

Landsorganisationen i Sverige. Kongress (18th, 1971, Stockholm). *Lönepolitik: Rapport till LO-kongressen 1971*. Stockholm, 1971. (LO 1971c)

Landsorganisationen i Sverige. Kongress (19th, 1976, Stockholm). *Kollektiv kapitalbildning genom löntagarfonder: Rapport till LO-kongressen 1976*. Stockholm, 1976. (LO 1976a)

Landsorganisationen i Sverige. Kongress (19th, 1976, Stockholm). *Löner, priser, skatter: Rapport till LO-kongressen 1976*. Stockholm, 1976. (LO 1976b)

Landsorganisationen i Sverige. Kongress (20th, 1981, Stockholm): *LO 80-rapporten: Rapport till LO-kongressen 1981*. Stockholm, 1981. (LO 1981a)

Landsorganisationen i Sverige. Lönepolitiska utredningen. *Lönepolitik för 80-talet: Rapport till LO-kongressen 1981*. Stockholm, 1981. (LO 1981b)

Landsorganisationen i Sverige. Näringspolitiska kommittén. *Näringspolitik för 80-talet: Arbetsrapport till LO-kongressen 1981 från LOs näringspolitiska kommitté*. Stockholm, 1981. (LO 1981c)

Landsorganisationen i Sverige. Utredningen om arbete. *Gemensamt ansvar för arbete: Rapport till 1986 års LO-kongress från LOs utredning om arbete*. Stockholm, 1986. (LO 1986)

Landsorganisationen i Sverige. *Lönepolitisk delrapport*. Stockholm, 1987. (LO 1987)

Larsson, Sven-Erik. *Regera i koalition: Den borgerliga trepartiregeringen 1976–1978 och kärnkraften*. Stockholm, 1986.

Lewin, Leif. *Planhushållningsdebatten*. Stockholm, 1967.

Liljeström, Rita, and Edmund Dahlström. *Arbetarkvinnor i hem- arbets- och samhällsliv*. Stockholm, 1981.

Lindbeck, Assar. *Svensk ekonomisk politik: Problem och teorier*. Under medverkan av Marianne Biljer-Ahnmarker och Lars Calmfors. Stockholm, 1975.

Lindberg, Göran. *SABO-företagens beroende av sin omvärld*. Stockholm, 1982.

Lindbom, Tage. *Den socialdemokratiska ungdomsrörelsen i Sverige: En historik*. 2d uppl. Stockholm, 1952.

Lindeberg, Sven-Ola. *CSA och arbetslöshetspolitiken*. Stockholm, 1983.

Lindensjö, Bo. *Högskolereformen: En studie i offentlig reformstrategi*. Stockholm, 1981.

Lindensjö, Bo, and Ulf P: Lundgren. *Politisk styrning och utbildningsreformer*. Stockholm, 1986.

Lindgren, John. *Svenska metallindustriarbetare förbundets historia: 1888–1905*. Stockholm, 1938.

Lindgren, John. *Per Albin Hansson i svensk demokrati*. Stockholm, 1950.

Lindhagen, Jan. *Socialdemokratins program*, 2 vols. Stockholm, 1972–74. Vol. 1, *I rörelsens tid 1890–1930*, 1972. Vol. 2, *Bolsjevikstriden*, 1974.

Lindskog, Claes. *Sydsvenska Dagbladet Snällposten 100 år*. Malmö, 1948.

Lindström, Ulla. *I regeringen: Ur min politiska dagbok 1954–1959*. Stockholm, 1969.

Lönebildning och samhällsekonomisk stabilisering. Lars Calmfors et al. Stockholm, 1985.

Lönnroth, Erik. *Den svenska utrikespolitikens historia: 1919–1939*. Stockholm, 1959.

Lundberg, Arne S. *Är det gammalmodigt med "community centers"? Plan*, 1977, no. 4.

Lundberg, Bengt. *Jämlikhet? Socialdemokratin och jämlikhetsbegreppet*. Lund, 1979.

Lundberg, Erik. *Konjunkturer och ekonomisk politik: Utveckling och debatt i Sverige sedan första världskriget*. Stockholm, 1953; 3d tr., 1955.

Lundberg, Erik. *Är vi verkligen solidariska?* En kritisk granskning. In *Lönepolitik och solidaritet: Debattinlägg vid Meidnerseminariet den 21–22 februari 1980*. Stockholm, 1980.

Lundberg, Erik. *Gunnar Strängs ekonomiska filosofi: Personliga iakttagelser och erfarenheter*. In *En bok om och till Gunnar Sträng*. Sammanställd av Frans Nilsson. Stockholm, 1981.

Lundberg, Erik. *Ekonomiska kriser förr och nu*. Stockholm, 1983.

Lundberg, Harald. *Broderskapsrörelsen (s) i svensk politik: Studier rörande ståndpunkter och praktiskt politiskt handlande under åren 1930–1980*. Stockholm, 1988.

Lundh, Christer. *Den svenska debatten om industriell demokrati 1919–1924*, 2 vols. Lund, 1987–. Vol. 1, *Debatten i Sverige*, 1987.

Lundkvist, Sven. *Folkrörelserna i det svenska samhället 1850–1920*. Stockholm, 1977.

Lundvik, Bertil. *Solidaritet och partitaktik: Den svenska arbetarrörelsen och spanska inbördeskriget 1936–1939*. Uppsala, 1980.

Makt och internationalisering. Göte Hansson, Lars-Göran Stenelo, red. Stockholm, 1990.

Malmström, C. Gösta. *Samverkan, slagkraft: En krönika över 50 SIF-år*. Stockholm, 1970.

Malmö arbetarekommun 50 år. Edited by Eric Holmqvist, Gotth. Sjölander, and Gösta Netzén. Malmö, 1951. Omslagstitel. *Arbetets söner*.

Malmö—Vår stad: kommunal studiehandbok. Utgiven av Malmö ABF. Malmö, 1962.

Marklund, Sixten. *Skolsverige 1950–1975*, 6 vols. Stockholm, 1980–. Vol. 1, *1950 års reformbeslut*, 1980. Vol. 2, *Försöksverksamheten*, 1982. Vol. 3, *Från Visbykompromissen till SIA*, 1983. Vol. 4, *Differentieringsfrågan*, 1985.

Meidner, Rudolf. *Samordning och solidarisk lönepolitik under tre decennier*. In *Tvärsnitt: Sju forskningsrapporter utgivna till LO:s 75-årsjubileum 1973*. Stockholm, 1973.

Meidner, Rudolf. *Samordning och solidarisk lönepolitik*. Stockholm, 1974.

Meidner, Rudolf. *Löntagarfonder*. I samarbete med Anna Hedborg, Gunnar Fond. Stockholm, 1975.

MHF 1932–1942: "Hyresgästerna." Malmö, 1942.

Michels, Robert. *Organisation och demokrati: En sociologisk studie av de oligarkiska tendenserna i vår tids demokrati*. Stockholm, 1983.

Millbourn, Ingrid. *Strejken kan väl inte i alla himlars namn börja i Trosa! Om socialdemokrater och 1902 års strejker*. In *Över gränser: Festskrift till Birgitta Odén*. Redaktion Ingemar Norrlid et al.; övriga deltagare i festskriftsarbetet Anna Gora (teckning). Lund, 1987.

Minnesskrift 1901–1926: Malmö arbetarekommun. Malmö, 1925.

Misgeld, Klaus. *Den nordiska arbetarrörelsens fredsmanifest 1951: Ett fredsdokument från Koreakrigets dagar*. *Scandia*, 1985: no. 1/2.

Molin, Björn. *Tjänstepensionsfrågan: En studie i svensk partipolitik*. Göteborg, 1967.

Molin, Karl. *Försvaret, folkhemmet och demokratin: Socialdemokratisk riksdagspolitik 1939–1945*. Stockholm, 1974.

Molin, Karl. *Planläggning inför efterkrigstiden*. In *Norden under andra världskriget*. Copenhagen, 1979.

Möller, Gustav. *Trygghet och säkerhet åt Sveriges folk! Ett socialdemokratiskt program inför valen.* Stockholm, 1928.
Möller, Gustav. *Kilbommarna och socialdemokratin.* Stockholm, 1932.
Möller, Gustav. De planerade socialreformerna. In *Tiden,* 1946, no. 2.
Möller, Gustav. Hågkomster. *Arbetarrörelsens årsbok,* 1971.
Möller, Gustav, and P. Albin Hansson. *Stormklockepolitiken under kritisk granskning.* Stockholm, 1916.
Möller, Yngve. *Östen Undén: En biografi.* Stockholm, 1986.
Murray, Mac. *Utbildningsexpansion, jämlikhet och avlänkning: Studier i utbildningspolitik och utbildningsplanering 1933–1985.* Göteborg, 1988.
Myhrman, Johan, and Hans Tson Söderström. Svensk stabiliseringspolitik: Erfarenheter och nya villkor. In *Svensk ekonomi: Ett samlingsverk.* Redigerad av Bo Södersten. 3d, omarb. uppl. Stockholm, 1982.
Myrdal, Alva. Internationell och svensk socialpolitik. In *Ett genombrott: Den svenska socialpolitiken: Utvecklingslinjer och framtidsmål.* Stockholm, 1944.
Myrdal, Alva, and Gunnar Myrdal. *Kris i befolkningsfrågan.* Stockholm, 1934.
Myrdal, Alva, and Gunnar Myrdal. *Kontakt med Amerika.* Stockholm, 1941.
Myrdal, Gunnar. *Jordbrukspolitiken under omläggning.* Stockholm, 1938.
"Nagelapan": Metallarbetare i Malmö under 100 år. Edited by Anne-Louise Kemdal. Malmö, 1984.
Nej! till svenska atomvapen. Av Ernst Wigforss et al. Stockholm, 1959.
Nestor, Per. *Boligpolitikken og OBOS gjennom 50 år (1929–1979).* Oslo, 1979.
Nielsen, Kåre H. Det norske arbeiderparti og befolkningsspørsmålet i mellomkrigstida. *Historisk tidsskrift* (Oslo), 1979.
Nilsson Hoadley, Anna-Greta. *Atomvapnet som partiproblem: Sveriges socialdemokratiska kvinnoförbund och frågan om svenskt atomvapen 1955–1960.* Stockholm, 1989.
Niva, Matti. *Bostad, politik och marknad: En jämförande studie av bostadspolitiken i efterkrigstidens Sverige och Finland.* Stockholm, 1989.
Norden dagen derpå: De nordiske økonomisk-politiske modellene og deres problemer på 70- og 80-tallet: Sluttrapport fra økonomisk politikk-prosjektet. Lars Mjøset, red. Oslo, 1986.
Nordlander, Carl Henrik. *Jordbrukets framtid: En redogörelse för 1942 års jordbrukskommittés betänkande.* Stockholm, 1946.
Nordström, G. Hilding. *Sveriges socialdemokratiska arbetareparti under genombrottsåren 1889–1894: Bidrag till det svenska partiväsendets historia.* Stockholm, 1938.
Norman, Birger. *Ådalen 31: En berättelse.* Stockholm, 1968.
Norman, Torbjörn. Hjalmar Branting och Folkens förbund. *Arbetarhistoria,* 1985, no. 1.
Norman, Torbjörn. Slutakt med efterspel: Ålandsuppgörelsen, Sverige och Nationernas förbund. In *Väster om Skiftet: Uppsatser ur Ålands historia.* Edited by Sune Jungar and Nils Erik Villstrand. Åbo, 1986.
Norrlid, Ingemar. *Demokrati, skatterättvisa och ideologisk förändring: Den kommunala självstyrelsen och demokratins genombrott i Sverige.* Lund, 1983.
Nu gäller det tjänstemännen. Stockholm, 1946.
Nuder, Ants. *Byggnadsrättens fördelning: Teoretisk diskussion av fördelningens konsekvenser för byggandets teknik och ekonomi.* Stockholm, 1971.
Nycander, Svante. *Kurs på kollision: Inblick i avtalsrörelsen 1970–71.* Stockholm, 1972.
Nyman, Olle. *Svensk parlamentarism 1932–1936: Från minoritetsparlamentarism till majoritetskoalition.* Uppsala, 1947.

Nyman, Olle. *Parlamentarismen i Sverige: Huvuddragen av utvecklingen efter 1917.* 2d uppl. Stockholm, 1955.

Nyström, Sture, and Bengt Månsson. *Malmö kommunala bostadsaktiebolag (MKB), 1946–1966.* Foto Åke Hedström. Malmö, 1966.

Odhner, Clas-Erik. Principer för den framtida jordbrukspolitiken. *Tiden,* 1946, no. 8.

Odhner, Clas-Erik. *Jordbruket vid full sysselsättning.* Stockholm, 1953.

Odhner, Clas-Erik. *Sverige i Europa.* Utgiven av Landsorganisationen och Kooperativa förbundet. Stockholm, 1962.

Odhner, Clas-Erik. *Nytt grepp på jordbrukspolitiken.* Utgiven av Konsumentkommittén för jordbruksfrågor. Stockholm, 1966.

Ohlin, Bertil. *Memoarer.* Stockholm, 1972–75. Vol. 2, *1940–1951: Socialistisk skördetid kom bort.* 1975.

Ohlson, Björn. Tillkomsten av arbetarrörelsens efterkrigsprogram. *Statsvetenskaplig tidskrift för politik, statistik, ekonomi,* 1958, no. 1.

Öhman, Berndt. Krispolitikens förhistoria. *Tiden,* 1969, no. 1.

Öhman, Berndt. Solidarisk lönepolitik och löntagarfonder. In *Två expertrapporter från Utredningen om löntagarna och kapitaltillväxten.* Stockholm, 1982.

Olofsson, Gunnar. *Mellan klass och stat: Om arbetarrörelse, reformism och socialdemokrati.* Lund, 1979.

Olsson, Reinhold. *En krönika om Sundsvalls arbetarkommun.* Sundsvall, 1972.

Östberg, Kjell. *Byråkrati och reformism: En studie av svensk socialdemokratis politiska och sociala integrering fram till första världskriget.* Lund, 1990.

Östman, Lena. *Lönepolitik: Företagets och chefens styrinstrument.* Stockholm, 1987.

Palm, August. Hvad vil socialdemokraterna? August Palms tal i Malmö 6 november 1881 enligt talarens manuskript. Med kommentarer av John Lindgren. In *August Palm: Biografisk skildring.* Av John Lindgren. Ny utg. Solna, 1981.

Palm, Irving. *Frikyrkorna, arbetarfrågan och klasskampen: Frikyrkorörelsens hållning till arbetarnas fackliga och politiska kamp åren kring sekelskiftet.* Uppsala, 1982.

Palme, Olof. *Med egna ord: Samtal med Serge Richard och Nordal Åkerman.* Pocketuppl. Uppsala, 1978.

Palme, Olof. *En levande vilja.* Urval Hans Dahlgren et al. Stockholm, 1987.

Palme, Sven Ulric. *På Karl Staaffs tid.* Stockholm, 1964.

Palmstierna, Erik. *Ett brytningsskede: Minnen och dagboksanteckningar.* Stockholm, 1951.

Palmstierna, Erik. *Politiska dagboksanteckningar,* 3 vols. Stockholm, 1952–54. Vol. 2, *Orostid: 1917–1919,* 1953.

Paulsson, Gregor. *Svensk stad,* 2 vols. Ny utg. Lund, 1972. Vol. 1, *Liv och stil i svenska städer under 1800-talet.*

Petersson, Olof. *Väljarna och valet 1976.* Stockholm, 1977.

Peterson, Tomas, Mikael Stigendal, and Björn Fryklund. *Skånepartiet: Om folkligt missnöje i Malmö.* Lund, 1988.

Pfannenstill, Bertil. *Sociologisk undersökning av Augustenborgsområdet i Malmö.* Malmö, 1953.

Pierre, Jon. *Partikongresser och regeringspolitik: En studie av socialdemokratiska partikongressens beslutsfattande och inflytande 1948–1978.* Lund, 1986.

Prawitz, Gunnar. *Jordfrågan: Jord- och fastighetsbildningspolitiken på den svenska landsbygden under förra hälften av 1900-talet.* Stockholm, 1951.

Den produktiva rättvisan: LO-ekonomerna gör en kritisk granskning av 1984 års långtidsutredning. Stockholm, 1984.

Qvist, Gunnar. Statistik och politik: Landsorganisationen och kvinnorna på arbetsmarknaden. In *Tvärsnitt: Sju forskningsrapporter utgivna till LO:s 75-årsjubileum 1973.* Stockholm, 1973.

Qvist, Gunnar. Ett perspektiv på den s. k. kvinnoemancipationen i Sverige. *Historisk tidskrift,* 1977, no. 2.

Ramström, Dick. Målstyrning i utbildningen—Skåpmat eller en reell förnyelsekraft. *Forskning om utbildning,* 1988, no. 2.

Rehn, Gösta. Ekonomisk politik vid full sysselsättning. *Tiden.* 1948, no. 3.

Rehn, Gösta. Lönepolitiken och fullsysselsättningen: Replik till professor Erik Lundberg. *Ekonomisk tidskrift,* 1950, no. 1.

Rehn, Gösta. Idéutvecklingen. In *Lönepolitik och solidaritet: Debattinlägg vid Meidnerseminariet den 21–22 februari 1980.* Stockholm, 1980.

Richardson, Gunnar. *Kulturkamp och klasskamp: Ideologiska och sociala motsättningar i svensk skol-och kulturpolitik under 1880-talet.* Göteborg, 1963.

Richardson, Gunnar. 1950 års enhetsskolebeslut: En politisk nebulosa. *Statsvetenskaplig tidskrift,* 1967, no. 5.

Richardson, Gunnar. *Svensk skolpolitik 1940–1945: Idéer och realiteter i pedagogisk debatt och politiskt handlande.* Stockholm, 1978.

Richardson, Gunnar. *Drömmen om en ny skola: Idéer och realiteter i svensk skolpolitik 1945–1950.* Stockholm, 1983.

Richardson, Gunnar. *Svensk utbildningshistoria: Skola och samhälle förr och nu.* 3d rev. uppl. Lund, 1984.

Ricknell, Lars. Studier rörande politisk struktur i fyra norrlandslän 1911–1920, speciellt med avseende å 1917–1920 års val. Umeå, 1971. Stencil.

Rothstein, Bo. *Den socialdemokratiska staten: Reformer och förvaltning inom svensk arbetsmarknads- och skolpolitik.* Lund, 1986.

Rudberg, Eva. Från grannskapsenhet till bilsamhälle. *Att bo,* 1976, no. 5.

Rudberg, Eva. Fyrtiotalets reform- och bostadsprogram. *Att bo,* 1976, no. 4.

Rudberg, Eva. *Uno Åhrén: En föregångsman inom 1900-talets arkitektur och samhällsplanering.* Stockholm, 1981.

Rudberg, Eva. Funktionalisterna och bostadsfrågan. *Meddelande från Arbetarrörelsens arkiv och bibliotek,* 1982, no. 2.

Rudling, Anna. *Kampen mot atomvapen.* Stockholm, 1975.

Ruin, Olof. *Kooperativa förbundet 1899–1929: En organisationsstudie.* Stockholm, 1960.

Ruin, Olof. *I välfärdsstatens tjänst: Tage Erlander 1946–1969.* Stockholm, 1986.

SAMAK. Arbetarrörelsens nordiska samarbetskommitté. *Solidaritet för tillväxt och sysselsättning: Rapport.* Utarbetad av ekonomisk-politisk grupp inom SAMAK. Stockholm, 1985.

Samuelsson, Kurt. *Minnen.* Malmö, 1983–. Vol. 1, *1921–1958,* 1983.

Sandahl, Rolf. *Bostadspolitiska styrmedel: En studie av statsmakternas styrning av bostadsstandarden.* Stockholm, 1983.

Sandberg, Nils-Eric, and Ingemar Ståhl. *Svensk bostadspolitik: Varför det blev så: Vad man kan göra.* Stockholm, 1976.

Sandler, Rickard. *Ett utrikespolitiskt program: Anföranden 1933–34.* Stockholm, 1934.

Sandler, Rickard. *Strömväxlingar och lärdomar: Utrikespolitiska anföranden 1937–39.* Stockholm, 1939.

Schiller, Bernt. *Storstrejken 1909: Förhistoria och orsaker.* Göteborg, 1967.
Schiller, Bernt. LO, *paragraf 32 och företagsdemokratin.* In *Tvärsnitt: Sju forskningsrapporter utgivna till LO:s 75-årsjubileum 1973.* Stockholm, 1973.
Schori, Pierre. Tydlighet, tradition, trovärdighet. In *Boken om Olof Palme: Hans liv, hans gärning, hans död.* Edited by Hans Haste, Lars Erik Olsson, and Lars Strandberg. Stockholm, 1986.
Schori, Pierre. Alliansfrihet och Europasamarbete. In *Sverige och den västeuropeiska integrationen: Anföranden vid AICs seminarium i Stockholm den 29–30 januari 1988.* Stockholm, 1988.
Schüllerqvist, Bengt. Kampen om Ådalsbilden och motsättningarna inom det socialdemokratiska partiet 1930–1931. Uppsala, 1988. Stencil.
Sidenbladh, Göran. Idédebatt och praxis i efterkrigstidens samhällsplanering. *Plan.* 1977, no. 4.
Simonson, Birger. *Socialdemokratin och maktövertagandet: SAP:s politiska strategi 1889–1911.* Göteborg, 1985.
Sjölund, Maivor. *Statens kaka: Lönepolitik i förändring.* Stockholm, 1987.
Sjölund, Maivor. *Statens lönepolitik 1966–1988.* Stockholm, 1989.
Sköld, Per Edvin. Jordbrukets organisationsproblem: Några synpunkter främst med avseende på småbruket. *Tiden,* 1926, no. 4. (1926a)
Sköld, Per Edvin. Ökad jordbruksnybildning: Särskilt med hänsyn till kronojordens upplåtande för egnahemsändamål. *Tiden,* 1926, no. 3. (1926b)
Socialdemokratin och svensk utrikespolitik: Från Branting till Palme. Edited by Bo Huldt and Klaus Misgeld. Stockholm, 1990.
Söderpalm, Sven Anders. *Arbetsgivarna och saltsjöbadspolitiken: En historisk studie i samarbetet på svensk arbetsmarknad.* Stockholm, 1980.
Sogstad, Per Egeberg. *Ungdoms fanevakt: Den sosialistiske ungdomsbevegelses historie i Norge.* Oslo, 1951.
SOU 1929:28. *Betänkande angående moderskapsskydd.* Avgivet den 26 september 1929 av inom Kungl. Socialdepartementet tillkallade sakkunniga.
SOU 1935:66. *Betänkande om folkförsörjning och arbetsfred.* Vol. 2, *Specialutredningar.*
SOU 1936:7. *Utkast till ett principbetänkande: Socialiseringsproblemet.* Vol. 1, *Allmänna synpunkter.*
SOU 1939:50. *Promemoria rörande bostadsbyggnadsverksamheten och bostadsförsörjningen.* Av Bostadssociala utredningen.
SOU 1941:4. *Utredning angående byggnadskostnaderna: Betänkande.* Avgivet av 1940 års byggnadskostnadssakkunniga.
SOU 1942:3. *Promemoria rörande bostadsförsörjningen.* Utarbetad av Alf Johansson.
SOU 1944:20. *1940 års skolutrednings betänkanden och utredningar.* Vol. 1, *Skolan i samhällets tjänst: Frågeställningar och problemläge.*
SOU 1944:57. *Utredningar angående ekonomisk efterkrigsplanering.* Vol. 7, *Framställningar och utlåtanden från kommissionen för ekonomisk efterkrigsplanering.*
SOU 1945:63. *Slutbetänkande.* Avgivet av Bostadssociala utredningen. Vol. 1, *Allmänna riktlinjer för den framtida bostadspolitiken, förslag till låne-och bidragsformer.*
SOU 1946:42, SOU 1946:46. *Riktlinjer för den framtida jordbrukspolitiken: Betänkande.* Avgivet av 1942 års jordbrukskommitté.
SOU 1948:27. *1946 års skolkommissions betänkande med förslag till riktlinjer för det svenska skolväsendets utveckling.*

SOU 1955:29. *Samhället och barnfamiljerna: Betänkande.* Av 1954 års familjeutredning.

SOU 1956:47. *Stöd åt ofullständiga familjer: Promemoria.* Avgiven av familjeberedningen. Bilaga: *Sammanfattning av familjeberedningens olika förslag till familjestödjande åtgärder.*

SOU 1961:38. *Stöd åt barnaföderskor: Betänkande.* Socialpolitiska kommittén.

SOU 1961:42. *Mål och medel i stabiliseringspolitiken: Betänkande.* Avgivet av Stabiliseringsutredningen.

SOU 1964:36. *Ökat stöd till barnfamiljer: Promemoria.* Avgiven av Familjeberedningen.

SOU 1965:22. *Dagstidningarnas ekonomiska villkor: Betänkande.* Av Pressutredningen.

SOU 1967:52. *Barnbidrag och familjetillägg.* Familjepolitiska kommittén.

SOU 1972:34. *Familjestöd: Betänkande.* Avgivet av Familjepolitiska kommittén.

SOU 1973:2. *Högskolan: Betänkande.* Av 1968 års utbildningsutredning.

SOU 1975:18. *Förtroendevalda och partier i kommuner och landsting: Rapport.* Utredningen om den kommunala demokratin.

SOU 1980:49. *Tomträtt: Betänkande.* Av tomträttskommittén.

SOU 1987:19. *Varannan damernas: Slutbetänkande från utredningen om kvinnorepresentation.*

SOU 1989:33. *Reformerad inkomstbeskattning: Betänkande.* Av Utredningen om reformerad inkomstbeskattning (RINK). Vol. 1, *Skattereformens huvudlinjer.* Vol. 2, *Inkomst av kapital.* Vol. 3, *Inkomst av tjänst, lagtext och kommentar.* Vol. 4, *Bilagor, expertrapporter.*

SOU 1989:34. *Reformerad företagsbeskattning: Betänkande.* Av Utredningen om reformerad företagsbeskattning (KLF). Vol. 1, *Motiv och lagförslag.* Vol. 2, *Expertrapporter.*

SOU 1989:35. *Reformerad mervärdesskatt m.m.: Betänkande.* Av Kommittén för indirekta skatter (KIS). Vol. 1, *Motiv.* Vol. 2, *Lagtext och bilagor.*

SOU 1989:38. *Det nya skatteförslaget: Sammanfattning av skatteutredningarnas betänkanden.*

SOU 1990:44. *Demokrati och makt i Sverige: Maktutredningens huvudrapport.*

Staaff, Karl. *Politiska tal samt några tal och inlägg vid skilda tillfällen,* 2 vols. Utgivna av Kristian Setterwall och Erik Staaff. Stockholm, 1918.

Stenkvist, Jan. Sven Hedin och bondetåget. In *Heroer på offentlighetens scen: Politiker och publicister i Sverige 1809–1914.* Kurt Johannesson et al. Stockholm, 1987.

Stråth, Bo. *Varvsarbetare i två varvsstäder: En historisk studie av verkstadsklubbarna vid varven i Göteborg och Malmö.* Göteborg, 1982.

Strömberg, Thord. *Kommunalsocialismen inför verkligheten.* Malmö, 1984.

Strömberg, Thord. *Mönsterstaden: Mark och bostadspolitik i efterkrigstidens Örebro.* Örebro, 1989.

Sund, Bill. *Nattens vita slavar: Makt, politik och teknologi inom den svenska bagerinäringen 1896–1955.* Stockholm, 1987.

Svensk inkomstfördelning i internationell jämförelse: Rapport till Expertgruppen för studier i offentlig ekonomi. Stockholm, 1986.

Svensk ordning och nyordning: En orientering. Av Mauritz Bonow et al. Stockholm, 1943.

Svenska arbetsgivareföreningen. *Rättvis lön: Lönepolitiskt program: Utgångspunkter, grundsatser: Antaget på SAF:s stämma 1979.* Stockholm, 1979. (SAF 1979)

Svenska arbetsgivareföreningen. *Lönen: Ett verktyg för chefen.* Stockholm, 1986. (SAF 1986)

Svenska atomvapen? Fakta och problem: Sex fackmannauppsatser. Edited by Per Edvin Sköld. Stockholm, 1959.

Sveriges socialdemokratiska arbetareparti. *Framstegens politik.* Utgiven av Socialdemokratiska partistyrelsen. Stockholm, 1956. (SAP 1956)

Sveriges socialdemokratiska arbetareparti. Socialdemokratiska partistyrelsens kommitté för studium av atomvapenfrågan. *Neutralitet, försvar, atomvapen: Rapport till Socialdemokratiska partistyrelsen.* Stockholm, 1960. (SAP 1960)

Sveriges socialdemokratiska arbetareparti. Kongress (23th, 1968, Stockholm). *Organisation, verksamhet, stadgar: Organisationskommitténs betänkande.* Stockholm, 1968. (SAP 1968)

Sveriges socialdemokratiska arbetareparti. Kongress (24th, 1969, Stockholm). *Ökad jämlikhet.* Stockholm 1969. (SAP 1969)

Sveriges socialdemokratiska arbetareparti. *Arbetarrörelsen och familjepolitiken: Barn- och familjepolitiskt program.* Stockholm, 1978. (SAP 1978a)

Sveriges socialdemokratiska arbetareparti. Kongress (27th, 1978, Stockholm). *Arbetarrörelsen och familjepolitiken: Rapport från barn- och familjepolitiska arbetsgruppen.* Stockholm, 1978. (SAP 1978b)

Sveriges socialdemokratiska arbetareparti. Kongress (27th, 1978, Stockholm). *Jämställdhet mellan kvinnor och män: En rapport om arbetet för jämställdhet.* Stockholm, 1978.(SAP 1978c)

Sveriges socialdemokratiska arbetareparti. *Jämställdhet mellan kvinnor och män: Program för arbetet för jämställdhet.* Stockholm, 1978. (SAP 1978d)

Sveriges socialdemokratiska arbetareparti. *Framtid för Sverige: Förslag till handlingslinjer för att föra Sverige ur krisen.* Programmet är utarbetat av en arbetsgrupp och antaget av partistyrelsen vid dess sammanträde den 16 juni 1981. Stockholm, 1981. (SAP 1981)

Sveriges socialdemokratiska arbetareparti. Kongress (29th, 1984, Stockholm). *Facklig-politisk samverkan: Rapport från arbetsgruppen angående det lokala facklig-politiska samarbetet: Förslag.* Stockholm, 1984. (SAP 1984a)

Sveriges socialdemokratiska arbetareparti. Kongress (29th, 1984, Stockholm). *Partiets inre arbete: Rapport från arbetsgruppen för partiets inre arbete: Förslag.* Stockholm, 1984. (SAP 1984b)

Sveriges socialdemokratiska arbetareparti. Kongress (30th, 1987, Stockholm). *Partistyrelsens förslag: Riktlinjer och utlåtanden,* 10 vols. Stockholm, 1987. Vol. 9, *Demokratin i framtidssamhället: Riktlinjer: Motionsutlåtanden om partiprogrammet.* . . . (SAP 1987)

Sveriges socialdemokratiska kvinnoförbund. *Familjen i framtiden: En socialistisk familjepolitik.* Stockholm, 1972. (SSKF 1972)

Sveriges socialdemokratiska kvinnoförbund. *6 timmars arbetsdag.* Stockholm, 1974. (SSKF 1974)

Sydow, Björn von. *Kan vi lita på politikerna? Offentlig och intern politik i socialdemokratins ledning 1955–60.* Stockholm, 1978.

Sydsvenske män: Ett porträtt- och autografalbum. Malmö, 1906.

Thagaard, Anna-Margrethe. *Livet på Backarna: Att växa upp i en förstad i början på 1900-talet.* Under medverkan av Anna Kristina Ribbing. Malmö, 1985.

Therborn, Göran. Socialdemokratin träder fram. *Arkiv för studier i arbetarrörelsens historia,* 1984, no. 27/28.

Therborn, Göran. *Nationernas ofärd: Arbetslösheten i den internationella krisen.* Lund, 1985.

Therborn, Göran. En dansk-tysk import: Det moderna Sverige och dess social-demokrati. *Arbetarhistoria*, 1986, no. 1/2. (1986b)

Therborn, Göran. Hur det hela började: Hur och varför det moderna Sverige blev vad det blev. In *Sverige—Vardag och struktur: Sociologer beskriver det svenska samhället*. Edited by Ulf Himmelstrand and Göran Svensson. Stockholm, 1988.

Thomson, A. Gammal och ny arbetslöshetspolitik. In *Ett genombrott: Den svenska socialpolitiken: Utvecklingslinjer och framtidsmål*. Stockholm, 1944.

Thullberg, Per. SAP och jordbruksnäringen 1920–1940: från klasskamp till folkhem. *Arbetarrörelsens årsbok*, 1974.

Thunberg, Ivar Thor. *Det brinner en eld: Svenska landsbygdens ungdomsförbund*. Stockholm, 1942.

Tingsten, Herbert. *Den svenska socialdemokratiens idéutveckling*, 2 vols. Stockholm, 1941.

Tingsten, Herbert. *Svensk utrikesdebatt mellan världskrigen*. Stockholm, 1944.

Tingsten, Herbert. *Den svenska socialdemokratins idéutveckling*, 2 vols. Ny utg. Stockholm, 1967.

Torstendahl, Rolf. *Mellan nykonservatism och liberalism: Idébrytningar inom högern och bondepartierna 1918–1934*. Stockholm, 1969.

Tufte, G. *Holdinger til boligenes eierforhold 1918–1974*. Oslo, 1975.

Uhlén, Axel. *Facklig kamp i Malmö under sju decennier: Historik*. Malmö, 1949.

Ullenhag, Jörgen. *Den solidariska lönepolitiken i Sverige: Debatt och verklighet*. Stockholm, 1971.

Undén, Östen. Neutralitet och solidaritet. *Tiden*, 1945, no. 1.

Unga, Nils. *Socialdemokratin och arbetslöshetsfrågan 1912–34: Framväxten av den "nya" arbetslöshetspolitiken*. Stockholm, 1976.

Utrikesfrågor: Offentliga dokument m. m. rörande viktigare svenska utrikespolitiska frågor. Stockholm, 1952–.

Valen, Henry. *Valg og politikk: Et samfunn i endring*. Oslo, 1981.

Välfärd i förändring: Levnadsvillkor i Sverige 1968–1981. Edited by Robert Eriksson and Rune Åberg. Stockholm, 1984.

Vi bygger vårt bor på Augustenborg. Utgiven av Malmö kommunala bostadsaktiebolag. Malmö, 1950.

Wallin, Erik. Om målstyrnings bekymmer. *Forskning om utbildning*, 1988, no. 3.

Wannfors, Erik. Stadsplanelagen 1907. In *Hundra år under kommunalförfattningarna 1862–1962: En minnesskrift*. Utgiven av Svenska landskommunernas förbund, Svenska landstingsförbundet, Svenska stadsförbundet. Stockholm, 1962.

Westerståhl, Jörgen. *Svensk fackföreningsrörelse: Organisationsproblem, verksamhetsformer, förhållande till staten*. Stockholm, 1945.

Westman, Karl Gustaf. *Politiska anteckningar september 1939–mars 1943*. Utgivna genom W. M. Carlgren. Stockholm, 1981.

Westman, Karl Gustaf. *Politiska anteckningar april 1917–augusti 1939*. Utgivna genom W. M. Carlgren. Stockholm, 1987.

Wigforss, Ernst. Allmän överblick av den industriella demokratiens problem. In *Den industriella demokratiens problem*. Stockholm, 1923. Vol. 1, *Betänkande jämte förslag till lag om driftsnämnder* (SOU 1923:29).

Wigforss, Ernst. *Den ekonomiska krisen*. Stockholm, 1931.

Wigforss, Ernst. Arbetare och bönder under krisen. *Tiden*, 1932, no. 6.

Wigforss, Ernst. Socialismen i socialdemokratin. *Tiden*, 1949, no. 4.

Wigforss, Ernst. *Minnen*, 3 vols. Stockholm, 1950–54. Vol. 3, *1932–1949*, 1954.

Wigforss, Ernst. *Skrifter i urval*, 9 vols. Redaktionskommitté Villy Bergström et al. Stockholm, 1980.
Wulz, Fritz C. *Wien 1848-1934: En arkitekturpolitisk studie av en stad i förändring*. Stockholm, 1979.
Zennström, Per-Olov. *Axel Danielsson: En biografi*. Omtr. Lund, 1983.
Zetterberg, Kent. Bostadspolitik på förändrade villkor: En studie i den bostadspolitiska debatten i dagspress och tidskrifter 1945-1960. Stockholm, 1978. Stencil.

List of Contributors

Klas Åmark   (b. 1944), Ph.D., professor of history at Stockholm University. Publications include *Makt eller moral* (Power or Morals) (1973); *Facklig makt och fackligt medlemskap* (Trade Union Power and Trade Union Membership) (1986); *Maktkamp i byggbransch* (Power Struggle in the Building Trades) (1989); *Makt och arbetsskador under 1900-talet* (Power and Work-related Injuries During the Twentieth Century), together with Bill Sund (1990).

Gøsta Esping-Anderson   (b. 1947), Ph.D., professor of sociology at the European University Institute, Florence. Previously at Harvard University and Wissenschaftszentrum in (West) Berlin. Publications include *Politics Against Markets* (1985); *Power and Social Citizenship* (1989); *The Three Worlds of Welfare Capitalism* (1990).

Villy Bergström   (b. 1938), Ph.D., senior research fellow, visiting professor in economics at Uppsala University, and director of the Trade Unions' Institute for Economic Research in Stockholm. Publications include *Den ekonomiska politiken i Sverige och dess verkningar* (Economic Policy in Sweden and Its Effects) (1969); *Kapitalbildning och ekonomisk demokrati* (Capital Formation and Economic Democracy) (1973); *Studies in Post-War Industrial Investment* (1982).

Peter Billing   (b. 1958), B.A., researcher in history at Lund University. Publications include *Människovärdet vi fordra tillbaka* (The Human Value We Reclaim) (1986).

Gullan Gidlund   (b. 1945), Ph.D., associate professor of political science, University of Umeå. Publications include *Partistöd* (Party Support) (1983); *Det kommunala partistödet* (Local Party Support) (1985).

Alf W. Johansson   (b. 1940), Ph.D., senior research fellow in history at Stockholm University, commissioned to write a history of *Dagens Nyheter*. Publications include *Finlands sak* (Finland's Cause) (1973); *Den nazistiska utmaningen* (The Nazi Challenge) (1983); *Per Albin och kriget* (Per Albin Hansson and the War) (1984; 1988); *Europas krig* (Europe's War) (1989).

Bo Lindensjö   (b. 1944), Ph.D., senior research fellow in political science at Stockholm University. Publications include *Högskolereformen* (The University Reform) (1981); *Politisk styrning och utbildningsreformer* (Political Rule and Educational Reforms), co-authored with U.P. Lundgren (1986).

Klaus Misgeld   (b. 1940), Ph.D., senior research fellow in history at Uppsala University; staff member of the Labor Movement Archives and Library in Stockholm. Publications include *Die "Internationale Gruppe demokratischer Sozialisten" in Stockholm 1942–1945* (The "International Social Democrats" in Stockholm 1942–1945) (1976); *Sozialdemokratie und Aussenpolitik in Schweden, 1945–1955* (Social Democracy and Foreign Policy in Sweden, 1945–1955) (1984).

Karl Molin   (b. 1944), Ph.D., senior research fellow in history at Uppsala University. Publications include *Försvaret, folkhemmet och demokratin* (Defense, "The People's Home" and Democracy) (1974); *Hemmakriget* (Domestic War) (1987); *Omstridd neutralitet* (Disputed Neutrality, 1948–1950) (1992).

Torbjörn Norman   (b. 1933), M.A. in history, archivist and university lecturer. He has published a number of studies of twentieth-century Swedish foreign policy.

Clas-Erik Odhner   (b. 1921), M.A. in agriculture, Stockholm, former director of research at the Swedish Trade Union Federation. Publications include *Jordbruket vid full sysselsättning* (Agriculture at Full Employment) (1953); *Framtidens socialism* (Socialism in the Future) (1959); *Nytt grepp på jordbrukspolitiken* (New Attitudes Toward Agricultural Policy) (1966).

Ann-Sofie Ohlander   (b. 1941), Ph.D., senior research fellow in history at Uppsala University. Publications include *Reaktionen mot utvandringen* (Reactions to Emigration) (1972, under the name Kälvemark); *More Children of Better Quality?* (1980, under the name Kälvemark), and *Kärlek, död, frihet* (Love, Death, Freedom) (1986).

Lars Olsson   (b. 1945), Ph.D. senior research fellow in history, Lund University. Publications include *Då barn var lönsamma* (When Children Were Profitable) (1980); *En typ bland typer i Lund* (One Type Among Other Types in Lund) (1983); *Gamla typer och nya produktionsförhållanden* (Old Types and New Conditions of Production) (1986).

Mikeal Stigendal   (b. 1957), B.A., researcher at Lund University. Publications include *Skånepartiet* (The Skåne Party), co-authored with Tomas Peterson and Björn Fryklund (1988).

Thord Strömberg   (b. 1943), Ph.D. in history, lecturer at the University of Örebro. Publications include *Kommunalsocialismen inför verkligheten* (Local Socialism in the Face of Reality) (1984).

Göran Therborn   (b. 1941), Ph.D., professor of sociology, Gothenburg University (previously at Lund and Nijmegen). Publications include *Science, Class and Society* (1976); *The Ideology of Power and the Power of Ideology* (1981); *The Calamity of Nations* (1986).

Tim Tilton   (b. 1947), Ph.D., professor of political science, Indiana University. Publications include *Nazism, Neo-Nazism and the Peasantry; The Case for the Welfare State: From Social Security to Social Equality*, with Norman Furniss (1977); *The Political Theory of Swedish Social Democracy* (1990).

Index

490   INDEX

tives and, 17–18; SAP opposition split of
1917, 377–83, 386
legostadgan, abolishment of, 179
Lehmann, H. G., 186
Level of Living data, middle-class welfare
state and, 51
Lewin, Leif, 192
Liberal Club (Frisinnade Klubben), 382
Liberal party (*Folkpartiet*): agricultural policy, 181, 185–86, 191–92; bourgeois political bloc and, xxii–xxiii; collective
agreement legislation and, 73; disarmament proposals, 381–83, 399–401; educational policy, 309–13, 323–25; erosion
of class politics and, 441–43; foreign policy and, 4, 341; Haga Agreements, 85;
housing policies, 244–45, 248; industry
support of, 115; insurance proposals, 41;
Malmö social democracy, 281–82; modern coalition politics, 430, 436–37; origins of, xix; parliamentarianism and, xx;
party politics and, xix, 11, 22, 24; popular movements and, 14–15; SAP coalition
with, xx–xxi, xxiv–xxv, 131, 381–83; sexual equality issues in, 232; tax reform
proposals, 432–34; workers organization
and, 100
Liedberg, Gösta, 203–204
lillsvensk ("Little Swedish") ideology, 352
Lindberg, Göran, 257–58
Lindberg, Nils E., 290
Linders, Sven, 181, 188–89
Lindgren, John, 111
Lindhagen, Carl, 139, 365; agricultural
policy, 204–205; land policies, 181–83,
185, 193; neutrality stance of, 340; own-
your-own-home movement, 183–
84
Lindman, Gunnar, 190, 291, 304n.63
Lindström, Rickard, 271
Lindström, Ulla, 215, 227–29, 231, 395
"lineman socialism," 100
literature/pamphlet distribution, as campaign tactic, 111, 120
livestock production, 182–83, 189
living standards: welfare policy and, 37, 51–
53, 155
Ljungbeck, Carl, 293. *See* Swedish Confederation of Trade Unions

local government, role of, in housing policy,
244–48, 253–60
Local Government Act, 245–46
Löfberg, Bertil, 398
Lövbom, Arvid, 156
Lundberg, Erik, 200

Malm, Stig, 118, 436–37
Malmö: Augustenborg housing project in,
290–92; "dis-community" in, 296–97;
early family policy programs in, 218–23;
geographical information, 272; industrial
decline in, 298–300; map of, 274–75; as
model of Social Democracy, 271–301;
municipal socialism in, 288–90; neighborhood community in, 273–79; Rosengård housing project, 295–96; SAP
election victory, 1988, 300–301
Malmö Bricklayers Association, 280–81
Malmö Byggnadsgille (Malmö Building
Workers Guild), 289–93
Malmö Hyresgästförening (Tenants' Association), 289–90
Manpower Commission (AMS), 45
manufacturing, wage differences in, 9
market economy: "framework legislation,"
416; postwar housing proposals and,
253–66; social-democratic ideology and,
418–19. *See also* labor markets
Marklund, Sixten, 321
marriage, changing trends in, 216–17, 219–
20
Marshall Plan, 359
Marxism: agricultural policy and, 177–86,
210n.20; housing policy and, 241; influence of, on Social Democracy, xvii, 63;
Postwar Program and, 149
mass politics, absence of, in nineteenth century Sweden, 8
Månsson, Fabian, 140
maternal aid, as replacement for maternity
benefits, 225–26
maternity benefits: history of, 213–15, 220–
23; modern reforms of, 228–29; vs. population policy, 215–16; transition to parental insurance, 231–35
MBL law (Medbestämmandelagen), 59, 86
means testing, Postwar Program agricultural
reforms, 200–201
meat prices, 189–90

Printed in the United States
798100002B